KT-405-060

The **Rough Guide** to

# Cyprus

written and researched by

## Marc Dubin

ROUGH
GUIDES

NEW YORK • LONDON • DELHI

www.roughguides.com

# Contents

3

## Introduction to

# Cyprus

**Cyprus, the Mediterranean's third-largest island after Sicily and Sardinia, defers only to Malta as the newest state in the region, having come into existence on August 16, 1960. For the first time, following centuries of domination by whatever empire or nation held sway in the eastern Mediterranean – including, from 1878 to 1960, Great Britain – the islanders seemed to control their own destiny. Such empowerment proved illusory: no distinctly Cypriot national identity was permitted to evolve by the island's Orthodox Christian Greek and Muslim Turkish communities. Within four years, tension between these two groups had rent the society asunder, followed in 1974 by a political and ethnic division of the island imposed by the mainland Turkish army.**

However, **calm** now reigns on the island, and for British visitors there's a persistent sense of déjà vu in Cyprus, perhaps more than with any other ex-Crown Colony. Pillar boxes still display "GR" and "ER" monograms near zebra cross-ings; grandiose colonial public buildings jostle for space with vernacular mud-brick and Neoclassical houses; Woolworth's, Next, TGIF, M&S, KFC, Pizza Hut and McDonalds are all present in the largest towns of the South; and of course driving is on the left. Before the recent founding of universities in both South and North, higher education was pursued abroad, preferably in the UK, and **English** – virtually the second, if unofficial, language in the South – is widely spoken. Despite the bitterness of the independence struggle against the UK, most is forgiven

Limassol market

(if not exactly forgotten) a generation or so later.

Even the most ardent Cyprus enthusiast will concede that it can't compete in allure with more exotic, airline-poster destinations, yet the place grows on you with prolonged acquaintance (as evidenced by the huge expat/immigrant population in the South, estimated at 60,000, mostly British but also east European and south Asian). There's certainly enough to hold your interest inland once you tire of the **beaches**, which tend to be small, scattered coves on the south coast, or longer, dunier expanses on north-facing shores. Horizons are defined by one of two **mountain ranges**: the convoluted massif of the Tróödhos, with numerous spurs and valleys, and the wall-like escarpment of the Kyrenia hills, seemingly sculpted of papier-mâché.

In terms of **special-interest** visits, archeology buffs, wine-tasters, flower-sniffers, bird-watchers and mountain-bikers are particularly well catered for, though state-of-the-art nightlife and cultural diversions can be thin on the

## Restoration accommodation

The rapid urbanization of Cyprus since the 1950s has meant wholesale abandonment of many attractive hill-villages, particularly in Páfos and Limassol districts. Since the late 1980s, a number of stone-built rural houses of varying sizes have been restored as unique accommodation. Facilities range from small cottages with perhaps two studio units to rambling complexes, essentially small inns, around a shared courtyard with a pool. Traditional architectural features, such as fireplaces and soaring arches in the main room, are often preserved. The idea is that guests will both interact socially with the remaining villagers and spend locally, rather than down at the coastal mega-resorts.

5

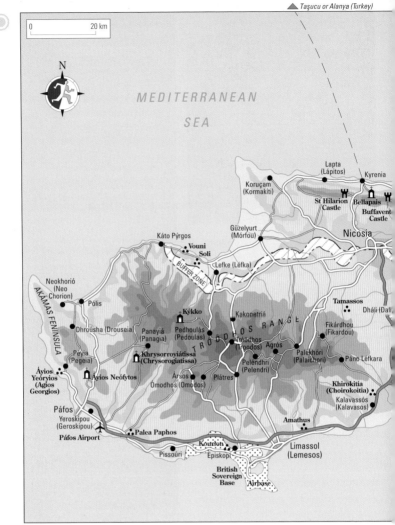

ground outside Nicosia, Limassol and Ayía Nápa, in keeping with the predominantly forty- and fifty-something clientele, and the island's enduring provincialism. This has both cause and effect in the overwhelming presence of the **package industry**, supported by law in the South, and by circumstance in the North, which has effectively put at least two of the bigger resorts plus numbers of hotels off-limits to independent travellers. But for an undemanding, reasonably priced **family holiday** most months of the year, Cyprus is still a good bet.

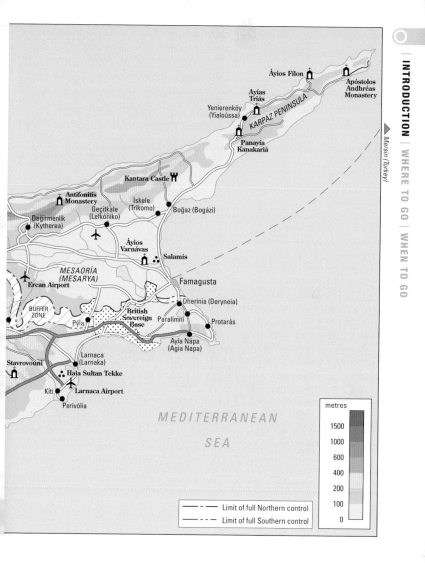

Mesrin (Turkey)

metres

| | |
|---|---|
| | 1500 |
| | 1000 |
| | 600 |
| | 400 |
| | 200 |
| | 100 |
| | 0 |

— · — · Limit of full Northern control

— - — - Limit of full Southern control

# Divided Cyprus

ong-dormant rivalry and resentment between Cyprus's two principal ethnic groups was reawakened late in the 1950s by the Greek-
Cypriot campaign for *énosis* or **union with Greece**. Following
independence, disputes over the proper respective civic roles of
the Greek- and Turkish-Cypriot communities, and lingering advocacy of

## Fact file

- Cyprus is the easternmost island in the Mediterranean, with a **surface area** of 9251 square kilometres (3572 square miles). The total **population** is 870,000, comprising 650,000 Greek Orthodox, Greek-speaking islanders, 80,000 Sunni Muslim, primarily Turkish-speaking natives, and 140,000 foreign-born immigrants or seasonal residents. All these figures are debatable as there has been no island-wide census since 1960. After 1974 Cyprus was divided into two zones: the South, comprising 68 percent of the land and predominantly Greek Cypriot-inhabited, the balance largely populated by Turkish Cypriots and an undetermined number of settlers from mainland Turkey. The **capital** of both regions is Nicosia.

- The **Southern republic** is a stable democracy, with regular, keenly contested elections, and since May 2004 a member of the EU. The head of state is the president; there is no prime minister. The House of Representatives has 56 seats; 24 more are reserved under the 1960 constitution for Turkish-Cypriot deputies who have not, however, occupied them since 1963. Instead they sit in the fifty-seat assembly of the North.

> [The Cypriot] is entering in thousands that trough – of how many generations? – between peasant honesty and urban refinement. "To be civilised," a Nicosia friend told me, "our people must first be vulgar. It is the bridge between simplicity and culture."
>
> **Colin Thubron**

*énosis,* or *taksim* (**partition of the island** between Greece and Turkey) by extremists in each camp, provoked widespread, ongoing communal violence.

Abetted by interested outsiders, these incidents – and a CIA-backed coup against the elected government – culminated in the 1974 landing by the Turkish army which effectively **partitioned** the island, with both Greek and Turkish Cypriots on the "wrong" side of the ceasefire line compelled to leave their homes. Nicosia, the capital, approximately at the centre of Cyprus, was divided like Cold War Berlin, and remains so at present; much of Famagusta, formerly home to about seven percent of the island's current population, lies abandoned. If this all sounds eye-rollingly familiar in the wake of events in former Yugoslavia and the Russian Federation, there was during the 1960s and 1970s a relative novelty to the crises that repeatedly convulsed Cyprus.

In the **aftermath** of 1974, the two zones of Cyprus nursed grievances against each other that were difficult for many outsiders to fathom, and for nearly three decades North and South remained mutually isolated, developing over time into parallel societies, destined in the view of some never to converge again. The island's division was compared by many to that of pre-1990 Germany, though as Cyprus is a far more intimate place the scale of human tragedy has been more visible. Any sort of **reunification** is bound to be hedged with conditions, and fraught with pitfalls similar to the German experience: while South and North are both avowedly capitalist, a prosperity gap compounded by the long-enforced segregation may prove difficult to bridge. Linguistic and religious differences are less likely to be problematic; many older people from each community still speak the "other" language, and Turkish Cypriot Islam must be one of the most easy-going variants in existence.

**Negotiations** between representatives of each community have taken place sporadically since well before 1974, but have never borne fruit, with many false dawns. The result of the island-wide referendum on the UN-devised "Annan Plan" for reunification in April 2004, decisively approved by the Turkish Cypriots but resoundingly rejected by the Greek Cypriots, dealt a serious, but by no means fatal, blow to such efforts. The sudden opening of the

▶ Road-hazard sign

• The **Northern system** provides for both president and prime minister, and on paper has all requisite democratic trappings, but only since 2000 has there been a serious challenge to the consolidation of power in the hands of an oligarchy, and a relaxation in repression of their opponents.

• **Tourism** constitutes the island's number-one **industry**: around two million vacationers in recent seasons to the **South**. Government dreams of attracting four million in future are neither logistically nor environmentally sustainable. British visitors make up roughly half the number, with Scandinavians, Germans, Greeks and Russians following in that order. By contrast, the **North** gets just 30,000–60,000 guests annually, with Brits again leading the way. Fresh produce, juices and wines are the principal **agricultural exports** of the South; shipping, banking services and medical care are other significant **foreign-currency earners**. Since 2000, the North's economy has effectively imploded, with its only significant money-spinners being higher education offered at a number of small universities, and remittances from the thousands of Turkish Cypriots who commute to work daily in the South.

9

## Basketry

Wicker-work in general is the Cypriot craft and souvenir par excellence. Flat woven trays or deep baskets, called *panéri* or *tséstos* in Greek (from the Italian *cesta*), or *sesta* by the Turkish-Cypriots, are a staple of restaurant decor: converted into lampshades, or hanging on the wall where their dyed, vaguely Amerindian designs catch the eye. They're fashioned by women and are completely hand-made, with only an awl as a tool. "Wicker" is used here generically; willows are almost non-existent on Cyprus, and the main raw materials are certain kinds of wheat straws, grasses and palm fronds.

"border" across the island a year previously has created its own, probably unstoppable momentum towards a settlement, and the odds are now that some solution will be cobbled together by the islanders themselves, if not one to the complete satisfaction of the EU or UN.

# Where to go

Because of the mutual hostility of South and North, you formerly had to choose which side of Cyprus to visit on any given trip, as there was extremely limited provision for crossing between them. All this changed radically in April 2003, when various political and economic factors compelled the North to open the "border" (nobody in the South will use the term other than in inverted commas, as the present situation is viewed as an interim one pending any definitive peace settlement). There is still disinformation deliberately promulgated by interested parties, but in effect EU nationals with proper ID are free to cross the line in either direction and stay as long as they wish; see p.35 for all pertinent details.

The package industry remains orientated to taking you to one or other side of the island, and either portion has plenty to keep you occupied. When the **South's** busiest beaches east of sleepy **Larnaca** pall, there's the popular hill village of **Páno Léfkara**, unique sacred art at the Byzantine churches of **Áyios Andónios** and **Angelóktisti** or the nearby Lusignan "**Chapelle Royale**", plus the atmospheric Muslim shrine of **Hala Sultan Tekke** to the west. **Ayía Nápa**, in

the far southeast, briefly enjoyed a reputation as a Mediterranean clubbing destination second only to Ibiza, and is still the liveliest summer-spot on the island. Beyond functional **Limassol**, the Crusader tower of **Kolossi** guards vineyards as it always has, while still-being-excavated ancient **Kourion** sprawls nearby atop seaside cliffs, which subside at the sandy bays of **Pissoúri** and **Evdhímou**. Inland from these, rolling hills shelter the **Krassokhoriá** or "Wine Villages", many of these attractively stone-built and little changed outwardly over the past century.

Of the three main south-coast resorts, **Páfos** has most recently awoken to tourism, and with its spectacular Roman mosaics and early Christian relics has perhaps the most to offer. The hinterland of Páfos district belies its initial bleak appearance to reveal fertile valleys furrowing ridges sprinkled with brown-stone villages and, to either side of the **Akámas peninsula**, the last unspoiled stretches of coast in the South. If you don't require lively nightlife, then **Pólis** and **Latchí** make good, comfortable overnight bases in this area, serving too as possible springboards into the foothills of the Tróödhos mountains. Magnificently frescoed ancient churches and monasteries abound, best of these **Áyios Neófytos** and the **Paleá Énklistra**, rock-cut rural shrines, **Ayía Paraskeví** in Yeroskípou, and **Áyios Kírykos** in Letímbou.

Inland from Páfos or Limassol, the **Tróödhos mountains** themselves beckon, covered in well-groomed forest, lovingly resuscitated from a nadir of the nineteenth century. **Plátres**, the original Cypriot "hill-station", makes a logical base on the south side of the range; to the north, more authentic village character asserts itself at **Pedhoulás** or **Kakopetriá**. Scattered across several valleys, a dozen or so magnificently **frescoed late-Byzantine churches** provide an additional focus to itineraries here if the scenery and walking opportunities aren't enough. If time is limited, the most important churches are **Asínou**, **Áyios Ioánnis Lambadhistís**, **Áyios Nikólaos tís Stéyis**, **Panayía toú Araká** and **Stavrós toú Ayiasmáti**.

## The Orthodox church

Southern Cyprus is one of the most religiously observant corners of the Orthodox world. Although women are more scrupulously devout, per head of population Cyprus sends more monks to Mount Áthos, the monastic republic in northern Greece, than any other Orthodox country. If you're used to the foul-mouthed blasphemies of metropolitan Greece, you'll notice that Cypriots for the most part keep a decorous tongue in their heads. Indeed, the Church used to all but run the show socially, ensuring that women kept to their allotted social place, that any other "creed" (this even meant yoga classes) was highly suspect, and that non-conformists – particularly communists in rural villages – soon sought exile in England or elsewhere. But two factors have steadily eroded clerical power in the last two decades: EU membership for Cyprus, which has meant the end of opposition to civil marriage and homosexual rights, and the Church's own involvement in a series of bizarre scandals (see p.454).

While not immediately appealing, south **Nicosia** – the Greek-Cypriot portion of the divided capital – can boast an idiosyncratic old town in the process of revitalization, and, in the Cyprus Museum, one of the finest archeological collections in the Middle East. North Nicosia, on the other side of the now-porous 1974 ceasefire line, is graced with most of the island's Ottoman monuments – and also introduces the Frenchified ecclesiastical architecture bequeathed by the Lusignan dynasty.

For the majority of tourists in the **North**, however, **Kyrenia** is very much the main event, its old harbour the most sheltered and charming on Cyprus. Mushrooming residential and resort development is threatening to outpace the town's limited infrastructure, but despite the recent boom the Kyrenia area still lags behind the South in that respect. The hills looming above support three medieval castles – **St Hilarion**, **Buffavento** and **Kantara** – whose views and architecture rarely disappoint. Add villages in picturesque settings north of and below the ridgeline, and it's little wonder that outsiders have been gravitating here longer than anywhere else on the island.

The **beaches** north of Famagusta are Kyrenia's only serious rival for tourist custom in the North, and hard to resist in tandem with **Salamis**, the largest ancient site on Cyprus. **Famagusta** itself is remarkable, another Lusignan church-fantasy wrapped in some of the most imposing Venetian walls in the world – though churches and ramparts aside there's little else to see or do, the town having lain devastated since the Ottoman conquest. North of the beach strip, the **Karpaz peninsula** points finger-like towards Syria, its fine beaches and generous complement of early churches – most notably at **Áyios Fílon** and **Ayía Triás** – a favourite target of Greek-Cypriot weekenders since the "border" opened.

# When to go

Because of a situation as much Middle Eastern as Mediterranean, Cyprus repays a visit in almost any month; the overall mildness of the **climate** allows citrus to grow at altitudes of 450m, grape-vines to flourish up to 1000m and frost-tender cedars to sprout at 1500-metre elevations in the Tróödhos. Such plant-zone limits would be unthinkable even on nearby Crete, despite an identical latitude of 34 degrees north. There's a local saying in the South that even the bad weather comes from Greece, arriving on the back of the prevailing west-southwest winds; the northerners say the same about Turkey, with cold midwinter storms trundling over from the mountains of Anatolia.

If you're coming for the **flora and birdlife** – as many people do – then **winter and spring**, beginning early December and late February respectively, are for you. Rain falls in sporadic bursts throughout this period and into April, leaving the rare spectacle of a green, prairie-like Mesaoría, the central plain which most tourists only know as a parched, stubbly dustbowl. March in particular is often very fine, if cool at night; April can curiously be more unstable, with heavy downpours. You'll also **cut costs** significantly by showing up in the off-season.

As the months progress and the mercury climbs, you can either brave the multitudes at the seashore – consider-able in the South – or follow the wild flow-ers inland and up the slopes of the Tróödhos

Arabis purpurea, Mount Adhelfi

mountains, veritable havens of **coolness** and relative solitude. In the coastal South, **midsummer** is a bit too hot for comfort (though Páfos tends to be 1–2°C cooler than Limassol or Larnaca, and less humid, thanks to the prevailing winds), and of course incurs **high-season** prices (June–Sept). During July or August you're probably better off in the **North**, where the seaward, damper slope of the Kyrenia hills

▼ Gothic tracery, Kihyseléoussa window

especially offers a refuge from crowds, though humid heat here can be trying. Many aficionados of the North choose to show up in September or October, when hotel space is at a premium.

**Autumn** everywhere is delightful, with the sea at its warmest, forays into the hills benefiting from **stable weather**, and the air (around Limassol and Páfos especially) heavy with the fumes of fermenting grapes. And if it's **resort life** you're after, the coastal strips don't completely wind down until November. This month, especially the latter half, can be wetter and gloomier than December, and Christmas/New Year's breaks are popular.

## Average daily temperatures and rainfall

|  | Jan | Mar | May | July | Sept | Nov |
|---|---|---|---|---|---|---|
| **Nicosia** | | | | | | |
| Max °C | 15 | 19 | 30 | 37 | 33 | 24 |
| Min °C | 6 | 7 | 14 | 22 | 18 | 10 |
| Days of rain | 14 | 8 | 1 | 0 | 0 | 6 |
| **Kyrenia** | | | | | | |
| Max °C | 17 | 18 | 26 | 32 | 31 | 23 |
| Min °C | 9 | 9 | 15 | 24 | 21 | 14 |
| Days of rain | 13 | 7 | 1 | 0 | 0 | 7 |
| **Tróödhos foothills** | | | | | | |
| Max °C | 8 | 12 | 21 | 29 | 25 | 15 |
| Min °C | 2 | 4 | 11 | 18 | 15 | 8 |
| Days of rain | 14 | 9 | 2 | 0 | 0 | 6 |

## things not to miss

*It's not possible to see everything that Cyprus has to offer in one trip – and we don't suggest you try. What follows is a selective and subjective taste of the island's highlights: superb ancient sites, outstanding buildings and natural wonders. They're arranged in five colour-coded categories to help you find the very best things to see, do and experience. All highlights have a page reference to take you straight into the guide, where you can find out more.*

**01** **Salamis** Page **394** • The gymnasium colonnade is one of many highlights at ancient Salamis, just north of Famagusta.

**02** **"Golden Beach"** Page **412** • Sea turtles and humans alike flock to Nangomí or "Golden Beach", one of the best on the remote Karpaz peninsula, and indeed the island.

**03** **Paleá Énklistra** Page **183** • The fifteenth-century ceiling frescoes of this rock-cut church are unique on the island for showing the Holy Trinity.

**05** **Cyprus Museum** Page **288**
• A bronze nude statue of Roman Emperor Septimius Severus is a highlight of the superb Cyprus Museum, the national archeological collection in South Nicosia.

**04** **Avgás (Avákas) Gorge**
Page **191** • The narrows of the Avgás Gorge are a natural wonder of the uninhabited Akámas peninsula, and a popular trek-through venue.

**06** **Byzantine Monastery of Panayía Absinthiótissa** Page **370** •
On the south side of the Kyrenia range, Panayía Absinthiótissa is like most churches in the North: attractive from afar but gutted inside.

17

**07** **Kyrenia harbour** Page **348** • Ringed with medieval buildings and flanked by a castle, this easily ranks as the most picturesque harbour on the entire island.

**08** **North Nicosia's Arabahmet district** Page **327** • This imposing mansion stands among terraces of well-restored vernacular houses in the Arabahmet district.

**09** **Hala Sultan Tekke** Page **104** • Palm trees and the mosque near Larnaca combine in an orientalist's fantasy.

18

**10** **Roman mosaics, Káto Páfos** Page **169** • Winter personified, in the "House of Dionysos", is just one of dozens of late Roman mosaics which adorn Káto Páfos.

**11** **Asprókremos** Page **208** • On the northeast flank of the Akámas peninsula, this is one of the least-spoilt beaches in the South.

**12 Caledonian Falls** Page **235** • The so-called Caledonian waterfall is among the beauty spots accessible by maintained hiking trails around Mount Olympus.

**13** **Lófou** Page **142** • The best-preserved of a score of stone-built villages in Limassol district's wine country.

**15** **Turtle hatcheries** Pages **192** & **377** • Loggerhead and green turtles return every summer to lay eggs on remote beaches of Páfos district and the Karpaz peninsula.

**14** **Ancient Soli** Page **334** • A swan mosaic constitutes the main attraction at ancient Soli on the island's north coast.

**17** **Scuba diving** Page **104** • The wreck of the *Zenobia* off Larnaca is ranked as one of the best dives in the Mediterranean.

**16** **"Cyprus delight"** Page **63** • *Loukoúmi* to the Greek Cypriots, *lokum* to the Turkish Cypriots, this makes a popular gift to hosts island-wide.

## 18 Lala Mustafa Paşa Camii
Page **389** • Literally and figuratively over-the-top, the facade of the Lala Mustafa Pasa mosque – once the cathedral of St Nicholas – is the pride of Famagusta.

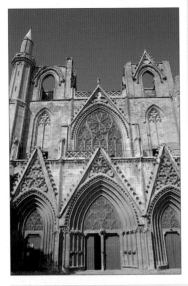

## 19 Bedesten
Page **324** • The north portal of the Bedesten, formerly the medieval church of St Nicholas, is representative of abundant ornamental Gothic carving in Nicosia.

## 20 Arkhángelos Mikhaïl church, Pedhoulás
Page **242** • The exquisite UNESCO-recognised frescoes adorning foothill churches of the Tróödhos range are typified by these vivid fifteenth-century examples at Pedhoulás.

**21** **Ayía Nápa nightlife** Page **120** • It might not have the buzz it once had, but Ayía Nápa is still the island's number-one after-dark destination.

**22** **Tróödhos mountains** Pages **234–239** • April, with its cherry-blossom display is an excellent time to visit the Tróödhos.

**23** **Áyios Mamás** Page **300** • This Gothic abbey-church at Áyios Sozómenos village is arguably the loveliest rural ruin in the South.

**24** **Abbey of Béllapais** Page **368** • The former Augustinian abbey of Béllapais forms the heart of the Kyrenian hill-village which grew up around it.

**25** **Monastery of Ayía Nápa** Page **118** • The graceful fountain-house and medieval church at Ayía Nápa's monastery stand in stark contrast to the resort excesses outside.

# Basics

# Basics

# ✈ Getting there

Almost all UK visitors to Cyprus, South or North, arrive by air as part of an all-inclusive package; frequent scheduled and chartered year-round flights operate from London and several regional airports. There are at present no non-stop flights between North America and any point in Cyprus; thus getting to the island is best considered as an adjunct to a wider European or Mediterranean tour. The same is true for reaching Cyprus from Australia or New Zealand, despite the sizeable expatriate Cypriot community in Australia.

The South is easy to reach by air from most **neighbouring countries**, except Turkey, from where you can fly only to the North. Similarly, there is only passenger boat service between Turkey and the North at present.

**Airfares** to Cyprus from Europe, North America and Australia always depend on the season. With minor variations for each market, "high season" means June to late September (plus Christmas/New Year week and October half-term), "low season" means October to early December and January to late March, with "shoulder season" fares usually applicable otherwise, including around both Western and Orthodox Easter. The cheapest published fares, designated by a bewildering "alphabet soup" of capital letters, require a minimum stay of three days away, and over a Saturday night, with a typical maximum period of thirty or sixty days, and make you liable to penalties (including total loss of ticket value) if you miss your outbound departure or change your return date.

You can often cut costs by going through a **specialist flight agent** – either a consolidator, who buys up blocks of tickets from the airlines and sells them at a discount, or (in the UK) an agent specializing in **charter flights and package deals**, which is much the most common (and usually least expensive) way of visiting Cyprus.

Don't overlook the possibility of using **Frequent Flyer miles**. From the UK, direct flights on Cyprus Airways or BA require 25,000 points, though some indirect carriers such as Swiss and Lufthansa only need 20,000 miles. From North America, most airlines require 70,000–80,000 miles. You'll still have to pay all taxes (around £55 from Britain), but a major advantage is that these types of tickets are usually date-changeable for a small fee.

## Booking flights online

Many airlines and discount travel websites offer you the opportunity to book your tickets **online**. Even if you don't end up actually buying your ticket online, websites can give you an indication of the prevailing published economy fares. However, the airlines' own sites tend to give you a choice only of nonchangeable/nonrefundable and full economy fares – for the numerous options in between, you'll still have to ring them. When exploring a quoted fare on a website, always click the "Rules" link – all conditions will be spelled out in small print. Some of the general travel sites, like Expedia and Travelocity, offer substantially discounted "special bargain" fares – the problem is that sometimes you don't get to see the scheduling, or the airlines used, until after you've bought the ticket. Any reputable site will have a secure, encrypted facility for making credit-card payments – if it doesn't, you're better off not using the site to purchase.

### Online booking agents and general travel sites

ⓦ **www.cheapflights.co.uk** (UK & Ireland), **www.cheapflights.com** (US), **www.cheapflights.ca** (Canada) or **www.cheapflights.com.au** (Australia & New Zealand). Not a booking site itself, but maintains links to the travel agents offering the deals.
ⓦ **www.cheaptickets.com** Discount flight specialists (US only).

Ⓦ **www.etn.nl/discount.htm** A hub of consolidator and discount agent web links, maintained by the nonprofit European Travel Network.

Ⓦ **www.expedia.co.uk** (UK & Ireland), **www.expedia.com** (US) or **www.expedia.ca** (Canada). Discount airfares, all-airline search engine and daily deals.

Ⓦ **www.kelkoo.co.uk** Useful UK-only price-comparison site, checking several sources of low-cost flights (and other goods and services) according to specific criteria.

Ⓦ **www.lastminute.com** (UK & Ireland), **www.lastminute.com.au** (Australia) or **www.lastminute.co.nz** (New Zealand). Good holiday-package and flight-only deals available at very short notice.

Ⓦ **www.opodo.co.uk** Popular and reliable source of cheap UK airfares. Owned by, and run in conjunction with, nine major European airlines.

Ⓦ **www.priceline.co.uk** or **www.priceline.com** Bookings from the UK/US only. Name-your-own-price auction website that can knock around forty percent off standard website fares. You can't choose the airline or flight times (although you do specify dates) and the tickets are nonrefundable, nontransferable and nonchangeable.

Ⓦ **www.skyauction.com** Bookings from the US only. Auctions tickets and travel packages using a "second bid" scheme. The best strategy is to bid the maximum you're willing to pay, since if you win you'll pay just enough to beat the runner-up regardless of your maximum bid.

Ⓦ **www.travelocity.co.uk** (UK & Ireland), **www.travelocity.com** (US) or **www.travelocity.ca** (Canada). Destination guides, hot web fares and deals for car rental, accommodation and lodging as well as fares.

Ⓦ **www.travelselect.com** A subsidiary of lastminute.com that is useful and fairly easy to use, but without most of the guff and banner adverts of the better-known sites.

Ⓦ **www.travelshop.com.au** Australian website offering discounted flights, packages, insurance and online bookings.

Ⓦ **www.travel.co.nz.** Comprehensive online travel company, with discounted fares.

Ⓦ **www.zuji.com.au** Destination guides, hot fares and great deals for car rental, accommodation and lodging.

## Flights from Britain and Ireland

**Scheduled flights** to either part of Cyprus are somewhat overpriced for the number of air miles involved; in season you might get better value from a charter (available to the

South only), though see the warning under "Packages" in this section. With the entry of the southern Republic into the EU, and the opening of the "border", the strategy of flying into Larnaca (in the South) for **access to either side** of the island has grown in popularity.

### Scheduled flights to the South

Larnaca and Páfos on the coast are the southern Republic's two international airports, each some four and a half to five hours distant from UK start-points.

**Cyprus Airways**, the national carrier scrambling to avoid bankruptcy as of writing, offers **summer** (late March to late Oct) service to **Larnaca** from London Heathrow (2 daily, morning and evening), London Stansted (3 weekly, afternoon), Birmingham (2 weekly, night) and Manchester (3 weekly, afternoon). Summer frequency to **Páfos** is markedly lower from London Heathrow (1–2 weekly, afternoon), London Stansted (2 weekly, afternoon), Manchester (3 weekly, afternoon) and Birmingham (1 weekly, night). In **winter**, departures for **Larnaca** dip marginally to 2 daily for Heathrow, 2 weekly from Stansted and Manchester, and 1 weekly from Birmingham. For **Páfos**, winter frequency is typically once weekly apiece from Heathrow and Birmingham, but twice weekly from Stansted and Manchester.

**Helios Airways**, the first private Cypriot airline, is beginning to outstrip Cyprus Airways, from the UK at least. Their website, however, is notoriously buggy; fortunately their offerings show up on general travel sites. During summer there's a daily late-morning service from **London Luton** to Larnaca, two midday weekly services London Luton to Páfos, five weekly night-time scheduled services from **London Heathrow** to Larnaca, two weekly (morning and late night) **Birmingham** to Larnaca, one weekly morning flight from **London Gatwick** to Páfos and then on to Larnaca, one weekly morning service from **Manchester** to Páfos/Larnaca, and three weekly (late-night or noon) from **Dublin** to Larnaca. Winter frequencies are daily from Luton to Larnaca, four weekly Heathrow to Larnaca, one weekly Gatwick to Páfos, two weekly Luton to Páfos, one weekly Manchester to Larnaca via Páfos, one weekly Dublin to Larnaca via Páfos, and one weekly Birmingham to Larnaca. Helios also functions as a charter carrier from Bristol, Newcastle, and Humberside.

**British Airways** offers just a daily morning service from Heathrow to Larnaca year-round, with additional late evening services April to October.

**Indirect** flights via a European hub are unlikely to appeal except at high season when direct services fill; they tend to have long layovers and not be conspicuously cheaper.

### Fares

**Fares** from the UK and Ireland to either Cypriot airport have become something of an unpredictable free-for-all since the entry of Helios (and various quasi-charter airlines like Excel) into the fray. However, from December to March (excluding the holiday period) you shouldn't ever have to pay over £200, and special offers in the region of £160–170 are common. Even in springtime fares clock in at £180–235, and buying far enough in advance you can even find high-summer fares for about £210 – though you can pay £270, or over £300, at short notice. Prices to Páfos and Larnaca are identical, as the airports are common-rated; with Cyprus Airways, it is also possible to fly into one airport and out of another for little or no extra charge (indeed you may find that planes out of Larnaca touch down at Páfos to pick up more passengers). For fully date-changeable or long-stay tickets you're looking at fares of over £500.

### Charter flights

**Charter companies** such as First Choice (ex-Air2000), Eurocypria, British Airways Charter, Monarch, Thomas Cook, TUI and Britannia also provide air links from Britain, but owing to Cypriot law (see "Packages" below) seats are difficult to get on a flight-only basis. In addition to the major airports, charter flights also leave from Bristol, Humberside, East Midlands, Cardiff, Luton, Glasgow and Newcastle for both Larnaca and Páfos. Although charters tend to have more family-friendly departure and arrival

hours, such tickets are utterly inflexible and rarely available for more than two weeks' duration. They are usually, however, noticeably **cheaper** than scheduled flights: perhaps £169 London–Larnaca at Easter time, £179 Gatwick–Páfos in May, £188 Manchester–Páfos in June, £255 Birmingham–Páfos in July.

### Scheduled flights to the North

Because of the IATA boycott of north Nicosia's airport at **Ercan**, North Cyprus has direct air links only with Turkey, where northern European planes must first touch down (at İstanbul, İzmir or Antalya). About half the time you will be required to change aircraft, usually being shuttled straight across the runway rather than entering the terminal. Reports of "direct" flights should be treated with healthy scepticism; at present this is permitted only during extreme weather conditions in Turkey, on an emergency basis. Even if a federal settlement is reached, and one of the North's airports declared licit, the simple economics of the situation will continue to dictate stopping flights. Despite the lengthening of travel time from five to seven or eight hours by the obligatory stopover, frequent scheduled flights start from several UK airports; with very few exceptions, they arrive between 9pm and midnight.

**Cyprus Turkish Airways** (*Kıbrıs Türk Hava Yolları,* KTHY), the official state airline, flies three days weekly from Heathrow to Ercan via İzmir all year; three days weekly from Gatwick via Antalya; twice daily from Stansted via Antalya, Dalaman or İzmir; twice weekly (weekend and midweek) from Manchester via Dalaman; and once weekly from Glasgow via Antalya. However, travellers' chat websites are full of horror stories about KTHY and, despite an uncivilised departure time returning from Ercan, regular fliers still reckon it worth paying the (often substantial) difference and flying with the far more professional **Turkish Airlines**. They offer year-round through service from Manchester five days weekly, and daily midday service from Heathrow and Stansted, to İstanbul, where you can expect a fairly long layover until their single daily evening flight to Ercan.

Otherwise, **Onur Air** has either dawn or mid-afternoon service from Stansted via İstanbul two days weekly, Thursday and Sunday in winter, Friday and Sunday in summer. They also have one weekly afternoon service from Manchester, usually Saturday. Onur Air has, however, quickly acquired a reputation for changing flight days with little warning – and if you can't or won't fly on the newly designated day, you lose the value of your ticket.

**Fares** from London start at just under £220 return during winter on KTHY (£270 on Turkish Airlines), with substantial hikes to about £270 in summer on KTHY (up to £400 on Turkish Airlines); allow £20–30 extra for Manchester departures. Subject to the caveat noted above, Onur Air works out rather cheaper: £149 in the pit of winter, up to £299 at peak season. You're pretty much expected to purchase tickets to the North through an agent; Onur doesn't have a website at present, and neither the KTHY nor THY websites are authorised to sell fares to Ercan (though you can sometimes find tickets to Ercan – code ECN – on general travel websites in the UK).

## Airlines

### Airlines serving the South

**British Airways** ☎0870 859 9850, in Republic of Ireland ☎1800/626 747, ⓦwww.ba.com.
**Cyprus Airways** ☎020/8359 1333, ⓦwww.cyprusairways.com.
**Helios Airways** ☎0870 750 2750, ⓦwww.flyhelios.com.

### Airlines serving the North

**Cyprus Turkish Airlines** ☎020/7930 4851, ⓦwww.kthy.net.
**Onur Air** c/o TWI Flights ☎0870 116 2211, ✉twi@flightcabin.com
**Turkish Airlines** ☎020/7766 9300, ⓦwww.thy.com.

## Flight and travel agents

**Andrews Travel** ☎020/8882 7153,🖷8886 8720. Long-established flight-only, fly-drives and tailor-made holiday specialists for Cyprus.
**Avro** ☎0870 458 2841, ⓦwww.avro.co.uk. Seat-only sales on flights to Larnaca and Páfos from major UK airports, on Monarch, First Choice and Flyjet, among others. The site is good about finding flights around, not just on, the date you specify.

**Delta Travel** ☎0161/273 7511, 0151/708 7955, 0121/471 2282, ⓦwww.deltatravel.co.uk. Flight specialists and members of Association of Greek Cypriot Travel Agents.
**Excel Airways** ☎0870 169 0169, ⓦwww.xl.com. Flight-onlys to Larnaca and Páfos, mostly from Gatwick, Birmingham and Manchester but also Glasgow and East Midlands; easy-to-use site gives a range of alternatives in terms of dates, airports and even other airlines besides Excel.
**Greece & Cyprus Travel Centre** ☎0121/355 6955, ⓦwww.greece-cyprus.co.uk. Competent flight consolidator with a myriad of fares to suit every need, including one-ways.
**Independent Aviation Group** ☎0871 222 3903, ⓦwww.iagflights.com. Charter brokers who regularly offload unsold seats (out of London Gatwick only) on a flight-only basis at good rates; website tells you instantly what's available, which can be quite cheap indeed. Typically one- or two-week duration, also one-ways.
**Joe Walsh Tours** Dublin ☎01/676 0991, ⓦwww.joewalshtours.ie. General budget fares and holidays agent.
**North South Travel** ☎01245/608291, ⓦwww.northsouthtravel.co.uk. Friendly, competitive flight agency, offering discounted fares worldwide – profits are used to support projects in the developing world, especially the promotion of sustainable tourism.
**Rosetta Travel** Belfast ☎028/9064 4996, ⓦwww.rosettatravel.com. Flight and holiday agent, specializing in deals direct from Belfast.
**STA Travel** ☎0870 160 0599, ⓦwww.statravel.co.uk. Worldwide specialists in low-cost flights and tours for students and under-26s.
**Thomas Cook** ☎0870 750 5711, ⓦwww.thomascook.com. Selection of complete packages and flight-onlys to Larnaca and Páfos, not just on Thomas Cook airlines; much better than you'd expect.
**Thomson Flights** ☎0800 000 747, ⓦwww.thomsonflights.com. Limited flight-only deals to Páfos on TUI, its parent-company airline; website's less than brilliant.
**Trailfinders** UK ☎020/7938 3939, ⓦwww.trailfinders.com, Republic of Ireland ☎01/677 7888, ⓦwww.trailfinders.ie. One of the best-informed and most efficient agents for independent travellers; branches in all the UK's largest cities, plus Dublin.

## Packages

Cyprus ranks as the most packaged destination in the Mediterranean after Malta, a status mandated by law in the **South**. Current regulations stipulate that only holidaymakers on fully inclusive packages may board charter craft flying out of Luton, Birmingham and Manchester, while at other UK airports, only fifteen percent of charter seat capacity is allowed to be sold on a seat-only basis; offending airlines are heavily fined. The message is clear – budget travellers need not apply – and has been reiterated by stiff, repeated hikes in package **prices** since the early 1990s. Expect to pay £650–800 per person assuming double occupancy, flight inclusive, for a two-week high-season package in a three-star hotel (the lowest grade now marketed as a package), or up to £1000 for two weeks at a four-star hotel; £1300–1600 for a detached villa with pool, including a rental car; £600–800 for a more traditional village house with or without a pool, again with a car provided; and a minimum of £220 for a week in a self-catering "hotel-apartment" studio in a less desirable area. From Ireland, typical prices are €499–589 per person a week in a three/four-star hotel, flights included.

Peak season is reckoned as late June through late October, but each tour operator seems to have their own system of assessing this, and autumn departures in particular can be more expensive than spring or very early summer.

All brochures also heavily promote adjunct activities such as scuba diving, golf, wedding packages and (especially) 36-to-60-hour **cruises** to Egypt and/or Lebanon – you basically get a full day out in each country with the longer option. Except in high season when availability may be limited, it is almost always preferable (and cheaper) to arrange these after arrival in Cyprus. Sample per-person prices for a cruise to one country only start at £130, for both £200, and it's fun if you don't take it too seriously: cheesy floor-shows on board, plenty of drinking, whirlwind tours of the sights (and souvenir bazaars), with a retinue of numerous, persistent touts throughout.

Package prices in the **North** run about twenty percent lower than those in the South for broadly equivalent facilities, with somewhat less fluctuation between low- and high-season prices, and far less availability of "character" villas. Again, high season is nominally rated as early July to early October, but subject to individual agency quirks. Recent years have seen a spate of **"winter specials"**, whereby two weeks' half board, flight included, have been sold for £299 (or even less) per person on double occupancy basis, with sometimes a few days' car rental thrown in for good measure. Such offerings should be treated warily; at these prices, the hotels concerned have little incentive to provide service or decent meals, and you may find yourself, for example, without hot water for most of the day or confronting table d'hôte suppers that make airline meals seem gourmet in comparison. With a demonstrable oversupply of both hotels and restaurants in the North, there's absolutely no reason to tolerate shoddy service in either.

**Two-centre holidays** – a week in Turkey plus a week on Cyprus – are popular and heavily promoted, making a virtue of the necessity of stopping over in Turkey.

## Package operators

### General operators to the South

**Amathus Holidays** ☎0870 443 4388, ⓦwww.amathusholidays.co.uk. A good selection of properties all over the south, including a token selection in the mountains.

**Argo Holidays** ☎0870 066 7070 ⓦwww.argoholidays.com. Strictly top-end hotels at the major resorts, including the Tróödhos; designated consolidator for BA and Cyprus Airways.

**Cyplon Holidays** ☎020/8340 7612, ⓦwww.cyplon.com. More of a generalist for beach-resort accommodation, representing nearly every hotel of three stars and above.

**Libra Holidays** ☎0870 246 0446, ⓦwww.libraholidays.co.uk. Another generalist, which also includes self-catering, two-star properties. Has controlling interest in Helios Airways.

**Planet Holidays** ☎0870 066 0909, ⓦwww.planetholidays.net. Direct competitor to Argo, again with the poshest hotels in all coastal resorts.

### Specialist operators to the South

**Cyprus Villages** ☎01202/485 012, ⓦwww.cyprusvillages.com.cy. Accommodation in restored or traditionally built houses and flats in Tókhni, Kalavassós and several other villages across Larnaca, Limassol and Páfos districts; also hosts special interest courses.

**Sunvil Holidays** ☎020/8568 4499, ⓦwww.sunvil.co.uk. By far the best operator for quality villas and restored village houses throughout Páfos district – they're the exclusive reps for Laona Project properties in the UK – plus a few elsewhere. Also restored village inns and small hotels in the Tróodhos, fly-drives, yacht charter, plus selected larger hotels in most coastal resorts.

### General operators to the North

**Anatolian Sky Holidays** ☎0870 850 4040, ⓦwww.anatolian-sky.co.uk. Offering many of the better-quality bungalow complexes around Kyrenia, plus an almost unique selection of "private villas"; also two hotels in or near Famagusta. Best bet for a two-centre holiday, as they're established Turkey specialists.
**Cricketer Holidays** ☎01892/664242, ⓕ01892/662355. Limited but carefully chosen accommodation offerings in conjunction with special-interest tours (wildflowers, Crusader castles, etc).
**CTA Holidays** ☎0870 600 1123, ⓦwww.ctaholidays.com Subsidiary of Cyprus Turkish Airlines which represents (rather indiscriminately, you take your chances) about two-thirds of all the major holiday complexes around Kyrenia and Famagusta.
**Cyprus Paradise** ☎020/8343 8888, ⓦwww.cyprusparadise.co.uk. Easily the best range of hotels and self-contained resorts in and around Kyrenia, selected for proven customer service; expanding winter programme (about half of the 30 or so properties represented in summer).
**Green Island Holidays** ☎020/7637 7338, ⓦwww.greenislandholidays.com. Close competitor to the foregoing, with a broad mix of up-market and mid-range facilties around Kyrenia.

### Specialist operators to the North

**Interest and Activity Holidays** ☎020/8251 0208, ⓦwww.holidaywalking.co.uk & ⓦwww.scubaholiday.co.uk. Offers early spring, one-week tours with easy walking (mostly tracks) in the Kyrenia range; also scuba diving holidays all season.
**Ramblers Holidays** ☎01707/331133, ⓦwww.ramblersholidays.co.uk. Walking in the Kyrenia hills, 8–11 days in early spring and mid-autumn; also has a 15-day tour of southwestern Cyprus (ie in the South), spring and late autumn.

## Flights from North America

Because there are no direct flights between North America and any airport in Cyprus, you will find that fares found through a website or walk-in travel agencies will have at least one and (especially for Canada) as many as three stops on route. Searches are most usefully

directed towards Larnaca; entering the code for the North's airport at Ercan (ECN) on online booking sites will either draw a blank, or a ridiculous quote running to several thousand dollars.

**From the USA**, low season fares from the east coast (eg New York) to Larnaca run about $750, high season $950–1100; from the west coast (eg Los Angeles) it's $1050 and $1600 respectively. Low-season fares New York–İstanbul cost about $550, or $950–1000 in peak season, with another $100 or so set aside for the final leg to Ercan in northern Cyprus, which should preferably be purchased in İstanbul itself. From Los Angeles, the applicable fares are just over $700 low season, just under $1400 high season.

**From Canada**, fares out of Toronto to Larnaca range from just under C$2000 in low season to C$2650 in peak season. The substantial Cypriot community in western Canada gets little joy from tickets out of Vancouver pegged at C$2550 low season, C$3150 high season. Toronto–İstanbul runs C$800 in winter, C$1750 in winter, while Vancouver–İstanbul can be much the same all year (ca. C$2550), presumably owing to skiing traffic in British Columbia. Again, allow about C$250 for the final journey to Cyprus from İstanbul.

## Airlines

**Air Canada** ☎1-888/247-2262, ⓦwww.aircanada.com.
**Air France** US ☎1-800/237-2747, Canada ☎1-800/667-2747, ⓦwww.airfrance.com.
**Alitalia** US ☎1-800/223-5730, Canada ☎1-800/361-8336, ⓦwww.alitalia.com.
**American Airlines** ☎1-800/433-7300, ⓦwww.aa.com.
**British Airways** ☎1-800/AIRWAYS, ⓦwww.ba.com.
**Continental Airlines** domestic ☎1-800/523-FARE, international ☎1-800/231-0856, ⓦwww.continental.com.
**Cyprus Airways** ☎718/267-6882 (authorized agent, Kinisis Travel, New York).
**Delta Air Lines** domestic ☎1-800/221-1212, international ☎1-800/241-4141, ⓦwww.delta.com.
**Iberia** ☎1-800/772-4642, ⓦwww.iberia.com.
**Lufthansa** US ☎1-800/645-3880, Canada ☎1-800/563-5954, ⓦwww.lufthansa.com.

Northwest/KLM domestic ☎1-800/225-2525, international ☎1-800/447-4747. ⓦwww.nwa.com, ⓦwww.klm.com.
Olympic Airways ☎1-800/223-1226 or 718/896-7393, ⓦwww.olympicairlines.com.
Swiss ☎1-877 FLY-SWISS, ⓦwww.swiss.com.
Turkish Airlines ☎1-800/874-8875, ⓦwww.thy.com.
United Airlines domestic ☎1-800/241-6522, international ☎1-800/538-2929, ⓦwww.united.com.
Virgin Atlantic ☎1-800/862-8621, ⓦwww.virgin-atlantic.com.

## Flight and travel agents

Air Brokers International ☎1-800/883-3273 or 415/397-1383, ⓦwww.airbrokers.com. Consolidator and specialist in RTW tickets.
Airtech ☎212/219-7000, ⓦwww.airtech.com. Standby seat broker; also deals in consolidator fares.
Flightcentre US ☎1-866 WORLD-51, ⓦwww.flightcentre.us, Canada ☎1-888 WORLD-55, ⓦwww.flightcentre.ca. Rock-bottom fares worldwide.
TFI Tours ☎1-800/745-8000 or 212/736-1140, ⓦwww.lowestairprice.com. Consolidator with global fares.
Travel Avenue ☎1-800/333-3335, ⓦwww.travelavenue.com. Full-service travel agent that offers discounts in the form of rebates.
Travelers Advantage ☎1-877/259-2691, ⓦwww.travelersadvantage.com. Discount travel club, with cashback deals and discounted car rental. Membership required.
Travelosophy US ☎1-800/332-2687, ⓦwww.itravelosophy.com. Good range of discounted and student fares worldwide.

## Specialist agent

Amelia International Tours ☎1-800/742 4591, ⓦwww.ameliainternational.com. Mediterranean specialist agency with a small south Cyprus programme – specifically an overpriced, one-week, Limassol-based package or a 13-day tour, paired with six days in Malta.

# Flights from Australia & New Zealand

Because of the way Australians and New Zealanders travel, most fares quoted by travel agents or booking websites will be valid for either six months or a year. One cost-effective strategy may be to get to Athens, İstanbul or London, and purchase an "add-on" fare from there; this depends, however, on the deals being offered at the time for through fares to Cyprus – for the South in particular this may not be necessary, with direct flights to Larnaca via the Middle East.

From Australia the shortest Sydney–Larnaca services are on Alitalia via Milan, Emirates via Dubai, and Egyptair via Cairo. The cheapest fares vary by season, but might be anything from just under A$2000 with Gulf Air (2 stops via Singapore and Bahrain), around A$2200 with Emirates via Dubai, or A$2300 with Cathay Pacific and BA via Hong Kong and London. Since the barriers came down it's no longer strictly necessary to fly into the North, and, as in the case of North America, 'ECN' (the code for the North's airport at Ercan) will either not be recognized by travel websites or some crazy amount will be quoted. For the record, you'll pay somewhere between A$1750 and A$2200 to get to İstanbul, probably on Emirates, and will have to budget another A$250 or so for an onward flight to Ercan.

From New Zealand, the best fares again tend to be two-stop relays on Emirates, with prices ranging NZ$1900–2600 depending on season.

## Airlines

Air New Zealand Australia ☎13 24 76, ⓦwww.airnz.com.au, New Zealand ☎0800 737 000, ⓦwww.airnz.co.nz.
Alitalia Australia ☎02/9244 2445, New Zealand ☎09/308 3357, ⓦwww.alitalia.com.
British Airways Australia ☎1300 767 177, New Zealand ☎0800 274 847, ⓦwww.ba.com.
Egyptair Australia ☎02/9241 5696, ⓦwww.egyptair.com.eg.
Emirates Australia ☎1300 303 777 or 02/9290 9700, New Zealand ☎09/377 6004, ⓦwww.emirates.com.
Gulf Air Australia ☎02/9244 2199, New Zealand ☎09/308 3366, ⓦwww.gulfairco.com.
Lufthansa Australia ☎1300 655 727, New Zealand ☎0800 945 220, ⓦwww.lufthansa.com.
Qantas Australia ☎13 13 13, New Zealand ☎0800 808 767 or 09/357 8900, ⓦwww.qantas.com.
Singapore Airlines Australia ☎13 10 11, New Zealand ☎0800 808 909, ⓦwww.singaporeair.com.
Thai Airways Australia ☎1300 651 960, New Zealand ☎09/377 3886, ⓦwww.thaiair.com.

Turkish Airlines Australia ☎ 02/9299 8400,
ⓦ www.thy.com.

### Flight and travel agents

Flight Centre Australia ☎ 13 31 33, ⓦ www
.flightcentre.com.au, New Zealand ☎ 0800 243
544, ⓦ www.flightcentre.co.nz.
STA Travel Australia ☎ 1300 733 035, New
Zealand ☎ 0508/782 872, ⓦ www.statravel.com.
Student Uni Travel Australia ☎ 02/9232 8444,
ⓦ www.sut.com.au, New Zealand ☎ 09/379 4224,
ⓦ www.sut.co.nz.
Trailfinders Australia ☎ 02/9247 7666, ⓦ www
.trailfinders.com.au.

### Specialist agent

Sun Island Tours Sydney ☎ 02/9283 3840,
ⓦ www.sunislandtours.com.au. Fly-drives, lots of
hotels for the major resorts, cruises beginning and
ending on the island.

## Flights from neighbouring countries

**Larnaca** in the South has air connections from most neighbouring countries, with flights on Cyprus Airways from Amman (at least 2 weekly year-round), Athens (3–4 daily all year), Beirut (daily), Cairo (at least 2 weekly year-round), Damascus (3 weekly), Iráklio, Crete (3 weekly, March–Oct only), Rhodes (2 weekly, March–Oct only) and Tel Aviv (daily in summer, 4 weekly in winter). Olympic Airways also flies into Larnaca from Athens four times daily most of the year (and from Thessaloníki 4 times weekly), while Aegean Air does 5 daily flights from Athens (some code-shared with Helios Airways). Helios will also soon provide a few weekly services from Hánia, Crete to Larnaca. Royal Jordanian, El Al and Egyptair contribute a couple of flights each, weekly, from Amman, Tel Aviv and Cairo respectively. **Páfos** is also served from Athens by Cyprus Airways (2 weekly in summer, 1 weekly in winter), for the same price as Larnaca (the two airports are common-rated). It's worth asking for student discounts if eligible; otherwise, you'll pay a somewhat overpriced €170 return from Athens, the longest haul in.

Flying **from Turkey to the North**, you can choose from a number of routes, though be aware that all of these can be fully booked far in advance at weekends.

Cyprus Turkish Airways flies in from Adana (3 weekly), Ankara (daily), Antalya (1–3 daily), İstanbul (3 daily) and İzmir (1–3 daily except Wed). Turkish Airlines offers a daily evening service (plus an extra later flight Fri & Sun) from İstanbul year-round – more for political than economic reasons, as it can't be profitable. Return fares from İstanbul to the North are periodically offloaded for as little as £53/\$100 round trip – if you don't have a car, this is a far better option than the ferry from southern Turkey (see below).

## By boat to the North

Despite the fact that Cyprus is an island, sailing there on scheduled ferry services (as opposed to a short cruise) is not a popular option. Only the North receives passenger services, and since only Turkey recognizes the Turkish Republic of Northern Cyprus, these leave from one of three **Turkish ports**: Taşucu, Mersin and Alanya. Fares, currently subsidized by the Turkish government, are relatively reasonable. This may change, of course, in the wake of any peace settlement, with unrestricted movement to the South for foreigners and a sharp hike in ferry tariffs equally likely. Sample figures below are converted from the Turkish lira and are intended only as guidelines.

### Shipping companies, routes and fares

**Mersin–Famagusta** is the most reliable and weather-proof crossing owing to the large size of the ships on line, and is favoured by many local residents even though it's longer and more expensive than the trip via Kyrenía (see below). The only company on this route is the Turkish state-run TML, represented by KTDI in Famagusta; departures from Mersin take place on Tuesday, Thursday and Sunday evenings, returning from Famagusta the next day after a ten-hour journey. There's only one class of passenger fare, at around £36 equivalent each way in pullman seats; transporting a car costs much the same.

**Taşucu–Kyrenia** looks temptingly short on a map but the standard of car ferries in particular can be pretty poor (they've historically been demoted from more profitable lines in western Turkey). Nominal crossing time for conventional boats is claimed to be four hours, but effectively five hours, sometimes stretching to six or seven owing to storms in the straits, Turkish navy manoeuvres, malfunctioning engines and the working hours of the Kyrenia customs (captains are fined for docking before opening time). The more attractive alternative for the carless is a **catamaran** (*deniz otobüsü* in Turkish), whose reported two-hour crossing time is more realistically three hours.

There are currently just two **companies** serving this route, each with a conventional ferryboat carrying vehicles, and a catamaran or two. Fergün's ferry leaves Taşucu daily at midnight, arriving in Kyrenia the next morning, returning at noon. During low season, the Friday and Saturday crossing from Taşucu may be missed out. By contrast, their "Express" catamaran (foot passengers only) leaves Taşucu every day at the nominal time of 11.30am, having first crossed from Kyrenia at 9.30am, plus there are two weekly midday departures from Alanya. Akfer's ferry sails daily at midnight from Taşucu, returning at 11am from Kyrenia; their catamaran follows much the same schedule as the competition, and additionally there are three weekly noon departures from Alanya (3hr claimed, best allow 4hr).

**Prices** charged by each company, including taxes, are virtually identical for each class of craft. One-way passenger fares on car-ferries run to about £22, though there are significant discounts for return trips or student status. A medium-sized car costs £37 to ferry, campers £45, again with a substantial return discount. Express catamarans from Taşucu cost £24 one way, £34 return, full fare; from Alanya, £22/£33.

## Shipping line agents

**Akfer Shipping**
Taşucu ☎ 324/741 4033
Alanya ☎ 242/512 8889

**Fergün Shipping**
Taşucu ☎ 324/741 2323
Alanya ☎ 242/511 5565
ⓦ www.fergun.net

**Turkish Maritime Lines**
ⓦ www.tdi.com.tr

# Moving between the North and the South

Since April 23, 2003, when the Turkish Cypriot authorities opened various barred roads along the Green and Attila Lines without any notice, it has become possible for most individuals to **cross between the two sectors** of Cyprus with little formality. All you need are a valid passport and (if you're bringing your own car) a certain amount of cash in hand to pay for supplementary insurance (see p.51).

At first the authorities on both sides attempted to enforce "Cinderella" rules by which people had to return to "their" side by midnight – but this was quickly dropped in the face of massive civil disobedience, and the realization that such strictures were pretty much unenforceable (though in theory Greek Cypriots are still limited to five days at a time in the North). It is now commonplace for Greek Cypriots to take weekend breaks in the North, and (to a lesser extent, owing to economic realities) Turkish Cypriots to stay over in the South.

Although the Republic of Cyprus continues to describe Ercan airport, Kyrenia harbour and Famagusta harbour as "illegal ports of entry", under EU rules there is in fact nothing they can (or will) do to **EU nationals** who land in the North and then head to the South – certainly on foot or by taxi; driving one's own foreign-registered car could prove trickier, and entry in a hire car with northern plates is not (yet) allowed, though ordinary northern Cypriot cars are allowed South. **Non-EU citizens** attempting the same could be given a hard time, up to and including denial of entry or deportation depending on where they are detected, but we've yet to hear of any instances of this.

With the new freedom of movement, many people fly into Larnaca, pay a round-trip taxi fare to Kyrenia or Famagusta, then fly out again at the conclusion of their holiday in the North; they reckon this worth it for the greater choice of flights and reduced flying time, though in fact they save little money once the taxi fare is figured in. Conversely, travel agents in the North openly sell tickets out of Larnaca to all comers.

At time of writing there are four legal **crossing points between the North and**

**South**: Ledra Palace (pedestrians only), Áyios Dhométios, Pýla/Beyarmudu and the Four-Mile Crossing through SBA territory, between Famagusta and Xylotýmvou. Eight more have been proposed, at least some of which are likely to open during the lifetime of this edition, despite wrangling between North and South over details. From west to east, they are: Pakhýammos–Káto Pýrgos direct via the Kókkina enclave coast road, Káto Pýrgos–Gemikonağı (Karavóstasi), Astromerítis–Güzelyurt (Mórfou), Leofóros Athinás–Áyios Kassianós in Nicosia, Ledra Street–Girne Caddesi (pedestrians only), again in Nicosia, Leofóros Kantáras–Mía Mília in the northeast of Nicosia, Dháli–Akıncılar (Louroujína), and Dherínia–Famagusta.

Although Turkey has yet to recognize the Republic of Cyprus, since May 2003, **Republic of Cyprus passport holders** have been allowed to travel there provided they first get a visa at the Turkish embassy in north Nicosia. There's the rather notorious case of a Greek-Cypriot man who went to İstanbul on a weekend break, flying on KTHY out of Ercan. He was prosecuted by his own authorities for using an "illegal" airport upon his return; a conviction was duly obtained, and a fine imposed, but never enforced as the gentleman in question threatened recourse to the EU Court of Human Rights in Strasbourg, where he'd surely win his case – and compensation. Since then other EU nationals have imitated him.

# Red tape and visas

Most foreign nationals require only a valid passport for entry into either the southern or northern sectors of Cyprus. Canadian, New Zealand, Australian and US nationals do not require a visa for either half of the island, and get a three-month tourist-visa stamp in passports upon arrival. EU nationals no longer have their passports stamped upon arrival in the South at either of the two airports.

The **southern Republic** has long declared all seaports and airports in the North "prohibited ports of entry and exit", but since the Republic joined the EU in May 2004 there is in fact nothing they can do to stop EU nationals entering the South if they've entered the North first (see our fuller remarks in the preceding section, "Moving Between the North and the South").

Upon **arrival in the North**, however, whether at a seaport, airport or land-crossing, it is still customary for a free visa to be stamped on a separate, loose slip of paper. Most Turkish-Cypriot officials speak good English but, if in doubt, the Turkish for "On a loose sheet, please" is *Lütfen gevşek kağıtda*. Staff at Ercan airport are used to such requests and keep a stack of loose visa slips handy.

The other potential sticking point on entry to the South is the ban on any imported **perishables**; eat those apples on the plane in, or the customs officers will eat them for you. However, the previous ban on bringing in produce from the North is set to be substantially relaxed. Additionally, when transitting from the North to the South, you are at present **limited** to €135 worth of gifts and personal purchases, 400 cigarettes and a litre of spirits. Car boots will be opened and inspected at the Áyios Dhométios crossing by Cypriot customs officials, and at Pýla/Beyarmudu or the Four-Mile Crossing by SBA police deputizing for the Republic. As a reciprocal measure, the Northern authorities announced in February 2005 low limits on the value of routine shopping that Northern residents could bring back from trips to the South.

# Health

In general, you're unlikely to experience any problems in Cyprus other than a spell of constipation brought on by initial contact with potentially stodgy food. Water is fit to drink almost everywhere except Famagusta and its environs (where the sea has invaded well bore-holes), though not always so tasty; bottled water is widely available. No inoculations are required for any part of Cyprus, though as ever it's wise to keep your tetanus booster up to date.

## Health hazards

Most routine threats to your health have to do with overexposure, the sea and flying insects. To avoid the danger of **sunstroke** wear a hat and drink plenty of fluids during the hot months. **Jellyfish** are rare, **sea urchins** more common. If you are unlucky enough to tread on, or graze, one of the latter, a sterilized sewing needle, scalpel and olive oil are effective aids to removing spines; left unextracted, they will fester. A pair of swim goggles and footwear for walking over tidal rocks should help you avoid both. In sandy-bottomed bays, **rays** and **skates** are fairly common; they have a barbed tail which is capable of inflicting nasty wounds with one swat. When entering such waters, make a bit of commotion so as to send on their way these creatures who have a habit of burrowing in the sand, with just the eyes visible.

In terms of dry-land beasties, there are **scorpions** about – tap out your shoes in the morning – and one stubby, mottled species of **viper**; antivenins for it are available at local pharmacies. Those enormous, two-metre-long black **whip** or **Montpellier snakes** which you'll see on the road are usually harmless to humans, and were in fact imported by the British to hunt both rodents and other venomous serpents. **Mosquitos** (*kounoúpia* in Greek, *sivrisinek* in Turkish) can be troublesome in summer, especially between Famagusta and the Karpaz (Kárpas) peninsula; solutions offered by hotels include pyrethrum incense coils, electrified vapour pads, and air-conditioned rooms with closed windows. In the South, insect-repellent-vaporizing units with a 30ml refill bottle on the bottom (eg, Aroxol brand) are popular and effective, allowing you to sleep with the windows ajar on hot nights. **Sand flies** are almost invisible, but their bites pack a punch, and itch nearly as badly as mossies – insect repellent is the answer.

There are few stray animals on Cyprus and thus (uniquely for this part of the world) **rabies** is not much of a danger. Indeed one of the few things the Greek- and Turkish-Cypriot communities agreed on before 1974 was to round up and put down most stray dogs, since many carried **echinococcosis**, a debilitating liver fluke which could spread to humans. Adherence to the practice is laxer now in the North, but overall the canine population is still not up to previous levels.

## Medical attention

The standard of health care is relatively high in Cyprus, with many English-speaking and -trained doctors; indeed provision of health care to residents of surrounding Middle Eastern nations has recently become a highly successful hard-currency earner. The fancier hotels can generally recommend local practitioners, and may even post lists of them. General **hospitals** in both sectors of the island have walk-in casualty wards where foreigners can have cuts sewn up and broken bones set at no cost.

**Minor ailments** can be dealt with at **chemists** (*farmakío* in Greek, *eczane* in Turkish); pharmacists are well trained and can often dispense medicines which in Britain would only be available on prescription. In the South, you can dial the operator on ☎192 to ask for the rota of night-duty chemists (and see contact list below); in both North and South, this is also published regularly in the English-language newspapers.

### Night-duty chemists

Nicosia district ☎ 1412
Limassol district ☎ 1415

# Insurance

The southern Republic at least is now an EU member, which means provision of public health care to other EU nationals on the same basis as locals upon presentation of Form E111 (or the "smart card" which will eventually supersede it). The surplus of doctors drives down private clinic consultation fees to about C£12, and virtually halves the cost of even fairly major surgical procedures compared to northern Europe or the US. All that said, it's still essential to take out some form of travel insurance.

Just about any travel agent, bank or insurance broker will sell you comprehensive cover, which includes not only medical expenses but also loss or theft of belongings. Rough Guides offers its own insurance policy, details of which are given in the box below.

If you intend to rent an off-road vehicle or motorbike, or engage in **special activities** such as parasailing, bungee-jumping, horse-riding or scuba-diving, you may need a more specialized policy: be sure to check with your insurers when getting cover.

When taking out medical coverage, ascertain whether benefits will be paid as treatment proceeds or only after return home, whether there is a **24-hour medical emergency number**, and how much the deductible is (sometimes negotiable). When securing baggage cover, make sure that the **per-article limit** – typically well under £500 in the UK – will cover your most valuable possession. Otherwise, it may have to be claimed on using your household effects policy (if any).

If you have anything stolen, go to the nearest police station, report the theft and get a copy

---

### Rough Guides travel insurance

**Rough Guides Ltd** offers a low-cost travel insurance policy, especially customized for our statistically low-risk readers by a leading British broker, provided by the American International Group (AIG) and registered with the British regulatory body, GISC (the General Insurance Standards Council). There are five main Rough Guides insurance plans: No-Frills for the bare minimum for secure travel; Essential, which provides decent all-round cover; Premier for comprehensive cover with a wide range of benefits; Extended Stay for cover lasting four months to a year; and Annual multi-trip, a cost-effective way of getting Premier cover if you travel more than once a year. Premier, Annual Multi-Trip and Extended Stay policies can be supplemented by a "Hazardous Pursuits Extension" if you plan to indulge in sports considered dangerous, such as scuba-diving or trekking. For a policy quote, call the Rough Guides Insurance Line: toll-free in the UK ☎ 0800/015 0906 or +44 1392 314 665 from elsewhere. Alternatively, get an online quote at ⓦ www.roughguides.com/insurance

of the report or the identification number under which it has been filed: you will need this when **making a claim** back home. Incidentally, following a rash of fraudulent claims, the police in the South are extra-vigilant for funny business, and will prosecute offenders.

# Information, maps and websites

Before leaving home it's worth stopping in at the tourist office of whichever part of Cyprus you intend to visit, since their stock of brochures and maps is invariably better than what's to be found once you're on the island. The Cyprus Tourism Organisation (CTO, ⓦwww.visitcyprus.org.cy) of the internationally recognized Republic of Cyprus (the South), with longer experience of such things, not surprisingly showers you with an avalanche of professionally presented and often useful material on every conceivable topic; the North Cyprus Tourist Office's offerings (ⓦwww.go-northcyprus.com), while both less slick and far less substantial, are recommended mainly because they include the only existing town plans with current Turkified street names.

## Useful free publications: South

Among **CTO titles** to look out for are the *Guide to Hotels and Other Tourist Establishments*, a massive but often elusive compendium of virtually every licensed hotel and hotel-apartment in the South, plus travel agencies and car-rental firms, supposedly published each March but often delayed; *Agrotourism: Traditional Holiday Homes*, for restored, high-standard houses in the interior; *Cyprus, 10,000 Years of History and Civilisation*, summarizing points of interest; the not necessarily annual *Cyprus Travellers Handbook*, containing nuts-and-bolts facts, rules, handy addresses and fairly up-to-date site and museum opening hours; a *List of Events*, a yearly calendar of festivals and cultural manifestations which may be supplemented by a more current and detailed monthly cyclostyle available in Cyprus; and *Domestic Transport Services*, a complete tally of bus and taxi schedules and fares between the major towns and resorts, appearing in theory each May.

The CTO has **tourist offices** in the Republic of Cyprus at Nicosia, Limassol, Larnaca, Páfos, Ayía Nápa, and (April–Oct) Plátres.

Hours are typically Monday to Friday 8.15am to 2.30pm, plus Monday, Tuesday, Thursday and Friday 3 to 6.15pm, and Saturday 8.15am to 1.30pm, with small local variations; exact addresses and schedules are given in the text.

## Useful free publications: North

Essential **North Cyprus publications** include some sort of folding map, which in addition to being a free printed source showing all villages as renamed in North Cyprus, also indicates most of the southern villages from which the refugee Turkish Cypriots came. There's also either the annual *Guide to Hotels and Other Tourist Services*, or (when it's produced) the smaller *Pocket Tourist Guide*, each of which profile all licensed hotels, as well as including bits of other useful information. At the time of writing no detailed city plans for Girne, Lefkoşa and Gazimağusa, as Kyrenia, Nicosia and Famagusta are called in Turkish, were available.

North Cypriot **tourist offices** are found only in Kyrenia, Famagusta, Nicosia and (seasonally) Yenierenköy; theoretical hours are given in the *Guide* but, especially during the off-season, they are often shut when they shouldn't be. If you want to take advantage of the North Cyprus Tourist Office's services, it's essential to call at their closest overseas branch before departure.

## Cyprus tourism offices abroad

### The Republic of Cyprus

**UK** CTO, 17 Hanover St, London W1S 1YP ☎020/7569 8800, ⓕ7499 4935
**USA** CTO, 13 East 40th St, New York, NY 10016 ☎212/683-5280, ⓕ683-5282, ⓔgocyprus@aol.com.
**Netherlands** Cyprus Verkeersbureau, Prinsengracht 600, 1017 KS Amsterdam ☎020/624 4358, ⓕ638 3369, ⓔcyprus.sun@wxs.nl.
**Sweden** Cypriotiska Statens Turistbyrå, Birger Jarlsgatan 37, 11145 Stockholm ☎08/105025, ⓕ106414, ⓔcypern@telia.com.

### North Cyprus

**UK** North Cyprus Tourist Office, 29 Bedford Square, London WC1B 3EG ☎020/7631 1930, ⓔinfo.uk@holidayinnorthcyprus.com.
**USA** 821 United Nations Plaza, 6th Floor, New York, NY 10017 ☎212/687 2350; 1667 K Street, Suite 590, Washington DC 20006 ☎202/887-6198, ⓕ467-0685, ⓔinfo@rncwashdc.org.

## Cyprus on the internet

With the exception of a few good sites under "General and bicommunal", the division of Cyprus is reflected as starkly in its presence on the internet as in its print and broadcast media (see p.68), with many websites propagandizing (subtly or otherwise) on behalf of one side or the other. North Cyprus has no country code of its own; anything with the suffix 'cy' is based in the South.

## The South

ⓦ**www.kypros.org** aka Kypros-Net; news, weather, exchange rates, on-line Greek lessons, and TV/radio listings from the southern Republic.
ⓦ**www.pio.gov.cy** The official web page of the southern Republic, maintained by the Public Information Office; essentially the utterances, and comings and goings, of officialdom.
ⓦ**www.cyprus-mail.com** The online version of the South's longest established English-language paper.
ⓦ**www.cyprusweekly.com.cy** As above, for the competing weekly newspaper; very slow-loading.

## The North

ⓦ**www.trncwashdc.org** The official voice of the North, though US-originated and maintained; with good general information and news.
ⓦ**www.hamamboculeri.org** The main opposition on-line forum in the North, with links to *Afrika* newspaper and articles in English and Turkish.

## General and bicommunal

**http://www.aegeantimes.net/** An excellent, Greek, Cypriot and Turkish-coordinated digest of current Cyprus-, Greece- and Turkey-related stories, some of them truly bizarre, from around the world. You have to register to post comments on the often-bruising discussion forum (not for the thin-skinned).
ⓦ**www.cyprusmedianet.com/EN/** Translated digest of all interesting press articles published across the island. Unfortunately, coverage stopped in January 2005 when the site lost its UN/US funding – hope for it to come back.
ⓦ**www.cia.gov/cia/publications/factbook/geos/cy.html** The online CIA World Factbook, with statistical information on the geography, population, economy and political situation of both halves of the island; though much improved in recent years, many of the "facts" are still one to three years old (perhaps that's why US policy on the island is usually in a muddle).
ⓦ**www.peace-cyprus.org** A hopeful, bicommunal site striving for reconciliation.

## Maps – and place-name problems

There are vast numbers of complimentary and commercial maps available for Cyprus, but no single one is entirely satisfactory and most handle the fact of the island's division awkwardly.

## Road maps

It's wisest to get an overall touring map of the island before leaving home, since most of the better ones are banned for sale in the South for political reasons. The best **small-scale road map** is the **Mairs** (formerly Marco Polo/Shell) 1:200,000 folding map, which alone of currently available commercial products shows all paved (and many unpaved) roads accurately, including the South's motorway system. There are two similarly priced products at the same scale; you want the one which cites both

Turkish and Greek names for places in the North, and gives Greek lettering (but no stress accents) plus "official" transliteration for spots in the South. It is also one of the very few commercial maps to depict the buffer zone (see below) accurately, but has no town plans on the verso. Pretty much as good as this is the **Freytag and Berndt** product at 1:250,000, which shows the motorways fairly accurately, Turkish names in the north and Greek script with accents, with the lesser road network up to 2002 currency. A possible alternative to these is **Rough Guides'** rip-proof, waterproof map at 1:250,000; while it has Turkish place-names in the North and Greek script in the South, plus the buffer zone shown correctly, the motorway network is obsolete and the originally German cartography is excessively cluttered. The official *Survey of Cyprus Administration & Road Map* (1:250,000) dates from 1984, and employs the old transliteration system, but it does show contours, district boundaries and the ethnic composition of each village on Independence; road tracings are fairly accurate, though in many cases surfaces have been improved in the interim. A post-1995 version should be available in the South, but is currently out of stock in the UK. None of the other currently in-print products is worth serious consideration.

For detailed **town plans**, the **Selas** series, locally sold in the South, are the most accurate available for Limassol, Nicosia, Páfos and Larnaca (though annoyingly no scales are provided). Their countrywide sheet at 1:250,000 lacks detail and is only adequate for journeys on major roads.

The CTO gives out a number of **free maps**: *A Visitor's Map of Cyprus*, the entire island at 1:400,000; Nicosia city centre and suburbs; Limassol town and environs; Larnaca town and environs; Ayía Nápa and environs; Paralímni and Protarás; Páfos and environs; and the Tróödhos. Most of these are reasonably current and accurate, especially the Larnaca, Nicosia and Páfos sheets, though Limassol and the Tróödhos are showing their age. The island-wide map dates from the early 1990s, and fails to show the current motorway system.

## Topographical maps

Unless you plan to do some hard-core, cross-country exploration, the walking maps in this book are adequate to take you around safely. Otherwise, **topographical maps** are prepared in the South by the Department of Lands and Surveys. Availability of the 1:25,000 series from 1982 seems to depend on your face and how the folk responsible are feeling that day, and obtainable (if at all) only through special petition directly to the DLS in south Nicosia (corner Alásias and Dhimofóndon streets, ☎2230 4120). However, the 1:25,000 issue from 1969 is still on sale in the Republic of Cyprus – albeit featuring dense, highly coloured cartography, and Roman-alphabet lettering in the pre-1995 transliteration scheme (see pp.42–43). Also accessible, curiously, is the 1981 series at 1:5,000, covering the entire island in 59 sheets and a joy to behold, though much more practical for archeology and geology than hiking. At present, none of these maps is sold abroad. More easily found, both in the South and overseas, is the 1:100,000 DLS 18 series, last revised in 1997, which covers the whole island in four sheets, or the K717 series at 1:50,000, covering the island in forty sheets but unavailable overseas (and possibly, depending on security jitters, in the South). Each of these series should cost about C£5 per sheet.

Not surprisingly, the Turkish military occupying the North do not make available to the public anything they have prepared.

## Problems with boundaries

Most existing island-wide maps have limitations to usefulness owing to international non-recognition of the **Turkish Republic of Northern Cyprus** (TRNC) and poor documentation of the **Attila/Green Line**, the ceasefire line marking the Turkish Army's furthest advance in August 1974, and the attendant **buffer zone** just beyond it. This zone, also called the "dead zone" or No-Man's Land, is off-limits to everyone except UN personnel and local farmers, and varies in width from a few paces in Nicosia to a few kilometres at the old Nicosia airport and the Nicosia–Larnaca expressway. Greek-Cypriot depictions of the "border" tend to be optimistic, placing it at the limit of the Turkish advance rather than at the southern Republic's edge of the buffer zone. All chapter maps in this guide show the correct extent of the buffer zone, into which you should not venture unless (as at Pýla) specifically allowed or invited to do so by people in authority – despite a recent mine-clearing programme begun since April 2003, there are still plenty of "live" fields laid by both the Turkish Army and the Cypriot National Guard.

## Map outlets

### In the UK and Ireland

**Stanfords** 12–14 Long Acre, London WC2E 9LP ⌕020/7836 1321, ⍟www.stanfords.co.uk. Also at 39 Spring Gardens, Manchester ⌕0161/831 0250, and 29 Corn St, Bristol ⌕0117/929 9966.
**Blackwell's Map Centre** 50 Broad St, Oxford OX1 3BQ ⌕01865/793 550, ⍟www.maps.blackwell .co.uk. Branches in Bristol, Cambridge, Cardiff, Leeds, Liverpool, Newcastle, Reading and Sheffield.
**The Map Shop** 30a Belvoir St, Leicester LE1 6QH ⌕0116/247 1400, ⍟www.mapshopleicester .co.uk.
**National Map Centre** 22–24 Caxton St, London SW1H 0QU ⌕020/7222 2466, ⍟www.mapsnmc .co.uk.
**National Map Centre Ireland** 34 Aungier St, Dublin ⌕01/476 0471, ⍟www.mapcentre.ie.
**The Travel Bookshop** 13–15 Blenheim Crescent, London W11 2EE ⌕020/7229 5260, ⍟www .thetravelbookshop.co.uk.
**Traveller** 55 Grey St, Newcastle-upon-Tyne NE1 6EF ⌕0191/261 5622, ⍟www.newtraveller.com.

### In the US and Canada

**110 North Latitude** US ⌕336/369-4171, ⍟www.110nlatitude.com.
**Book Passage** 51 Tamal Vista Blvd, Corte Madera, CA 94925 and in the San Francisco Ferry Building ⌕1-800/999-7909 or ⌕415/927-0960, ⍟www .bookpassage.com.
**Distant Lands** 56 S Raymond Ave, Pasadena, CA 91105 ⌕1-800/310-3220, ⍟www.distantlands .com.
**Globe Corner Bookstore** 28 Church St, Cambridge, MA 02138 ⌕1-800/358-6013, ⍟www.globecorner.com.
**Longitude Books** 115 W 30th St #1206, New York, NY 10001 ⌕1-800/342-2164, ⍟www.longitudebooks.com.

**Map Town** 400 5 Ave SW #100, Calgary, AB, T2P 0L6 ⌕1-877/921-6277 or ⌕403/266-2241, ⍟www.maptown.com.
**Travel Bug Bookstore** 3065 W Broadway, Vancouver, BC, V6K 2G9 ⌕604/737-1122, ⍟www.travelbugbooks.ca.
**World of Maps** 1235 Wellington St, Ottawa, ON, K1Y 3A3 ⌕1-800/214-8524 or ⌕613/724-6776, ⍟www.worldofmaps.com.

### In Australia and New Zealand

**Map Centre** ⍟www.mapcentre.co.nz.
**Mapland (Australia)** 372 Little Bourke St, Melbourne ⌕03/9670 4383, ⍟www.mapland .com.au.
**Map Shop (Australia)** 6–10 Peel St, Adelaide ⌕08/8231 2033, ⍟www.mapshop.net.au.
**Map World (Australia)** 371 Pitt St, Sydney ⌕02/9261 3601, ⍟www.mapworld.net.au. Also at 900 Hay St, Perth ⌕08/9322 5733, Jolimont Centre, Canberra ⌕02/6230 4097 and 1981 Logan Road, Brisbane ⌕07/3349 6633.
**Map World (New Zealand)** 173 Gloucester St, Christchurch ⌕0800/627 967, ⍟www.mapworld .co.nz.

## Place names in the North

A major problem in the North is that all available maps except the TRNC's tourist handouts, and the Mairs, Freytag and Berndt or Rough Guides commercial products, continue to show **only Greek place names** in the North as it existed pre-1974, despite the fact that all Greek signposts have long since vanished there. The southern Republic considers this Turkification just one aspect of the "cultural vandalism and falsification of history", as they put it, which has taken place in the North since 1974. Even the Turkish Cypriots in the North, whether native or resettled refugees, are often nonplussed by the official village names imposed on them, since virtually every place had a Turkish form from Ottoman times – often phonetically related to the Greek rendition – which is still used conversationally in preference to the often clumsy official name. Only certain villages and towns which had always had Turkish names were exempted from the Turkification campaign.

In "The North" section of **this guide**, first the "new" name as it appears on road signs is cited, followed by the pre-1974 Greek name and finally (if known) any

## International English forms

Throughout the book the **internationally accepted forms** for five of the six largest towns – Nicosia, Limassol, Larnaca, Famagusta and Kyrenia – are used in preference to the official vernacular renditions, which are given just once for reference at the beginning of accounts.

Ottoman Turkish names in brackets. Maps also show first the post-1974 name, and then the internationally recognized name in brackets immediately following. Our use of this convention is intended to help readers find their way about, and should not be construed as an endorsement of the North's official nomenclature.

## Place names in the South

As in the North, so in the South: the orthography of place names has in recent years become hostage to ethno-political correctness. Considerable dismay was prompted, both on Cyprus and abroad, by the sudden and arbitrary introduction in late 1994 of a new nomenclature and transliteration system for all place names in the South. Despite the misgivings of Mayor Lelos Demetriades, the name "Nicosia" was officially abolished by a vote of councillors, to be replaced by Lefkosía even in English literature; those concerned believed that Nicosia was a colonial imposition of the British, though in fact the word dates back to Lusignan times. Similarly, Larnaca officially became Lárnaka on tourist bumph, Limassol woke up to Lemesós, and Paphos ended up as Páfos (the only instance this book conforms to, to distinguish it from ancient Paphos). Street names were also re-transliterated, wholesale, and in many cases renamed after EOKA heroes; political correctness truly disappeared up its own backside with such Roman-alphabet street-sign renditions as "Tzon Kenenty" and "Fragklinou Rousvelt". Even Cypriot personal names were affected,

with individuals being effectively commanded to change the Roman-alphabet spellings of a lifetime to the new "legal" forms (eg, Yiannis to Giannis). The changeover was largely the work of two Helleno-fanatic incumbents in the Ministry of Education and Culture, convinced of the manifest inferiority of Cypriot dialect compared to that of "Mother Greece", though Cypriot is arguably more venerable and truly "Greek" in retaining extensive vocabulary and pronunciation apparently unchanged since ancient times. It seems further ironic that the South's government should, on the one hand, castigate the North for its forcible name-changes, and then engage in a similar mutilation of cultural heritage on its own turf.

Barring a major political upheaval (or some clause of whatever federal settlement occurs), the new system is here to stay. But most foreign residents and native islanders alike remain strongly opposed to the new rules, not least because the old system gives non-Greek speakers a reasonably phonetic rendition of the local-dialect pronunciation. Organizations opting out of the new scheme include most UK tour operators, Friends of the Earth, the Laona Project, most wildlife conservation bodies, most foreign archeologists (who continue to produce works in the old scheme), listings mags *Time Out Cyprus* and *What's On*, the *Cyprus Mail*, most estate agents, as well as several municipalities. Latchí refused to be rechristened Lakki, but had to settle for Latsi; the Nicosia borough of Eylenjá ("too obviously Turkish", they were told) wasn't having Aglangeia, but as a concession only got 'Aglantzia' in brackets after the "official" signposting.

In this book, we place the **new forms in brackets following the old form, where different** (they aren't always). In the box-tables at the end of each of the first five chapters of the Guide, you will find the old phonetic rendition, accented; next the new "official" Latin-alphabet version; and finally the unaccented upper-case Greek-alphabet version as it appears on town-limits and highway signs.

# Money and banks

Unusually among travel destinations, Cyprus's low crime rate – South and North – and British affiliations make pound-sterling notes or plastic far preferable to travellers' cheques as a way of carrying your money. In general the Southern banking system is far more efficient, but by way of compensation you can pay for almost anything in the North directly with foreign cash.

## The South

The currency of the southern Republic of Cyprus is the **Cyprus pound** (C£), which though not traded internationally is a fairly strong, stable currency with a current unit value equal to roughly £1.20 sterling or US$2.25. The euro is supposed to be introduced at some point before 2008, but as yet no fixed conversion rate has been announced.

The Cyprus pound is divided into 100 cents (*sent*, singular or plural, in Cypriot Greek): there are coins of 1, 2, 5, 10, 20 and 50 cents, and paper notes of 1, 5, 10 and 20 pounds (only banks and post offices stock, or bother much with, 1- and 2-cent coins).

Before 1983 the pound was divided into 20 shillings; it was also divided into 1000 mils. Thus you still hear people referring habitually to a sum of 50 *sents* as *dhéka shillíngia* (ten shillings) or *pendakósia míl* (500 mils), so be prepared for such idioms.

### Banks and exchange facilities

Southern **banks** are open 8.30am–12.30pm, Monday to Friday, plus 3.15–4.45pm on Monday in winter; however, many branches in well-touristed areas offering a supplemental afternoon service, Tuesday to Friday, from 4–6pm (May–Sept) or 3.15–4.45pm (Oct–April). Banking and exchange facilities in the two airport arrival lounges are open for all flights; however, experience has shown that airport ATMs (particularly at Páfos) can seize up without warning, so have some sterling notes handy to exchange at the staffed booths. Plan funding needs ahead at Orthodox Easter, a popular time to visit: all banks will be shut from Holy Thursday noon until the following Wednesday morning, with most ATMs running out at some point during this period.

**Cash** can be changed easily (with no commission), while **travellers' cheques** are subject to fees, typically C£2 per transaction plus a few cents per cheque. However, it's worth noting that Thomas Cook travellers' cheques can be exchanged commission-free at any branch of the Bank of Cyprus, and the rate may be better than cash. **Plastic** (especially a **debit card**) is also extremely useful, as ATMs are ubiquitous: most machines accept any from among Visa, MasterCard, Cirrus, Maestro and Plus system cards, though American Express holders are restricted to the networks of the Alpha Bank and Laïki Bank. Screen instructions are given in English on request. **Credit cards** are widely accepted for purchases, but typically attract surcharges of 3–5 percent.

## The North

From 1983 until 2004, the legal tender in the Turkish Republic of Northern Cyprus was the **old Turkish lira** (TL) – a decision taken more for ideological posturing than sound economic reasons, and one with which few inhabitants were happy, given its habitual devaluation/inflation rate of close to eighty percent per year. As a result of this imported hyperinflation, prices quoted in old TL were fairly meaningless, so all northern prices tended – and still tend – to be given in pounds sterling. Following the 2002–2003 reigning-in of inflation through IMF bailouts and austerity programmes, the stage was set for a long-mooted currency reform, whereby the six final zeros of the old lira – which was typically well in excess of two million to the pound sterling – were knocked off and the new Turkish lira launched on January 1, 2005.

The **new Turkish lira** (YTL or *yeni türk lira*) comes in paper notes of 1, 5, 10, 20, 50 and 100 YTL. One YTL is subdivided into one hundred *kuruş*, a denomination last seen in 1980, and there are also coins in various denominations between one *kuruş* and one YTL inclusive. Old Turkish lira will be completely withdrawn after December 31, 2005, so readers of this guide should not accept any.

With any durable federal settlement, the Cyprus pound – or more likely by then, the euro – will be reintroduced as the uniform currency throughout the island. At the moment both, along with the pound sterling, are accepted as payment across the North. Sterling tends to be given a fair exchange rate, but the C£ tends to be discounted about 10–15 percent off its true value, while the euro is not much liked (despite numbers of German guests – and real estate purchasers). Don't even think about waving US dollars around as they're utterly disdained.

At present there are no strict **controls** on the amount of cash or travellers' cheques imported into the North, but you should leave with as few YTL as possible, for the simple reason that – despite the curbing of its historical instability – they're worth little outside Turkey or North Cyprus.

## Banks and exchange facilities

The various **banks** operating in North Cyprus are fairly inconvenient as tourist facilities for a number of reasons: the red tape involved in exchange is fairly off-putting, and most foreign-exchange tills keep hopelessly short working hours (8.30am–noon Mon–Fri).

There are no functioning banking facilities at Ercan airport; seven banks failed in summer 2001; and most of the rest have been kept going ever since by "artificial life support".

A much better bet, one used by virtually everyone involved in tourism, are the **money exchange houses**, at least one of which functions in each of the major towns. Open 8.30am to 1pm and 2 to 5pm Monday to Friday (6pm in summer), plus Saturday 8.30am to 1pm, they give speedy service and top rates for foreign cash and travellers' cheques without taking commission.

Foreign-currency **notes** are in many ways the best form in which to bring funds, the chance of theft being very slim. You can pay directly for hotel bills, car-rental surcharges, souvenir purchases, restaurant meals and hotel extras such as sauna or phone fees with overseas cash (in order of preference as noted above) – and you may well *have* to pay the airport cabbie in sterling, so keep some £5 and £10 notes ready. Even UK one-pound, and sometimes even fifty-pence, coins are widely accepted at exchange houses, as well as at many shops and hotel receptions. The only things that you have to pay for in YTL are such "official" purchases as postage stamps, museum admissions and phone cards; when you buy articles with pounds sterling, you'll be given change in YTL on a near-as-dammit basis.

Finally, **plastic** is very handy, both for large transactions such as car rental, and for use in the score of ATMs scattered across the North. Ones with foreign-language greeting messages accept some or all from among Visa, MasterCard, Cirrus, Maestro or Plus system cards. Locations are detailed in the *Guide*.

# Costs

The main Cyprus travel season begins early in spring and extends well into autumn, with July/August visits somewhat unappealing for a number of reasons. Obviously you'll save a lot on accommodation tariffs in either part of Cyprus if you're willing to go outside of midsummer (though September is also reckoned peak season), a sensible strategy whatever your budget. Some form of student identification is useful for discounted admission to archeological sites and museums, whose fees in any case are modest throughout the island.

## The South

The southern Republic of Cyprus has a somewhat unfair reputation for being expensive. This is a holdover from the days when it *was* vastly pricier than almost any other nearby country, but with steadily climbing prices the rule in both Greece and Turkey, costs in the South are beginning to seem normal in comparison. However, entry to the EU has hiked costs noticeably – about twenty percent compared to 2000–2002.

Travelling independently in the South, you should budget a **minimum** of around £30 per person a day. This assumes, however, exclusive reliance on bicycles, or **public transport** at £1.25–4 a go, staying in one of the limited number of basic village pensions or no-star hotels at about £12 per person a night and only one modest meal out for about £8.50 maximum, with the balance of food bought from shops.

To travel in some degree of **comfort** and style, though, you'll want at least £50 disposable per person, which should let you book a modest but acceptable hotel on double-occupancy basis and share the cost of a **rental car** (and petrol – slightly less than in Britain), as well as two full main meals. **Beer and wine** are good, and cheapish at £1.75 and £6.50 per large bottle respectively at restaurants; village wine from the barrel goes for as little as £2.50 per litre, while brandy sours run just over a pound.

**Winter visits** – or even extended residence, a popular strategy with British senior citizens – offer considerable savings. One-bedroom apartments can be found starting at £200 per month, two-bedroom ones from £300. Car rental can be 35 percent cheaper, and hotels nearly as much less, than normal. Full English breakfast at coastal resorts can be had for about £2.50, while a three-course set meal with wine can go for as little as £7. If you wear out your wardrobe, January–February sales for shoes and clothing take place as in northern Europe.

## The North

The economy of **Northern Cyprus**, both before and after it adopted the Turkish lira as official currency in 1983, has lagged behind that of the South, and consequently it is significantly cheaper – except in the confines of a four-star resort. You'll even find certain items less expensive than in Turkey, owing to a combination of subsidies and judicious direct imports from Britain.

> ### Tipping and taxes
>
> Since a ten-percent **service charge** is included on virtually all restaurant bills in the South, no extra amount need be left unless table-waiting was exceptional; in the North, where only the fancier places will tack on an identical fee, use your discretion. Taxi-drivers, especially in the South, expect a gratuity.
>
> **VAT** (Value Added Tax) is levied in the southern Republic; since EU accession it's fifteen percent. VAT in the North is also fifteen percent, often charged separately in fancy restaurants.

For various reasons it's paradoxically much harder to travel independently in the North despite its occasionally lower costs at street level. You're at a considerable disadvantage given the very limited number of hotels geared to a walk-in trade; at package-oriented hotels, theoretical over-the-counter prices are often higher than those granted to advance bookings and agencies. Owing to the historically unstable nature of the Turkish lira, accommodation rates are invariably quoted in hard currency, usually pounds sterling, and the *Guide* follows this example. There are a bare handful of small, attractive **pensions and hotels** in and around Kyrenia, for example, charging £8–12 per person a night, as well as a handful of small inns on the Karpaz peninsula; elsewhere in the North

you can count the number of such places on one hand.

**Eating out** can sometimes be less expensive than in Turkey, for example; even in the Kyrenia area or at major hotels it's difficult to spend more than £11 per person on a meal, plus a few pounds for imported Turkish wine. However, the recent influx of a Greek-Cypriot clientele has had its effect, and meal prices anywhere along the well-trodden routes, even in ostensibly remote areas, will rarely be below £7. **Car rental** is inexpensive, starting at about £12 a day during the off-season, though petrol prices are approaching European levels, at £0.58 a litre. **Overall**, budget about £35 a day per person (including accommodation) to live quite well.

# Getting around

Cyprus has fairly sparse bus services, though in the South the theoretically useful institution of the service (shared) taxi makes getting around fairly straightforward and cheap on the main routes – even if "service" is often the last thing on drivers' minds. Private taxis are relatively expensive; there has been no train service since the early 1950s. Car rental is reasonable by European standards, making it the best option for visitors to either side of the island – and something you should seriously consider, as it's often the only way to reach isolated points of interest.

## Local buses in the South

The most important **inter-urban routes** in the **South** are served by a number of private companies, whose terminals tend to be clustered at various points in the main towns: there's never really anything that could be singled out as a central bus station. Except on Saturday afternoons and Sundays, when services can be skeletal to nonexistent, departures are fairly frequent during daylight hours – up to nine times daily from Larnaca to Ayía Nápa, for example. **Fares**, sold at kerbside offices or on board, remain reasonable despite sharp 2004 hikes in diesel prices; crossing the island from Nicosia to Páfos, for example, won't set

you back much over C£5.50. If you make forays into the Tróödhos, however, you'll find frequencies dropping sharply, with the need to plan an overnight in the hills; to explore up there it's far simpler to have a car, using the coastal towns as jump-off points.

Worth just a mention are the old-fashioned villagers' **market buses** – essentially a Bedford truck chassis with a sort of multi-coloured charabanc mounted on top. They are marvellously photogenic institutions, but with their typical once-daily, 6am-out-2pm-back schedules – plus school-bus seating – they're unlikely to be of much practical use, though lately, large numbers of them are being refurbished by adventure companies for use in back-country safaris.

47

## Local buses in the North

In the **North**, local buses are more consciously modelled on the Turkish system, with coaches gathered at a single vehicle park and a ticket-sales/waiting building adjacent. With fewer cars in the poorer economy, locals are more dependent on buses and accordingly departures are more frequent: as much as quarter-hourly between north Nicosia and Kyrenia. **Fares** are also lower than in the South, but once again you'll find public buses inconvenient to do much adventuring. For the most part your fellow passengers will not be native Cypriots, but Anatolian settlers and soldiers returning to postings. Walking along roads, you may be tooted at by the drivers of oncoming buses in a bid to get your custom; wave them down if you want to ride.

## Urban buses

Of all the island cities, only Nicosia and Limassol are really big enough to sustain an **urban bus network**. With very few exceptions, however, these services run only from about 6am to 6pm (7pm in summer). Fares cost between C£0.50 and C£0.70, and route maps – worth snagging if you're staying a long time – are available from the relevant tourist office. In and around Larnaca and Páfos, a few routes are of interest to visitors, and detailed in the town accounts.

## Service taxis and dolmuşes

Another way of getting about Cyprus is the shared taxi or minibus, called a **service taxi** in the South and a **dolmuş** in the North. Service taxis have now been amalgamated into a single company, Travel and Express; stretch limos and small transit vans carrying four to seven passengers can be booked by phone, and will pick up and drop off at any reasonable point (eg a hotel or private dwelling). That's the theory anyway; tales of ignored bookings abound, and vehicle condition often leaves much to be desired. Ticket prices are little more than double the bus fare for the same route, and journey times can be quick, though sometimes drivers' styles may have you fearing for your life. Drivers are famous for swearing fluently in

Greek, English and Russian at other drivers (and passengers, especially those who delay them the least bit); local women scream at the drivers when they overtake on blind, hairpin curves – you'll be too petrified. Something to try once, perhaps.

In the South, some of the so-called scheduled **minibus services** up to the lonely northern beaches near Pólis seem to straddle categories a bit; they may offer a pick-up service and/or refuse to depart at all without a certain quota of passengers. Strictly speaking, there are few shared saloon cars in the North, but more often minibuses which dawdle, engines idling, in bus parks until they are full or nearly so, thus meeting the definition of *dolmuş* – "stuffed".

## Taxis

Privately hired **taxis** within urban areas in the **South** have rigidly controlled fares, not exorbitant by British or North American standards. The meter starts at C£1.38 (C£1.82 between 8.30pm and 6am); the meter ticks over at a rate of C£0.24 per kilometre (C£0.29 per kilometre during night hours as cited). Every piece of luggage weighing over 12kg incurs a C£0.24 charge. Pets are paid for at C£0.22 each, and the driver has the right to demand they be transported in a cage or carrier.

There also exist numbers of **rural taxis** providing service between Tróödhos resorts or foothill villages and nearby towns; for these trips you should know the going rate, as meters will not be used. The per-kilometre rate is C£0.20 ordinarily, but C£0.15 on an out-and-back trip, or C£0.20 between 11pm and 6am; one piece of baggage is carried free, otherwise it's C£0.20 per piece. As guidelines, Nicosia to Plátres will cost about C£20 per carful; from Limassol to the same place slightly less; from Larnaca to Páno Léfkara about C£12. From Larnaca airport to Kyrenia (an increasingly popular trajectory), budget a stiff C£50.

Around Christmas, New Year and Orthodox Easter, a C£0.66 tip is added mandatorily to your fare on both urban or rural taxis.

In the relatively small towns of the **North**, there's less need for urban taxis. Moving between population centres, fares for the same distance are comparable to those in the South, for example £15–20 from Ercan airport to Kyrenia or resorts around it.

## Driving

Almost three-quarters of visitors to either part of Cyprus end up driving themselves around at some time during their stay, and this is really the best way to see the country. Either a licence from your home country or an International Driving Permit is acceptable in the North, though in the South, non-EU drivers will be required to have an IDP in addition to their home licence.

### Road rules

Traffic moves **on the left** throughout the island, as in the UK and most Commonwealth nations. **Front-seatbelt** use is mandatory on the open road but discretionary in towns; children under five years of age may not occupy the front seats, and kids five to ten only if wearing seatbelts. **Drunk-driving** laws are strict, north and south, and if you're caught over the limit in the North, you'll pay a stiff fine *and* spend the night in a drying-out cell.

**Speed limits** in the South are 100km/hr (minimum 65km/hr) on dual carriageways, 80km/hr on other rural roads and 50km/hr in towns. Entry into urban zones is announced by big signs reading "*Katikómeni Periokhí*" (Built-up Area). In the North, limits are roughly the same, but may still be posted in miles per hour: 100kph/60mph on the Kyrenia–Nicosia–Famagusta highway, 60kph/40mph on smaller back roads and 50kph/30mph in built-up areas.

Urban boundaries aren't explicitly signposted in the North, but there are remarkable numbers of khaki-drill-clad policemen maintaining **speed traps** with hand-held radar devices at town outskirts. A particular stake-out, well known but still netting large numbers of victims, is just west of Kyrenia, near the military camp, especially on weekend nights. If you're caught, police are apt to be polite but firm. You have fifteen days to pay **citations** at the district police station; if you don't, your name might pop up on the airport computer at departure. Fines (£4–5) are geared to local salaries and therefore seem risibly low to outsiders. Radar speed

traps are now quite common on the motorways of the South, but they haven't yet made much of a dent on unsafe local driving habits, chief among which are tailgating and ambling down the centre of the road.

In the larger Southern towns, use the designated municipal lots for **parking**; they're not expensive – C£0.40 or C£0.50 for a half-day in Nicosia or Larnaca is the most you'll ever pay, though lots kept by private individuals can be much more. If you see a tempting-looking bit of waste ground and leave your car there, odds are that an attendant will appear as if by magic and dun you. Meters on some commercial streets take twenty-cent coins for each hour, and yellow lines at kerbsides mean the same thing as in Britain: single, no parking during business hours; double, no parking or stopping at all. No-parking zones are poorly indicated in the North, though a policeman may appear and politely tell you if you're being blatantly illegal.

### Road conditions

In the South, **roads** themselves come in four grades: in descending order of quality, A, B, E and F, cited as such on maps and highway signs. 'A' roads are the usually excellent, four-lane divided motorways linking Nicosia with Limassol, Larnaca, Páfos and Ayía Nápa, while 'B' roads are major, undivided highways provided as a rule with verges. At the other end of the scale, 'E' denotes a two-lane country road, while 'F' can mean either a one-lane paved drive or an appalling dirt track fit only for jeep or mountain bike. Even when paved, many 'F' or sub-F roads throughout the island are single-lane colonial relics with merely a thin layer of asphalt strewn over British cobbles. This makes them extremely bumpy, with very sharp edges over which you're forced to put two wheels by oncoming traffic. Lack of lane markings on 'E' and 'F' roads, and blind corners without mirrors, aggravate the effects of bad local driving.

Nearly ten years in the making, the Limassol–Páfos **A6 motorway** was completed in 2003. That said, the A6–A1 transition at Limassol is a bit of a joke, with no fewer than six roundabouts to disrupt your cruise-through; proper flyovers are finally being built at the westernmost two. The eastbound A3 was extended to Ayía Nápa in 2003 – surprisingly, the Cypriots had the right to take the highway across British Sovereign Base territory; in the event of a final federal settlement a spur will extend to Varósha. Across the South in general, the road system, whether 'A', 'B', 'E' or city-street, seems to be in a **permanent state of excavation**, and there are plenty of busy uncontrolled intersections, so beware.

In the **North**, the highways between Kyrenia–Güzelyurt–Gemikonağı, Güzelyurt–Nicosia, Nicosia–Famagusta and Famagusta–Boğaz are comparable to an undivided British 'A' route, and there are even stretches of four-lane, divided highway between the airport and Nicosia, or Nicosia and Kyrenia, built with Saudi funding. Elsewhere, however, most of the road network has been essentially unmaintained since 1974 and will be pretty slow going. The presence of **unlit military lorries**, lumbering along the Nicosia-Famagusta highway in particular, makes night driving in the North most inadvisable; there have been numerous fatalities, including Raif Denktaş, elder son of long-standing Northern leader Rauf Denktaş, from drivers rear-ending such poorly visible hazards. Another **hazard** in the North are cars with number plates beginning in **ZZ**, which should be treated with the utmost caution and deference. These temporarily imported cars usually belong to rich, spoilt Saudi, Gulf state and İstanbul Turkish students who rarely miss an opportunity to impress upon you – by running you off the road if necessary – just how flash and high-performance their buggies are. Involved in numerous smash-ups, these individuals have been the impetus for ongoing anti-drunk-driving campaigns in the North.

**Signposting** varies, too; village exits South or North are usually not obvious, so you'll get acquainted with the boys in the central café asking directions – otherwise you may well end up caught at the bottom of a steep cul-de-sac, with reversing the only way out. By contrast, the Tróödhos range forestry roads, despite their often horrific condition, are almost always admirably marked, with white lettering on a green background. In North Cyprus, however, many rural signs are badly faded, not having been repainted at all since 1974, though this has improved since the late 1990s in the more visited parts of the Kyrenia hills – and even more so since 2003, as bewildered Greek-Cypriot trippers are catered to with better signage.

All **road distances** are marked in kilometres in the South; accordingly, all rental car speedometers there indicate kilometres, as does the recommended Mairs map. Their signposting is often completely up the spout, however – yo-yoing up or down by several kilometres in the space of a few hundred metres, apparently a consequence of marking not keeping pace with road regrading and straightening. In the North, a transitional state exists: kilometres are signposted along major highways, but distances appear – if at all – in miles on secondary roads or forest tracks, where you might have to keep a sharp lookout for old colonial milestones. A typical rental car speedometer in the North will show readings in both miles and kilometres.

## Fuel

In the **South**, unleaded 95, 98 or 100 octane petrol costs C£0.46–0.50 a litre, while diesel is C£0.44 per litre, hugely increased since subsidies were removed upon EU entry – all prices considerably less than in the UK, though nearly double those in North America. Leaded fuel has been phased out with EU entry, though you can find lead-substitute fuel for those vehicles which need it.

**Filling stations** are normally open Monday to Friday 6am to 6pm (until 7pm Oct–March), with Saturday closure at 3pm, though they may also close Tuesday at 2pm (or Wednesday at the same hour within Nicosia district). On Sundays and holidays only about ten percent of the South's stations are open, on a rota basis; it's easy to run out if you're not careful, so plan ahead. To address this problem, large numbers of **automatic 24-hour stations** operate in all the major towns, with a consequent reduction in staffed stations; at these "automats" you feed C£1, C£5 or C£10 notes into a machine which then shunts that amount's worth of fuel to your pump. They generally work well, and instructions are given in English. However, these machines don't actually give change;

if your banknote exceeds the value of your fuel needs, hit the button marked "Receipt"; you'll get a sales slip showing actual sale, which you can exchange for a refund of the difference at the same station during daylight staffing hours. You can avoid this problem entirely by using plastic – most automats take the major **credit cards**, without surcharges.

Owing to the phasing out of various Turkish subsidies, fuel costs in **North Cyprus** have risen to much the same as in the South: £0.58 per litre for leaded or unleaded premium, £0.37 for diesel. Unleaded fuel is now widely, though not universally, available. Filling stations, especially in the Kyrenia area and Nicosia outskirts, are reasonably numerous and tend to be open until 9 or even 10pm, with near-normal service on Sunday. Credit cards are now accepted at most stations, but a dwindling few without on-line links to banks may demand a commission of 5.25 percent.

## Car rental

It's worth stressing that the **condition** of rental cars on either side of the Line can be appalling, with bad brakes the most common fault; if at all possible, take the candidate car for a spin around the block before accepting it. Most rental cars in the North – especially soft-top jeeps – have no radio-cassette/CD player; so many have been stolen that they are no longer fitted. Reputable chains in the South will furnish you with a list of their branches Republic-wide, to be contacted in the event of a breakdown. Rental cars in both South and North have distinctive red **number plates** beginning with a single "**Z**", and their drivers have historically been accorded every consideration by police – for example, a warning instead of a ticket for not buckling up – though speeding fines are now levied on one and all in the North.

Visitors may **cross the Attila Line** from South to North with a rental vehicle (but *not* at present from North to South), using one of however many legal checkpoints are open at the time you read this. All rental companies in the South will tell you that this is forbidden, because Republic of Cyprus insurance is not valid in the North. However, there is nothing to stop you turning up at one of the checkpoints and buying supplemental third-party insurance from a dedicated booth (price negotiable – ie, what they think you're good for – at C£10–12 for a minimum of 3 days, £C15 for up to a month). The reason southern hire companies don't like you to do this is the scandalously low level of coverage furnished by these policies: C£6000 at time of writing, though set to go up to about €30,000 now that EU accession negotiations for Turkey are about to start. There are also persistent, worrying reports that the companies involved don't pay out in the event of an accident. So the final word is, strictly at your own risk.

In the **South**, numerous agencies, including most international and several local chains, offer primarily A- and B-group Japanese and European compacts both at airports and in towns. If you have a choice, prefer the Opel Corsa, Toyota Yaris or the Fiat Polo to grossly underpowered Suzukis or Subarus, the latter in particular with a sewing-machine engine and an apparent top speed of about 80kpm/50mph. With a bit more to spend, consider a four-door Toyota Corolla or a Peugeot 206. Summer rates start at C£17 a day, unlimited mileage and VAT included, a figure which should be kept in mind as a yardstick when pre-booking an A- or B-group vehicle from overseas. In or near high season you should reserve in advance – not difficult since so many fly-drive packages are offered. You are virtually obliged to accept the additional daily fee of C£3–6 for Collision Damage Waiver (CDW); remember also that venturing onto dirt tracks with a non-4WD vehicle will usually void your insurance cover if you damage the undercarriage. During winter, rates for saloon cars drop to as little as C£12 per day, all inclusive (even the CDW). For most of the year, a **three-day minimum rental period** applies.

If you intend to do any backroad exploration of the Tröödhos or Akámas areas, then some sort of **4WD vehicle** is highly advisable. As a party of more than two, it's well worth considering the rental of a diesel-powered Mitsubishi or Shogun jeep, though daily rates for these are high (typically C£40). Otherwise, the lighter-weight Suzuki Vitara or Samurai jeeps can just about take two adults with their luggage, though their soft tops makes security problematic.

The **minimum age** for renting a car is generally 21; credit cards are the preferred method of payment in the South. An irritating quirk of Cypriot rentals, both South and North, is that you may be asked to deposit an inflated sum (eg, C£25 for a 40-litre tank), in cash or with credit card, covering the cost of a **full tank** of petrol; the idea is to return the car as empty as possible, rather than full as in other countries. It is an iniquitous and potentially dangerous practice, with the company benefiting to the tune of several tanks of petrol per season since no sensible person finishes up driving on fumes. In the South, if you return the car to a staffed office, rather than leaving it in the airport parking lot upon departure (much more likely), the company is supposed to refund the value of the fuel remaining in the tank. You will also be liable to a charge of about C£10 for either **one-way** rentals (pick up one town, drop off in another) or **"after-hours"** service – defined as picking up cars at airports before 8am or after 9pm.

Because the **North** is unrecognized internationally, none of the overseas chains has been represented there in the past, leaving the field clear for local entrepreneurs. There are no car-rental booths at Ercan airport, so you'll be stranded unless you've prearranged to have a car meeting your flight arrival. Arrange a fly-drive package through a tour operator, or contact (by fax) the agencies noted in Kyrenia, north Nicosia or Famagusta, directly from overseas – the latter strategy tends to be somewhat cheaper.

Left-hand-drive cars made in Turkey are invariably cheaper to rent than right-hand-drive vehicles, though they're rarely offered these days. On-the-spot **rates** for a bottom-end, left-hand-drive Renault 9 start at about £18 per day in high summer; expect to pay 33 percent less out of season, 15 percent more if booking through a package agent. Given the state of most roads off the main trunk routes, you'll probably prefer to splash out for a 4WD – the adequate Suzuki Vitara starts at about £19 a day in low season. Credit cards or foreign cash are preferred payment methods, though be aware that most companies slap a **surcharge** on the

use of cards, and an equal number require full advance payment of the estimated rental price in cash. A CDW premium, usually about £3 per day, is payable, often in cash upon delivery of the car.

## International car rental chains

### Britain

Avis ☎0870 606 0100, @www.avis.com.
Budget ☎0800 181 181,
@www.budget.com.
Europcar ☎0870/607 5000, @www.europcar
.co.uk.
Hertz ☎0870 844 8844, @www.hertz.com.
National ☎0870 536 5365, @www.nationalcar
.co.uk.
Sixt/Kenning @www.e-sixt.com.
Suncars ☎0870 500 5566, @www.suncars.com.
Transhire ☎0870 789 8000, @www.transhire
.com.

### Ireland

Avis Northern Ireland ☎028/9024 0404, Republic of Ireland ☎01/605 7500, @www.avis.ie.
Budget Republic of Ireland ☎09/0662 7711,
@www.budget.ie.
Europcar Northern Ireland ☎028/9442 3444,
Republic of Ireland ☎01/614 2888, @www
.europcar.ie.
Hertz Republic of Ireland ☎01/676 7476, @www
.hertz.ie.
Sixt Republic of Ireland ☎1850 206 088, @www
.irishcarrentals.ie.

### North America

Alamo ☎1-800/462-5266, @www.alamo.com.
Avis US ☎1-800/230-4898, Canada ☎1-800 272-5871, @www.avis.com.
Budget ☎1-800/527-0700, @www.budget.com.
Europcar US & Canada ☎1-877/940 6900,
@www.europcar.com.
Hertz US ☎1-800/654-3131, Canada ☎1-800 263-0600, @www.hertz.com.
National ☎1-800/962-7070, @www.nationalcar
.com.

### Australia

Avis ☎13 63 33 or 02/9353 9000, @www.avis
.com.au.
Budget ☎1300/362 848, @www.budget.com.au.
Europcar ☎1300/131 390, @www.deltaeuropcar
.com.au.
Hertz ☎13 30 39 or 03/9698 2555, @www.hertz
.com.au.

National ☏ 13 10 45, ⓦ www.nationalcar.com.au.

### New Zealand

Apex ☏ 0800 93 95 97 or 03/379 6897, ⓦ www .apexrentals.co.nz.
Avis ☏ 09/526 2847 or 0800 655 111, ⓦ www .avis.co.nz.
Budget ☏ 0800/652-227, ⓦ www.budget.co.nz.
Hertz ☏ 0800 654 321, ⓦ www.hertz.co.nz.
National ☏ 0800 800 115, ⓦ www.nationalcar. co.nz.

*Local chain outlets and one-offs are given in "Listings" of each major town.*

## Bringing your own car

Cars brought over on boats **from Turkey to northern Cyprus** are allowed to stay for six months, and for the immediate future will very likely encounter difficulties in crossing the Attila/Green Line from North to South, irrespective of the nationality of their owner. No foreign insurance is valid in the North; you can be insured on the spot for exceedingly basic, third-party cover as you roll off the boat, at approximately the rates cited for the land-crossings from the South. It is much more economical to buy coverage for a month, or a year, like the Greek-Cypriots do. Should you be able to cross into the South, you will find your North policy inapplicable, and will have to buy another policy for about C£17 per month.

There are two cargo services a week from Keratsíni (a satellite port near Piraeus) in **Greece to Limassol** in the South, on which cars or motorcycles (but not their owners) can be put – you have to fly out to meet the vehicle. Cyprus is a signatory to the MGA (Multilateral Guarantee Agreement), whereby Cypriot cars can now circulate within the EU without customs formalities, with reciprocity for EU cars within Cyprus; this means that EU nationals with EU-registered vehicles should encounter no difficulties on docking. Green cards or EU-contracted insurance are now recognized in the South, but only up to minimum statutory limits; you'll probably want to contact your insurer about supplementary coverage.

Non-EU drivers/cars, judging from past practice, can expect considerable hassle upon arrival in Limassol, where you will only

be granted up to twelve months' circulation in the Republic (beyond that you would have to officially import the vehicle). Entry controls tend to be strict, in the wake of stolen-vehicle scams; declaration forms may ask you to minutely document all accessories and extras.

**Mechanics** in the South are largely geared to the Japanese models which have virtually captured the market, but other European makes are represented. A breakdown in the North used to mean days or even a week of waiting for parts, though the situation is much better now for the more common Japanese or Italian makes, with growing numbers of authorized representatives in north Nicosia for the flash sedans and 4WDs which are rapidly replacing the antique British and Turkish models of yore. However you'd still be foolish to bring anything unusual such as a Volkswagen van.

## Scooters and cycles

In the coastal resorts of the South, you can rent small **scooters** for C£4–7 a day (or even C£15 a week); few people will want to take them further than the beach, as you will get scant respect from four-wheeled motorists on curvy mountain roads. Crash helmets are compulsory in the South for anything over 50cc, and this law has been systematically enforced since 2000. Rental motor-scooters and pedal-bikes have made a limited appearance in the North, restricted to a few outlets in downtown Kyrenia in the summer only.

By contrast, the uplands of either South or North are ideal for **mountain biking**. Both the Tróödhos range and the Kyrenia hills are laced with a network of dirt forest tracks which would be extremely tedious for hiking but constitute a mountain-biker's dream. With some planning or guidance (group bike tours are beginning to be advertised) you could cover either range from end to end in a matter of a few days. Mountain bikes are for sale in south Nicosia and Limassol, and for rent in the main Tróödhos resort of Plátres. Incidentally, few rented bikes are supplied with pumps or tyre repair kits. The CTO publishes a useful A4-format pamphlet, "Cyprus for Cycling", detailing nineteen back-country routes for cyclists.

Additionally there are less specialized, general bike sales and repair shops in most of the South's larger towns, which you will almost certainly take advantage of, if only to buy patches or replace a pump worn out from constantly pumping up flat tyres. Plentiful thorns on the road ensure a steady incidence of punctures, and there's the usual hot-country problem of the sun melting the rubber solution, so repair jobs won't last if you leave the bike in full sun. Cypriot car drivers tend to regard bicyclists as some lower form of life – on a par with the snakes found deliberately run over everywhere – and can be very aggressive, so pedal defensively.

# Accommodation

The majority of visitors to Cyprus arrive on some sort of package that includes accommodation. That's not to say that independent travel is impossible: most of the Southern hotel listings in the *Guide* are for establishments that are more geared for walk-in trade, and not block-booked by foreign operators.

Following a run of slack seasons, overbooking in the South is much less of a problem than it was. The limited number of pensions and rooms in private houses are mostly in the Tróödhos or Páfos district, often occupied by Cypriot holiday-makers. Northern Cyprus, on the other hand, has only about seventy resort-standard hotels or self-catering establishments, which used to be rarely if ever full – not too surprising when you consider that scarcely forty thousand English-speaking tourists show up in a typical year. However, since 1997 the advent of Turkish gambling tours has periodically placed many of the more luxurious outfits off-limits to Europeans, and in September – the busiest season – there are rarely enough beds to go around at the quality outfits.

Most of the tourist industry in the North was formerly carried on in hotels abandoned by Greek Cypriots and let out on a concession basis by the government-run Cyprus Turkish Tourism Development Corporation, but with one or two exceptions these inefficiently run and poorly maintained properties have now been "privatized" (ie, bought up by mainland Turks). Only after the late 1980s did numbers of privately funded, purpose-built and professionally managed resorts spring up under Turkish Cypriot ownership. Our accommodation listings show a preference

---

## Accommodation prices in the South

All hotel and apartment-hotel prices in the South have been categorized according to the price codes given below. These categories represent the minimum you can expect to pay in the high season for a double room or a two-person self-catering unit. Single rooms will normally cost fifty to eighty percent of the rates quoted for a double room. Rates for dorm beds in the very few existing hostels, where guests are charged per person, are given in Cyprus pounds.

| | | |
|---|---|---|
| ❶ under C£20 | ❹ C£41–50 | ❼ C£91–120 |
| ❷ C£21–30 | ❺ C£51–70 | ❽ C£121–150 |
| ❸ C£31–40 | ❻ C£71–90 | ❾ over C£151 |

for these, and it is worth making an effort to book into them.

## Hotels, guest houses and private rooms in the South

The CTO grades and oversees most accommodation outfits in the South, be they hotels of zero to five stars, guest houses or "hotel-apartments" (self-catering units). Their names, locations and current prices are shown in the *Guide to Hotels* issued yearly, but this can be hard to find, and does not distinguish between the relatively few establishments which welcome independent travellers and the vast majority which are pitched at package bookings. Neither does it distinguish between the more modest listings which are geared for conventional tourist trade, and some which double up as brothels. There are also a small number of "furnished apartments and tourist houses" which, while licensed by the CTO, are not allowed by law to be marketed by overseas tour operators, but are intended for walk-ins, whether Cypriot or foreign. They are currently undocumented in official tourist literature.

### Hotels

All **hotels** of one star or over, and some of the unstarred ones, have en-suite baths. Hotel rooms are most frequently offered on a bed-and-(continental) breakfast basis; charged separately, breakfast rarely exceeds C£3 in humbler establishments, but frankly if you're having to pay extra, it's often better to go out and find a full English breakfast for roughly the same price. Desk staff are almost universally from central Europe or somewhere in the Indian subcontinent, the latter recruited assiduously for their English-language skills.

Single occupancy **prices** tend to be well over half the double rate, and maximum rates must be posted either in the room itself or over the reception desk on a CTO-validated placard. Generally there won't be any fiddling in this regard, and except between early July and early September you may have some scope for bargaining, again stipulated by CTO rules. Travelling **independently** outside peak season, it's usually possible to find comfortable if modest hotel rooms for less than C£30 double; if you insist on arriving in summer, then you're probably wisest to book in advance from Britain on a package basis.

### Agrotourism: restored inns and village houses

Faced with continued, gradual depopulation of some of the more attractive hill villages, the CTO during the mid-1990s established the **Cyprus Agrotourism Company** to implement the restoration of old buildings, mostly in the Tróödhos foothills, as character accommodation. The idea is that guests staying in hitherto little-visited villages will confer a bit of much-needed prosperity on these moribund communities scattered across Páfos, Limassol, Larnaca and Nicosia districts. There are now over fifty such properties, either entire houses or inns divided into conventional rooms or self-catering suites. It is a worthy and increasingly popular programme, if inevitably limited in numerical impact – and with expansion reportedly bogged down in bureaucratic muddles. There is some overlap in membership between the CAC and private initiatives such as the **Laona Project** (see p.194) and **Cyprus Villages** (see p.107). The CAC publishes its own useful brochure, *Agrotourism: Traditional Holiday Homes*, and in the CTO's *Guide to Hotels and other Tourist Establishments* you will find most of them – ie, those that have gained official CTO certification – in the section entitled "Traditional Houses". Few official double occupancy prices exceed C£30, and many studios are C£24 or under – outstanding value for often exquisitely executed restoration facilities. Among package companies in the UK, Sunvil and Amathus currently represent the best selection of these properties (see p.31).

### Guest houses and private rooms

**Guest houses**, typically charging C£6–10 per person, are a numerically dwindling feature of life in the centres of the larger Southern towns and certain Tróödhos resorts. Some, as in Páfos, are reputable; others (in Limassol and Nicosia especially) are pretty grim or dodgy in some respect. We've made distinctions clear in the town accounts.

The CTO disavows all knowledge of, or responsibility for, **unlicensed rooms** in boarding houses and no-star hotels which have let their CTO certification lapse; similarly for those unofficial rooms in private rural houses, but the latter do exist in some numbers, particularly in the villages of Páfos district and the Tróödhos foothills, both north and south slopes. The going rate currently is about C£7–8 per person, and this often includes some sort of breakfast. They can offer quite a good look at country domestic life, and are recommended at least once – particularly welcoming families may lay on an evening meal at little or no extra cost, feeding you far better than at the nearest tour-

ist grill. If there are no advertising signs out, the best strategy is to contact the *múkhtar* (village headman) and have him arrange something.

## Hotels in the North

Choice is more limited in Northern Cyprus: the broad middle ground between luxury compounds and soldiers' or migrant workers' dosshouses is somewhat thinly inhabited, and many establishments are block-booked by the operators of package tours, making just showing up on the off-chance a risky endeavour between June and October. The North's tourism authority nominally exercises some control over hotel standards and prices, though in practice things tend to be considerably more free-wheeling, not to say Wild West – proprietors have been known to

### Real estate sales on Cyprus

Since the early 1990s, **property** in both northern and southern Cyprus has been assiduously marketed to foreigners, especially Brits, interested in either a holiday/retirement home or an investment opportunity. Since the advent of EU membership for the South, a steady stream of purchases has become a flood. UK ownership numbers in the South are now well into five figures, with a concentration in Páfos district but a presence everywhere along the south coast; in the North, the figure is estimated at about seven thousand. **Real estate development** has drastically affected the landscape and infrastructure of both sides of the island, and in terms of money changing hands now far outstrips conventional tourism. There are scores of estate agents in every resort, though most of the projects are the work of the biggest half-dozen developers on each side of the island.

What both sides have in common is the fact that something of a bubble is developing, and **infrastructure** has simply not kept pace with construction; water shortages are a fact of life, roads are in a continual state of excavation, and high-speed internet connections are generally not available in the hills. Moreover, Cyprus real estate is **overpriced** compared to other popular Mediterranean destinations and a correction is probably overdue, though expect prices to rise for the immediate future.

In the **South**, Larnaca is cheapest, Páfos the most expensive, with Limassol somewhere in between. It is assumed that many purchasers will engage in buy-to-let, though foreigners are restricted to one freehold piece of property up to 43,200 square feet. In the **North**, the bulk of development is in the Kyrenia area, though villas are sprouting near Salamis, on the Karpaz peninsula, and even around Cape Koruçam (Kormakíti). Isolated areas (plus cheap-and-nasty blocks in central Kyrenia) are not surprisingly the least expensive, Bellapais and the coastal plain immediately west of Kyrenia the most expensive zones.

Comparing like with like, it appears initially that the North is about a third less costly than the South, but the savings could prove illusory and the strongest possible warnings apply about **security of title**. The overwhelming majority of apartment blocks and bungalow complexes here are built on what was, before 1974, Greek-Cypriot land. The titles issued since by the northern government to displaced

quote double (or half) the "official" price for a given season without so much as batting an eyelash.

A relatively recent development aggravating this profile has been the rise of North Cyprus as a Turkish **gambling** and **sex-tourism** destination after the closure of Turkey's casinos in 1997 prompted the organized-crime and money-laundering interests involved to shift their attentions to North Cyprus. Nightclubs attached to, or near, several hotels remain havens for prostitution, and many hotels (even away from the clubs) see themselves obliged to accept patronage by the hour, especially during the slow season. Gambling weekends used to be all the rage; mainland Turks would have their flights, accommodation and meals laid on free provided they wagered a certain amount per day. Under the circumstances, the management had little incentive to provide assiduous service or maintenance, and desk staff often spoke no foreign languages. With both the Turkish and North Cypriot economy still in recovery from their 2000–01 crash, there is less pressure of this sort on local accommodation, but several formerly well-regarded complexes – including the *Salamis Conti*, the *Celebrity*, and the *Chateau Lambousa* – got the boot from most UK tour operator brochures in the late 1990s and never found their way back in. With Turks still staying away, these (and other) big resort-hotels in the North now actively tout for a Greek-Cypriot gambling (and whoring) clientele, as hoardings and billboards on the Nicosia-Kyrenia highway leave in little doubt. Accordingly, with a few exceptions where the

Turkish-Cypriots, or Turkish settlers, using these properties, have never been recognized as valid outside of the North – something reiterated by the European Court of Human Rights. When momentum for a settlement began to build in 2002–2003, these title-holders – now living abroad – sensed that the former Greek-Cypriot owners might demand some sort of compensation and/or that the post-1974 titles would soon be worthless. The northern title-holders quickly sold their holdings to mostly London-based developers, who overnight threw up the constructions now visible, flogging them just as rapidly (often over the internet and off-plan) to Brits (plus a few Germans and Israelis).

When the southern republic alone joined the EU in May 2004, affected Greek Cypriots were not slow in **recourse to EU-wide law** to get satisfaction. One, Meletis Apostolidis, took a British couple, David and Linda Orams, to court over a house built on land to which Apostolidis still has the original titles. In late 2004, a Greek-Cypriot court ordered the house demolished and the land returned to the plaintiff; because the edict is not enforceable owing to the Turkish military occupation of the North, there is a possibility that under EU law the Orams' UK home could be seized and sold to compensate Apostolidis. As of writing, the Orams' appeal is pending, but should they lose, the entire bottom could fall out of the northern real estate market, and a procession of other, similar court cases follow.

So the best advice when property-hunting in the North is to buy only where **pre-1974, Turkish-Cypriot titles** are demonstrable – such properties are in fact rare and relatively expensive (ie, at Southern levels), because such transactions will never be challenged in court. Otherwise, wait until a final political settlement permits the establishment of a property compensations board and an orderly, legitimate transfer of titles between North and South against payment. By the same token, you should not buy any property in the South which has a pre-1974 Turkish-Cypriot owner – unless they appear at your solicitor's personally with legitimate titles – or one that is still owned by the *vakıf* (Muslim benevolent fund). Already a number of resourceful Turkish-Cypriots have imitated their compatriots and taken the southern government to court for building refugee housing, roads, etc on their land, and they may well do the same to a private buyer or developer.

## Accommodation prices in the North

Hotels and apartment-hotels in the North which can offer rooms to independent travellers (ie, those which are not monopolized by package-tour operators, whether British or Turkish) have been categorized according to the price codes given below. These categories represent the minimum you can expect to pay in the high season for a double room or a two-person self-catering unit. As prices quoted in the new Turkish lira remain an unknown quantity, the codes are based on the pound sterling, the most widely recognized foreign currency in the North, which can always be used to pay hotel bills.

❶ under £20
❷ £21–30
❸ £31–45
❹ £46–60
❺ £61–80
❻ over £81

facility does not dominate the character of the hotel, this book does not recommend establishments with a casino on-site.

### Apart-hotels, villas and longer stays

An increasing percentage of Cypriot accommodation, in both the South and the North, is **self-catering** in so-called tourist apartments or **apart-hotels**, or the more appealing semi-detached **villas**. (Incidentally, you shouldn't utter the word "villa" to non-English speakers – it means the male generative organ in Cypriot Greek slang.) In the southern Republic the best of these tend to be concentrated in Páfos district, with more scattered around Larnaca and Ayía Nápa; in Northern Cyprus they are almost exclusively in and around Kyrenia, though numbers of true self-catering facilities have levelled out, as the latest wave of tourists – including Greek-Cypriot trippers – seems to want the full-service treatment of a hotel. The majority of villas have good kitchen amenities and are well maintained by Mediterranean standards, the odd water shortage or power cut aside, though furnishings (in the North especially) tend to be spartan. See the "Getting There" sections above for specialists offering something out of the ordinary.

If you intend to **stay longer** in the South it's worth scanning adverts in one of the literally thousands of estate agency windows and in the real estate supplements of the two main English-language newspapers. In a reasonably desirable area, rents for one-bedroom furnished flats start at about C£180 a month; two-bedrooms fall in the C£230–400 range, with Larnaca and Páfos tending to be

cheaper than Limassol or Nicosia. In Northern Cyprus such lettings are done almost exclusively through the dozens of estate agencies in Kyrenia, with rents at near-parity with levels in the South. With the new interest in hotels (and outright house ownership) as opposed to self-catering villas, many of the latter formerly marketed by overseas tour companies are being offered for rent medium-term.

### Hostels and campsites

Neither the South nor the North was ever really on the backpackers' trail, and this is even more true since passenger ferry service between Greece and Israel (with impecunious backpackers bound to or from a kibbutz) was suspended. In the South, hostels are frankly on the way out, while campsites (with one or two sterling exceptions) are grim caravan parks for Cypriots hankering after a cheap weekend residence.

In the **South**, there are simple, variably clean **hostels** in Nicosia, Larnaca and on Mount Olympus in the Tróödhos; an official IYHF card is generally not required, and bunk charges won't exceed C£5, plus another pound for sheets if needed. There is also the extremely popular forestry lodge at Stavrós tís Psókas in the Tillyrian hills. In the **North**, you'll find a number of workmen's and soldiers' dosshouses in Kyrenia, Famagusta and (especially) Nicosia, but these are in general pretty unsavoury and only for desperate solo males.

The South has four official **campsites**, at Governor's Beach (near Limassol), Coral Bay and Yeroskípou (both near Páfos), and Pólis; most of them are open March to October inclusive, with fees of C£1–1.50 daily per person, with similar charges per tent or caravan. In addition, the forestry department runs over thirty more or less amenitied **picnic sites**, mostly in the Tróödhos; at some camping is expressly forbidden, while at others signs announce that "Camping is Allowed Here".

The North can muster just a bare handful of **picnic grounds**, for example at ancient Salamis and in the Kyrenia hills, where overnighting would probably garner you the unwelcome attentions of the Turkish army; there are at present no authorized, maintained areas for **camping**.

# Eating and drinking

Food throughout Cyprus is generally hearty rather than refined, and on the middle-of-the-road tourist circuit at least can seem monotonous after a few days. In many respects resort food – especially in the South – is the unfortunate offspring of generic Middle Eastern, and British, cooking at its least imaginative; the (under)fried potato is the tyrant of the kitchen, resulting in a "chips with everything" style of cuisine. If all else fails you can seek solace in the excellent beer, brandies and wine of the South. Restaurant fare in the North is a bit lighter and more open to outside influences, especially mainland Turkish, but is still heavily Anglicized.

All this is unfortunate, since once off the beaten track, or in a private home, meals are consistently interesting and appetizing, even if they'll never get a single star from Michelin. Less obvious, vegetable-based delights derived from such home cooking are featured in the food glossary on p.525.

## Breakfast

In the **South**, the breakfast (*próyevma*) offered at less expensive hotels tends to be minimum-effort continental, with tea/coffee, orange juice and slices of white toast with pats of foil-wrapped butter, jam and (if you're lucky) a slice of processed cheese or *halloúmi*. If you crave more, you'll have to pay extra for bacon-and-eggs-type English breakfasts, either at the hotels or at special breakfast bars in town. Comfortable hotels above two stars in rating will generally provide a more substantial buffet breakfast.

**Northern Cyprus** has embraced the mainland Turkish breakfast, which means untoasted bread, jam, *beyaz peynir* or white cheese, *kaşar* (kasseri) cheese, olives and either tea or coffee plus inexpensive (typically orange) juice. In the better hotels, these will be presented as a buffet with hot or cold meats, some sort of egg dish, a choice of bread products and fresh fruit as well.

## Snacks

Cypriots are not as prone to eating on the hoof as continental Greeks or Turks. On both sides of the island small British-style cafés sell sandwiches and drinks, but local solutions are less numerous.

Stuffed baked goods in the **South** include *eliópitta*, olive-turnover; *tashinópitta*, a pastry with sesame paste; and *kolokótes*, a triangular pastry stuffed with pumpkin, cracked wheat and raisins. Around Easter time you'll repeatedly be offered *flaoúnes*, dough steeped in an egg-and-cheese mixture, then studded with raisins. *Aïráni* (*ayran* to the Turkish Cypriots) is a refreshing street-cart drink made of diluted yoghurt flavoured with dried mint or oregano and salt, though the dwindling number of vendors seems restricted to Larnaca and Nicosia. *Soushoúkou* (sometimes rendered *soudzoúki*), a confection of almonds strung together and then dipped like candle wicks in a vat of *paloúza* (grape molasses) and rosewater, are sold everywhere in the South for about C£5 a kilo and make an excellent food to consume on trail-walks; so does *pastelláki*, a sesame, peanut and syrup bar costing about the same. Other less elaborate dried seeds and nuts are easily available in markets.

In the **North**, street vendors also offer *börek*, a rich, flaky layered pastry containing bits of meat or cheese. You'll have to sit down in a *pideci* or "pizza parlour" for a *pide* (Turkish pizza); usual toppings are *peynirli* (with cheese), *yumurtalı* (with egg), *kıymalı* (with mince), *sucuklu* (with sausage) or combinations of the above. Usually a small bowl of *çorba* (soup) is ordered with a *pide*. *Pidecis* may also offer *mantı* (central Asian ravioli, stuffed with mince) or *pirohu* (similar but stuffed with cheese), either topped with yogurt, garlic and chilli oil. *Tatar böreği*, broadly similar to *mantı*, is traditionally served with grated *halloúmi* cheese and mint.

## Fruit

Cypriot fruit, especially from the South, has a well-deserved reputation. Because of the long growing season, varieties tend to appear much earlier than their counterparts in Europe – for example strawberries in April, watermelons in June. Until 2003, everything was grown locally in the South, since the government bans imported products – ostensibly to keep the island relatively pest-free but also to economically protect the local farmers and specifically exclude smuggled-in goods from the North. In February 2005, restrictions on northern produce were relaxed, so you can expect to see citrus from Mórfou across the island in the future.

*Froutaría* is Greek for a **roadside fruit-and-vegetable** stall, *manav* the Turkish word. The central covered bazaars of all the major towns also usually have a good selection, though in the North much comes from Turkey, since the orchard potential of the Kyrenia hills and the Mórfou plain is limited.

Strawberries are increasingly available in the South all year round. Medlars and loquats ripen in mid-spring; their large pips and papery husks may have you wondering why people bother until you taste them. Apricots are next up, followed by peaches, which are imported from Turkey into the North. Watermelons grown in Páfos district and around Nicosia are on sale everywhere from June on, followed by dessert melons. Plums are also excellent in early summer; cherries, solely from the Tróödhos villages of the South, are delicious in their several varieties.

Towards autumn prickly pear fruit presents an exotic challenge, tasting like watermelon once you penetrate its defences. Table grapes of marketable quality are confined to the South, an adjunct of the wine industry. Wonderful strawberry guavas – allegedly the late President Makarios' favourite fruit – arrive in October and November. Citrus, specifically oranges, mandarins and grapefruit, is ready in winter. The longest established eating oranges (see p.150 for a thumbnail sketch of citrus cultivation in Cyprus) are called Jaffa, something of a misnomer as they're elongated rather than round, juicy and almost seedless. Valencias and Merlins ("navel" in the US) are also available, as is an old, non-acid but seedy variety called *sherkérika*, good for sweet juice. Since the late 1980s, subtropicals such as avocados, bananas, mangoes, kiwis and starfruit have been introduced in the warmer corners of Páfos district.

## Food shopping

Shopping for yourself, it's easy to find your way around the supermarkets and corner stores **in the South**. Labelling is always in English as well as Greek. Local dairy products in all flavours and sizes are conspicuous, as are smoked breakfast and picnic meats; the best types are listed on p.525. Because of Cyprus' many immigrant communities, it's easier than in many European countries to find exotic spices and condiments. In all of the major towns of the South (except Larnaca), central market halls are excellent sources of farm produce and meat; additionally there are often lively street markets immediately around them, for example in Páfos on Saturdays.

**In the North** things aren't so self-explanatory, nor abundant, but English labelling is on the rise, and you certainly won't starve if self-catering. There are central market halls for produce in Kyrenia and north Nicosia, and largish markets in central Kyrenia much like a medium-sized corner shop in North London – where many of the proprietors are likely to have spent time. The biggest supermarket chain is Lemar, with particularly convenient ones at both the western and eastern edges of Kyrenia.

## Restaurants

It takes some diligence to avoid the bland, often over-fried stodge dished out to undiscriminating tourists at most restaurants. Generally this means going slightly upmarket, to restaurants with more imaginative menus; to a remote village setting, especially to the **exokhiká kéndra** or country tavernas of the South which cater to locals with limited but consistent-quality offerings; or to a midtown *ouzerí* (Greek; often referred to as a **mezé-house**) or **meyhane** (Turkish), where local delicacies are served to accompany drink. Both *meyhane*s and *mezé*-houses are at their best from November to April, when rains nurture the wild greens and mushrooms which are a staple of their menus, and hunters bring in game.

A watered-down version of the **mezé** (*meze* in Turkish) is a succession of up to twenty small plates served in succession, along with a couple of grilled mains, until you're sated. Unfortunately, many purveyors opt to go for gut-busting quantity over quality, such that you reckon the establishment should have a Roman-style vomitorium next to the toilets. Another all-too-common failing of "touristy" *mezé/meze* is the indiscriminate mingling of fish and meat platters, to even more nauseating effect. Such establishments have completely lost sight of the fact that, in the original Persian, *meze* means "titbit" or "taste". All this acknowledged, such gargantuan *bouffes* are, if nothing else, decent value at C£6–9 each, drink extra, though in the South there is a minimum party of two (sometimes four) persons.

As a rule main-dish portions are generous (if a bit too heavy on the chips), somewhat offsetting the increasing highness of the **prices**. Main courses cost between C£4 (vege- or meat-based) and C£10 (pricey fish), with menu prices usually including a ten-percent service charge and VAT (currently fifteen percent). Prices in the North are much the same, in sterling.

Restaurant **hours** are somewhat restricted, at least compared to Greece or Turkey; **lunch** is generally available only from 12.30 to 2.15pm across the island, **dinner** from 7 to 10pm, even 9.30pm out of peak season. The main exceptions to this are South/North Nicosia, and beachside tavernas, at which you can get lunch pretty much all afternoon. *Exokhiká kéndra* may be open most of the day or evening in summer, but tend to serve weekend lunch only in spring and autumn, and often close completely in winter owing to their outdoor seating.

## Meat and fish

**Meat** dishes tend to predominate, both on and off resort menus. *Kléftiqo* (Gr) or *küp kebap/fırın kebap* (Trk) is arguably the national dish, a greasy, sometimes gristly slab of lamb or goat roasted with vegetables until tender in an outside domed oven with a small opening – you see these next to virtually every farmhouse. However, it has begun to go out of fashion, with Cypriots in the South preferring the less fatty *soúvla*, large chunks of lamb or goat on a rotisserie spit. Lamb chops – *payidhákia* (Gr) or *pırzola* (Trk) – are small by British or North American standards but tasty. *Souvláki* or *şiş* is pork or lamb arrayed in chunks on a skewer and grilled; you'll be asked how many *smíles* (skewers) you want. In the North, you will frequently encounter the set-price **full kebab**, where succulent grilled titbits – sausage chunks, lambs' kidneys, baby lamb chops – are relayed to your table piping hot.

The Venetians introduced domesticated pigeons to the island, and they're much tastier than you'd imagine; quail (*ortíchia*) is the gamier alternative, and both seem much more common than chicken. *Afélia* – pork chunks in red wine and coriander seed sauce – is, unsurprisingly, found only in the non-Muslim Greek community; *sheftália/ şeftalya, şeftalı kebap* – small rissoles of mince, onion and spices wrapped in gut casing – are found all over the island. *Moussakás/musaka*, aubergine and potato slabs overlaid with mince and white sauce in its truest form, is better on the Greek side;

*karnıyarık* is a meatier Turkish aubergine dish without the potato or sauce.

**Fish** is not as plentiful as you'd think around the island, nor as cheap. The best places to get it are around Pólis in the South and on the Karpaz (Kárpas) peninsula, or at Boğaz, in the North; otherwise you can safely assume, even at the most expensive restaurants, that all seafood has been **flash-frozen and shipped in** from elsewhere. Squid and cod, for instance, come from the North Sea, king prawns from farms in Thailand or Bangladesh; the fraudulent passing off of shark as swordfish is not unknown, and farmed bass and gilt-head bream are indistinguishable from those on offer in British supermarkets. If you want to be sure of having fresh, local fare, best stick to the humbler species such as *sorkós/sargoz* or *wóppes/woppa*. *Marídhes*, the least expensive fish in the South, are traditionally sprinkled with lemon slices, rolled in salt and then eaten whole, head and all. Barracuda and *sokan* are best grilled, and either full-sized grouper or its smaller cousin *lágos/lahoz*, usually batter-fried, must be well done to be appetizing. In North Cyprus, *sokan*, *mercan*, *karagöz* and *barbun* are the best-value species. Across the island, squid and octopus are also standard budget seafood options.

## Vegetarian food

**Vegetarians** may have limited options at times, especially in the South, where some restaurateurs think that offering overpriced plates of chips and tomatoes justifies claims of catering to meat-avoiders. *Mezé* opening courses, fortunately, are largely meat-free, consisting principally of *húmmos/humus* (chickpea paté), *tahíni/tahin* (sesame puree), olives, fried *halloúmi/helim* cheese and other titbits; explicitly vegetarian *mezé* is now offered. Unfortunately, inferior rubbery *halloúmi* – full of added yeast and powdered (cow) milk, squeaking on the teeth when chewed – abounds; when you finally get the real thing (from sheep or goat milk, with the butterfat oozing out to the touch) you'll never willingly go back to the other. In the North, *tahin* is often served with lemon juice on top, in the style known as *eşeksiksin*; originally this was *ekşisi* ("sour"), but in a story illustrative of the coarse Cypriot sense of humour, a

Greek Cypriot diner failed to get his tongue around the term and it came out as *eşeksiksin* ("may a donkey fuck it"). The *meyhane*-keeper and the customer came to blows over the perceived insult, but the name stuck forever after.

**Salads** are offered with all entrees, usually a seasonal medley of whatever's to hand: lettuce, tomatoes, parsley, cucumbers, cheese and onions (the latter served on a separate plate). Chefs who try harder may treat you with *rokka* (rocket) greens with their pleasant peppery taste, coriander sprigs or purslane weed (*glystrídha*) – this last much tastier than it sounds. Caper plants are served pickled whole, thorns and all; artichokes – for which the main season is December to April – are typically served raw. Other spring greens, especially popular amongst the Greek Cypriot community as Lenten garnishes, include *khristagáthi* (dock), *strouthondhiá* (wild baby spinach) and *pangáli*. Northern specialities include *gömeç* (mallow greens), said to help settle the stomach, and *molohiya*, (sometimes *mulihiya* or *melokhia*), another steamed, flavourful leaf of the mint family, originally introduced from Egypt some time in the nineteenth century. In the South, fava beans are pureed into *louvána* soup, not to be confused with *louviá* (black-eyed peas); *óspria* is the general term for any **pulse dish**, and what vegetarians should always ask for – it's often not on the menu, considered unfit to sell to foreigners. In winter especially *trakhanás/tarhana*, a soup of grain soaked in yoghurt, is prepared, though it is often made with chicken stock. Healthier **starch** sources than the ubiquitous potato include chunks of mild-flavoured *kolokássia/kolokas* (taro root) brought to the island from Egypt or Syria over a thousand years ago, and *pourgoúri* (cracked or bulgur wheat). Sliced *kouloúmbra* or kohlrabi root is a refreshing, slightly sweet garnish found in many *mezé* arrays.

## Desserts and sweets

**Ice cream** is everywhere, made by small local dairies, and far more prominent than the traditional Levantine sweets; Turkish or Italian style is invariably better than imitation British. In the South, P&P (Papaphillipou & Patisserie Panayiotis) and Iraklis are generally accepted as the best local ice cream brands; in the North there's Mr Bob's, sold on the main highway at Ortaköy in north Nicosia, and Geye in central Kyrenia. Crème caramel and European-style pastries are also well represented. Again in the North, fırın sütlaç (baked rice pudding) is delicious, and through Ramazan the novelty sweet aşure is very popular. In the South, palouzé (grape-must pudding with rosewater) is a common autumn treat.

Among oriental **sticky cakes**, you'll most often find baklavás/baklava, filo pastry layers alternating with honey and nuts; galaktopoúreko/su böreği, filo pastry filled with custard; and kataïfi/kadayıf, similar to baklava but in a "shredded wheat"-type winding. Katméri/katmer is a sort of crêpe filled with banana, honey and sometimes clotted cream, a common dessert in mezé houses/meyhanes. Glyká/macun, preserved candied fruit (and vegetables) of assorted types, is another village speciality occasionally sold to outsiders. Last but not least, you can't miss the island-wide **"Cyprus" Delight**, varying formulas of sugar, rosewater, pectin, nuts and fruit essences – there's no need for anything else (E-numbers, preservatives, etc), so scan ingredient lists carefully.

## Drinking

Traditionally Cypriots drink only as accompaniment to food, and prefer brandy or raki; inebriated north European louts staggering down the streets are apt to offend local sensibilities in either community.

### Wine

Owing to near-ideal climate and soils, Cypriot experience in wine-making stretches far back into antiquity, and the tradition has been carried on with pride – indeed **wine-drinking** can be one of the highlights of a vacation here, though with a few exceptions the vintages aren't yet up to French, Italian or even Greek quality. The industry is based almost entirely in the South, and largely dominated by four major wineries headquartered in Limassol: KEO, ETKO, LOEL and SODAP. However, there are also a number of independent microwineries across the island whose products are usually superior; the best examples are listed below.

Cyprus Trade Centre booklets have listed close on fifty labels of wine, sherry and brandy, quite a total for a medium-sized island, with more being added slowly as the result of research and new varietal planting. You would have to be a pretty dedicated toper to get through all of them during a short stay, so the evaluations below should give you a head start.

Arsinoë is a very dry **white** offering from SODAP, while Danae (also SODAP) is slightly less dry, light white, though by no means fruity or sweet. LOEL's Palomino is a dry white, smoky in colour and taste; ETKO's White Lady is another contender in the dry-white market. Bellapais (KEO), a medium-dry, light sparkling wine a bit like Portuguese vinho verde, comes in white and **rosé** versions. Afrodhite (KEO), an acceptable medium-dry cheap white, and LOEL's Saint Hilarion, are about as sweet as you'd want to drink with food; Saint Panteleimon (KEO), essentially a dessert or mixer white, is too sugary for most tastes. Sódha is the lingua franca for plain soda water – useful for making wine spritzers of those sweeter varieties.

KEO's Rosella is a very dry, dark rosé; the same company makes Othello, a full-bodied **red** not unlike a Cabernet Sauvignon. Hermes is for those who like a rough, dry red, while ETKO's Semeli is a bit more refined. LOEL's Mediterranean, made from actual Cabernet, isn't at all bad as a mid-range product.

Every major vintner (KEO and SODAP are reckoned the best) has a version of **Commandaria**, a red dessert wine related to Madeira, with an interesting pedigree going back to antiquity. Cyprus's first (1990) AOC wine, it's produced by just fourteen villages in the Limassol foothills, and made largely from white Xynisteri grapes, with dark Mavro for colour and balance. These are sun-dried for a week, part-fermented, and then sent down the hill to major wineries, who age it for a minimum of two years in oak barrels and then fortify it to 15 percent alcohol.

Each major label also produces dry, medium and sweet cream **sherries**, most famous of these being ETKO's Emva line. However, following objections from Spain, all the Cypriot players are going to have to call it something else, as "sherry" is now a protected AOC of the Jerez region.

In the Tróödhos foothill villages, it's worth asking for the local **bulk wine**: cheaper, often very good (if not decanted plonk from tetra-pak cartons) and sold in half- or full-litre measures.

Amongst **microwineries**, the Khrysorroyiátissa monastery bottles an excellent dry white, Ayios Andronicos, and a pale red, Ayios Elias. Most wine from the Fikardos winery in Mesóyi is worthwhile, though not easily available outside of Páfos district. Their products include the Amalthia Xynisteri, a very crisp but easy-drinking white, the Ayia Irini white, the Ravanti red from Mataro grapes, and a Cabernet Sauvignon. Other proven products to keep a lookout for include Pampella rosé and Alina white, from Vouni in Panayía; Agravani and Ambelidha, two organic wines from Oekologiki Oenotechnia in Áyios Amvrósios village; Ayios Onoufiros, a dry blended red from Vasilikon in Káthikas; Cava Rotaki, from the Linos winery; anything from Perati, in the Limassol foothills; the Yiaskouris blended red or Shiraz from the eponymous winery in Pákhna; the Domaine Nicolaides rosé, from Anóyira; and the Kilani Village red or white, from the Ayia Mavri winery. Among more recently established players, the Domaine Vlassides (Kiláni) Shiraz and Cabernets are excellent, while almost anything from the Kyperounda, Vasa and Tsiakkas wineries is worthwhile.

## Beer

**In the South**, Carlsberg is currently the best-selling locally brewed beer, available in small 333ml or large 645ml bottles at 4.6 percent; the same brewery makes an "Ice" variety, worth getting but available in supermarkets only. Rival KEO's pilsener, along with its sub-label Leon, comes in the same sizes and alcohol strengths, though KEO in particular is dismissed as watery and insubstantial. **In North Cyprus**, your choices are the Turkish mainland Efes label; Gold Fassl, an Austrian lager made locally under licence; or the strong (5.2 percent) local pilsener, Altınada. There is now quite a variety of imported beers on both sides of the border, especially at theme pubs in Ayía Nápa and Páfos.

## Spirits and liqueurs

Stronger local **firewater** includes zivanía, nearly pure grape alcohol produced greatly in excess of local requirements, and nearly identical to the marc of France, the tsípouro of Greece and the arak of the Arab world. Some is flavoured with botanical agents for home use; the rest is sold to the Southern government or exported to fortify weak drink as far away as Russia. **Oúzo**, as in Greece, is increasingly popular in the South, mostly KEO but also made by a few smaller labels.

KEO also makes a range of **hard liquor**, though imported booze is easily available. As for **brandy**, independently bottled Peristiany 31 and KEO VSOP 12 are fine, though locals prefer to tipple either KEO's Five Kings, Hadjipavlu Anglias or VO 43, all historically smuggled into the North (along with Peristiany). The North's 1975 edict outlawing Greek-Cypriot-produced brandy was deeply unpopular, as brandy-drinking was (and is) one of the few shared tastes of the two communities – doubtless with the "border" porous the trade is less furtive now. **"Brandy sour"**, brandy spiked with lime or lemon juice and Angostura bitters, is effectively the national aperitif in both communities and beloved of holiday-makers; unfortunately, use of premixed citrus base, which can't really substitute for fresh ingredients, is on the increase. Among the more bizarrely flavoured **liqueurs** are Filfar, a sickly sweet orange aperitif, and Mosphilo, made from hawthorn fruit.

## Wines and spirits in the North

In North Cyprus, one lonely distillery near Famagusta makes raki – an aperitif similar to ouzo – and a decent 35-proof brandy called Antique, but Aphrodite, the single red/white wine from straggly grapes in the Kyrenia hills and the Karpaz, is laughable and eminently worth avoiding. Most wine at restaurants in North Cyprus, red or white, is imported from Turkey; Turasan and Peribacası, two quality labels from Cappadocia, are about the best of those commonly available, edging out Kavaklıdere's rougher, more acid Yakut red.

## Tea, coffee and soft drinks

**Tea** in both communities comes in somewhat expensive packs of bags, though in the North, Anatolian settlers have introduced, in the villages at least, the practice of brewing loose tea in a double-boiler apparatus known as a *çaydanlık*. The favourite island-wide **herbal** tea is *spadjá*, made from a variety of sage.

Traditional Middle Eastern **coffee**, fine-ground, boiled without filtration and served in small cups, comes in three grades: plain, medium-sweet and very sweet. Rombout's instant coffee may be preferable to Nescafé in the South, but if you're in a villa with drip-filter coffee-making apparatus, packs of Jacobs pre-ground are widely available and better than either. Incidentally, it's not possible to get a proper espresso or cappuccino in the North – it will be made with instant coffee!

**Juices** throughout the island come in a rainbow of flavours and are usually excellent, available at markets in either litre cartons or bottles. Fresh citrus juice goes briskly at most resort bars. Among brands of **mineral water** in the South, Agros might have an edge, not least because of its packaging in 665ml glass bottles, but Ayios Nikolaos is considered the best and purest.

# Post, phones and the internet

Both the postal and phone systems of post-independence Cyprus were modelled on those of Britain, but since the events of 1974 these facilities have diverged considerably in North and South. Both offer fairly reliable services (the South, as ever, more efficient), though outgoing mail invariably travels faster than incoming. There are plenty of ISPs in both the South and North, but they tend to change identity or go bust with alarming frequency.

## Post

Post offices in the **South** are generally open Monday to Friday 7.30am to 1.30pm plus Thursday 3 to 6pm except in July and August; in the four largest towns, a limited number of branches, listed in the *Guide*, are open every weekday afternoon except Wednesday from 3 to 6pm (4–7pm May–Sept; 3–5pm only in Plátres), as well as Saturday 8.30am to 10.30am.

**Outgoing mail** is reliable, though postage is not especially cheap. Stamps can also be purchased from newsagents, but they may not know the exact rates for your destination. Count on five to seven days for post to arrive in the UK. Numbers of quaint colonial **pillar-boxes** survive, the royal monograms "GR" and "ER" still visible through coats of fresh yellow paint. The same central post offices which have afternoon services also

## Sending mail to North Cyprus

Because of the international postal union boycott of North Cyprus, both incoming and outgoing mail is initially routed through Turkey. When writing to anyone in North Cyprus, you must add a special post code – **Mersin 10, Turkey** – to the last line of the address (this designates the tenth county of Mersin province – further support for the contention that North Cyprus is being subject to creeping annexation by Turkey). If you fail to do so, the letter may be misdirected to the South or more likely to the "addressee unknown" bin.

usually have **poste restante** and **parcel** facilities.

In **Northern Cyprus**, most post offices are open in summer 7.30am to 2pm and 4 to 6pm Monday to Friday, 8.30am to 12.30pm Saturday, while in winter, hours are 8am to 1pm and 2 to 5pm Monday to Friday, 9am to noon on Saturday. **Outgoing mail** is tolerably quick (five to eight days to the UK), considering that it has to be shuffled through Turkey to get around the international postal union boycott; despite this, North Cyprus issues its own stamps. As in the South, look for kerbside pillar-boxes, now a distinctly faded yellow. Parcels are easily sent from Nicosia, Famagusta or Kyrenia. **Poste restante** service is theoretically available in these three towns.

## Phones

Cyprus has a good-to-excellent phone service, though call boxes are fewer than in the UK or North America throughout the island, verging on non-existent in the North. Southern services are modelled on UK prototypes, right down to the model of phoneboxes used; those in the North (not surprisingly) were until recently duplicates of the mainland Turkish system, though now there are models apparently imported from the US and UK.

### The South

Phones in the Republic of Cyprus are administered by the Cyprus Telecommunications Authority, **CYTA** for short. Town- and village-centre **call boxes** should have detailed calling instructions in English, but if not, to **phone overseas from Cyprus**, dial ☏00 – waiting for changes in tone – and then the country code. There are automatic direct-dial connections with virtually everywhere, including the North, which however is treated as a separate country – dial ☏00 392 before the ten-digit number (see below for a discussion of northern phone schemata).

All (often noisily situated) call boxes are now **card-operated**; you may have to keep your thumb on the back end of the card to keep it from popping out. You can purchase C£3, C£5 and C£10 **telecards** from CYTA offices, certain banks, post offices, corner kiosks

and wherever you see the telecard logo displayed. Rates are slightly higher than from fixed phones (see below). Countertop **coin-op** phones in hotel lobbies and restaurants take 5-, 10-, 20-cent and 50-cent coins. Use 5-cent coins for fixed-phone calls, 10- and 20-cent ones for ringing local mobiles; for international calls you're better off using a card-phone or buying a local mobile plan (see below).

Basic subscriber **rates** are currently among the cheapest in the EU. At all hours, from a fixed phone there's a minimum charge of C£0.02 for two minutes to all national numbers, a tad more for local mobiles, C£0.05 per minute to the US, Canada, Greece and the UK, and C£0.06 to the rest of the EU. Calls **from your hotel room** will attract a minimum surcharge of a hundred percent on the basic long-distance rates – luxury hotels bump up overseas rates by factors of four or five.

Almost all Southern **phone numbers**, whether fixed or mobile, are a uniform eight digits, with previous internal area codes becoming mere prefixes (consult the box opposite for prefixes which still show where your callee resides). All numbers starting with 2 are fixed lines; those beginning with 99 are mobiles; 8000 for the first four digits means a free-phone service; while 900 or 909 signals a premium-rate service. Six-digit numbers beginning with 77 are so-called "universal access" numbers, analagous to the UK's 0845 or 0870 codes. To **ring the Republic of Cyprus from overseas** you'll need to dial the country code ☏357, followed by all eight digits.

It's theoretically possible to bring your **mobile phone** from home and roam whilst in the South, but with an extortionate price-fixed cartel applying within the EU (£0.70 per minute plus VAT to anywhere), and with Cyprus offering some of the cheapest mobile rates in the world, you'd be mad to do this for any stay of over a week. Upon arrival, pop your home SIM card out – having the apparatus unblocked if necessary at any corner telecoms shop – and buy one of the two **pre-paid plans** available at present. Cytamobile-Vodafone's "So Easy" costs C£15 plus VAT to get started, with a few pounds' worth of call-time included and top-ups (C£5, C£10 and C£20) valid for a year, so you can keep your SIM if you plan to return to the island next season. Rates for any other phone on the island are 8–8.6 cents/min, while calling overseas it's the CTYA fixed-subscriber rate plus 5.5 cents per minute.

The alternative is Areeba, which for £15 all-in offers much cheaper tariffs of 3.6 cents a minute to any Cypriot fixed or mobile phone, and comparably economical calls to international numbers. The main catch is that the initial credit (and the phone number itself) expires if not re-topped up within 30 days, and top-ups (C£4, C£8 and C£16) have 60, 120 and 240 days of validity respectively.

If you're planning to stay quite a long time, you might consider Cytamobile-Vodafone's **contract plan**: C£10 for the number, plus a monthly subscription fee, with call fees ranging from 2.4 cents/min for fixed phones to 7.6 cents/min for other mobiles.

### The North

Fixed phones in the Turkish Republic of Northern Cyprus are handled by the *Telekomünikasyon Dairesi* or Telecom Division. The system features grey card-phone **call boxes** accepting so-called "smart" *telekart*s, available only from the *Telekomünikasyon* offices. A hundred-unit card costs roughly £1.50 equivalent, enough for just five minutes' chat to the UK. These call boxes are so rare that we've pinpointed them in the *Guide*; working ones tend to have long queues of students and soldiers.

You may get more joy from a so-called **kontürlü telefon** (metered counter phone), which costs about double the *telekart*-phone rates but still about half as much as using a hotel-room phone (see below). These phones are prominently signposted and fairly common in central Kyrenia – you pay after completing your call. Alternatively, there are a bare handful of peaceful booths or counter phones in the equally scarce (and limited-hours) **Telekomünikasyon offices** themselves, where again you pay after you've finished your call.

Despite manifestly outrageous surcharges (at least quadruple the basic *telekart* rate), some users still prefer to place calls from their **hotel room**, reckoning it worth the extra convenience and privacy. Once clear of the hotel circuitry, dial ☏00 to get an **international line**, followed by the usual repertoire of country and area codes. Calls to local fixed-line calls can cost 30p/min, 55–60p/min to local mobiles and a whopping £1.10–1.20/min to any foreign number.

**Mobile phone users** will find that their UK service provider has a reciprocal agreement with the local subsidiary of Turkey-based Telsim or Turkcell. Coverage is excellent but charges to dial anywhere in the EU (including the South) are outrageous – £1.40–1.50 per minute depending on the length of call, ie worse than hotel surcharges. Fees for dialling locally to either fixed or mobile lines are still inflated at £0.60–£1 per minute (and fixed lines are not necessarily cheaper).

It should be evident now that Turkish Cypriot phone services are a rip-off, especially dialling overseas; any local who needs

### Useful telephone numbers and codes

**The South**
International operator (reverse-charge calls, from private or hotel phones only) ☏198
Inland directory assistance ☏192
Overseas directory assistance ☏194
Speaking clock ☏193
Police, fire and ambulance ☏199 or 112
Forest fire reporting ☏189 or ☏1407

Fixed-phone numbers in ... start with:
Nicosia district ☏22

"Free Famagusta" district ☏23
Larnaca district ☏24
Limassol district ☏25
Páfos district ☏26

**The North**
Directory assistance ☏118
International operator ☏115
Police ☏155
Ambulance ☏112
Fire ☏199
Forest fire reporting ☏177

to do this a lot simply buys a Cytamobile-Vodafone or Areeba subscription. From anywhere on the Mesarya with a clear line of sight to the South's antennae – basically half the country – you too can take advantage by just logging into CYTA-Mobile or Areeba and dialling away – it's treated as a roaming call within the EU, and billed as such on your home statement. Better yet, just cross the "border" and get an actual plan.

It is also now a simple matter to call **across the Attila Line** on a fixed line; simply precede the 8-digit number in the South with 00 357. As with calling in the opposite direction, it's charged as an international call, though negotiations are proceeding to get this down to something like local CYTA rates.

Since 1993, North Cyprus has shared the ten-digit Turkish phone number convention: a three-digit area code, ☎392, which applies to fixed phones in the entire country, followed by a seven-digit subscriber number. Mobile numbers are prefixed with ☎0542, 0533 or 0535. When dialling a land line within North Cyprus, omit the ☎392, but when ringing mobiles you must include ☎0542, 0533 or 0535. When **ringing from overseas**, preface these ten digits (leaving off the initial zero of mobile codes) with the international code for Turkey, ☎90; as in matters postal, Turkey effectively "fronts" for North Cyprus in the international arena.

## Internet access

With about half the adult population in the South owning a computer, and a growing proportion in the North, **internet cafés** are not a big thing on either side of the island. If you have a lightweight laptop, it's probably better to consider bringing it. Along with the modem cable, bring any necessary plug adaptors; hotel phone sockets in the South tend to be flat, UK-type, whilst those in the North are either RJ11-type – or an antiquated triple-pin variety for which no adaptor is available.

Any shop that sells you a mobile phone plan can also set you up with a short- (or long- ) term **subscription** CD to a **local ISP**, if your home provider does not have an access number on Cyprus. Minimum periods are two to three months, for an equivalent of C£8/month (plus low phone charges) – about what you'd spend in an internet café after a few hours.

# The media

For a modest-sized island, Cyprus is served by a disproportionately large number of printed publications and TV and radio channels. Part of this is a result of non-market factors, such as sponsorship of print media by political groups on both sides of the Attila Line, and also to its critical position in the eastern Mediterranean, enabling the island both to tap the airwaves from, and beam to, neighbouring countries.

## Newspapers and magazines

While the vernacular-language print media will be inaccessible to most visitors, there are a number of informative, locally produced English-language publications aimed primarily at expats. A very few foreign newspapers are available – at a price.

### The South

Nearly a dozen Greek-language newspapers, many toeing a particular party line, cater to native readers in the South. Among **English-language papers**, *The Cyprus Weekly* (Fridays) and the daily (except Mon) *Cyprus Mail* are both part-colour but design-challenged. The *Mail*, one of the oldest publications in the Middle East and considered a paper of record, is far more intelligent, worth a read for Patroclos' Sunday-only "Tales from the Coffee Shop" scandals-and-corruption column alone. More native Cypriots than care to admit are known to take a furtive look at it, and at the paper as a whole. The standard of journalism at the *Weekly*, a Turkophobic, nationalist fishwrap, is far lower. Editorial content aside, both have news, extensive small ads, real estate pullouts, and daily/weekly programmes for most radio and TV stations. The *Mail* features brief weekday sections for films and exhibitions, airport timetables and chemist rotas, though the Sunday edition is particularly valuable for its "What's On" pull-out section giving the week's listings of film, TV, radio and live events. Chemist and Sunday petrol-station opening times appear in the *Weekly*, along with a more extensive, pull-out arts-review section called "Lifestyle", which includes a "TV and Cinema" listings section. **Foreign newspapers** are generally limited to *The Times*, the *International Herald Tribune*, *The Guardian* and the *Daily Mail*.

## The North

You'll see only very occasional, overpriced copies of the *Financial Times* or *Sunday Times* in the North, the rather turgid *Turkish Daily News/Probe* from the mainland, plus the Asil-Nadir-owned weekly *Cyprus Today* (Saturday) in English; this has radio and TV listings, plus the rota of late-night chemists and complete Ercan airport flight info. There are also around a half-dozen Turkish-language papers, mostly daily, nearly all affiliated with a political party. *The New Colonial* (monthly) is a bilingual, glossy mag published by and for expats, much improved since it stopped being a freebie advertiser.

## The whole island

If you really get involved with Cyprus, one of the best objective publications is the yearly (autumn) **Report of the Friends of Cyprus**, a British lobby of parliamentarians, Euro-MPs and other public figures pushing for an equitable settlement to the island's division. In addition to a summary of the previous year

on Cyprus, it has a mix of technical articles on law and statecraft along with memoirs, poetry and book reviews. To subscribe (£5 plus postage per issue), contact Mary Southcott ☎0117/924 5139, ✉friends ofcyprus@hotmail.com.

## Radio, TV and cinema

The advantages of having your own electronic media for propaganda purposes are not lost on either of Cyprus's two main communities; accordingly there's an ongoing "battle of the transmitters". **Bayrak**, the North's radio voice, dangles lengthy Greek-music and -language programming to reel in Southern listeners (plus the latest UK styles), as a prelude to news broadcasts presenting the South in a bad light, overrun with mafiosi, graft, terrorism and unreconstructed Enosis-ists. For its part, the Southern station **CyBC** (Cyprus Broadcasting Corporation), even in its Turkish-language programming, studiously refers to the North as "Turkish-occupied territory", and Denktaş plus his successor as "leader of the Turkish-Cypriot community". In recent years, programming hours have lengthened and (at last count) two dozen **private stations** have emerged, mostly on the FM dial, to challenge the government monopoly, a sharp break from the past where meagre advertising revenues and a limited audience dictated just a few hours' broadcasting per day.

## Radio

On the **radio**, CyBC's strictly Greek Programme 1 can be found at 97.2 and 90.2FM and/or 693 AM, 6am to midnight. CyBC's Programme 2, at 91.1, 92.4 and 94.2 FM during the same time slot, has a more cosmopolitan line-up with news in English at 1.30pm and 8pm, and all-English programming from 6pm to midnight. The BBC World Service broadcasts at 1323 AM more or less around the clock; reception is usually very strong, since the transmitter for the whole Middle East sits on the coast between Larnaca and Limassol. The British Sovereign Bases operate the British Forces Broadcasting Service (BFBS), in English with Western music programming, on Programme 1 (24hr) at 92.1 (Limassol),

89.7 (Nicosia) and 99.6 (Larnaca) FM, and features, news and serials (including almost-daily doses of *The Archers*) on Programme 2 (6am to 9pm) at 91.7 or 95.2 (Nicosia), 85.3 (Larnaca) and 81.9 FM (Limassol). Skipping along the dial you'll also find several private, local English-language stations, for example Radio Napa at 90.9FM and Kiss at 89FM. Among Cypriot channels, Kanali 6 at 107.1FM is excellent for quality Greek music, especially on Sunday.

In **the North**, the official Bayrak Radyo (87.8 and 105 FM) functions from about 6.30am to midnight; English-language programming was expanded in 1999, and there tends to be quality Western music at night, also listened to by numbers of folk in the South. Most people listen to Metro at 104 FM, with a good range of Western pop, and widely available as it's beamed in by powerful transmitters from Turkey. The most reliable BFBS-2 frequencies are 95.2, 91.7 (Nicosia) and 89.9FM, and 1089 or 1503AM.

### Television

CyBC 1 and 2 (RIK 1 and RIK 2 in Greek) beam TV from **the South** daily from about 7am to 1am and from 8am to 3.30am respectively (subject to daily variations); programming is a lively mix of soaps, films, music, sports, talk shows and documentaries. There's a lot of foreign material with its original soundtrack, and even the Greek transmissions have English and Turkish subtitles. Otherwise people tune in to the Greek stations ET1, Mega and Antenna from Rhodes, Paphos TV in Páfos district, or private local stations Logos, Sigma, Lumiere

(alias LTV, mostly films; subscriber only), Alfa or Fred-TV. Satellite dishes pick up BBC World and CNN.

In **the North**, Kıbrıs TV will have at least one foreign film nightly, starting between 8.30 and 10.40pm, with original soundtrack; BRT2 has films and variety shows, plus occasional news in English, from 5.30pm until almost midnight. Otherwise people make do with TRT from Turkey, or a host of private Turkish channels such as ATV, Show, Star, Kanal Altı, NTV and Kanal D.

### Cinema

In terms of **cinema in the South**, there are fourteen regularly functioning commercial screens in Nicosia, ten in Limassol, eight in Larnaca and three screens in Páfos; films tend to be first-run caper/action releases. For art-house and retrospective fare, there are cinema clubs in Nicosia, Limassol and Páfos (often a special night at the commercial movie-houses), while the British, French and Russian cultural centres in south Nicosia also screen their share of such.

Prints are generally in the original language, with Greek subtitles. Screening times are usually given in the foreign-language press. Producing a student ID often nets you C£1 off admission.

There are now thirteen movie screens in the **North**: three two-plexes in Nicosia, a two-plex in Famagusta, four screens in and around Kyrenia, and even one in Güzelyurt. Movies tend to be up to a year old, but of reasonable print quality. Programmes are given on the "What's On at the Cinema" page of *Cyprus Today*'s centre pullout section.

# Opening hours, holidays and festivals

Business hours throughout the island are scheduled around the typical Mediterranean midday siesta. Generally the South's public holidays have a religious focus, reflecting the Greek Orthodox Church's pre-eminent position in the culture, while the North – technically a secular society – has more commemorations of salient events in Turkish communal history. In recent years many special events have been developed by the Southern tourism authorities, with a view to a foreign audience, to supplement the bedrock of traditional religious festivals.

## Opening hours

Town shops in **the South** are meant to be open daily in summer (June to mid-Sept) from 8am to 1pm and again from 4 to 7.30pm, except for Wednesday and Saturday when there are no afternoon hours. During spring (April–May) and autumn (mid-Sept to Oct), afternoon hours end at 7pm. Winter (Nov–March) hours are daily 8.30am to 6pm, except for Wednesday and Saturday when everything shuts at 2pm.

Both mountain village stores and establishments in tourist resorts are likely to keep longer hours. Food shops along roads leading to dormitory/suburb villages around major towns will be open beyond 7pm, often until 9.30pm. In August, all filling stations close down for a week, with a rota so that a very few are open at any given time.

Office-based private professionals work nominally 8am to 1pm and 3 to 6pm (mid-Sept to May), 8am to 1pm and 4 to 7pm (June to mid-Sept).

In **the North**, summer hours are supposedly 8am to 1.30pm and 2.30 to 6.30pm Monday to Friday, plus a morning session on Saturday. In winter, shops are meant to be open continuously 8am to 6pm Monday to Saturday. Observance of schedules may be haphazard, with midday summer closures extending until 4pm. Some office-based professionals are taking to closing by 5pm, especially in winter.

## Public holidays in the South

In the South, there is near-complete overlap between religious and bank **holidays**, so of the dates below official business is only conducted (after a fashion) on *Kataklysmós*. When these dates fall on a Sunday, the subsequent Monday is usually a public holiday – in the case of Easter, the following Tuesday is also a bank holiday, as is Good Friday and part of Maundy Thursday. Shops do stay open on Good Friday and Holy Saturday morning, but then remain shut until Wednesday morning except in tourist areas, so beware.

## Religious holidays in the South

**New Year's Day** in Cyprus is the feast day of **Áyios Vassílios** (St Basil), and the evening before, most homes bake a *vasilópitta* or cake containing a coin bringing good luck to the person finding it in their slice. The saint is also the Orthodox equivalent of Santa Claus, and gifts are exchanged on this day, though see the note below about Christmas.

In the Orthodox Church, **Epiphany** marks the baptism of Christ in the Jordan, and the conjunction of the Holy Trinity; the Greek name *Ta Theofánia* refers to the resulting inner illumination. Holy water fonts in churches are blessed to banish the *kalikándzari* demons said to run amok on earth after Christmas. As a finale at seaside locations, a local bishop hurls a crucifix out over the water, and young men swim for the honour of recovering it.

**Clean Monday** comes at the end of the ten days of **Carnival**, the occasion for fancy-dress balls and parades, most notably in Limassol. In rural areas, the day also signals the beginning of a strict seven-week abstention from animal products for the devout.

## Public holidays in South Cyprus

| 2006 | 2007 | 2008 | |
|------|------|------|---|
| 1 January | same | same | Áyios Vasílios (New Year's Day) |
| 6 January | same | same | *Theofánia* (Epiphany) |
| 6 March | 19 March | 10 March | Clean (Lent) Monday |
| 25 March | same | same | Annunciation |
| 1 April | same | same | Southern Republic Day |
| 21 April | 6 April | 25 April | Orthodox Good Friday |
| 23 April | 8 April | 27 April | Orthodox Easter Sunday |
| 1 May | same | same | Labour Day |
| 12 June | 28 May | 16 June | *Kataklysmós* (Flood Festival) |
| 15 August | same | same | Assumption of the Virgin |
| 1 Oct | same | same | Cyprus Independence Day |
| 28 Oct | same | same | Greek National Day |
| 25/26 Dec | same | same | Christmas/Boxing Day |

March 25 is usually billed as "Greek National Day", but is more properly the feast of *Evangelismós* or the **Annunciation**.

Observance of **Easter** starts early in **Holy Week**, and the island's small Catholic and Armenian communities celebrate in tandem with the Orthodox majority. The most conspicuous customs are the dyeing red of hard-boiled eggs on Maundy Thursday, the baking of special holiday cakes such as *flaoúnes* (which actually transgress the Lenten fast with their egg-and-cheese content) and on Good Friday eve the solemn procession of the *Epitáfios* or Christ's funeral bier in each parish, whose women provide its elaborate floral decoration. In Páfos town, for example, at least two of these are paraded solemnly through the streets, preceded by an intimidating military escort and youth bands playing New-Orleans-ish cortège themes, until they meet near the central park at about 10.30pm, where the local bishop presides over a brief service.

On Saturday evening, huge bonfires (*lambrádjia*) are set – giving rise to the word **Lambrí**, the alias for Easter in Cypriot dialect – before the spectacular midnight *Anástasi* or Resurrection mass. Not everyone will fit into the confines of a typical village church, so crowds gather in the courtyard, around the embers of the fire. Observance is pretty casual, even by Greek rural standards; the noise of high-decibel fireworks set off by teenagers – everything from Roman candles to dynamite left over from the Límni mine in Tillyría – all but drowns out the liturgy, such

that in one year early in the 1990s the priest at Neokhorió village on the Akámas peninsula refused to proceed with the service.

Things calm down temporarily at midnight, when the officiating priest appears from behind the altar screen bearing a lighted candle and the news of eternal life for believers, and soon church interiors and courtyards are ablaze with the flame passed from worshipper to worshipper. The skyline of the larger towns will be illuminated now by spectacular fireworks displays – the wealthier the municipality the better. It is considered good luck to get your candle home still alight, to trace a soot-cross over the door lintel; then the Lenten fast is broken with *avgolémono* soup, and family members crack their red-dyed eggs against each other (owner of the last unbroken egg "wins").

**Kataklysmós** or the **Festival of the Flood**, fifty days after Easter, is unique to Cyprus; elsewhere in the Orthodox world it is merely Whit Monday or the Feast of the Holy Spirit, but here it's a pretext for several days of popular events. At all coastal towns people crowd into the sea and sprinkle each other with water; the festival ostensibly commemorates the salvation of Noah and his family from the Flood, but it's likely a vestige of a much older pagan rite in honour of Aphrodite's birth, or perhaps her purification after sleeping with Adonis.

**Christmas** (*Khristoúyenna*) is relatively subdued in Cyprus, though inevitably European-style commercialization – including house illuminations and plastic Santas – has made inroads. The most durable old custom is that of the *kálanda* or carols, sung by children going door-to-door accompanying themselves on a triangle. It's worth noting that many establishments (restaurants and KEO brewery tours, for example) seem to shut down between Christmas and New Year, opening only sporadically between January 1 and 6.

## Other events in the South

In addition to the strictly ecclesiastical holidays, municipalities and tourist boards lay on a number of other events, with a steady eye on the foreign audience. The most reliable of these include the May *Anthistíria* or **Flower Festivals**, best in mid-May at Larnaca and Páfos; the **Shakespeare Festival** preceding **Cyprus Music Days**, at Kourion's ancient theatre during late June/early July; the Limassol and Larnaca municipal festivals in July; the **Páfos festival** of music, theatre and dance staged in the ancient *odeion* and medieval castle from July to September; the **Ayía Nápa festival** in late September; and the **Limassol Wine Festival,** with free tasting sessions in the central park, during the first half of September. If you're determined to coincide with any or all of these, get a copy of the CTO's annual *List of Events* or the monthly update produced at each local tourist office.

## Public holidays in the North

In the **North**, the holiday calendar is again a mix of religious holidays and official, patriotic commemorations, many imported from Turkey. All religious feasts recede eleven days yearly in the western calendar (12 in a leap year) because of the lunar nature of the Muslim calendar; however future dates of festivals as given on Islamic websites are provisional, owing to factors such as when the moon is sighted and the international dateline, so you should expect variance of up to a day in the ranges given in the box. Unlike in the South, there's just not the budget or inclination for laying on big-theme secular bashes. Surviving, reliable and prestigious **cultural festivals** include the Bellapais Music Festival (late May to late June), with performances by name artists in the eponymous abbey, and the Famagusta International Festival, featuring more varied acts from late June to mid-July. Additionally, there are occasional folkloric performances at the castles of Famagusta and Kyrenia, and festivals on the Mesarya (Mesaoría) linked to the harvest of various crops, especially the Güzelyurt Orange Festival in mid-May.

The official holidays of the North are fairly self-explanatory, though a word on the movable **religious feasts** is in order. **Şeker Bayramı** marks the end of the **fasting month of Ramazan** (Ramadan), and is celebrated with family get-togethers and the distribution of presents and sweets to visitors. At the northern outskirts of Nicosia, there's a fun-fair on purpose-built grounds, with "luna-park" rides for kids, and traditional foods and crafts on sale. **Kurban Bayramı** commemorates the thwarted sacrifice of Ishmael by Abraham – a Koranic version of

### Public holidays in the North

| 2005 | 2006 | 2007 | |
|------|------|------|---|
| 1 January | same | same | New Year's Day (*Yılbaşı*) |
| 20–23 Jan | 9–12 Jan | 29 Dec '06–1 Jan '07 | *Kurban Bayramı* |
| 22 April | 11 April | 1 April | *Mevlûd* (Muhammad's Birthday) |
| 23 April | same | same | National Sovereignty & Children's Day |
| 1 May | same | same | Labour Day |
| 19 May | same | same | Youth and Sports Day |
| 20 July | same | same | Peace Operation Day |
| 1 August | same | same | TMT Day |
| 30 August | same | same | *Zafer Bayramı*(Victory Day) |
| 29 October | same | same | Turkish Republic Day |
| 3–5 Nov | 23–25 Oct | 12–14 Oct | *Şeker Bayramı* |
| 15 November | same | same | TRNC Foundation Day |

the Abraham-and-Isaac story – and used to be distinguished by the dispatch and roasting of vast numbers of sheep; the custom is now on the wane in Cyprus, among native-born Turkish Cypriots anyway.

By their own admission, Turkish Cypriots are among the laxest Muslims world-wide in terms of observance – few set foot in a mosque on any given Friday – but almost everybody makes some effort to observe Ramazan by swearing off booze for the duration (a major sacrifice, given some pretty hard drinking habits) and food during daylight hours, which means outside of Kyrenia many restaurants shut at midday, especially if the

fasting month falls during the tourist off-season. This, and the fact that everyone eats in to save up money for expensive nights out on **Arife**, the first evening of the Şeker Bayramı festivity, makes Ramazan a rather dull time to travel. Restaurants are particularly empty on the fifth evening before Şeker Bayramı, known as **Kadir Gecesi** or the night the Koran was revealed to Muhammad. Most people stay home then, reading the Koran and praying; it's believed that prayers on this night have a special efficacy. Many, if not most, Turkish Cypriots do attend mosque services on Şeker Bayramı and Kurban Bayramı.

# Sites, museums, churches and mosques

Archeological sites and museums throughout the island have user-friendly opening times, though you may find certain Northern museums and monuments shut (when they're supposed to be open) without explanation owing to staffing problems. Admission fees are modest, especially compared to neighbouring countries, and in the South at least, polite signs instructing you to "Please ask for your ticket" are a far cry from the typically growling human Cerberus blocking the way in Greece or Egypt. Churches and mosques of interest to visitors have less established visiting hours and operate on a "donation" basis.

## Opening times and admission fees

The more popular ancient sites in the **South** are fenced but accessible from roughly 9am to near sunset all year, though even during long-day months they're never open past 7.30pm. Most major museums shut weekdays at 4.30 to 5pm, and by 1pm on Saturday and Sunday. On most public holidays (see previous section) outdoor sites are unaffected, but many museums keep short – or no – hours, and everything closes on Easter Sunday, Christmas and New Year's Day. No entrance fee for state-run facilities exceeds C£1.50, and most are currently C£0.75–1; children under 10 usually get in free, but student discounts are not the rule. Since Cyprus's entry to the EU, many (though

not all) sites are free to all EU nationals on Sundays.

Operating hours at the limited number of museums and sites in **Northern Cyprus** are vaguely similar; admission fees cost £0.75–£2.50, depending on the attraction, and properly identified students almost always get a two-thirds discount.

## Churches

Most of the famous **frescoed churches** of **the South** are still used in some sacred capacity, and kept locked to protect them from thieves and the elements; accordingly they often don't have set visiting hours. Part of the experience is locating the key-keeper, not always a priest, who may live or work some distance away. A donation (of C£0.50

## Churches in the North

Since the events of 1974 only a bare handful of **churches in the North** continue to function as houses of Christian worship. The rest have been either converted into mosques or museums, or desecrated in various ways, mostly by the Turkish army but also by Anatolian settlers or Turkish Cypriots.

This behaviour is naturally seized on by the outraged Greek Cypriots as further proof of (mainland) Turkish barbarism, and used to good effect in their sophisticated "public relations" efforts. The Southern government pointedly contrasts the treatment of these buildings with the relative consideration accorded to mosques in the South, which are held in trust by a Religious Affairs Department, provided with a tiny budget to maintain the buildings.

For their part, the Northerners either tend not even to acknowledge that injury has been caused or to justify it as the understandable venting of frustrations and aggressions on the most tangible, helpless reminders of the atrocities perpetrated on the Turkish Cypriots by EOKA, which included the dynamiting of mosque minarets on certain occasions. Moreover, it is claimed that the ringing of church bells often signalled the start of an anti-Turkish-Cypriot pogrom in formerly mixed villages.

What this means to a visitor is that the Northerners are touchy about requests to visit churches not specifically prepared for public use. You will often find abandoned churches off-limits as military depots, and/or appallingly vandalized, sometimes with their entrances bricked up to prevent further damage. In any case it's a depressing exercise visiting these battered buildings, empty of the devotion which the Greek Cypriots lavished on them, and something most people will only do once or twice.

to C£1) to the collection box, if not the person himself, is required; some of them can be impatient, to say the least, with non-Orthodox, and will begin fidgeting or muttering if in their view too much time is spent in gawping irreligiously at the frescoes. Since all but one or two of these churches are still consecrated, men may not usually enter in shorts, nor women in trousers or culottes of any sort, and neither sex in sleeveless tops – wraps for the indecently attired are not provided, so bring suitable garb. Photos, especially with flash or tripod, are usually not allowed.

### Mosques

Most **mosques** in the South are now kept locked, presumably awaiting the hypothetical return of their Turkish-Cypriot users. One apiece still functions in south Nicosia, Limassol and Larnaca, meeting the spiritual needs of the Republic's sizeable population of Arabs, Pakistanis, Bangladeshis and Iranians – as well as the slowly growing numbers of remaining (and returning) Turkish Cypriots in the South. The Hala Sultan Tekke near Larnaca is also still an active place of pilgrimage for both island and foreign Muslims.

Some rules of **etiquette** apply to any mosque throughout the island. Contrary to what you may read in other sources, shoes must be removed at the entrance, and one does not enter scantily clad – this in effect means the same guidelines as for churches (see above). Native Cypriot Muslims are remarkably easy-going (eg, their tolerant attitudes towards drinking and dogs) and flattered at any attention to their places of worship, so you would have to do something fairly insensitive to irk them. As a minimum, don't enter mosques when a service is in progress, and try not to walk in front of a praying person.

# Police, trouble and harassment

In general, Cyprus is one of the safest Mediterranean travel destinations: assault and theft are almost unknown, and the atmosphere is so unthreatening that you catch yourself feeling silly for locking a rental car. What crime there is tends to be fraud, extortion and smuggling, though since the mid-1990s there has been a series of grisly killings inside the Cypriot underworld.

Civilian authorities and police in both communities usually go out of their way to make tourists feel welcome, and the most likely occasion for misunderstandings will be the various **military zones** – far more numerous in the North than in the South. It is best to give any military installation in the North a very wide berth; do not park or halt cars, "loiter" (ie, walk slowly past), read, write or photograph *anything* within sight of a command post, barracks, officers' apartments, military hospital, canteen, etc. Sentries are apt to be twitchy and over-zealous, especially since the September 11 incidents and the İstanbul UK consulate bombing (Turkish forces are considered lackeys of the US by Al Qaeda and thus a tempting target). The Turkish army is a law unto itself – no civilian authority will intervene on your behalf – and you could find yourself detained for an hour or more by a trigger-happy conscript, until a commanding officer and interpreter are found to help ascertain that you are not in fact a suicide bomber or something similar.

Unless you are actually visiting someone living in the **buffer** (demilitarized, "dead") **zone**, or are escorted by authorized UN personnel, you'll at least raise an eyebrow or two by driving into it – certainly in the North – and could provoke a major incident by using any roads marked as blocked-off on our maps. With more legal crossings expected to open in the future, you'll have little excuse for being found in such places.

Do heed the **"no photography"** signs near military bases throughout the island, as well as along the Attila Line (called the Green Line in Nicosia). If you are caught photographing, even inadvertently, a military installation anywhere in Cyprus, your film

may be confiscated – politely, and possibly returned after processing and screening, in the South; more brusquely by the Turkish army in the North. In the southern Republic some or all of certain monasteries are now off-limits to cameras, since the monks grew tired of being zoo-animal-type attractions. Similarly, don't sneak snaps of the interiors of the South's frescoed churches – caretakers accompany you inside to prevent this, among other reasons.

For years, casual visitors were unlikely to see much evidence of **organized crime** on the island. But late in 1995, a spectacular scandal broke, implicating the higher ranks of the South's police force in a spate of gangland shootings, car bombings, apartment arson and torture of suspects in detention with UK-supplied stun-batons. Things have not let up much since then, as mafia dons – now largely *Russopóndi* or Caucasians of Greek ethnic origin – fight an ongoing turf war for control of these lucrative ventures. Though it all sounds lurid, as long as you avoid cabarets, massage parlours, gambling dens and unwise purchases of controlled substances, you should avoid being caught in crossfire or getting on the wrong side of the police.

Of late, the influence of organized crime has become almost equally pervasive in the burgeoning brothels and casinos of the North, but violent scores tend to be settled in mainland Turkey, where most of the big bosses remain. An exception – and the most "illustrious (Cypriot) corpse" resulting to date – was Sabri Tahir, dubious (anti)hero of Lawrence Durrell's *Bitter Lemons*, who early in 2001 was gunned down (on the second attempt) at the helm of his Orient Brothel-Casino, ironically just opposite the Ministry of

Tourism. It seems he had not made payoffs to "associates" in a timely manner.

If you have anything **stolen**, it is still worthwhile – despite all the foregoing – to report the theft at the nearest police station and get a copy of the report or the identification number under which your report is filed: you will need this if you intend to make an insurance claim once you get back home. Be prepared, however, to be scrutinized carefully by the Southern police, as there have been numbers of fraudulent claims – and prosecutions of offenders.

## Sexual harassment and prostitution

Both Greek- and Turkish-Cypriot men are more reserved than their mainland counterparts, though as throughout the Mediterranean, resort areas support numbers of underemployed Romeos. Told to desist in no uncertain terms, Cypriot men usually will. In the more traditional inland areas, unescorted women will generally be accorded village courtesy.

The traditional, home-grown red-light districts of Limassol and Nicosia may have been wound up since the millennium, but they were long since eclipsed in any case, on both sides of the line, by veritable armies of eastern European prostitutes. Over 1500 "natashas" who work the brothels and "nightclubs" of the **North** pay large "sureties" against future taxes, plus fees for residence permits, to the governing regime which is in effect pimping from them. Since the "border" opened in April 2003, their former Turkish mainland clientele has been largely replaced by a Greek-Cypriot one.

In the **South**, the focus of the industry is Limassol, where an undisclosed number of Russians, Moldavians, Bulgarians, Ukrainians and Romanians staff the "gentlemen's clubs" or patrol the hotel strip. The **cabarets** are to be avoided as a nightlife option; the bill for three or four beers can run to C£300–400, and reluctant payers will be frog-marched by bouncers to the nearest cash dispenser and "persuaded" to withdraw the necessary funds.

# Sports and outdoor activities

Because of its mild climate, Cyprus is a good place to indulge in assorted open-air athletic activities. The CTO even devotes an entire six-page, large-format leaflet to the subject, detailing indoor facilities as well. In terms of spectating, football and tennis – for which the South hosts major international tournaments yearly – are the big events.

## Water sports

Virtually all resorts in the South cater well to any water sport you could mention, from kayaking to parasailing by way of waterskiing. **Windsurfing** boards are available everywhere, but you only get strong breezes around the island's capes: in the far southeast, between Ayía Nápa and Protarás; around Páfos; and occasionally on the exposed coast west of Pólis. Small sailcraft can be rented from the marinas at Larnaca,

Limassol and Páfos. In North Cyprus, windsurfing and sailing facilities concentrate west of Kyrenia, and at the luxury hotels near ancient Salamis.

Perhaps the biggest attraction is underwater; unusually for the eastern Mediterranean, where submerged antiquities are prone to theft, **scuba** is encouraged by the tourism authorities and actively promoted by numerous dive operators – we've listed at least one in each major resort. In the North, at least two (in some years three) scuba schools operate in or near Kyrenia, plus there's often an operator trying its luck near Famagusta. As a general rule, diving off the island's north coast – whether from Greek Cypriot or Turkish Cypriot territory – tends to be more exciting, and sheltered, than off the south coast, with the outstanding exception of the *Zenobia* wreck near Larnaca.

## On land

Cypriots are big **tennis** buffs, participatory as well as watching, and most hotels over three stars in either the North or the South will have their own courts. Otherwise, courts are open to the public in all the big Southern towns.

**Mountain-biking** has already been noted as a possibility in "Getting Around", but there are also some bona fide marked trails – as opposed to vehicle tracks – in the Tróödhos, prepared expressly for **hiking** by the CTO in conjunction with the forestry division. The *Guide* covers all of them, though the longest itinerary will fill just a single day. The only long-distance, GR-type route, between the Akámas and Ayía Nápa, is the European long-distance trail E4, though much of it is

a bad joke, relying extensively on jeep tracks and even stretches of paved road – hardly the point of such a route. It's more difficult, but still possible, to walk in the steeper Kyrenia hills as long as you steer clear of military areas, though a catastrophic 1995 fire has detracted considerably from the appeal of the countryside.

Southern Cyprus can boast the exotic attraction, for the Middle East, of a **ski** resort. There's a single complex of four lifts serving seven runs on the northeast face of Mount Olympus, the island's summit. The season, in a good year, lasts approximately from January to late March; don't come specially.

Since 1995 **golf**, focused on the new golf courses at Tsádha, Secret Valley and Aphrodite Hills in Páfos district (plus the Elias near Limassol, and the twelve-hole course at Víkla), has been heavily promoted to visitors (see box p.197 for some background). Most package-tour operators offer the option of pro booking green fees, which, depending on the company and time of year (high summer is cheapest) vary from £15–26 per day.

# Shopping

Cyprus, North or South, is not a souvenir hunter's paradise, but while you're travelling around there are certain items worth looking out for. See also the note on bargaining in the "Directory", following.

## The South

The South is most famous for **lacework**, produced principally at Páno Léfkara, equidistant from the three largest towns. Strictly speaking this is a misnomer, as it is more like drawn-thread work and not bobbin lace, with a sewing needle being used. Local cotton or linen is no longer used, light or dark Irish linen now being the raw material. Be aware of machine-made tape lace from the Far East fraudulently labelled as "hand-made".

More reliable and affordable is the Léfkara **silverware**. Arguably more attractive, colourful, **loom-woven items**, also more likely to be indigenous, are available at Fýti in Páfos district. Reed **basketry** is another distinctive product, especially in Páfos district; of particular interest are the almost Amerindian-looking, bi- or tri-colour **circular mats and trays** (called *tséstos* in Greek), which adorn the walls of many tavernas. You can find reed products at the central covered markets of Nicosia, Páfos and Limassol, as well as at Yeroskípou and Liopétri villages. Another taverna-decor staple which can still be purchased are *kolótzia* or **etched gourds**, embossed with designs either painted or burned on.

More urban specialities include **shoes, silver jewellery** and (in particular) **optical goods**. High-quality sunglasses at the numerous opticians cost about the same as in North America, owing to direct importation, and thus much less than in Britain. Moreover, speciality products such as high-diopter plastic lenses for registered blind persons can be obtained reasonably and quickly from warehouse stock (often within 24 hours), as opposed to a month on special order in Britain. Since entry to the EU, however, savings compared to northern Europe have been sharply eroded, starting with the five-percent hike in VAT.

The government-run **Cyprus Handicraft Service** has several fixed-price retail outlets, which gather together under one roof "approved" examples of each craft. It's worth stopping in to gauge quality and cost at the very least; addresses are given below.

### Cyprus handicraft centres

**South Nicosia** Athalássas 186 ☎ 22305024; Laïkí Yitoniá ☎ 22303065.

**Larnaca** Kosmá Lysióti 6 ☎ 24630327.
**Limassol** Themídhos 25 ☎ 25330118.
**Páfos** Apostólou Pávlou 64 ☎ 26240243.

## The North

There is rather less on offer in the **North**, though the basketry products (*sesta* or *paneri* in Turkish) seem more refined, and comparatively expensive; you can find very strong, large **baskets** suitable for clothes hampers in north Nicosia and the village of Edremit, though as in the South the items tend to be made elsewhere, in the remote villages of Serdarlı, Gönendere and Görneç. Junk and antique dealers in Nicosia and Famagusta have a limited and expensive stock of **old copper** and **household implements**.

Otherwise you are faced with the task of sifting through a fair amount of second-rate kitsch (garish backgammon sets, thin-gauge copper lanterns, onyx eggs, ceramic ashtrays, frankly bad carpets), offloaded from Syria and Turkey, lying in wait for tourists insisting on something "Oriental".

# Directory

**Addresses** In the Greek-Cypriot sector, addresses are written either in Greek or in English. When in Greek, the number follows the street name, for example "Leofóros Faneroménis 27". The same place in English is cited as "27, Faneromenis Avenue". Post codes exist but are not yet used much; more often a district within the municipality is cited.

In Northern Cyprus, addresses are generally given bilingually (Turkish/English) on visiting cards and bumph, but if not, *Caddesi*, abbreviated to Cad, means avenue; *Bulvarı* (Bul) is boulevard; *Meydan/Meydanı* (Meyd) is plaza; *Sokak/Sokağı* (Sok) means street; and *Çıkmazı* (Çık) is a dead-end alley. *Karşısı* means "opposite from", as in *PTT karşısı*, "opposite the post office".

**Bargaining** Not a regular feature of Cypriot life, except in the case of any souvenir purchase where price is not marked. Don't expect the vendor to come down more than twenty percent from their opening bid, however. Hotels and pensions in the

South have prices prominently displayed, and there is generally no upward fiddling in this respect. At slow times you can get rooms for twenty to forty percent less than posted rates; the same applies to car rental, at least with local chains and one-offs. In the North things are more flexible; written rates and prices are not so conspicuous, but again expect only small discounts.

**Bring...** a water container for hot-weather ruin-tramping; a torch for dark corners of same, and for outlasting power cuts in Northern Cyprus; bath/sink plugs (rarely supplied) for washing clothes, 37mm and 44mm diameter best; a line and clips for hanging said clothes; a Swiss-Army-type knife with screwdriver and tweezer attachments; a small alarm clock; some form of flying/biting-bug repellent (sold in the South, though) or netting; and sunscreen cream with a protection factor of over 25 (difficult to find). In the North you'll want all of the above, plus slide photo film and contact lens solutions from home.

**Children and babies** They are sacred in both communities, and should present few problems travelling; in most resorts geared for the package trade on either side of the island, family-sized suites are easy to come by. Baby formulas and nappies are available in pharmacies and supermarkets everywhere. Fresh, full-fat milk is easy to get in any supermarket; organic and salt-free products can be found in the South with some diligence. Child seats, not necessarily up to UK standards, are available in rental cars if booked well in advance. Many hotels in the South offer child-friendly programmes; we've singled out a few in accounts, and such outfits are usually clear about this in brochures.

**Cigarettes and smoking** In the South there is a small homegrown tobacco industry, plus hoardings and ashtrays everywhere, but despite this locals are light puffers compared to all the surrounding countries, and non-smoking areas and campaigns are gaining ground – including all hotel diners and on Cyprus Airways, much to the consternation of native island passengers. Nicotine habits are a bit more pronounced in Northern Cyprus, based almost entirely on rough Anatolian brands, but again you

won't die of asphyxiation if you're a non-smoker.

**Contraceptives** The Greek for condoms is *profylaktiká*, the Turkish is *preservatif*.

**Departure tax** Included in the price of air tickets out of the southern Republic; in the North, various annoying chits may be dispensed upon check-in at the ferry harbour, whose total cost (payable in Turkish lira) equals about C£5.

**Disabled travellers** Hotels in the South are excellent for the wheel-chair-bound, with plenty of ramps and lifts; the North is less equipped, but many of the low-rise bungalow complexes are intrinsically well suited for people with mobility problems. Both sides rate less well in catering for those with sight problems: too many shiny marble bank floors, not enough stripes at stair edges, or audio-pips at pedestrian crossings (these last nonexistent in the North). That said, post-1997 Cyprus pound notes have a tactile coding of narrow, parallel raised bumps at one end: one for the C£1, two for C£5, three for C£10, four for C£20.

**Electric current** Throughout the island, this is 220–240 volts AC, with triple, rectangular-pin plugs as in Britain: hence you don't need any sort of adaptor to run electrical appliances. In very old buildings, however, you may still encounter the closely spaced, triple, round-pin, Chelsea system sockets. Two-to-three pin adaptors are often furnished in better hotels and villas for use by continental (ie Greek or Turkish) customers; if not, they are easily purchased in corner shops.

Visitors from mainland Europe or North America may well want to come equipped with a two-to-three adaptor suitable for dual-voltage hair dryers or irons, as they are expensive and not as easily found. Continental plug-owners can easily and cheaply prepare one by replacing the 1-amp fuse in a two-to-three unit marked "for shaver only" with a 5-amp fuse.

**Gay life** This is still almost non-existent, at least above ground, in the tight-knit, family-oriented Cypriot society – in either community. In the South homosexual acts between men used to be illegal, with offenders liable in theory to five years in prison; even "attempts to commit" homosexual acts (that is, propositioning somebody) potentially faced a sentence of three years. During the process of applying for full EU membership, various European authorities pointed out that this was at major variance with standards in other member countries; initially the South only undertook not to prosecute "overt" acts, rather than decriminalizing homosexual behaviour on the statute books, though in the face of vociferous opposition from the Orthodox Church, formal repeal of the offending statutes went forward in 1998. The North, while having no specific legislation, shares the same attitudes, and both communities will often be hostile to any public display of gay affection between foreigners. Contact is thus low-key: the few bars, and beaches, in and around Limassol or Páfos, that have reputations as gay meeting places are mentioned in the text.

**Laundry** Most major towns in the South have at least one laundrette.

**Lottery** The South has a national lottery using instant-winner, scratch-cards (*xystó* in Greek); supposedly 121,348 players per million win back at least the purchase price of C£1.

**Naturism** Unisex topless is the rule in the busier resorts of the South, and with some discretion in North Cyprus. And that's about as far as you'll prudently go.

**Time** Two hours ahead of GMT, and seven hours ahead of EST. Clocks go forward for summer time at 2am on the last Sunday in March and back again at 2am on the last Sunday in October. A recorded time message can be heard by dialling ☎193 in the South.

**Toilets** In the South, these are found in parks, on coastal esplanades, etc; sometimes there's a five- or ten-cent fee. They tend to close by 5pm from October to April. In the North, pay toilets are well signposted in strategic crannies of Kyrenia harbour, Famagusta old town and Nicosia, but you're more likely to be using restaurant and hotel loos. When present, bowl-side baskets are for collecting paper which would block temperamental drains.

**Weather report** In the South, the RAF base at Akrotíri maintains a call-in line (☎25266577) with a regularly updated recording on weather conditions; this tends to emphasize the Limassol coast and the Tróödhos, where most British military installations are, but it's useful nonetheless. Otherwise, 🌐 http://weather.yahoo.com has weather forecast sites for Nicosia and Larnaca, which will give you a fair idea of the maximum temperatures to expect on the island's lower-lying portions. In the North, you can obtain three-day forecasts from the weather station at Ercan airport by dialling ☎166.

**Weights and measures** The southern Republic went completely metric in 1987, while North Cyprus clings stubbornly to many imperial units. There are two Ottoman holdovers on both sides of the Line: the *dönüm* (Tr)/*skála* (Gr), a measure of land equal to about a third of an acre, and the *oka* (same Gr/Tr) equal to 2.8 pounds in weights and still occasionally met with in food markets.

**Work** Despite a growing labour shortage in the tourism and agricultural sectors of the **southern Republic**, a job for non-EU nationals is only strictly legal if arranged before you leave home. Your prospective employer will apply on your behalf for either a three- or six-month permit, though positions in hotels sometimes merit a two-year permit. In recent years many jobs have been taken by Bulgarians, Latvians, Estonians, Ukrainians, Romanians, Moldovans, Russians, Egyptians, Lebanese and Sri Lankans, to name only the most conspicuous nationalities. Other foreigners you see at work in resorts are invariably tour-group couriers recruited and paid from abroad, or those with special skills (eg, scuba-diving instructors). Native teachers of English are of a sufficiently high standard that you are unlikely to land an ESL/TEFL-type job. Unions are well organized and aggressive in looking after their own; employers can only hire foreigners (except as bar-girls) after having satisfied the authorities that the help cannot be recruited locally. So it's best, if showing up on spec, not to bank on anything other than an informal spell of picking grapes for a rural family, as the vineyards are always short-handed in September.

Opportunities for work in **Northern Cyprus** are even more limited; your only chance is to start a business with imported capital, such as a windsurfing or ballet school, which stakes out a patch in which locals can't or won't compete. Economic stagnation is the overriding issue here, and a likely consequence of any final federation settlement is the repatriation of as many Anatolian settlers as is mutually agree-able and a general consolidation by the North Cypriot authorities to protect locals in their jobs. However, some foreigners are regarded as more equal than others; it's apparent that Pakistanis, for instance, have little trouble getting established in the hotel or restaurant trade, and as "fellow Muslims" face few obstacles to naturalization.

# The South

# The South

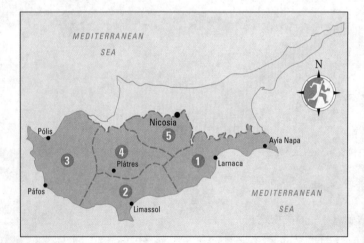

# Introduction

Foundation of the island-wide **Republic of Cyprus** in 1960 was a compromise solution to a Gordian knot of imperial, regional, Cold War and ethnic problems. Independence was the alternative to remaining a British colony, rule by a NATO condominium, union (*énosis*) with Greece or a double partition between Greece and Turkey reflecting the **mixed Greek and Turkish population**. Like most compromises it left few happy, least of all the Turkish-Cypriot minority community – and the more intransigent pro-*énosis* guerrillas in **EOKA** (*Ethnikí Orgánosis Kypríon Agonistón* or "National Organization of Cypriot Fighters"). Conflict was almost inevitable, and by 1974 control of the northern 38 percent of the island had passed nominally to the Turkish Cypriots, but effectively to the Turkish army. Yet for most of the world, Cyprus still means the Greek-Cypriot-inhabited, southern Republic of Cyprus.

If you're used to Greece, you'll find South Cyprus somewhat more civilized: things work better; administratively, there's less wasted motion; drivers are marginally more courteous to pedestrians and each other. People in general – often educated abroad and multilingual – seem relatively cosmopolitan, a useful trait when hosting thousands of tourists. Scratch this veneer, though, and island society proves paradoxically more traditional than in Greece: the social scale is cosy, with much of the population acquainted on sight if not exactly on first-name basis. Unlike in Greece, prevailing mores frown on certain kinds of conspicuous consumption; those who wish to gamble or spend a night on the town go to Greece or northern Cyprus, away from the censorious tongues of kin and neighbours. Many Cypriots are too busy working two jobs to "get ahead" – and educate their kids privately – to really enjoy life.

People who know both islands say that until the 1980s Cyprus was very much like Ireland, both in the bipolar ethno-religious conflict and a suffocating provinciality. The village was historically the core social unit; women were expected to "know their place"; and, until recent scandals brought it into disgrace, the **Orthodox Church** remained enormously influential, tapping a vein of uncomplicated, fervent faith co-existing with the worldliness.

Despite a politically motivated Hellenization campaign that has been running in the South since the early 1990s, and the dominance of Greek franchises in banking, petrol stations and fast-food outlets, there is in fact little love lost between Greek Cypriots and continental Greeks. The latter are generally referred to in Cyprus as *kalamarádhes*, and the mainland dialect as *kalamarística*. These terms first arose early in the nineteenth century, when schoolmasters from peninsular Greece first introduced "proper" Greek to the island; these purveyors of linguistic rectitude were dubbed *kalamarádhes* (quill-wielders), after the main tool of their trade. Over time, the word came to apply, in a mixture of opprobrium and affection, to all mainlanders, especially the corps of Greek army officers on the island during the 1960s. Some wear the label as a badge of honour, but it's most often prefixed indivisibly by *poústi* (literally "sodomite", in effect "untrustworthy bastard").

## The troubled republic

Both parochialism and internationalism were exhibited to destructive effect over the **fourteen turbulent years** between independence in 1960 and the catastrophe of 1974. Power-sharing between the two communities, regulated by a meticulously detailed constitution, had by 1964 collapsed in an orgy of recriminations and violence orchestrated by EOKA and its Turkish counterpart **TMT** (*Türk Mukavemet Teskilati* or "Turkish Resistance Organization"). The island was further destabilized through meddling by "mother" countries Greece and Turkey; soon the superpowers and the UN were inextricably involved.

Cyprus limped along as a unitary state for ten more years, albeit with a thoroughly poisoned civic life: Turkish Cypriots withdrew from the mainstream into a series of TMT-defended **enclaves**, while the Greek Cypriots retaliated by severely restricting traffic in goods or persons across their boundaries. Feeble reconciliatory overtures alternated with fresh incidents, but Cypriot society was already split, with Turkish Cypriots relegated to second-class citizenship in their laagers.

When **all-out war** erupted in July 1974, only the exact timing and details came as a surprise. At the instigation of the military junta then ruling Greece, **EOKA-B**, successor to EOKA, staged a coup aimed at effecting *énosis*; in response the Turkish army, technically acting as guarantor of the island's independence, landed on the north coast and, instead presided over de facto **partition**. The Greek Cypriots fled, or were expelled, from the North, the population of the scattered Turkish-Cypriot enclaves soon replacing them.

In the immediate **aftermath of the war**, all Cyprus was prostrate, with both ethnic communities demoralized and fearful, the economy in tatters. The South was particularly hard hit: about 160,000 Greek Cypriots had immediately fled the North, to be followed within a few years by 20,000 more. The Turkish army held the most productive portions of the island, assiduously developed since 1960: the Greek Cypriots lost the fertile citrus groves around Mórfou, the busy port of Famagusta with its bulging warehouses, and lucrative tourist facilities in Kyrenia and Varósha. Southern unemployment stood at forty percent until 1976, with the added burden of providing emergency shelter for the refugees.

## South Cyprus today

Since 1974, the South has wrought an **economic miracle** – but at a price. Developing the hitherto untouched southern coast for tourism, with few zoning restraints and maximum financial returns, was seen as the quickest fix for a dire predicament. Over three decades later, with **tourism** the country's biggest foreign-currency earner, the results are all too plain: hideous strips of uninterrupted low-to-medium-rise tower blocks on the coast around Larnaca, Limassol, Ayía Nápa and Páfos.

Inland, crash programmes rehoused the refugees in often shoddily-built **housing estates**, with only a rising standard of living diminishing the appeal of a return to the North. The relocation of nearly a third of Cyprus's population has meant overcrowding (artificial, given the relative emptiness of North Cyprus) and inflated property prices. Private, speculative development took precedence over delayed and underfunded public works. Much of the countryside is now for sale to the highest bidder, and phalanxes of **villas** sprout virtually uncontrolled at any spot that is in the least desirable. Since 1998, road-improvement works have extended to the remotest corners of the South, either serving villas already there or encouraging more to take root. The momentum for this is the huge loans taken out by the developers, which must be repaid to the exigent banks – sales of apartment and villa developments keep the cash flowing during years of sluggish conventional tourism, and indeed **residential tourism** is seen as the future as ground-breaking for hotels slows or even stops as a matter of official policy.

All this has threatened not only the visual **environment** but the ecological one, too: on an island permanently short of water, with most of it trapped in the North, supplies barely suffice for residential and agricultural needs, let alone tourism and leisure – yet somehow water is found for the "water-parks" at Limassol and Ayía Nápa, and several golf courses near Limassol and Páfos. Lately there have been signs of a token rethink, as conservationists organize to protect remaining unspoiled landscapes and to promote human-scale tourism; they also managed to elect a single Green MP, the island's first, in the 2001 elections. The government has provided muddled direction: while one agency proposed national parks, the tourism authority long adhered to a policy of encouraging five-star, high-impact tourist installations. In 1995, a moratorium was declared on new construction of most types of accommodation, both on the coast and inland, essentially freezing the number of licensed tourist beds in the South at just over 80,000 – though this had been rescinded by 1998. Cut-rate package tourism is seen as damaging to the social and environmental fabric, but during recent recessions there have not been enough customers at luxury facilities to justify their multiplication. The compromise – Green "**agrotourism**", mostly in Páfos district and the Tróödhos foothills, and comprising just a few hundred beds – has had merely a symbolic effect on the direction of organized tourism. Many long-standing fans of Cyprus are staying away, as the "product" goes increasingly mass-market despite protestations of "quality" by the Cyprus Tourism Organization. The new wave of clients often opt for one-week stays rather than two, feeling that they've "been there, done that" after seven days – or make a beeline for one of the thousands of estate agents and join the ranks of part-time residents.

By way of balance to this dependency on volatile tourism patterns, the demise of nearby Beirut as a business centre came as a welcome windfall for Cyprus. The South is now established as a popular venue for **international conferences**, and – thanks to its taxation policies and reliable infrastructure – as a base for **offshore companies**, though EU membership has put a stop to the dodgier among these. Liaisons begun in the heyday of the non-aligned movement, and the traditional importance of AKEL (the local Communist Party), continue to pay dividends in trade relations with eastern Europe, Africa and the Middle East. Starting in the 1990s, Russian "investment" – mostly money in need of laundering – flooded into the country, reflected in a rash of restaurant menus, estate agent signs and tourist literature printed in Cyrillic. For the most part, Cypriots welcome these big spenders, no questions asked; tales abound of Russians buying villas off-plan with a suitcase full of $100 bills.

Light **industrialization** resumed after 1976, much of it geared towards export markets. High-quality **medical care** at the main hospitals is successfully pitched at neighbouring countries as a hard-currency earner; it has also been developed as a matter of local need, since – like many isolated island populations – Cyprus is a massive incubator for debilitating genetic diseases such as thalassaemia.

Spurred by well-trained and -paid workers, economic growth since 1977 has been impressive, producing, during the 1990s, an unskilled **labour shortage**. As a result, the South is now a veritable Tower of Babel, with a huge (and growing) foreign workforce. Almost without exception, low- and mid-ranking staff at hotels and restaurants are Sri Lankan, Pakistani, Indian or from various countries in eastern and central Europe. Largely unrepresented by local unions, they're often treated appallingly, with sexual harassment and other sorts of abuse the norm. This reaches its apotheosis in the vast numbers of cabaret *artistes* (essentially a code word for **prostitutes**), who are brought here on six-month visas, renewable once. The lucky ones save enough for down payments on property back home, or manage to escape the brothel system by marrying (or becoming the mistress of) a Cypriot. The EU wasn't willing to tolerate the Russian "funny money" banks, but it has acquiesced in incorporating a country that's a destination of choice for white slavers.

While all credit is due to the Greek Cypriots for reviving their part of the island, there's no denying that much of the recovery has been subsidized by **foreign aid**. Only the southern Republic has membership in such multinational bodies as UNESCO, the EU and the World Bank, and has thus been eligible for direct assistance from those organizations.

Despite retaining its original name, the contemporary Republic of Cyprus is a fundamentally different country: all but mono-ethnic (if you disregard the burgeoning foreign population), yet with *énosis* completely eclipsed by the quasi-*énosis* with Greece afforded by joint EU membership; its 1960 constitution a dead letter; and public life preoccupied with *Tó Kypriakó* (**Cyprus Question**) – the imposed partition of the island. Until the dramatic events of 2003–04 (see below), posters and graffiti referred obsessively to the events of 1974, as did periodic heartfelt demonstrations, with little need of stage-managing (though inevitably exploited by nationalist ideologues). The theoretical right of Greek Cypriots to return to their homes in the North has been the most emotionally charged issue, though it seems that fewer than half would actually do so. Nostalgically named refugee clubs attempt to link the generation born in exile with ancestral towns, and maintain community solidarity for a possible day of repatriation. Telephone directories still list numbers in the North as they were before July 1974, and the official hotel guide pointedly cites Famagusta and Kyrenia hotels as named before the Turkish intervention, without, however, giving any practical details.

## Strategies and prospects for reconciliation

Without the military means to expel the Turkish army, the South has instead exploited its monopoly in world forums to mount a relentless propaganda campaign against, and **boycott** of, the Turkish Republic of Northern Cyprus (TRNC) in an attempt to bring it to heel. Ire is directed at Turkey too, in overseas court cases demanding that vanished property or persons be accounted for. When advised that this was unlikely to create a favourable climate for reconciliation, the South retorted that giving North Cyprus more breathing space would remove any incentive for it to come to terms.

With the benefit of hindsight, some Greek Cypriots have assimilated bitter political lessons and recognize the wisdom of generous gestures towards the Turkish Cypriots, initiatives unthinkable before 1974. Despite the official campaign against the TRNC, many (in private, anyway) willingly admit past errors: in particular, there's widespread revulsion at the activities of EOKA-B, which during its brief 1974 reign killed more Greek Cypriots than Turkish Cypriots. A retrospectively rosy view of intercommunal relations before 1960 prevails in the South, but whether this is genuine or promulgated to counter Northern pessimism is debatable.

Officially the southern Republic is still **bicommunal**, though fewer than three thousand island-born Turks – less than half a percent of the population – continue to live there (albeit significantly increased since the late 1990s, and dwarfed by the estimated 10,000 Turkish Cypriots who now commute to work daily from North to South). Banknotes and many public signs remain trilingual in Greek, Turkish and English; radio and TV broadcast Turkish-language programmes; the official languages of instruction at the university are Greek and Turkish (not English, as in the North); the eighty-seat parliament currently functions with only 56 deputies, the balance reserved for hypothetical Turkish-Cypriot representatives as per the 1960 constitution. In its propaganda and negotiating position the government proposes generous constitutional concessions on condition that Turkish Cypriots embrace federation and abandon their insistence on separate states. But the best-case model held out – that of Belgium – is hardly one to emulate, given the barely suppressed ethnic tensions there and the fact that these lead to Brussels being one of the worst administered cities in Europe: remarkably reminiscent, in fact, of Nicosia from 1960 to 1963.

The Southern government tried to prevent the 44,039 **Turkish Cypriots** in the South from departing – voluntarily or otherwise – to the North in early 1975, correctly fearing that the Turkish side would deem this a quid pro quo for the involuntary expulsion of Northern Greeks. It is increasingly common for Turkish Cypriots to return to the South, which they do as much to escape misery in the North as out of any "patriotic" feeling. Once in the South, their reception can be ambivalent: while theoretically welcome as a tiny reversal of the island's apartheid, they are also distrusted as potential spies, and many become restricted to living on the margins of society, involved in off-the-record or low-level work with little job security and smuggling of contraband back to the other side.

All standing property of Southern Turkish Cypriots is technically held in trust by the government, which now stands accused of not adequately protecting the interests of the true owners. Current Greek-Cypriot occupiers have only rental agreements with their departed true owners, but commercial rents in particular are set at risibly low levels, and many city-dwellers illegally squat and renovate Turkish-Cypriot country houses as weekend retreats. There have been several instances of vacant Turkish-Cypriot land being built over by the government to house refugees, and court cases have been filed by aggrieved Turkish-Cypriot owners, mirroring the more famous suits pursued by dispossessed Greek Cypriots.

## The events of 2003–04

All existing parameters were in part overtaken by the milestone events of April 2003 to May 2004. In chronological order, but not necessarily ranked in significance, they were the sudden **opening of the "border"** dividing the island, on April 23, 2003, to pretty much unrestricted travel by all parties; an island-wide **referendum** on April 24, 2004, on the UN-promulgated **Annan Plan** for a federal solution; and the **accession to the EU** of the Republic of Cyprus on May 1, 2004. Freedom of movement permitted a reality check for all concerned, after years of nostalgia and demonization; vast numbers of people (on both sides) went back to look at their ancestral properties and consider "what to do if…", while interaction between Greek and Turkish Cypriots as "tourists" in the others' territory was remarkable for its civility. However, despite widespread reconciliation on a personal level, this did not translate into a political solution. For reasons analyzed on pp.461–462, the Annan Plan was approved in the North by a margin of 2:1 – but was defeated in the South by a staggering 3:1 (both communities had to vote "yes"). EU officials, hoping to welcome an island on the path to integration, were incandescent, feeling the Republic had manoeuvred itself into the "Europe of 25" on false pretences. As the Turkish Cypriots had often complained about in the past, the South would once again presume to speak for the whole island in an important multinational body – a core example of the long-running gap in understanding as to what constitutes the appropriate roles of communities and central government on Cyprus. Indeed there's a widespread feeling that EU membership has come prematurely for the Republic, which is somewhat ungraciously toeing the line on myriad matters ranging from the trivial to the fundamental: no more eating songbirds, tormenting homosexuals, making Turkish Cypriots queue separately from Greek Cypriots when crossing from North to South, or prosecuting Greek Cypriots who choose to fly out of the North to İstanbul for the weekend – and no more fuel subsidies, which has caused petrol and heating oil prices to skyrocket.

# Larnaca and around

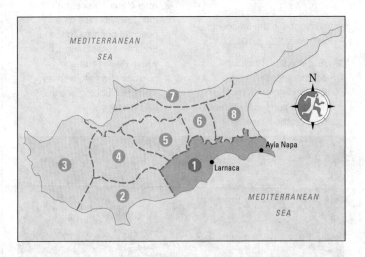

CHAPTER 1 — # Highlights

✳ **Pierides Museum** The collection at this privately run museum in central Larnaca overshadows those at many of the state-run archeological museums. See p.100

✳ **Hala Sultan Tekke** This stereotypically Middle Eastern tomb and mosque is further enlivened in winter and spring by thousands of flamingos in the adjacent salt lake. See p.104

✳ **Angelóktisti** The sixth-century mosaics in this Byzantine church are the finest in-situ work of their type on the island. See p.105

✳ **Khirokitia** The largest and most completely excavated Neolithic town on Cyprus. See p.109

✳ **Áyios Andónios, Kelliá** This hilltop church contains some of the oldest and most unusual Byzantine frescoes on the island. See p.114

✳ **Ayía Nápa** The central monastery serves as a peaceful contrast to the South's liveliest resort, where daytime beach pursuits alternate with an all-night clubbing scene. See p.116

△ Áyios Andónios church

# Larnaca and around

The southeastern flank of Cyprus, centred on Larnaca, is still – recent development at Páfos notwithstanding – the most touristed portion of the island: a consequence of the 1974 Turkish invasion, and the subsequent conversion of hitherto sleepy Larnaca airfield into the southern republic's main international airport. Except for its hilly western part, the district isn't particularly scenic – not that this bothers many of the patrons of the burgeoning resorts, who seldom venture far from the clear, warm sea and their self-contained hotels.

Despite lying a short motorway drive from two mega-resorts at the southeastern tip of the island, the district capital of **Larnaca** still claims its share of local tourism, though increasing industrialization – and the possibility that Varosha (see p.392) might soon be rehabilitated – casts some doubt on its future as a holiday destination. However, just southwest of the town lie two of the most appealing, and most easily accessible, monuments in the area: the Muslim shrine of **Hala Sultan Tekke** by Larnaca's salt lake, and the mosaic-graced Byzantine church of **Angelóktisti** at Kíti. **Perivólia**, on the approach to **Cape Kíti**, is perhaps the last human-scale resort in this part of the island, but the coast beyond will reward only the most determined explorers; at the end of the line, little **Zíyi** port with its fish tavernas is more easily reached from the main Nicosia–Limassol expressway.

**Inland** and west in Larnaca district, a number of attractions are scattered to either side of this highway. Neolithic **Khirokitia** is one of the oldest known habitations on the island, and a visit can be easily twinned with one to **Páno Léfkara**, a picturesque village in the Tróödhos foothills, renowned for its handicrafts. More directly approached from Larnaca along a secondary road, the **Chapelle Royale** at Pýrga houses a rare example of Lusignan sacred mural art, and nearby **Stavrovoúni** is an equally unusual instance of a strictly penitential Cypriot Orthodox monastery. To the southwest of Pýrga, **Kofínou** village has a reputation as a pottery centre, though it's more famous for a particularly ugly intercommunal incident during the days of the unitary republic – as is **Tókhni**, near **Kalavassós** on the far side of the A1 expressway, both now popular holiday bases on account of some imaginative accommodation schemes.

**East of Larnaca**, there is little specifically to recommend along the coast: the sandy crescent of Larnaca Bay and the British Sovereign Base Area of Dhekélia are each compromised in their own way. Things only look up at the two overgrown resorts to either side of **Cape Gréko**: though by no means the largest permanent community, **Ayía Nápa** mushrooms in season to become the busiest hard-core clubbers' resort in the area, while the strip at **Protarás** on the northeast coast is slightly more upmarket.

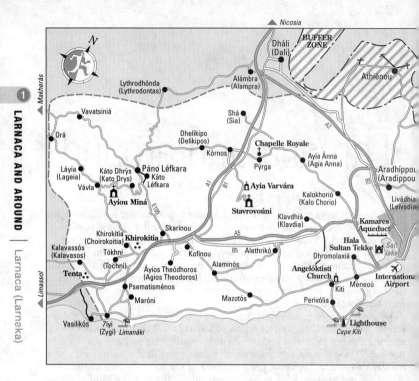

With the city as a base, it's easy to make several full- or half-day trips to the surrounding attractions. To do this with any degree of flexibility, you'll need a car, for while public transport links the city with the majority of the sites detailed, there are few connections between them. Outside Larnaca, Ayía Nápa and Protarás, **accommodation** can be found at Perivólia, Kalavassós, Tókhni, Vávla and Páno Léfkara.

## Larnaca (Larnaka)

**LARNACA** (officially **LARNAKA** since 1996) has little tangible evidence of its eventful history, and is today a visibly moribund tourist centre and minor port forgetful of its past. Gone is the romantic town depicted in eighteenth-century engravings, with only furnace-like summer heat, an adjacent salt lake and palm trees to impart a nostalgic Levantine touch.

Such recent growth as has occurred is primarily due to regional catastrophe; numbers were first swelled by Greek refugees from Famagusta in 1974, and a year or two later by Lebanese Christians fleeing the strife in their homeland. With a permanent population of about 75,000, Larnaca is just half the size of Limassol, and more encroached upon by downmarket, town-based tourism, though the coastal hotel "ghetto" of Voróklini to the northeast is also increasingly important.

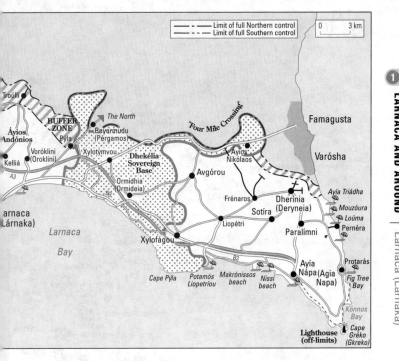

## Some history

The site of Larnaca was originally colonized by Mycenaeans in the thirteenth century BC, but had declined, like many other Mediterranean towns, by about 1000 BC. It emerged again as **Kition** two centuries later, re-established by the Phoenicians, and resumed its role as a port exporting copper from rich deposits at Tamassos and elsewhere in the eastern Tróödhos. A subsequent period of great prosperity was complicated by the city's staunch championing of the Persian cause on Cyprus: Kimon of Athens, heading a fleet sent in 450 BC to reduce Kition, died outside the wall in the hour of what proved to be a transient victory. Persian influence only ended with the Hellenistic takeover of the whole island a century later, a period which also saw the birth of Kition's most famous son, the Stoic philosopher **Zeno**.

Christianity came early to Kition, traditionally in the person of **Lazarus**, the man resurrected by Christ at Bethany. Irate Pharisees tried to dispose of the evidence of this miracle by casting Lazarus adrift in a leaky boat; he supposedly landed here to become the city's first bishop and, following his (definitive) death, its patron saint. After an otherwise uneventful passage through the Roman and early Byzantine eras, Kition suffered the same seventh-century Arab raids as other Cypriot coastal settlements. It didn't really recover until the end of the Lusignan era, when the Genoese appropriation of nearby Famagusta prompted merchants to move here to take advantage of the small port; by now the anchorage was called **Salina** or **Les Salines**, after the salt lake just inland.

The name **Larnaca**, derived from *larnax* (a sarcophagus or urn, of which there were plenty to hand from various periods of the town's past), only gained

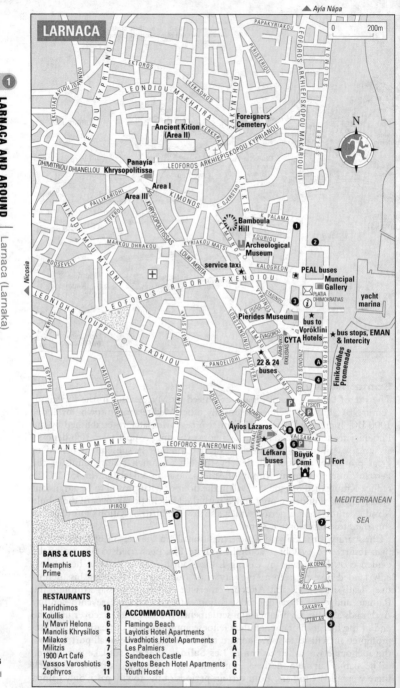

# LARNACA

▲ Ayía Nápa

0 — 200m

N

**Ancient Kition (Area II)**

**Foreigners' Cemetery**

**Panayía Khrysopolítissa**

Area I

Area III

**Bamboula Hill**

**Archeological Museum**

service taxi

**PEAL buses**

**Muncipal Gallery**

PLATIA DHIMOKRATIAS

yacht marina

**Pierides Museum**

bus to Voróklini Hotels

CYTA

22 & 24 buses

bus stops, EMAN & Intercity

Finikoúdhes Promenade

**Áyios Lázaros**

Léfkara buses

**Büyük Cami**

Fort

**MEDITERRANEAN SEA**

▲ Nicosia

---

**BARS & CLUBS**

| | |
|---|---|
| Memphis | 1 |
| Prime | 2 |

**RESTAURANTS**

| | |
|---|---|
| Haridhimos | 10 |
| Koullis | 8 |
| Iy Mavri Helona | 6 |
| Manolis Khrysillos | 5 |
| Milakos | 4 |
| Militzis | 7 |
| 1900 Art Café | 3 |
| Vassos Varoshiotis | 9 |
| Zephyros | 11 |

**ACCOMMODATION**

| | |
|---|---|
| Flamingo Beach | E |
| Layiotis Hotel Apartments | D |
| Livadhiotis Hotel Apartments | B |
| Les Palmiers | A |
| Sandbeach Castle | F |
| Sveltos Beach Hotel Apartments | G |
| Youth Hostel | C |

Airport, Hala Sultan Tekke, Angelóktisti & ⑩ ▼        ⓔ, ⓕ, ⓖ, ⑪, Fishing Port (100m) & ▼ MacKenzie Beach (40

wide currency at the start of Ottoman rule. By the eighteenth century Larnaca was the premier port and trade centre of the island, briefly eclipsing Nicosia in population, with numerous foreign consuls in residence. Britain's consul often simultaneously administered the English Levant Company, a trading organization analogous to the British East India Company. Around the consuls gathered the largest foreign community on the island, leading lives of elegant and eccentric provinciality, the inspiration for reams of travel accounts of the time. In 1878 the British landed here to take over administration of Cyprus, and it was not until after World War II that Larnaca again fell behind Famagusta and Limassol in importance.

## Arrival, orientation and information

Landing at Larnaca **airport**, you'll find a **CTO** office open for all arrivals – which means pretty much around the clock – and ample exchange facilities, including two bank **ATMs**. Quite likely you'll have a rented car awaiting you as part of a fly-drive arrangement; if not, there are a half-dozen rental booths in the arrivals area. **Municipal buses** #22 or 24 (the former labelled "Makenzy-Tekkes-Airport") run into town up to eleven times daily in season (Mon–Sat 8am–6pm; not Wed or Sat pm), dropping you on Ermoú. Alternatively, a taxi into town shouldn't cost much more than C£5 at day rates – as ever, make sure the meter is switched on.

Larnaca's street plan is confusing, with numerous jinks, one-ways and name changes, though the sea is always due east, with two north–south boulevards paralleling it. The **Finikoúdhes** or palm-tree esplanade, officially **Leofóros Athinón**, has always been the focus of the tourist industry and, towards its north end, hosts a few important inter-city **bus terminals**. The large **Platía Dhimokratías** (often known by its English name, "King Paul Square", and still Vassiléos Pávlou on most maps) is home to the not wildly helpful **CTO office** (Mon–Fri 8.15am–2.30pm, Sat 8.15am–1.30pm, plus Mon, Tues, Thurs & Fri 3–6.15pm). From here, **Leofóros Grigóri Afxendíou** is the main avenue out to the Nicosia and Limassol roads. Running parallel to the sea front, **Zínonos Kitiéos** leads south to the diagonal junction with **Ermoú** and, via the alleyways of the bazaar, indirectly to **Platía Ayíou Lazárou**, home to its ornate namesake church and more bus stops. **Odhós Ayíou Lazárou**, later **Stadhíou**, reaches the roundabout that gives onto both the Nicosia road and **Leofóros Artemídhos** to the airport and beyond along the coast.

For drivers the one-way system can prove to be a nightmare. Moreover, **parking** in the centre, on a pay-and-display basis, is pretty well confined to a large purpose-built structure on Valsamáki, about 200m inland from the Finikoúdhes, plus a few open-air lots nearby – which may appear to be unattended, but as ever wardens appear suddenly to demand fees.

## Accommodation

The **hotel and pension** situation in Larnaca for those showing up on spec is not great, though slightly better than in Limassol or Ayía Nápa. For budget rates you can pretty much forget about a room with a sea view; with a bit more outlay you'll get a relatively quiet sleep and some sea breeze some way south of the town centre along Piyale Paşa towards Mackenzie Beach, the rather meagre strip of sand preceding the airport. Other hotels (from three to five stars) are located at Voróklini, 5km along the coast to the northeast (see p.116).

**Flamingo Beach** Piyale Paşa 152, 400m past the fishing port, just opposite the start of Mackenzie Beach ☎ 24828224, ⓦ www.flamingobeachhotel .com. One of Larnaca's better in-town three-star hotels: there's a rooftop pool, air con and on-site cafeteria, while all rooms have an oblique balcony view of the sea. ❺

**Layiotis Hotel Apartments** Artemídhos 31 ☎ 24624700, ⓕ 24626152. Comfortable one-bedroom units, located inland in a residential area. ❷

**Livadhiotis Hotel Apartments** Nikoláou Róssou 50 ☎ 24626222, ⓔ livadhiotishotapts@cytanet.com .cy. Studio, one- and two-bedroom apartments, with air con, TV and friendly management, in a modern building overlooking nocturnally illuminated Áyios Lázaros church. ❷–❸

**Les Palmiers** Athinón 12, corner with Pierídhi ☎ 24627200, ⓕ 24627204. Good-value two-star on the Finikoúdhes promenade, with some sea-view rooms and a copious buffet breakfast. ❸

**Sandbeach Castle** Piyale Paşa, past the fishing port ☎ 24655437, ⓦ www.castlehotel.com.cy. The only Larnaca town hotel with its feet (and lovely dining terrace) in the sea, this small, mock-castle outfit was originally built in the 1930s as the colonial district commissioner's residence. Half the main-wing rooms face the sea, as do four newer bungalow units and a self-catering house (sleeps 4). ❸

**Sveltos Beach Hotel Apartments** Piyale Paşa, south of the fishing port ☎ 24657240, ⓕ 24658334. Beachfront hotel apartments just south of the city limits; no pool. Studio ❷, two-bedroom apartment ❸

**Youth Hostel** Nikoláou Róssou 27 ☎ 24621188. Housed partly in the disused Zuhuri mosque, this has kitchen facilities, but also the usual Cypriot-hostel problems with hot-water reliability and cleanliness. C£4 per person, plus one-off C£1 sheet fee.

## The City

Larnaca's minuscule old town is clearly in decline, with numerous vacant shop-fronts close to a bar-lined, pedestrianized "Laïkí Yitoniá", optimistically – or rather, ominously – modelled on the one in Nicosia. Promoters tout the shore esplanade as an echo of the French Riviera, but lately they must overlook all-you-can-eat specials at *McDonald's*, *KFC*, *Goody's*, *Pizza Hut* and other assorted pubs and "snacks" and the botched renovation of the *Four Lanterns*, dowager empress of the in-town hotels. Worse still, the old covered market *halle* just inland was demolished on scanty pretext in 1997 to make way for an open-air car park, leaving the only positive recent development the restoration of several former customs warehouses on harbourfront Platía Evrópis as the **Larnaca Municipal Gallery** (Tues–Fri 9am–2pm, Sat 9am–noon, plus Oct–April Sun 9am–noon; free), which has a changing programme of exhibitions by local and overseas artists.

The remaining sights – a much-revered church, a handsome mosque, two museums and an archeological zone – can be seen in a leisurely day, preferably a cool one, as they're scattered in such a way as to make use of the minimal city bus service difficult and a walking tour appealing.

### Áyios Lázaros church

The most obvious place to start a tour is the landmark church of **Áyios Lázaros** (daily: April–Aug 8am–12.30pm & 3.30–6.30pm; Sept–March 8am–12.30pm & 2.30–5pm). Poised between the former Turkish and bazaar quarters, it was erected late in the ninth century to house the remains of Lazarus, fortuitously discovered here. The church is distinguished by its grace-ful Latinate belfry, part of a thorough seventeenth-century overhaul and a miraculous survival of Turkish rule; the Ottomans usually forbade the raising of such structures, considering their height a challenging insult to the mina-rets of Islam, and (more practically) fearing they would be used to proclaim insurrection. Indeed the church had to be ransomed from the Turks in 1589, and was used for joint worship by Roman Catholics and Orthodox for two centuries after – as evidenced by Greek, Latin and French inscriptions in the

Gothic-influenced portico, in addition to the earlier Byzantine and Lusignan coats-of-arms near the main south door.

The spare stone interior (consequence of a fire in 1970) is a relief after the busy decoration of many Cypriot churches. Three small domes are supported on four pillars slit into doublets, with narrow arches springing from wedged-in Corinthian capitals. The celebrated carved *témblon* (altar screen), partly restored after the fire, and a Rococo pulpit on one pillar (for Latin use) are some three hundred years old; on another pillar hangs a filigreed icon of Lazarus emerging from his tomb, an image reverently paraded in the presence of the bishop of Kition every Easter Saturday evening.

The low-ceilinged crypt under the altar supposedly housed the relics of Lazarus only very briefly – they were taken to Constantinople by the Byzantine emperor Leo VI in 901, whence they were stolen, turning up later in Marseilles. But his purported tomb eventually formed part of a catacomb of general use, as witness several sarcophagi lying about here. In the northeast corner of the outside compound are more graves in a gated but usually open enclosure – this time of foreign consuls, merchants and family members who died in Larnaca's unhealthy climate during the sixteenth to nineteenth centuries.

### The former Turkish quarter

Stretching from Áyios Lázaros almost to the fishing port, the extensive **Turkish quarter** has retained its old street names, but is now home to Greek Orthodox refugees from Famagusta and the Kárpas villages. Judging from some impressive houses and bungalows, the Turks here seem to have been wealthier than in Páfos – but there are "chicken shacks" as well. Originally the late medieval church of the Holy Cross, the porticoed, flying-buttressed **Büyük Cami** (Cami Kebir), at the north end of the quarter, now sees regular use by the local Egyptian/Syrian/Iranian population. Bowing to the demands of tourism, the mosque is open in daylight hours, except during services, allowing you a glimpse of its arcaded, three-aisled interior, complete with wooden gallery. One could formerly climb the minaret, but this is now visibly cracked and scaffolded against imminent danger of collapse. The nearby **fort** (June–Aug Mon–Fri 9am–7.30pm; Sept–May Mon–Fri 9am–5pm; C£0.75), a 1625 Turkish refurbishment of a Lusignan castle, stands mostly empty at the south end of the Finikoúdhes, but its upper storey hosts a small museum of oddments from Hala Sultan Tekke and ancient Kition. The place is also the occasional venue for evening functions, when you can inspect the courtyard, and ponder the fact that before World War II the British used the fort as a prison.

### The beach and bazaar area

Immediately north of the fort stretches the pedestrian-only **Finikoúdhes** promenade. This in turn is fronted by the town beach – some 800m of gritty, hard-packed sand, well patronized despite its mediocre condition. If it's not to your taste, you'll find somewhat better beaches to either side of town, at Perivólia and around Ayía Nápa.

The bulk of the **bazaar** sprawls north of Áyios Lázaros, but it effectively had its heart torn out by the demolition of the covered central market; the best remaining shopping options in Larnaca are discussed on p.103. Though you're unlikely to be tempted to stay here, stop in a moment at the youth hostel to examine the mosque that houses it, the unusual nineteenth-century **Zuhuri Cami** (literally, "Clown Mosque") with its double dome and truncated minaret.

### The Pierides Museum

Conveniently situated just off Platía Dhimokratías, the **Pierides Museum** (Mon–Thurs 9am–4pm, Fri & Sat 9am–1pm, plus Sun peak season 11am–1pm; C£1) shares an old wooden house at Zínonos Kitiéos 4 with the Swedish consulate, and was renovated to good effect in late 1994, though there are still a few unsorted, unlabelled display cases. The building was originally the home of Dhimitrios Pierides, who began his conservation efforts in 1839, using his wealth to salvage discreetly what archeological treasures he could from tomb plunderers, including the infamous Luigi Palma di Cesnola, first US consul at Larnaca.

Unlike Cyprus's state-run archeological museums, the well-lit collection, which was expanded by Pierides' descendants, ranges across the whole island, and is simply the best and most digestible ensemble for a complete overview of Cypriot culture through the ages. That said, it's strongest on Archaic terracottas, plus other unusual small objects that have escaped the attention of the official district museums. The half-dozen exhibition rooms are arranged both by theme and by period, with the earliest artefacts to the left as you enter.

Among the oldest items are some greenish picrolite idols from the Chalcolithic period (c.3000 BC), and the famous **"Howling Man"** of the same era from Souskiou, in the first gallery to the left. Liquid poured through his hollow head pees out of a prominent member; the mechanics give little clue as to whether he had a religious or secular function. Less unexpected are the Archaic female statuettes brandishing drums and other votive offerings, which were left in shrines as "permanent worshippers".

There are numerous notable examples of painted **Archaic pottery**, especially one decorated with a so-called "astronaut" figure (beloved of Erich von Däniken and other extraterrestrial-visitation enthusiasts), bouncing on what appear to be springs or other mechanical devices, though they are described as a "stool". Among the imported **painted Attic ware**, you'll find Theseus about to run the Minotaur through with his sword, while on another pot in the same glass case, two centaurs, emblems of lust, flank a courting couple; note also the dish emblazoned with two scaly fish and a cuttlefish.

The collection of relatively rare Classical and Hellenistic **terracottas** includes a funerary reclining man from Marion, in perfect condition down to the fingers, and a model sarcophagus with three pull-out drawers; other oddities include a surprisingly delicate spoon among a trove of Early Bronze Age black incised ware.

A room to the right of the main corridor – which itself houses a superb collection of **antiquarian maps** of Cyprus and the Aegean – is devoted to **Byzantine and Lusignan pottery**, in particular brown- or green-glazed *sgraffito* ware. Perhaps the drollest etched-in design is a rampant Lusignan anthropomorphized lion, seemingly prefiguring Picasso.

In the "folklore" wing on the right at the rear of the building, you'll find assorted jewellery, embroidery and household utensils, as well as a finely carved polychrome desk and *armoire*. Featured also are numerous works by the "naive" painter **Mikhaïl Kashalos**, killed aged 89 by the Turkish army in his village studio in 1974. Particularly topical is a canvas of the Green Line in 1964, complete with UN personnel.

### The Archeological Museum

Larnaca's other significant collection, the **Archeological Museum**, stands a ten-minute walk away, north of Grigóri Afxendíou (Mon–Fri 9am–2.30pm, Sept–June also Thurs 3–5pm; C£0.75). It's purpose-built, with excellent labelling and explanatory panels, but you get a feeling that the collection comprises pickings and leavings when compared to Nicosia's Cyprus Museum or the Pierides itself. It's certainly the impression you get when you step into the entry hall, where the management has been reduced to displaying copies of a famous statue of Artemis and funerary stele (the originals in Vienna and Berlin respectively).

Pre-eminent in the early part of the collection is a reconstruction of a **Neolithic tomb** from Khirokhitia, complete with a stone atop the corpse's chest indicating a fear of revenants from the dead. Later exhibits clearly illustrate how Late Bronze Age pottery, especially the so-called "white slip ware", prefigured the decorated dishes of the Geometric era. The fact that the latter were painted only on the outside (discounting the possibility that any inside designs were worn off by use) may indicate that they were meant to be hung up by their handles as decoration, like the woven *tsésti* or trivets of today.

Vast amounts of **Mycenaean pottery** in the so-called "Rude" (ie rustic) Style, dug up at adjacent Kition, demonstrate Argolid settlement around 1200 BC; the prize exhibit is a fish *krater* (large wine goblet) from Áyios Dhimítrios near Kalavassós. Cypriot literacy dates to at least two centuries earlier, as evidenced by a display of Cypro-Minoan inscriptions (so far undeciphered), while a case of items imported towards the end of the Bronze Age demonstrates trade links at the same time; notice an ivory lamp in the shape of a fish. Back among indigenous ware, there's an unusual clay torch from Pýla, and a clay brazier-pan from Athiénou – perhaps meant to heat bedclothes or a small room. Terracotta highlights in the Archaic section include a horse and rider with emphasized eyes, plus a couple – possibly royal or divine – in a horse-drawn chariot.

## Ancient Kition

Most of **ancient Kition** lies under modern Larnaca, and thus cannot be excavated, though the Swedes under Einar Gjerstad began to make attempts during the 1920s. The British had made matters worse in 1879 by carting off much of what had survived above ground – "rubble" as they called it – to fill malarial marshes. Their depredations were severest at the ancient acropolis on Bamboúla hill, directly behind the Archeological Museum in fenced-off parkland; consequently there's little to see except for a nearby dig site – possibly the Phoenician port, far inland from today's shoreline – next to the municipal tennis courts on Kilkís street. So-called Areas I and III, at the north end of Kímonos opposite the weird, top-heavy belfry of Panayía Khrysopolítissa church, are Late Bronze Age holes in the ground – of essentially specialist interest now that they have disgorged their treasures.

The one exception to this inaccessibility is the so-called **Area II**, beyond Arkhiepiskópou Kypriánou, from which you turn up Kérkyras to reach the gate at the northwest corner of the site (Mon–Fri 9am–2.30pm, Sept–June also Thurs 3–5pm; C£0.75), where a wooden catwalk is provided for an overview of ongoing excavations. The Phoenician resettlement sits atop Late Bronze Age foundations, abutting the mixed mud-brick and stone wall which bounded Kition to the north. The main structures are a large ashlar-based shrine, rededicated to the fertility goddess Astarte in Phoenician times, and four smaller earlier temples, one of them linked to the smelting workshops found here, suggesting, if not worship of a copper deity, then at least a priestly interest in copper production. In another of the shrines, thought to be that of a masculine seafaring god, a pipe for the ritual smoking of opium was discovered. Few Hellenistic or Roman artefacts were found, making the site unusual and archeologically important – as well as politically delicate, since Greek Cypriots are often less than enthusiastic about remains indicating Asiatic cultural origins.

# Eating

It doesn't take much nous to work out that you're going to get ripped off at the glittery purveyors of "international" stodge on the Finikoúdhes, many of which are being displaced in any case by even less admirable fast-food outlets. However, a little foraging about away from the obvious will turn up a number of good, reasonably priced eating and drinking venues in Larnaca.

**Haridhimos Taste of Paradise Steak House** On the road southwest from Hala Sultan Tekke, northeastern edge of Meneoú village, 7km from town ☎24424148. Never mind the silly name, this popular place offers very good and abundant carnivorous *mezé* for under C£8, plus grills and fish. Reservations advised at weekends.

**Koullis** Piyale Paşa 5, corner of İstiklar. A decent taverna specializing in fish and catering overwhelmingly to a local clientele. C£10 will get you a starter, octopus and a beer, C£14 a grilled fish meal, while two can eat well on less glamorous species (cuttlefish, *marídhes*) for C£22.

**Iy Mavri Helona** Mehmet Ali 11, near Áyios Lázaros ☎24650661. Most of the rough edges of this durable little upstairs *ouzerí* have been filed smooth over the years, and the menu has got blander and more expensive (C£8 per person, drink extra). However, it remains popular with nearly as many locals as tourists, and in season you'll probably have to book. On Wed, Fri and Sat nights there's somewhat touristy *bouzoúki* and accordion music. Dinner only; closed Sun & Mon.

**Milakos** Petrolina Building, Arkhiepiskópou Makaríou 23, 1st floor ☎24664472. The influx of Lebanese Christians into Cyprus has borne fruit in this excellent restaurant, where Milos and his Cypriot wife serve up a wide range of vegetarian dishes, meat and sausages, a nice *tursí* (pickled veggie) plate, and the increasingly rare *mahallebí* (rice-flour and rosewater pudding). There's a 17-platter *mezé* for C£8 each, otherwise allow C£12–13 per person á la carte, booze (such as Lebanese *arak*) extra. Post-prandial hubble-bubble with flavoured tobacco (eg, strawberry) on request.

Dinner only; reservations necessary Fri & Sat; closed Mon.

**Manolis Khrysillos** Faneroménis, opposite Áyios Lázaros. Workers' and shoppers' hole-in-the-wall canteen doing excellent, home-style dishes like rabbit stew, bean dishes, *afélia* and the like at budget prices. Lunch only.

**Militzis** Piyale Paşa 42, 250m south of the fort. Limited menu, and sometimes offhand service, but what they do – baked or grilled meat, casserole dishes – they do well, generously and without grease. Allow C£10 per head.

**1900 Art Café** Stasínou 6 ☎24653027, @www .artcafe1900.com.cy. Housed in an early twentieth-century mansion, and run by a local radio-journalist and an artist. There's a downstairs bar-café, but the highlight is the civilized upstairs salon-restaurant, which attracts a mix of locals and foreigners – there's art on the walls, a good selection of taped music, winter fireplace and attentive service. The menu is limited, mostly chicken dishes and a token vegetarian presence, though supplemented by fine homemade desserts and good house wine; count on C£10 per head. Open 6pm–midnight; closed Tues.

**Vassos Varoshiotis** Piyale Paşa 7, corner of Sakarya. More plushly appointed than its rival *Koullis* next door, with terracotta floors, wall-to-wall aquariums and swishing fans, plus excellent, if slightly pricey, fare: salad, their famous seafood soufflé, a dessert and wine comes to about C£16. It's always crowded, especially at Sunday lunch when service gets erratic under pressure.

**Zephyros** Piyale Paşa 37 ☎24657198. Well-regarded seaside fish taverna.

# Nightlife and entertainment

Visitors in search of a drink gravitate towards several adjacent **bars** in the pedestrianized Laïkí Yitoniá, just inland from the Finikoúdhes, though locals tend to avoid the place. They instead patronize *Memphis* at Athinón 76, the premier Larnaca **club** with its stunning, high-tech interior and name DJs laying on techno, house and trance events. Honourable mentions go to *Prime* at Filíou Tsingarídhi 2–4, with an aquarium for interest and mostly Greek soundtrack, and the smaller *Venue* at Thermopýlon 8, with a mix of Greek pop and trance-dance, and frequent theme/party nights.

Watch the hoardings of the municipality for details of more formal events, especially during **Kataklysmós**, the five-day Festival of the Flood, usually held in June (see p.72). Most years, one of the commercial sponsors or the *Cyprus Weekly* publishes a full programme of events; the evening singing, dancing and verse competitions are heavily subscribed. Vendors' stalls, normally forbidden on the Finikoúdhes, return at this time to sell everything from canaries to plastic toys.

There are two **cinemas** around Larnaca, showing first-run "family entertainment": the central *Othellos 1 & 2* (☏24657970) at Ayías Elénis 13, and – a short drive out of town near the Kamáres aqueduct – the six-screen *K-Cineplex* at Peloponnísou 1 (☏24819022). It's best to check English-language newspapers or on-site posters for screening times, as these phone numbers have Greek-only recordings.

## Shopping

In the former Turkish quarter, just inland from Piyale Paşa and five blocks south of the fort, are the studios of several leading Cypriot **ceramicists**, all of Famagusta origin. On the adjoining lanes called Ak Deniz and Bozkurt, the workshops of Efthymios Symeou, Akdeniz 18 (☏24650338), Stavros Stavrou, Akdeniz 8 (☏24624491), and Fotini Kourti-Khristou, Bozkurt 28 (☏24650304), turn out a wide variety of thin stoneware and raku ware, either practical or decorative, in both traditional and innovative designs.

In what remains of the tradesmen's bazaar on Kaloyéra are a few coppersmiths, wood-restorers and **antique dealers**, plus another (Antique Emporium) on Valsamáki near the enclosed car park. Connoisseurs of slightly more mundane second-hand items should gravitate towards Bags of Fun in the Christos Demetriou Commercial Centre, or the Larnaca Thrift Shop, Prótis Aprílíou 67.

## Listings

**Airlines** Helios Airways, Nietzsche 22, Ria Court 9, 1st floor ☏24815700; Cyprus Airways, Arkhiepiskópou Makaríou 20 ☏80000008.
**Airport information** ☏24643300.
**Banks and exchange** The most convenient bank branches with ATMs (eg Bank of Cyprus, Hellenic Bank) are immediately around the CTO, plus a few more on Ayíou Lazárou and Zínonos Kitiéos.
**Bookshop** Academic & General, Ermoú 41, is one of the best in Cyprus, with a large English-language stock on all subjects, including travel (some Rough Guides), magazines and Cypriana, including the hard-to-find Trigraph backlist (see "Books" in *Contexts*).
**Bus companies** Principal outfits include Intercity, to Nicosia, Limassol, Ayía Nápa and Protarás, and EMAN, to Ayía Nápa, both departing from terminals on the Finikoúdhes opposite the *Four Lanterns Hotel*. Municipal PEAL buses to Paralímni, Kíti (for Hala Sultan Tekke and Angelóktisti church), Perivólia and Voróklini leave from a stop on Arkhiepiskópou Makaríou, near the police station. The single daily service to Páno Léfkara village goes from Platía Ayíou Lazárou.

**Car rental** Agencies at the airport include: Andreas Petsas, Astra/National, Budget, Europcar, Hertz and Sixt. Very few licensed companies maintain in-town outlets any longer; the exceptions are GDK (Budget), Arkhiepiskópou Makaríou 61A ☏24629170, and Theodoulou Self Drive, Leonídha Kiouppí 13 ☏24627411.
**Internet** Alto Café, Grigóri Afxendíou (daily 10am–2am); Replay, Finikoúdhes (daily 10am–1am).
**Laundry** Artemis Speed Queen, Armenikís Ekklisías 12.
**Post offices** Main post office is next to the CTO on Platía Dhimokratías (Mon–Fri 7.30am–1.30pm, also Mon, Tues, Thurs, Fri 3–6pm in winter, 4–7pm in summer, plus Sat 8.30–10.30am); also a small branch opposite Áyios Lázaros church (Mon–Fri morning hours only, plus Thurs 3–6/4–7pm).
**Scuba school** Best in-town outfit is Dive-In, Piyale Paşa 132 ☏24627469, ⌐www.dive-in.com.cy, with the considerable advantage of their own boat moored at the nearby fishing marina rather than at the main port. They're normally open April–Nov (plus winter by arrangement), offering triox and nitrox programmes in addition to the usual PADI/

## The wreck of the *Zenobia*

Far and away the best scuba destination in Cyprus is the wreck of the *Zenobia*, an enormous car-ferry some 1400m outside Larnaca commercial port. She was almost brand-new when a computer malfunction flooded a ballast tank as she was leaving the harbour; the *Zenobia* listed fatally to port, constituting a stationary navigational hazard, and the decision was made to tow the ship out to the present locale and scuttle her. Over a hundred lorries are still trapped on board, along with an aquarium's worth of resident sea-life. Water temperature varies from 16°C to 27°C by season, and visibility in calm conditions can approach 50m.

The wreck depth ranges from 16m to 42m, so this isn't a beginner's dive; some of the chains holding the lorries in place are also distinctly corroded, so caution must be exercised. The former monopoly on diving the *Zenobia* has been broken, and several island operators anchor in an orderly and fairly amicable fashion at various points along the 172-metre length of the wreck. Usually you'll have a two-dive day, the first to about 35m, the second (after lunch taken on board the dive boat) shorter and shallower. Some local outfitters, such as Larnaca's Dive-In, offer "Three Wrecks in a Day", including a sunken private yacht, and the British patrol boat *HMS Cricket*, as well.

If you're not scuba-certified, you can still see the wreck and its tenants on the Sadko tourist submarine operating out of Larnaca Yacht Marina (℡24642588 for information).

BSAC courses, and welcome disabled and under-age divers. Octopus Diving Centre, opposite *Palm Beach Hotel* on the Voróklini strip ℡24646571, ⍟www.octopus-diving.com, also comes recommended. See also the box above.

**Service taxis** Combined services to Limassol and Nicosia run by Travel & Express operate out of a single terminal at Kímonos 2 ℡24661010.

# Southwest of Larnaca: the coast

Larnaca is conveniently situated at the centre of its administrative district, with a number of archeological sites, handicraft-producing villages and less popular resorts scattered in a broad arc all around. The main expressways to Limassol and Nicosia are routed well inland west of the city, leaving the coastal plain to the southwest relatively untravelled except for local village traffic. This is one patch of Cyprus, though, where the best bits are the easiest to reach.

## Hala Sultan (Umm Haram) Tekke

The **Hala Sultan (Umm Haram) Tekke**, 5km southwest of Larnaca and just past the airport, is quite possibly the first thing of note that you'll see on arrival in Cyprus, since it's clearly visible from jets coming in to land. According to the foundation legend, Muhammad's paternal aunt, accompanying her husband on an Arab raid of Cyprus in 649, was attacked by Byzantine forces here, fell from her mule, broke her neck and was buried on the spot. A mosque grew up around the grave on the west shore of a salt lake, surrounded today by an odd mix of date palms, cypress and olives. Rain permitting, a tank and a series of channels water the grove, adding to the oasis feeling of this peaceful, bird-filled place.

*Tekke* literally means a dervish convent, but this was always merely a *marabout* or saint's tomb. Despite the events of 1974, heavy-gauge fencing and a nocturnal police guard to prevent vandalism, it's still a popular excursion target for Greek Cypriots and **place of pilgrimage** for both Cypriot and foreign Muslims, for Hala Sultan ranks as one of the holiest spots of Islam, after Mecca, Medina, Kairouan and Jerusalem. The twin name is Turkish/Arabic: *Hala Sultan* means "the Ruler's paternal aunt", while *Umm Haram* or "Sacred Mother" seems an echo of the old Aphrodite worship.

Having left your shoes at the door, you're ushered inside the present nine-teenth-century mosque (daily: summer 7.30am–sunset, winter 9am–sunset; may close an hour before dark; donation) to the **tomb recess** at the rear, behind the *mihrab*. Beside the presumed sarcophagus of the Prophet's aunt, there's a recent (1930) tomb of the Turkish wife of King Hussein of the Hejaz. Above, shrouded in a green cloth, you'll see three slabs of rock forming the dolmen that probably marked the grave until the mosque was built. The horizontal slab, a fifteen-ton meteorite chunk, is said to have been suspended miraculously in mid-air for centuries, before being forcibly lowered into its present position to avoid frightening the faithful who prayed underneath.

The dolmen and the mosque were by no means the first permanent structures here; remains of a **Late Bronze Age town**, west of the access road and car park, have been excavated since the late 1970s, yielding various treasures. The wealth of material from Egypt confirms that the island's links with North Africa and the Near East go back long before the Ptolemies.

Flamingos and other migratory birds stop over at the **lake** during winter and early spring (see p.490). Like the *tekke*, the lake has a foundation legend, too: lately resuscitated Bishop Lazarus, passing by, asked a woman carrying some grapes for a bunch; upon her rude refusal, he retaliated by turning her vine-yard into the salty lagoon, now three metres below sea level. Post-resurrection Lazarus indeed comes down in legend as a rather grim figure; it is said that he never smiled while bishop, a result of what he'd seen during his brief sojourn in the realm of the dead.

The Kíti-bound PEAL municipal **bus** from Larnaca (Mon–Fri 11 daily 8am–7pm, Sat 5 daily 8am–1pm, reliable summeronly) can take you to within 1km of the *tekke*; have the driver set you down at the signposted side road, just the far side of the causeway over the salt lake.

On the north shore of the lake near the Limassol-bound road is the so-called **Kamares aqueduct**, built in 1747 by Abu Bekir, the only popular Ottoman governor of the island. The 75 surviving arches, illuminated at night to good effect, were in use until 1930.

## Angelóktisti church

The above-noted bus continues to **Kíti**, 10km from Larnaca. At a prominent three-way junction in the village, where roads head shorewards for Perivólia or on to Mazotós, stands the Byzantine **church of Angelóktisti** (Mon–Sat 8am–noon & 2–4pm, Sun 9.30am–noon & 2–4pm; donation). If necessary, the key can be fetched from the nearby snack bar, and smocks are provided for the "indecently" dressed; since this is still Kíti's main church, visits during Sunday morning liturgy are problematic.

Most of the church dates from the eleventh and twelfth centuries, having replaced an original fifth-century sanctuary destroyed by the Arabs. What today serves as a narthex and display area for old icons (signs in Greek warn the faith-ful not to kiss them if wearing lipstick) began life as an apsed and rib-vaulted Latin chapel in the thirteenth or fourteenth century. The main nave has three aisles, a single apse and no true narthex, though there's a large *yinaikonítis*, and painted-on, all-seeing eyes to either side of the *témblon*.

But the highlight of Angelóktisti is the **mosaic** (illuminated on request) in the conch of the apse, probably the last surviving section of the original building. Inside a floral/vegetal border, the Virgin – labelled unusually as *Ayía María* or "Saint Mary" – lightly balances a doll-like holy infant on her left arm as she gazes sternly to a point just left of the viewer. The pair is attended by two dissimilar archangels with fish-scale wings – Gabriel, on the right, is fleshier and more masculine than the damaged portrayal of Michael – proffering celestial orbs and sceptres in the direction of the Infant. The date of the mosaic is controversial, but the Ravenna-esque artistic conventions, especially Mary's stance on a jewelled pedestal and inclination to the left, would suggest the sixth century. Yet it is far more refined than the purportedly contemporaneous mosaic in the North Cyprus church of Kanakariá, which was the only other complete Cypriot ecclesiastical mosaic *in situ* until its desecration.

## Perivólia and Cape Kíti

Just 2km southeast of Kíti, **PERIVÓLIA** is developing as a resort because of its proximity to the beaches on **Cape Kíti**, almost 3km further in the same direction (and also reachable from Meneoú – follow signs for "Meneoú Beach"). These beaches, to either side of the lighthouse, are mostly scrappy, narrow and sharply shelving, with large pebbles on a sand base. Nonetheless, self-catering hotel apartments are springing up on the outskirts, ever-burgeoning villas and apartments overlooking the beaches are for sale, and "Flats to Let" signs abound in the village.

If you have a rented car, Perivólia or its beach annexes could be a good, relatively quiet base, considerably less tatty than Larnaca itself. Out by the lighthouse, there are two comfortable, moderately priced beachfront **hotels**, both with tennis courts, pool and similar facilities: *Three Seas* (℡24422901, ⓦwww.3seashotel.com.cy; ❹), and *Faros Village* (℡24422111, ⓦwww.farosvillage.com; ❺), a plusher, landscaped bungalow complex represented by a few UK package companies. Numerous **tavernas** in the village centre also make it a possible destination for a night out from Larnaca, but the most authentically Cypriot fish taverna is the *Akrogiali* (aka *Panikos'*), out at **Kíti Beach** – pretty much the last building before the salt marsh and airport, with seating over the sand. It's pleasant and salubrious, though not particularly cheap at C£11 for a plate of *lithríni*, salad, assorted dips and a beer.

A restored sixteenth-century **Venetian watchtower** looms conspicuously on a knoll just over a kilometre north of the modern lighthouse. Dirt tracks converge there from all directions, and it's always in sight – though not especially compelling once you get there.

## Westwards to Maróni and Zíyi

Returning to Kíti village, it's possible to follow the coast **westwards** by forking left, away from Mazotós. Despite the paved road running alongside, the shore thus far remains little developed except for farms and Cypriots' weekend villas, and frankly there's not much to justify any exploitation; the few beaches are rocky and difficult to reach, though once you are in the water the seabed is sandy enough.

If you persevere along this road, you eventually return to civilization at either Zíyi or Maróni, though either is, in fact, simpler to reach along the old, inland trunk road or the newer, parallel expressway. Spread appealingly over several hills, **MARÓNI** is a major hothouse-vegetable centre. Its atmospheric old town, like that of Psematisménos, 2km north, is home to numerous expatriates, and a taverna or two takes advantage of this market. Despite (or perhaps because of) its status as a mixed village before 1974, its Greek-Cypriot inhabitants were claimed to be among the most virulently nationalist in the district, and, in the words of one former resident, "made Nikos Sampson (see p.443) look like a Communist sympathizer". When the Turkish Cypriots left in late 1974, the remaining villagers bulldozed their houses and claimed their fields, rather than distribute them to refugees from the North.

ZÍYI (Zygi), 3km southeast of Maróni, sprang up in the nineteenth century as the first Cypriot port dedicated to shipping out carob pods; the Greek name, like the Turkish moniker *Terazi*, means "weighing scales". The Cypriot republic inherited two military bases here from the British, their radar masts overshadowing the regional BBC transmitter – and acting as a magnet for would-be spies, with two Israelis arrested and jailed for several years in 1998.

Today, Zíyi has a newer role as a minor local resort, with seaside villas for Cypriots and a baker's dozen of fish **tavernas** drawing in crowds from as far away as Nicosia. However, quality is questionable, with imported/farmed seafood the rule, so we make no specific recommendations at present.

The lack of beaches in the area doesn't seem to deter local day-trippers and weekend apartment-owners. The nearest approximation to one is at **Limanáki**, about 3km east of Zíyi: look for a side track (signposted as "Maroni Beach") to seaward just west of the turn-off for Maróni, beside an enormous beached wooden caïque. This little bay has the only patch of sand for miles around, but the cove is jetsam-prone, and the taverna behind has been derelict since the early 1990s.

# Western Larnaca district

Compared to the parched, rather barren land close to Larnaca and the low-rise excesses of outer Limassol, the gently rolling country at the western end of Larnaca district presents a welcome change, with trees, streams and a hint of the Tróödhos foothills further west. Several points of interest flank the Limassol–Nicosia expressway, suitably provided with exit roads across and onto the old highway, which in many respects is better for travelling short distances here.

## Kalavassós

If you're seized by an urge to stay in the area – and it does have the considerable virtue of being roughly equidistant from Nicosia, Larnaca and Limassol – cross the expressway from either Maróni or Zíyi to ravine-nestled **KALAVASSÓS** (Kalavasos), where frogs croaking in the nearby stream-bed are likely to be the only noise to disturb you at night. Until 1972, the village lived off copper mines just up the valley, the proceeds from which funded the extravagantly ornate north portal of the church. One of the little locomotives which used to haul the ore-cars out of the hills to the coast has been poised on an isolated stretch of narrow-gauge track over the Vasilikós River, and is creatively illuminated by night.

Kalavassós – along with adjacent Tókhni – is the original focus of an admirable **accommodation** scheme based in a dozen well-adapted village houses, plus a few new stone-clad structures, run by Cyprus Villages (T 24332998, W www.cyprusvillages.com.cy). Studio, one- and two-bedroom units are available at daily rates (summer rates ❷–❸ and ❹ respectively; advance bookings essential), but they're generally let as part of a one-week package with car rental and airport transfers included, arranged through various British, German and Scandinavian tour companies. Cyprus Villages is affiliated with the Swiss- and English-run Drapia Farm (℗99437188), a **horse-riding centre** just north of the village; prices range from two-hour rides for C£20 per person to ten hours on horseback for C£80, spread over a week. Mountain-biking and sailing (out of Larnaca) are also available.

It is possible to find other accommodation in Kalavassós that's not part of Cyprus Villages. This includes the *Kontoyiannis House* (℗25580306, Ⓦwww .kontoyiannis.com; ❷), with four modernized units in an old building, and *Stratos House* (℗24332293 or 25346588; ❺ for 4-bedded apartments), somewhat more sympathetically restored.

Kalavassós nominally has five **tavernas**, but only two operate reliably outside high season. Gregarious Stavros lays on a good Friday-night *mezé* in his *Tenta Restaurant* at the north end of the village, but just fish or meat fry-ups and bulk wine on other nights. The *Bridge House Tavern* at the village entrance provides standard, inexpensive (under C£7 a head) Cypriot meals, enlivened by their home-made cheesecake, and there's a convivial bar with both indoor and outdoor seating.

## Tókhni

**TÓKHNI** (Tochni), in the next valley east, is even more appealing scenically, but it's as well to know that this was the site of a particularly ugly intercommunal atrocity in summer 1974, when all of the Turkish-Cypriot men over 16 were killed by an EOKA-B detachment (see p.445 in *Contexts*). The Turkish quarter was on the easterly hillside; besides many derelict houses, slowly being restored, the only traces of it are a sturdy mosque (without minaret) and the old graveyard near the turning for the Cyprus Villages office. Down in the central ravine, the arcades of a coffeehouse neatly frame the belfry of the church, which straddles the watercourse.

Among the eight separate Cyprus Villages properties (see "Kalavassós" above), the *Myrto* complex of five studios – at the southwest edge of the village – is particularly worth singling out for its high standard of restoration, peaceful setting and private pool. Up by the *Tokhni Taverna*, there's an eponymous cluster of stone-clad, 2003-built studios and one-bedroom apartments with another, less private pool. As at Kalavassós, there are also several "independent" **accommodation** options, though a few don't operate outside of peak season. The most conventional is *Sokratis House Hotel* (℗24333636, Ⓕ24332536; closed Nov–March; ❸), on the slope west of the central church, with a taverna on-site (dinner only), though the rooms are a bit small. **Self-catering** outfits include *Danae House* (℗24662123 or 99682276, Ⓔdanae@spidernet.com.cy; ❷), comprising eight studio or one-bedroom units on the highest hilltop, adjacent to the Cyprus Villages office; *Vasilopoulos House* (℗24332531, Ⓕ24332933, Ⓔavasifa@spidernet.com.cy; ❸), a courtyard complex of studios and one-bedroom units on the east side of the village; and *Niovi's House* (℗99468446, Ⓦwww.niovi-agrotourism.com.cy; ❷), a three-bedroom hillside house with courtyard that's suitable for families.

For **eating out**, *Tokhni Taverna*, managed by Cyprus Villages, purveys adequate if somewhat unadventurous fare, with the setting (balcony in summer, fireplace in winter) being the biggest plus. Other options, including the taverna at *Sokratis House* (see above) and *Nostos* opposite the church, are not always open outside of peak season.

# Tenta (Ténda)

Close to Kalavassós and Tókhni are two important excavated ancient sites. The nearest is the Neolithic village of **Tenta** (Mon–Fri 10am–4pm; C£0.75, detailed guidebook £3 extra), smaller than roughly contemporary Khirokitia (see below), but sharing its cultural features. To get here head south out of Kalavassós, then bear right (west) onto "Tenta Street", which leads up to an unmissable "teepee", supported by girders, on a natural hillock next to the expressway. The canopy protects mud-and-stone-rubble structures culminating in the largest **roundhouse**, "Structure 14", at the summit, just glimpsing the sea; there are smaller round huts just to the east, with a ditch and **perimeter wall** at the edge of the settlement. This appears to have numbered some 45 to 50 dwellings, both flat- and dome-roofed, sheltering at most 150 people. Burial practices seem to have been a bit more casual than at Khirokitia, with about half the skeletons found outside dwellings, mixed with rubbish. The original name of the place is of course unknown; the modern one arises from a local legend asserting that Saint Helena, mother of Constantine the Great, pitched her tent (*ténda*) here upon returning from Jerusalem with a portion of the True Cross, en route to founding the monastery of Stavrovoúni.

Between Tenta and the motorway lies **Áyios Dhimítrios**, an important Late Bronze Age town with a large ashlar building, possibly a palace, but it's still being excavated and not yet open to the public.

# Khirokitia

Some of the earliest traces of human settlement in Cyprus, from around 6800 BC, are found at Neolithic **Khirokitia** (Choirokoitia), roughly halfway between Larnaca and Limassol on the modern expressway. The proper name of the site is Khirokitia-Vouni, but it's most often called simply Khirokitia after the modern village to the northwest.

Despite noisy distraction from the motorway, Khirokitia ranks among the most rewarding of Cypriot ruins, with ongoing excavations likely to increase its allure. The excavated area forms a long ribbon on a southeast-facing slope dominating a pass on the age-old highway from the coast to Nicosia. It's not always open during the prescribed **opening hours** (Mon–Fri 9am–5pm, summer until 7.30pm, Sat & Sun 9am–5pm; C£0.75, explanatory pamphlet available for a small extra charge), and at weekends at least it's unwise to show up after 1pm. The only nearby amenity is a taverna on the access road from the main highway, on the east side of the bridge over the Maróni creek.

### The site

The combination of arable land below and an easily defensible position proved irresistible to the settlement's founders, who were thought to have come from the Levantine coast or Anatolia. Archeological investigations are continuing in the earliest inhabited sector, a saddle between the two knolls at the top of the slope; despite the limited area uncovered to date, it seems certain that most of the hillside was inhabited.

What's visible thus far are housing foundations – most substantial and recent at the bottom of the slope – and a maze of lanes, dictated more by the placement of dwellings than any deliberate planning. You walk up on what appears to be the main street, in fact a defensive **perimeter wall**, something that becomes more obvious at the top of the hill; the very few houses that were built outside it were later enclosed by a secondary outer wall.

The sixty-odd circular *tholos* (beehive-type) **dwellings** exposed to date are single-storey structures that probably had a mixture of domed and flat roofs.

Interior walls were lined with stone benches doubling as sleeping platforms, with scanty illumination provided through slit windows. The largest dwelling, an egg-shaped chieftain's "**mansion**" with an inner diameter of just under six metres, had two rectangular piers supporting a loft. As the structures deteriorated, they were flattened into rubble and built over by the next generation (it was this practice that prompted the now-discarded theory that the perimeter wall was in fact the main street, its elevation constantly raised to keep pace with the level of the new houses). This "urban-renewal" method has greatly complicated modern excavations, which began in 1936, two years after the site's discovery; these have yielded vast troves of small Neolithic objects, undisturbed by vandals and now to be seen at the Cyprus Museum in Nicosia. Several concrete replicas have been erected to give an idea of how claustrophobic life in one of the original houses must have been.

Estimates for the maximum **population** of Khirokitia run as high as two thousand, an astounding figure for the time. Wheel-less pottery techniques were known only in the local culture's latter phases; during the so-called **Aceramic** period, the inhabitants worked strictly in stone, turning out – for example – relief-patterned grey andesite bowls and rather schematic idols. Flint sickle blades, grinders hollowed out of river boulders, and preserved cereal grains provide proof of the community's largely agricultural basis, though hunting, particularly for deer, and the herding of goats was important too.

The Khirokitians **buried their dead** in the fetal position under the earth floor, or just outside the entrance, of some of the round-houses – a rather convenient, if unhygienic form of ancestor reverence; beneath one dwelling, twenty-six graves on eight superimposed levels were discovered. The deceased were surrounded by offerings and personal belongings, exquisite stone-and-shell necklaces being found in female graves; more ominously, the corpses usually had their chests crushed with a grinding quern to prevent the dead returning. As at Tenta, infant mortality was high, and adult skulls show evidence of ritual deformation – surviving infants would have been tightly bound on a cradle-board to flatten the back of the head.

## Hill-villages: the long way to Páno Léfkara

Rather than proceed from ancient Khirokitia along the expressway to the most direct side road for Páno Léfkara, a rewarding detour can be made through some little-visited hill-villages. The first of these, **KHIROKITÍA**, straddles a ridge 2km west of the ruins and offers a foretaste of **VÁVLA**, a depopulated village 9km to the northwest, where an array of beautiful old houses is slowly being restored. Families and groups may stay in the baronial, three-bedroom *Papadopoulou House* (☎24656327 or 24342698; ❹ minimum two-room rental), usually available through at least one UK package operator; at weekends snacks are offered at the lone *kafenío* here.

Vávla marks the turning for **Ayíou Miná convent** (Sun–Fri 9am–noon & 3–6pm), one of several such functioning in the South, but so far among the least visited despite its proximity (7km) to Páno Léfkara. The Byzantine-Gothic church, probably founded by the Dominicans during the fifteenth century and reworked two hundred years later, provides the main focus of interest; the friendly nuns produce icons and honey, both offered for sale.

The main valley road from Vávla continues up through less distinguished Láyia (Lageia) and Orá, beyond which the surface abruptly deteriorates as you crawl over a saddle towards **VAVATSINIÁ**, nestling in a fold of Mount Kiónia at the top of the valley that drains towards Ayíou Miná. Above the central church, an *ayíasma* (holy spring with curative powers) issues from a deep shaft; below the church the *Pefkos* taverna, packed out at weekends, looks across the gorge towards a typical peaked-roof hill-country chapel: fresco-less but with a carved-wood interior. As you leave the village in the direction of Páno Léfkara, you pass another pair of enormous **tavernas** (*Stavros* and *Maria's*) on the outskirts, also jammed at warm-weather holidays with Cypriot day-trippers.

## Páno Léfkara

**PÁNO LÉFKARA**, 700m above sea level on the fringes of the Tróödhos, is reached along an easy climb from its own exit of the motorway onto the well-made E105. A retreat of the Orthodox clergy in Lusignan times, it's now almost a small town and a very handsome one to boot: arches make veritable tunnels in the streets, and fine door-frames and balconies complete the picture. Many of the old houses are being restored by Cypriots and foreigners, though prices are high owing to equidistance from the South's three largest towns. There was a small Turkish quarter here, too, down at the low end of the village by the mosque.

The usual reason for visiting is to sample the **lace and silver** for which the place is famous; it is claimed, somewhat apocryphally, that Leonardo da Vinci purchased a needlepoint altarcloth for Milan cathedral when he came to Cyprus in 1481. The silver jewellery and silverware, men's work, are more reasonably priced than the women's lace. Both are sold in over half a dozen shops devoted to each craft, mostly on the main commercial street.

That said, constant "shopping tours" have had their effect, and everyone from petrol-pump attendant to café owner will happily trot out the work of relatives at the first opportunity – if you don't want to be almost ceaselessly hustled (having parking fees waived in exchange for "just a look" is a common ploy), you may as well not show up. It's also as well to know that the "lace" to be embroidered is actually imported Irish linen. On the whole, lace prices are inflated in Páno Léfkara, so bargain hard, or seek out better deals in surrounding villages. The **Patsalos Folklore Museum** (Mon–Thurs 9.30am–4pm, Fri & Sat 10am–4pm; C£0.75), devoted largely to the two crafts, might be a useful first stop before going on a shopping spree. Páno Léfkara is also noted for its "Turkish" delight (*loukoúmia*), and if you're lucky you might catch a demonstration of its manufacture.

### Practicalities

As you approach, it's best not to take the first signposted turn-off into the village – there's no **parking** on this side and it leaves you with a fair hike into town. It's easiest instead to leave a vehicle at the northeast end of the village by the post office, where a line of arched, wooden-floored *kafenía* opposite the school offers a marvellous tableau of the village elders playing at cards or dice. Páno Léfkara has just one surviving **hotel**: the 1994-constructed *Agora* (☎24342901, ℱ24342095; ❹), with its pool-courtyard and large, bland rooms available through at least one UK package company, but otherwise not terribly good value. In a not very illustrious field of candidates, the diner at the *Agora* is the best place to eat in the village.

## Káto Léfkara and Kátho Dhrýs

Páno Léfkara's lower neighbour, **KÁTO LÉFKARA**, 1500m down the road, is also architecturally of a piece, but much less frequented – here too, however, there is a snack bar and several trinket shops. The real sight in Káto is the largely twelfth-century **church of the Arkhángelos** (always unlocked), by itself in a field to the southwest of the village car park. Although the preservation and quantity of its **interior frescoes** cannot rank it with the best examples of painted churches in the high Tróödhos, what remains is well worth the slight detour. The oldest and best surviving images decorate the apse, with *Christ's Communion with the Apostles* (six of whom are missing) above five early Fathers of the Church. Over the south door, the *Mandylion* (*Holy Kerchief*) is essentially a *Pandokrátor* superimposed on a shawl, just below a badly deteriorated *Baptism*. A much later (fifteenth-century) *Resurrection* in the arch of the west vault looks suspiciously like the *Healing of the Leper*.

Lace-making endeavours are also evident 2.5km to the southwest at **KÁTO DHRÝS** (Kato Drys), on the road between Káto Léfkara and the convent of Ayíou Miná, and claimed to be the village immortalized on the unnumbered, unsigned side of the Cypriot one-pound note. There are a few shops here, plus two **tavernas**, including the *Platanos* at the outskirts, with seating under the namesake tree.

## Pottery villages: Kofínou and Kórnos

Back on the route towards Nicosia, you can detour almost immediately to **KOFÍNOU**, which has just a single pottery workshop, Skutari Craft Pottery, near the ugly prefab church. The present villagers are refugees from the North; this was among the largest, nearly all-Muslim villages in the South, attacked on scanty pretext by EOKA on November 15, 1967. Before a truce was arranged two days later, 25 local Turkish Cypriots had died, and the incident nearly precipitated a Greek–Turkish war. Scars of the battle are still evident in the old Turkish quarter, now abandoned, boarded up and signposted as "Government Property". The incoming Greek Cypriots were housed in a grid-plan prefabricated development to the west. Kofinou is well-known locally for its **kléftigo** houses: if you're in the mood for a good-value lunch, check out the *Pentadaktylos Kleftigo House*, one of several such that lie adjacent to the Larnaca-bound motorway; just under C£6 should see you to a small beer, a very creditable *kléftigo* with not much gristle, and a caper-garnished salad. The closest alternative with vegetarian fare lies about 3km southwest along the B1 at **SKARÍNOU**, where the courtly Achilleas' *Happy Valley House* (☎24322544) offers such delights as bean soup, or just coffee and dessert, to a mixed Cypriot and expat clientele in what was originally a staging-post on the old Larnaca–Limassol road. Sunday lunch is particularly popular and must be pre-booked.

**KÓRNOS**, 11km north on the other side of the highway, is a more cheerful place, set in a tree-lined stream valley, and also occupies itself with pottery (*kórnos* means "clay" in Cypriot dialect). Again there's just one "proper" shop, with a phone number to call in the (likely) event they're shut, but they do come if summoned. There are also a few more informal kilns operating in back gardens, with portable wares priced at C£4–7 per item.

## Stavrovoúni monastery

Proportionate to its small population, Cyprus contributes more monks to the monastic enclave of Mount Áthos in northern Greece than any other Orthodox country. You can get a glimpse of the reasons why at **Stavrovoúni monastery**, perched atop an isolated, 689-metre crag that dominates this corner of the island.

Its foundation legend places it as the oldest religious community on Cyprus: Saint Helena, mother of the eastern Roman Emperor Constantine, supposedly came through here in 327 on her way back from Jerusalem, leaving a fragment of the True Cross (plus the entire cross of the penitent thief). Previously home to a temple of Aphrodite, the peak took its modern name from this event (*Stavrovoúni* means "Cross Mountain"), and a religious community quickly sprang up around the holy relics.

In Lusignan times, Benedictine monks displaced Orthodox ones, but despite an imposing fortified design, both monastery and revered objects were destroyed after the 1426 rout of King Janus nearby (see "Pýrga" below). Today's silver reliquary crucifix, which supposedly encases the venerated sliver of the True Cross, dates only from the late fifteenth century; perhaps the contents are identical with the purported cross of the penitent thief which a wandering Dominican friar claimed to have seen here, still intact, by the altar in 1486.

After the Turkish conquest the monastery was burned again, and only during the nineteenth century was Stavrovoúni rebuilt, on the old foundations, and repopulated – by both monks and dozens of cats, the latter a scourge of snakes here as at the Cape Gáta nunnery at Akrotíri. But by the late 1970s the place was in decline once more, with just two elderly monks besides the abbot. It had given up its once-extensive holdings to surrounding villages, a process doubtless completed by the pressure of refugees from the 1974 invasion, though it retained the convent of Ayía Varvára at the base of the hill as a dependency.

## Monastery life

Today about twenty very committed, mostly young monks follow a rota: six or seven up in the citadel, the rest down at Ayía Varvára at any given time. They are on an **Athonite regimen** (as on Mount Áthos in Greece), the strictest on the island, which entails a day divided into roughly equal thirds of prayer and study, physical labour, and rest. "Rest" means only two frugal, meat-less meals, just before midday and an hour or so before sunset, taken together in the tiny refectory, plus sleep interspersed between the nocturnal devotional periods. There is a minimum of four communal liturgies each day in the courtyard church: matins before dawn, the main liturgy after sunrise, vespers before the evening meal and compline afterwards.

Life has been eased somewhat since the 1980s by the paving of the steep, twisty road up and provision of mains water and electricity, but winters on top are severe, and the monks still do a full day's work on the surrounding agricultural terraces in addition to their devotions. Honey and sultanas, the latter legendarily having their first Cypriot cultivation here, make up some of the harvest. The icon-painting studio of the elderly Father Kallinikos at well-restored **Ayía Varvára** (closed noon–3pm) is well signposted; he is claimed (rather controversially, since some consider him vastly overrated) to be one of the finest living practitioners of the art, and his work is accordingly expensive.

## Visits

Strict conditions apply for **visiting the upper monastery**. In accordance with Athonite rules, no women are admitted at all, not even female infants; no entry is allowed from noon to 3pm (11am–2pm in summer – the monks don't observe daylight-saving time); and photos are forbidden – cameras must be left at the guard house at the foot of the long stairway up from the car park. In short, you don't come here to gawp – except perhaps at the amazing views, since there's little remaining of artistic or architectural merit after the pillaging, fires and the bishop of Kition's ham-handed 1980s restoration – but on pilgrimage, possibly to stay the night on invitation.

A Greek sign in the entry hall sums up the monastic creed: "If you die before you die, then when you die you won't die." In other words, he who has renounced the world gains eternal life. When a monk *does* die bodily, he is interred for the five years prescribed by Orthodoxy and then exhumed for display in the ossuary, his religious name emblazoned across the forehead of his skull.

## Pýrga: the Chapelle Royale

Near the centre of **PÝRGA** village, just 3km from Kórnos and east of the expressway, stands the **Chapelle Royale** (signposted as "Medieval Chapel"), a small, frescoed Lusignan shrine actually dedicated to Saint Catherine (open daylight hours according to keeper's whim; C£0.75). It owes its alias to a fine wall-painting of **King Janus**, who, together with his queen, Charlotte of Bourbon, built the chapel in 1421. "Good King Janus" was among the last of Cyprus's Crusader monarchs, as respected as he was ineffective; just a few kilometres south, below Khirokitía village, runs the Maróni stream where his armies were defeated by the Mamelukes in 1426. Janus was held prisoner in Cairo for two years before being ransomed, and this little church is his only surviving legacy.

The building itself is quite plain, merely a single-vaulted structure with three doorways. By 1426 all the inside surfaces had been decorated by a Greek-Cypriot painter effecting a unique synthesis of Byzantine and Latin iconographic elements; unhappily only a small fraction of the paintings survive. Janus appears, along with Queen Charlotte, as a tiny, kneeling figure at the foot of a fragmentary *Crucifixion* on the east wall. On the northeast ceiling you can make out *The Raising of Lazarus* and a *Last Supper*, the latter the best-preserved image here and – unusually in Cyprus – identified in medieval French. Opposite these frescoes, also tagged by French inscriptions, an *Ascension* and *Pentecost* are just recognizable.

## Kelliá: the church of Áyios Andónios

The Byzantine **church of Áyios Andónios**, a mere 5km north of Larnaca via Livádhia, makes a satisfying complement to the two preceding sites. It's just west of **KELLIÁ**, formerly inhabited wholly by Turkish Cypriots and named for the hermits' cells which existed here long before the village. The church enjoys a commanding position atop a man-made hillock and was originally erected in the ninth century, though what you see now is an engaging medley of eleventh- to fifteenth-century styles, plus an eighteenth-century west arcade. The building's current ground plan is that of a multi-vaulted cross-in-square, with three aisles and apses, plus a fifteenth-century narthex. Since whitewash and extraneous buttressing were removed, the value of Áyios Andónios's early Byzantine **frescoes** has been recognized and the church is now kept scrupulously locked; to gain access to the interior (donation to the offerings box) – and it's well worth it – you must track down the caretaker Mikhalis, a lovely man who lives in the white house with a vast courtyard, opposite the main *kafenío*.

The paintings exposed thus far decorate four interior pillars and the west wall. On the right front (southeast) pier, the faces of the *Crucifixion*, the earliest known fresco on the island, are strangely serene and wide-eyed in the Middle-Eastern, paleo-Christian manner; just above this, a surviving fragment of the eleventh-century *Betrayal* clearly shows Peter lopping off the ear of the high priest's servant. On the rear left (northwest) pier, the figure of an equestrian Saint George is twelfth-century, but the slightly mismatched legs of his horse date from the tenth century; from the south face of the same pier, another, tenth-century, George gazes out, a heavy-lidded, slightly foppish Byzantine prince. Facing this pier, on the west wall, is a figure of Saint Pandelimon (often misidentified as either saint Kosmas or Damian), from the early eleventh century, with his gaze oddly averted to his right. On the southwest pier, facing the narthex, a *Virgin Enthroned*, thought to date from the tenth century, is superimposed on a geometric background, the latter possibly a holdover from the Iconoclastic period. Immediately opposite this on the west wall are two versions of the *Sacrifice of Isaac*, from the early eleventh and twelfth centuries; the later, lower rendition, is more intact, complete with the angel admonishing Abraham not to do the deed.

# East of Larnaca: the resort coast

As you head out of the city, the bight of Larnaca Bay bends gradually from north to east. It takes nearly 5km to outrun the oil refineries and tankers to

## Special uses for the Dhekélia Sovereign Base

The existence of the **Dhekélia Sovereign Base** (see also box on p.148), and its inviolability even in the wake of the 1974 invasion, gave rise to some anomalies in the supposedly hermetic, pre-2003 separation of Cyprus North and South. Both Turkish and Greek Cypriots continued to hold jobs on the base; access from the South was unrestricted, and with the right paperwork from their own authorities Northerners could enter along the so-called "Four Mile Crossing" from Famagusta, or (more usually) at the Beyarmurdu/Pérgamos–Pýla crossing. Turkish Cypriots wishing to make clandestine visits to the South, especially for nightlife, merely left their Northern numberplate cars in the base or Pýla, and had Greek-Cypriot friends with suitable cars waiting for them.

**Pýla**, entirely within the buffer zone near a point where the boundaries of the North, the South and the Dhekélia base meet, acquired special notoriety as one of only two remaining bi-ethnic villages in the southern Republic (the other is Potamiá, near Nicosia, though only about thirty Turkish Cypriots remain there now). Preserved here is an approximate microcosm of island life between 1963 and 1974: Greek (67 percent) and Turkish (33 percent) Cypriots live in proximity but not together, with two opposing coffeehouses (one – guess which – is called *ly Makedhonia/Macedonia*), two sets of flagpoles and separate communal schools. Disputes over Turkish-Cypriot-owned property boundaries often require the mediation of the local UN post, currently manned by civilian Australian and Irish policemen; in theory the writ of neither the Northern nor Southern authorities runs here. A medieval tower, bespattered with pigeon droppings, looms beyond the minaret, both overawed by a ring of modern Turkish army watchtowers on the crags just above – hence no photos anywhere in the village.

Before April 2003, the only tacit intercommunal co-operation involved the **smuggling** of vast amounts of goods from the North, just 5km away across Sovereign Base territory at Pérgamos (Beyarmudu). This loophole made a mockery of the Republic of Cyprus's prohibition on "foreign" agricultural produce, with even fruit and seafood from hated Turkey entering via this corridor. Particularly on the access road in from Larnaca, numerous shops did a roaring trade in "duty-free" jewellery and designer clothing, though by the late 1990s most of these had been driven out of business by harassment from the authorities and price-cutting elsewhere. Since the two-way opening of the checkpoint at the southern edge of Pérgamos/Beyarmudu, there is in fact nothing much to distinguish this road from any of the other legal ways between North and South – though as with any of them you're still liable to have your car searched for contraband (see p.36) when returning from the North.

reach the paragliders and hotels of **VORÓKLINI** (Oróklini) shore annexe, served by PEAL municipal bus from Larnaca. The beach here is acceptable for a dip, but nothing to rave about: the tidal zone is often reefy, the water interrupted by rock jetties and breakwaters. Most of the ten or so **hotels** clustered south of the motorway boast three or four stars. The most consistently well-regarded are the four-star *Palm Beach* (℡24846600, Ⓦwww.palmbeachhotel.com; ❾), refurbished in early 2003; the four-star *Sandy Beach* a couple of kilometres to the east (℡24646333, Ⓦwww.sandybeachhotel.com.cy; ❼); and the five-star *Golden Bay* (℡24645444, Ⓕ24645451, Ⓔgbadmin@goldenbay.com.cy; ❾), three self-contained complexes with beachfront locations, available through virtually any package operator. For a smaller, more affordable choice, still with most amenities, try the *Lenios Beach* (℡24646100, Ⓔlenios@cytanet.com.cy; ❹).

Beyond the hotel strip, there's even less to stop for as the route curls east, and halting is awkward once inside the **Dhekélia Sovereign Base**, home to the British Forces and an enormous, ugly power station between the highway and the sea. The only real bright spot hereabouts is the *Kantara Taverna* (℡24645783) near Dhekélia village, popular with Cypriots for its fish, steak and unusual starters, served in an upmarket environment and priced accordingly.

Once clear of the Sovereign Base, your first detour might be to **Potamós Liopetríou**, a long, narrow creek-inlet that's a genuine, rare fishing anchorage. The only facilities are two **tavernas**, the *Potamos* and the *Demetrion*, both mobbed for weekend lunches, despite slightly bumped-up prices, average-to-good fare and slow service. At *Demetrion*, closer to the mouth of the inlet, C£8 will get you a portion of fresh grilled squid, a salad and a beer. The place itself is attractive, if beachless, though some sand has been hopefully strewn at a suitable bathing spot near the mouth of the inlet. It appears that the French poet Rimbaud stopped in, too, working as a quarry foreman in 1879 before supervising the construction of the governor's residence in the Tróödhos.

# Ayía Nápa

In his book *Journey into Cyprus*, Colin Thubron describes cooking a fish, in the summer of 1972, on the empty beach below the then-fishing village of **AYÍA NÁPA** (Agia Napa), and later being awoken by sandflies. Were he today to find an unpoliced stretch of sand, he would be lucky to sleep at all over the din of nearby clubs. Any local identity has been utterly swept aside since Thubron's visit, with Ayía Nápa press-ganged into service as one of the South's largest package resorts, replacing the lost paradises around Famagusta. The beach is still obvious enough, a crescent swath extending east hundreds of metres from the fishing harbour, but it's packed to the gills in mid-summer. Strictly speaking, you don't need a guidebook to find your way about here – all is pretty self-explanatory – but rather a fat wallet, a large liver capacity and boundless stamina for physical and/or nocturnal exploits.

The resort was put firmly on the map by Channel 4's "Fantasy Island" series, tracing the rise of UK garage music in Ayía Nápa during the 1999 season. From then until 2001, Ayía Nápa ranked as the Med's second hottest clubbing destination, after Ibiza. That, however, is now history; 2004 in particular was pretty listless after dark and, for club-owners and music promoters alike, it's now a case of hunkering down and retrenching, hoping that fashions will again waft substantial numbers of visitors their way.

The bursting of the bubble had a number of causes besides a notoriously fickle scene simply moving on. The place had long had a reputation for testosterone-fuelled brawls amongst holidaying lager-louts, their numbers sometimes augmented by British servicemen. Following their involvement in various incidents of rape, affray and murder, squaddies from both Dhekélia and the UN contingent were banned from local bars and clubs. Trouble continued amongst the "civilians", however, with another fatal stabbing after a UK Radio-1-sponsored event in July 2000. But the biggest factor, perhaps, in Ayía Nápa's decline was local racist hostility to the growing number of black visitors, many from South London, and the hardline attitude taken towards drugs. Although controlled substances in general were never as abundant as on Ibiza, a "zero tolerance" policy towards drugs of any sort was instituted, undercover agents

**AYÍA NÁPA**

▲ Paralimni

0 — 200 m

**Town Hall & Marine Life Museum**

**Ayía Nápa Monastery**

Park

*(i)*

N

**KAFKALLIA**

**EMAN Bus Terminal ★** B

*Limanáki Beach*

*Limanáki Port*

▲ (1) 100m/, ⓐ, Nissi & Makronissos Beaches
▶ Cape Gréko
▶ ⓑ & Kryo Neró Beach

**CLUBS**

| | |
|---|---|
| Black & White | 9 |
| Car Wash | 8 |
| Castle | 13 |
| Club Abyss | 12 |
| Insomnia | 19 |
| Jurassic Bar | 5 |
| River Reggae | 11 |
| VIPs | 16 |

**BARS**

| | |
|---|---|
| The Africa Pub | 3 |
| Bedrock Inn | 4 |
| Guru Ethnic Bar | 2 |
| Luke Kelly | 7 |
| Maïstrali | 18 |
| Minos | 10 |
| Napa Dreams | 6 |

**RESTAURANTS**

| | |
|---|---|
| Clarabel | 15 |
| Markos | 21 |
| Pagoda | 17 |
| Stamna Tavern | 1 |
| Taste of India | 14 |
| Vassos | 20 |

**ACCOMMODATION**

| | |
|---|---|
| Aereas | A |
| Grecian Sands | C |
| Leros | B |
| Limanaki Beach | E |
| Okeanos Beach | D |

abounded, and being caught with even a single spliff or a few Ecstasy tablets earned a number of people a few months in the slammer.

## The Town

Around the central **Platía Seféri** and its pedestrian zone, notional centre of the old pre-tourism village, anything not related to nightlife is likely to be a clothing boutique or overpriced fast-food outlet. Aside from the monastery, don't expect to find any other manifestations of high culture in Ayía Nápa. By day the place can seem eerily quiet, since most visitors (predominantly British and Scandinavian, few of them over 35) sleep until noon, then soak up some sun on the beach before a long evening nap. People next emerge for dinner, before partying until dawn.

### The monastery of Ayía Nápa

The beautiful Venetian-style **monastery of Ayía Nápa** (always open) comes as something of a surprise after the commercialisation of the adjacent *platía*. The monastery's arched cloister encloses an irregularly shaped, flower-decked courtyard, in the middle of which sits an octagonal **fountain**, its sides decorated with reliefs and the whole surmounted by a dome on four pillars. Across the way burbles a boar's-head spout, the terminus of a Roman **aqueduct** whose spring-fed waters were the impetus for sporadic settlement here since Hellenistic times – and the focus of the monastery's foundation legend.

During the sixteenth-century Venetian heyday in Cyprus, some hunters had a mangy dog whose coat improved markedly after visits to a hidden spring. Curious, the hunters followed the wet dog, finding not only the source of the abandoned aqueduct but also an icon of the Virgin hidden here for seven hundred years since the Iconoclastic crisis, when Byzantine zealots outlawed the adoration of such images. News of the waters spread, with humans availing themselves of its healing powers, and soon a monastery was founded around the lower end of the refurbished aqueduct. Work was scarcely completed when the Turks conquered the island, expelling the Catholics from the complex and replacing them with more tractable Greek Orthodox monks; they too soon departed, but a village sprang up around the abandoned monastery.

The **church**, off to the right (west) of the sloping courtyard, is partly subterranean and has a magnificent fanlight-cum-rose window over the door. In the gloom at the base of the stairs down, you'll find a supplementary Latin chapel, from the time of the monastery's original dedication, though the miraculous icon has long since vanished. Back outside you can look from the south façade towards the sea over a cistern brimming with carp, and two giant sycamore figs said to be six centuries old. The Venetian designers built the hefty **perimeter wall** to keep pirates at bay; it now has the unforeseen, though happy, effect of cordoning off the place from drunken revellers.

The monastery was restored during the early 1970s and made available, ironically in light of Ayía Nápa's eventual fate, to the World Council of Churches as a conference centre; delegates, and a few Arab Christians acting as volunteer co-ordinators, are the only people in residence now. From April to December the church itself stays busy on Sundays: Anglican services at 11am, Catholic vespers at 5pm, followed by local baptisms (prestigious monastic churches are highly popular for this purpose among Cypriots).

### The Marine Life Museum

Besides the monastery, the only other real "sight" in Ayía Nápa is the **Tornaritis Pierides Municipal Marine Life Museum**, housed in the town hall at

Ayías Mávris 25, next to the namesake church (May–Sept Mon–Sat 9am–2pm, plus Thurs 3–6pm; Oct–April Mon–Sat 9am–2pm, plus Thurs 3–5pm; C£1, children C£0.50). Funded, like the eponymous museum in Larnaca, by the Pierides Foundation, it consists largely of the seashell and fossil collection of naturalist George Tornaritis, plus stuffed or preserved specimens of larger marine species in dioramas.

Incidentally, this museum should not be confused with the rip-off "Marine Park" at Nissí Beach: C£6 for one sea lion, two trained dolphins and a bar.

## The beaches

Some 2km west of central Ayía Nápa on its namesake avenue, **Nissí Beach** is for once as attractive as touted – but in high season it's hopelessly crowded as the four or five hotels here disgorge their occupants onto the few hundred metres of sand, or into the handful of snack kiosks above the tidemark. At such times you can retreat by wading out to the islet which lends the beach both definition and its name (*nissí* means "island"). The rocky shore between Nissí and "Sunny Bay" is a popular gay hangout. Nissí and the adjacent **Makrónissos Beach**, some 5km from the centre, are both linked to Ayía Nápa proper by cycle paths, of which (to its credit) the resort has many.

Otherwise, the big attraction at Nissi is **bungee-jumping**, organized by Bungee Downunder (June–Sept daily 9am–6pm; bookings on ☎99684789). As the outfit's name implies, they're Australian-based and -trained, with one of the sport's pioneers still involved; a fifty-metre plunge, with the option of dipping your hair in the sea, will set you back C£45. For more water and less air, there's **Waterworld**, a waterpark at the west end of town (May–Oct daily 10am–6pm; day-pass C£14, children C£7).

## Practicalities

Orientation is straightforward: **Nissí** is the initial name of the main E309 road west to Nissí and Larnaca, 39km distant; **Arkhiepiskópou Makaríou** links the central square, **Platía Seféri**, with the harbour; and **Krýou Neroú** heads out east towards Cape Gréko. Above Platía Seféri, the trunk routes fray into a welter of narrower streets on the hillside, but if driving, persist to find the big roundabout at the top of town funnelling traffic to Paralímni.

EMAN **buses** from Larnaca will drop you either down at the main ticket office near the base of Arkhiepiskópou Makaríou, or up at a stop next to the Cyprus Airways office. The none-too-enthusiastic **CTO** (Mon–Sat 8.30am–2pm, plus Mon, Tues, Thurs & Fri 4–6.30pm) is around the corner at Krýou Neroú 12, near the five-way junction. The **post office** keeps limited afternoon and Saturday morning hours, while numerous **banks** are liberally furnished with ATMs. **Car-rental** franchises cluster near the town-centre end of Nissí avenue – for example Ham Yam at no. 17 (☎23721825) and Andreas Petsas at no. 20 (☎23721260) – with Hertz at Krýou Neroú 4 (☎23721836). Best of several **internet** cafés is IntenCity Media Networks, at Belloyiánni 10 (24hr), with 32 multi-media terminals.

### Accommodation

If you're staying here, it's 99 percent certain that you've come on a package. Choosing from a brochure, **hotel** properties to go for include the five-star *Aeneas* behind westerly Nissí beach (☎23724000, ⓦwww.aeneas.com.cy; ⑧), with a huge pool and excellent sports facilities, or the four-star *Grecian Sands* (☎23721616, ⓦwww.grecian.com.cy; ⑦), set in tiered gardens behind easterly

Krýo Neró beach. One of the few exceptions amongst hotels in terms of target audience is the one-star *Leros* (☏ 23721126, ℱ 23721127; ❷) conveniently opposite EMAN bus terminal on Makaríou, overhauled in 1994 and pitching itself since then to winter long-stay patrons. If you want a beachfront but still fairly central location, the two-star *Okeanos Beach* (☏ 23724440, ℱ 23724441; ❺) and three-star *Limanaki Beach* (☏ 23721600, ⓦ www.ayianapahotels.net; ❻) are both small-scale operations with reasonable amenities, just northeast of Limanáki harbour, and not commonly marketed by UK operators. Most other affordable on-spec accommodation in Ayía Nápa is **self-catering**, with studios and one-bedrooms starting at C£25–30, two-bedroom units at C£40; the CTO office keeps complete lists of licensed premises.

## Eating

Despite its incredible range – everything from Thai to Mexican, by way of Italian and Danish – cuisine in Ayía Nápa usually plumps for shallow depths. The best that can usually be said is that it's hot, abundant and looks vaguely like the glossy picture on the menu outside. Perhaps the most authentic food is to be had at the fish tavernas down at pedestrianized Limanáki port, where Cypriots can be found dining at off-season weekends despite the bumped-up prices.

**Clarabel** Arkhiepiskópou Makaríou. Does the best *mezédhes* in town. Meat is prepared on a beguiling outdoor barbecue and the menu proposes seductive treats such as "scallops on a bed of rice". Open 5–11pm, much of the year.

**Markos** Limanáki Port. The "right-hand" taverna, the first (1955) established here; open all day, with an ever-popular courtyard.

**Pagoda** Nissí 29. Part of the chain which first brought Chinese fare to Cyprus in 1969, this makes a reliable fist of Szechuan and Peking dishes such as chicken in black bean sauce and shredded beef in chilli sauce.

**Taste of India** Arkhiepiskópou Makaríou 8, just below Platía Seféri. The best surviving Indian in town, with an intriguing *mezé* including prawn *puri* and butter chicken with *roti* and Kashmiri rice.

**Stamna Tavern** Stone's throw from Platía Seféri. Authentically rustic, and grumpy service actually highlights the excellence of the food, with remarkable *loúntza* jostling for attention next to succulent *halloúmi*, jumbo-size local olives and sweet tomatoes.

**Vassos** Limanáki Port. Among several local fish tavernas, this (adjacent to *Markos*) is the second oldest (1962), one of the most reliably open and typically the busiest – always a good sign.

## Drinking and nightlife

Most of the brashest watering-holes congregate just uphill from the town's monastery, around Platía Seféri and the pedestrian zone above it and to the west, particularly along Louká Louká Street (universally nicknamed "The Look" Street for reasons soon obvious). **Bars** are licensed between 9am and 2am during the week, with half-hour extensions at weekends – but the music must be shut off at 1.30am, which sees the *platía*'s "pre-clubbing" outfits empty rapidly in favour of the numerous **clubs**, which can hold up to two thousand revellers. Clubs open at 1.30am and close between 4 and 4.30am; entry in these lean times runs C£3–5, and a few venues were free in 2004. Promotions often change venue from year to year, or even mid-season, but the quality of the venue dictates the type of promoters it attracts. Garage and House are not, contrary to image, the be-all and end-all of Ayía Nápa; they have lately yielded to Trance, R&B plus nostalgia tracks from the 1960s to the 1980s.

The **nightlife** venues listed below are those most likely to survive the current lull, though no guidebook can hope to keep abreast of seasonal trends; for that you're best off consulting the free, monthly listings-and-adverts mag, *What's On* (ⓦ www.wocy.com), available all over the southeast of the island.

## Bars

**The Africa Pub** Eleftherías, just uphill from the *platía*. A mother-and-daughter team have a late licence until 6am and triple-for-double-measure deals on their spirits which render mixers largely irrelevant.

**Bedrock Inn** Louká Louká, corner of Ayías Mávris. Check out this hilarious Flintstones-themed bar for karaoke and its feet-through-the-floor car.

**Guru Ethnic Bar** Odhyssás Elýti 11, ⊛ www.gurubar .com. Occupying a house with terraced gardens, this is the most upmarket spot in town (ie, smart dress code), vaguely hankering after the Parisian *Buddha Bar*; gourmet snacks, flavoured tobaccos in chillled hubble-bubbles, three outdoor bars, mood-enhancing "global" music, even massages on request.

**Luke Kelly** Ayías Mávris 26–28, opposite town hall. Irish brews on tap, live music and sports on the big screen make this a perennially crowded success.

**Maïstrali** Krýou Neroú, opposite the *Napa Mermaid Hotel*. A more family-orientated venue which affords an excellent view of the beach and horizon. You can also book a table for snacking.

**Minos** Platía Seféri. One of the oldest, and most exciting of the resort's bars, with excellent resident DJs playing Hip-Hop, R&B and Garage – an ideal vantage point from which to watch the madness go by, if you get there early enough.

**Napa Dreams** Louká Louká. Rivals *Minos* for quality, but adds podiums and poles to the mix. Its minimally chic decor and pounding House music will keep you on your feet until closing time.

## Clubs

**Black & White** Louká Louká 6. Probably the best of the smaller venues, a spartan and intense underground venue perfect for grinding Hip-Hop, soul and smouldering R&B – plus it's open most of the year.

**Car Wash** Ayías Mávris 24. Where you go when head-banging music begins to pall; popular with an older crowd who bop to a 1970s/1980s

soundtrack, including (of course) music from the eponymous film. Busy even in these lean seasons, thanks in part to unsurpassed sound system and lighting effects, and open most of the year.

**Castle** Grigóri Afxendíou. Merits a look for its ridiculous drawbridge/moat decor, and is ideal if you're part of a larger group with different tastes, as disco and R&B rub shoulders with Drum 'n Bass and House in this three-room club (plus outdoor "chill" area). At 3000 capacity, it's one of the largest clubs, but tends to fill because tour reps steer their charges here.

**Club Abyss** Grigóri Afxendíou 17, ⊛ www .clubabyss.co.uk. Housed in a sumptuous three-level, four-room setting, Ayía Nápa's "first purpose-built superclub" attracts the big DJ Garage and House names, installed in a pulpit. Ownership is set to change for 2005, but expect much the same format.

**Insomnia** Nissí 4, ⊛ www.clubinsomnia.tv. Late-night (4–7am) operation which has the most popular Garage after-parties. Cuban cigars and a bottle of French champagne are mandatory fashion articles here.

**Jurassic Bar** (formerly *Ice Club*) Louká Louká 14. Amuses by its dogged pursuit of innovation – aside from the inevitable foam nights, 1970s revivalists Club Fantastic hold a weekly popcorn party here, flooding the club via air cannons with 200 kilos of freshly popped corn.

**River Reggae** Access through Rio Napa Apartment Complex on Mishaoúli ke Kavazóglou. Probably the best pre-dawn venue in Ayía Nápa. Its spectral "Apocalypse Now" jungle setting boasts two winding pools for night-swimmers, a basement House club and beaten-up pool tables. A mix of reggae and lovers' rock is the ideal backdrop for its hidden alcoves and sweeping rock faces, where exhausted clubbers can grab a ledge and watch the sun rise in each others' arms. Open midnight–7am.

**VIPs** Arkhiepiskópou Makaríou. The "Scandi" club; brace yourself for lots of Abba.

# Around Ayía Nápa

Inland from Ayía Nápa and the south coast, the gently undulating terrain is dotted with the **Kokkinokhoriá** or "Red Villages", so called after the local soil, tinged red by large amounts of iron and other metallic oxides. This is the island's main potato-growing region, the little spuds irrigated by water drawn up by the dozens of windmills – the only distinguishing feature of an otherwise featureless region – and harvested in May to appear subsequently in British corner shops. (Since 1990 the overdrawn aquifer has been invaded by the sea, and fresh water must be brought in by pipeline from the Tróödhos.) Less savoury is the area's longstanding reputation for the trapping of songbirds for food, particularly at

Paralímni; *ambelopoúlia* are small fig-eating blackcaps (often known by their Italian name, *beccafico*), pickled whole and mostly exported to the Middle East. The practice is now illegal, as per EU law.

Other than this, there is little to be said for or about the hinterland as a tourist attraction, and even the CTO admits as much in its earnest, rather desperate promotion of the handful of unheralded late medieval churches scattered in and around the various relentlessly modern villages. Despite their inland location, however, they are too close to the seashore fleshpots to have entirely escaped the notice of visitors and expatriates, so at **Dherínia** and **Paralímni** in particular there is a smattering of necessary infrastructure and recommendable restaurants. East of Paralímni is a cluster of tiny coves arrayed around **Pernéra** resort, which is dwarfed by the massive development of **Protarás**, extending south to **Cape Gréko**, which enjoys some protection as a natural reserve.

## Dherínia

**DHERÍNIA** (Deryneia) is visited mainly for its hilltop setting just south of the Attila Line and overlooking the "dead zone" towards Famagusta and its modern suburb Varósha. Disconnected windmills spin aimlessly, or stand devaned and idle in the abandoned fields to the north. A cluster of cafés, installed in the last Greek-Cypriot-civilian-occupied buildings before the dead zone, charge small sums for the privilege of using their binoculars or telescopes to take in the sad tableau of **Varósha** crumbling away, its rusty construction cranes frozen in their August 1974 positions. Since the violent nearby incidents of 1996 (see p.453 in *Contexts*), videos and posters at the viewing platforms propagandize local and foreign visitors alike.

In the event of an official settlement and the reoccupation of Varósha by its original inhabitants, these cafés will doubtless lose most of their raison d'être. Much more likely to survive is an excellent **taverna** between the main old church and a little chapel, *Misohoro* (aka *Makis*) at Dhimokratías 32 (☎23743943; closed Tues), a popular *mezé* house charging about C£5 per head, drink extra.

## Paralímni and nearby beaches

After the events of summer 1974, **PARALÍMNI**, a few kilometres south of Dherínia, became the de facto administrative capital of "Free Famagusta" district, and as such has a concentration of banks, petrol pumps, shops and cultural venues – as well as the most northerly access to the strip of Greek-Cypriot-controlled coast below Famagusta. Beachfront development extends well northwest of Ayía Triádha cove, past the roundabout funnelling traffic west to Dherínia, and becoming more low-key before fizzling out just before the buffer zone. There are some fine, more or less normally priced **tavernas** here too: *Ikaria*, featuring metropolitan Greek (as opposed to Cypriot) fare, and *Tony's* (aka *O Xenykhtis*) near the CYTA telecom tower, purveying great bean dishes, snails, fish, imported game and own-made dips, and featuring one of the largest wine cellars on the island.

The coast itself has a number of beaches, divided by little headlands. Working southeast from **Ayía Triádha** (Agias Trias), there's tiny Mouzoúra and then the larger beach of Loúma at **PERNÉRA**. A number of self-catering **apartments** can be had early or late in the year on a walk-in basis, both just northwest of Ayía Triás and at Pernéra. One in particular to try is Irini Koumoulli's peaceful *Sirena Bay Inn* (☎ & ☎23823502; closed Dec–Feb; ❸), an eight-room B&B outfit right on the water near Ayía Triádha.

# Protarás

Pernéra merges south into the formerly pristine stretches of **PROTARÁS**, aka "Fig Tree Bay", which is a developmental disaster of some thirty wall-to-wall hotels and self-catering facilities, packed out from mid-May onwards with relatively well-behaved Scandinavian (and a few British) families. The rather narrow sandy beach is not even indicated from the inland bypass road, lined by a dozen restaurants – only the hotels themselves are signposted. Thus if you don't know that the *Salparo Hotel Apartments* mark the north end of the bay, and the *Nausicaa Beach Hotel Apartments* the southern extreme, it's quite easy to drive right past Protarás resort without ever seeing the sea. Once you do figure it out, you'll find that big shoreline lawns and swimming pools, substantial enough to accommodate the crowds, supplement the lack of sands – conveying a clear message that, unless you're actually staying at one of the behemoths or using their manifold recreational facilities (water-skiing, paragliding and so on), you're not exactly welcome here. At least the sea, if you do manage to reach it, is as clear and warm as you'd hope for.

It's difficult to imagine a setting less appropriate for non-package visitors, but Nicosians come here in some force at weekends, and (unlike Ayía Nápa) much of the resort stays "open" in winter. A good bet for anyone showing up on spec is the three-star *Pernera Beach* (℡ 23831011, ⓦ www.pernera.com.cy; ❺), which, as the name suggests, is just above that stretch of sand and at slow times can be bargained down considerably from the rack rate. The area's commercial hub is **Eden Square**, opened in 2004, a mini-mall of bars and restaurants. Other worthwhile, scattered eateries include *The Raj* on the main drag in Protarás, with tandoori dishes a strength, and fish-and-steak specialists *Nissiositis Beach* at so-called Flamingo Bay.

## Cape Gréko

Chances for a quiet, free-access swim are better south of Protarás, where the road along the mostly rocky shoreline passes through a brief patch of forest en route to **Cape Gréko** (Gkreko), Land's End for this corner of the island.

Tiny beaches offer good snorkelling in the vicinity of Kónnos Bay, though even here excursion boats tend to arrive by noon. **Kónnos** itself is the only stretch of sand south of Protarás, but it's tiny and ridiculously gently shelving, plus the presence of a water-sports centre and café means it's not exactly peaceful.

Despite the area's status as a national reserve, the tip of the cape remains off-limits owing to a lighthouse, Cypriot military installations and the Radio Monte Carlo International relay station. Reefy coves to either side of the final isthmus see some yacht traffic, though swimming is difficult if the wind is up, as it frequently is.

A favourite landlubbers' activity in the area is to **hike the coastline** from Protarás to Ayía Nápa (or vice versa), following a dirt track that runs parallel to the shore; this three-to-four-hour outing will take you past impressive cliff-scapes, sea caves (with the local rubbish tip scandalously adjacent), a natural rock arch and a Roman quarry. You'll also see lots of cross-country racers and cyclists using the same path – though it's rough, and could easily shred the tyres of a touring bike. All told, however, the area's intrinsic merits are sufficiently limited to make you wonder just how much it would have been developed for tourism had the considerably better beaches from Famagusta northwards remained under Greek-Cypriot control.

# Travel details

## Buses

Ayía Nápa to: Nicosia (Mon–Sat 1 daily, early morning, on EMAN; 1hr 30min); Paralímni via Protarás (May–Oct Mon–Sat, half-hourly 9am–8pm, hourly 8–11pm; Sun service half-hourly 9am–noon & 4–8pm, hourly noon–4pm; Nov–April Mon–Sat 8 daily; 20min).

Larnaca to: Ayía Nápa (high season Mon–Sat 9 daily, Sun 5, otherwise Mon–Sat 6 daily, Sun 2, on EMAN; 40min); Limassol (Mon–Fri 4 daily, Sat 3, on Intercity; 1hr 15min); Nicosia (Mon–Fri 6 daily, Sat 3, on Intercity; 1hr); Protarás via Ayía Nápa on Intercity (summer 4 daily, winter 2; 50min); Protarás via Paralímni (Mon–Fri 6 daily, Sat 3, Sun 1; 1hr).

## Greek place names

| Old system | New system | Greek lettering |
| --- | --- | --- |
| Angelóktisti | Angeloktisti | ΑΓΓΕΛΟΚΤΙΣΤΗ |
| Ayía Nápa | Agia Napa | ΑΓΙΑ ΝΑΠΑ |
| Áyios Lázaros | Agios Lazaros | ΑΓΙΟΣ ΛΑΖΑΡΟΣ |
| Ayíou Miná | Agios Minas | ΑΓΙΟΥ ΜΗΝΑ |
| Cape Gréko | Cape Gkreko | ΑΚΡΩΤΗΡΙ ΓΡΕΚΟ |
| Dherínia | Deryneia | ΔΕΡΥΝΕΙΑ |
| Hala Sultan | Hala Sultan | ΧΑΛΑ ΣΟΥΛΤΑΝ |
| Kalavassós | Kalavasos | ΚΑΛΑΒΑΣΟΣ |
| Káto Dhrýs | Kato Drys | ΚΑΤΩ ΔΡΥΣ |
| Káto Léfkara | Kato Lefkara | ΚΑΤΩ ΛΕΥΚΑΡΑ |
| Khirokitía | Choirokoitia | ΧΟΙΡΟΚΟΙΤΙΑ |
| Kíti | Kiti(on) | ΚΙΤΙ |
| Kofínou | Kofinou | ΚΟΦΙΝΟΥ |
| Kórnos | Kornos | ΚΟΡΝΟΣ |
| Larnaca | Larnaka | ΛΑΡΝΑΚΑ |
| Maróni | Maroni | ΜΑΡΩΝΙ |
| Páno Léfkara | Pano Lefkara | ΠΑΝΩ ΛΕΥΚΑΡΑ |
| Paralímni | Paralimni | ΠΑΡΑΛΙΜΝΙ |
| Perivólia | Perivolia | ΠΕΡΙΒΟΛΙΑ |
| Pernéra | Pernera | ΠΕΡΝΕΡΑ |
| Protarás | Protaras | ΠΡΩΤΑΡΑΣ |
| Pýla | Pyla | ΠΥΛΑ |
| Pýrga | Pyrga | ΠΥΡΓΑ |
| Stavrovoúni | Stavrovouni | ΜΟΝΗ ΣΤΑΥΡΟΒΟΥΝΙ |
| Tókhni | Tochni | ΤΩΧΝΙ |
| Vavatsiniá | Vavatsinia | ΒΑΒΑΤΣΙΝΙΑ |
| Vávla | Vavla | ΒΑΒΛΑ |
| Zíyi | Zygi | ΖΥΓΙ |

# Limassol and around

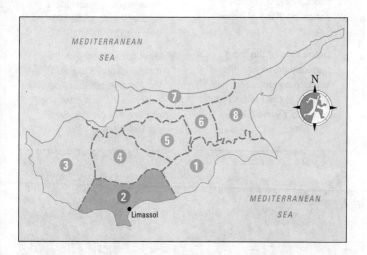

CHAPTER 2 **Highlights**

✳ **Limassol** The old town attracts visitors with its mix of contemporary shopping, restored nineteenth-century architecture and cutting-edge restaurants. See p.133

✳ **Voúni Donkey Sanctuary** Elderly donkeys get a second lease of life at the sanctuary just outside the peaceful village of Voúni. Soo p.130

✳ **Lófou** One of the most perfectly preserved, yet least commercialized, hill-villages in the foothills of Limassol's wine country. See p.142

✳ **Panayía Iamatikí** An intriguingly hybrid Byzantine-Lusignan church in Arakapás village. See p.144

✳ **Kolóssi** The single, but imposing, legacy of the crusading Knights of St John. See p.149

✳ **Kourion** Extensive Roman and early Christian structures enjoy a magnificent setting atop coastal cliffs. See p.152

✳ **Beaches** Koúrion, Evdhímou, Pissoúri and Pétra toú Romíou are four fine beaches in the western half of Limassol district. See pp.155–157

△ Kourion, Margareites-Ellinikos combat

# Limassol and around

**L**imassol, the island's second largest city, is a brash, functional place, with little to recommend it other than gritty authenticity, a wide range of dining options and sophisticated nightlife. More than anywhere else in the South, it has acted as a magnet for extensive and debilitating urban drift from the poor, low-altitude hill-villages just north, and was a major focus of Greek-Cypriot refugee resettlement after 1974.

The city continues to expand a hundred or so metres annually to the east along the coast (westward growth is blocked by a British Sovereign Base), and a similar distance up into the barren, shrub-clad foothills of the Tróödhos, whose nearer settlements are now scarcely other than commuter dormitories. The most interesting spots, such as **Ayía Mávra**, **Ómodhos**, **Vouní** and **Lófou**, might not rate a special detour, but are easily visited en route to the high Tróödhos. Other half-inhabited hill-hamlets, like **Arakapás** with its fine Italo-Byzantine church, **Akapnoú** and **Odhoú**, see few outsiders from one month to the next; reaching them requires considerable energy, not to mention your own vehicle, as there's effectively no public transport in the backcountry.

Along the coast east of Limassol, you have to outrun 16km of fairly horrific hotel and apartment development before the tower-blocks halt a little past the small but evocative ancient site of **Amathus**. Just before the coast road veers inland towards Nicosia, there's access to **Governor's Beach**, the last remaining (relatively) unspoilt stretch of sand in the district. The adjacent bay of **Áyios Yeóryios Alamánou** is better for dining, while **Pendákomo** just inland is perhaps the most interesting of the villages in this direction.

Heading out of Limassol in the opposite direction holds more promise. A long beach fringing the **Akrotíri peninsula**, home to one of the island's three British Sovereign Bases, ends near the legend-draped convent of **Ayíou Nikoláou tón Gáton**. On the far side of the lagoon, orange and eucalyptus groves soften the landscape en route to the atmospheric crusader castle of **Kolossi** and the clifftop ruins of **Kourion** – together with its associated **sanctuary of Apollo Hylates**, one of the most impressive ancient sites in the South. You can swim at the beach below the palisades, but it's probably better to wait until reaching the more secluded bays at **Evdhímou** and **Pissoúri**, both favourite hideouts of British expats.

## Limassol (Lemesós)

Although its old centre of Levantine stone buildings and alleyways lends the city some charm, **LIMASSOL** (*Lemesós* in Greek, now the official name) is

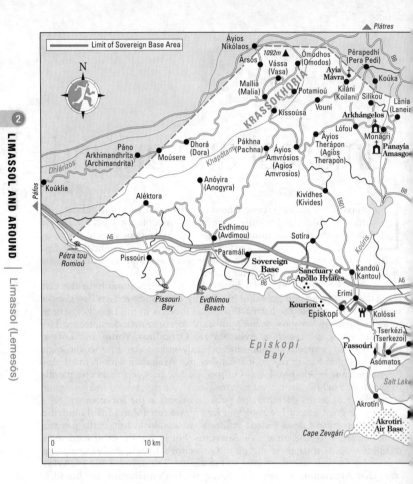

primarily the industrial and commercial capital of the southern coast, special-izing in wine-making, citrus processing and canning. Since 1974 and the loss of Famagusta, it has also become the South's largest port, with container ships at anchor near the seafront esplanade throughout the year.

With about 160,000 inhabitants, Limassol basks in its reputation as a mini-Texas of conspicuously consuming, gregarious *nouveaux riches* – and this was true even before a massive, mid-1990s influx of Russian *biznismen* who briefly dominated the "offshore banking" industry here. Large sums are still frittered away at "exclusive" nightclubs just off the expressway to Larnaca, and at topless "gentlemen's clubs" closer to the centre. Along with the laundering of money smuggled out of the Russian Federation, prostitution is now a major local enterprise, and has spilled out from the confines of its traditional central red-light zone.

Most of the conventional tourist industry is ghettoized in a long, unsightly ribbon of development east of the town, in the areas known as **Potamós Yermasóyias** (Potamos Germasogeias) and **Amathus** (Amathous). This

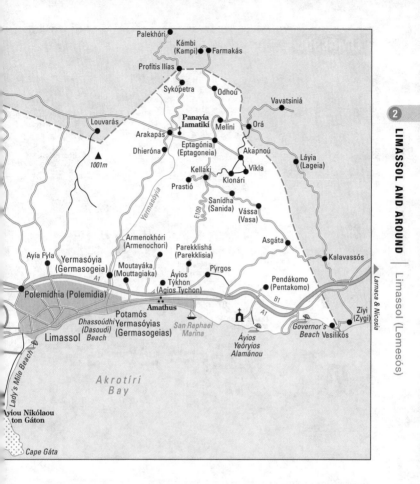

consists of 15km-plus of intermittent roadworks and traffic diversions, crumbling, faded, rabbit-warren hotel and apartment buildings, neon-incandescent bars, naff restaurants and "waterparks", all abutting a generally mediocre beach. Jewellery and furs are assiduously pitched at the Russian market – judging from the fact that every fourth sign is in the Cyrillic alphabet – while many (though by no means all) of the hotel entrances are closely patrolled by eastern European prostitutes.

All is not frowsiness and vulgarity, however; under a new mayor, extensive areas of the old commercial centre have been rehabilitated. The giant Anexartisías shopping mall just off the eponymous street, the refurbished central market and the Lanitis Carob Mill project, constitute the main foci of this urban renewal. Native Lemessans do their utmost to uphold the city's reputation as the party town of Cyprus, with some lively music venues, quality restaurants and stylish nightspots. And if you're considering a winter-sun break in Cyprus, Limassol (or at least its environs) makes an excellent choice – as a "real" town, it most emphatically does not close down off-season the way Ayía Nápa does.

## Some history

A near-complete lack of significant monuments attests to the relative youth of the town. Limassol hardly existed before the Christian era, being for centuries overshadowed by Amathus to the east and Kourion to the west. It burst into prominence in 1191, when Richard the Lionheart's fiancée, Berengaria of Navarre, and his sister were nearly shipwrecked just offshore. Isaac Komnenos, self-styled ruler of the island, refused to send them provisions. Hearing of this insult to his intended, Richard landed nearby in force, married Berengaria on the site of the present-day Limassol castle, and went on to claim the island after defeating Isaac in battle.

Two centuries of prosperity followed, with both the Knights Hospitallers and Knights Templars having extensive holdings around Limassol after the loss of the Holy Land. However, an earthquake and devastating raids by the Genoese, Mamelukes and finally the Turks combined to level the settlement by the beginning of the Ottoman era; it's only since the end of the nineteenth century that the town has grown again.

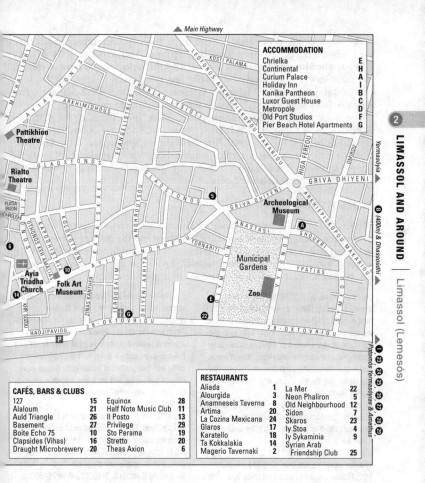

▲ Main Highway

**ACCOMMODATION**
| | |
|---|---|
| Chrielka | E |
| Continental | H |
| Curium Palace | A |
| Holiday Inn | I |
| Kanika Pantheon | B |
| Luxor Guest House | C |
| Metropole | D |
| Old Port Studios | F |
| Pier Beach Hotel Apartments | G |

Pattikhion Theatre

Rialto Theatre

Archeological Museum

Municipal Gardens

Zoo

Ayia Triadha Church

Folk Art Museum

Yermasóyia ▶
(400m) & Dhassoúdhi ▶
Potamós Yermasóyias & Amathus

**CAFÉS, BARS & CLUBS**
| | | | |
|---|---|---|---|
| 127 | 15 | Equinox | 28 |
| Alaloum | 21 | Half Note Music Club | 11 |
| Auld Triangle | 26 | Il Posto | 13 |
| Basement | 27 | Privilege | 29 |
| Boite Echo 75 | 10 | Sto Perama | 19 |
| Clapsides (Vihas) | 16 | Stretto | 20 |
| Draught Microbrewery | 20 | Theas Axion | 6 |

**RESTAURANTS**
| | | | |
|---|---|---|---|
| Aliada | 1 | La Mer | 22 |
| Alourgida | 3 | Neon Phaliron | 5 |
| Anamneseis Taverna | 8 | Old Neighbourhood | 12 |
| Artima | 20 | Sidon | 7 |
| La Cozina Mexicana | 24 | Skaros | 23 |
| Glaros | 17 | Iy Stoa | 4 |
| Karatello | 18 | Iy Sykaminia | 9 |
| Ta Kokkalakia | 14 | Syrian Arab | |
| Magerio Tavernaki | 2 | Friendship Club | 25 |

## Arrival, orientation and information

Since early 2002, all passenger-ferry services to Limassol have been suspended and show no sign of resuming; the Cypriots are unwilling to terrorist-proof the port terminal, 4km southwest of the town centre, to the satisfaction of the Israelis who shared the boat-line. Bus #30 still runs into town from the port via the seafront, its route extending along the coastal boulevard down to the hotel strip, all the way to the marina; the service runs roughly every 20 to 25 minutes from 7.30am to 7pm, then half-hourly from the old port until 11.30pm. The less far-ranging #6 links only the market area with the marina, approximately every 20 minutes from 7am to 7pm.

Arriving by **long-distance bus** or **service taxi**, you'll be dropped at one of the terminals shown on our map and detailed in "Listings" (p.138). If you're driving, make for the public pay-and-display **car parks** on the seafront promenade, or various privately operated ones inland along Elládhos. There are a very limited number of uncontrolled spaces around the municipal gardens.

The town centre is defined by three main thoroughfares: the coastal boulevard, which changes its name first from **Spýrou Araoúzou** to (very briefly) **Khristodhoúlou Hadjipávlou**, then to **28-Oktovríou** as you head northeast; the main shopping street, **Ayíou Andhréou**, which runs roughly parallel to it just inland as far as the Municipal Gardens and Archeological Museum; and **Anexartisías**, which threads though the central downtown area.

The main **tourist information** office (Mon, Tues, Thurs & Fri 8.15am–2.30pm & 4–6.15pm, Wed 8.15am–2.30pm, Sat 8.15am–1.30pm) sits on the ground floor of the *Continental Hotel* building on Spýrou Araoúzou, but their stock of leaflets is not the greatest – English-language material in particular can disappear quickly. There's also a branch near Dhassoúdhi beach at Yeoryíou toú Prótou 22, keeping the same hours.

## Accommodation

Moderately priced accommodation in Limassol itself remains scarce, with little in between the frowsy guest houses of the bazaar and the pricey package digs of the resort strip. Certain no- or one-star hotels, here and in the red-light district, are best avoided. Recent years, however, have seen the emergence of some decent and affordable hotel-apartments within the town limits.

**Chrielka** Olymbíon 7 ☎25358366, ⓦwww
.chrielka.com.cy. These superbly appointed 2000-built A-class hotel-apartments represent the best standard in town. The units, many with safe and fax machine, are pitched at a business clientele; bathrooms and kitchens are large, though breakfast is also available on the ground floor. Limited sea views, but there's a pool, and front rooms face the Municipal Gardens. ⑤

**Continental** Spýrou Araoúzou 137 ☎25362530, Ⓕ25373030. Atmospheric, old-fashioned two-star relic that's popular with the business trade. ③

**Curium Palace** Výronos 11 ☎25891100, ⓦwww.curiumpalace.com. One of Limassol's first, 1930s-era, orientalized Art Deco hotels, this was thoroughly refurbished in 2002 to four-star standard, without altering the listed exterior. Vast common areas make it an enduringly popular wedding and conference venue; there's also a pool, sauna, gym and tennis court tucked away in the deceptively large back garden. There are three grades of rooms, all with tubs in the baths and somewhat low ceilings; junior and executive suites are aimed at business travellers. Advantageous on-site car rental. Standard ⑤, executive ⑦

**Holiday Inn** City/Potamós Yermasóyias boundary, 2km east of the town centre ☎25851515, ⓦwww.holiday-inn.com/limassolcyprus. Four-star beachfront outfit with watersports, pools, gym and better-than-average hotel food. You can get higher standards further out of town, but this is the most luxurious choice close to the centre. Rates are often heavily discounted. ⑤

**Kanika Pantheon** 28-Oktovríou, corner of Ioánni Metaxá, 400m from the Municipal Gardens ☎25591111, ⓦwww.kanika-group.com/pantheon. Along with the *Curium Palace*, the most comfortable digs within the city limits; not seafront – that's five minutes distant – but a well-priced three-star outfit with two pools and health club. Rooms have oblique sea views, and for a few pounds extra you can get an "upgraded" room with desk and modem hookup. ⑤

**Luxor Guest House** Ayíou Andhréou 101 ☎25362265. On the pedestrianized portion of the shopping street, which is barred to night-time traffic, so it's quiet. Doubles are fair-sized if non-ensuite, though singles are dingy. ①

**Metropole** Ifiyenías 6 ☎25362686 or 25362330. Former dosshouse in the bazaar extensively redone in 2001, though most of the money went into the ground-floor bar and snack-café. En-suite rooms upstairs can be a bit airless, but this is still a good budget option. ①

**Old Port Studios** Dhimitríou Mitropoúlou 7 ☎25760776 or 25260079. Excellently sited near the castle and Carob Mill complex, these simple rooms and self-catering units are upstairs from a café which provides snacks and breakfast. ①, self-catering ②

**Pier Beach Hotel Apartments** 28-Oktovríou 261A, corner with Riyénis ☎25749000, Ⓕ25749005, ⓔpierhot@logos.cy.net. High-quality B-class studios and one-bedroom units, redone in 1997, most with sea view. Run more like a standard hotel, with an on-site restaurant and pavement terrace bar; parking at the rear. ④

# The City

Limassol presents a number of isolated points of interest rather than a town-scape to savour: from 1974 until it was outstripped by Ayía Nápa in 1994 this was, numerically speaking, the number-one tourist base in the South, but you won't need more than a full day to take in all there is to see. After looking in at the **castle**, the **carob mill** area, several **museums** and one of the **wineries**, perhaps taking a stroll around the **bazaar** and having a good meal or two, many visitors will probably be ready to move on, at least in summer.

## Limassol castle

Unassuming from the outside, **Limassol castle** stands in a pleasant garden immediately north of the old port. What you see today is a careful restoration of Byzantine foundations, Venetian vandalism, Ottoman adaptation for military purposes and traces of British justice (it was a jail during the colonial period). Somewhere under the existing walls stood the long-vanished Byzantine chapel of Saint George in which, tradition has it, Richard the Lionheart married Berengaria on May 12, 1191. Anticipating his rout of Isaac, Richard also had himself crowned king of Cyprus and his bride queen of England, in the presence of assorted Latin clerics and nobility.

Currently, the castle houses the **Cyprus Medieval Museum** (Mon–Sat 9am–5pm, Sun 10am–1pm; C£1), though the building, with its musty, echoing vaults, air shafts and masonry ribs, is as interesting as any of the exhibits, most of which are on the upper floor. The emphasis is on metalware, heraldry and sacred art, including bas-reliefs and pottery with Christian designs; the best bits are silver Byzantine plates showing events in the life of David, part of the Lambousa Treasure (see p.357), and a suit of armour from the Lusignan period (twelfth–fifteenth century). The roof terrace and secondary tower are sometimes open and afford excellent views over the town.

## The Lanitis Carob Mill and Time Elevator

In 2002, the row of stone-built industrial and commercial premises bounding the castle on two sides was rescued from long-standing dereliction by its owners, the Lanitis Group. The **Lanitis Carob Mill** on the northwest side was restored both as a free museum to the processing of the pods into syrup, animal feed-pellets and culinary powder, which only ceased in the 1970s, and as the home of the **Time Elevator** (daily 9am–8pm, shows more or less hourly; C£7, children C£5), Limassol's most heavily touted tourist attraction. Some five thousand years of Cypriot history are compressed into 25 minutes of tendentious, hokily scripted highlights as you're strapped into a lurching, ten-seater "car" and buffeted by surround-sound, 3D visuals and various other sensory phenomena (scuttling-mice effects, wind in your hair, etc).

The warehouses occupying the southwesterly row of buildings have, almost without exception, been colonized by cutting-edge bars, cafés and restaurants, for which see p.135.

## The bazaar

The neighbourhood surrounding the castle was once the Turkish commercial district, as street names will tell you, and its lanes are still worth a brief wander. The **Cami** (pronounced "Jami") **Kabir**, its minaret visible from the castle roof, is still used by Limassol's Arab and remaining Turkish Cypriot population, though the **Cami Jedid** (also known as the Köprülü Hacı Ibrahim Ağa mosque), at the far end of Angýras nearer the former Turkish residential quarter, is firmly locked. The apses of a much older Lusignan church which once stood here have been excavated and exposed to view in the lane immediately east of the Cami Kabir, while immediately south the Ottoman **hamam**, with a calligraphic inscription over the door, still functions from 2 to 10pm. Also on Angýras at no. 45, identifiable by a huge, fragrant eucalyptus in the yard, is a café that's much more genuine than the fast-food joints immediately around the castle. The latter alternate with tacky souvenir stalls; the covered **central market**, an attractive, late-nineteenth-century stone-built structure, may appeal more, especially after its recent refurbishment. A few minutes' walk past the Cami Kabir, beyond the hideous early-twentieth-century cathedral of Ayía Nápa, the old *mitrópolis* of **Áyios Andhrónikos**, built in mock-Byzantine style during the 1870s, hides in a cul-de-sac accessible only by a single alley from the waterfront.

## Winery tours

The city's four **wineries** – ETKO, KEO, LOEL and SODAP – are strung out in a row on Franklin Roosevelt, west of the old harbour; each lays on a free tour at 10am, though ETKO also has a somewhat broader schedule of tours (Mon–Fri 9.30am–1.30pm). Parking is available in front of the wineries, but the brief walk from the castle area or the bus ride along Franklin Roosevelt (#19 or #30) are perhaps better options after the final tasting session. Incidentally, you're advised to do the tours on your own, as described, since group coach tours actually have to be paid for (and are exactly the same).

To join the daily tour at **KEO**, the largest drinks manufacturer on the island, just show up at 9.50am (except in summer when you should book on ☏25362053) in the reception area of the administration building, just behind the parking lot. In the space of about half an hour you're rather perfunctorily shown the cellars for the heavy, sweet Commandaria (see p.63) where a third of each barrelful is retained as the *mána* or "mother" ferment for the next cycle; the distillery for *zivanía* (grape-mash spirit), used to fortify KEO's liqueurs; the 40,000-litre oak ageing barrels for brandy; and barrels of sweet and cream "sherry" – no longer allowed to be labelled as such, owing to objections from Spain – ageing out in the sun (the dry stuff stays in a dark cellar). The tasting session provides a wonderful opportunity to familiarize yourself with Cypriot wine types and to lessen the likelihood of getting stuck with a grim vintage in a taverna.

## The Folk Art Museum

At the opposite end of Ayíou Andhréou, near the corner of Óthonos kéh Amalías at no. 253, the **Folk Art Museum** (June–Sept Mon–Fri 8.30am–1.30pm & 4–6.30pm; Oct–May Mon–Fri 8.30am–1.30pm & 3–5.30pm; closed Thurs pm all year; C£0.50) has filled a grand old mansion with rural and domestic knick-knacks, woodwork, traditional dresses and jewellery. The lighting and labelling aren't good, however, and you're virtually obliged to buy the guide booklet to make much sense of the exhibits.

## The Municipal Gardens and Archeological Museum

A little way beyond the Folk Art Museum spread the **Municipal Gardens** (daily 8.30am–8pm/7pm), a couple of acres of well-tended greenery fronting the sea, with an expensive restaurant within. The gardens are the venue for the **September Wine Festival** (10 days during the first half of the month); there's also a **mini-zoo** (daily: summer 9am–noon & 3–7pm; spring/autumn 9am–6.30pm; C£0.50), mostly comprising an aviary, though it has a zebra and a few cheetahs.

The district **Archeological Museum** (Mon–Sat 9am–5pm, Sun 10am–1pm; C£1), just north of the gardens, is strongest on Archaic, Geometric and Bronze Age artefacts. The left-hand gallery is ninety percent pottery, best of which are the Geometric-era dishes – an obvious inspiration for the modern *tsésti* or woven circular wall-hangings you see everywhere in tavernas. Archaic terracotta figurines also abound, with what are thought to be toys scattered amongst the animal-drawn chariots and other votive offerings. Highlights include a *rhyton* in the form of a bull, and a headless torso with unusually detailed hands holding a bird to its chest. Female figures, possibly offerings for fertility, clasp their breasts or a mirror (a symbol of Aphrodite/Astarte), and one plays a frame-drum. A column capital in the guise of Hathor demonstrates the introduction of Egyptian gods to the island. Bird-necked zoomorphic Bronze Age pots with vestigial noses and ears round off the hall's exhibits.

The smaller, central Classical room is sparsely stocked except for some gold and precious-stone jewellery; there's also a curious anthropomorphic lampstand, with ears for an oil wick and the head hollowed to accommodate a candle or incense. The Roman section on the right contains the usual painted and multi-coloured glass; the rainbow/oil-slick effect is the result of sodium and potassium ions leaching into the alkaline soils in which the objects were embedded before discovery.

## Eating and drinking

The plastic-fantastic, steak-and-chips eateries interspersed among *McDonald's* and *KFC* along the waterfront and in Potamós Yermasóyias are pretty dismissible, but a short walk, or even a brief drive, will be amply rewarded. Bear in mind also that Lemessans eat late, as in metropolitan Greece, from about 9.30pm onwards – though this is much less true on the tourist strip.

### Restaurants: centre

**Aliada** Irínis 117 ☎25340758. One of the more consistent and best-value of several "old house" tavernas hereabouts. For about C£12 you get soup, cold self-service buffet, a hot main course and the run of the very fancy (Western) sweet trolley, plus *zivanía* as an aperitif (wine extra). Dinner only; closed Sun; reservations essential at weekends.

**Alourgida** Eleftherías 52 ☎25763636. Rival to nearby *Aliada*, in a similar converted mansion, but with arguably more choice in its range of starters and mains. Reserve at weekends.

**Anamneseis Taverna** West end of Angýras, well-signposted behind the Cami Jedid ☎25746290. Very popular locally for its fresh ingredients and reasonable prices, though some of the Cypriot country fare – snails and offal – may put off the squeamish; there's more stress on seafood of late. C£13 a head includes drink, good salads and no chips; reservations advisable Fri & Sat evenings.

**Artima** Lanitis Carob Mill buildings, Vassilíssis Street. Generic Mediterranean-cum-Italian fare in stylish surroundings: antipasti, pasta and fish or meat mains for about C£20 per head.

**Glaros** Ayíou Andoníou, 700m west of the old harbour ☎25357046. Fish restaurants – especially close to the old port – are generally overpriced in Limassol; this one, perched above the sea and favoured by locals although quality is not superlative, is one of the more reasonable at about C£11 per person, plus drink. Open evenings and weekend lunchtimes only; evening reservations recommended.

**Karatello** Lanitis Carob Mill buildings, Vassilíssis Street. An upmarket take on the traditionally *mezé* house, in suitably industrial-minimalist surroundings. Tick off your choices on the menu and eat well (with local wine) for about C£23 for two.

**Ta Kokkalakia** Ayíou Andhréou 239. The name means "little bones" and hopefully that's all that will remain on your plate after you demolish fair portions of meaty South African dishes like spare ribs, piri-piri chicken livers, Boerewors sausage and ostrich steak. Budget C£17 per person, drink extra.

**Magerio Tavernaki** Eleftherías 121. Homestyle lunchtime fare (meat-and-veg stews) is average-to-good in quality, at average prices, yet this spot is enduringly popular and far cozier than *ly Sykaminia* (see below). There's live *rebétika* music at night, when the menu is more conventional for Cyprus.

La Mer 28-Oktovríou 127. One of the most pleasantly set, and best, local fish tavernas, where you dine à la carte or mezé format.

Neon Phaliron Gládstonos 135 ⓦwww .neonphaliron.com. Considered one of the top, and top-priced restaurants in Limassol, founded in 1960. Arguably best in winter, when game (mostly imported) comes to the fore in nouvelle incarnations. Closed Sun dinner.

Old Neighbourhood Ankýras 14. Looks like a tourist trap, in a touristy area, but purveys some of the best fish in Limassol.

Sidon Saripólou 71–73, opposite the covered market ⓣ 25342065. Quite a cavernous interior behind a deceptively small storefront at this elegant Cypro-Lebanese eatery. Decent appetizers (turnovers, chicken livers) precede a mains list strong on lamb and chicken dishes, topped off by the increasingly rare mahallebí as dessert. Portions are adequate, though not huge; count on C£14 per person with a modest amount of local drink, avoiding the pricey foreign wine list. Dinner only.

Iy Stoa Enóseos 5. Not much to look at, but excellent, cheap Cypriot country fare, with outdoor seating across the way in fair weather.

Iy Sykaminia Eleftherías 26. Classic working-man's canteen, where you can fill up very inexpensively on lamb with spinach, assorted ósprià, and other home-style dishes. Open Mon–Sat lunch only.

### Restaurants: Yermasóyia/ Potamós Yermasóyias

La Cozina Mexicana Profítis Ilías 28, Potamós Yermasóyias, 4km east of the centre; turn off the strip at the Louana kiosk. Surprisingly authentic Tex-Mex fare – the fajitas and tacos al carbon are

excellent – with friendly service and pool-side seating in the warm months. Budget about C£10 per person, plus drink.

Skaros North end of Yermasóyia village, opposite a municipal car park ⓣ 25325080. Fish and seafood here is fifty percent dearer than the norm – starting with a mezé at C£11 – but the quality is high, with an attractive environment for both indoor and outdoor seating. Ring for reservations and opening hours.

Syrian Arab Friendship Club Iliádhos 3, opposite Apollonia Beach Hotel, Potamós Yermasóyias, 5km east of the centre. The same, outstanding, 15-platter Arabic mezé as its sister branch in Nicosia (see p.293), which is recommendation enough.

### Cafés and bars

Draught Microbrewery Lanitis Carob Mill buildings, Vassilíssis Street. Very popular in the early evening for its own-brewed beer, but the snack-food here (aside from nibbles) is overpriced.

127 Elénis Paleoloyínas 5, opposite Solomonides stores. Combination bar and snack-café offering imaginative sandwiches and salads, fruit shakes and home-made desserts. Or just come for a drink amidst a decor of distressed 1940s–1970s chairs, or (during warmer months) sit out in the rear garden. Food served until midnight, drinks to 1am.

Il Posto Ifiyenías 32. A favourite meeting point, despite its vast size militating against any sort of coziness; light snacks, desserts, coffees, backgammon boards.

Stretto Lanitis Carob Mill buildings, Vassilíssis Street. Ultra-trendy café with exposed stonework, squishy sofas, fat candles and a long wine list.

# Nightlife and entertainment

The resort strip of Potamós Yermasóyias, defined by its main drag Yeoryíou toú Prótou, has the expected complement of foreign-orientated **bars and clubs**, most of which close down in the off-season. Town-centre venues tend to have much greater patronage from locals, and stay open all year. There's a scattering of gay, or at least gay-friendly, clubs among them – Limassol was always the hub of Cyprus's **gay life**, even before the late-1990s relaxation of laws against homosexual practices.

As part of the revival of downtown Limassol, the **Rialto Theatre** (ⓣ77777745, ⓦwww.rialto.com.cy) at Andhréa Dhroushióti 19, on the corner of Platía Iróön, has been gloriously refurbished and pressed into service as the city's main venue for serious musical, dance and dramatic acts, about evenly split between Greek and foreign names. This local renaissance has had the effect of partially reclaiming Platía Iróön, the historical heart of Limassol's traditional red-light district, from the sin merchants – there are now even "respectable" places for theatre patrons to have a coffee before or after performances. The former shack-like brothels, complete with proverbial red bulb over the doorway, at the fringes of the square have all closed down, but sleazy **cabarets** just around the corner from the Rialto have paradoxically multiplied.

The **Pattikhion Theatre** on Ayías Zónis (☎25343341) is the city's longest-running quality music and drama venue, and still offers a crowded programme. Limassol can also muster three **cinemas**: Othellos 1 & 2, Thessaloníkis 19 (☎25352232 and ☎25363911); the Rio at Elládhos 125, corner Navarínou (☎25352232); Pallas, Evklídhou 2 (☎25362324); and the K-Cineplex 1–5 at Ariádhni 8 in Potamós Yermasóyias (☎778383). There's also the much cheaper **Limassol Film Society**, housed in the Praxis Theatre on Mikhaïl Mikahelídhes (☎25357570), which shows art-house movies on Mondays at 8.30pm (not July/Aug).

### Centre

**Alaloum** Loutrón 1. Limassols's longest-running gay club, housed in stone-built, arcaded premises, with proprietor Stelios laying on a mixed Greek/European soundtrack and making a mixed clientele (including transvestites and lesbians) feel at home.

**Clapsides (Vihas)** End of Ayíou Andoníou. Come-as-you-are dance club, with an open-air dance floor in summer. Greek and foreign sounds week-day nights, Latin (including lessons) as weekends. Usually no cover.

**Half Note Music Club** Sokátous 4, corner with Saripólou ⓦ www.halfnotemc.com. Busiest on Fri and Sat nights, for the sake of taped Latin sounds; occasional live acts.

**Ikho Evdhomindapende/Boite Echo 75** Ayíou Andhréou 259. Pub-like atmosphere, enhanced by a pool table. The place also does duty as the headquarters of GAIA, an "ancient culture club". Occasional live music; open 6pm to midnight.

**Sto Perama** Zík Zák. Dance club with occasional live acts near the *hamam*, which received a thorough overhaul in 2003/04.

**Theas Axion** Elénis Paleoloyínas 40. Reasonably priced, classy wine (and beer) bar, with large snack platters available, imbued with the personality of ex-actor owner Kostas, who has set up shop in his parents' former house, an unmistakable round-fronted 1930s-vintage structure. The atmosphere of a private party; an excellent choice before or after attending an event at the nearby Rialto Theatre.

### Potamós Yermasóyias

**Auld Triangle** Yeoryíou toú Prótou 89. Four alternating resident DJs mean an exceedingly varied play list, enjoyed by a friendly, mixed crowd (mostly tourists and British servicemen) – theme parties as well.

**Basement** Yeoryíou toú Prótou 91. Small and usually very busy, playing mainstream pop through a state-of-the-art sound system.

**Equinox** Yeoryíou toú Prótou. The sound here is predominantly Garage, R&B and Hip-Hop.

**Privilege** By the *St Raphael* hotel, 18km east of the centre. The largest and most locally patronized of the clubs here, with lots of different dance areas (including outdoor), a mix of Greek and north-European hits, and meals available as well.

## Shopping

Central Limassol is in the grip of a restoration craze, as fine Neoclassical buildings are being steadily rehabilitated for business and residential use. This has created a ready market for **antiques** to furnish the interiors, and dealers abound in the commercial district. The plushest, installed in a former candy factory, is Hermal's Auction House at Gládstonos 48 (ⓦ www.hermalsauction.com), which also hosts sales of international art.

More affordable, locally produced art – primarily **painting** – is on view at Morfi Gallery, Ankýras 84 (Tues–Sat 10am–1pm & 4–7pm, Mon 10am–1pm; ⓦ www.morfi.org). For **ceramics**, Kerameas, nearby at no. 55, has a selection of portable, yet unusual, objects.

At the Ergastiri Keramikis Tekhnis (Workshop of Ceramic Art) on Khrístou Sózou, between Ayíou Andhréou and Spýrou Araoúzou, you'll find highly idiosyncratic, often eerie, large-scale work by Pambos Mikhlis, displayed in an old house just behind the seafront.

## Listings

**Banks and exchange** Plenty of banks in the bazaar, all with ATMs.

**Bicycles** Kostakis Aristidhou on Irínis does reasonable, quick repairs and servicing; Kaittanis Hire Centre, Khristáki Kránou 2, rents pedal-cycles as well as scooters.

**Bookshops** Travelers' Tales Internet Café Bookstore, Ayíou Andhréou 4, in the Stoa Fylaktou (linking the street with the covered fruit market), is a combination internet café and bookshop. Otherwise, try Ioannidhes, Athinón 30–32, the best in town for books on Cyprus and also for Department of Lands and Surveys maps, or Kyriakou, an English-oriented general-purpose bookstore at Gríva Dhiyení 3.

**Bus companies/terminals** Useful long-distance outfits include Intercity ☎24643492, from the old port, for Larnaca; ALEPA ☎99625027, by Panikos Kiosk on Spýrou Araoúzou, for Páfos; LLL ☎22665814, from the municipal market, for Nicosia; PEAL ☎99742310, by the municipal market, for Plátres in the Tróödhos. Buses for Episkopí village and the turning for Kourion ruins depart from beside the castle.

**Car rental** ASG/Europcar, Yeoryíou toú Prótou, Belmar Complex, Shop 1, Potamós Yermasóyias ☎25322250; Hertz, Yeoryíou toú Prótou 61

☎25323758; Andreas Petsas, Yeoryíou tou Prótou, Sea Breeze Court, Suite 1, Potamós Yermasóyias ☎25323672; St George's, Arkhiepiskópou Makaríou 62 ☎25562808, ⓦwww.tgeorges-carhire.com; Sixt, Yeoryíou toú Prótou, Belmar Complex, Shop 5, Potamós Yermasóyias ☎25312345.

**Laundry** Anastási Shoúkri 20 (formerly Kánningos), Lordos Court, near the Archeological Museum (Mon–Fri during normal shopping hours; service wash C£4).

**Post offices** The main branch, with late afternoon hours and parcel/poste restante service, is somewhat inconveniently located on Gládstonos; there's a more central branch for outbound letters on Kyprianoú in the bazaar, also open Mon, Tues, Thurs & Fri 3–6pm & Sat 9–11am.

**Scuba schools** Dive-In has a branch operating out of the *Four Seasons Hotel*, 12km east of the centre; see Larnaca "Listings" for details (p.103).

**Service taxis** Travel & Express is at Thessaloníkis 21 ☎0777474.

**Travel agent** Becky's Travel at Arkhiepiskópou Makaríou 95, Shop C ☎25386032, ⓦwww.beckystravel.com, are tops for air tickets, being able to secure advantageous fares as very short notice.

# The Limassol foothills

Inland from Limassol, the foothills of the Tróödhos range are home to a substantial number of Cyprus's commercial **vineyards**, set amid infertile terrain covered in maquis vegetation. With little other significant economic activity, however, many of the villages are moribund, with futures only as weekend retreats for city-dwellers, holiday homes for foreigners or artists' colonies.

The rise to the highest peaks of the Tróödhos is not uniform: roads going inland roller-coaster past the first set of barrier ridges into hollows and hidden valleys that contain the bulk of the attractions described below. At one time or another most of these places were fiefs of the Hospitallers or other Lusignan nobility; they lie primarily between 600 and 800 metres above sea level, which results in a pleasant climate even in high summer.

Outsiders will probably pass through the various settlements just off the two main highways up towards the Tróödhos, the **E601** and the **B8**, which begin at Erími and Polemídhia respectively on the Limassol coastal plain. The British first opened a "Wine Road" (later the E601) as far as Ómodhos at the beginning of the twentieth century to facilitate the shipping out of the grape harvest.

## The westerly Tróödhos approach: the Krassokhoriá

The large villages clustered near the top of the westerly route towards the Tróödhos are collectively labelled the **Krassokhoriá** (wine villages) in CTO promotion, but known as "Commandaria villages" on some maps; in any event, they are indeed renowned for both their dry and sweet-dessert wines. At vintage time in autumn, huge lorries groaning with grapes lumber along the narrow roads, and signs warn of grape-juice slicks on the pavement.

## Vouní

Your first likely detour from the E601 is just beyond Áyios Amvrósios, a seven-kilometre drive towards partly abandoned but highly picturesque **VOUNÍ**, where the remaining elders sit at a few *kafenía* on the Paliostráta, the old high street. Since the mid-1990s the village has been listed as a protected architectural showcase, and is quite striking seen against its hillside from the southwest, though some jarring Hellenic-blue balustrades and a few illicit brickings-up have crept in amongst the traditional materials and methods supposed to be used for renovations.

Vouní (or rather the Stená ravine, well-signposted just west) is home to the **Vouní Donkey Sanctuary** (summer Mon–Sat 10am–4pm, winter Mon–Sat 8.30am–4.30pm; C£1) run by the Cyprus-registered charity "Friends of the Cyprus Donkey" (effectively Mary and Patrick Skinner), which plays host to around a hundred elderly and not-so-elderly beasts who can no longer be cared for by their former owners. Until the mid-twentieth century Cyprus was famous for the quality of its donkey breed, but today they are only used at grape-harvest time to work terraces inaccessible to farm machinery, and instances of animal abuse or abandonment have increased sharply. The aim of the sanctuary is not only to serve as a "retirement home" and riding zoo for children, but to provide veterinary care on an "out-patient" basis, and a bank of strong, healthy animals which can be hired out for a few weeks yearly during the vintage season. There is also a café, visitors' centre and gift shop on site.

Along with the gentrification have come a few **tavernas**. Best of these is *Iy Orea Ellas / Beautiful Greece* in the village centre (closed Mon; ☎25944152), which stresses metropolitan Greek rather than Cypriot food, as the proprietor's from Thessaloníki. Dishes like *spédzofaï* (sausage and pepper stew) and *yígandes* (white haricots in sauce) are washed down with purple local bulk wine; portions are smallish but so are prices (C£8 per head), and the place is popular with a trendy Limassol clientele.

### Kiláni and Ayía Mávra

**KILÁNI** (Koilani), 5km northeast of Vouní along a much better road than maps imply, is architecturally less of a piece but a bit livelier; there's a pedestrianized area with several *kafenía*, one of which serves *mahallebí* as a sweet. If you're taken with the place, you can **stay** at one of two apartments in the *Mavrikios House* near the square, managed by Cyprus Villages (☎24332998, ⓦwww.cyprusvillages.com; ❸). There are also several excellent local **wineries**, though visits are by appointment only: Erimoudes (☎25470669), Vardalis (☎25470261), Ayia Mavri (☎25470225) and Domaine Vlassides (☎99441574), of which the last is perhaps the most renowned for the sake of its excellent Cabernet Sauvignon and Shiraz reds.

Behind the modern church of Panayía Eleoússa, the Limassol archbishopric has set up an **ecclesiastical museum** (admission by keeper's whim) of items scoured from crumbling churches round about. It's a better-than-average collection housed in two rooms, with a stress on intricately crafted sacred objects as well as icons. Kiláni was chosen as the location because of its past importance in church affairs; nearly half a dozen bishops of the sixteenth to eighteenth centuries hailed from here, and indeed the archbishopric of

Limassol itself was based here for some years during the seventeenth century, when Limassol was at its nadir.

Continuing a kilometre up the valley of the Krýos stream from Kiláni, past the Ayia Mavri winery on Kiláni's outskirts, you can't miss the twelfth-century chapel of **Ayía Mávra** (sometimes Ayía Mávri; always open), set in the river gorge by some trees and a handful of rural weekenders' **tavernas**. The little church is all that remains of a much larger monastery, and a spring still burbles from the apse; according to legend the water flows from a cleft in the rock created when Mavra, pursued against her will by her father and proposed fiancé, appealed to the Virgin to preserve her vow of chastity – and was promptly swallowed by the low cliff. This tale, told with variations around the Greek Orthodox world, is a revamping of the pagan legend of Daphne pursued by Apollo; in fact, the historical Mavra is supposed to have married Saint Timothy.

Inside are some smudged fifteenth-century frescoes, rather late in the day for Cyprus and not really of the first rank, but engaging nonetheless. Áyios Timothéos (Saint Timothy) and Mávra herself have been cleaned, and face you as you enter; just above are the remains of the *Dormition*. A *Virgin Enthroned* graces the conch of the apse, flanked by the *Ascension* (left) and *Pentecost* (right). The central vaulting is occupied by indistinct scenes from the *Life of Christ*, with the *Pandokrátor* in the dome; unusually, one squinch bears the *Annunciation* rather than one of the Evangelists, which would be the norm for this position.

### Potamioú and Vássa

A right turn off the E601 after Kissoúsa leads up to **POTAMIOÚ**, nearly the equal of Vouní in architectural distinction and graced by the sixteenth-century Ayía Marína church. The ruins of Byzantine Áyios Mnáson lie outside the village, down in the valley of the Khapótami.

Staying with the E601 brings you to **VÁSSA** (Vasa), 35km from Limassol and, like its neighbours, a hive of renovation activity. There is no longer any short-term accommodation here, but a pair of **tavernas** operates in the cobble-paved village centre during the warmer months. However, much the best and most reliable local eating is well south of town near the bypass road: *Iy Ariadhni* (☎25944064). This offers excellent homestyle fare such as *koupépia* with farm-fresh sheep's yoghurt, *keftédhes*, *bourékia* with *anári* cheese, good grills and a couple of dishes of the day, all washed down with decent bulk wine. For something better, order products of the local Vasa winery, particularly their Cabernet Sauvignon.

Spare a moment for the fifteenth-century **church of Áyios Yeóryios**, in the ravine just north of the village, by the roadside, with slightly later frescoes. Among these, of special note are the *Evangelists* on the squinches, including Saint John the Divine with his disciple Prohoros; an *Annunciation* over the main door; and a *Deposition* on the central arch.

### Ómodhos

Three kilometres beyond either Potamioú or Vássa brings you to the more heavily promoted **ÓMODHOS** (Omodos), unusually laid out around its **monastery of Timíou Stavroú** (the Holy Cross), with a vast cobbled square leading to it – probably an instance of Lusignan town planning, since rarely in the Greek world is a monastery the core of a settlement. Although of Byzantine foundation, what you see now dates entirely from the early and mid-nineteenth century. Dositheos and Khryssanthos, sponsors and abbots of the monastery during its late eighteenth-century revival, were hanged by the Ottoman authorities along with sundry others in 1821 when news of the mainland Greek rebellion reached the island. Since 1917 the monastery has been empty of monks, and Orthodox pilgrims visit principally for the sake of purported Crucifixion relics kept inside the otherwise undistinguished church. The gallery of the upper storey is sporadically open, and worth the climb up for its intricate woodwork. This includes carved lattice railings along the walkway past wooden cell doors; at the northeast corner of the enclosure, wood ornamentation reaches new heights in the fantastic bishop's room, with its carved ceiling and cabinets lining the east wall.

The **village** itself is pleasant enough, if rather commercialized, with a sprinkling of Visa and MasterCard signs and a few touts inveigling you to visit rather bogus traditional houses. Much the best interior is that of the originally Lusignan *linós* or old **wine press** (free, always open) just north and downhill from the monastery; find the light switch to view the mammoth boom of the press, embedded *kioupiá* (urns) for holding the grape mash, and the copper *zivanía* still. The best souvenir buys are bottles of the red and white local wine – Linos is particularly recommended – or *loukoúmia* ("Turkish" delight); only some of the basketry and lace displayed here are locally crafted. A number of simple **cafés** alternate with the souvenir displays on the plaza that slopes down to the monastery's portal. The liveliest time to visit is September 14, when the monastery church becomes the focus of the festival of the Holy Cross, which spills out onto the square outside.

Among half a dozen or so full-service **tavernas**, *Katoi* (dinner only) – around the corner from the old wine press – is as good as any, though Friday and Saturday evenings sees fairly genuine Cypriot music and dance at *Makrinari* just north of the village, with locals in conspicuous attendance.

## Malliá, Ársos and the ridge route to Páfos

**MALLIÁ** (Malia), overlooking a major junction near the end of the E601, once had the largest Turkish-Cypriot population in the Limassol hills; the graves of six original villagers, killed in the troubles of early 1964, lie by the mosque in the western clifftop neighbourhood, whose houses are slowly being squatted and renovated as weekend retreats (houses lower down have been sparsely occupied by Greek-Cypriot refugees). Malliá is the highest in altitude of the Commandaria-producing villages – there is still a large KEO plant at the outskirts – and before 1974 the inhabitants used to barter their dessert wine for dry wine from Ársos. Just at the main entrance to the village an old *kafenío* has been refurbished as a **taverna**, the *Platanos Malias* (☏25944944), featuring good wine from Ársos, though their C£6 *mezé* is better quality than their *kléftigo*.

**ÁRSOS**, 3km north, is much the biggest of the wine villages, but while it's an imposing, stone-built place, there's nothing in particular to see other than the Nikolettino micro-winery. There's **accommodation** at *Dia's House* (☏25372368; ❹ for minimum of two rooms), a restored nineteenth-century arcaded stone dwelling at the northwest edge of "town". The *Moustos* (☏99679788, ℻25313022, ⓔadonis.sh@cytanet.com.cy; 1-bedroom unit ❹, 2-bedroom ❺) has a huge salon and is exceptionally well restored, while the central *Cornaro House* (☏25358836, ℻25358257, ⓔcornaro@cytanet.com.cy; studio ❹,1-bedroom units ❺) is more suitable for couples.

From Ársos you can carry on to Áyios Nikólaos, near the head of the Dhiárizos valley (see p.222), or backtrack slightly to follow an interesting ridge route along the eastern flank of the valley into Páfos district, with spectacular views west to the Páfos hills. **DHORÁ** (Dora), the remotest of the *Krassokhoriá*, is an attractive place on the brow of a ridge whose narrow lanes repay exploring on foot; there are two tavernas. The district boundary lies 2km southwest at tiny

**MOÚSERE** hamlet, half-abandoned in greenery and doubtless the next target for weekend-retreat-restorers.

The road continues 5km to Arkhimandhríta in Páfos district, from where it's plain sailing down to Koúklia on the main Limassol–Páfos highway; this route is entirely paved and often bona fide two-lane, and until or unless the dug-up Dhiárizos valley road gets a new contractor to fix it, this remains the fastest way down to Páfos from the Tróödhos.

## The easterly Tróödhos approach

The more heavily used of the two main highways to the Tróödhos, the B8 up from Exit 28 of the coastal expressway, is less immediately appealing than the western route, but off the main road some attractive old villages and monastic churches cling to the vine-clad hillsides.

### Lófou

The first worthwhile detour, 18km out of Limassol, is the side road up to **LÓFOU**, an extraordinarily photogenic village built on several hills, as its name (*lófos* is "hill" in Greek) implies – though the outskirts are beginning to straggle a bit untidily with modern villas. Most visitors make it up here for the sake of Kostas Violaris' *Iy Lofou* **taverna**, well signposted near the top of the village (reservations usually needed on ☎25470202 or 99468151; open lunch/dinner Tues–Sun, though tends to run out of food Sun pm). A rich *mezé* and bulk wine from Peléndhri are served in a well-converted arcaded house, at its best in the cooler months when a fire blazes in the hearth; Kostas and friends provide acoustic musical accompaniment later in the evening. If you're utterly taken with the village, you can stay in one of the nicely restored **rooms** above the restaurant (②).

Lófou can also be reached by paved roads from Perá Pedhí to the north, Áyios Amvrósios to the west, or Monágri (see below) via Áyios Yeóryios to the east.

### Monágri, Arkhángelos and Panayía Amasgoú

There's little to prompt another halt until the short turning left to **MONÁGRI**, about 21km out of Limassol. Immediately beyond the village stands the **monastery of Arkhángelos**, surrounded by vineyards and overlooking the Koúris river valley. Originally founded in the tenth century on the site of an ancient temple, it was rebuilt after a disastrous fire in 1735 and, since 1989, both church and the grounds have been meticulously restored by the Monagri Foundation and the Department of Antiquities. The foundation, currently headed by Richard and Alison Sale, maintains a worthwhile permanent exhibition showing the traditional building techniques used in the restoration.

Visits (ring ☎25434165 first) begin with the **monastic church**, whose fine eighteenth-century frescoes (including some by Filaretos, who painted the interior of Áyios Ioánnis in Nicosia – see p.284) have been cleaned by the Courtauld Institute of London University. Uniquely in Cyprus, the interior retains geometric *mihrab* decoration over the south window from the church's time of use as a mosque (Monágri was apparently once a Linovamváki village – see box on p.430 – which later openly espoused Christianity). The front porch is supported by two Corinthian columns apparently recycled from a Roman-era temple. In 2004 the icons and *témblon* were cleaned by the bishopric of Limassol. The gallery and exhibition space, in the main outbuilding and former priest's residence, incorporates a **Roman olive mill**, the only known one on the island.

The twelfth-century monastic **church of Panayía Amasgoú**, 3km downriver from Monágri on the west bank, has fine if only partly cleaned fresco fragments from four periods up to the sixteenth century; the nuns of the surrounding convent will show you the interior (Tues, Thurs and Sat mornings only). However a hyperactive building programme initiated by a former bishop of Limassol has resulted in new, tall structures all around and a consequent reduction of available light in the church.

### Silíkou and Lánia

A little further up the Koúris valley and the B8 are two other villages of interest. Attractive **SILÍKOU**, west of the B8 and actually reached directly from Monágri, can offer an **olive-mill museum**, though the taverna here has changed hands and is no longer noteworthy.

East of the B8, via a one-kilometre side road, stands **LÁNIA** (Laneia), another atmospheric village popular with expats (a quarter of the population), including a few artists; one, Michael Owen, runs the Mediterranean Bookshop. There is just one surviving **taverna**, the *Lania*, run by a young couple whose good cooking makes up for somewhat limited opening hours (lunch only weekdays, plus dinner weekends).

## Eastern hill-villages

The cluster of villages straddling the border with Larnaca district are among the most isolated and forlorn in the Limassol foothills – which in the Cyprus of today is an attraction in itself, though the region isn't quite the miniature Tuscany that the CTO once made it out to be in its publications. The main problem, from a tourist-development standpoint, is that just enough cash has trickled in to finance unsightly "improvements" which ruin the architectural homogeneity of these places. Easiest access to this area is via either the Yermasóyia (Germasogeia, Exit 24) or Parekklishá (Parekklisia, no. 21) exits of the Limassol–Nicosia expressway.

### Kelláki to Akapnoú

The road in from Parekklishá emerges after 16km on a knoll at **KELLÁKI**, with a grand view of the ridges of Pitsyliá – and the sea – on the far side of the valley. A few villas have gone up, and progressively more local land is for sale. But otherwise neither Kelláki nor its neighbour Prastió, downhill to the west, offers much to casual visitors, despite a hopeful sign "Area Tourist Information Here" at the Kelláki *kafenío*. Most of these hamlets now have a seasonal taverna of sorts.

You'll get a fair idea of the original vernacular architecture by detouring east of Kelláki. **KLONÁRI** hamlet, some 6km east, has a fine church of Áyios Nikólaos, bare inside, though built in the standard pitched-roof Tróödhos style (see p.244), but the tenants of the smelly dovecotes far outnumber the remaining humans. The dozen houses of **VÍKLA**, a couple of dirt-road kilometres further, are completely abandoned despite a fine setting, though this will probably change now that the twelve-hole **Vikla Golf Club** (☏22761333; one-day greens pass C£8–10) has been laid out nearby; it's very informal, with no golf shoes or specialist clothing required.

From either here or Klonári, fairly rough dirt roads head for **AKAPNOÚ**, to the north on a hillock surrounded by relatively fertile and well-watered land. This has retained about thirty friendly inhabitants and a few attractive houses which are now benefiting from restorers' attentions, as well as some flagstoned pedestrian lanes. Besides the rather bare *kafenío* by the square, with its recently built but appealing church of Áyios Yeóryios, there's also an *exokhikó kéndro* in the fields west of the village, near the small chapel of **Panayía tou Kámbou**. Among the sixteenth- and seventeenth-century frescoes inside, above roundels of saints on the south wall, are preserved an *Annunciation*, Joseph scolding Mary for her surprise pregnancy, and part of a *Nativity*; worth seeing if the key is in the door, but not worth a special detour.

## Eptagónia to Odhoú

You return to the main road at **EPTAGÓNIA** (Eptagoneia), a relatively busy place; west, on the road between here and Arakapás, a newish purpose-built primary school serves the region's children, the individual village schools having long since closed down. **MELÍNI**, 4km north, has another standard-issue gabled church and marks the start of the impressive climb up to **ODHOÚ** (Odou), at the edge of the high Tróödhos and actually just over the border into Larnaca district. Marvellously set amid 850-metre-elevation crags overlooking the canyon, the village itself is a rather unhappy architectural hotch-potch, modest prosperity having prompted some cheap and easy renovations; it enjoys some summer day-trip trade owing to its cool climate.

Beyond Odhoú a steep but paved road climbs to a 1100-metre pass in the Pitsylian ridges; once onto the watershed, you've a view down onto handsomely spread-out Farmakás and Kámbi (see p.263). If you're headed towards Pitsyliá, you can also use the route north which begins at Arakapás (see below). This is narrower but asphalted as far as ravine-hugging Sykópetra and **PROFÍTIS ILÍAS**, improbably set amid bare, rocky spurs and not shown on most maps; there's a **taverna** here. The 7km between here and Palekhóri on the main Tróödhos ridge route, despite pessimistic depictions on many maps, are now paved.

## Arakapás and Panayía Iamatikí

Using the side road from Exit 24, you'll run quickly through Yermasóyia, then past its eponymous dam, before slowing down for some scenic ridge-driving until reaching Dhieróna (Dierona) and Arakapás (22km from the highway). Along with Eptagónia, these villages are the closest things to going concerns hereabouts, with olive and mandarin orchards providing a precarious living. Low-lying **ARAKAPÁS** sits in a natural depression, lower and warmer than any of its neighbours (thus the citrus), with plenty of cafés and snack bars in its centre.

The big local attraction is the much-modified cemetery **church of Panayía Iamatikí**, on the outskirts as the road turns east towards Eptagónia. Originally a Latin foundation of the sixteenth century, it was rebuilt in 1727, preserving only the westernmost transverse arch of the original, plus two fine triple arcades which divide the present church into three aisles. Architecturally, it is almost unique in southern Cyprus, having only the ruined Gothic church at Áyios Sozómenos (see p.300) as a peer. The wonderful, mysterious interior repays the small effort of getting access; the presiding priest appears every evening, or you can seek him out at one of the cafés.

The Italo-Byzantine style of the interior's **frescoes** is similarly rare in Cyprus. In the soffit of the arches closest to the west door are some finely sketched angels, inside roundels. Images on the north arcade, dating from the 1600s, include the four Evangelists in the spandrels, plus Áyios Ioánnis Dhamaskinós (Saint John Damascene) attended by a miniature figure of the Virgin. Frescoes on the somewhat damp-damaged south arcade are a bit earlier; these include the monk Zozimas spoon-feeding the withered desert ascetic Osia Maria, a former courtesan who repented of her ways, and Áyios Mámas riding on his trademark lion, a flowing robe giving a tremendous sense of motion.

# East of Limassol: the coast

The town beach at Limassol, stony and flanked by intermittent breakwaters and stationary tankers, is pretty forgettable; recognizing this, the CTO has improved a beach at **Dhassoúdhi (Dasoudi)**, about 4km east of town near the edge of Potamós Yermasóyias. But you really need to travel further towards Larnaca before reaching any patches of fairly natural coastline.

## Amathus (Amathoús, Amathoúnda)

Some 13km east of Limassol town centre, just before the end of the resort strip, **ancient Amathus** (daily: June–Aug 9am–7.30pm; Sept–May 9am–5pm; C£0.75) is signposted just inland from the coast road. In the Cypriot-ruin sweepstakes low-lying Amathus does not perhaps rank among the most evocative, but its presence has kept resort hotels at a healthy distance, and as excavations proceed there is progressively more to see. Limassol city **buses** #6 and #30 pass the site, but the nearest official stop is about 800m west; some find it more enjoyable to follow the coastal walkway which runs along the resort strip from near the *Poseidonia Hotel*, with an underpass allowing access to the site.

### Some history

Amathus is among the oldest of Cyprus's city-kingdoms, purportedly founded by a son of Hercules, who was revered as a god here. The legend seems to indicate settlement by the original island colonists, with a later Phoenician religious and racial overlay. In some versions of the myth, Ariadne, fleeing from the labyrinth on Crete, was abandoned here and not on Aegean Naxos by Theseus; she then died in childbirth, and was buried in a sacred grove, where her cult melded easily with that of Aphrodite. Lightly Hellenized, and prone to worshipping Egyptian gods like Bes as well as Asiatic ones, Amathus sided with Persia against Salamis and the other Cypriot kingdoms during the fifth- and fourth-century BC revolts, though it later declared for Alexander the Great.

The Romans made it capital of one of the four administrative districts of the island; this anticipated a bishopric in Byzantine times, and it was the birthplace of Saint John the Almoner, patron of the Order of the Knights Hospitaller. But decline and destruction ensued after the repeated Arab raids of the seventh century, and a destructive visit from Richard the Lionheart in 1191, and the city was largely forgotten until the eighteenth century, when its tombs to the west were looted; shortly after, some of its dressed stone was taken to Egypt to line the locks of the new Suez Canal, though in fact the contractors mostly used fresh-cut stone from a nearby quarry. The first systematic excavations occurred in 1862, 1893 and 1930, though there was no lack of plundering and pilfering in between.

### The site

The remains of the city, fetchingly illuminated at night, are dominated by a vast paved **agora**, studded with a dozen restored and re-erected columns, including three spiral-fluted and two square ones. In the middle of the area there's a square foundation filled with rubble and masonry fragments; its original function is uncertain, though it was probably a fountain. Under a corrugated-roof shelter, more column chunks and pediments, all found since excavations resumed in 1975, await final disposition. To make any sense of the place, consult the site plan on the raised viewing dais near the Hellenistic baths.

Backed into the bluff at the northwest end of the marketplace is what appears to be an elaborate **waterworks system**, the terminus of an aqueduct which supplied the city from the north. The flow of a niche-spring was diverted through tunnels to sluices, feeding a small basin at the head of more channels running to a pair of large cisterns. Some water appears to have run through open gutters, but you can still see a conspicuous large water-main which, exposed, leads some way out into the marketplace. A stepped street leads up the partly excavated slope past rows of Hellenistic-era **houses**. At the seaward end of the agora, a round precinct with pebble mosaics in chequerboard and rosette patterns represents the foundations of **Hellenistic baths**.

Up on the bluff is the ancient **acropolis**, with stretches of defensive **walls** to seaward, the remains of Amathus's main **temple**, jointly dedicated to Aphrodite and Hercules, plus one of the more important of the Byzantine city's **Christian basilicas** superimposed upon this, retaining extensive patches of *opus sectile* and *champlevé* flooring. Across the road, towards the sea, are more sections of wall and traces of the ancient port, now submerged to a distance of several hundred yards from the shoreline; earthquake and subsidence have laid them low. It is claimed that Richard the Lionheart landed at this bay in May 1191 to begin his march on Limassol.

## Áyios Yeóryios Alamánou and Pendákomo

Beyond Amathus, you can continue east along the old B1 road or take the A1 motorway to Exit 18, which gives access to both the bay of Áyios Yeóryios Alamánou and the inland village of Pendákomo.

As you head seawards down the pleasant, narrow valley here, unlikely to ever be developed like its neighbour (see below), you should probably shun the turning up and right to the convent of **Ayíou Yeoryíou Alamánou**, an uninteresting modern construction and a "working" institution, not a tourist attraction.

Fork left instead; soon the narrow lane dwindles to dirt surface, and some 1600m from the junction you'll arrive at the bay of **Áyios Yeóryios Alamánou**. The short beach here sports coarse pebbles verging on melon-size, but to either side is some of the most impressive white-cliff scenery in Cyprus, with the occasional sea-cave to explore. At road's end is a single, popular **taverna**, the *Paraliako Kentro* (☎99624376), featuring sustaining seafood grills and fry-ups without airs or graces; budget C£10 per person for fish, a large salad and a beer.

Some 2.5km inland, **PENDÁKOMO** (Pentakomo) is the last village before the border with Larnaca district and arguably the first community east of Limassol with an existence other than that of a dormitory suburb. It's attractive enough to have spawned a restoration complex, *George's Houses*, at present marketed exclusively through Sunvil Holidays. In the centre, just up from the church, is the *Kafé-Theatro Iris* (evenings only; closed Mon). Food there is, but the emphasis is on **musical and theatrical events** held regularly in the covered courtyard; call ☎25633737 for the current programme.

## Governor's Beach (Aktí Kyvernítou)

The area's most appealing beaches can be found 29km east of Limassol at **Governor's Beach (Aktí Kyvernítou)**, just a few kilometres off the express-way at Exit 16. Despite the singular name, Governor's Beach consists of several coves of fine dark sand, contrasting dramatically with the low, chalk cliffs which back them. The beaches fill quickly on warm weekends, and each cove is lorded over by spruced-up **tavernas**, each having manicured lawn-gardens sloping down to the sand, with steps or a ramp for access, and often flats to rent – though these are now outnumbered by vast numbers of villas proliferating just inland.

The road from the expressway forks almost immediately, and where the right-hand turning splits again (actually either bearing joins to form a loop), a signboard locates the half-dozen tavernas schematically. Bearing right first leads to the broadest, cleanest stretch of sand and sunbeds, with the *Akti Sofroniou, Adamos* and *Faros* tavernas adjacent. From the rocky lighthouse cape beyond, looking towards the ugly industrial installations at Vasilikós which mar the area, it's possible to walk west over white-rock cliffs, which have a reputation as a gay hangout. The coves on the far left are narrower and more secluded, served by the revamped *Panayiotis* ttaverna (which rents flats) and overlooked by a rather bleak and shadeless **campsite** that's popular with permanently anchored Cypriot caravans but not really suitable for tents.

# The Akrotíri peninsula

At the southwest end of Limassol, near the entrance to the new port, two routes leave the city: the minor road, paved part way only, that parallels the **Akrotíri peninsula**'s east shore, and the better, paved road heading roughly west across the base of the peninsula to the Fassoúri plantations.

## Lady's Mile Beach (Aplóstra)

Now officially signposted as **Aplóstra**, but still popularly known as **Lady's Mile Beach** in honour of a mare named Lady that a British officer used to exercise here, the east shore is, in fact, closer to four miles of grey, hardpacked sand. No permanent development has taken place because it remains the property of the British Ministry of Defence and also because, with a mosquito-plagued salt lake behind, it's not very good as a beach (though the bird life in the lake is rewarding; see p.490). The barely sloping tidal flats are better for jogging (and dune-buggying, popular with locals) than sunbathing. Every few hundred metres there's a shack-like café or taverna catering for the weekend crowds, but, as signs warn you, various activities, including camping, are prohibited since, surprisingly, parts of the beach are a turtle-nesting area.

## Ayíou Nikoláou tón Gáton and Akrotíri

At the south end of Lady's Mile, the dirt track takes a bend inland to follow the southern shore of the salt lagoon; after about a kilometre a signposted driveway on the left wiggles through a gate in the fence and past hedgerows to the grounds of the convent of **Ayíou Nikoláou tón Gáton** (St Nicholas of the Cats).

The peculiar name springs from a wonderful Byzantine **legend**, according to which Saint Helena imported hundreds of cats from Egypt or Palestine, at the time of Saint Nicholas's fourth-century foundation, to control the population of poisonous snakes which infested the place. The monks (at what was originally a monastery) would summon the cats to meals by the tolling of a bell, and another bell would send them out into the surrounding fields to battle

## The British Sovereign Bases

One of the conditions of Cypriot independence in 1960 was the retention of a certain percentage of the island as a British military reserve, known as the **Sovereign Base Areas** or SBAs for short. Indeed, the date of nationhood was delayed by disputes over the SBAs' exact size, which eventually resulted in a figure of about 99 square miles. Most of this area consists of the Episkopí Garrison; the adjoining Akrotíri Air Field; and the Dhekélia Base between Larnaca and Ayía Nápa. Base borders were drawn in such a way as to exclude almost all private land and villages – the only exception being Akrotíri village (whose inhabitants have dual Cypriot and British nationality), and Áyios Nikólaos hamlet near Famagusta, omitted from most maps. In addition to these main bases, fifteen "retained sites" (annexes) lie scattered across the South; the most conspicuous of these include the RAF/NATO radar domes on Mount Olympus, the BBC transmitters at Zíyi and an artillery range (currently unused) on the Akámas peninsula.

Technically the bases form British Dependent Territories administered by a military governor, though the population of about eight thousand (roughly half servicemen, the rest their dependants and other civilians) is subject to a civil legal code based closely on Cypriot law – provided the alleged offence(s) occurred on SBA territory, and not in Cyprus proper. As a result of ongoing Greek-Cypriot-nationalistic protests against the continuance of the SBAs, internal security is now quite tight; vehicles are liable to be stopped and checked by the distinct SBA police force, and photography is strictly forbidden. Otherwise, there is no formal border control: the main indications that you've entered a base are a sudden outbreak of UK-style street signs, with names like Mandalay Road or Agincourt Lane, and cat's-eye reflectors in the middle of the road. Southern Cypriots as well as foreigners circulate freely across SBA boundaries, and more than two thousand Greek Cypriots have jobs on the two largest bases.

About three hundred Turkish Cypriots also continue to work at the Dhekélia Base; before the thaw of April 2003, they entered strictly via the "Four Mile Crossing", a thin sliver of British territory abutting the outskirts of Famagusta, and the Attila Line. After August 1974, almost 10,000 Turkish Cypriots from the Limassol area, escaping

---

the serpents, so that, in the words of a visiting Venetian monk of 1484, "nearly all were maimed: one has lost a nose, another an ear; the skin of one is torn, another is lame; one is blind of one eye, another of both."

The habit of keeping cats to fend off the island's numerous snakes spread quickly to most other Cypriot monasteries, and also to Rhodes; when the Knights Hospitallers of Saint John moved there, they are said to have taken a whole shipload of cats with them. More recently, the Greek Nobel laureate George Seferis used the inter-species struggle as a metaphor for opposition to the dictatorship then in power in Greece, in one of his last published poems "The Cats of Saint Nicholas":

Wildly obstinate, always wounded,
They wiped out the snakes, but in the end they were lost,
They couldn't endure so much poison...

The contemporary reality of Ayíou Nikoláou is not so lofty: a working cloister, brashly remodelled since 1990 and of little architectural interest other than a fine coat of arms over the door of the thirteenth-century church; an enormous, brick-paved forecourt dwarfs the buildings. Today the convent is home to a handful of aged nuns and – still – dozens of cats, many as ragged-looking as

reprisal attacks by EOKA-B, sought refuge in the Episkopí base for six months, until they were airlifted out to Turkey – and from there to the North.

The official rationale for the bases' establishment and continued existence asserts their importance to British strategic interests as listening posts, east Mediterranean airfields and warm-winter training areas. Indeed Britain's 1878 acquisition of Cyprus, and stubborn retention of the island in the face of nationalist agitation, was premised on such logic. But it is more an irony of history than a demonstration of accidental foresight that only since the late 1950s, with the winding-up of empire and successive Middle Eastern crises, have the SBAs come to play the role originally envisaged for the whole island.

It is often asserted that the Americans have a secret base somewhere on Cyprus. This is half-true, since they in fact get total co-operation from the British and do not require facilities of their own. The American air force continues to fly U2 surveillance missions over the Middle East out of the Akrotíri airfield, and used to send supplies to the US embassy in Beirut on low-altitude Blackhawk runs which touched down momentarily, for reasons of protocol, at Larnaca. The conspicuous sixty-metre-wide electronic dish beside the Four Mile Crossing gathers information shared among the NATO allies, while emitting dangerous levels of radiation. Indeed, construction of a new, 190-metre-high radio mast at Akrotíri stirred long-simmering Cypriot resentment to boiling point in early July 2001. Incensed by the arrest of long-time ultra-nationalist MP Marios Matsakis on charges of trespass and criminal damage, over a thousand violent demonstrators trashed the Episkopí police station, set 35 British military vehicles alight and caused over UK£300,000 of damage in a single night. Ironically, base sources claim that the new antennae would emit far less radiation at ground level than the ones they were replacing.

The original extent of base territory would seem to be surplus to current requirements, as the British – as a sweetener to Cypriot voters in the unsuccessful April 2004 Annan Plan referendum – offered to cede about half of the area of the SBAs to the mooted federal republic (90 percent of this to the Greek-Cypriot unit). It remains to be seen if the offer will be repeated in the event of a new plan being formulated.

those seen by the Venetian. They stalk about like the denizens of a temple to the Egyptian cat-god which may once have stood here, and Cape Gáta (She-Cat), out past the runway of the Akrotíri airfield, is named after them, too.

# Kolossi

From near Limassol's modern harbour, a good road signed towards Asómatos and Fassoúri runs west to the Crusader castle of Kolossi and beyond to the stunningly sited ancient city of Kourion (see below). The route is no longer, and far less dangerous, than either of the inland highways, the steep, winding B6 and the high-speed A6. It's also the most scenic: giant cypresses, planted long ago as windbreaks, have grown up to form lofty tunnels over the road; eucalyptus clumps drained the swamps here and allowed extensive **orange groves** to flourish, most of them originally planted by Jewish settlers at the end of the nineteenth century, about a dozen families of them staying on after independence (and now living in Nicosia). At roadside stalls near the Red Seal Phassouri Plantation, you can buy giant sacks of the fruit, the cheapest in the South.

Cultivation originally started with Jaffas during the 1870s; Valencias from South Africa followed in the 1930s, with Merlins after World War II. One particular, old-fashioned variety to look out for are the sweet *sherkérika* or sugar oranges, the name derived (say some) from Tserkézi (Tserkezoi) village en route, but equally likely from the Turkish *shekerli*.

Long before citrus arrived, sugar cane and grapes were cultivated in this area; the **castle of Kolossi** (daily: June–Aug 9am–7.30pm; Sept–May 9am–5pm; C£0.75), just south of the village of that name, still stands evocatively amid the vineyards that helped make it famous. Frequent #16 or #17 **buses** run here from Limassol's central market (Mon–Sat only; journey time 20min).

The story of Kolossi is inextricably linked with the **Knights Hospitallers**, whose *commanderie* it was – the name was later bestowed on the rich dessert wine, Commandaria, still made from vines in the Limassol foothills. The Knights were first granted land here in 1210 by the Lusignans, and the castle that grew up became their headquarters after the Crusaders' final loss of the Holy Land. Even after the Order shifted to Rhodes exactly a century later, the Knights kept Kolossi as the headquarters of their local fiefs, which included dozens of foothill villages. Mameluke raids of the fifteenth century virtually levelled the original castle, later rebuilt on a smaller scale; in 1488 the Venetians appropriated it, along with the Order's other holdings. The Ottomans allowed the place to fall slowly into disrepair until the British restoration of 1933.

Today's three-storey, keep-style structure stands among the ruins of a much larger castle; from the **coat of arms** of the Grand Master Louis de Magnac, set into the east wall, a date of approximately 1450 has been deduced for the earlier restoration. Modern stairs have replaced a retractable defensive ramp up to the door; the ground level with its vital well, in effect a three-chambered storage basement, originally had no entrance from outside. In the left-hand, vaulted room of the middle storey, probably the kitchen, you'll see the first of several huge **fireplaces**, more appropriate to northern European chateaux and not equalled on the island since. By the spiral stairway in the other room, a glass plate protects a damaged **fresco** of the *Crucifixion*. The upper storey has thinner walls, and two grand halls at right angles to those below – presumably the quarters of de Magnac, as his heraldry again appears on one of the two back-to-back fireplaces. Benches flanking most of the window niches add a homely touch. Steps continue to the flat roof-terrace, where machicolations over the gate permitted the pouring of noxious substances onto uninvited guests.

The other roofed building in the precinct is the **sugar factory**, a barn-like vaulted structure also buttressed externally; first the Knights and later the Venetians produced sugar locally, though the establishment of slave-worked plantations in the Caribbean put paid to the Cypriot industry early in the Ottoman occupation. The still-visible cane-crushing millstone outside was watered by sluices fed in turn by a huge aqueduct, now shaded by a giant pepper tree, at the northeast corner of the grounds. Evidently the springs still ran until recently, as modern, metal-sheathed extensions of the spillways snake through burgeoning flower gardens. Within sight of the castle, to the northeast, the usually locked twelfth-century church of **Áyios Efstáthios** was the Knights' place of worship.

If you crave a meal after your visit, the *Kolossi Steak House* in the adjacent village of **KOLÓSSI** is recommended not only for tender steaks, but also for seafood. A bill for two won't exceed C£22 with drink. Reservations for the ever-popular Sunday lunch are suggested (☎25932570).

△ Apollo Hylates temple

# Kourion (Curium)

Perched dramatically on a sheer bluff overlooking the sea, **Kourion** (Latinized as "Curium") is easily the most spectacular of the South's archeological sites – even though close up some of its individual attractions may be out of bounds or incoherent while excavations continue. Kourion consists of two sites, entirely contained within the Episkopí Sovereign Base: the ancient city, closer to Kolossi, and the sanctuary of Apollo Hylates, a few kilometres west – you'll want half a day to see them both. The ruins lie about 5km west of Kolossi, but are served by a separate **bus service** originating at Limassol castle.

## Some history

Despite discouraging water-supply problems, this easily defensible clifftop may have been first settled in Neolithic times, but a recognizable city only emerged following Mycenaean colonization between the thirteenth and twelfth centuries BC. Kourion played a leading – negative – role in the **Cypriot rebellion against Persia**; at a critical moment its king Stasanor defected to the enemy with a considerable body of troops, guaranteeing the island's resubjugation. Like Amathus, however, it later championed Alexander against the Persians, and remained an important town throughout the Roman and early Byzantine periods; indeed, most of what can be seen today dates about evenly from those two eras. Following a cataclysmic earthquake in 365 AD, the city was utterly destroyed, and only tentatively rebuilt and resettled over the next few decades. After the seventh-century Arab raids, Kourion, like many other coastal settlements on Cyprus, was abandoned for good, and its bishop moved to nearby Episkopí.

The notorious American consul-turned-antiquarian **Luigi Palma di Cesnola** began excavating (or rather plundering) in 1865, and eleven years later claimed to have chanced on several untouched hoards of gold, silver, bronze and objects inlaid with precious stones, suggesting that Kourion had been far wealthier than anyone imagined. Even at the time many doubted his story, accusing him of doctoring the evidence and assembling the collection from his activities at various sites scattered across the island. Whatever the truth, the troves were shortly sold en bloc to the New York Metropolitan Museum and came to be known as the **Curium Treasure**.

Between 1933 and 1954, George McFadden of the University of Pennsylvania carried out rather desultory **archeological excavations** at both the ancient city and the nearby sanctuary of Apollo. But while popular locally, he was not a particularly systematic or effective archeologist, and after his untimely death by drowning just below the site, more important work was undertaken by a Cypriot team. In the early 1980s they were succeeded by the American David Soren and assistants, who soon dramatically established not only the exact date of the mid-fourth-century quake which had levelled Kourion, but also – from jewellery found on skeletal remains of several victims – that its population was already substantially Christian. Soren's account of these discoveries (see p.502) is invaluable for making sense of the ruins and placing the city in some historical context.

## The ancient city

More than usual, it's imperative to visit the site of the **ancient city** (daily: June–Aug 8am–7.30pm; Sept–May 8am–5pm; C£1) early or late, since coach tours of cruise-ship patrons clog the walkways between 10am and 3pm and

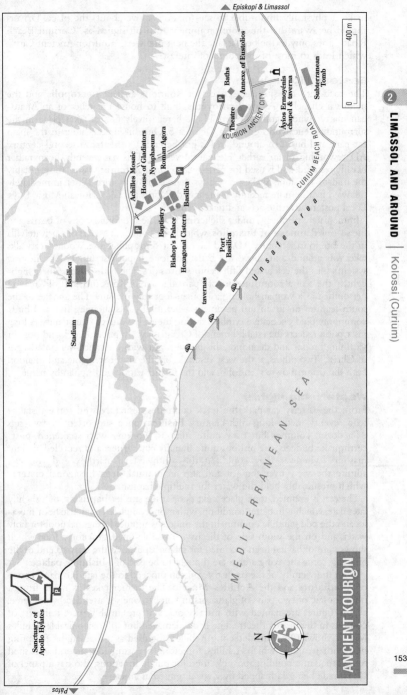

Episkopí & Limassol

400 m

Baths
Annexe of Eustolios

Theatre
KOURION ANCIENT CITY

Áyios Ermoyénis
chapel & taverna

Subterranean
Tomb

CURIUM BEACH ROAD

Achilles Mosaic
House of Gladiators
Nymphaeum
Roman Agora

P

Baptistry
Basilica

Bishop's Palace
Hexagonal Cistern

Basilica

Port
Basilica

tavernas

Unsafe area

Stadium

MEDITERRANEAN SEA

Páfos

P

Sanctuary of
Apollo Hylates

N

ANCIENT KOURION

make it physically impossible to see (or even move about) the place. Drivers should be aware that the more prominent turn-off signed as "Curium Beach Road" goes only to the beach; take the next one west, "Kourion Ancient City", which leads to most of the points of interest.

## Eastern highlights

The road into the site passes traces of Kourion's ancient **necropolis** and the medieval chapel of **Áyios Ermoyénis**, built to house the relics of an Anatolian martyr whose coffin floated ashore here; a lively festival takes place in the surrounding eucalyptus grove on October 5. Once inside the site gate, the main car park and bus turn-around area is just behind the **theatre**, a second-century AD reworking of an earlier Hellenistic version. This has recently been rather brashly restored, and is used for performances in high tourist season, most notably the mid-to-late-June Shakespeare plays (held every year since 1961), immediately followed by the more recently inaugurated Cyprus (Jazz & Classical) Music Days. Local posters advertise acts and ticket venues.

Immediately northeast, under sheltering roofs, lie the foundations of **baths** and the so-called **annexe of Eustolios**, which were both built as part of a private villa in the late fourth century AD, and later donated for public use. Wooden catwalks take you around and above the baths' intricate hypocaust (underfloor heating system), plus the celebrated fifth-century **mosaics**. The baths have as their highlight, in the central room, mosaics of a partridge and of Ktisis, the spirit of Creation personified as a woman holding a Roman-foot rule measure. The annexe to the south features on its atrium pavement a beautiful panel showing fish and birds, commonly used decorative symbols during the early years of Christianity. A long inscription reflects the establishment of Christianity: "In place of rock and iron, or gleaming bronze and diamonds, this house is girt with the much-venerated signs of Christ." Two others, at the west vestibule, bid the visitor welcome and mention both the original owner Eustolios and the former patron god Apollo by name.

## Western highlights

From the easterly car park the track continues hesitantly west some distance to a seventy-metre-long fifth-century **basilica**, once supported by two sets of a dozen columns but now quite ruinous. Working with straitened, post-earthquake budgets, the bishops quite literally cut corners and recycled ancient masonry wherever they could. At the southwestern, narthex end you can admire the view over the sea and also an unusual, deep hexagonal **cistern**, which presumably held the water for multiple baptisms.

These, it is assumed, took place next door at the smaller **baptistry**, of a slightly later date, which is in better condition, with more complete geometric floor mosaics and the odd standing column. In the middle is another hexagonal pool for holy water, and on the south side of the nave a marble-lined, cruciform font which shows signs of having been modified for infant baptism. At the seaward end of the building, some surviving arches are thought to be part of a **bishop's palace**.

From the vicinity of the baptistry you can proceed to the late Roman **House of Gladiators** and the **Achilles Mosaic**. The former takes its name from a floor mosaic of two pairs of gladiators in combat, one set attended by a referee; all the figures are named with inscriptions, and presumably were stalwarts of contests in the nearby theatre. The badly damaged but still recognizable Achilles Mosaic shows Odysseus detecting Achilles disguised as a maiden, by tempting him with weapons which Achilles, forgetting his assumed gender, has rushed to try; the same building, possibly used for public functions, also has a panel of Ganymede being kidnapped by Zeus disguised as an eagle.

Now that excavations have been completed, there should be no access problems for the Roman **agora**, with its stretch of re-erected second-century colonnade. This is flanked by the **nymphaeum** (fountain-house), once fed by an aqueduct which also must have supplied some conspicuous **baths**.

## The beach

The **beach** southwest of the ruins is reachable either by the link road past Áyios Ermoyénis and its attendant *exokhiko kéndró*, or "Curium Beach Road" proper, which passes a ramp descending to a large **subterranean tomb**, its entrance kept locked. Once you're clear of the prominently marked unsafe area, the water is cleaner and deeper (beyond the pink buoys) than the 800m of hard-packed sand suggests. The swimmable end of the beach is dotted with three impromptu **tavernas**, all of them unabashedly commercial and much of a muchness. Immediately inland from the road's end are the prominent remains of the sixth-century, so-called **Port Basilica** with tessellated flooring, which presumably served the spiritual needs of those working in the ancient port near here. Only discovered in 1994, it's currently being excavated.

## The sanctuary of Apollo Hylates

About 2km west of Kourion proper, at the large sacred complex (same hours as Kourion; separate C£0.75 admission) surrounding the **sanctuary of Apollo Hylates** – sometimes cited as Ylatis or Ylatou – Apollo was worshipped as the god of the surrounding woodland and as protector of the pre-Christian city. Today a huge RAF antenna farm west of the sanctuary distracts somewhat from the atmosphere, but it is still an attractive archeological site.

The sacred precinct was consecrated during the eighth century BC, but the present buildings are early Roman, flattened by the great earthquake of 365 AD. The two ancient **gates**, that of Paphos on the west and of Kourion on the east, are no longer intact, though the path from the ticket office passes the stumps of the former. On the right, before reaching the Kourion gate, you'll see the **palaestra** area, in one corner of which still stands a large water jug, used by athletes to cool off. Beyond, to the northeast, the **baths** sprawl under a tin shelter protecting piles of hypocaust stones.

The **processional way** starts at the extensive **xenon** or inn for pilgrims, with its restored Doric colonnade, and passes the presumed **priests' quarters** and precinct walls as it climbs a slight slope to the partly restored **temple of Apollo**. Two columns, a wall corner and an angle of the pediment enclose the altar area, open to the sky even in its day, and most holy; unauthorized individuals profaning it even with an inadvertent touch were hurled off the Kourion cliffs to appease the god's wrath. On the west side of the grounds, near the site of the Paphos gate, are the foundations of the **display hall** for votive offerings; between it and the processional way hides a curious round structure or **vothros**, not yet completely excavated, where it is surmised the priests discreetly disposed of old and surplus gifts to the god.

A curious and ubiquitous feature of the sanctuary is a series of broad **stone channels** hacked out of the strata. Once thought to be aqueducts, current theory identifies them as planter boxes used by the priests of Apollo for landscaping the grounds in a manner befitting a woodland god.

Not much is left of the imperial Roman **stadium** (access unrestricted), 500m to the east; it once seated six thousand, but now only a few rows of seats, and three gaps where the gates were, can be distinguished. On a knoll still further east, fenced but with its gate always open, a sixth-century **basilica** has a huge well in the floor and traces of floor mosaic in the altar area. Much of the flooring, however, was found in 1974 to be marble plaques pilfered from the nymphaeum in the city, laid face down so that bas-reliefs of pagan mythological scenes would not offend Christian sensibilities.

### Episkopí

The **Kourion site museum** (Mon–Fri 9am–2.30pm, also Sept–June Thurs 3–5pm; C£0.75) is 2.5km from the old city, in the large village of **EPIS-KOPÍ**, which shares the same bus service from Limassol as the site. Follow signs through Episkopí to the church of Ayía Paraskeví; the museum, in the old rambling house once lived in by archeologist George McFadden, stands opposite. The collection, occupying two wings, consists largely of terracotta objects from Kourion, the sanctuary of Apollo and two minor sites nearby.

Episkopí has become something of a popular overnight base, especially for Brits visiting relatives in the military here, though beware of Saturday nights, when the village centre serves as the venue for loud bands of variable quality accompanying wedding celebrations. Much the best-value local **accommodation** is *Antony's Garden House* (✆25933910; closed Jan & Feb; ❸), a modernized stone-built pension with a lovely courtyard and pool. You can **eat** at the *Episkopi Village Inn*, centrally located opposite the Bank of Cyprus, though à la carte is much better than the *mezé*.

# West towards Páfos: beaches

The limits of the Episkopí Sovereign Base extend almost to the boundary of Páfos district, again having the happy if unintended side effect of protecting the local coast from gross despoliation. Some 27km west of Limassol on the old road, watch for a sign seawards pointing to **Evdhímou Bay**, not to be confused with the inland village of Evdhímou (Avdimou; own motorway exit), which like its three western neighbours was Turkish-Cypriot-inhabited before 1974. A paved side road from either the old B6 road or the motorway exit leads to the sand-and-pebble **beach**, one of the best in the South, with little inland other than ruined carob warehouses just behind the site of the long-vanished jetty.

Two **restaurants** stake out respective ends of the beach: the long-hours, more Cypriot *Melanda* on the west (separate access road; closed Mon evening) for inexpensive, savoury seafood-and-chips lunches, and the *Kyrenia* to the east, more of an expats' hangout, run like a pub diner with restrictive meal hours, featuring a mix of Cypriot and British dishes and a good line in Western puds (sticky toffee pudding, strawberries and cream).

One of the closest places to **stay** is **ANÓYIRA** (Anogyra), some 10km inland on the hillside, a fairly lively place offering *Nicolas and Maria's Cottages* (✆25331963 or 99525462; studio ❷, family suite ❸), a restored old house opening onto a courtyard. Just outside town there's a well-regarded winery, Domaine Nicolaides (✆25221709 to arrange visits), now under the direction of the third generation of this family.

### Pissoúri

The only really sizeable coastal settlement between Episkopí village and the Páfos border is **PISSOÚRI**, draped appealingly over a ridge a bit south of the highway, though disfigured by too many new buildings to be really attractive close up. Owing to relative calm and proximity to the Episkopí Sovereign Base, it's a favourite with service families, and has numerous places to **stay** and **eat**. Among these, the *Victoria Hotel* (℡25221182; ❷), just off the main square, is mid-1990s-built, reasonably priced and has a pleasant snack bar attached. *Hillview* (℡25221972, 🅦 www.hillview.com.cy; studio ❷, 2-bedroom apartment ❸) at the northwestern edge of the village lives up to its name, and has an excellent restaurant (closed Mon) with dishes ranging from Cypriot to gourmet international. Occupying a converted two-century-old farmhouse, the long-established *Bunch of Grapes Inn* (℡25221275, ℻25222510; ❸) passed into Cypriot management in 2002, with a salutary effect on the food in the courtyard restaurant.

Pissoúri's **beach**, 3km below the village along a good but twisty road, is a lot longer (nearly 1km) than it appears from above, well protected and sandy, though somewhat blighted by jet-skis in peak season. (There is quieter and more commendable **windsurfer** rental through Surfcyprus, 🅦 www .surfcyprus.com.) You could do worse than base yourself here, though like the upper village the place has really taken off since the mid-1990s, with vast numbers of villa developments and hotel-apartments springing up along the paved road in. The wood-ceilinged *Kotzias Apartments* (℡25221014, ℻25222449; ❷, but usually monopolized by at least one UK package company) are attractively set in well-maintained gardens; if you really want to push the boat out, go for the well-run *Columbia Pissouri Beach* (℡25833333, 🅦 www .columbia-hotels.com; ❼), virtually on the sand and available through almost any UK tour operator. This comprises a conventional three-star hotel with a main wing and garden suites (offering more like four-star amenities), and a mock-traditional five-star bungalow complex of "resort suites" (C£275), about which nary a peep of complaint has been heard. Four or five bars and a like number of **restaurants** surround the central beachfront car park; favourites include the *Vine Leaf*, with floor shows on summer Fridays and a log fire in winter; the *Monte Beach* at the western end of the strand, with inexpensive lunches including a salad bar; and friendly *Pepis*, with high standards and vegetarian options.

## Pétra toú Romíou

Beyond Pissoúri, both motorway and old road run through desolate countryside until, just over the boundary in Páfos province, the imposing shoreline monolith of **Pétra toú Romíou** invariably prompts drivers to slam on their brakes at a strategic viewpoint and fish for the camera. Parking on the old B6 is on the uphill side of the road, with pedestrian access to the beach via an underpass; avoid the café-restaurant in the CTO souvenir pavilion just inland, which offers inexpensive, but almost inedible, snacks.

In legend this was the spot where Aphrodite, ancient patron goddess of Cyprus, emerged from the sea foam, though the formation actually takes its name (Rock of Romios) from the Byzantine folk-hero Dhiyenis Akritas, aka Romios, who used this and other boulders as missiles against pirates. A longish **beach** of pebbles and coarse sand extends to either side of the largest rock and its satellites, though it must be said that its popularity is due mostly to its mythic associations and ease of access; the high-speed traffic whizzing by just overhead hardly makes it alluring, though this blight has lessened slightly since the expressway opened a bit inland. Further local change is inevitable with impending new phases of the massive, ever-expanding *Aphrodite Hills* five-star resort and second-home project just inland, the largest such Cyprus has seen to date, complete with an 18-hole golf course and a "Beach Club" which encroaches on part of the shoreline near Pétra toú Romíou.

# Travel details

## Buses

Limassol to: Agrós (Mon–Sat 1 daily at 12.20pm with Agros Bus, from corner Enóseos and Irínis; 1hr); Kourion (Mon–Sat 3 daily on Episkopí village bus; 10am, 12.30pm, 1.30pm Mon–Fri, 10am, 11am, 1pm Sat; returns Mon–Sat 11.50am, 2.50pm, plus 4.50pm summer; 20min); Larnaca (Mon–Fri 4 daily, Sat 3 with Intercity; 1hr); Nicosia (Mon–Fri 10 daily, Sat & Sun 4, with LLL, Mon–Sat 1 daily with ALEPA; 1hr 15min); Páfos (Mon–Sat 1 daily with ALEPA; 1hr 15min); Plátres (Mon–Fri 1 daily at 9.30am with PEAL; 1hr 30min).

## Greek place names

| Old system | New system | Greek lettering |
| --- | --- | --- |
| Akapnoú | Akapnou | ΑΚΑΠΝΟΥ |
| Akrotíri | Akrotiri | ΑΚΡΩΤΗΡΙ |
| Aktí Kyvernítou (Governor's Beach) | Akti Kyvernitou | ΑΚΤΗ ΚΥΒΕΡΝΗΤΟΥ |
| Amathoúnda | Amathounta | ΑΜΑΘΟΥΝΤΑ |
| Amathus | Amathous | ΑΜΑΘΟΥΣ |
| Anóyira | Anogyra | ΑΝΩΓΥΡΑ |
| Aplóstra | Aplostra | ΑΠΛΩΣΤΡΑ |
| Arakapás | Arakapas | ΑΡΑΚΑΠΑΣ |
| Ársos | Arsos | ΑΡΣΟΣ |
| Áyiou Yeóryiou | Agios Georgiou | ΑΓΙΟΣ ΓΕΩΡΓΙΟΣ |
| Alamánou | Alamanou | ΑΛΑΜΑΝΟΥ |
| Ayíou Nikoláou ton Gáton | Agiou Nikolaou ton Gaton | ΑΓΙΟΥ ΝΙΚΟΛΑΟΥ ΤΩΝ ΓΑΤΩΝ |
| Dhorá | Dora | ΔΟΡΑ |
| Episkopí | Episkopi | ΕΠΙΣΚΟΠΗ |
| Eptagónia | Eptagoneia | ΕΠΤΑΓΩΝΕΙΑ |
| Evdhímou | Avdimou | ΑΥΔΗΜΟΥ |
| Kelláki | Kellaki | ΚΕΛΛΑΚΙ |
| Kiláni | Koilani | ΚΟΙΛΑΝΙ |
| Klonári | Klonari | ΚΛΩΝΑΡΙ |
| Kolossi | Kolossi | ΚΟΛΟΣΣΙ |
| Kourion (Curium) | Kourion | ΚΟΥΡΙΟΝ |
| Lánia | Laneia | ΛΑΝΝΕΙΑ |
| Limassol | Lemesos | ΛΕΜΕΣΟΣ |
| Lófou | Lofou | ΛΟΦΟΥ |
| Malliá | Malia | ΜΑΛΛΙΑ |
| Melíni | Melini | ΜΕΛΙΝΗ |
| Monágri | Monagri | ΜΟΝΑΓΡΙ |
| Moúsere | Mousere | ΜΟΥΣΕΡΕ |
| Odhoú | Odou | ΟΔΟΥ |
| Ómodhos | Omodos | ΟΜΟΔΟΣ |
| Panayía Amasgoú | Panayia Amasgou | ΠΑΝΑΓΙΑ ΑΜΑΣΓΟΥ |
| Pendákomo | Pentakomo | ΠΕΝΤΑΚΩΜΟ |
| Pétra toú Romíou | Petra tou Romiou | ΠΕΤΡΑ ΤΟΥ ΡΩΜΙΟΥ |
| Pissoúri | Pissouri | ΠΙΣΣΟΥΡΙ |
| Potamioú | Potamiou | ΠΟΤΑΜΙΟΥ |
| Potamós Yermasóyias | Potamos Germasogeias | ΠΟΤΑΜΟΣ ΓΕΡΜΑΣΟΓΕΙΑΣ |
| Profítis Ilías | Profitis Ilias | ΠΡΟΦΗΤΗΣ ΗΛΙΑΣ |
| Silíkou | Silikou | ΣΙΛΙΚΟΥ |
| Vássa | Vasa | ΒΑΣΑ |
| Víkla | Vikla | ΒΙΚΛΑ |
| Vouní | Vouni | ΒΟΥΝΙ |
| Yermasóyia | Germasogeia | ΓΕΡΜΑΣΟΓΕΙΑ |

# Páfos and the west

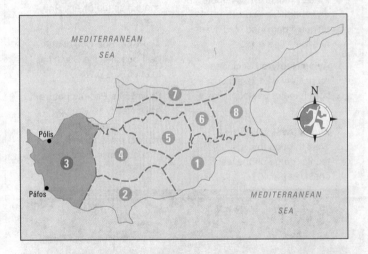

MEDITERRANEAN
SEA

Pólis

Páfos

MEDITERRANEAN
SEA

N

CHAPTER 3 # Highlights

**✳ Roman mosaics, Páfos**
These extensive Roman mosaics are some of the best in the eastern Mediterranean. See p.169

**✳ Tombs of the Kings, Páfos** A subterranean tomb complex carved from living rock. See p.172

**✳ Paleá Énklistra** This remote cave-hermitage boasts unique if damaged medieval frescoes. See p.183

**✳ Áyios Neófytos** Secluded monastery with its superb hermitage of St Neophytos. See p.185

**✳ Avgás (Avákas) gorge** Walk through this spectacular gorge on the west coast. See p.191

**✳ Lára Turtle Hatchery** On summer nights you may be able to witness turtles laying or hatching at the protection station at Lára. See p.192

**✳ Akámas peninsula** An uninhabited wilderness, popular with walkers, mountain bikers and (off its shores) scuba divers. See p.208

**✳ Asprókremos** One of the best beaches the South has to offer. See p.208

**✳ Stavrós tís Psókas nature trails** Nearly 1000m up in the mountains, these marked paths thread through dense, cool forest. See p.219

△ Pólis Khrysokhoú Bay, Akámas

# Páfos and the west

Since Cyprus passed out of Byzantine control late in the twelfth century, the western end of the island has traditionally been its most remote and least-developed region. Following the Ottoman conquest, the district of Páfos also became the most Turkified part of the island, with close to a third of the population being Turkish Cypriot before the events of 1974. These conditions inevitably had a profound effect on local customs and speech, with the accent and dialect of both communities strongly influencing each other – and becoming all but incomprehensible to outsiders. Another result of the area's relative isolation was the Greek community's retention of a large vocabulary of Homeric Greek, a heritage of the original Mycenaean colonization that further complicated the linguistic profile. Other Cypriots labelled the Pafiots as backward, mongrel bumpkins and told (and still tell) scurrilous jokes about them; the Pafiots retorted that this was simply jealousy at work, since they were more intelligent than the other islanders. With the departure of the Turkish commmunity in 1975, and the opening of Páfos international airport in 1983, local idiosyncrasies have inevitably diminished, and the level of touristic development is rapidly approaching that of the other coastal districts. But big chunks of the region are still exhilaratingly wild, its villages characterful, and the beaches arguably the best in the South. Towards off-islanders the Pafiots continue to display an extroverted bluntness, which might cause offence if you didn't realize they generally mean well.

The district capital of **Páfos** is showing all the signs of too-rapid growth, but it still makes for a comfortable overnight stay and has much to offer in the way of antiquities and dining opportunities. Strike out in any direction from Páfos and rolling, well-tended hills and deep river valleys provide relief from the occasional tattiness of the town, as do the tantalizing ruins of its ancient predecessor **Palea Paphos** and the middle- and late-Byzantine monuments at **Yeroskípou**, **Émba**, the **monastery of Áyios Neófytos** and the cave-church of **Paleá Énklistra**.

Northwest of Páfos, the **coast** is surprisingly deserted once past the last gasp of resort and villa development; the beaches leading up to the **Lára** area, itself protected, remain the focus of battles between developers and conservationists, the latter steadily losing ground as the former buy up every scrap of available private land. The recent growth of tourism, both short-term and residential, on the coast has halted the depopulation of the closer hill villages, but chances of traditional livelihoods surviving in the remoter settlements are pretty slim, especially when selling up your marginal fields will get you more income than thirty years of goat-grazing. Accordingly, the rural areas are favourite

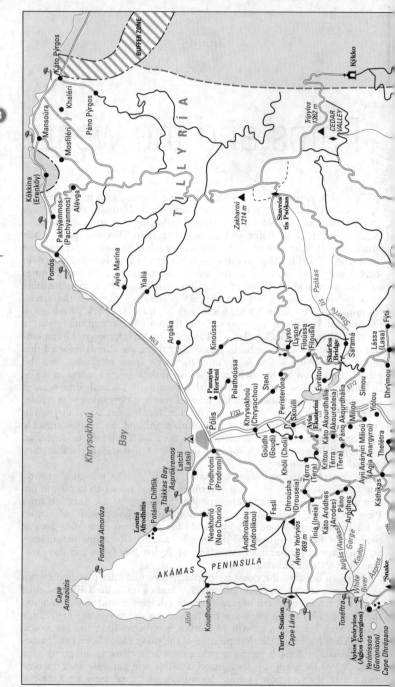

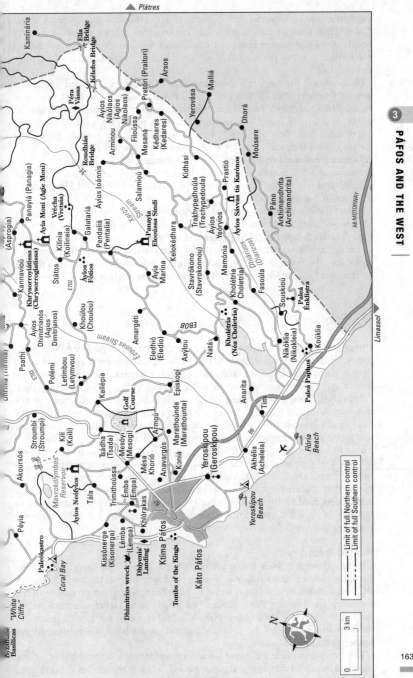

▲ Plátres

Kamináiria

Elia Bridge
Kélefos Bridge

Péra Vássa

Pretóri (Praitori)

Ársos

Áyios Nikólaos (Agios Nikolaos)

Arminou

Roudhiás Bridge

Filoússa

Mesaná

Kédhares (Kedares)

Yerovása

Malliá

Dhorá

Moúsere

Panayiá (Panagia)

Ayia Moní (Agiá Moní)

Vrécha (Vretsia)

Áyios Ioánnis

Salamioú

Kídhasi

Páno Arkhimandhrita (Archimandrita)

A6 MOTORWAY

Kannavioú

Khrysorroyiátissa (Chrysorrogiatissa)

Galatariá

Kilínia (Kilineia)

Pendaliá (Pentalia)

Panayia Eleoússa Sindi

Trakhypedhoúla (Trachypedoula)

Áyios Yeóryios

Áyios Sávvas tis Karónos

(Asprogia)

Státos

Áyios Fótios

Ayiá Marína

Stavrókono (Stavrokonnou)

Mamónia

Kholétria (Choletria)

Fasoúla

Souskioú

Paleá Énklistra

Áyios Dhimítrios (Agios Dimitrianos)

Khoúlou (Choulou)

Amargéti

Eledhió (Eledio)

Axýlou

Natá

Kholétria (Néa Choletria)

Nikóklia (Nikokleia)

Koúklia

Paleá Páphos

Limassol

Psathí

Polémi

Letímbou (Letymvou)

Kallépia

Kelokédhara

Xerós Stream

Mesógi (Mesogi)

Ármoú

Marathoúnda (Marathounta)

Anavargós

Episkopí

Anaríta

Timí

Tímí

Akoursós

Stroúmbi (Stroumpi)

Kilí (Koili)

Tsádha (Tsada)

Mésa Khorió

Koniá

Yeroskípou (Geroskipou)

Akhélia (Achelia)

Mavrokólymbos Reservoir

Áyios Neófytos

Trimithoússa

Émba (Empa)

Fióría Beach

Péyia

Kissónerga (Kisonerga)

Lémba (Lempa)

Khlórakas

Paleókastro

Ktíma Páfos

Coral Bay

Dhimítrios wreck
Dhiyenís' Landing

Káto Páfos

Tombs of the Kings

Yeroskípou Beach

"White Cliffs"

Byzantine Basilicas

163

N

0 ————— 3 km

– – – Limit of full Northern control
– · – · Limit of full Southern control

targets for foreign second-home hunters, and it's estimated that there are about 17,000 Brits resident full- or part-time in the entire district, as well as a nearly equal number of eastern European immigrants, legal or illegal – an astonishing proportion in a total population of just over 70,000, a figure itself doubled since the late 1990s.

Head towards the northerly shore lapped by Khrysokhoú Bay, and – for a few years yet anyway – you're seemingly on a different island. The district's second town, **Pólis** provides a peaceful retreat, with uncluttered beaches stretching in either direction, though the coast to the west in particular is finally succumbing to large-scale development. Pólis and surrounding resorts make good bases for jeep, boat, mountain-bike or foot explorations along the rugged tip of the **Akámas peninsula** to the west – thinly vegetated, slashed by ravines, and (so far unsuccessfully) proposed as the South's only national park. This almost uninhabited area can be reached from the large villages of **Péyia** and **Dhroúsha** at the base of the peninsula.

East of the main road lies some of the emptiest country on Cyprus, essentially abandoned after 1974 or reduced to a backwater by the proximity of the Attila Line. The landscape becomes gentler and the pace of life slower in the villages en route to the showcase monastery of **Khrysorroyiátissa**, but there's still scope for adventure (and good hiking) in the uninhabited forests of **Tillyría**, or the equally isolated **Xeró** and **Dhiárizos river valleys**.

# Páfos

Perhaps the most noteworthy feature of the district capital **PÁFOS** is its layout. Two distinct settlements – the harbour, archeological zone and hotel strip at **Káto Páfos**, and the true town centre of **Ktíma**, 3km up the hill – are jointly and confusingly referred to as Néa (New) Páfos, to distinguish it from Palea (Old) Paphos, now by the village of Koúklia, 16km to the east. For the moment, Káto and Ktíma together still form a fairly pleasant provincial capital of around forty-five thousand permanent inhabitants, but the upper town, first settled by the Byzantines as a haven from coastal attacks, seems in danger of losing its separate identity, as the blank spaces between it and the lower resort area are being steadily filled in by ready-mix concrete lorries and their highrise offspring. Development, frankly, has got out of hand; the only bright spot of the inconvenient excavations and traffic diversions – which continue as a new access road to the airport is built – was the discovery of a considerable quantity of buried Roman and Hellenistic antiquities, which should eventually find their way into the archeological museum.

## Some history

The foundations of **Néa Páfos** are obscure; in legend Agapenor, leader of the Arcadian contingent to Troy, was shipwrecked near here in the twelfth century BC and decided to stay. But it seems to have been only a minor annexe to the sanctuary and town at Palea Páphos (see p.181) until Hellenistic times, when the last independent Pafiot king, **Nikoklis**, laid out a proper city. Its perimeter walls enclosed much of the headland behind the harbour, which shipped out timber from the hill-forests.

The Ptolemies made Páfos the island's rather decadent administrative centre, which it remained during the Roman period, when it rejoiced in the pompous title of **Augusta Claudia Flavia Paphos**. Cicero was proconsul here for two years, as was one **Sergius Paulus**, the first recorded official convert to Christianity, at the behest of apostles Paul and Barnabas. Acts 13: 6–12 records the event, and verse 9 is in fact the first time that Paul is referred to as such (rather than as Saul of Tarsus). A Jewish sorcerer named Elymas attempted to distract the proconsul, at which Paul temporarily blinded Elymas. Sergius Paulus was so impressed that he embraced the True Faith forthwith. Despite this success, Paul seems to have had a hard time combating Aphrodite's love-cult here, and was reputedly scourged for his trouble on the site of the Byzantine basilica.

Successive earthquakes, including two in the fourth century, relegated Páfos to the status of a backwater, and the Cypriot capital reverted to Salamis (Constantia), though Páfos was designated – and has since remained – an important bishopric. The **Arab raids** of the seventh century completed the process of desolation, however, and for more than a millennium afterwards visitors were unanimous in characterizing the shabby port as a hole – that is, if they were lucky enough to survive its endemic diseases and write about it.

Under **British administration** Páfos's fortunes perked up: the harbour was dredged and the population began to climb from a low point of less than two thousand to about nine thousand at independence. During the late 1950s, when Páfos district was a hotbed of EOKA activity, the British ran a major interrogation and confinement centre in the town. But when in 1974 **Archbishop Makarios** took refuge here following the EOKA-B coup, it was the British who saved his bacon by airlifting him out by helicopter to the Akrotíri air base, and thence into exile.

## Arrival and information

There is no bus service to or from the **airport**, 15km southeast of Káto Páfos, but taxi fares shouldn't be more than C£10 to Ktíma, perhaps C£12 to Káto Páfos; strenuously resist those drivers who demand C£15–20. Facilities in the arrivals lounge include three or four relatively pricey car-rental booths, a part-time tourist information booth, a bank ATM and a money-exchange counter. (There are no banking facilities in the big, shiny departures hall.) However, Páfos airport is set to undergo further expansion, specifically the addition of a second terminal, between now and 2007, so you can expect changes in layout and amenities.

---

### Municipal bus services

Near the main car park and old market in Ktíma is the central stop for ALEPA **municipal bus services** (fares C£0.60–70 depending on destination), with several useful lines along the main drags: Káto Páfos and Ktíma (often cited as "Agorá" on bus schedules) are linked during daylight hours by bus #11, which plies Leofóros Apostólou Pávlou, connecting the two districts, and Posidhónos, the shorefront road of Káto's southerly hotel ghetto. The #10 bus – which actually stops down in the car park – goes further afield, diverging from Apostólou Pávlou at Leofóros Táfon tón Vasiléon and heading out past the northwesterly resort strip en route to Coral Bay; the #10A variant includes Áyios Yeóryios several times daily in summer; the #15 plies a similar route to the #10 every 15–20min, beginning from Yeroskípou beach, and unusually offers evening service until 11pm from May until November.

Other numbered ALEPA routes to the **suburb villages** of Yeroskípou, Khlórakas, Lémba, Kissónerga, Émba, Tála, Péyia, Tsádha, Kónia, Mesóyi and Trimithoússa begin at the Karavélla parking lot off Andhréa Yeroúdhi in Ktíma. Ask at the central kiosk here for your bus, as they tend not to have their route numbers or destinations prominently displayed.

Long-distance **buses** and **service taxis** arrive at the points detailed on our Ktíma Páfos map (and see "Listings"). **Driving** into Káto Páfos, you'll probably end up in the enormous, free, paved lot behind the waterfront – nominally an archeological site – or the dirt lot immediately behind this; in high season the narrow streets of the hotel "ghetto" will be out of the question (unless you're booked into accommodation with parking space). Up in Ktíma you're best off using the enormous free car park at the foot of the bluff on which the bazaar and old Turkish quarter of Moúttalos are built.

Páfos's **tourist information office** (Mon–Fri 8.15am–2.30pm, Sat 8.15am–1.30pm, plus Mon, Tues, Thurs & Fri 3–6.15pm), which has a fairly complete stock of maps and handouts, can be found in Ktíma on Pávlou Melá. The street is still cited as Gládstonos on many maps and is home to various other tourist services such as estate and travel agencies.

## Accommodation

Páfos, upper and lower, has outstripped Limassol as the South's second-largest resort and there are now nearly 20,000 guest beds available. However, since the recent wave of gentrification and development, little decent accommodation remains, especially in Káto Páfos, that is not part of the pre-booked package scene. Many of the places below are no exception, but at least are used to being approached individually.

### Káto Páfos

**Alexander the Great** Leofóros Posidhónos ℡ 26965000, ⓕ 26965100, ⓔ alexander1@cytanet .com.cy. Four-star resort with a prime setting just above a semi-natural beach (and incorporating an archeological site) in the heart of the tourist strip; all the expected facilities including a conservatory pool, and available through most package operators. **❼**

**Annabelle** Near northwest end of Leofóros Posidhónos, seaward side ℡ 26938333, ⓦ www .thanoshotels.com. Páfos' most established five-star option, looking to the sea over exotic water-gardens (including a "swim-in" grotto). Several on-site restaurants, a spa, a gym and a range of rooms from standard to family studios complete the picture. Discounts often available. **❾**

**Apollo** Ayíou Lambrianoú, just off Apostólou Pávlou ℡ 26933909, ⓕ 26937174, ⓔ eleonora112@hotmail.com. Intriguing fake stone-ruin decor at this small, quiet two-star hotel, used to British birding groups, and with a view of the lighthouse from its rear rooms and pool area; closed in winter. **❸**

**Paphian Bay** Leofóros Posidhónos, 3km south-east of central Káto Páfos, near Yeroskípou Beach ℡ 26964333, ⓦ www.paphian-cbh .com. Well-priced three-star, a bit remote but quiet, attractively landscaped and set on a well-groomed patch of natural beach. Good for families, as lots of childrens' activities and areas are provided. **❻**

**Pioneer Beach** Leofóros Posidhónos, 3km south-east of central Káto Páfos ℡ 26964500, ⓦ www .pioneer-cbh.com. The beach of the name is okay, but the big pluses here are a lush garden setting and the fact that this four-star outfit is now adults-only (over age 16). **❼**

**Porto Paphos** Northwest end of Leofóros Posidhónos ℡ 26942333, ⓦ www.portopaphos .com. Simple, clean, excellent-value three-star hotel, renovated in 2003, with pleasant pool area, unbeatable harbour views and good breakfasts. **❺**

### Ktíma Páfos

**Agapinor** Nikodhímou Mylona 24–28 ℡ 26933926, ⓦ www.agapinorhotel.com.cy. The best standard available in the upper town at this 2001-renovated, smallish three-star with large pool, on-site restaurant/coffee shop, non-smokers' rooms and dedicated secure parking – plus knock-out views as long as you get a room on the escarpment side. **❺**

**Axiothea** Ívis Malióti 2, a stair-street off Apostólou Pávlou ℡ 26232866, ⓕ 26245790. Strategically located on Moussalás hill, the ancient acropolis, the bar/breakfast lounge and terrace of this congenially run two-star hotel have unbeatable views over the town and coast. The rooms themselves are on the small side, and furnished to a higher standard in the preferable new wing. **❸**

**Kinyras** Arkhiepiskópou Makaríou 91 ℡ 26941604, ⓦ www.kiniras.cy.net. The town's finest surviving restoration inn, seven of whose high-ceilinged rooms have balconies – all have fridges, air con and clock radios. There's a well-regarded courtyard restaurant on the ground floor, where breakfast (included in rates) is served. Gets some German packages, but walk-ins welcome. ❹

**New Olympus** Výronos 12 ☎ 26932020, ⓦ www.newolympus.co.cy. This unmistakable three-storey Art-Deco/Neoclassical hybrid, the first (1953) hotel built in Páfos, has an exceptionally quiet location at the east edge of town, with spacious ground-floor common areas (including restaurant), a pleasant pool-garden and easy parking. The energetic management plans to upgrade the frankly anachronistic rooms, which have already been provided with air con. It's popular with walking groups, and packed lunches are available. ❸

## Káto Páfos

The main resort strip in **Káto Páfos**, east of Apostólou Pávlou and the harbour, consists of opticians, estate agents, ice-cream parlours, fast-food franchises, more estate agents, indistinguishable restaurants, nightclubs, still more estate agents, clothes shops, souvenir kiosks, banks and travel agencies, the characterless pattern repeating itself every couple of hundred metres along **Leofóros Posidhónos**, the shoreline boulevard. It's a fairly lacklustre sequence, the only "sight" being the **Paphos Aquarium**, at Artemídhos 1 (daily 9am–7pm; C£3.50 adults, C£2 children, or C£10 family ticket) with numerous tanks containing sea creatures (including a few alligators), plus an on-site snack bar.

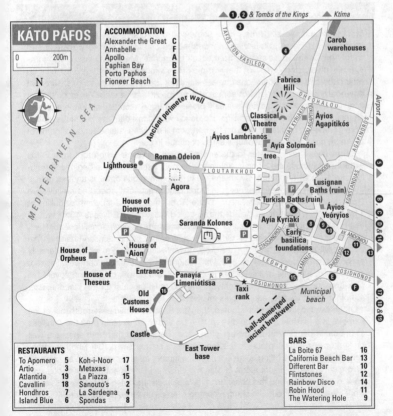

**KÁTO PÁFOS**

0  200m

N

MEDITERRANEAN SEA

**ACCOMMODATION**

| | |
|---|---|
| Alexander the Great | C |
| Annabelle | F |
| Apollo | A |
| Paphian Bay | B |
| Porto Paphos | E |
| Pioneer Beach | D |

& Tombs of the Kings    Ktíma

Carob warehouses

Fabrica Hill

Ancient perimeter wall

Classical Theatre

Áyios Agapitikós

Áyios Lambrianós

Ayía Solomóni

tree

Lighthouse

Roman Odeion

PLOUTARKHOU

Agora

Lusignan Baths (ruin)

Turkish Baths (ruin)

House of Dionysos

Saranda Kolones

Ayía Kyriakí

Áyios Yeóryios

Early basilica foundations

House of Orpheus

House of Aion

Entrance

House of Theseus

Panayía Limeniótissa

Old Customs House

Taxi rank

POSIDHONOS

Municipal beach

half-submerged ancient breakwater

LEDHAS

Castle

East Tower base

**RESTAURANTS**

| | | | |
|---|---|---|---|
| To Apomero | 5 | Koh-i-Noor | 17 |
| Artio | 3 | Metaxas | 1 |
| Atlantida | 19 | La Piazza | 15 |
| Cavallini | 18 | Sanouto's | 2 |
| Hondhros | 7 | La Sardegna | 4 |
| Island Blue | 6 | Spondas | 8 |

**BARS**

| | |
|---|---|
| La Boite 67 | 16 |
| California Beach Bar | 13 |
| Different Bar | 10 |
| Flintstones | 12 |
| Rainbow Disco | 14 |
| Robin Hood | 11 |
| The Watering Hole | 9 |

However, much the best place to begin a tour of the lower town is the **harbour**, near which are found traces of the ancient and medieval town, as so often in Cyprus placed cheek-by-jowl or converted for use by later occupiers. The harbour-mouth **castle** and its inland counterpart **Saránda Kolónes** are originally Lusignan, while the early churches of **Ayía Kyriakí** and **Ayía Solomóni** both show signs of previous use, and the Hellenistic **Tombs of the Kings** eventually saw service as Christian catacombs. But the glory of Káto Páfos, and the chief motive for a visit if you're not actually staying here, is the series of **Roman mosaics** found northwest of the harbour; having been buried and forgotten over centuries, they were never subsequently modified or adapted.

Local **beaches** extend east of the little port, fronting the row of resort hotels which has sprung up since 1983. They are serviceable at best and, like the municipal beach at the east edge of our map, have to be artificially supplemented with sand from elsewhere.

### The harbour and castle

The **harbour** area was "improved" during the early 1990s, with the quay pedestrianized and the old customs house restored. However, it seems the

## Scuba diving off Páfos

Most four- and five-star hotels have some sort of in house dive school, but Páfos harbour is still home to a few independent scuba operators. In theory, there are up to fifty **dive sites**, near and far, from which to choose. Many are classed as morning-only dives, since much of the year prevailing winds from the southwest pick up after noon and make conditions unpleasant, if not downright nauseating; ensure that any boat you're boarding is of sufficient size, ideally with a stabilizer or prominent keel. Obviously dive sites are jealously preserved trade secrets, with preferred ones changing from season to season in accordance with storm damage, oversubscription from competing outfits, or divemaster boredom. Following is a selection of some of the more common destinations, likely to continue in use.

**Shore dives**, with transfer to the site by transit van (or even on foot from Páfos waterfront), include the Roman Wall in the harbour itself, the usual beginners' training site at under 6m depth. Cynthiana, near the eponymous hotel, is another novice favourite (10m); Moray Cove, north of Coral Bay, is especially good as a night dive (15m depth); while The Maze, near "White River" beach, is a labyrinth of gullies at 11m maximum. **Boat dives** include the so-called Valley of the Caves (9–15m), though this is rather underwhelming as the grottoes barely rate as overhangs; Janchor Reef, a popular morning dive with an old anchor and (often) groupers seen near the 27m bottom; Mismaloyia, a "reef" (gentle drop, no real wall) at 26–32m for the moderately experienced, where amberjack and (with luck) loggerhead turtles can be glimpsed; and Manijin, a classic multilevel site (6–22m) with a drop-off, caves (one covered in pink-and-purple algae) and an archway. The sea must be calm for this last one, as a 40-minute boat transfer each way is involved.

Of the two local **wreck** dives touted, the *Vera K,* some 25min east-southeast of the harbour, is a feasible afternoon dive at 10–11m and more exciting than the *Achilleas* at the same depth west-southwest of the port; be advised that both ships are well broken-up and can't compare to the *Zenobia* near Larnaca (see p.104). Another potential wreck dive in the offing is the *Dhimitrios*, a lumber freighter which ran aground off Khlórakas during a violent storm in March 1998. It is in imminent danger of breaking up and spilling oil along this coast; local dive schools are trying to get permission to work it free, pump it out and scuttle it properly as an underwater attraction.

refurbishing will not continue, as the local authorities refuse to co-operate with the CTO, which was behind the plan. For now, the quay esplanade consists of a half-dozen indifferent patisseries and tavernas, trading largely on their position. On the waterfront, **cruises** in glass-bottomed boats are on offer according to demand: reckon on paying C£5 for a short hop to a wreck, C£10 up to Lára Bay, or C£18 all the way around the Akámas peninsula. Keep a beady eye out, however, for the weather, especially on the so-called "fishing trips" – departing in choppy seas is an expensive way of seeing your breakfast again.

The foundations of the Byzantine church of **Panayía Limeniótissa**, destroyed like so much else during the seventh century, can be seen a few paces inland from the esplanade; the Danish crusader Eric the Good, one of many who died here, was supposedly buried inside the ruins.

The diminutive **castle** (daily 9am–5pm; till 6pm in summer; C£0.75) guarding the harbour entrance is reached by a small stone bridge across a narrow moat. You can climb up to the roof for unrivalled views over the port and town, though the building itself is currently empty – it's the occasional venue for events like the early September opera evenings during the Pafos Aphrodite festival. The existing structure is merely the reworked western tower of a much larger Lusignan castle dating from 1391, which the Venetians demolished nearly a century later. The stump base of the easterly tower is still visible about seventy metres along the modern mole, itself pointing towards the ancient breakwater, now half submerged. The Ottomans repaired what was of use to them in 1592; the ground floor served as their dungeons, which the British used as a salt warehouse till 1935.

## The Paphos mosaics

Whatever else happens in Páfos, the entire headland between the harbour and the lighthouse will remain open space, as it's suspected that as much archeological wealth lies buried as has so far come to light. The most spectacular finds unearthed to date are the **Roman mosaics** (daily: June–Aug 8am–7.30pm; Sept–May 8am–5pm; C£1.50), discovered accidentally by a ploughing farmer in 1962. Subsequent Cypriot and Polish excavations revealed an extensive complex of Roman buildings fitted with exquisite floor mosaics, showing episodes from ancient mythology and considered among the best in the eastern Mediterranean. Nowhere is the wealth and opulence of imperial Roman Paphos better suggested than in these vivid floorings, new stretches of which seem to be discovered every few years. Mosaics have always been an expensive medium, far more so than frescoes, requiring not just the retainer of master craftsmen and several assistants, but often the application of gold leaf as well as paint to the tiny glass cubes or tesserae which make up the images. (Other, less costly, tesserae were chipped from stones of the appropriate colour.) Modern shelters protecting many of the mosaics are naturally lit and provided with catwalks for viewing – though often the colours are far from dazzling, since the tesserae are not kept polished as they were when new.

### The House of Dionysos

The largest building in the mosaics complex, next to the ticket booth, is the **House of Dionysos**, so called because of repeated representations of the god, and probably built in the late second or early third century AD as the villa of a wealthy merchant. However, a much earlier Hellenistic pebble-mosaic, showing the monster Scylla, has been relocated to a previously undecorated floor, and is the first thing you see on entering. Towards the rear of the building Zeus as an eagle abducts Ganymede, while Dionysos frolics with Ariadne, attended by Cupid and a hunting dog.

But the most famous panels ring the main atrium, on the west side of which Apollo pursues Daphne, while her father the river-god Peneios reclines below; in a nearby panel Poseidon chases after the nymph Amymone with more success, as evidenced by Cupid hovering over the sea-god's quarry. The *Triumph of Dionysos*, with the god riding in a chariot pulled by two she-leopards and flanked by satyrs, slaves and bacchantes, reflects the decadence of the Roman town.

Another long panel shows first Dionysos proffering a bunch of grapes to the nymph Akme – as her name implies, the personification of perfection (in this case a good vintage); next is King Ikarios, legendary first manufacturer of wine, with a bullock-drawn cart of the new elixir; and on the far right, two lolling, inebriated shepherds are rather redundantly labelled "The First Wine-Drinkers". The First Piss-Up apparently ended badly – in the unshown sequel, friends of the shepherds, thinking them poisoned, murdered Ikarios. Left of this group the tragedy of Pyramus and Thisbe unfolds, the lion escaping with Thisbe's mantle, and Pyramus shown erroneously as the god of the eponymous river in Anatolia.

Around the other three sides of this atrium, there is fine animal detail in a series of hunting scenes; elsewhere a peacock dominates the central square of one of several excellent geometrical floors. At the edge of several panels, including that of the Four Seasons personified (near the entrance), visitors are exhorted to "Rejoice" (*Khairei*), presumably with liberal quantities of wine – from these inscriptions it's deduced that these panels formed the floor of a banqueting hall or a reception room.

## The House of Aion

In the **House of Aion**, uncovered in 1983, the mosaics are later (mid-fourth century) and more sophisticated in theme and execution. In the lower right panel, Apollo sentences the silenus Marsyas, who dared challenge him to a musical contest, to be flayed. In the next scene above, the result of a beauty contest between Cassiopeia and several nereids is depicted; the latter, the losers, ride sulkily away on an assortment of sea monsters. Still on the right, the topmost frame shows Hermes offering baby Dionysos to the centaur Tropheus for rearing, surrounded by nymphs preparing a bath. The left-hand scenes are less intact; of the god Aion, from whom the building takes its name, only the head is visible, and a version of Leda preparing to meet the swan is somewhat damaged. Except for the statue niche in the west wall, the building itself is a purpose-built reconstruction, though of old masonry.

## The House of Theseus

The next precinct, the unroofed **House of Theseus**, takes its name from a round mosaic of coarse tesserae that portrays Theseus brandishing a club against the (vanished) Minotaur, while Ariadne and personifications of Crete and the Labyrinth look on. In the next area west, a very late (fifth-century) mosaic, *The First Bath of Achilles*, is shown: a nursemaid carries him firmly in the presence of the three Fates and his parents. Its arrangement strongly prefigures the iconography of early Christian portrayals of the Nativity, wherein the Virgin reclines in the same way as the nymph Thetis, and the three Magi replace the Fates. It is speculated that this building, or a vanished adjacent one, was the location of Sergius Paulus's interviews with the apostles.

## The House of Orpheus and House of the Four Seasons

Sheltering by the sea under a temporary tent at the west edge of the archeological zone, the **House of Orpheus** features Orpheus charming a naturalistic bestiary with his lyre, in an exceptionally large floor panel. A smaller panel shows a naked Hercules about to strangle the charging lion of Nemea with his bare hands.

The **House of the Four Seasons**, a relatively new area discovered early in 1992, was provisionally named after personifications of the seasons, though only Autumn has survived. Most of the images in what was evidently another sumptuous mansion are engagingly realistic hunting scenes: a tiger claws the haunches of a wild ass, and a hunter faces off with a marauding lion, while a deer runs away from the melee. On the floor of what was possibly the banqueting hall are more animal portraits, including a dog chasing a hare, and a goat shown, unusually, full-face – in both pagan and Christian mosaic and fresco imagery, animals are usually depicted only in profile (later to be joined by non-Christians and the wicked), with the frontal view reserved for humans.

## The Roman odeion

From the northerly access path to the mosaics, a short lane leads up to the **Roman odeion** (gate open dawn to dusk; included in mosaics admission fee), a workmanlike 1970s restoration of the theatre and not very compelling except during the July/August ancient drama evenings. Just south of the contemporary agora, beyond the stage to the east, extensive ancient building foundations await excavation. From the odeion a pedestrians-only dirt track leads west to the picturesque **lighthouse**, beyond which are the most intact stretches of the city's **perimeter wall**.

## Saránda Kolónes

Just north of the exit road from the municipal car park, the fortress of **Saránda Kolónes**, signposted as Byzantine, is actually a Lusignan structure built atop its predecessor (same hours as mosaics; included in fee). Almost as soon as it was completed, it was destroyed by an earth tremor in 1222, and until excavation (1957–1983) the only objects visible above ground here were numerous tumbled columns – hence the Greek name which means "Forty Columns".

It's still a confusing jumble of moat-ringed masonry. Some well-worn latrines, near the remaining arches, are the only obvious items – they were fitted with doors, in deference to Christian modesty. The pavement is riddled with sewer tunnels, vaults and stables, some interconnecting and offering rather claustrophobic scrambling (strictly at your own risk). For a supposed stronghold, an improbable number of sally ports fitted with stairs breach the roughly square walls. The ramparts were originally entered by a gateway on the east, and sported eight mismatched towers.

## Ayía Kyriakí (Khrysopolítissa)

Crossing busy Apostólou Pávlou, pedestrianized Stassándhrou leads directly to **Ayía Kyriakí (Khrysopolítissa)**. This late (eleventh- or twelfth-century) Byzantine church, with a later belfry, is dwarfed by the vast foundations of an earlier, seven-aisled basilica and an archiepiscopal palace, both destroyed by the all-scouring Arab raids. What's left are extensive fourth-century floor mosaics, mostly geometric, and a scattering of probably contemporary columns, including one dubbed "St Paul's Pillar" after the apocryphal tradition that the apostle was tied to it and scourged.

Though still being excavated, much of the fourth-century zone, considerably below modern ground level, is now open to close-up viewing. Highlights include a **figural mosaic** of a brimming wine *krater* accompanied by an inscription: "Wisdom Inside This (Vessel)" – not, as in the pagan villas, an exhortation to drunkenness, but part of a series of allegories in this vehemently Christian terrain. Nearby panels show a deer (today with its head missing) drinking under the remains of the opening to Psalm 42: "As the hart panteth after the springs of water, so panteth my soul after thee, O Lord...", and, just above some grape clusters, the intact inscription "I am the True Vine" (John 15: 1).

A catwalk gives access to Ayía Kyriakí itself. The small **church** is bare of any decoration inside, and was ceded early during the 1990s by the Orthodox bishop of Páfos to the Catholic and Anglican expatriate communities for their use – perhaps the first time that heterodox rites have been celebrated here since the Lusignans displaced the Orthodox with a Catholic diocese in 1220. To the north are scattered the domed Ottoman baths and the Lusignan baths, which the Turks heavily modified, as well as a Byzantine church converted to a mosque and a tiny, cottage-like modern mosque used by local Turks until 1975.

### Ayía Solomóni catacombs and Fabrica Hill

Ayía Kyriakí lies near the easternmost circuit of ancient walls, and other points of historical interest lie up Apostólou Pávlou. The **catacombs of Ayía Solomóni**, just east of the pavement, are overshadowed by a huge **terebinth tree** festooned with knotted-together votive rags or kerchiefs, a practice common to both Christians and Muslims throughout the Middle East and similar in efficacy to the prayer flags of the Buddhists. Steps lead down to a multi-chambered, sunken sanctuary honouring one of those obscure, weirdly named saints in which Cyprus seems to specialize – in this case a Jewish woman whose seven children were martyred by one of the Seleucid kings of Palestine. It's thought that the subterranean complex was once the synagogue of Roman Paphos, and doubtless a pagan shrine before that. The frescoes in the small chapel are a mess, first vandalized by the Crusaders; more curious is a sacred well, accessed by a separate flight of stairs, with water so clear that you'll step into it unintentionally even though you've been warned. Just up Apostólou Pávlou is the similar catacomb-shrine of **Áyios Lambrianós**.

The rock outcrop just north, known as **Fabrica Hill**, contains more tunnelled-out tombs and churches, including those of Áyios Agapitikós and Áyios Misitikós. These two shrines honour saints even more shadowy than usual, and pointedly unrecognized by the Orthodox Church. According to legend, dust gathered from the floor of the former can be used as a love charm (*agápi* means "love" in Greek), but from the latter has the opposite effect (*misós* means "hate"): useful magic that presumably ensures the saints' long-running veneration. Ongoing Australian excavations since 1995 on the south slope of Fabrica hill have uncovered almost the entire extent of a **Classical theatre** – hacked, like everything else here, out of the living rock, and bidding to rank as the largest on the island, even bigger than the one at Salamis.

## The Tombs of the Kings

From the vicinity of Fabrica Hill, a well-signed major road, Leofóros Táfon tón Vasiléon, leads 2km northwest to the so-called **Tombs of the Kings** (daily: summer 8.30am–7.30pm; winter 8am–5pm; C£0.75). Rock outcrops near the shore – called *Paleokástra* ("Old Citadels") for their similarity to castles – conceal dozens of tombs hacked out of the soft strata, since this was a permissible distance outside the city walls for a necropolis. There's no evidence of royal use, merely that of the local privileged classes, starting in the third century BC. Their design, curiously, is not strictly indigenous but heavily indebted to Macedonian proto-types, passed on from Alexander's legions to the Ptolemies who ruled Cyprus.

△ Tombs of the Kings

Eight complexes of tombs are singled out for you by number (nos. 3, 4 and 8 are the most elaborate), and include several reached by stairs down to sunken courts, ringed by peristyles of rough square, or round fluted, Doric columns carved from the living rock. Beyond the colonnades, passages lead to rooms with alcoves or niches provided for each corpse. At anniversaries of the death of the deceased, relatives would troop out to the tomb for a *nekródhipno* or ceremonial meal, with the leftovers deposited near the actual sepulchre; variants of this custom still prevail in Greek Orthodox observance. Carved crosses and traces of fresco pigment in a few tombs suggest their use as catacombs in early Christian times. Later they were systematically looted (have no fear of encountering skeletons, or hopes of artefacts) and scholarly excavations only began in 1977. Today it's still an eerie place, the drumming of the distant sea and chirps of nesting birds the only sounds.

## Ktíma Páfos

Looking down from the edge of the escarpment on which **Ktíma Páfos** is built, you can appreciate the Byzantines' defensive reasoning: it's nearly a sixty-metre drop to the coastal plain, with the harbour castle assuming toy-like dimensions at this distance. The main thoroughfares of Pávlou Melá and Pallikarídhi subdivide the upper town: to the east lies a cantonment of broader avenues containing the courts, police station, archbishop's house, various schools with their grand Neoclassical façades, the municipal gardens, tourist facilities and **museums**, while on the west the more vernacular neighbourhood forms a warren of narrower, denser gridded streets encompassing the bazaar and the old Turkish quarter of **Moúttalos**.

### The bazaar and Moúttalos

Heading west on Agorás, the continuation of Makaríou, you quickly reach a relatively ornate, early-twentieth-century building – the **covered market**, where a selection of local souvenirs has almost entirely pushed out vendors of fresh produce. South of this, over the edge of the palisade, you'll spy a medieval **"Turkish" hamam** down by the car park, restored early in the 1990s but kept firmly locked; in fact it appears to have originally been a Latin, or even Byzantine church before its use as a bath-house, which only ended during the communal troubles of the 1960s.

Further northwest lie the narrow alleys of the former Turkish quarter of **Moúttalos** – before 1974 this was a guarded enclave, with many refugees from outlying Pafiot villages. The sole architectural monument here is the **Cami Kebir** or "Great Mosque" (always closed), once the Byzantine church of Ayía Sofía and still a handsome building.

Finally, near the end of the clifftop neighbourhood, where the original street signs in Turkish still survive, there's a *platía* flanked with kebab houses and clubs used by the locals, all Greek refugees from the North. After the often conspicuous wealth of urban Greek Cyprus, the meanness of the bungalows here may come as a shock – you are not merely looking back nearly forty years in time, but also at the consequences of both a TMT-enforced prohibition on doing business with Greek Cypriots, and retaliatory government measures against the enclaves, whereby a long list of materials deemed "militarily strategic" were forbidden to be brought in.

### The museums

The southeastern cantonment of Ktíma is home to the three most important museums of Páfos district, collectively worth a half-day of your time. First stop

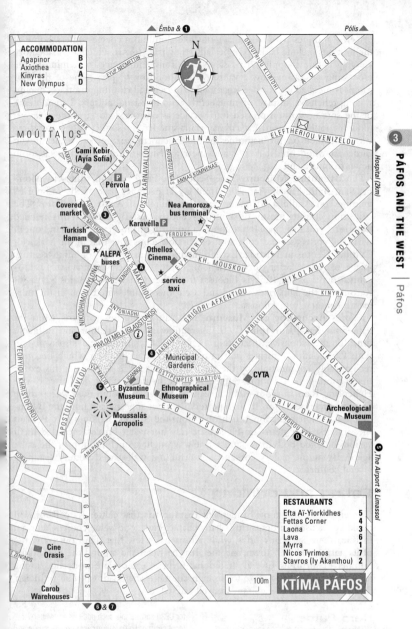

**ACCOMMODATION**

| | |
|---|---|
| Agapinor | B |
| Axiothea | C |
| Kinyras | A |
| New Olympus | D |

N

② MOÚTTALOS

Cami Kebir (Ayía Sofía)

P Pérvola

Covered market ③

"Turkish" Hamam ★

P ALEPA buses

Nea Amoroza bus terminal ★

Karavélla P

Othellos Cinema

★ service taxi

ANTONIADHI

ⓑ PAVLOU MELA (GLADSTONOS)

ⓘ

④ Municipal Gardens

ⓒ Byzantine Museum

Moussalás Acropolis

Ethnographical Museum

CYTA

Archeological Museum

ⓓ

Cine Orasis

Carob Warehouses

▼ ⑥ & ⑦

**RESTAURANTS**

| | |
|---|---|
| Efta Aï-Yiorkidhes | 5 |
| Fettas Corner | 4 |
| Laona | 3 |
| Lava | 6 |
| Myrra | 1 |
| Nicos Tyrimos | 7 |
| Stavros (Iy Akanthou) | 2 |

0     100m

**KTÍMA PÁFOS**

might be the privately run **Ethnographical Museum** at Éxo Vrýsis 1, south of the municipal gardens, occupying two floors of the Eliades family mansion (March–Nov Mon–Sat 9.30am–5.30pm, Sun 10am–1pm; Dec–Feb Mon–Sat 9.30am–5pm, Sun 10am–1pm; C£1). Although the rooms are labelled after a fashion, you might snag the guide booklet (C£3) available at the entrance to make complete sense of the ground-floor rural collection, which intermingles priceless antiques with recent cast-offs like aluminium cheese-graters. Some of the best bits include basketry, especially straw trays (*tsésti*), which are mandatory viewing before shopping trips; sieves and irons; and devices pertaining to the processing of cotton, now a vanished livelihood on Cyprus. One of the four rooms is mocked up as a bed-chamber, with lace and clothing; another contains a comprehensive display of nineteenth-century island pottery. Larger items, of the sort now often pressed into service as taverna decor, include *pinakótes* (dough-moulding boards), *dhoukánes* (flint-studded threshing sledges) and three wagons parked on the flagstones of the cruciform passageway. In the sunken garden, a wood-fired bakery stands near a genuine third-century rock-tomb hewn from the cliff.

The **Byzantine Museum** (June–Sept Mon–Fri 9am–5pm, otherwise Mon–Fri 9am–4pm; Sat all year 9am–1pm; C£1) occupies part of the bishopric's premises on Andhréa Ioánnou, near the church of Áyios Theódhoros. The collection consists mostly of sixteenth-century, post-Byzantine **icons** rescued from local country chapels; though of a uniform quality, few really stand out in what is Cyprus's second collection of portable icons after that in the Makarios Cultural Centre in Nicosia. Exceptions include an eighth- or ninth-century image of Ayía Marína, the oldest icon known on the island; a late twelfth-century icon of the Panayía Eleoússa from the monastery of Áyios Sávvas tís Karónos in the Dhiárizos valley; and a curious double-sided icon of the thirteenth century from Filoússa.

Ktíma's **Archeological Museum**, well east of the town centre (Mon–Fri 9am–5pm, Sat 10am–1pm; C£0.75), requires a special detour and sufficient time for the extensive, interesting exhibits. The chronological displays begin with Chalcolithic figurines and rather wild abstract pottery, which becomes recognizably zoomorphic by the time the Bronze Age is reached; this exotic trend continues, in a more refined manner, in the Archaic display case. The Hellenistic-Roman room, as usual, features myriad glass objects, as well as more figurative representation, though pottery does not appear again until the Byzantine and Lusignan section, much of it from the Saránda Kolónes fort. Perhaps the strangest later items are Hellenistic clay hot-water bottles, moulded to fit various afflicted body parts, and a finely wrought crouching lion of the same age. A Byzantine gallery contains colourful and well-glazed pottery spanning several centuries.

## Eating and drinking

Contemplating the knots of identikit **restaurants** that clutter Káto Páfos, you could be excused for despairing of any characterful, good-value choices. Yet even in Káto there are many finds, while Ktíma has a few that stand out by virtue of its status as a "real" town, and the areas between and around the two hold a number of surprises. Overall, traditional Cypriot eateries are in decline, losing ground to an ongoing craze for foreign cuisine – aficionados of Italian, Indian, Thai, Chinese and French fare are well catered to.

### Káto Páfos

**To Apomero** Ikárou 25 ☎ 26944832, ⊛ www
.homestead.com/apomero/ApomeroMain.html. The name means "off the beaten track", and despite burgeoning villa construction nearby it still is (relatively). It's also one of the better surviving *mezé* houses; forgo their set C£7.50 meals in favour of à la carte, on which three can dine (and drink beer)

for C£30 and sample such oddities as *tsamarélla* (goat salami), *kouloúmbra*, caper greens, snails and decent *sheftália*. Gets varying proportions of locals and expats by season; outdoor terrace in summer. Dinner only; closed Mon.

**Atlantida** Yeroskípou "Tourist Beach", at the southeast end of Káto Páfos' hotel row ☎ 26964525. Upmarket seafood specialist with good service set behind the lawn of its "private" strand, serving a wide variety of palpably fresh fish and shellfish. About C£14 will get you greens garnish, a mini-*mezé*, fruit, coffee and a beer along with your fishy mains.

**Cavallini** Leofóros Posidhónos 65, corner of Dhanáïs ☎ 26964164. Fairly authentic northern Italian cuisine, in formal surroundings. Antipasti, meat dishes and pasta all feature in sizeable portions, though service can be uneven. Reckon on C£13–17 apiece for two courses and dessert, plus booze. Dinner only; closed Sun.

**Hondhros** Apostólou Pávlou 96. Consistently well-executed, moderately priced Cypriot standards, plus fish; allow C£8–9 each if you stay away from seafood, and always ask about the off-menu specials. Pleasant outdoor seating, especially at lunch, and a congenial bar indoors, decorated with old photos and the statuary of Andy Adamos (his widow Jenny and changing shifts of four children run the place). Closed Feb.

**Island Blue** Pafías Afrodhítis 14 ☎ 26818015. Strictly fish and seafood (plus excellent desserts), with nouvelle presentation and modern environment; pricey at about C£20 a head.

**Koh-i-Noor** Klioús 7 ☎ 26965544. Páfos' longest-running north Indian: all the tandoori favourites, plus vegetarian dishes and boneless lamb or chicken curries. Budget C£15 for three courses and dessert, drink extra. Dinner only; closed Mon.

**La Piazza** Alkminís 11–12, just off Posidhónos ☎ 26819921. Very upmarket Italian with a Venetian flair, its menu and recipes vetted once yearly by a north-Italian professor. A good balance between seafood, pasta and meat dishes, and you can eat well (and drink, sparingly) for about C£20 each.

**Spondas** Ayías Anastasías 6 ☎ 26934131. Genuinely family (mother and son)-run fish taverna, popular with Cypriots as well, that's incongruously classy for the neighbourhood. Some ingredients can be hit or miss, but a fish *mezé* pieced together from small à la carte platters shouldn't top C£23 for two, drink extra. Live music Fri/Sat eves in winter; reservations advisable at weekends year-round.

## Between Káto and Ktíma

**Artio Brasserie** Pyrámou, off Táfon tón Vasiléon ☎ 26942800. Chic without being snooty, with cutting-edge décor and well-trained staff, this is the most exclusive see-and-be-seen spot in town. The cuisine is nouvelle/minceur Mediterranean, accompanied by a wide-ranging Cypriot/French/New World wine list. You could keep the bill down by just ordering mains and one of the superb desserts, otherwise three courses and Cypriot wine will set you back C£25–30 each.

**Lava (ex-Vezouvios)** Agapínoros 31, 350m inland from *Nicos Tyrimos*. Very popular among locals in the know for a quick, real-charcoal-grilled meal at the six pavement-conservatory tables (or a takeaway). Only fresh (not frozen) materials, so there's superb swordfish in April and May (if that); otherwise kebab, *sheftália* or *lougániga* with side salad, *tahíni*, *talatoúra*, *toursí* and chips at C£4 will probably be too much for one person to finish. Serves daily until 11pm, so a good first choice for anyone arriving on a late flight.

**Metaxas** Amfitriónos 8, quiet side street opposite *Tasmaria Hotel Apartments* on Táfon tón Vasiléon ☎ 26945923. Eccentric, sub-kitsch decor and hearty westernized food, cooked up by a returned South African Cypriot restaurateur, with gracious service from wife Ewa and son Martin. Specialities include avocado croquettes, good steaks, red snapper in shrimp sauce and *halvás*-flavoured ice cream. Not cheap (C£15–16 a head, plus drink) but consistently high quality. Weekend reservations advised. Dinner only; closed Mon.

**Nicos Tyrimos** Agapínoros 71, behind the old carob warehouses on Apostólou Pávlou ☎ 26942846. This is arguably Páfos's best fish restaurant, though it's grown slightly pricey of late. Offers a wide, fresh selection, preceded in spring by unusual, abundant *mezédhes* like *agrélia* (wild asparagus – may be charged extra), *kírtamo* (rock samphire) and fried baby crabs. About C£13 per head *mezé* format, with wine from a good wine list, and service charge; going à la carte, budget £20 for two fair-sized fish, plus another £13 for assorted extras (garnish, drink, service). Open noon–midnight, dinner reservations advised; closed Mon.

**Sanouto's Meze House** Ayías Théklas, between Koráï and Theodhórou Zenónos, Káto Pervólia district ☎ 26941528. To find it (slightly tricky), turn off Koráï onto Stylianoú – there's a supermarket on the corner – then look for a grove of trees in an open area on the left; *Sanouto's* is amidst this. A Scots (Kathleen)-Cypriot (Agathokleous, "Ali") duo present unusual *mezédhes*, mostly own-grown vegetarian with a strong herbal flavouring (Ali is a botanical expert) but also a couple of meat platters, and wine from the barrel. C£9 gets you the twelve-plate works and though portions aren't huge, it's worth it. The convivial old house has only twenty seats, so reservations are essential in the cooler months; there's more capacious garden seating in summer. (Sanouto, by the way, was the name of their old donkey.) Evenings only, by arrangement, from 6pm in winter, 7pm in summer; closed Sun and one random month in off-season.

**La Sardegna (da Gino)** Apostólou Pávlou 70, Shops 6–7 ☎ 26933399. Excellent wood-oven-fired pizzas are the big hit here, purveyed by native Sardinian Gino Sechi. On the menu, small means medium by most standards, medium means large – you have been warned. About C£11 a head with salad or starter, drink extra (curiously, there are no desserts); booking suggested at busy times. Dinner only; closed Tues.

## Ktíma Páfos

**Efta Aï-Yiorkídhes** Anthypolohagoú Yeoryíou M Sávva 37, at the Ktíma Páfos-Yeroskípou border, off Dhanáïs ☏ 99655824, ⓦ www.7stgeorgestavern.com. The congenial "Seven Saint Georges" mezé house has acquired a cult following since opening in 1997. The dialect name comes from an episode when seven lads named George battled Saracens scaling the cliffs here; they were all killed, but their resistance allowed the villagers to escape. A guaranteed chip-free zone: instead, there are imaginative dips, pickled veg or meat-based platters, while typical dishes include flash-fried *agrélia*, yellow lentils, *tsamarélla*, cured fish, smoked pork fillet, chicken with mushrooms, wild greens and goat-and-cumin *tavás*, plus preserved fruit and home-made liqueurs to finish off. All vegetables are either organically grown or self-gathered. Indoor–outdoor seating, wonderful taped music, and stimulating conversation (when they're not too busy) from proprietors George and Lara; count on about C£15 a head with wine, dessert and coffee

(the basic *mezé* is C£9). Dinner reservations advisable; closed Mon and random weeks in winter.

**Fettas Corner** Corner of Iakovídhi and Ioánnou Agróti, opposite the fountain roundabout. Well-regarded, evening-only eatery offering just salad, *halloúmi*, *loúntza*, *tahíni*, grills and a few oven dishes, but very reasonable (allow C£7–8 each including a beer) and decent quality. Welcoming management and jolly atmosphere, with locals outnumbering tourists, plus limited outdoor seating until November.

**Laona** Vótsi 6. This *kafestiatório* is the best venue in town for an inexpensive, traditional cooked lunch (Mon–Sat 10am–4pm) in salubrious surroundings – a 110-year-old *mosaïkó*-floored room, plus pavement seating. Bank employees packing out the place on Mondays particularly tell you you're on the right track; plenty of bean-based dishes for veggies, plus stews like pork with *kolokássi*, and home-style sweets including *kaló práma* and *palouzé*.

**Myrra** Neapóleos 37, corner of Lámbrou Sépi ☏ 26936009. Established in 1974, this ramshackle old-house taverna (also with outdoor seating) does a decent C£8 *mezé* (wine extra). Dinner only.

**Stavros (Iy Akanthou)** Platía Mouttálou. A well-loved local where the busy, focal-point bar is on an equal footing with the food service; not many foreigners come here, especially off-season. The *mezé* is good value at about C£8 each, and meat platters in particular are four-star.

# Nightlife and entertainment

Conventional local nightlife is concentrated down in the hotel district of Káto Páfos, with most **bars and clubs** found along Posidhónos or just inland on Ayíou Andoníou, aka "Nightlife Street" – all the venues reviewed below are marked on the map on p.167. One word of warning: the parts of Táfon tón Vasiléon with cabarets and attendant pimps, touts and street hassle are worth avoiding, especially by unescorted women. Among **cinemas**, the Cine Orasis two-plex at Apostólou Pávlou 35 tends to have more first-run foreign fare in English than Othellos at Evagóra Pallikarídhi 41; it also has a Thursday-night art-film club. The **Pafos Aphrodite Festival** (early September) and the **Akamas Festival** (late March) see concerts and other events in the larger hotel venues or Páfos castle. Other classical performances are regularly staged at the Markidion Theatre, on Andhréa Yeroúdhi in Ktíma.

**La Boite 67** Káto Páfos harbour. Students from the Lemba art school and Páfos trendies tend to be found drinking between or after meals at this long-running pub, though its heyday has long passed.

**California Beach Bar** Ayíou Andoníou. Run by a returned California Cypriot named Jimmy, this features DJs on rotation playing various sounds; get hammered with "fish bowl" cocktails and vodka slush puppies.

**Different Bar** Ayías Nápas 6–7, near corner of Ayías Anastasías. The local gay bar, but gets a mixed clientele for the sake of its tasteful soundtrack, cool interior and friendly, informative owner.

**Flintstones** Dhionysíou, off Ayíou Andoníou. Run by three brothers as an annexe of their house, this attracts a mix of locals and tourists, with music at a level to permit conversation, and a good atmosphere engendered by the landlords.

Rainbow Disco Ayíou Andoníou. Káto's oldest and most prestigious dance-hall, with big-name DJs typically poached from London, Ibiza or Ayía Nápa.
Robin Hood Pub Ayíou Andoníou. (In)famous pick-up bar (Cypriot men picking up foreign women for the most part), with 1960s to contemporary

sounds, a dance floor, and sixty claimed kinds of beer.
The Watering Hole Ayías Anastasías, corner Ayías Nápas. A no-nonsense bar with DJ sounds, footie on the TV, a small dance space and reasonably priced drinks; one of the most popular early-evening spots.

# Listings

**Airlines** British Airways rep is Leda in Káta Páfos, opposite *Hondhros* restaurant on Apostólou Pávlou ☎26935675; Cyprus Airlines is at Gládstonos 37–39, Ktíma ☎26933556.

**Airport flight information** Ring ☎26422833 and ask for the extension of your airline.

**Backcountry expeditions** Guided hiking excursions have very nearly died out around Páfos – thanks to track-bulldozing and a change in clientele – and all jeep safaris offered are much of an (environmentally destructive) muchness; they won't take you anywhere that your own rental jeep, used in conjunction with this book, can't visit. For a sterling exception to the above rule, contact Welsh-educated Simon Demetropoulos ☎99427152, ⓔchelonia@logos.cy.net, one of the top naturalists in Cyprus, who can arrange hiking trips and quality bespoke jeep safaris to less frequented areas.

**Banks and exchange** About half-a-dozen banks, up around Platía Kennedy in Ktíma or along Arkhiepiskópou Makaríou, all have ATMs.

**Bookshops** Romos Christodoulides' Terra Books, in two premises in the arcade at Ayíou Kendéa 31 in the heart of town, has a good mix of Greek and English titles, both new and second-hand, as well as large-scale DLS maps – well worth a look, and a chat with Romos. Moufflon Books, Kinýra 30, run by Frances and Ken Carter, has a large stock of new books on Cyprus (both coffee-table and guides), fiction and fine art. One or other is likely to stock this guide if you're reading someone else's.

**Bus companies** Long-distance companies in Ktíma are limited to ALEPA at the Karavella car park ☎26934252, with services to Limassol and Nicosia; and Nea Amoroza, Evagóra Pallikarídhi 79 ☎26936740, to Pólis and Pomós.

**Car rental** ASG/Europcar, Leofóros Posidhónos, Natalia Court, Shops 19–20 ☎26936944; Andreas Petsas, Apostólou Pávlou 86, Green Court ☎26935522; Budget/GDK, Leofóros Táfon tón Vasiléon, Dora Complex ☎26953824; Hertz, Leofóros Apostólou Pávlou 54A ☎26933985; Holiday Autos Cyprus, Leofóros Táfon tón Vasiléon, Aristo Court Shop 3 ☎26221321; Sixt, Leofóros Táfon tón Vasiléon 58, Aristo Royal Complex Shop 8 ☎26936991.

**Internet** Most central are the two branches of Maroushia (Mon–Sat 9am–11pm, Sun 3–11pm), in Káto at the Myrra Complex Shop no. 15 on Posidhónos, and up in Ktíma at the central junction, above the Hellenic Bank. There's also Webst@tion C@fé in Káto at Ayíou Andoníou 12 (daily 11am–2am).

**Mobile phones** At Andy's Telecom Centre, Evagóra Pallikarídhi 30, Andy Georgiou (late of London) will unblock overseas mobiles and will set you up with a CYTA or Areeba pay-as-you-go plan.

**Motorbike rental** Shikkis, Leofóros Posidhónos 2, opposite the defunct SODAP plant ☎26965349; CyBreeze Pentaras, Táfon tón Vassiléon 4, Shop 3 ☎26943810.

**Post offices** The nominal main branch, in an old colonial building on Nikodhímou Myloná (Mon–Fri 7.30am–1.30pm, plus Thurs 3–5.30pm), has been effectively supplanted for things like parcels and poste restante by the new district sorting office on the corner of Eleftheríou Venizélou and Vassiléos Konstandínou (Mon–Fri 7.30am–1.30pm, plus Thurs 3–5.30pm; Sat 9–11am). The Káto Páfos branch next to *To Apomero* keeps the same hours as the Nikodhímou Myloná branch.

**Rugby** This has a big following locally amongst both Cypriots and expats, as the Paphos Tigers are reckoned the best of the three civilian sides on the island (there are also four British military squads). Games are on Saturdays, late October to early February (cup competition thereafter), at the Cypria Maris stadium near Yeroskípou. For more information, call ☎99522226.

**Scuba diving** CyDive, in the Myrra Complex shopping centre at Posidhónos 1, Káto Páfos ☎26934271, ⓦwww.cydive.com, the longest-established school in the district, has a good reputation and operates most of the year out of their own boats. They offer a range of morning or afternoon shore and boat dives, mostly quite shallow but including archeological remains, caves and some wrecks, as well as full days out. For qualified divers, C£25 per dive (C£42 2-tank dive) for all equipment, transport and dive master; basic PADI courses C£210, Advanced Open Water certification C£150. Alternatively, try Abyss Dive Center, by the *Helios Hotel* out in Argáki district ☎26910500 or

99622774, ⓦ www.abyss-diving.com. For a summary of diving opportunities near Páfos, see the box on p.168.

**Service taxi** Travel & Express is at Evagóra Pallikarídhi 8, Ktíma ☎ 26932424. Direct service to Limassol only; journeys to Nicosia or Larnaca are via Limassol.

**Shopping** The Cyprus Handicraft Service show-room is at Apostólou Pávlou 64, Ktíma. Mikis Antiques, Fellahoglou 6, Ktíma, displays some wonderful Belle Epoque phonographs, rural impedi-menta and furniture. There simply isn't, however, the variety of shops that one finds in Limassol and Nicosia.

**Travel agencies** Iris Travel, 10 ☎ 26948933, across from the CTO, is recommended for interna-tional air tickets; try also Ricky's, just downhill at Gládstonos 17 ☎ 26935233.

# Southeast from Páfos

The A6 motorway has siphoned off much of the traffic heading southeast from Páfos, making the B6 road far more manageable and pleasant than before. It's probably the better bet for short-haul touring as it passes over a trio of rivers, the lower reaches of streams beginning far up in the Pafiot corner of the Tróodhos range (exploring the Xéros and Dhiárizos valleys is described on pp.220–222). The resulting fertility (notably in melons) softens the usual·mineral, parched yellowness of the south Cypriot coast, and seems to be in sympathy with the age-old worship of the island's patron goddess, Aphrodite, at **Yeroskípou** and **Palea Paphos**. Little tangible remains of her shrines, but her worship continues faintly in Christianized forms. One emphatically Byzantine site which doesn't seem to owe much to pagan antecedents is the remote painted cave-shrine of **Paleá Énklistra**.

## Eastern beaches

The Páfos town beaches, specifically those fringing the eastern hotels, aren't up to much; to reach anything moderately attractive you have to get a little way out of town. The first substantial strip is the maintained and improved beach in **Yeroskípou**, between the *Atlantida* seafood restaurant and the last hotel, though most locals content themselves with the kilometre or so of natural shingle shore just east from the *Ricco Beach* snack bar. The bottom's sandy once you're in, the water's clean, and there's a well-established gay nude-bathing scene here after dark in summer, especially around the full moon. A bit inland lies the *Zenon Gardens* **campsite** (daily fees C£1 per site, plus C£1.50 per person), which tends to get buzzed by low-flying aircraft and run out of mains water. The other easterly beach is **Flória**, seaward of Tími village, about halfway along the airport spur road – follow signs pointing to the dirt drive that leads to some ramshackle tavernas and the first hints of development. There's also the official Tími picnic ground in a eucalyptus grove nearby.

## Yeroskípou

**YEROSKÍPOU** village (Geroskipou, pronounced "Yerostchípou") is now virtually a suburb of Páfos, beginning just a kilometre or so beyond the district archeological museum, and linked with Ktíma (Karavélla parking lot) by the regular ALEPA **buses** #1 and #(2)1. The name is a modern rendition of the ancient *Hieros Kipos* or "Sacred Garden and Grove", consecrated to Aphrodite, which grew in the fertile plain below towards the sea.

These days, Yeroskípou has a reputation as a crafts centre, as reflected by numerous stalls on the main road peddling basketry, Cyprus delight (they bristle if you call it "Turkish" delight) and pottery (Savvas at the east edge of the village is considered tops for that). The craft theme is highlighted in the Yeroskípou **Folk Art Museum** (Mon–Fri 9am–2.30pm, plus Sept–June Thurs 3–5pm; C£0.75). This, on Leondíou just south of the through road, is lodged in the former house of a certain Andreas Zoumboulakis, the British vice-consul here in the early nineteenth century, who is better known as Hadji Smith, having adopted his sponsor's surname. The museum, on two storeys, is probably the best of its kind on the island, emphasizing domestic implements on the ground floor and local costumes upstairs, plus decorated gourds, including one fashioned into a stringed instrument.

Among a handful of **tavernas and snack bars** around, or just off, the central square, most distinctive by far – and doubling as a butcher's shop – is *Khristos Pitsillis Ofton Kleftiko*, some 80m east of the square on the north side of the highway. You can enjoy some of the best *kléftigo* on the island (with the traditional raw-onion-and-lemon garnish) at a few rickety outdoor tables, for about C£4 plus drinks.

### Ayía Paraskeví church

Nothwithstanding its name, the village proper is probably of Byzantine origin, and the best demonstration of this is the renowned church of **Ayía Paraskeví** bang in the middle (nominal hours May–Oct daily 8am–1pm & 2–5pm; Nov–April closes 4pm; free).

The damaged frescoes in the altar dome are non-representational, dating construction to the ninth century, when the veneration of icons was banned by the Iconoclasts who then held sway in the Byzantine Empire. The church is unique on the island in having six domes, including that of the reliquary under the nineteenth-century belfry. Most of the surviving frescoes date from the fifteenth century and were cleaned in the 1970s, but unfortunately something has gone awry since and many are now prevented from sloughing off only by temporary protective gauze. Up in the central cupola hides a crude but engaging *Virgin Orans*; opposite the south door, and the first images seen upon entering, are the *Last Supper*, the *Washing of the Feet*, the *Betrayal* – where figures in Lusignan armour date the images – and Pilate washing his hands. Across from these you see the *Birth and Presentation of the Virgin*, complete with a set table in the former scene, plus the *Raising of Lazarus* and the *Entry into Jerusalem*. Back on the north wall arch, between the western and central domes, there's an unusual representation of Simon carrying the Cross for Christ while a Roman soldier drags Jesus along by a rope, with a *Nativity* and *Baptism* diagonally opposite, in the niche closest to the altar screen. The church itself was originally cruciform with a single nave, but had an ungainly narthex added to the south side in the nineteenth century (though a *yinaikonítis* or women's gallery in the rear was removed in the late 1990s). July 25–26 marks the **feast** of the patron saint; this is also a good spot to participate in the Greek Easter Resurrection Mass.

## Palea Paphos and Koúklia

Approaching the boundary of Limassol district, some 11km east of Yeroskípou, you can't help noticing a large, solidly built structure on a prominent rise. This is **La Cavocle**, a fourteenth-century manor that's the inevitable marker-cairn and introduction to both the ancient city of **Palea Paphos** and the large village of **KOÚKLIA** just to the north. Once an ethnically mixed community, Koúklia remains a pleasant if unremarkable place of low houses, whose meandering lanes converge on a small *platía* with a church and some coffeehouses. Indifferent to the trickle of tourists visiting the nearby ruins, it has changed little – except for the departure of its Turkish Cypriots – since independence. Of the **tavernas** in the village centre, the most accomplished (and renowned for its non-touristy *mezé*) is *Dhiarizos*, though you'll have to contend with a constantly blaring TV.

Incidentally, the **road** from Koúklia over the district border via Moúsere to Dhorá (see p.141) is currently the shortest, easiest and best-condition route from Páfos to the high Tróödhos – as well as giving access to the Paleá Énklistra (see below).

## The site

The ancient temple stood on a knoll about 2km inland, overlooking the sea but probably not the orchards and gently sloping fields which have appeared since. Despite the hoariness of the cult here, there's little above-ground evidence of it or of the city which grew up around, and the archeological site itself is really of specialist interest. The courtyard-type **sanctuary of Aphrodite** (June–Aug Mon–Fri 9am–7pm, Sat & Sun 9am–5pm; Sept–May daily 9am–5pm; C£0.75), with rustic, relatively impermanent buildings, was common in the pre-Hellenic Middle East; thus, little has survived other than low foundations to the north as you enter. Matters were made worse for posterity when a wealthy Roman chose to build a private villa (bits of its mosaic floor still visible) next to the Archaic shrine in its last years, and the medieval placement of sugar-milling machinery atop the convenient stone foundations was extremely destructive to anything remaining above knee level. Finally, the nearby villagers, from Byzantine times onwards, treated the ruins as a quarry – virtually every old building in Koúklia incorporates a cut stone or two from the shrine area.

In one corner of the precinct a sign points along the short path to the "**Leda Mosaic House**", where you're informed that the central figure, Leda baring her behind to the lustful Zeus-swan, is a copy. The replica was installed here after the second- or third-century AD original was stolen by art thieves, then luckily recovered, to be lodged in the relative safety of Nicosia's Cyprus Museum.

Outside the sacred precinct, there's even less to see until the Swiss-sponsored excavations are completed. To the northeast, off the road towards Arkhimandhríta, are the remains of a **city gate**, and a **siege ramp** built by the Persians in 498 BC to breach the city walls. The defenders burrowed under the ramp in a vain attempt to collapse it and thus the Persian war-engines atop; two of the tunnels are now open for public inspection. The **necropolis** (still under investigation) lies to the southeast of the hill, and appears to have escaped the notice of tomb robbers.

Just east of the precinct stands the usually locked twelfth-to-sixteenth-century church of **Panayía Katholikí**, new goddess of the local cult. Should you gain admission (best chance of this weekdays 10am–noon), there are traces of fourteenth-century frescoes inside, the most curious being gargoyle-like personifications of the rivers Tigris and Euphrates on the west wall. Until recently Koúklia village women used to light candles nearby in honour of the Panayía Galaktariótissa – the Virgin-Who-Gives-Milk-to-Mothers.

## La Cavocle and the local museum

The most obvious and worthwhile item in the main archeological zone is the four-square Lusignan manor of **La Cavocle**, whose name is a rendering of (take your pick) the Greek *kouvoúkli*, "canopy"; *kovoukuleris*, the royal bodyguard; or more likely the Latin *cubiculum*, "pavilion" – corrupted in whichever case to Koúklia, the name of the modern village. La Cavocle was the headquarters of the Crusaders' surrounding sugar plantations, and continued to serve as the "big house" of a large farm in Ottoman times. Only the east wing survived the Mameluke raid of 1426; the rest, including a fine gate tower, is a Turkish reconstruction. Because the courtyard level has risen over the centuries, you descend slightly to the ground floor of the east wing, where a purported thirteenth-century banquet room has a groin-vaulted ceiling.

This fine specimen of domestic Crusader architecture is being prepared for use as part of an expanded **local museum** (same hours as the site), at present housed entirely upstairs. Among the few exhibits in Gallery I is one of several existing *betyls* or phallic cult monoliths (the biggest one is in Nicosia), which, not unlike Hindu Shiva *lingams*, used to be anointed with olive oil by local women well into modern times. Gallery II contains finds of all eras from the site, in chronological order. Best is the huge chalk bathtub of the eleventh century BC, complete with a soap dish. Most of the other items are painted pottery, with some bronze work, much of which was found in the rubble piled up by the Persians to support their siege ramp.

## Paleá Énklistra

Just outside Kouklá, hollowed out of a cliff, is the Byzantine cave-hermitage of **Paleá Énklistra**, so called (*énklistra* = enclosure) by locals who mistook it for St Neophytos's (see p.186) first hermitage. The grotto and its frescoes are in fact mid-fifteenth-century, 250 years too late to have sheltered Neophytos. Although the faces of the figures were mutilated during the 1960s by shepherds from the nearby village of Souskioú, diminishing their impact, it's still emphatically worth the trip out. From the centre of Kouklá, drive 3.5km east–northeast on the F612 road bound for the Tróödhos, then turn left onto a dirt track towards the visible medieval chapel of Áyios Konstandínos (signposted in blue-on-white Greek lettering), 500m further. Leave cars here, and then continue on foot along a narrower track which drops to the stream-valley floor before becoming a path up to the north-facing cliff opposite. You'll find the cave here, behind an unlocked door.

The **iconography** of the Paleá Énklistra is quite unusual, dictated in part by the irregular surfaces, but even more so by the doctrinal conventions of the time, which help date its frescoes to shortly after 1439, when the eastern and western Churches were briefly united and the Holy Ghost held to proceed from the Son as well as the Father. Accordingly, instead of the expected *Pandokrátor* on the ceiling there's a rare late-Byzantine depiction of the Holy Trinity, ensconced in two diamond-shaped mandorlas. All three figures bear a I C X C monogram, including the Holy Spirit, perching as a dove on the Gospel; of the pair of lower figures each labelled "O ΩN" (Being, or Existence), the rather hairier figure on the viewer's right, with ethereally delicate hands, is God the Father. Around them are arrayed the heavenly guardians: cherubim, seraphim (with eyed, sextuple wings) and the Archangels, including the seldom-shown Rafael and Uriel in addition to the usual Gabriel and Michael. In the next circle out, evangelists Mark and Luke share a desk, while opposite sit John the Divine, his scribe Prokhoros and Matthew with their respective scrolls. Still lower down, note the ascetic Saint Onófrios (Humphrey) by the entrance, his long beard hiding his nakedness, and Saint Anastasía east of Mark and Luke, holding her fabled antidotes to poison.

To vary a return to Páfos, take – shortly before the turning for Paleá Énklistra – the signed, cobbled track bound for **Souskioú** in the Dhiárizos valley; it's a scenic 3km there, with partridges dashing every which way. The village itself is ex-Turkish Cypriot and abandoned save for goat pens and a modern church, but lies just east of the F616 road (currently not recommended for travel up-valley).

# North from Páfos

North of Páfos the landscape is initially flattish and uninspiring, dotted with large villages that are essentially dormitories for the district capital, and increasingly for long-term foreign residents. Only as the terrain begins tilting gently up at the first outriders of the Tróödhos mountains does development diminish and the mystique of the country reassert itself.

Most of the inland settlements immediately north of Páfos town can boast some late-Byzantine church or remains, but with the exception of the following two monuments, all have had their appeal compromised by ill-advised additions or renovation.

## Émba: Panayía Khryseléoussa

In the middle of **ÉMBA** (Empa), 3km north of Páfos, the twelfth-century church of **Panayía Khryseléoussa** sits in a small park whose greenery burns to a crisp by June, just uphill from a horrible, hangar-like modern church. A dome perches at each end of the double-cruciform ground plan, and the narthex with stairs up to vanished monks' cells on the mortared roof is an eighteenth-century addition. Loiter about purposefully and a guardian will appear with the key, but only if you're suitably dressed; he may prove even more elusive, in which case enquire in the arcaded municipal office building opposite, or in the *kafenía* up the road.

Inside, late fifteenth- or early sixteenth-century frescoes were cleaned during the 1970s, but they'd been badly retouched during the late nineteenth century, and some were damaged by the quake of 1953. Anything that remained out of reach of the "restorer", however, is still worth scrutiny: the *Apocalypse* and the *Second Coming* on the right of the main nave's vault, for example, is very fine high up but mauled below. Funds permitting, the cruder overpainting will eventually be removed by the archeological services, so visits should become progressively more rewarding with time.

The *témblon* (altar screen) dates from the sixteenth century, and just as the guard says, the eyes of St John the Divine (on the panel left of the main icon) seem to follow you around the room. The revered icon of the Virgin is unique in that both she and the Child are crowned; there is also a sixteenth-century icon of the apostles.

ALEPA urban **bus** #4 from Ktíma's Karavélla car park passes through Émba on its way to Tála.

# The monastery of Áyios Neófytos

Nine kilometres from Páfos and five from Émba, at the head of a wooded canyon, the **monastery of Áyios Neófytos** (Agios Neofytos, sometimes Ayíou Neofýtou) appears suddenly as you round a curve. Twice each weekday, mid-morning and at about noon, the ALEPA #4 **bus** extends its route beyond Tála to call in here.

The hermit Neophytos, born in 1134 near Léfkara, moved here from the monastery of Khrysostómos near Nicosia at the age of 25, seeking solitude in this then-desolate region. His plan backfired badly; such was Neophytos's reputation that he became a guru of sorts to numerous disciples who gathered around his simple cave-hermitage, founding the monastery here long before his death in 1219 or 1220. Unusually for a "desert ascetic", Neophytos was a scholar and commentator of some note, and a few of his manuscripts have survived. Among these are the *Ritual Ordinance*, a handbook for monastic life, and a historical essay on the acquisition of Cyprus by the Crusaders in 1191, deeply disparaging of the two protagonists Isaac Komnenos and Richard the Lionheart. That he could write this with impunity is perhaps a measure of the respect in which he was held during his lifetime.

### The katholikón and the énklistra of Neophytos

The enormous monastery compound, home now to just seven monks, consists of a square perimeter cloister enclosing a garden and aviary, with the **katholikón**, or central church, on its own terrace. At the rear of the vaulting over the *katholikón*'s south aisle, the best remaining of various early sixteenth-century frescoes is a pensive *Prayer of Joachim in the Wilderness*, depicting an angel descending with the tidings that Anna shall bear the Virgin. Westernized decoration above the north aisle is much more fully preserved, consisting of a complete cycle of the Akathistos Lenten hymn (each stanza beginning with one of the 24 letters of the Greek alphabet), glorifying the Virgin and Christ. Especially noteworthy – and well-lit – are the *Nativity* (stanza H), with unusually no bath for the Holy Infant but plenty of shepherds and angels in attendance; the *Adoration of the Magi* (stanza I); and the *Flight into Egypt* (stanza Λ), while opposite these are *Christ Minded to Save the World*, leading a troupe of angels (stanza Σ) and near the end, *Christ Enthroned* (stanza Y). But interesting as they are, the *katholikón* and the monastery grounds are not the main reason visitors come up here.

On the far side of the car park with its café (lively during the feasts of January 24 and September 27), at the very head of the ravine, cave-niches form the **énklistra** or **hermitage of Neophytos** (daily: April–Sept 9am–1pm & 2–6pm; Oct–March 9am–4pm; C£0.50). This has parallels most obviously with the roughly contemporary man-made cave-shrines of Cappadocia, and of course the much later, nearby Paleá Énklistra; the hermit supposedly dug many of the cavities himself, and it is conceivable that a few of the oldest frescoes are by Neophytos, though most were merely done under his supervision. At least two other painters, one signing his work as that of Theodore Apseudes, were involved.

Visits begin with stairs mounting to a pair of chambers on the left comprising a chapel, dedicated to the Holy Cross and completely decorated by 1196. These frescoes, of a "primitive" Syrian/Cappadocian style, were redone in 1503 and cleaned in 1992, so in the **nave** it's easy to make out a complete, clockwise cycle of Passion scenes such as the *Last Supper* (complete with Judas reaching over the carrots and radishes of the Hebrew Passover to snatch the fish of the Believers), the *Washing of the Feet* (with various disciples engaged in undoing their sandal-straps) and Roman soldiers portrayed as Crusaders in the *Betrayal*, and in the *Descent from the Cross* the figure of Joseph of Arimathea, thought to be a portrait of Neophytos himself, about to wrap the dead Christ in a shroud. Everything culminates in the *Ascension* of the dome, cleverly hacked from the soft rock so that Christ seated on his trademark mandorla (borne by two angels rather than the usual four) appears to be disappearing up a small hole in the ceiling, through which Neophytos, from his quarters upstairs, used to hear confessions and issue edicts (he only emerged once a week to preach).

In the **ierón** or central sanctuary, two archangels seem like celestial policemen (as they indeed are in Orthodox belief), escorting Neophytos to the ranks of angels in a ceiling painting in the style of the more fashionable Constantinopolitan school. Flanking the doorway to the hermit's cell is an exceptionally fine *Annunciation*, with the Archangel Gabriel's cloak swept back in his own wake as he delivers the good news.

A third chamber off to the right (north) was Neophytos's earlier private **cell**, with benches, niches and a desk carved for his use, as well as his sarcophagus – appropriately presided over by an image of the *Anastasis* or Resurrection, which can be compared to a slightly later one on the east wall of the nave, unusual for including the Hebrew kings David and Solomon, plus John the Baptist with a prophetic scroll. The hermit himself left instructions that his quarters be walled over at his death "that none may know where I have been buried; there my worthless body shall stay in quietness until the common Resurrection." This command was predictably disregarded in 1756, when the sarcophagus was prematurely emptied so that Neophytos's bones might serve as relics; today pilgrims to the *katholikón* kiss his skull in its silver reliquary.

The upper caves of the cliff-face are undecorated and currently inaccessible. Neophytos retreated there in 1197 after the lower levels became unbearably busy with his followers; he is said to have ensured his privacy with a retractable ladder.

# Northwest along the coast

Leaving Páfos and heading towards the **northwest**, the avenue past the Tombs of the Kings continues as a fairly broad road for some kilometres, passing phalanxes of modern hotels and villa projects. It's strange to reflect that in the 1950s this rugged coast was so deserted that EOKA chose it as a landfall when smuggling in arms and men from Greece. Today, signs for Chinese and Indian restaurants lend the only exotic touches, along with the banana plantations just inland that testify to the mildness of the climate. But although this route seems to offer little promise of seclusion and beauty (other than the "**Baths of Adonis**" at the head of the Mavrokólymbos valley), you are heading towards one of the most unspoiled stretches of shoreline in the South, past **Áyios Yeóryios** with its small basilica and reptile park, and up towards the **Akámas peninsula**. This in turn can offer excellent beaches at **Toxéftra** and **Lára**, just beyond the sculpted **Avgás** gorge. **Buses** run as far as Coral Bay and very sporadically to Áyios Yeóryios, but there's no public transport any further along the coast.

## Lémba

An inland route from Ktíma, which joins up with the coast road beyond Kissónerga, brings you after 4km to **LÉMBA** (Lempa); ALEPA bus #3 runs here regularly from Ktíma's Karavélla parking lot. An outrageous (and controversial) roadside *objets-trouvés* sculpture, the 45-metre-long (and growing) "Great Wall of Lempa", indicates your approach to the **Cyprus College of Art** (Ⓦ www.artcyprus.org), a fully accredited institution offering a three-year or post-graduate programme in fine art. Visitors are welcome at the dozen or so studios, and there is a small gallery of finished work for sale. Two independent **potteries** within sight of the college, particularly George and Sotiroulla Georgiades' *Lemba Pottery* (Ⓣ 26943822), are also well worth calling in at.

Conspicuously signposted at the downhill end of town, the Lémba **prehistoric site** (unrestricted entry) was founded in about 3500 BC and flourished for over a thousand years, courtesy of the nearby spring and stream (not potable today, alas). The well-labelled **Lemba Experimental Village**, a thorough reconstruction of a half-dozen Chalcolithic dwellings, courtesy of the University of Edinburgh excavation team, lends considerable interest, and in terms of architectural appeal compares rather favourably with the appalling tower blocks visible to seaward. Most of the finds from the actual prehistoric site can be found in the Páfos archeological museum.

The only nearby **taverna** is the eponymous *Lemba* (Ⓣ 26271451), out on the Khlórakas-Kissónerga bypass road. Their speciality is *soúvla* and *gourounópoulo*, and despite an emphasis on quantity over quality, and zero atmosphere in the shed-like conservatory (softened in winter by a fire), it's reasonable value and popular with locals, such that booking is wise at weekends.

## The Dhiyenis' Landing museum

Some 4km out of Páfos along the coast road, the site of George Dhiyenis Grivas's disembarkation on November 10, 1954 to begin co-ordination of the EOKA uprising is now prominently marked below the village of Khlórakas as "**Dhiyenis' Landing**", one of the many manifestations of an upsurge in nationalist fervour in the South since the mid-1990s (for more information on Grivas, see p.284). Right by the sea at Rodhafiniá cove, just south of the enormous *St George Hotel* and eponymous church (the latter constructed by the bishopric of Páfos to commemorate the landing), a purpose-built **museum** houses the gun-running caïque *Ayios Yeoryios* (open daily all day; free). This was captured by the British along with its Greek crew of five, and eight local EOKA activists who had come to meet them, on January 25, 1955. On the walls are archival photos of the capture and trial of the thirteen, along with their deadly cargo, though British testimonials to the bravery of many of these men during the recent world war – subtly reiterating the long-standing Greek-Cypriot position that they were virtually owed independence in return for their faithful service to the Allies – have vanished since the millennium.

## Mavrokólymbos Reservoir and the Baths of Adonis

About 1km before Coral Bay (see below), signs point inland to the **Mavrokólymbos (Mavrokolympos) Reservoir**, an increasingly popular picnic and angling spot, especially in the heat of summer – though between September and January, the water level is likely to be markedly down. Even at the best of times, swimming is not an option; for that, and for frankly more alluring scenery, there are the so-called **Baths of Adonis** considerably upstream, though the much-touted connection with Adonis and Aphrodite is utterly spurious.

There's a choice of two **access** routes: for jeeps, the more direct but steep (and in spring, muddy) dirt track taking off from the Akoúrsos road, or the longer (10.7km) but well signposted way in from Kissónerga via Tála and the Leptos Kamara housing estate, the only sensible choice for saloon cars. However you arrive, just beyond the car park lies the attractively restored **watermill** and snack-bar of actor and self-styled arts personality Pambos Theodhorou (his grandfather was the last miller here). Here you pay an admission charge of C£3.50 – not strictly legal since rivers and the shore for a width of 12 feet are public land in Cyprus. Once inside the grounds, you'll find two sets of impressive **waterfalls**, each feeding sizeable **pools** with water temperature at a brisk 17°C. The lower one is about 6m deep at the centre, and fitted with a rope swing; daredevils jump in from the ledge above (strictly at your own risk). The upper pool is shallower (2–3m) but more secluded, with discreet skinny-dipping tolerated. From Kíli (Koili) village further upstream it's possible to walk in direct and "free" to the upper pool, but you will probably be detected and ejected if you venture down to the lower one.

Possibly the best method of visiting the area is with Paddocks Horse Farm in Kissónerga (☏99603288, ℻26244467, ✉ioloarch@spidernet.net), run by a Mancunian Greek-Cypriot named Ari, with much more attention to safety and animal welfare than the norm. He offers a three-hour ride to the dam for moderately experienced **horse riders**, and a six-hour all-day trip to the Baths of Adonis for veterans.

## Coral Bay

With the coast hitherto inaccessible, unsafe (see below) or overrun by hotels, the first place that might tempt you to stop is **Coral Bay** (officially Kólpos Koralíon in Greek), 11km out of Páfos and blessed with a public-access beach, for once not monopolized by hotels. A sandy, 600-metre crescent is hemmed in by a pair of headlands, with two snack bars and sunbed-rental places behind. The only real sight, on the northwesterly headland, are traces of **Paleókastro** (Máa), a Bronze Age settlement excavated before 1985 and claimed to be the Myceneans' first landfall in Cyprus, coming from present-day Greece. Although the site itself is somewhat neglected and unfenced, there's an adjacent **Museum of the Mycenean Colonization of Cyprus** (Mon–Sat 10am–3.45pm; C£0.75), housed in an Italian-designed "beehive" intended to mimic the architecture of the tholos tombs at Argolid Mycenae in Greece.

Down on the main bay, the water is not always the cleanest, but the bay is at least safe from currents, which can't be said for the tempting-looking cliff-backed beach, with anglers and a few sunbeds, at **Kissónerga** 2km south. Every summer there are drownings here owing to strong undertow and lateral currents; explicit warning notices to this effect are often defaced or removed by interested parties (the sunbed concessionaires).

### Practicalities

Coral Bay is the end of the line for the ALEPA #10 and #15 **bus** routes from town. Atop the promontories and along the access road is an estate of summer homes for wealthy Nicosians and expats, a cluster of hotels, and a single commercial high street that's a perfect miniature of the "strip" down in Káto Páfos.

Top **accommodation**, overlooking the superior sandy bay beyond the northwest headland, is the self-contained five-star *Coral Beach Hotel* (☎26621601, Ⓦwww.leptos-hotels.com; Ⓞ), set in its own gardens. Though owned by the Leptos clan of developers, a special *bête noire* of local conservationists, it has to be admitted that once inside, the resort is in better taste than many, with arts and crafts exhibitions and other token concessions to traditional Cypriot culture. There's a little marina too, the base for watersports and shared with the few local fishermen who've been allowed to stay. Since mid-2004, there's been a rival of sorts in the adjacent five-star *Thalassa Hotel* (☎26623222, Ⓦwww.thalassa.com. cy; Ⓞ), sharing the headland with the archeological site. Also a Leptos property, it's not much to look at from the outside – it was originally planned as a three-star hotel – but impressions change dramatically once inside what's claimed to be Cyprus's first boutique hotel, and supposedly the only "butler-concept" lodging in the Mediterranean (one member of the bewilderingly multinational staff is dedicated to discreetly shadowing you and gratifying your every whim during your stay). All the designer units have at least a partial sea view, and vary from "mini-residences" (C£175) to true suites of 84 square metres and above (C£700 and up), though the most common option is the "double residence" (C£380), with two bathrooms and a lounge. The public areas include the main *Ambrosia* restaurant and several bars (including a cigar lounge), plus the spa, yoga studio and gym; the spa in particular lies at the heart of the hotel's appeal and – compared to rooms and meals – is surprisingly reasonably priced. The only demerit is that the rock lido immediately south of the hotel is not that appealing, but guests are free to use the *Coral Beach* beach and all its facilities.

**Villas** are a popular option around Coral Bay; one of the best, offered by Sunvil, is spacious *Villa Hilarion*, ideal for families of up to five – there's no pool, but there are plenty of verandahs and it's walking distance to the beach. There's also a small **campsite** behind the beach, *Feggari* (C£1 per site, C£1.50 per person), which – given the area's transport connections – would make a more practical base than the site near Yeroskípou.

In terms of **restaurants**, *Corallo* (traditional Cypriot) and *La Vigna* (Italian) on the main "strip" are tolerable, but much the best local eating is at south-Indian-run *Keralam* (☎26622877) northwest of the main public beach in the Aristo Coral Bay Complex. As the name suggests, Keralan food is featured; portions aren't huge, and it's not cheap for Cyprus, but the fare is deceptively rich and the quality high. There's a less expensive buffet lunch on Sundays only.

## Áyios Yeóryios

Just past Coral Bay, developments begin to taper off amidst vineyards and grain fields; the road, while still asphalted, dwindles too. The Roman town on **Cape**

**Dhrépano**, 8km beyond, has been supplanted by a modern Christian church at **ÁYIOS YEÓRYIOS** (Agios Georgios), with a nearby offering-tree like that at Ayía Solomóni in Káto Páfos, next to a medieval chapel dedicated to Saint George. Prayers are still said here for the recovery of lost objects and people (hence the tree).

Some 200m southeast of the modern church sprawls an enormous Byzantine sixth-century **basilica complex** (summer daily 9am–1pm & 2–6pm, winter Mon–Sat 9am–3.45pm; C£0.75) with extensive panels of geometric and animal floor mosaics, admittedly not as vivid as those in Káto Páfos but still worth a stop. In the nave, behind the *synthronon* or semicircular bishop's throne (on the left as you face it), an octopus is surrounded by birds, fish and even a turtle; two panels right of this, a crustacean and a snail appear. Such bestiaries are common enough in pagan art, but rare in Christian iconography; it has been theorized that they refer to the pre-lapsarian Golden Age evoked in Isaiah 11:6–9. The most vivid geometric mosaics, a trellis pattern of interlocking curved squares, are at the southwest corner, in the elevated baptistry. Another later, smaller basilica lies to the south, with attractive column capitals but no mosaics.

Aside from the basilica mosaics, and a few rock-cut tombs (accessible by footpath down the cliff), the headland has little allure other than spectacular sunsets, and a possible role as a base for exploring the Akámas peninsula. American-sponsored archeological digs on the little offshore islet of **Yerónissos (Geronisos)** have discovered a stone inscribed to Apollo at the bottom of a sacred well, and Byzantine-era remains. This is explained by the fact that **Moudhális**, the little port opposite, was an important halt on the trade route between Byzantium and Egypt; if you follow the road down to modern Moudhális, you'll find an anchorage still used by the local fishermen, but artificially strewn (and often littered) sand, and water hardly more salubrious.

More secluded swimming alternatives and a more attractive shore are found by going south along the dirt track beginnning from the "Stop" sign on the curve of the road down to Moudhális. Spurs off the main track lead to the area called "**White Cliffs**", where sculpted chalk formations offer good sunbathing and conceal miniature sandy coves as far down as Manijín islet. They're well known to locals, however, and getting into the water can be problematic, what with reef underfoot. It is also possible to **walk** back to Coral Bay, some 6km through countryside that is rapidly being filled with villa projects; however the coastal track is a public right-of-way.

### Practicalities

Several **hotel-tavernas** are scattered about the cape within walking distance of each other. Setting aside the brutalist two-star *Macarthur*, others include the *Yeronisos* (T & F 26621078; ❶), a one-star hotel, slightly inland by the access road, with friendly British-Cypriot co-management; and the *West End Rooms & Restaurant* (T 26621555; ❷), opposite, the best value here, with immaculate en-suite doubles. *Saint George* (T 26621306; ❷), the sea-view establishment, has a limited number of basic rooms and is most regarded for its terrace **restaurant**, always packed at weekends (booking advised) for the sake of its fresh, reasonably priced fish and unbeatable views; your platters come from the anchorage just below, and with starters and a beer won't run to much over C£12 a head.

### The "Snake George" Reptile Park

Signs direct you inland from the Eko filling station to the "**Snake George**" **Reptile Park** (daily 9am–sunset; C£1 adults, C£0.50 kids), the brainchild of one Hans Joerg Wiedl. An Austrian who first came to Cyprus as a UN peace-keeper in 1973, he settled permanently on the island in 1986 and promptly dedicated himself to educating the Cypriots *not* to kill every snake they saw. The exhibit humanely houses at least one specimen of every Cypriot endemic species, including a vital captive breeding population of the aquatic "grass" snake, long feared to be extinct but rediscovered in 1992 (and just barely hanging on in its one natural island habitat, see p.256). More spectacularly, in September 2000 a female specimen at the exhibition dispelled 242 years of misconception by proving that the Cypriot blunt-nosed viper lays eggs rather than giving birth to live young. Hans Joerg, if he's about, makes an enthusiastic guide to his beloved snakes and turtles, in particular the captive-bred grass snakes hunting minnows in special ponds.

## Beaches and gorges: Avgás and around

At the intersection 500m inland from Áyios Yeóryios, the northbound option signposted "Akámas Peninsula, 18km" takes you towards the finest canyons and beaches on this coast. The road is paved only until "White River Beach", and beyond that point is apt to be badly chewed up by British military vehicles; you can usually wrestle an ordinary car as far as the junction 8km beyond Cape Lára (see next section), but for guaranteed passage – and any forays beyond – you really need a 4WD vehicle.

### "White River" and Toxéftra beaches

The first attractive sandy bay, signposted as "**White River Beach**" (Áspros Pótamos in Greek), lies about a kilometre north of the junction, at the mouth of the Áspros gorge; access from the road is now controlled with a chain, locked at dusk, perhaps to prevent folk absconding with the "sunbets" and "ubmrellas" (sic). Just inland of the road here stands *White River Snack Bar*, whose proprietor has seen to the illicit paving of the road to his doorstep (but no further, of course). Most drivers will press on another 1500m towards unamenitied **Toxéftra Beach**, far sandier and lonelier.

### The Avgás (Avákas) and Koufón gorges

Toxéftra is essentially the mouth of the Avgás gorge system, "Avákas" in dialect and increasingly signposted as such. With your own vehicle, you can bear right, following a wooden forestry department sign, to the point where the valley, initially given over to grapefruit and banana plantations, splits into the two notable ravines. After parking near the more spectacular left-hand (northerly) one, which is the **Avgás/Avákas Gorge** proper, you can start off on the trail which quickly appears. The canyon walls soar ever higher, and before June at least there's plenty of water, duly tapped by irrigation piping for the thirsty orchards downstream. Some fifteen minutes along, the gorge narrows into a spectacular gallery where the sun rarely penetrates, before opening again, about half an hour along, at the foot of a scree-and-boulder slope loosened further by a 1996 earthquake.

Avoid this, and carry on straight upstream through the canyon, where **streamside vegetation** abounds: juniper, plane and pine trees, terebinth, mastic, oleander and fragrant storax shrubs, plus (at ground level) orchids, cyclamen and a rare endemic centaury. The receding cliffs to either side are alive with birds, and on the foliage close by, Savigny's tree frog can often be sighted. You emerge, an hour to an hour and a half later, in the Lípati pastures just below the vineyards of Aródhes, with some track-tramping separating you from that village.

The right-hand (southerly) gorge of **Koufón** seems initially less impressive, but after about twenty minutes past weirdly eroded rocks you reach a point where rock-climbing and/or abseiling skills are required. You would eventually reach the Lípati tableland which separates Koufón from Avgás.

## Cape Lára and beyond

The symmetrical cape at **Lára**, just over 5km north of Avgás and nearly 28km from Páfos, shelters large sandy beaches on either side, which you choose according to how the wind is blowing. The slightly overpriced but beautifully set **café-snack bar** overlooking the kilometre-long southerly beach is so far the sole facility (closed Nov–April).

The smaller northerly bay, signposted as "**Lara Turtle Hatchery**", is one of several local nesting grounds for green and loggerhead sea turtles. Gently shelving, and thus warm enough for dips early in spring, this is even more scenic than its neighbour, backed by low cliffs and buffeted by the surf which wafts the turtles in on midsummer nights to lay their eggs. Accordingly the whole area is fenced, with no access to the coast allowed on nesting-season evenings (June–early Oct), when the station towards the north end of the beach is staffed by volunteers. At other times access is uncontrolled, the only evidence of the midsummer activity being stacked wire-mesh cages used to protect the turtle nests from marauding foxes – and a helpful, informative exhibit-board by the car-park area.

**Beyond Lára**, the coastal track continues past more tiny coves on its way to Joni and former British Army firing range (see p.210). Aside from completely retracing steps to Páfos, there are three alternative ways out of the Lára area. The

### Sea turtles and their conservation

The western coast of Páfos district is one of the last Mediterranean nesting grounds of green and loggerhead turtles, both endangered species. Although ocean-going reptiles, the turtles require dry land to lay eggs, gravitating late at night towards long, fine-sand, gentle-surf beaches for the purpose.

In Cyprus, the turtles nest every two to four years from late May to mid-August, laying clutches of about a hundred round eggs at a depth of 50 to 70cm every two weeks during this period. The hatchlings emerge after dark some seven weeks later, instinctively making for the sea, which they recognize by reflected moon- or starlight. Thus any artificial light sources behind "turtle beaches" (flashlights, bonfires, tavernas, hotels, etc) disorientate the baby turtles, who head in the wrong direction to die of dehydration. Similarly, if the females are disturbed by light or movement, they will return to the sea without depositing their eggs properly. Because of these factors, green turtles have ceased to breed at now-developed coasts near Coral Bay and around Ayía Nápa; loggerheads still attempt to nest on beaches fringed by light sources, which usually results in death for the hatchlings.

It is thought that sea turtles reach maturity between fifteen (for loggerheads) and thirty years (greens) after hatching, and by an imperfectly understood imprinting process return to the very beach of their birth to breed. Perhaps one in a thousand hatchlings survives to adulthood. Predators, particularly foxes, dig up the eggs on land; a high surf can literally drown the eggs; and until they attain sufficient size at about ten years of age the juveniles are easy prey for sharks, seals, and large fish.

Surveys taken in 1976 and 1977 showed an alarming drop in Cypriot turtle populations, to barely a hundred green turtle females in the Lára region, and a slightly larger number of loggerheads (which also nest in the Pólis area). Accordingly, in 1978 the Lara Turtle Conservation Project and its field station were established in an attempt

most adventurous involves heading 8km north to **Koudhounás junction**, then climbing for 5km more through thick forest to the ridge track above the Smiyiés picnic grounds. Some years this is feasible in an ordinary car, but most seasons you'll need a jeep – always enquire locally before committing yourself. Otherwise, the more northerly ("Ineia 16km, Drouseia 13km") of two signposted dirt tracks heading inland from behind the southerly Lára Beach winds up to a point on the main ridge road between Faslí and the two villages cited. The southerly track ("Ineia 8km"), mostly cemented now if still one-lane, is an easier climb **up to Ínia village**, a rise in altitude of 500m past the outcrops of Áyios Yeóryios peak, which should present no problems to an ordinary rental car.

# Villages of the Akámas heights

The Akámas peninsula begins north of an imaginary line joining Áyios Yeóryios and Péyia village. Named after a legendary lover of Aphrodite, this is the most desolate, and (except for Tillyria) the most thinly populated portion of Cyprus. An inclined plane of sparsely vegetated chalk and reef limestone atop sharp volcanic peaks, it drops off sharply to the east and north but falls more gradually west towards the sea, furrowed by ravines that hide precious water. At its centre the land climbs to a spine of hills nearly 700m high, now supporting the bulk of permanent habitation in the area, though in ancient times the coastline was more important.

Several of the **villages of the Akámas heights** were partly or wholly Turkish Cypriot before 1974, and either the prior troubles or the subsequent exodus

to reverse this decline. Each summer, volunteers search this and nearby beaches for the telltale tracks that females leave behind when returning to the sea; nests are assessed for viability, and if poorly sited, the eggs are dug up, transferred to Lára for reburial, and protected by wire anti-fox mesh. Turtle gender is determined by incubation temperature, which in turn is a function of nest depth: 29–30°C results in an even sex balance, lower temperatures in more males, higher temperatures in excess females. Since its inception, the Lára programme has resulted in a quadrupling of the yearly survival rate for hatchlings, and staff scientists have also begun experimenting with raising young turtles in tanks to further reduce mortality.

Despite financial support by the government's Department of Fisheries since 1978 and (more recently) the EU, the turtle conservation project may ultimately be futile if development battles raging over this deceptively peaceful place go the wrong way. The designation of the entire coast from "White River Beach" to a point several kilometres north of Lára as a "specially protected area" in 1989 did not prevent 25 lorry-loads of sand being illegally carted away from Toxéftra Beach by minions of the bishop of Páfos in early 1995, for use in the Tsádha golf-course; the archdiocese still hopes to put up a luxury resort within sight of Lára, and in 1997 refused an offer of C£40 million compensation from the World Bank in exchange for dropping opposition to the establishment of a national park here, which would incorporate some of its property. Almost the only non-governmental groups opposing such development schemes are Friends of the Earth, the Cyprus Conservation Foundation, and the Laona Project (see p.194 for the latter). The news is not all bad, however; sand-filching seems to have definitely been stopped, and in 2003 the turtle-hatching beaches at Pólis and Límni (east of Pólis) gained some statutory protection.

left them almost empty: their lands, however extensive, were generally too poor to attract refugees from the North, and silk-cocoon culture – the major traditional earner – had already withered away by the 1960s. Other, wholly Greek-Cypriot communities have shrunk as well – thanks to the usual emigration overseas or to Cypriot towns, often no further than the service-sector jobs of the Páfos resorts. Mostly the old remain, some wondering why the "miracle" of Ayía Nápa shouldn't be repeated here.

Virtually the only organization to suggest otherwise is the **Laona Project** (PO Box 257, Limassol ☎ 25369475, ℻ 25352657), supported by the European Commission and the philanthropic Leventis Foundation. Theirs is a two-pronged programme: to secure protection for the natural environment of the wildest parts of the Akámas, and to revive the dying villages by introducing "sustainable tourism" – specifically the restoration of selected old properties for use as visitor accommodation, and the involvement of tourists in the day-to-day economies of the villages. So far Sunvil Travel, a quality British tour operator, has been the main taker, being the exclusive UK representative for a variety of Laona-restored accommodation between Páfos and Pólis. If already in Cyprus, you can call the Laona Project directly (ask for Artemis Yiordamli or her assistant) to book any of the 26 properties available to date. The village houses and inns, in Milioú, Páno and Káto Akourdhália, Krítou Térra and Káthikas, cost from C£25 per day for two.

## Péyia, Akoúrsos and Káthikas

Some 4km above Coral Bay, along the well-graded E709 road, the large village of **PÉYIA** (Pegeia) tumbles down a hillside overlooking the sea. After the excesses of Káto Páfos, the place's very ordinariness counts as an asset, but identity has shifted considerably since it became a dormitory community for vast numbers of expats buying purpose-built villas or renovating old houses. The villagers had already amassed considerable wealth from selling off landholdings closer to the shore at the start of the Pafian tourist boom, with the funds reflected in the not always sympathetic "updating" of Péyia dwellings.

Most **accommodation** around Péyia is between the village and Coral Bay, in fairly expensive, purpose-built villas with pools. For longer-term (by the month) lodging in the village, the local Agridiana Company is recommended (☎ 99764344 or 99696956). It's worth coming to Péyia proper just to eat at one of several decidedly carniverous **tavernas** grouped around the cistern-fountain square; *Peyia* is one of the most consistent and popular, a cheap-and-cheerful option where meals (drink extra) run about C£6 whether *mezé* or à la carte. The adjacent *Kyrenia*, which serves a fixed *mezé* (C£6 a head, house wine extra), is renowned for its Wednesday- and Sunday-evening magic-trick cabaret and dance contests. The *Jail Pub*, just downhill from these, was indeed the regional British police station, magistrate's court and prison from 1916 to 1953; prison decor abounds, along with billiards, darts and a steady expat clientele. Péyia is important enough to rate its own ALEPA **bus** connection on line #7.

The E709 road from Péyia curls west, then east as it climbs scenically through dense pine forest, and then photogenic vineyards, on its way to Káthikas, up on the Akámas watershed at the very edge of the commercial grape-growing zone. However, if you're starting from Coral Bay, the minor F704 is shorter (though not faster) and more relaxing, threading en route through the goatherds' village of **AKOÚRSOS**, which has one seasonal taverna – and a small population of Turkish Cypriots who refused to leave in 1975.

**KÁTHIKAS** has long been noted for its wine, particularly any which isn't sent downhill to the mass-market wineries. The best local **microwinery** is Vasilikon (☎26633237) on the western bypass road, noted for its Ayios Onoufrios red and Vasilikon white. There's a rather listless **information centre** in the old school (Tues–Sun 11am–4pm) behind the church, but the main highlights in Káthikas are three excellent **tavernas**. *Araouzos* (☎26633035 or 26632076), 150m west of the church on the through road, is famous for its homestyle dishes – *kolokássi* (taro root) with pork, *domátes me avgá* (sun-dried tomatoes with egg), rabbit stew, *spanagórizo* (spinach pilaf), *goutsiá* (broad beans), *pastítsho* (macaroni pie) and beets served with their greens. The menu changes daily – you'll never get all the delicacies cited, sometimes just roast chicken or roast lamb – but it's indisputably good value since a set-price (about C£6.50) covers all you can eat and drink. Not surprisingly, it's packed with a mix of Cypriots and tourists on most weekend nights, when reservations are virtually mandatory; lunch is much calmer.

*Taverna Imoyeni/Imogen's Inn* (☎26633269 or 26632954; dinner only, closed Dec–Feb), just east along the same street, also offers an abundant C£7-a-head *mezé* with a slight Egyptian flair (proprietress Eleni lived there many years), plus excellent red or white house wine to wash it down. There's attractive courtyard seating in summer, while during the cooler months the interior can be crowded and loud with a loyal following who attend as much for the sake of the kindly London-Cypriot couple at the helm as for the food. The third, and most recent, entrant in the Káthikas eating sweepstakes is *Farmyard Tavern*, out on the eastern bypass road (☎26632745 or 99421706; closed Sun eve). The food's a bit Anglicized, and the management makes the common error of mixing fish and meat dishes, but the good-quality C£6.50 *mezé* is abundant (go hungry), and there's a pleasant environment and reasonable wine list.

Káthikas has a fair amount of short-term **accommodation**, for example *Chelidona* (☎26233358, ℻26244467, ✉ioloarch@spidernet.net; ❷), which has three one-bedroom apartments in a house restored as part of the agrotourism initiative. Slightly newer possibilities include *Loxandra's House* (☎26632150 or 25336673, ℻25335734; studio ❷, 1- bedroom ❸), a restored but smart complex with four one-bedroom or studio units, and *Anogia tou Mikhali* (☎26944229, ℻26943286, ✉papanna@cytanet.com.cy; ❷), another restoration project at the start of the road to Akoúrsos, with a walled courtyard and two split-level units.

## The ridge route to Pólis

At Káthikas the E709 turns north to track the spine of Akámas; it's a drive worth doing at least once for its own sake, as opposed to the main valley route (the B7) which is in fact no quicker (and far more dangerous). All the villages along here require slight detours – bearing left initially takes you onto the parallel access road for the two Aródhes settlements, Ínia and Dhroúsha.

**PÁNO ARÓDHES** (Arodes) is still mostly inhabited, despite being rocked by an earthquake on February 23, 1995; many damaged buildings around the handsome square, including the church, have been repaired in exemplary fashion, and in the process tourist **accommodation** created – including the *Themokrini Studio* (☎26332148; ❷) and the *Karythia Cottage* (☎99659928 or 24634680, ℻24641838; ❺), the latter a three-bedroom house with pool, available through Sunvil.

**KÁTO ARÓDHES** was also badly hit by the quake, but before that was a sad casualty of 1963–1974; a few cracked houses emblazoned with the Turkish star and crescent still stand empty, the fields and vineyards around largely abandoned, with their terrace walls slowly being toppled by vaulting goats. But such is the pressure of tourism and second-home hunger that here, too, a high proportion of the dwellings have been renovated.

Humbler **ÍNIA** (Ineia), in the shadow of craggy Áyios Yeóryios peak, roof of the Akámas, once cultivated cotton, flax and winter wheat all the way down to the Lára shore; now the villagers only concern themselves with goats and a few vines. The Laona Project has helped establish a private **basket-weaving museum** here (℡ 26332562 for information). Ínia can also offer the friendly *Dionysos Taverna* (aka *Eleni and Marios*) advertising "home-made food", and it's very good and inexpensive indeed; since the place doubles as the main coffee-house, you may be able to get served until about 3pm.

### Dhroúsha

**DHROÚSHA** (Drouseia), with its sturdy stone dwellings, magnificent views and winding streets, is still perhaps the best single target along this ridge, despite incipient gentrification. There are just four hundred current inhabitants, but local boosters claim fifty times that many loyal emigrants and descendants live abroad; their simultaneous appearance at holiday times puts such a strain on resources that the locally staffed, three-star *Dhroushia Heights* **hotel** (℡ 26332351, ℻ 26332353; ❾) is the result. With sweeping views, plus a small pool and tennis court, this is also popular with foreign walking groups, and represented by various UK tour operators. Both above and below the central junction are half-a-dozen *kafenía* and **tavernas**; *Christos* at the top of the grade attracts groups, *Phinikas* at the bottom tends to serve dinner only, and many of the others only operate in peak season.

The evocative rock pinnacles of **Áyios Yeóryios peak** (669m), just to the west, offer scope for rock-climbing, mostly ascents of around twenty metres at all grades of difficulty – but no bolts in the rock to clip your rope to.

**Beyond Dhroúsha**, head north to rejoin the main ridge road, which brings you to Prodhrómi, just west of Pólis, without any complications. Alternatively, you could cut eastwards from Dhroúsha across the main ridge road, to reach Krítou Térra and its ex-Turkish-Cypriot neighbour, Térra, a kilometre north down the same valley.

### Krítou Térra and Térra

**KRÍTOU TÉRRA** (Kritou Tera) – supposedly dating from Roman times – is a lot bigger and more handsome than initial impressions suggest, with old houses lining the lush, upper banks of the ravine and covering the ridge beyond. The Laona Project has restored the trough spring at the village entrance and established just opposite a **café-taverna**, *Kefalovryso*, which has worked erratically in recent years. On the same plaza is the Environmental Studies Centre, an introduction to the natural history and ecology of the area. There are three places to **stay**: the three-unit *House of Anastasia* on the east side of the village (℡ 26332209, ℻ 25369679; ❷), available through the Laona Project in Limassol; the agrotourism project's three-studio-unit *Makrynari* (℡ 26232522, ℻ 26949163; ❷), at the west entrance to Krítou Térra, near the café-taverna; or the similar *Konatzi tis Kritou* (℡ 22766336, ℻ 22762890; studio ❷, 1-bed ❸), up on the "ridge" of the village.

Krítou Térra also marks one possible approach to the late Byzantine church of Ayía Ekateríni (see below): proceed through the village, past the single central *kafenío* (not the *Kefalovryso*) and the *House of Anastasia*, exiting the village on a cement drive descending south into a canyon; follow this paved track as it bends north–northeast to reach the lonely church after 4km.

**TÉRRA** (Tera), 1km down the hill, was for years occupied only by a few Greek-Cypriot refugees but in recent years a large proportion of its fine dwellings have been occupied by Nicosians keen on a squattable weekend retreat. It's worth seeking out the handsome, buttressed, eighteenth-century mosque and the arcaded (but now dry) fountain just south and down the hill.

# Along the Páfos–Pólis highway

The busier, **B7** route north out of Páfos to Pólis, the district's second town, climbs to a saddle near Tsádha and then rollercoasters through the gentle hills around Stroumbí and Yiólou, two of several local villages devoted to winegrapes. The hummocky terrain is softened, too, by fruit trees and the occasional hedge of artichokes, budding until May. Don't get too distracted by the beauty of the surroundings, though – the road is dangerous, with bends, sharp grades and plenty of slow trucks; rumour has it that a motorway will be built from Páfos to Pólis in due course.

## Milioú and the Akourdhália villages

Beginning the gradual descent to Pólis, a detour 2km west leads to the calcium-sulphate spa of **Áyii Anáryiri Milioú (Agioi Anargyroi Miliou)**, set in a secluded, citrus-planted valley. However, the one-star *Ayii Anargyri* hotel here (℡26632318; ❷) is overpriced, and the cool, mineral-water pool is for guests only. **MILIOÚ** village itself, 1km further, was badly hit by the February 1995 quake (the two fatalities were recorded here) but still has an oasis feel; there's a single taverna-coffee-shop which – if it's open – can often be persuaded to

---

### Golf in Cyprus

In April 1994, Cyprus's first **golf course** (excluding the two reserved for British Forces, at Dhekélia and Episkopí) opened 1500m southeast of Tsádha village. It occupies land which formerly belonged to the late medieval monastery of Stavrós tís Mýthas, now marooned in the middle.

At first thought, a golf course might seem a strange idea for an island perennially short of water that ought perhaps to be reserved for agriculture and urban use. The new course has also depleted equally scarce local beaches; its traps/bunkers were allegedly filled with sand stolen by night from the Toxéftra turtle-nesting area. The haulier, working for the bishop of Páfos, was caught red-handed, and both men were fined wrist-slap amounts; subsequently the good bishop, who had authorized the alienation of monastic lands to lay out the course, announced that he considered his debt to society fully discharged.

For its part, the family now managing the **Tsádha golf course** has claimed that their sand is *not* from Toxéftra, and that the lawns are irrigated with water unfit for other purposes. They also argue that, with the EU (of which Cyprus is now a member) avalanched with oranges and tomatoes, as well as drowning in a wine lake, the country has no choice but to opt for upmarket tourism of this type. In 1998 another course, **Secret Valley**, opened, with two more – **Vikla** near Limassol, and **Aphrodite Hills** near the district boundary – commencing operations since then. But the pivotal issue, in light of the recent tendency to market Cyprus as a lowest-common-denominator tourism destination, and generally falling arrival numbers, is whether enough four- or five-star hotel patrons and villa guests will pay the going rates to keep such outfits alive.

prepare good-value homestyle meals, with some local tangerines thrown in at the right time of year (Dec–Jan).

A direct onward road from Milioú to Páno Akourdhália shown on most maps does not really exist. You actually emerge at **KÁTO AKOURDHÁLIA** (Kato Akourdaleia), blessed with a "Folk Art Museum" in the former school, 300m west of the village centre (the headman Mr Sofokleous has the key and can often be found working in the dog-guarded farm a little way down the track to Ayía Paraskeví). Just before the folk museum, a signposted cement – later dirt – track leads west to reach after 1500m the jewelbox-like chapel of **Ayía Paraskeví**, perched opposite a ruined watermill on the flank of the Kyparísha gorge. Restored in 1991, its original construction date is uncertain – estimates vary by nearly a thousand years – but some time between the twelfth and fifteenth centuries seems likely. Though completely bare of decoration, it is well worth the special trip, not least for its magical setting above the ravine.

Káto offers ample **accommodation**: the restored, if somewhat eccentrically managed *Amarakos Inn* (☎26633117 or 22313374, ⓦwww.amarakos.com, or through Sunvil/Laona Project; ❹), whose en-suite units are furnished to a high standard. There's an attractive breakfast courtyard, though the restaurant itself is not up to much. For more privacy or families, they have an adjacent three-bedroom villa, which comes with pool (which inn guests can use). Nearby there's the family-oriented *Olga's Cottage* (☎99571065; ⓦwww.olgascottage.com; ❸ for 4 people, ❺ for 6).

**PÁNO AKOURDHÁLIA** (Pano Akourdaleia), when you finally reach it by continuing southwest on the main road through Káto, has a sixteenth-century church as attractive as its modern replacement is hideous, and a Laona-instigated herb centre in the old school.

Páno Akourdhália and Milioú can be enjoyably visited together **on foot**, by leaving vehicles in either Milioú or Páno Akourdhália and then following Walk 4 from the recommended *Discover Laona* booklet (available most easily from Terra Books in Páfos). We will not plagiarize or even paraphrase this excellent little regional guide, but merely note some important changes since publication in 1993. The initial track west out of Milioú is now completely cemented, retaining no cobbled or earth surface; turn right onto a dirt track after 500m, the trail now starts between walls at the end of this. The spring near the hybrid lemon/orange tree has run dry. Returning from Páno Akourdhália, the reportedly overgrown zigzags in the path are now cleared, but the path from the water tank down to Milioú has become a messy bulldozer track. The walking time of about two hours is still correct.

## Ayía Ekateríni

About 1km short of Skoúlli village on the B7, a black-lettering-on-white sign points the way towards **Ayía Ekateríni**, the best-preserved late-Byzantine church in the Akámas, 1500m along a side road to the left. Set in the middle of vineyards, the church is unusual for its southwest-to-northeast orientation, its lofty central cupola and (betraying Lusignan influence) its arcaded, domed narthex of the sixteenth century. There was apparently once another structure similar to the narthex on the north side, also with three domes, hence Ayía Ekateríni's local nickname of "Seven-Domed" (counting the central one). Currently, the existing domes are brightly plastered, and visible from afar. Since the 1953 earthquake, only traces of frescoes remain, but the masonry is largely intact, and the setting, looking across the Stávros tís Psókas stream valley to the

Tillyrian Tróödhos, is enchanting – try to be here towards the end of the day, as the sun sets on the hills opposite. Inside (the centre narthex door is usually open) the church is triple-aisled, these set apart by delicate arcades of three pointed arches; since 1999 a stone-tiled floor has replaced the former one of tamped earth, and judging from tended oil lamps, cheap icons and votive offerings, the church is still actively used. The onward road up to Krítou Térra is also paved.

## Khóli, Goúdhi and Khrysokhoú

Just before the Skoúlli bridge, a narrow, inconspicuous road leads west towards **KHÓLI** (Choli), remarkable for two beautiful post-Byzantine churches. The late fifteenth- or early sixteenth-century **Arkhángelos Mikhaïl church** is actually predated by half a century by its belfry, which was built by James II as a watchtower to monitor the Ottoman threat. Inside the barrel-vaulted, single-ribbed church a number of frescoes survive, betraying Italianate influence. The north side of the vault is devoted to the life of the Virgin, with a particularly good *Blessing of the Infant Mary by the High Priests* on the lower right. Below this is a recognizable fragment of Osia Maria being spoon-fed by the abbot Zozimadhos; Maria was an Alexandrine courtesan who, repenting of her ways, fled to the desert and performed extreme penances, being found at the point of starvation by the good abbot. The south wall is reserved for the Life and Passion of Christ; particularly vivid scenes include the *Transfiguration* behind the altar screen, with one apostle covering his mouth in awe, and a well-preserved *Crucifixion* at the far west end, with the Virgin and friends on the left of the Cross, and St John and the Good Centurion on the right. There are also some frescoes in the nearby fifteenth-century chapel of the **Panayía Odhiyítria**; the keys for both churches are found in the combination *kafenío*-dwelling of the priest and his wife, just uphill from the phone box. You're expected to donate a candle, and the keepers are apt to get tetchy if, as a non-Orthodox, you linger too long.

There's **accommodation** in Khóli, namely an exceptional restored four-unit complex with a pool, *Ta Palatia* (available exclusively through Sunvil). The adjacent hamlet of **GOÚDHI** (Goudi) has an even larger restoration complex, the popular *Kostaris* (☎99626672 or 26270440, ☏26242339, ©kostaris@cytanet.com.cy; 1-bed ❹, 3-bed ❺), consisting of seven variably sized units, again with a terrace-pool; Cyprus Villages (☎24332998, ⓦwww.cyprusvillages.com.cy) maintains a presence here, too, at *Spanos House* (❷), divided into three small apartments, sharing a pool.

Some of the best *mezé* in Páfos district – C£10 per head for the works, including wine – is just across the valley from Goúdhi at *George and Nitsa's* (☎26991031 or 99655617); seating is limited so booking is essential, particularly on Fridays. To find them, descend to the B7 along the Goúdhi slip road, then keep going on the minor road opposite for about 50m, then 100m right to what's essentially a private house with a large verandah taking in the view.

Approaching Pólis, you can't help but notice the forlorn mosque, once a Byzantine chapel, of **KHRYSOKHOÚ** (Chrysochou) village, abandoned like many other Turkish settlements to the south and east of Pólis in 1975. In this case the surrounding farmland was fertile enough to attract a full complement of Greek-Cypriot refugees. The disused mosque is open for visits to its plain interior, and its stone minaret was carefully restored in 1998–99.

# Pólis

Set back slightly from the Stavrós tís Psókas stream as it enters Khrysokhoú (Chrysochou) bay, **PÓLIS** remains (just) the most easy-going of the island's coastal resorts, and the only one that still makes much provision for independent travellers. The Berlin backpacker-hippies who "discovered" the place in the

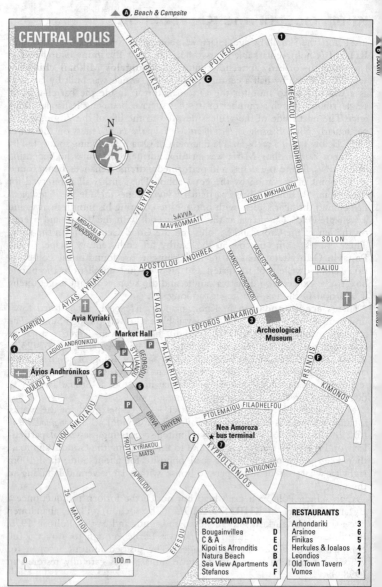

▲ **Ⓐ**, Beach & Campsite

**CENTRAL POLIS**

THESSALONIKIS
DHIOS POLIEOS **Ⓒ**
**❶**
MEGALOU ALEXANDHROU

N

**Ⓓ**
YERYINAS
VASILI MIKHAILIDHI
SAVVA MAVROMMATI
SOFOKLI DHIMITRIOU
MISIAOULI & KAVAZOGLOU
SOLON
APOSTOLOU ANDHREA **❷**
MANOLI ANDRONIKOU
VASILEOS FILIPPOU
IDALIOU
AYIAS KYRIAKIS
**Ⓔ**
✝ **Ayia Kyriaki**
EVAGORA
LEOFOROS MAKARIOU **❸**
**Market Hall**
PALIKARIDHI
**Archeological Museum**
25 - MARTIOU
AGIOU ANDRONIKOU
GEORGIOU STYLIANOU
**Ⓕ**
ARSINOIS
**←  Áyios Andhrónikos**
✉
✝
**❺**
**❻**
KIMONOS
IOULIOU 9
AYIOU NIKOLAOU
GRIVA DHIVENI
PTOLEMAIOU FILADHELFOU
PROTOU
KYRIAKOU MATSI
**(i)**
**Nea Amoroza ★ bus terminal**
**❼**
KYPROLEONDOS
ANTIGONOU
25 - MARTIOU
APRILIOU
EFESOU

**ACCOMMODATION**
| Bougainvillea | D |
| C & A | E |
| Kipoi tis Afronditis | C |
| Natura Beach | B |
| Sea View Apartments | A |
| Stefanos | F |

**RESTAURANTS**
| Arhondariki | 3 |
| Arsinoe | 6 |
| Finikas | 5 |
| Herkules & Ioalaos | 4 |
| Leondios | 2 |
| Old Town Tavern | 7 |
| Vomos | 1 |

0 ——— 100 m

▼ *Prodhrómi & Latchí*  ·  *Páfos* ▼

early 1980s have long since moved on, or traded up, so that gentrification (and increasing commitment to the package industry) have definitely set in. Indeed, the locals are positively licking their lips at the prospect, and feel that the area has thus far not been properly "promoted" in Britain. Since the late 1990s, Pólis has been growing at a rate of knots, and not always gracefully; extensive road works and building sites are the order of the day. Gone is the small, strictly linear town straggling along a ridge and the road down to the shore – now there's a huge, featureless extension sprouting on the flatlands to the east, and apartments and villas slowly displacing citrus on the surrounding coastal plain. The scenery, whether looking west towards the tip of Akámas, or out to sea, is still magnificent, and nearby beaches, if not always brilliant, are more than serviceable.

Pólis Khrysokhoú – to give the complete historical title – occupies the sites of ancient Marion and Arsinoë, the former a seventh-century BC foundation which grew wealthy from the nearby copper mines until being destroyed by Ptolemy I, leaving little evidence of its existence other than thousands of tombs. A later member of the dynasty founded the replacement town of Arsinoë slightly to the west, and it came to be called Pólis in Byzantine times, though Arsinoë lives on in the title of the local bishop. Recent decades were not as peaceful as present appearances suggest; Turkish villages on the coast and in the valleys to the northeast and southeast got on poorly with the pro-*énosis* Greeks of the town, with a UN post required to keep order until the evacuations of 1975.

## The Town

There are few specific sights in Pólis other than an old town centre of stone buildings, with their ornate doorways and interior arches. The outstanding exceptions are a museum of archeological finds, inaugurated in 1999, and a late Byzantine church.

The **Archeological Museum** (July & Aug Mon–Fri 8am–2pm, Sat 9am–5pm; Sept–June same hours plus Thurs 3–6pm; C£0.75) consists of two galleries' worth of grave finds from Marion and Arsinoë, which flank the modern town to the northeast and southeast respectively. The most noteworthy exhibits include Archaic *amphorae* and *kraters* painted with chariot-racers, birds and geometric designs; two finely modelled female heads of the same era, plus slightly later terracotta statuettes in "Attic" style; and spiral hair-rings and plaque-like earrings of the Classical era. These last contrast sharply with a limited quantity of Hellenistic and Roman gold or silver jewellery, looking startlingly modern with its fine detail and careful stone-settings.

The little sixteenth-century church of **Áyios Andhrónikos** (admission in groups only, escorted by museum guard) lies west of the pedestrian zone, in the midst of a landscaped park. Long the central mosque for the local Turkish-Cypriot community, since their departure it has been examined by archeologists, and the cleaning of extensive, previously whitewashed frescoes has been completed. They share an affinity with the roughly contemporary wall paintings in Arkhángelos Mikhaíl in Khóli, though here it's the north vault that's devoted to the events of the Passion and Christ's post-Crucifixion appearances, whilst the south vault chronicles the life of Mary. On the north, from west to east, Eve unusually stands at the left of Jesus, in his mandorla; the angel greets the myrrh-bearers at the empty tomb (Matthew 28:5); Christ appears to Mary Magdalene (Mark 16:9), sups at Emmaus with Kleophas and Luke, who initially fail to recognize him, addresses his disciples, ascends to heaven, and bestows the Holy Spirit at Pentecost (these latter events as related in Luke 24:13–35). The south vault, alas, is in far worse condition, with only the *Kiss of Joachim and Anna*, and the *Birth of the Virgin*, recognizable, but despite this – and sundry gouged-out eyes and dagger-marks on the surviving images – Áyios Andhrónikos is well worth a visit, and the museum staff apt to be more patient than the keeper at Khóli.

## Practicalities

The town is well provided with pay-and-display **car parks** – or you can park for free in the streets north of the archeological museum. **Minibuses** from Ktima Páfos stop at the Nea Amoroza booking office (℡26321114) near the southern edge of town on Kyproléondos. There's a **CTO office** more or less opposite, at the entrance to the town centre (in season Mon, Tues, Thurs, Fri 9am–4pm, Wed & Sat 9am–2.30pm). Other amenities include a **post office**, several **banks** with ATMs and the municipal **market hall**, which is the best place to buy fruit and meat for miles around. There's also a rash of **scooter-rental** agencies, such as Tsaggaros (℡26322973) just before the Latchí turning by the Nea Amoroza office.

### Accommodation

This used to be one place in the South where you could just drive up and find accommodation on the spot, but this is no longer a good idea, at least in peak season. There are plenty of "rooms to let" signs lining the highway, especially in the direction of Latchí, though many of these remain unlicensed by the CTO. As an alternative to "urban" Pólis, the "suburb" of **Prodhrómi** (Prodromi), just 1km west, makes a good base with its abundant self-catering accommodation. Few are especially worth singling out, though, and many are in thrall to UK package operators.

Within the town itself, licensed **self-catering** choices include the *C & A* at Megálou Alexándhrou 3 (℡26321881, Ⓦwww.ca-tourist-apts.com.cy; ❷), with a pool and extensive provision for disabled customers; the *Sea View Apartments* (℡26321276; ❷), on a small turn-off from the access road to the campsite; the fancier sea-view studio or one-bedroom units at *Bougainvillea* (℡26812250, Ⓦwww.bougainvillea.com.cy; ❸), also partway along the campsite road; and, best located of all, overlooking (for the moment) peaceful fields, the *Kipoi tis Afroditis* at Dhiós Póleos 8 (℡26322219, Ⓕ26322210; ❷). There are several more expensive **hotel-apartments** – like *Stefanos* at Arsinóis 8 (℡26322411, Ⓕ26322582; ❹) – which you can bargain down to half price during the off-season.

Among very few bona fide **hotels**, the best is found 1km east of town between citrus and olive groves – the 1999-built, three-star *Natura Beach* (℡26323111, Ⓦwww.natura.com.cy; ❺), separated from a turtle-nesting beach by a broad sweep of lawn. It's a low-rise complex, nothing special architecturally, but the rooms (two-thirds ocean view, one-third mountain) are tasteful, if rather spartan. Meals are good, with a wide choice for vegetarians and many ingredients grown by the hotel; there's also on-site bicycle and scooter rental.

The **campsite** (March–Oct), by far the best in Cyprus, is magically set in a jungle of eucalyptus and calamus 1500m north of town, at the east end of the long beach that stretches all the way from Latchí. At C£1.50 per tent/caravan, and C£1 per person, plus an on-site snack-bar, it can't be faulted except for its relative remoteness, though the road back up to Pólis is lined with a few tavernas, grocers, the hospital and an excavated patch of ancient Arsinoë.

**Eating and drinking**

Most **restaurants** in the compact town centre are on the expensive or touristy side, though the quality and value on offer at *Finikas*, on the pedestrian zone, belie its dubious appearance. Universally praised *Arsinoe*, also on the pedestrian zone, specializes in fish and homemade wine, though it's open evenings only. Marginally less expensive is its worthy rival *Leondios*, on the corner of Apostólou Andhréa and Evagóra Pallikarídhi, its menu restricted to salads and palpably fresh fish; budget C£11 per person with drink, or go for the C£7 seafood *mezé*. Carnivores are well seen to at either *Herkules & Ioalaos*, in a pleasant indoor/outdoor environment by the park, or at friendly, homely *Vomos*, out at the intersection of Dhíos Poliéos and Megálou Alexándhrou, with some of the best *kléftigo* in town. For a special blow-out, try either the *Old Town Tavern* near the turning for Latchí, dear at C£15–19 à la carte (booze extra), but worth it; or, next to the archeological museum, *Arhondariki* (☎26321328), set in an old mansion as the name suggests, with attentive service and good-value food – most nights, you'll need to book here.

**Nightlife** – such as it is – revolves around a pedestrianized three-way junction, now the triangular central plaza, where a dozen self-styled "café-bar-snacks" vie for your attention.

# Northeast of Pólis

There's relatively little traffic up the coast towards Káto Pýrgos, partly because its backwater status was reinforced in 1974 by the ceasefire line just beyond – the former direct route to Mórfou and Nicosia can no longer be used, though it is very likely that this will be opened as an additional legal crossing point by 2006. The area only comes alive in summer, when the environs of **Pomós** and **Pakhýammos** become retreats of some importance for Cypriots who haven't the appetite or the wallet for the purpose-built hotel strips and restaurants elsewhere in the South. Public transport is rare along this stretch, so you really need your own wheels, and a fair bit of spare time for the arduous detour around the **Kókkina enclave**.

## Pomós and Pakhýammos

The first twenty-odd kilometres towards Pomós parallel the little-developed but exposed shoreline, though villas are sprouting here too, and this will definitely increase when the crossing point finally opens. The one facility of note, on the highway near Argáka, is the *Halfway House* **grill**, notable for its pork chops. **POMÓS** itself has a few self-catering apartments, but the village is quite featureless, and the obvious main beach not up to much. Indeed, the best pretext for a visit is a handful of **tavernas**, including *Kanali*, on the promontory east of the village centre, overlooking the fishing anchorage, which serves no-nonsense seafood at eminently reasonable prices, with views from the terrace across to the Kormakíti peninsula and the Kyrenia hills. Up on the main road, the more seasonal *Sea Cave* sees less trade but straddles access to a small, sheltered beach.

Both, however, defer to *Paradise Place* (closed Jan & Feb, plus some weekdays off-season), about 1km west of the village centre (look for the unmissable verandah), which purveys "Home made and improvised food and drink" to an "alternative" clientele of Cypriots and foreigners. Sokratis the proprietor worked in Athens for 25 years, which has had a salutary effect on the food – it's excellent, abundant and features at least one vegetarian main dish each day; budget C£8 a head. It's open from 10am till late, with no set meal hours (though it's okay to just have a drink); there's a salsa/jazz/Greek soundtrack, plus occasional live sessions, culminating in a more regular **jazz festival** for three days in late September. The promisingly named "**Paradise Beach**" (as pictured on the restaurant's business card) is well hidden and just downhill from some greenhouses across the road; the final trail approach is slippery, so flip-flops are inadvisable.

Things improve scenically as you round the prominent cape and bounce along the deteriorating road into aptly named **PAKHÝAMMOS** (Pachyammos) – "Broad Sand"; here the settlement tilts downhill towards the huge (if occasionally wave-battered and seaweed-littered) beach. Organized amenities here are limited to a taverna at the local pilgrimage shrine of Áyios Rafaélos, and a mini-market.

## Around the Kókkina enclave to Káto Pýrgos

Beyond Pakhýammos the narrow road which climbs sharply inland through forested hills was resurfaced in 1999, but it's still a tedious twenty-kilometre, 45-minute detour to avoid the problematic enclave of **KÓKKINA** (Erenköy). Until that year, the local administration hadn't bothered to improve the bypass, partly because it was always assumed that Kókkina and the old coast road would be ceded to the South in any settlement, and indeed this was envisioned in the failed Annan Plan (though see the box below for a different view). Along the way, Greek-Cypriot and Turkish-Cypriot watchtowers face each other, a few hundred metres apart; the single **UN post** towards Pakhýammos is currently manned by Argentines, often to be seen jogging along the road. You'll pass through long-abandoned Turkish-Cypriot hamlets such as Alévga and Áyios Yeorgoúdhi, and surviving Greek Mosfiléri, before reaching the coast again at ex-Turkish-Cypriot **MANSOÚRA**, its houses finally being renovated by squatters as weekend retreats. Otherwise, there's just a Greek-Cypriot military

### The Kókkina enclave

The **Kókkina enclave** was off-limits to Greek Cypriots years before the Turkish Army occupied it in 1974. Beginning in 1962, the Turkish-Cypriot TMT made it a beachhead, using it to off-load supplies from Turkey, just as their EOKA opposite numbers had previously used the then-empty westerly Páfos coast for receiving shipments from Greece. Over 500 TMT fighters – mostly young students, some of them returning directly from life in London – filtered into the handful of Turkish-Cypriot villages here, to stiffen morale; the Greek Cypriots not surprisingly sealed the area off from any further land approaches. Effectively besieged, the civilians and young garrison did without bathing and subsisted on stale bread and wormy olives as 1964 wore on.

Matters came to a head on August 3, 1964 when 3000 National Guard troops under the command of General George Grivas (see box on p.284) attempted to throttle the only tenable coastal landing-point from Turkey by attacking Kókkina and several surrounding Turkish hamlets. According to witnesses, Archbishop Makarios, communicating by field telephone from Káto Pýrgos, attempted to dissuade Grivas from proceeding, but was rebuffed. The outnumbered Turkish-Cypriot defenders were forced back into Kókkina itself; on August 8, as they were at the end of their tether, dozens of Turkish jets appeared from the mainland, bombing and strafing nearby Greek villages (including Pólis) for two days, with the use of napalm and consequent heavy casualties. Among these were coachloads of Greek students who were being bused in to gloat over the impending TMT surrender. One of the jets was shot down; the pilot bailed out, but on landing was beaten to death by outraged Greek-Cypriot villagers.

outpost, a small beach with taverna and the beautiful medieval bridge that carries the old road just upstream.

Set among peach orchards beside the buffer zone, **KÁTO PÝRGOS** proves to be a surprisingly large place, which, despite mediocre beaches to either side and a certain scruffiness, is well equipped for guests, with no fewer than three largish hotels and numerous self-catering units pitched mainly at Nicosians, who can barely conceal their eagerness for the "border" crossing here to open. Among the hotels, one-star *Tylo Beach* is the most central and comfortable (☏ 26522348, ℻ 26522136; ⑤). Other than going swimming, eating fish and watching Greek-Cypriot or UN troops, however, there's little to do here, though the potential for excursions inland has been improved of late by the paving of a road through the Tillyrian mountains to Kýkko monastery (see p.243).

# West of Pólis: Latchí, Neokhorió and the coast

Once beyond Prodhrómi, the road west hugs the so far little-developed, but often windswept, beach on its way to the emphatically developed resort of **Latchí**. Beyond here, you've a choice between excursions inland to **Neokhorió**, one gateway to the Akámas region, or following the coast to the excellent beaches at **Asprókremos** and **Ttákkas**.

## Latchí

The most celebrated "fishing village" of Páfos district, **LATCHÍ** (Latsi) has acquired a distinctly tatty air since the mid-1990s, at least as seen from the

Outright war between Greece and Turkey was only narrowly avoided through UN intervention, but the Kókkina episode marked a turning point in two ways. Had EOKA succeeded in overrunning the place, all further Turkish-Cypriot militancy would probably have collapsed; in any event, the estrangement of the two island communities, which had begun the previous year, was now virtually complete. Until 1974, Turkish Cypriots from the hills around continued to enter the fortified enclave; after the invasion, all civilians were relocated to Yenierenköy on the Kárpas peninsula, and Kókkina became strictly a military base, which it remains – there's one Turkish Army garrison, and one UN contingent in the buffer zone towards Pakhýammos. During the months of the battle, the Swedes manned the UN camp here, and one soldier, moved by the predicament of the defenders, elected to breach neutrality by supplying them. He was denounced by his commanding officer and spent two years in jail; he spent subsequent years living in northern Cyprus, fêted as a hero. Once a year, on August 8, the villagers and surviving members of the TMT garrison make a pilgrimage (by boat, of course) from the balance of the North, and visit the graves – tended as shrines – of the thirteen students who fell. Whatever the other details of a final peace settlement, the North is unlikely to give Kókkina up gracefully; it's too potent a symbol of Turkish-Cypriot resistance, despite its current lack of any strategic significance – other than playing host to a powerful transmitter for Bayrak, the north Cypriot television and radio station.

## Diving near Latchí

**Latchí Watersports Centre**, on the waterfront (☎26322095, ⓦwww.divecyprus
.com; closed Jan), offers motorboat and sailboat rental, as well as windsurfing
hire and tuition. Most of their energies, however, are devoted to **scuba-diving**,
taking in various underwater highlights along the northeast Akámas shore; the
main sites are around Áyios Yeóryios island, a protected marine reserve, and
further out towards Cape Arnaoútis. Conditions are typically better here than on
the Páfos side, as the coast is sheltered from the prevailing southwesterly winds.
Just southwest of **Áyios Yeóryios** there's a forty-metre wall, with lots of schooling
fish and scorpionfish to see, plus a cave (12m) which often contains octopuses.
Even shallow beginners' dive classes are likely to see brilliant orange moray eels,
groupers and perhaps a ray. Remoter (25-min boat transfer) but shallower dives
(9–15m) around **Cape Arnaoútis** include Pláka reef and Mazáki island, with caves,
gullies and even an arch or two, and grouper holes, wrasse and baby barracuda
during the summer; this area tends to maintain good visibility when other sites
are churned up.

Two introductory dives cost C£35, PADI-certification courses start at C£190 (BSAC
and nitrox tuition also available), or qualified divers can dive twice daily over five
days for C£180 (all equipment included). Unusually, Latchi Watersports will accept
paraplegics, and children aged 8 to 14, on its courses and dives, and their equip-
ment/instruction standard is excellent.

---

through-road, where a long succession of souvenir shops, groceries, banks,
hotels and apartments mimic in miniature Káto Páfos's seafront boulevard.
Latchí's seaward aspect is rather more appealing, with half a dozen fish tavernas
jostling to be close to the picturesque harbour – being extended in 2004–06.
At Latchí's good pebble **beach**, windsurfing or canoeing are on offer; however,
the beach itself improves as you head east towards Pólis, or west towards Loutrá
tís Afrodhítis.

### Practicalities

The best-value local **accommodation** is the two-star *Souli* (☎26321088,
ⓦwww.soulihotel.com; ⑨), just west of Latchí overlooking a clean patch of
beach; there's a pool too, as well as an attached restaurant serving good-value if
not terribly adventurous food. For a well-executed self-contained, self-catering
complex, available through most package companies (or on spec at slow times),
try the *Elia Latchi Village* (☎26321011, ⒻF26322024, Ⓔelialaki@logos.cy.net;
⑨), with two pools, lush gardens and a Club-Med-style programme for kids.
Alternatively, Sunvil has exclusive control of a number of excellent, secluded
villas a few kilometres inland, for example the *Arodaphne*, the *Kaneeta* or the
*Little Rocks*, all sleeping two to six people.

Although the Latchí waterfront promenade has been improved, many of the
**restaurants** here are much of a muchness. *Yangos and Peter's*, the oldest one with
the most local clientele, serves massive portions of fresh seafood-with-*mezé* for
under C£13 per person. At the opposite (east) end esplanade, the *Seafare* also
acquits itself well. The family-run *Psaropoulos Beach Restaurant*, about 1km east,
offers reasonable seafood, fresh salads and heated premises for the cooler months
(it's open all year); stick to fish and vegetarian *mezé* – what they do best – and
you should be all right. Just west of Latchí, about 50m before the *Hotel Souli*,
the *Periyiali* cooks more "upmarket" with a continental flair, but not so cheaply
– budget C£9 each, plus drink.

# Neokhorió

At the junction 1500m beyond Latchí, the inland turning leads to **NEOK-HORIÓ** (Neo Chorio), with a dramatic hillside setting for its stone houses. The place was moribund before 1985, but has been almost wholly renovated as the effects of tourism pulse uphill. There's a fair amount of self-catering **accommodation**, most of it fairly high standard, and several UK package companies can oblige; barring that, you can make local arrangements for a **room** in a family's house. No need to eat at sea level either, as there are several **restaurants**, including *Stone Taverna* and *Kouppas Stone Castle*, the latter with assorted oven dishes (including baby potatoes), roasts and a competent *mezé*. Neokhorió is also known for its lively **Easter Sunday festival**, with traditional games such as tug-of-war, street snacks and evening live music.

Neokhorió overlooks the **Petrátis Gorge**, famous for its bat cave (one of two caverns here) filmed by David Attenborough in 1985. The lower reaches of the canyon, clogged by boulders and vegetation, are really too rough for casual trekking; if you're interested, Simon Demetropoulos (see p.179) occasionally organizes expeditions here.

## Beyond Neokhorió: ghost hamlets and Smiyiés

Once clear of the village, if you bear left and down at the first junction, this scenic dirt track (4WD only if any mud present) crosses the shallow top of the Petrátis Gorge before reaching the former Turkish-Cypriot villages of Andhrolíkou and Faslí. Goat-patrolled **ANDHROLÍKOU** (Androlikou) is now uninhabited except for Hasan Mustafa (a "star" of the recommended film *Our Wall*; see *Contexts*) and his family; notwithstanding a reasonable amount of water by Akámas standards, the poor soil and lack of electricity failed to attract fleeing northerners after 1975. Despite a continuing absence of power, the abandoned houses are being done up as weekend retreats by Nicosians, and for their benefit a mostly paved road arrives directly up from Prodhrómi. A short, good dirt road leads from Andhrolíkou to **FASLÍ**, which has national-grid power and a sheltered position out of the prevailing winds; it too is served by a paved road from the south, along which you wind, under the antenna-and-military-radar-crowned crenellations of Áyios Yeóryios peak, summit of the Akámas, en route to Ínia.

The signposted road, bearing straight ahead just outside Neokhorió, leads, after just over 3km of occasionally rutted track (easily passable in a two-wheel-drive), to the prepared picnic grounds at **Smiyiés (Smigies)**, a pleasant, pine-forested spot, with a slightly sweet spring at one end of the eponymous nature trail (see p.212). Another 500m of careful driving brings you out onto the summit ridge, covered with yellow gorse and white rock rose in spring. Turn left and go another 500m or so to the well-signed top of the five-kilometre link road down to Koudhounás and eventually Cape Lára.

## The coast west of Latchí

The shoreline between Latchí and the Baths of Aphrodite (see p.210) once sheltered the last pristine stretch of really good beach in southern Cyprus, but since the mid-1990s that's history. Just west of the turning for Neokhorió, the five-star **Anassa Hotel** could, until the *Thalassa* opened at Coral Bay, claim to be the South's most luxurious complex. Ground for it was broken in 1997, in stark contravention of the government's "master plan" for the Akámas area.

Like the five-star *Annabelle* in Káto Páfos, it is partly owned by Alekos Mihai-lides, the ex-foreign minister obliged to resign under a cloud of scandal; full opening was delayed almost a year, to 1999, because the *Anassa* was found to have infringed its permit conditions – lip service to the "master plan". (The hotel was also obliged to remove permanently installed sunbeds on the beach, which implied that it was private). Were it a one-off, not even conservationists would mind, but the *Anassa* has served as the thin end of the wedge for villa projects which will eventually fill in all the empty coastal space between Latchí and Loutrá tís Afrodhítis, and compromise local beach quality with their inevi-table cesspit leakage. The monk seals (and bats) who apparently used to nest in caves in the bluff here have already taken their business elsewhere, as have the sea turtles whose eggs have been crushed by the assiduous dredger-grooming of the beach below the hotel.

### Asprókremos Beach and Ttákas Bay

Staying with the paved coast road below Neokhorió, you'll pass first the *Anassa*, and shortly after, the turning for the four bunker-blocks of the contrastingly modest, two-star *Aphrodite Beach Hotel* (℡26321001, ℻26322015; ❹); the site, however, is superb, and the hotel good value. The namesake beach just below – officially **Asprókremos** – is claimed to be the "best in Cyprus"; certainly it's the best in Páfos district, at least until the cement mixers start churning again up on the bluff. The unaffiliated, somewhat pricey snack-bar and sunbed-rental booth down on the beach is thus far one of only two developments actually at sea level.

The other, reached by the next side-turning, is the friendly *Ttakkas Bay Restaurant* (℡26321087; closed Nov–March), which has a loyal return clien-tele who like the good seafood (C£15 feeds two on bream and little crabs) and superb setting. Table capacity is limited so booking is advisable in high season. The little **bay** in question, just out front, has a serviceable beach of coarse sand and pebbles, with showers and more rental sunbeds/umbrellas, but carry on east around some rocks and you'll find access to the west end of Asprókremos's two-to-three-kilometre extent – ending more or less under the *Anassa*.

# The Akámas peninsula

Neokhorió is the last bona fide village before the final, tapering tip of the **Akámas peninsula**. Except for dense pine groves along the summit ridge, the region is largely deforested, though there are springs and tiny streams tucked into relatively lush hollows and gorges. The coast drops off fairly sharply, espe-cially on the northeast shore, and there's very little sandy shoreline anywhere. It's a severely impressive rather than calendar-page beautiful landscape, much of its appeal residing in the near-absence of human activity (except during the hunting season); in spring and autumn appearances of migrating cranes, herons and storks add to the allure.

Un-green as this may sound, it's territory often best explored from a boat (Latchi Watersports Centre – p.206 – can help), in a 4WD or on some sort of very sturdy two-wheeler. The few marked trails are summarized below, but a plethora of unmarked jeep tracks go almost everywhere else. The often shade-less terrain is not conducive to aimless wandering on foot, especially between June and September.

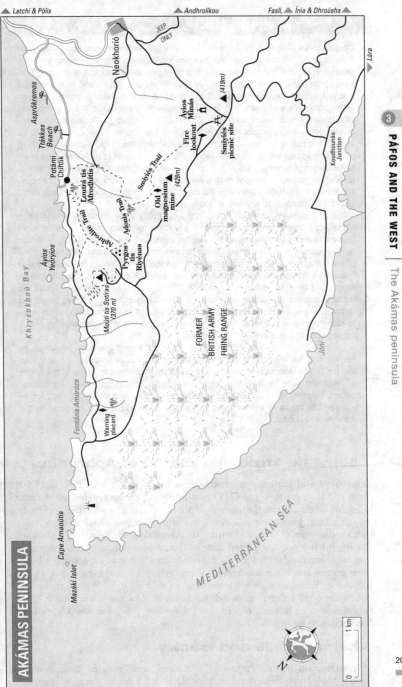

AKÁMAS PENINSULA

Despite years of special international commissions, expert reports and lobbying by Cypriot environmental groups, the **Akámas peninsula** still has no comprehensive protection regime, but remains a crazy quilt of private land (both Greek- and Turkish-Cypriot-owned) and state forest. A 1995 World Bank/EU report recommended that isolated patches of state forest be joined up, land-owners compensated, and buffer zones created, with land uses incrementally restricted to those compatible with the aims of a natural reserve. In March 2000, the Cyprus Government Council of Ministers instead proposed the extension of the "tourist development zone" for several kilometres northwest beyond Loutrátís Afrodhítis, thus allowing Carlsberg brewing magnate and property developer Photos Photiades to realize his long-cherished dream of building a major holiday complex, complete with paved-road access (asphalt at present is banned from state forest territory). Hunting is barely, if at all, controlled, with Wednesdays and Sundays from autumn to spring the designated (and thus hazardous to walkers) shooting days.

The only positive developments of the late 1990s were a ban on goat-grazing within state forest land, the continued prohibition of motor rallies, a moratorium on new licences for "jeep safaris", and the cessation, late in the 1990s, of British military exercises at their artillery firing range west of the Akámas watershed. (One of the conditions of Cypriot independence was the reservation by the UK of various "retained sites" on the island other than the Sovereign Bases, and this was one of them.) Led by such characters as DIKO MP (now Euro-MP) Marios Matsakis, an unlikely coalition of environmentalists and nationalists agitated for years to get the British to leave, exploiting lingering resentment against the UK for failing to do more to stop the invasion of 1974, though ironically the British military presence may have helped keep the area in a relatively pristine state.

Since Cyprus's accession to the EU in May 2004 (and the extra infrastructure funding that will ensue), the declaration of some sort of park seems probable, but this potential outcome has speeded up a race by developers to nibble at the edges of proposed park territory, thus compromising its final value. The latest hopeful potential development is that Mr Photiades may be offered a deal he can't refuse – prime beachfront land near Pólis – in exchange for quitting his holdings on the north Akámas coast.

## Loutrá tís Afrodhítis (Baths of Aphrodite)

The paved road along the northern side of the peninsula from Pólis and Latchí ends at a large car park and **CTO pavilion** just past the few houses of Potámi Chíftlik hamlet. Here, the named "Aphrodite" nature trail, diverging from a rough coastal jeep track at a distinctive wooden canopy and archway, begins with a five-minute walk to **Loutrá tís Afrodhítis**, the "Baths of Aphrodite". In legend the goddess retired here to bathe before (and after) entertaining assorted lovers; today's reality is a flagstoned area beside an attractive pool about four metres across, the headspring of the irrigated oasis below, fed by rivulets off the rock face of a grotto smothered in wild fig trees. Signs forbid you to succumb to the temptation of bathing in the shallow water, drinking it, climbing the trees or hanging objects from them (see p.172 for why Cypriots feel compelled to do so).

## Akámas trails and tracks

A combination of the "Aphrodite", "Adonis" and "Smiyiés" trails described below would give you the best possible transect of the Akámas watershed, though upon reaching the Smiyiés picnic grounds you'd face an additional 45 minutes' walk to get to Neokhorió, the closest habitation. The dirt road there can be rough and/or muddy after rainy winters – starting from the village, an ordinary car will make it, but a taxi-driver might refuse the trip or charge you dearly.

In order to make any sense of the Aphrodite or Adonis nature-trail labelling, you need the 28-page **key booklet** "Nature Trails of the Akamas", distributed free by the CTO and widely available both on the island and overseas. However be aware that some of the plants detailed may have died since publication, and some species are highlighted repeatedly. The Smiyiés trail is not as yet so documented. The best **map** available is Marengo Publications' "Akamas Walkers' Map", packaged as part of their pocket guide *Walks in the Akamas Area* (see p.508).

To access the trails from the Baths of Aphrodite pool, proceed downstream on a narrower path to rejoin the coastal track; just inland of this is a placard warning that the track is hazardous for any standard of vehicle, and that you proceed at your own risk.

### The Aphrodite trail

Just before the warning placard, you head up the continuation of the **Aphrodite trail**, climbing from carob, mastic and eucalyptus near sea level up to juniper, pine and other species labelled in Greek and Latin; in May, white *Cistus* (rock rose) is everywhere. At the top of the first hard climb you get good views east over the Pólis coastal plain and nearby offshore islets, before a straight-marching trail heads west through an old firebreak. There are some waymarks, plus lots of shotgun shell-casings: birds, especially quail, love the phrygana (scrub biome), and most Cypriots are keen to bag them. Somewhat under an hour above Aphrodite's baths you'll arrive at a picnic area in a hollow shaded by a gigantic oak tree; a spring here is reasonably reliable. The adjacent **Pýrgos tis Riyénas (Rigainas)** archeological site – apparently the remains of a Byzantine monastery or Lusignan fort – is self-explanatory.

Walk about ten minutes west-northwest along a dirt track from the ruins and oak tree, before bearing right onto the trail's continuation (marked by a cairn), and again right onto a dirt track. The path is finally subsumed into the narrow, sharply climbing track, which ends some twenty minutes above the oak with an opportunity to detour left on a path to the viewpoint atop the 370-metre summit known as **Moúti tís Sotíras (Páno Vakhínes)**. There's a suicide leap out towards Cape Arnaoútis, the very end of Akámas, so you retrace your steps – for all of a ten-minute detour – down to the signed junction for the descending, onward footpath to the coast.

Ingeniously engineered into the seaward-facing slopes of the mountain, this offers one more bush-shaded viewpoint before meeting up with the coastal track within around half an hour. You can avoid a fair amount of track-walking on the way back to the car park by keeping to the slightly higher path system until it ends a few minutes before some smelly goatpens to seaward. You'll need to allow approximately two and a half hours for the entire loop out of the CTO pavilion.

### The Adonis and Smiyiés trails

From the oak-shaded picnic area by Pýrgos tís Riyénas, another nature trail, the **Adonis**, heads off south on a most interesting course. The path initially climbs for fifteen minutes over a saddle, then becomes a wider track heading southeast. After ten minutes on this, you bear left (east) again onto the resurgent trail, which in five more minutes reaches a reliable spring in a forested dell at the head of a canyon.

There's also an important marked junction here: northeast down the canyon back to Loutrá tís Afrodhítis along the Adonis trail, or south onto the **Smiyiés** path. Following the latter for just over five minutes brings you to the kiln stack and tunnels of a derelict magnesium mine, which is also accessible by jeep track along the ridge to the west. The path continues briefly east, then heads south again on a fairly level course before reaching the Smiyiés picnic site just over an hour after quitting Pýrgos tís Riyénas.

From the dell-spring, the continuation of the Adonis trail back towards the CTO pavilion descends northeast along the canyon, following a water pipe at first, before curling east. Next you bear north, away from the pipe, then east again across what is now a plateau along the much-widened track through the scrub. Rather suddenly there's a zigzag plunge down towards the coastal road, the route debouching under a now-familiar standard-issue nature trail canopy, about a kilometre southeast of the CTO car park at Loutrá tís Afrodhítis. From the spring-junction down to the coast road, count on a good hour.

### The Fontána Amoróza coastal track

The most straightforward – and arguably the least exciting – Akámas walk is the six-kilometre one leading to **Fontána Amoróza**, a popular excursion destination almost at Cape Arnaoútis. It's perhaps best done in conjunction with one of the inland nature trails, and is frankly more enjoyable on a mountain bike. If you intend to walk much of it, you'd do well to arrange a boat ride from Latchí to drop you off at Fontána Amoróza, and walk back along the route of your choice – it's very tedious both ways. A simple tramp back to the CTO pavilion takes about ninety minutes; just keep to seaward at every option. Some path shortcuts are possible, especially those mentioned above at the base of Moúti tís Sotíras. If Mr Photiades does not respond to blandishments to take his hotel business elsewhere, there may so be much more to contend with en route than the few bulldozer-scrapings and temporary caravans erected to date at his prospective building site.

Vegetation en route is mostly juniper and mastic bush, with scattered pines. The coast itself, disappointingly, is not very usable; the sea is quite clear, but a northern exposure means lots of debris in the coves of mixed sand and pebbles (if it's beaches you're after, there are better, if less private, ones at Ttákkas and Asprókremos).

The celebrated **spring** at Fontána Amoróza is a crashing non-event – diligent combing of the bushes turns up nothing more substantial than a tiny, murky well (now covered) on the cliff overlooking the protected bay. Mythological hype surrounding the "fountain of love" stems from the sixteenth-century Italian traveller and poet, Ludovico Ariosto, who confused it with Loutrá tís Afrodhítis, to the frustration of all who followed him. On the bright side, the best swimming along the route is just below, where a small sand and gravel beach at the base of the cliff lies out of the wind.

More marvellous than the *fontana* perhaps is the canyon track up behind an obsolete artillery-range warning sign ("Keep out when red flags are flying as (artillery) firing is then in progress. Do not touch any object [ie military debris] on the ground as it may explode and kill you.") just to the east; about 400m along this, in a stream gully, **drinkable water** trickles amid the greenery.

# Eastern Páfos district

East of the main Páfos–Pólis road, the severity of the Akámas yields to more forgiving, stereotypically beautiful countryside, largely devoted to vineyards and almond groves. The goal of most trippers here is the large village of **Panayiá**, birthplace of Archbishop (and first Cypriot president) Makarios, and the historic monastery of **Khrysorroyiátissa** just south, but there are various, arguably more worthwhile, halting points beforehand, including a frescoed church in **Letímbou**, the **Skárfos bridge** near Filoússa, and the crafts village of **Fýti**. Beyond Panayiá, it's possible to strike out north into the Tillyrian wilderness (see p.219) and, with some hard driving, the coast northeast of Pólis; or, with greater facility, to turn south to explore the valleys of the Xerós and Dhiárizos rivers.

## Routes from Páfos

You've a choice of **approach roads** into the hills. Coming from Páfos initially on the B7, you'll find the quickest route – on the broad E703 highway – is through Polémi, descending to Kannavioú, a negligible place except for the chance to pause at tree-shaded tavernas, before the final climb to Panayiá.

### Letímbou: Áyios Kírykos and Ayía Ioulíti

Alternatively, leave the B7 at Tsádha for the F719, then turn east on the E702, via **LETÍMBOU** (Letymvou), which can offer the twelfth-century **church of Áyios Kírykos and Ayía Ioulíti**; the key is kept in the house opposite the newer central church of Áyios Theodhóros. The Byzantine church is 350m away; beside the paved plaza with a double fountain, turn left (there may be a faded sign), and then almost immediately bear right – Áyios Kírykos should be visible on the brow of a hill just ahead. The building is strikingly unusual, with the apse facing northeast rather than east, the transept far longer than the nave in a modified cross-in-square plan; the dome is supported by four low symmetrical arches rather than piers. Late fifteenth-century frescoes are fragmentary and in need of cleaning, but enough remains for anyone to see that they were once remarkable and in many cases rare in subject matter, and well worth the effort of tracking down the key.

The west side of the south transept is taken up by scenes from the birth and life of the Virgin, in particular Joachim reading to Anna from the scriptures (written in cod-Hebrew script), kissing lip-to-lip in a very un-Orthodox manner, and the blessing of young Mary by three high priests at a table elaborately set with utensils and foodstuffs. Evangelists Mark and Matthew occupy their customary places up on the pendentives, while the northeast vault (in the *ierón*) is devoted to Christ's post-Crucifixion (dis)appearances. There the Angel at the Tomb surprises the Myrrh-Bearers, the Pentecost includes a rare personification of the World (*Kosmos*) holding the twelve scrolls over the assembled Nations, and – next to this – an almost unique portrayal of Christ "in another form" (Mark 16:12), standing in a six-pointed mandorla and raising his right hand in blessing, showing the nail-wound.

Beyond Letímbou, it's a straightforward matter to proceed to Panayiá via Ayía Moní and Khrysorroyiátissa, leaving the E702 at Áyios Fótios.

## Routes from Pólis

From Pólis two initially parallel roads look as if they would be the quickest ways going southeast; however the option for Pelathoússa dwindles to dirt track after that village. Just under 4km from town you might turn left (north) on the marked side track for the medieval chapel of **Panayía Horteni**; head 200m along and there it is, picturesquely perched at the mouth of a ravine, overlooking the sea. This single-naved, domed and vaulted country church (always unlocked) was well restored in the 1990s, but of its sixteenth-century frescoes only a ring of seraphs and angels in the dome, and part of the *Assumption of the Virgin* on your left as you enter, remain recognizable; damp and vandals have seen to the rest.

The next side road south, the F733, is more rewarding, and gives eventual access to both Panayiá and Stavrós tís Psókas. It's broad two-lane as far as Stení, then colonial-era one-lane cobble thereafter. Stení isn't up to much; **PERISTERÓNA**, the next village, has a single taverna, a nearby gorge (signposted as a 1950s EOKA lair) and the rather missable **Byzantine Museum of Arsinoë** (April–Oct Mon–Fri 10am–1pm & 2–6pm, Sat 10am–1pm; Nov–March Mon–Fri 10am–4pm, Sat 10am–1pm; C£1). Forking left above this village, the road improves considerably, continuing as one-and-a-half-lane surface to Lysó and then on much broader asphalt 17km to Stavrós tís Psókas.

## Lysó

**LYSÓ** (Lysos), the largest village in the Pólis foothills, offers a clutch of seasonal snack bars, some new villas and, on a terrace just below the centre, the handsome fifteenth-century **church of Panayía Khryseléoussa** (usually locked) defaced by a surpassingly hideous new free-standing belfry. In keeping with Lysó's importance, it was probably the place of worship for the Lusignan overlords of the area, and the building preserves strictly Gothic features rather than the Byzantine-Latin hybrids seen elsewhere in Cyprus. There's lovely tracery over the north window, a blind Gothic window at the apse, and the coats-of-arms of the Gourri and Neville clans above the north and south doors respectively. The interior is not so distinguished, but there is an elaborate wooden *yinaikonítis*, and behind the altar screen, in the niche of the blocked apsidal window, a post-Byzantine *Panayia Glykofiloussa*, the *Virgin Kissing the Child*, probably executed not long before the Ottoman conquest.

### Filoússa and the Skárfos bridge

Forking between Peristeróna and Lysó brings you shortly to back-of-beyond **FILOÚSSA** (Filousa), which has only the *Philousa Manor House* (bookable through Sunvil) to offer. The road, one-lane again, continues 2.5km south to the floor of the lush Stavrós tís Psókas stream valley, popular with birdwatchers in springtime, where you may also visit the remains of the Lusignan, single-arched **Skárfos bridge**, which carried the medieval Páfos–Pólis road. Once over the modern bridge downstream from the old one, the road surface turns to dirt and you bear left onto another signposted track along the south bank for 200m, until drawing about even with a watermill on the far side of the valley. You should be at the start of the short but faint path leading down the slope to the bridge – visible from many directions, but difficult to approach.

From the bridge turning it's another 2.6km south, mostly on single-lane dirt surface, up to the E712 just below Símou; you might visit Skárfos from this direction, as the turning off the E712 is now well signposted for both the bridge and Filoússa ("5.5km").

Starting from the B7 opposite derelict Loukrounoú (supposedly the natal village of northern leader Rauf Denktaş's mother), the E712 threads through the villages of Símou, Dhrýmou, Lássa and Dhriniá, all scattered on the south-bank ridge of the Stavrós tis Psókas stream canyon, before linking up with the E703 at Áyios Dhimitrianós, just below Kannavioú.

About 1500m along from the B7, the *Sa Buneri* **taverna**, in an isolated stone-built construction, makes a good touring halt – its verandah overlooks the reservoir and abandoned Turkish-Cypriot village of Evrétou. The kindly managing family provides simple, inexpensive fare: bean soup, *halloúmi*, salads at any hour, and grilled meat when there are sufficient customers.

### Fýti

At Lássa it's worth making a brief detour 1km east up to **FÝTI**, the most architecturally distinguished of this string of villages along the E712, where locally woven **lacework** and *plakotó* **wall hangings** are sold both out of the old houses and at the two restaurants on the main square. While there is little of the hustle that accompanies the trade in Páno Léfkara (see p.111), and it's commendable to see production (and buy) at source, you won't save much over the prices at Páfos market. Before purchasing, you might want to have a look at the free, privately run **Weaving Museum** (☎26732126 for information). The *Fyti Taverna* (☎26732540) across from the church is a restored coffee-shop and *mezé* house, whose energetic young chef Maria provides a full spectrum of dishes, including many vegetarian offerings and excellent home-made *loúntza* (smoked pork loin).

## Panayiá

Though shown on most maps as "Páno (ie Upper) Panayiá", no Káto (Lower) Panayiá is visible, and the town limits sign merely announces **PANAYIÁ** (Panagia), the largest of several settlements near the headwaters of the Ézousas stream. Here, 750m up, you're at the fringes of the Tróödhos mountains, with walnut trees and tufts of forest visible on the ridge behind. The village is famous as the birthplace of the late Archbishop and President Makarios III, honoured by two small museums and an enormous statue in the main square. At the rear of the plaza sits the grandiosely named **Makarios Cultural Centre** (Tues–Sun 9am–1pm & 2–5pm; free), devoted to photos and paraphernalia of the great man's activities. While the mock-up of the radio set over which Makarios broadcast his defiance of the July 15, 1974 coup is of some interest, the displays are in general pretty feeble, padded out with such vaguely pertinent items as the slippers and alarm clock of a cousin, and rosters of the 1974 war dead from the village.

More atmospheric, perhaps, is **Makarios's Childhood House**, well sign-posted south of and below the central *kafenío* crossroads. If the gate's locked when it should be open (nominally daily 10am–1pm & 2–6pm; tip to warden) try phoning ☎26722858 for Maria the key-keeper. With its pleasant garden and two interior rooms, it seems surprisingly large for a peasant house of the early twentieth century – until you realize that the livestock occupied the back room, with two adults and four children up front. Photos of crucial moments in Makarios's life – some duplicates of those in the Cultural Centre – and assorted household knick-knacks make up the exhibits.

### Practicalities

Since the mid-1990s a fair amount of **accommodation** has sprung up in Panayiá, with no fewer than four "agrotourism" facilities. The *Palati tou Xylari* (☎99614673, ℱ22339849, ℰpalati@cytanet.com.cy; studio ❷, one-bedroom ❸) comprises four self-catering units sharing a wood-and-stone lounge. The

President-Archbishop **Makarios III**, the dominant personality in post-independence Cyprus until 1974, was a contradictory figure. For a start, there's the apocryphal tale that he was really the illegitimate son of a Turkish-Cypriot father, accounting for his close relationship with long-time adviser Ihsan Ali, rumoured to be a blood cousin; in reality Makarios' perfect Constantinopolitan Turkish was the result of his years studying at the Orthodox seminary on Hálki (Heybeliada) near İstanbul. Both a secular and a religious leader, his undeniable charisma and authority were diminished by alternating spells of arrogance and naivety, plus a debilitating tendency to surround himself with pliant yes-men. Many observers, not least Turks and Turkish Cypriots, found it difficult to understand the fusion of his two roles as spiritual and political leader of the Greek Cypriots, in what was nominally a secular republic; they failed to recognize that such a strategy had been institutionalized in Greek communal history since the fall of Byzantium. Cyprus is still ambivalent about him: officially (though by no means universally) revered in the South, resented when not detested in the North, a balanced, homegrown appraisal of his life – including his alleged numerous relationships with women (and, more often, men) – seems unlikely in the near future.

One among four children of Christodhoulos and Eleni Mouskos, he was born **Michael Mouskos** in Panayiá on August 13, 1913. He herded sheep in the forest above the village before spending his adolescence as a novice at **Kýkko monastery** (see p.243) in the nearby mountains – where he made friendships later to prove invaluable. The monks paid his matriculation fees at the prestigious Pancyprian Gymnasium in Nicosia; after graduating in 1936, Mouskos proceeded to Greece, where he attended university and managed to survive the harsh wartime occupation. Postgraduate work in Turkey and Boston was interrupted in April 1948 by the news that he had been chosen Bishop of Kition (Larnaca).

Adopting the religious name **Makarios (Blessed)**, he also turned his attention to politics in his homeland. Soon after co-ordinating a plebiscite in early 1950 showing 96 percent support among the Greek Orthodox population for *énosis* or union with Greece, he was elected Archbishop of all Cyprus, which made him the chief Greek-Cypriot spokesman in future negotiations with the British colonial masters. With George Grivas (see box on p.284), in 1952 he co-founded **EOKA** (Greek Organization of Cypriot Fighters) to struggle for *énosis*. But Makarios initially balked at the violent methods proposed by Grivas, and for various reasons the rebellion did not begin until April 1955. Makarios's contacts at Kýkko proved essential, as both he and Grivas used the monastery as a hideout, recruiting centre and bank.

It didn't take the British long to determine who was lending moral if not material support to the revolt, and Makarios plus three other clerics were **exiled** to the Seychelles, but released after a year of house arrest on condition they didn't return to Cyprus. So Makarios was able to continue his tactic, evolved since 1948, of travelling around world power centres watching the strategies of others and drumming up support for his cause – particularly among the newly independent portions of colonial empires. Among tactics emulated were accepting help from whatever quarter offered – including AKEL (the Cypriot Communist Party) and the Soviet Union. In the short run this went some way towards uniting polarized Greek-Cypriot society and much of world opinion behind *énosis*, but in the more distant future would generate accusations of unscrupulousness – and earn him the undying, and ultimately destructive, enmity of the overwhelmingly right-wing membership of EOKA.

The last straw, as far as EOKA extremists were concerned, was his reluctant acceptance in 1959 of the British offer of **independence** for the island, rather than *énosis* (reputable sources have asserted that, faced with Makarios's hesitation, the British secret services confronted him with compromising photographs from his seminary days, in a clear threat of blackmail; the archbishop signed on the dotted line the next day). Grivas returned to Greece, soon to plot more mischief, while Makarios was elected first president of the new republic. He faced an unenviable task, not least convincing suspicious Turkish Cypriots that his abandonment of the cause of *énosis* was genuine. This he failed to do, most signally in 1963–64, by first showing considerable tactlessness in proposing crucial constitutional changes to the Turkish-Cypriot Vice-President, then by declining to decisively restrain EOKA appointees in his cabinet and EOKA gunmen in the streets, and finally by outright threats of violence against the Turkish-Cypriot community both before and during the Kókkina incident (see p.204).

It's conceivable that, during the early years of the Republic, Makarios was back-pedalling towards *énosis*, but following the colonels' coup in Greece of April 1967, he again saw the advantages of non-aligned independence, especially if the alternative were union with a regime he openly despised – and his own relegation in status to that of a backwater bishop. By early 1968 he had publicly proclaimed the undesirability of *énosis* (in favour of two "Greek" voices at the UN) and began looking for ways out of the impasse, specifically by reopening negotiations with the Turkish Cypriots and opting for a gradualist, assimilationist approach to the "problem" they represented. But these talks, which continued intermittently until 1974, were never marked by any sufficiently conciliatory gestures – though admittedly such actions would have exposed him to danger from EOKA extremists, which shortly materialized anyway.

To these vacillations on the relative merits of *énosis* and independence, and Makarios's continued espousal of the Non-Aligned Movement (not to mention his relations with communists at home and abroad) can be traced the roots of growing **US opposition** to the archbishop. US President Richard Nixon openly vilified him as "Castro in a cassock", while Secretary of State Henry Kissinger sought a discreet way to remove this obstacle to more malleable client-states in the Mediterranean. The Greek junta's views on Makarios matched his opinion of them, so they needed little encouragement to begin conspiring, through cadres planted in the National Guard and EOKA-B (a Grivas revival), for his overthrow. Despite repeated, unsuccessful **plots**, instigated by the junta and the CIA, to assassinate him between 1970 and 1974 – including the shooting down of his helicopter – Makarios unwisely agonized over how to handle their proxies, EOKA-B; by the time the archbishop and his supporters decided on firm suppression, in April 1974, it was too late.

On **July 15, 1974**, the EOKA-B-infiltrated National Guard, commanded by junta-appointed Greek officers, stormed the archiepiscopal palace in Nicosia – Makarios's residence – inflicting such comprehensive damage that a clear intent to kill him was evident. Makarios, actually in the presidential palace at the time, escaped, being spirited away by loyalists first to his old refuge at Kýkko and later to the archiepiscopal palace in Páfos, where he broadcast a message disproving announcements of his death. From here his old adversaries, the British, airlifted him onto the Akrotíri airfield and thence to London and exile. Neither the British nor the Americans initially bestirred themselves much to reinstate a leader whom they felt had received his just desserts for years of intriguing.

Yet Makarios's long practice as emissary to and of the Third World paid off, particularly at the UN, and late in 1974 he was able to **return to Cyprus**, addressing a huge rally in Nicosia with the consummate showmanship which came so naturally to him. He resumed office as president, but the multiple attempts on his life and the depressing fact of the island's division must have weighed on him. On August 3, 1977 Makarios suffered a fatal heart attack, and five days later was buried in an artificial grotto on Throní hill, near Kýkko.

Controversy surrounded even the unseasonable downpour at the time of his funeral: the Greek-Cypriot eulogists characterized the rain as the tears of God weeping for his servant, while the Turkish Cypriots – watching the proceedings on television in the North, to make sure their bogeyman was really dead – retorted with their folk belief that the sins of the wicked deceased were washed away by the rains before burial.

one-unit *Stelios House* (☎99433094, Ⓕ26722971; ❷) has a large courtyard; the four-unit *Arhontiko tou Meletiou* (☎26935011, Ⓕ26947395; ❷–❹) is almost a small inn, with a range of accommodation; while the combined two-bedroom and studio units of the *Liakoto* (☎26235597, Ⓕ29912366; ❷–❸) are particularly suitable for families. Any of these will probably appeal more than the massive *Oniro Hotel* at the north edge of the village (☎26722434, Ⓕ26722929; ❸), though the latter's rooms are spacious and comfortable.

There's a line of *tavernas* across the road from the statue *platía*, though the eateries all appear to be owned by the same family and we receive persistent reports of assorted rip-offs. Your best bet for **food** is probably the *Kentron Avramis*, outside Asproyiá on the main road up from Kannavioú, which serves good salads and *halloúmi*. In the same direction from the village, partway along, the **Vouni Panayia Winery** (daily: winter 8am–5.30pm, summer 8am–7pm) gives free tours, and samples of its excellent Pampela rosé, Alina white and Maratheftiko red.

## Khrysorroyiátissa and Ayía Moní

Just 3km south of, and slightly higher than Panayiá, the **monastery of Khrysorroyiátissa** (officially, Chrysorrogiatissa; in church Greek, Khrysorroyiatíssas) stands at a shady bend in the road, gazing out over terraced valleys to the west. Revisionist derivation of the unusual name, "Our Lady of the Golden Pomegranate", from an epithet of the Virgin as Golden-Breasted, seems to point suspiciously back in time to Aphrodite's similar attribute. A twelfth-century foundation legend centres on the hermit Ignatius, who retrieved a glowing icon of the Virgin from the Pafiot shore and, as so often when miraculous images make their wishes known, heard a celestial voice advising him to build a home for her here. Over the years this particular manifestation of the Virgin became the patroness of criminals, who prayed to avoid arrest or for a light sentence – probably a holdover of the safe haven granted to fugitives in certain pagan temples. Dating like the rest of the structure from 1770, with a 1967 repair of fire damage, the *katholikón* is plunked down in the middle of the triangular cloister dictated by the site. Its most interesting feature is not the *témblon* or the hidden icon, but the carved and painted wood-panel *yinaikonítis* in the rear of the nave.

Khrysorroyiátissa is ostensibly a working monastery – the reasonably priced products of the basement **Monte Royia winery**, including some selected aged vintages, are on sale in the shop, and the current abbot Dionysios is meticulously involved with icon restoration. But the few monks are chary of the tourist hordes, and the guest quarters, though well restored since the early 1990s, are reserved for religious pilgrims.

The courtyard seems open for visits all day, but the shop and *katholikón* close during summer from 12.30 to 1.30pm. Outside the walls a panoramic snack/drink bar is not grossly overpriced, and comes alive at the time of the local February 1–2 and August 14–15 **festivals**.

In comparison, the small monastery of **Ayía Moní**, 1500m beyond Khrysorroyiátissa and mostly dating from the seventeenth and eighteenth centuries, has little to offer the casual tourist. Restoration has been carried out in such a way that the church, originally built during the sixth century atop a temple of Hera and thus one of the oldest in Cyprus, now appears to belong to no particular period. Since 1997, Ayía Moní has been reoccupied by shy nuns, who are especially uncomfortable in the presence of men; a former note by the door which read "Not open to tourists [ie heterodox heathens]" has vanished, but neither is there any visiting information posted in English, so the message seems clear.

# The Tillyrian wilderness

North of Panayiá extends a vast, empty, wooded tract of hills, historically known as **Tillyría** (pronounced *Dillyrgá* in dialect), though strictly speaking the label doesn't apply until you're past the Stavrós tís Psókas forestry station. Unlike the highest stretches of the Tróödhos, the region is not and never has been appreciably settled, frequented in the past mainly for the sake of its rich copper mines (now worked out). If you're staying anywhere on the Pólis coast, a drive through here, and a ramble along the nature trails, satisfactorily completes a day begun in the Páfos hills.

## Cedar Valley

Leaving Panayiá on the route signposted for Kýkko monastery, follow the paved road, always veering towards Kýkko at the well-marked junctions, for 22km until the paving ends abruptly upon arrival at **Cedar Valley** (Kiládha tón Kédron in Greek). This is no more or less than that, a hidden gulch with thousands of specimens of *Cedrus brevifolia*, a type of aromatic cedar indigenous to Cyprus, first cousin to the more famous Lebanese variety and now principally found here. At a hairpin bend in the track, there's a picnic area and a spring, while a sign points to another track – wide but not suitable for vehicles – that leads 2.5km up to **Trípylos peak** (1362m). Strangely, the hike passes few of the handsome trees; they're mostly well downstream, and (perhaps intentionally) inaccessible.

Kýkko itself (see p.243), some 20km further along, is more usually and easily approached from Pedhoulás in the Tróödhos. If you're heading on to Stavrós tís Psókas and the coast, backtrack 4km from the picnic site to the junction marked "Stavros". Follow the sign right and you'll pass, after 6km, a labelled jeep track coming down from the Trípylos summit.

## Stavrós tís Psókas and beyond

Some 7km further along the paved road, there's another important junction: right goes down and north to the coast, left and south descends 3km more to the colonial-era forestry station and rest house at **Stavrós tís Psókas**. The name is that of a monastery, abandoned in the nineteenth century, which once stood here, and is usually politely translated as "Cross of Measles"; it actually means "Cross of the Mange", and in the days before pesticide lotions a spontaneous cure of scabies must have seemed well-nigh miraculous.

Facilities at Stavrós include a small and fairly useless **café** with overpriced snacks, the **forestry headquarters** for Páfos district and the extremely popular **hostel** (☏26332144 or 26722338; C£10), where space must be reserved in advance from June to August. Bunks are in simple rooms with en-suite bathrooms. The rangers will proudly assure you that this is the coolest spot in the district (950m up in deep shade, it's not hard to believe). Most visitors drive up the easiest ways, either on the wide, surfaced road taking off between Kannavioú and Panayía or (in 45min) along the equally broad route from Lysó.

### The nature trails

Some 200m along the road west towards Lysó stands an enclosure for Cyprus **moufflon**, only just saved from extinction – one is now the logo of Cyprus Airways. Wild members of the small herd also wander the surrounding ridges, but you're exceedingly unlikely to see any roaming free while hiking one of the two surveyed **nature trails**. It's unhappily difficult to hike these as a loop, though you can just about do them back-to-back, making the most of a day sandwiched in between two nights here. The first, heralded by the same distinctive archway and canopy as used on the Akámas peninsula, begins about 1.7km along the seven-kilometre stretch of paved road north of Stavrós towards Trípylos, and plunges off the ridge to end near the final side-turning into the station. The second one begins downstream from the station and climbs up the ridge towards Zakhárou peak (1212m), ending prominently in another archway up at the three-way saddle-junction called Selládhi toú Stavroú, where paved roads go either to the Cedar Valley and Kýkko, the coast or back down to the station.

### Out to the coast

The route **to the coast** is well signposted and paved, but it's curvy, slow going and littered with rockfall after rainstorms. You'll end up in Pomós, west of the Kókkina enclave (35km from Selládhi toú Stavroú) in an hour, or Káto Pýrgos (39km) via the inland salient of the Kókkina detour (25km) in well over an hour. En route you'll notice how the careful husbandry of the British and Republican forestry services was set back considerably by the Turkish Air Force, which set the trees alight with napalm during the summer of 1974; patterns of long reafforestation terraces are still some years from fully reversing this act of sabotage. The forest is, in fact, very monotonous; the views over successive ridges and down to the sea are the point of the drive.

# The Xerós and Dhiárizos valleys

The far southeast of Páfos district is taken up by two major river valleys, those of the **Xerós** and the **Dhiárizos**. They offer not only exciting landscapes and ample opportunities for walking, but monumental attractions in the form of abandoned monastic churches on the riverbanks and two ancient bridges over the streams. The latter formed an integral part of the **Venetian camel-caravan route**, the beasts transporting copper ore from the Tróödhos down to Páfos or Pólis. Not being as durable as the cobbled, round-island Roman road, the Venetian path can scarcely be traced any longer, but the bridges are still here to be enjoyed. Most of the villages hereabouts, however, lack the distinction of those further west, having been devastated by a great earthquake in 1953 and repaired in a utilitarian manner, if at all.

## The upper Xerós valley

The upper reaches of the **Xerós valley**, which contain the more interesting monuments, are easily reached from the vicinity of Ayía Moní (see p.218). From here it's 8km south, via Statós, to the ruins of old Áyios Fótios, abandoned in 1969; the ground is unstable and its houses are literally heading south. Here you turn east and then north for **GALATARIÁ** (*Galatargá* in dialect), where you should plan a lunch stop at *Family Restaurant / Ikoyeniaki Taverna Galataria*. Owner Kyria Susana is the soul of kindness and will stuff you silly for C£6 or so (booze extra): *louvána* greens, home-made *talatoúra*, *tahíni*, *halloúmi*, *pourgoúri* (on request), *païdhákia hiriní krasáta* (wine-marinated pork cutlets) and – assuming any room left – home-made sweets. In summer there's *kléftigo* as well, and the two terraces are packed; the place doubles all year as the village *kafenío*, so you'll meet all the local characters.

### Vrécha and the Roúdhias bridge

The narrow but still-paved road continues through Kilínia (Koilineia) to ex-Turkish **VRÉCHA** (Vretsia). Before 1974, this constituted a major enclave, something borne out by an empty UN post and abundant graffiti in favour of "Taksim" (partition of Cyprus between Turkey and Greece) and "Volkan" (the pre-TMT Turkish-Cypriot militants' organization); possibly in retaliation, the Republican administration never provided the place with electric current. Though it's one of the most beautiful spots in the district, with ample water and land, Vrécha remains abandoned except for a few sporadically occupied houses and a seasonal **taverna**.

From the lower, southern end of Vrécha it's under an hour's descent on foot to a derelict, single-arched **watermill** near the banks of the Xerós River; as in most such structures, the valuable millstone has been filched, recycled for use in modern olive presses. The medieval **Roúdhias** (*Roúthkias* in dialect) **bridge**, a simple, round-arched span hidden by trees, lies a ten-minute walk upstream from here; in the vicinity you'll find a deep, swimmable pool, which retains water most years into July or early August. The bridge is also accessible by a more direct jeep track from Vrécha, leaving the obvious track by the mosque, which crosses a modern bridge just above the older one. Once you're past this point, the track – now in better state – can be followed east, via Péra Vássa and the Kélefos bridge, for about 20km to Áyios Nikólaos (see p.223); walkers can use a 17-kilometre **nature trail** from Vrécha to Kaminária village.

### Panayía Eleoússa Síndi

Retracing your steps through Kilínia and Galatariá, you can proceed south to attractive Pendaliá, unfortunately plagued by landslips like Áyios Fótios (a new prefab village is being prepared nearby). From the old village centre, a south-easterly dirt track (passable to saloon cars depending on mud levels) just over 6km in length provides the usual approach point to the lonely monastery of **Panayía Eleoússa Síndi** (Panagia tou Sinti), at the mouth of a side stream on the west bank of the Xerós valley, here considerably wider than at Roúdhias. The main watercourse is flanked by defunct watermills, which once ground the monastery's corn. Síndi, a dependency of Kýkko monastery, was initially restored in 1994–1997 by the same team that saw to Ayía Moní, thankfully with a bit more sensitivity; in the next phase (indefinitely postponed), two wings of cells and outbuildings around the courtyard will be reconstructed with an eye to monastic rehabitation. The most striking feature here, once inside the walled compound (open all hours; free), is a wonderful fieldstoned courtyard; the very plain, high church with its new *témblon* and octagonal lantern dome dates mostly from the early sixteenth century.

### Out to the coast

From Pendaliá, it's easy enough to continue southwest towards the coast on the high-standard E606 road, via Amargéti, Eledhió and Axýlou. **AMARGÉTI** could be a touring base: the *Exohiko Kendro Zoodhohos Piyi* (☎26723212; ❷) has a few rooms to let upstairs, but the food and atmosphere are rather sani-tized compared to the *Galatariá* café, and you'll probably have to settle for the dreaded steak Diane and chips unless you ring ahead to arrange for their C£7-a-head *mezé*.

From the latter two communities (both grid-plan bungalow replacements for nearby, destroyed villages) you can either proceed straight to the coast at Akhélia, or detour down to Natá to **cross the Xerós River** just above the Asprókremos reservoir. The area is good for bird-watching, and this route – the only partially paved one to the far side of the valley – is a handy short-cut for getting to the Dhiárizos valley via old Kholétria, but the river could be too high to ford in very early spring; enquire in Natá before proceeding. **KHOLÉTRIA** is slowly being reoccupied by the renovation-minded, and can offer a seasonal, riverview **taverna** a few hundred metres north of the attractive, possibly sixteenth-century village **church of Áyios Pandelíomonas** (usually open).

## The Dhiárizos valley

The **Dhiárizos valley** is in general very appealing compared to the Xerós or the Ézousas further west. The easiest introduction to it, if you haven't got a jeep or haven't crossed the Xerós as described above, is via the turning off the B6 southeast of Páfos for **NIKÓKLIA** (Nikokleia), not to be confused with nearby Koúklia. Here, the *Vasilias Nikoklis Inn* (☎26432211, ⓦwww .vasilias-nikoklis-inn.com; ❸) is a restored medieval roadside hostelry with beamed ceilings and fairly modern rooms. The restaurant menu isn't very adventurous but provides reasonable value, served in appealing surroundings, and the last prepared food you'll see for a while.

Immediately downstream from Nikóklia, the road divides; the more westerly option, which traces the ridge dividing Xerós from Dhiárizos, has been comprehensively rehabilitated and now is the fastest way up the valley. Of the several villages en route, only **Néa Kholétria** early on – built to replace quake-shattered old Kholétria – plus **Salamioú** and **Armínou**, near the top of the valley, show many signs of life. From Armínou, the newish road swoops in well-graded arcs to cross over to the more scenic east bank of the river via Filoússa.

Heading upstream from Nikóklia to Áyios Nikólaos via the easterly road – currently a chewed-up mess, likely to remain so until the contract is re-tendered – you wind past **MAMÓNIA**, the only local Orthodox village lower down in the valley at independence; the *Mylos* tavern on the roadside just north of the village serves good light lunches and dinners. Old Prastió, on the east slope of the increasingly sheer valley, was, like Souskioú and Fasoúla downstream, shattered by the quake of 1953; the replacement, roadside prefab

△ Kélefos Venetian-era bridge

grid opposite had hardly been occupied before communal troubles dictated its abandonment.

## Áyios Sávvas tís Karónos
**Prastió** is the closest place to the intriguing monastic Byzantine-Latin church of **Áyios Sávvas tís Karónos**, with the best access from just downstream. Some 3km east of Áyios Yeóryios, keep an eye out for a black-on-white Greek-lettered sign reading "Pros Eklisaki Ayiou Savva", pointing to an initial cement track crossing the river (probably not passable late winter/early spring) which heads initially towards a modern chapel on a hillock. Go past this, on a well-surfaced dirt road, for 2km to reach the walled former monastery in its lovely setting. At first the rectangular, gable-roofed church, first erected in 1120, seems more like a carob warehouse than a monastery *katholikón*, but then you notice the twin Gothic arches over the north and south doors, the plaque over the west door commemorating the Venetian restoration of 1501, and the little grinning gargoyle just above this. Inside (one door always open), the double-ribbed vault is bare of decoration except for an intricately worked *témblon* with naive polychrome painting on the lowest level in geometric and floral designs. At both the west wall and apsidal end are small round windows, with delicate tracery. Extensive outbuildings, in ruins since the nineteenth century, include an arcaded meeting hall.

## Pretóri, Áyios Nikólaos and the Kélefos bridge
Beyond Kidhási, the last valley-bottom settlement of what was yet another Turkish-Cypriot enclave, the road crosses the Dhiárizos River and skims the district border as it climbs through more prosperous and scenic Kédhares and **PRETÓRI** (Praitori), where you can feast on tasty and abundant **snacks** in the coffee house. In an exquisitely microscopic bit of regional rivalry, the east-bankers of the Dhiárizos used to reproach the west-bankers, regardless of ethnic affiliation, with excessive stinginess – a grave insult in a peasant society. The worst, apparently, were the pre-1974 inhabitants of Áyios Ioánnis, a Turkish-Cypriot village descended from the peculiar Linovamváki sect (see p.430).

The end of the east-bank run, some 26km from Nikóklia, is **ÁYIOS NIKÓLAOS**, highest of the Dhiárizos villages, except perhaps for the much-maligned Áyios Ioánnis. Beautifully set amidst orchards and irrigation ditches, Áyios Nikólaos boasts the majority of the few **tavernas** in the Dhiárizos valley – the best of these being the *Rumeli* on the bypass road, where you can lunch on *louvána* and *kléftigo* for about C£6 per person, finishing up with their own candied fruits or *palouzé*. The village is also the easiest access point for the graceful **Kélefos bridge** ("*Tzílefos*" in dialect, and lately even on signage), which spans the upper Dhiárizos and is reached along a six-kilometre paved (after a fashion) road northwestwards; with its pointed arch, it's more photogenic than the Roudhiás bridge. It is also possible to reach Kélefos directly from Roudhiás via a dirt track passing **Péra Vássa** forestry station, which claims to harbour the largest tree in Cyprus (duly signposted).

From the Kélefos bridge, with a decent map to navigate by, you can either carry on 3km east, on a wide, paved road, to the Elía bridge (and thence to Kaminária village in the Tróödhos); retrace your steps to Áyios Nikólaos and cross the district border heading southeast to Ársos to visit the *Krassokhoriá*; or proceed from Áyios Nikólaos to Mandhriá and thence Plátres.

## Greek place names

| Old system | New system | Greek lettering |
| --- | --- | --- |
| Akámas | Akamas | ΑΚΑΜΑΣ |
| Akourdhália, Páno/Káto | Akourdaleia, Pano/ Kato | ΑΚΟΥΡΔΑΛΕΙΑ, ΠΑΝΩ/ ΚΑΤΩ |
| Amargéti | Amargeti | ΑΜΑΡΓΕΤΙ |
| Armínou | Arminou | ΑΡΜΙΝΟΥ |
| Aródhes, Páno/Káto | Arodes, Pano/Kato | ΑΡΟΔΕΣ, ΠΑΝΩ/ΚΑΤΩ |
| Asproyiá | Asprogia | ΑΣΠΡΟΓΙΑ |
| Avgás/Avákas Gorge | Avakas/Argaki tis Avgas | ΑΒΑΚΑΣ/ΑΡΓΑΚΙ ΤΗΣ ΑΒΓΑΣ |
| Ayía Moní | Agia Moni | ΑΓΙΑ ΜΟΝΗ |
| Áyii Anáryiri | Agioi Anargyroi | ΑΓΙΟΙ ΑΝΑΡΓΥΡΟΙ |
| Áyios Neófytos | Agios Neofytos | ΑΓΙΟΣ ΝΕΟΦΥΤΟΣ |
| Áyios Nikólaos | Agios Nikolaos | ΑΓΙΟΣ ΝΙΚΟΛΑΟΣ |
| Áyios Yeóryios | Agios Georgios | ΑΓΙΟΣ ΓΕΩΡΓΙΟΣ |
| Dhiárizos (valley) | Diarizos | ΔΙΑΡΙΖΟΣ |
| Dhroúsha | Drouseia | ΔΡΟΥΣΕΙΑ |
| Dhrýmou | Drymou | ΔΡΥΜΟΥ |
| Dhriniá | Thrinia | ΘΡΙΝΙΑ |
| Émba | Empa | ΕΜΠΑ |
| Filoússa | Filousa | ΦΙΛΟΥΣΑ |
| Galatariá | Galataria | ΓΑΛΑΤΑΡΙΑ |
| Ínia | Ineia | ΙΝΕΙΑ |
| Kannavioú | Kannaviou | ΚΑΝΝΑΒΙΟΥ |
| Káthikas | Kathikas | ΚΑΘΙΚΑΣ |
| Káto Páfos | Kato Pafos | ΚΑΤΩ ΠΑΦΟΣ |
| Káto Pýrgos | Kato Pyrgos | ΚΑΤΩ ΠΥΡΓΟΣ |
| Kholétria | Choletria | ΧΟΛΕΔ ΡΙΑ |
| Khóli | Choli | ΧΩΛΙ |
| Khrysokhoú | Chrysochou | ΧΡΥΣΟΧΟΥ |
| Khrysorroyiátissa | Moni Chrysorrogiatissas | ΜΟΝΗ ΧΡΥΣΟΡΡΟΓΙΑΤΙΣΣΑΣ |
| Kíli | Koili | ΚΟΙΛΙ |
| Kilínia | Koilineia | ΚΟΙΛΙΝΕΙΑ |
| Kissónerga | Kisonerga | ΚΙΣΣΟΝΕΡΓΑ |
| Koufón Gorge | Argaki ton Koufon | ΑΡΓΑΚΙ ΤΩΝ ΚΟΥΦΩΝ |
| Koúklia | Kouklia | ΚΟΥΚΛΙΑ |
| Krítou Térra | Kritou Tera | ΚΡΙΤΟΥ ΤΕΡΑ |

# Travel details

## Long-distance buses

**Ktíma Páfos** to: Limassol (Mon–Sat 1 daily on ALEPA; 1hr 15min); Nicosia (Mon–Sat 1 daily on ALEPA; 2hr 30min); Pólis (Mon–Fri 10 daily, Sat 6, with Nea Amoroza; 45min); Pomós (Mon–Sat 2 daily, via Pólis, with Nea Amoroza; 1hr 45min). **Pólis** to: Latchí/Loutrá tís Afrodhítis (June–Sept 3 daily; 20min).

## Local buses (ALEPA)

**Káto Páfos** to: Coral Bay (summer daily 8am–7pm every 15min, 7–11pm every 20min; winter daily 8am–7pm every 20min; 40min). **Ktíma Páfos (Karavélla terminal)** to: Áyios Neófytos (Mon–Fri 2 daily; 20min); Émba (Mon–Fri 5 daily, Sat 1; 15min); Lémba (Mon–Fri 9 daily, Sat 4; 15min); Péyia (Mon–Fri 4–5 daily, Sat 2; 30min);

| Ktíma | Ktima | ΚΤΗΜΑ |
|---|---|---|
| Lára | Lara | ΛΑΡΑ |
| Lássa | Lasa | ΛΑΣΑ |
| Latchí | Latsi, Lakki | ΛΑΤΣΙ, ΛΑΚΚΙ |
| Lémba | Lempa | ΛΕΜΠΑ |
| Letímbou | Letymvou | ΛΕΤΥΜΒΟΥ |
| Loutrá tís Afrodhítis | Loutra tis Afroditis | ΛΟΥΤΡΑ ΤΗΣ ΑΦΡΟΔΙΤΗΣ |
| Lysó | Lysos | ΛΥΣΟΣ |
| Mesóyi | Mesogi | ΜΕΣΟΓΗ |
| Milioú | Miliou | ΜΙΛΙΟΥ |
| Moútallos | Moutallos | ΜΟΥΤΑΛΛΟΣ |
| Natá | Nata | ΝΑΤΑ |
| Neokhorió | Neo Chorio | ΝΕΟΧΩΡΙΟ |
| Nikóklia | Nikokleia | ΝΙΚΟΚΛΕΙΑ |
| Páfos, Páphos | Pafos | ΠΑΦΟΣ |
| Pakhýammos | Pachyammos | ΑΧΥΑΜΜΟΣ |
| Panayiá | Panagia | ΠΑΝΑΓΙΑ |
| Panayía Eleoússa Síndi | Panagia tou Sinti | ΠΑΝΑΓΙΑ ΤΟΥ ΣΙΝΤΙ |
| Pendaliá | Pentalia | ΠΕΝΤΑΛΙΑ |
| Peristeróna | Peristereona | ΠΕΡΙΣΤΕΡΕΩΝΑ |
| Péyia | Pegeia | ΠΕΓΕΙΑ |
| Pólis | Polis | ΠΟΛΙΣ |
| Pomós | Pomos | ΠΟΜΟΣ |
| Prastió | Prastio | ΠΡΑΣΤΙΟ |
| Pretóri | Praitori | ΠΡΑΙΤΩΡΙ |
| Salamioú | Salamiou | ΣΑΛΑΜΙΟΥ |
| Skoúlli | Skoulli | ΣΚΟΥΛΛΗ |
| Smiyiés | Smigies | ΣΜΙΓΙΕΣ* |
| Stavrós tís Psókas | Stavros tis Psokas | ΣΤΑΥΡΟΣ ΤΗΣ ΨΩΚΑΣ |
| Stroumbí | Stroumpi | ΣΤΡΟΥΜΠΙ |
| Tála | Tala | ΤΑΛΑ |
| Térra | Tera | ΤΕΡΑ |
| Trimithoússa | Trimithousa | ΤΡΙΜΙΘΟΥΣΑ |
| Tsádha | Tsada | ΤΣΑΔΑ |
| Xerós (valley) | Xeros | ΞΕΡΟΣ |
| Yerónissos | Geronisos | ΓΕΡΟΝΗΣΟΣ |
| Yeroskípou | Geroskipou | ΓΕΡΟΣΚΗΠΟΥ |

Yeroskípou (Mon–Fri 8 daily, Sat 2; 10min). **Ktíma Páfos (market car park)** to: Áyios Yeóryios (Mon–Sat 4 daily 9am–4.30pm; 50min); Coral Bay (Mon–Sat every 10–15 min 6.30am–5.20pm; 35min); Káto Páfos (summer Mon–Sat 6.15am– 7pm every 10–15min, Sun 6.30am–7pm every 20–30min; winter Mon–Sat 6.15am–6.30pm every 10–15min, Sun 6.30am–1pm every 20–30min; 20min).

# The High Tróödhos

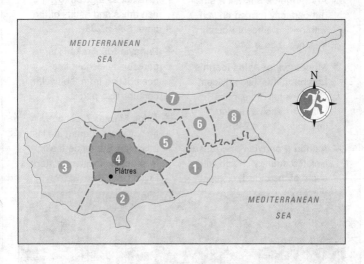

CHAPTER 4 **Highlights**

✳ **Mount Olympus** Nature trails provide good hiking around the summit of the island's highest mountain. See p.236

✳ **Tróödhos mountains** The high-altitude flora encompasses everything from spring cherry blossoms to orchids. See pp.236–242

✳ **Arkhángelos Mikhaïl** A small but perfectly formed church, with brilliant fifteenth-century frescoes. See p.242

✳ **Monastery of Áyios Ioánnis Lambadhistís** Two adjacent churches full of frescoes reflect extensive Western influence. See p.249

✳ **Asínou (Panayía Forviótissa)** Isolated country church with some of the oldest, clearest and most vivid frescoes in Cyprus. See p.243

✳ **Linos Inn, Kakopetriá** In the heart of the old quarter, this is one of the most successfully executed restoration inns on the island, with two affiliated restaurants. See p.251

✳ **Arkhángelos Mihaïl** Sixteenth-century frescoes here act as a guide to Venetian dress and habits of the time. See p.255

✳ **Panayía toú Araká** Has particularly elegant frescoes dating from the twelfth century. See p.256

✳ **Áyios Mámas** A deceptively tiny chapel featuring the last Lusignan-Byzantine-fusion frescoes by master painter Philip Goul. See p.262

△ The Ascension of Christ, Louvarás

# The High Tróödhos

R ising to nearly 2000m, the **Tróödhos** mountains (pronounced as three syllables, "*Tro*-o-dhos", rather than "True-dhos") – form the backbone of the southern Republic and occupy nearly a quarter of the island's surface area. This dense mass of igneous rock, the largest volume of ophiolite (mixed with serpentine) in the world, is thrust-up primordial seabed, allowing rare glimpses of geological strata normally hidden beneath lighter continental landmasses. It's also extraordinarily rich in mineral deposits and metallic ores, which were mined until recent decades. Too low and hummocky to be stereotypically alpine, the Tróödhos still acquit themselves as a mountain resort area, and their western part supports what is touted, with some justification, as the best-managed island forest in the Mediterranean. But this is by no means virgin, first-growth woods: ancient miners felled all of that to feed the copper-smelting furnaces of nearby Tillyría, and after centuries of neglect under the Lusignans, Venetians and Ottomans, the British found scarcely more trees growing when they arrived. In every era the range has been a barrier as well as a resource, and during the Christian era especially, a refuge for Hellenic culture. The devastating raids of middle Byzantine times left the hills untouched, and during nearly four centuries of Lusignan rule, when the Orthodox Church was humiliatingly subordinated elsewhere, the Tróödhos provided a safe haven for a minor renaissance in its fortunes – most strikingly evidenced in the famous collection of **frescoed rural churches** here. The Ottomans didn't bother to settle the region, and when the mainland Turks returned in 1974, the obstacle the mountains represented, as much as any ceasefire agreement, may have deterred them from overrunning the entire island. Among foreign occupiers, only the British, homesick and sweltering down in the flatlands, realized the recreational potential of the mountains, with a lacework of roads and assorted architectural follies.

From the south, the usual gateway to the region is the functional, though beautifully set, resort of **Plátres**, which has the largest concentration of hotels on that side of the watershed. Its higher neighbour **Tróödhos** has no village character whatsoever, but is the jump-off point for a day's walking around the highest summit, **Mount Olympus**. Good roads lead from either place to **Pedhoulás**, chief village and resort of the Marathássa valley – and also your introduction to the painted churches of the Tróödhos, both here and downstream at **Moutoullás** and **Kalopanayiótis**. Pedhoulás also offers the easiest access to **Kýkko monastery**, out by itself at the edge of the Tillyrian wilderness.

The next area east of Marathássa, **Soléa**, has as its "capital" the resort of **Kako-petriá**, with its preserved old quarter and unusually accessible concentration of

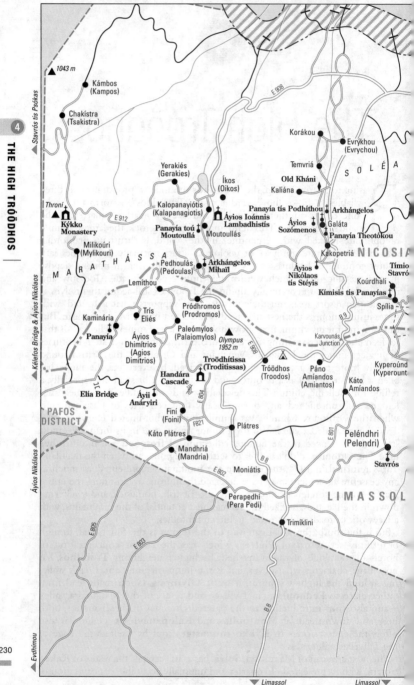

▲ Stavrós tís Psókas

▲ Kéletós Bridge & Áyios Nikólaos

▲ Áyios Nikólaos

▲ Evdhímou

▼ Limassol          Limassol ▼

▲ 1043 m

Kámbos (Kampos)

Chakístra (Tsakistra)

Korákou

Evrýkhou (Evrychou)

Temvriá

Old Kháni

S O L É A

Yerakiés (Gerakiés)

Íkos (Oikos)

Kaliána

Panayía tís Podhíthou    Arkhángelos

Throní

Kýkko Monastery

E 912

Kalopanayiótis (Kalapanagiotis)

Áyios Ioánnis Lambadhistís

Panayía toú Moutoullá

Moutoullás

Áyios Sozómenos

Galáta

Panayía Theotókou

Milikoúri (Mylikouri)

M A R A T H Á S S A

Pedhoulás (Pedoulas)

Arkhángelos Mihaïl

Kakopetriá

NICOSIA

Áyios Nikólaos tís Stéyis

Tímio Stavró

Lemíthou

Koúrdhali

Kímisis tís Panayías

Spília

Kaminária

Trís Eliés

Pródhromos (Prodromos)

B 9

Panayía

Áyios Dhimítrios (Agios Dimitrios)

Paleómylos (Palaiomylos)

▲ Olympus 1952 m

E 908

Karvounás Junction

Kyperoúnd (Kyperount)

Troödhítissa (Troditissas)

Handára Cascade

Tróödhos (Troodos)

Páno Amíandos (Amiantos)

Káto Amíandos

Elía Bridge

Áyii Anáryiri

E 804

Finí (Foini)

F 821

Plátres

Peléndhri (Pelendri)

E 801

PAFOS DISTRICT

Káto Plátres

Mandhriá (Mandria)

Moniátis

B 8

Stavrós

E 802

LIMASSOL

Perapedhí (Pera Pedi)

E 805

E 803

Trimíklini

B 8

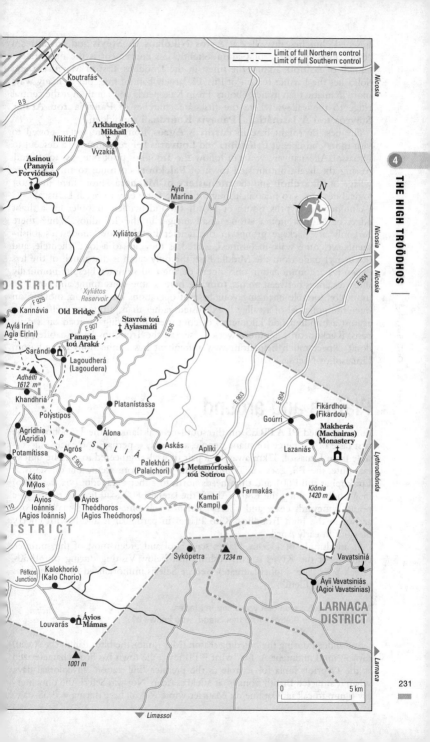

frescoed churches, up-valley at **Áyios Nikólaos tís Stéyis** and downstream at the adjacent village of **Galáta**. Slightly less convenient is the magnificent church of **Asínou**, among the finest in the Tróödhos. East of Marathássa and Soléa lies the harsher terrain of Pitsyliá, largely bare of trees but in many ways more dramatic than its neighbours. From Kakopetriá you climb over the central ridge to the valleys where the first-rate churches of **Panayía toú Araká**, **Stavrós toú Ayiasmáti** and **Panayía Koúrdhali** are hidden.

The best overnight base in Pitsyliá is **Agrós**, from where you're poised to visit more churches at **Peléndhri** and **Louvarás** before beginning a descent to Limassol. Alternatively, you can follow the Tróödhos peak line east to its end, passing the lively, untouristed town of **Palekhóri** en route to the showcase village of **Fikárdhou** and the **monastery of Makherás**. From here, the most logical descent is to Nicosia, though it is also fairly easy to reach Larnaca.

Uniquely in Cyprus, South or North, the independent traveller has a slight edge, or at least not a strong disadvantage, in the Tróödhos. While there certainly are package groups in the fancier **hotels**, more modest establishments welcome walk-in business, geared as they are to a local clientele, and (formerly) trade from the Middle East; the only catch is that much of the less expensive accommodation only opens during mid-summer. Despite nominally short distances between points, **touring** here is time-consuming, and you'll be more comfortable changing your base of operations on occasion, moving on once the potential of a valley is exhausted, rather than pitting yourself and car against a hundred-odd kilometres of contorted, often dug-up road on a daily basis. Reckon on a leisurely week to see all the Tróödhos have to offer, and don't expect much help from very infrequent bus connections to and from Limassol or Nicosia.

# Plátres and around

Forest-swathed **PLÁTRES** on the south-central flank of the Tróödhos is the first taste of the range for many people, and easily – perhaps too easily – accessible from Limassol, 37km away, by a pair of well-engineered roads. The quickest route, the B8, goes via Trimíklini; the other, more scenic option starts at Episkopí as the E601 and then heads north to either Perapedhí (via the E805) or Mandhriá (along the E803). Above the lateral E802 road linking these three points, vineyards cease and cherry orchards and pines begin, signalling your arrival in the high Tróödhos; Káto Plátres in particular is awash with cherry blossom in early April.

At an altitude of 1150m, Plátres stays cool and green most of the summer, courtesy of the Krýos stream rushing just below. Visiting during the 1930s, Greek poet (later Nobel laureate) George Seferis immortalized its nightingales in his poem "Eleni":

The nightingales won't let you sleep in Plátres.
And just what is Plátres? And this island, who knows it?

And indeed during the breeding season (May–June), the birds trill in the stream canyon until midnight. As for "what is Plátres?", the town has been characterized as the Cypriot Simla for its role as the premier "hill-station" in colonial days, when it attracted British from as far afield as Aden. Nor was Seferis the only literary figure to call in; Daphne du Maurier wrote *Rebecca* here during a 1938 stay.

Long after independence, Plátres remains a weekend haunt of expats and enlisted men – you can watch UK footie in one of several pubs, and many tavernas are tuned to British Forces radio. Comparisons with the more famous Indian hill-station were doubtless partly inspired by a few remaining villas with whimsical turrets and rooflines (all built, incidentally, by wealthy native Cypriots), but a staggering quantity of modern development pitched at locals and *nouveaux riches* foreigners (especially Russians) is dwarfing the "Raj days" architecture, especially at Plátres' south end. During summer the main drag becomes an unenticing uproar of double-parked buses, strolling day-trippers and tacky souvenirs.

## Practicalities

The extent of Plátres' commercial district is a single high street, with a combination **post/telephone office** (Mon–Fri 3–5pm only) and adjacent **CTO branch** (April–Oct Mon–Fri 9am–3.30pm, Sat 9am–2.30pm; closes 3/2pm in July/Aug), behind the large central car park doubling as the central square. From here depart the weekday **buses** to Limassol and Nicosia. You can also rent **mountain bikes** (look for the sign) to explore the myriad wide dirt tracks in the surrounding hills. Municipal fee **car parks** are numerous, taking advantage of the summer-season congestion, though only systematically enforced at that time. There are also two **bank ATMs**, just about the only ones in the mountains, so take advantage. The more village-like quarter, inhabited by locals and deceptively large, lies to the south, with a 24-hour **filling station** – again one of the very few in the Tróödhos.

### Accommodation

Plátres as a resort has lost favour with both the British and the islanders, and – notwithstanding new villa construction – is decidedly in decline, with a halving in the number of **hotels** since the late 1980s. Most local accommodation is scattered throughout the town, away from the high street; the location of the various establishments is shown on a helpful placard posted near the tourist office. However, many of these places only operate at peak summer season and have seen better days; at present just eight establishments have retained their CTO certification, though discreet enquiries out of season will turn up offers of unlicensed, modest **guest houses** for C£20 double or even less, for example at the *Village Restaurant* (☎25421741).

Pick of the **hotels** geared up for walk-in clientele has to be the two-star *Minerva* on the upper through road, open most of the year (☎25421731, ⓦwww.minervahotel.com.cy; ❸). Botanist Yiannis Christofides, an engaging and knowledgeable host, is the third generation of his family to run the hotel since 1947, and presides over excellent breakfasts (and has a no-smoking policy throughout). All rooms are heated, and some have balconies, some full bathtubs; the top-floor units were enlarged and completely redone in 1997. At the back there's an annexe of six superior, 2000-built wood- or tile-floored rooms with antique furnishings, gabled ceilings and large bathrooms – much the best-value facilities in the mountains – as well as a detached, self-catering villa for families. If the *Minerva* is full, try the two-star *Edelweiss* across the street (☎25421335, ⓔedelweiss@cytanet.com.cy; ❹), an acceptable, if slightly pricier, alternative, also centrally heated and open most of the year, with useful on-site car rental.

Among the hotels more usually booked as part of an all-inclusive holiday, the three-star *New Helvetia* (☎25421348, ⓦwww.minotel.com; ❺) is a magnificent period piece (1929) perched above the river at the north end of the resort, offering mountain-bike and car rental; the newer free-standing studio complex, however, has poor soundproofing. The four-star, modern, aptly named *Forest Park* (☎25421751, ⓦwww.forestparkhotel.com.cy; ⑥), at the southwest end of the upper through road, was extended in 1994 and offers every conceivable comfort, including indoor/outdoor pools, tennis court and fitness centre. Both of these hotels are available through most UK package companies.

### Eating and drinking

**Restaurant** prices are nearly identical across the board, often for mediocre fare. Honourable exceptions include the *Skylight*, on the main drag, doing good trout with vegetables and a starter plate for about C£10, or there are typical Cypriot dishes; the environment's pleasant, and includes a swimming pool (free use with meal). *The Village Restaurant*, towards the western end of the same street, has salubrious food, best in *mezé* format: ten starter platters plus a couple of mains for about C£8, in an equally savoury environment. Cypriots tend to gravitate towards *John's*, a bit up from the *Skylight* just opposite the Luna Park, for the sake of genuine home cooking, decent house wine, a warm welcome and a warm fire on cooler nights. Alternatively, just north of the developed area, the more brazenly touristy Psilódhendhro **trout farm** has heated indoor premises and outdoor seating under the trees, and claims to open every day of the year (but 11am–5pm only); budget C£8 for a trout-based meal. Káto Plátres has its own **microwinery**, Lambouri (☎25421329 to arrange visits), which makes a very decent white, worth asking for in local restaurants.

## Around Plátres

Three popular excursions – one riding, the other two walking – start from Psilódhendhro, 300m north of Plátres. If you're not up to an outing of several hours, there's also the **Mylomeri trail**, a half-hour (one way) stroll down to the base of the eponymous waterfalls, which starts halfway between the central church and Plátres' central plaza. Other excursion destinations are all shown on the map on p.237.

### Mesapótamos monastery

The remote **monastery of Mesapótamos** lies 7km east along a dirt track pelted hazardously by rock-falls. After years of abandonment and dereliction, the monastery has been reoccupied by Orthodox monks who, in the usual way of these things, are fairly zealous and not particularly welcoming to casual visitors. The streamside **Arkolakhaniá picnic site** about 1km before might be more compelling as a goal for your mountain bike.

### Pouziáris trail

The **Pouziáris trail** system, which starts on the east bank of the Krýos stream by the trout farm, offers meatier hiking and the possibility of loops, though at least one leg is probably worth avoiding for its dreary surface. You've an initial quarter-hour climb (signed as "1km") east-northeast through some oaks – and some severe landslide damage from 2004 which should soon be repaired – to a divide in the path and beginning of the loop system. At this junction bear left (north-northwest), crossing a firebreak-cum-jeep-track just over twenty minutes along. Continue climbing steadily in zigzags, east then north, up onto the shoulder of Pouziáris; the trail narrows, and you've your first grand views west to Páfos, and south to the sea. There's less shade now, though the basic vegetation profile of mixed pine and oak remains the same, albeit with small specimens unlabelled. Just under an hour from the start, veer onto what looks like a minor trail hairpinning back and right (straight on leads to the top of the Kalidonia trail, as described below); over the next ten minutes, the side turning zig-zags east-southeast through more imposing pines to the secondary, 1629-metre summit of Pouziáris hill (signed as the "shoulder"), with its small radar reflector, two benches and superb views south.

Here also is another marked intersection: left or north leads more or less levelly towards the British radar "golf balls" and the Makriá Kondárka path, for a longer loop returning via Tróödhos resort and the Caledonian Falls; or you can head down and right ("Kaminoudia 2km, Psilon Dendron 6km"). The latter option drops east in just over a quarter of an hour, along the south flank of the Arkoud-holahaniá ravine, to a point where it widens into a disused track; this alternates with surviving path shortcuts to another bench and a "Kaminoudia" signpost, about 1hr 45min into the walk. From here on the track system is unavoidable, and poorly marked; bearing down and left at the next Y-fork deposits you on the Mesopóta-mos–Plátres track in just over half an hour, whilst bearing up and right may (or may not) return you to the start of the loop just above Psilódhendhro. All in all, not brilliant marking or routing by the responsible authorities; there are frankly better paths higher up in the Tróödhos, especially around Spília (see p.260).

## Walk to Caledonian Falls

The most popular walk from Psilódhendhro is the one up to **Caledonian Falls**, designated as the "Kalidonia Nature Trail" by CTO signage. Begin on the wide track passing left of the trout farm as you face it; after 300m this dwindles to a marked trail, with the distance to the falls given as 1km. The impressive eleven-metre cascade, the highest on the island, indeed beckons twenty minutes later, in a pleasantly wooded ravine. En route you're obliged to change sides of the stream several times, and you'll get your feet wet in the springtime; more water crossings are involved in continuing upstream along the path.

Some 45 minutes beyond the falls you emerge at the opposite trailhead, marked by the familiar canopied noticeboard, about 1km from the Tróödhos resort (see "Mount Olympus" below). If you do this walk in the opposite direction, the access slip road off the Tróödhos-bound highway, just below that serving the "Katoikiai/Residences" of the president, is also well signposted, with yet another wooden nature-walk sign. Hiking downhill to the falls also takes about 45 minutes, owing to the roughness of the trail at some points – those with trainers beware.

The walk is short enough that retracing your steps is not so arduous; if you're vehicle-less and intent on leaving Plátres, it's worth noting that this trail, despite its steepness, is much the quickest way of getting up to the Tróödhos resort on foot. Alternatively, combine it with one of the Pouziáris trails, following the description above in reverse, to make a loop.

Before British administration began in 1878, the area was little visited except for shepherds based at Plátres and gatherers of snow (used for refrigeration), but shortly thereafter a military training camp was established near to the site of present-day Tróödhos, and a **summer residence** built for the British High Commissioner. Now the retreat of the president of the southern Republic, this stands just above the high end of the Caledonian Falls trail, and is also a touch-down point for one leg of the Pouziáris trail. Signs discourage entry at the start of the driveway, but you may want to stop in to read the rather startling plaque to one side of the door of what looks like an ordinary Highland shooting lodge. Written in French, it declares: "Arthur Rimbaud, French poet and genius, despite his fame contributed with his own hands to the construction of this

## Tróödhos range trails

Since 1981 the CTO, in conjunction with the forestry department, has laid out and marked a growing number of **nature trails** in the high Tróödhos. Actually, most of these paths existed long before then, used by mountaineers travelling between the highest villages and monasteries, but since the 1950s many had been overgrown and forgotten, while others had been bulldozed or even paved. Lately, those rights of way which have survived as paths have been cleared and rehabilitated as **hikers' routes**. The 1981-vintage 1:5,000 topographic maps (see p.41) show many of them correctly; guests at the *Minerva* or *New Helvetia* hotels in Plátres can ask to see map sets, kept by the management for consultation. The nature trails, in addition to being refurbished where necessary, have also been fitted with numbered wooden markers calling walkers' attention to selected natural features. The labelling, however, is pretty perfunctory, with only Latin species names given – if at all – and often specimens are embarrassingly dead or missing. To enjoy the trails as they were intended, it's essential to get the 28-page, periodically updated CTO publication *Nature Trails of the Tróödhos*, which contains the number keys for four of the more popular trails. These are variably available; if you intend to follow the markers, start looking for the booklet in English long before you reach Plátres; otherwise you may have to settle for a French- or German-language version – or no booklet at all.

At present there are four fully documented trails in the Tróödhos/Plátres area, most with fanciful names from Greek mythology. The **Atalante** nearly completes a circuit of Mount Olympus; the **Persephone** leads to a viewpoint known as Makriá Kondárka (Makrya Kontarka); **Kalidonia** links the presidential forest lodge with Caledonian Falls; while **Artemis** executes a complete loop of Khionístra summit at a higher contour than the Atalante. In addition to the as-yet undocumented Pouziáris trail, there are also several other trails, thus far sparsely labelled, along and across the Madhári ridge between Spília and Agrós, some kilometres east of Tróödhos. All of the South's prepared trails are described in a folding pamphlet, "Nature Trails", but this is strictly schematic, far from error-free and not suitable for navigation.

house, 1881." Rimbaud's two visits to Cyprus were sandwiched between time with the Dutch colonial army in Java, recuperation from typhoid in France and a stint in the Horn of Africa; he in fact merely supervised a work party here and did no actual manual labour – nor was he yet famous.

# Mount Olympus

At 1952m (6404ft), the Khionístra (lately Chionistra – "snow-pack" or "chilblain") peak of **Mount Olympus** (Olympos) is the highest point on Cyprus. It does not rise particularly dramatically from the surrounding uplands, which are cloaked in dense forest of hardy black and Austrian pine, with a smattering of Cypriot cedar and junipers. The trees keep things cool except perhaps in high summer, and provide much of the justification for five marked nature trails (two of them already mentioned above). In winter, the northeast-facing slopes are host to the island's only ski resort. The area is worth a visit at any time of year; however, the altitude and terrain can act as traps for sudden storms in most months, so don't step off unprepared onto the paths. When you do, you'll find them relatively empty, except perhaps on Thursdays, which is the designated "walk day" for large groups of German coach tours.

## The Tróödhos resort

The only thing resembling permanent habitation in the peak zone is a strip of development, called **TRÓÖDHOS** (Troodos), flanking the main road junction about 1700m above sea level. By no stretch of the imagination is this a village, merely a resort complex with the opportunity for some very tame horse-riding. All day long through much of the year it's beset by tour coaches whose clients barely venture off the single parade with its landscaped park. Public **buses** to and from here operate weekdays out of Limassol via Plátres, and also from Nicosia; the uphill morning leg of the Limassol-based bus is an excellent way for walkers to get from Plátres to here, though the downhill journey starts inconveniently early in the afternoon.

There seems little to recommend an overnight stay here other than the pine-scented air, with just one **hotel**, the two-star *Jubilee* (☎ 25420107, ☏ 22673991, ✉ jubilee@cytanet.com.cy; ⑤), which has an attached mountain-bike rental centre. Just north of the major T-junction, the **youth hostel** (closed Nov–April) asks a bit more than usual at C£6 per person, plus a C£1 sheet fee; alternatively, the congenial, popular if exceedingly basic **campsite** (May–Oct), 1km north-east of the intersection on the road to Nicosia, charges C£2 per tent and C£1 per person, though it functions primarily as a caravan park for Cypriots.

Spare a moment for a look at the **Tróödhos Military Cemetery**, a wonderful spot on the hillside just above the road between the campsite and the youth hostel. Most of the fatalities – infants and children as well as military personnel

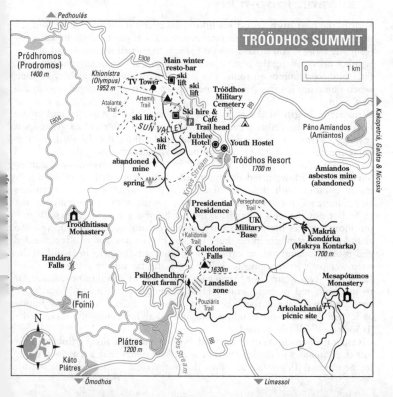

## Skiing on Mount Olympus

No one comes specially to Cyprus to ski, but if you're here between New Year and the end of March, you just might consider the slopes for their novelty value. Four T-bar lifts serve seven runs of 200 to 600 metres in length, none rated as difficult except one north-facing one, dubbed "Jubilee". **Snow** surface, alas, tends to be slushy or icy owing to warmish, sunny days alternating with freezing nights, even in the pit of winter. That said, on a good day immediately after a snowfall, you can get light, dry, Rockies-style powder. The shorter, more southerly Sun Valley runs are considered beginners' areas, and this is where equipment is rented and lessons given; the more advanced northern runs are often given over to competitions, with the main **restaurant/café** at the base well-poised to watch the action.

Lift tickets cost about C£12 a day, skis, boots and sticks rental C£10, with half off for Cyprus Ski Club members – temporary membership is available but only worth it if you'll be here a few days. Ninety-minute group **lessons** are C£10, or you can be humiliated in private for about C£25. For current information, contact the Ski Club in Nicosia (℡22675340) or the ski station itself for a **weather report** (℡25420104) – many winters there simply isn't enough snow. If you're planning way in advance, Ⓦwww.skicyprus.com is worth a look.

– date from the peacetime summers of 1879 and 1885, a reminder of just how unhealthy Cyprus was at the time.

## A summit loop-hike

Perhaps the **best high Tróödhos hike** is the circuit made possible by combining parts of the Atalante and Artemis nature trails. It can be done in half a day – slightly more if you make a detour towards the actual summit – and in clear weather offers among the best views of the island, as well as an attractive plant (and bird) community en route. The walk is most enjoyable in May or June, when numerous streams (and the one improved spring) are guaranteed to still be flowing.

Itineraries **begin** at the archwayed trailhead for the Atalante trail at the north end of the resort parade, just south of the *Jubilee Hotel*. A signpost reading "Chromio 8km" is somewhat misleading: the labelled path is approximately that distance, but you never actually end up at the abandoned chromium mine in question. Your first fork is some twelve minutes out; go left for now, following red-dot waymarks. The proper trail skims the 1750-metre contour with little significant height change. Some forty minutes along, there's a three-way junction; ignore a wide track up the ridge to the right but not the onward trail taking off behind a wooden bench. Within ten more minutes there's a masonry fountain, running much of the year. An abandoned chromium mine shaft 1 hour 25 minutes out is often flooded and probably dangerous to explore; here shun wider tracks in favour of the narrower path hairpinning back left along the far side of the creek valley. Just under two hours along, you've a first view of Pródhromos village far to the west, and its giant, empty Hotel Berengaria (see p.242). Soon a TV tower looms overhead, then the trail becomes a track through mossy pines about ten minutes before ending, two-and-a-half hours into the hike, on the Tróödhos–Pródhromos road.

Rather than emerging onto the road, bear up and right along a **link trail** for just three minutes to the intersection with the Artemis trail, a true loop closer to the summit. It's possible to follow this to the right (anti-clockwise), but for the quickest way back to the original trailhead, take a left turn, crossing the courses of two T-bar ski lifts. Once you're past the second lift, there's a fine view northeast over northern Cyprus, as you progress roughly parallel to the road back to Tróödhos. You soon meet the tarmacked side road up to Khionístra peak; cross to the nature-trail canopy opposite to stay with the path. At the next track junction bear left, keeping to path surface; three minutes along this bear left again at trees tacked with a yellow arrow and a red dot, forsaking both a track ahead down the ridge and the onward nature trail in favour of an older track dropping down into the valley on your left.

Rocks here are splashed with a few **blue dots**; followed in reverse up the hill, this blue-marked route passes a giant, labelled black pine and the top of the Sun Valley ski lift on its route to the summit area. This is a better detour than following the previously encountered paved drive. Resuming the descent, you drop through a defile, and then the narrowing track curls back to join the Atalante trail just below the *Jubilee Hotel*. You should be back at the starting point roughly an hour and fifteen minutes from the "Chromio" end of the same path (not counting any detours to the peak), for a total walking time of three hours 45 minutes.

## Khionístra summit

If you're intent on **visiting the peak**, it's better to arrive by car, a ten-minute drive from the resort. Scant ruins of a Venetian watchtower and an ancient temple of Aphrodite are all but invisible; what draws the eye are various elec-tronic/surveillance installations which have always figured prominently in the island's geopolitical status. The right-hand (easterly) compound is one of the UK "retained sites", with its famous RAF radar "golf ball", visible for miles around (there used to be two more but they've been moved over to Makriá Kondárka). The left-hand (westerly) compound is Cypriot, comprising civilian telecom and TV towers, plus a small "golf ball" built to guide the Russian SS-300 missiles (see p.456) which never arrived. There's a narrow corridor between the two bases, all of 100m long, which can be traversed for the view north, but this is sullied by electrified barbed wire and more military installations down the slope; obviously no photography is allowed.

## The Makriá Kondárka (Persephone) trail

This additional short walk is just the thing if you haven't had enough for the day, and can be optionally extended to get you back to Plátres, as you will have almost certainly missed the afternoon bus down the hill. The path begins inconspicuously at the southeast end of the Tróödhos resort, beyond the police station; if you end up at an off-limits British base, you'll know you've missed the trailhead. At a moderate pace, the out-and-back route should take just over ninety minutes; the destination is the viewpoint of **Makriá Kondárka** (Makrya Kontarka) at 1700m, allowing unobstructed views southeast over the Limassol foothills and coastal plain. On the way back you get to look at the incongruous radar domes and telecom tower on Khionístra, as well as the huge scar of the **Amíandos open-pit asbestos mine**, largest in the world, to the northeast. Owned by the bishopric of Limassol, it is not exhausted but has shut down owing to a sharp drop in demand for this carcinogenic material; the site is supposed to be filled with topsoil and planted with trees, but to date hasn't been. From the viewpoint, a path heads southeast towards Plátres, debouching on the track to Mesapóta-mos about 2.5km shy of Psilódhendhro.

# West of Plátres and Tróödhos

Rather than proceeding directly from Plátres or Tróödhos resort to the Marathássa valley, it's worth detouring slightly along one of three more roundabout, westerly routes, which converge at the alpine settlement of **Pródhromos**. The quickest of the three options, a direct, entirely paved route from Plátres, passes right by venerable **Tróödhítissa monastery**, now alas closed to the non-Orthodox. Closer to Plátres lies workaday **Finí** village, with a crafts tradition and better restaurants than at the neighbouring resort. Rather than proceeding due north from Finí via the pleasant but nondescript hamlets of Áyios Dhimítrios and Paleómylos, veering west along partly dirt roads could be justified by a trio of minor **medieval monuments** along the way.

## Tróödhítissa monastery

Nestled in orchards and pines 8km northwest of Plátres at about 1200m elevation, the **monastery of Tróödhítissa** (Panagia tis Trooditissas) is the highest working monastery in the land. It owes its thirteenth-century foundation to a wonder-working icon which, as ever, floated mysteriously over from Asia Minor at the height of the eighth-century Iconoclast controversy. Two hermits guarded it in a nearby cave for some years; after they had died and the memory of the relic faded, an unearthly glow alerted a succeeding generation to its presence, and a suitable home was built for the image. A marked three-minute trail up to the hallowed **cave** begins 300m east of the turn-off for the monastery; a sign in Greek reads, "to the cave in which the icon of the Virgin Tróödhítíssas was found". On arrival, you'll find the diminutive grotto has little palpable air of mystery, though at least it's not tastelessly gaudy; in the cascade-lashed gorge below, British forces often hone their abseiling techniques.

The present monastery buildings date mostly from 1730, and since 1996 have been absolutely out of bounds to the non-Orthodox; there's a notice to this effect at the start of the access road, and a gatehouse to vet visitors. A dozen or so monks live here, and the same austere regimen as at Stavrovoúni (see p.112) prevails. In the **katholikón** it's traditional for monks to encircle young women with a medallion-studded girdle, said to induce fertility – in the old days any resulting boy-child had to be dedicated to the church as a monk, or "ransomed" with a generous donation. Infidels obviously won't get to revere the marvellous icon, a silver-sheathed *Virgin Enthroned*, displayed to the left of the Holy Door in the fine *témblon*.

## Finí

A paved side road just 1km up the Tróödhítissa-bound highway, the F821, mysteriously never shown on maps, provides easy, fairly direct access to **FINÍ** (Foini), just 4km from Plátres. Unlike its near neighbour, this is a "normal" village with a functioning primary school, and its semi-arid landscape and domestic architecture attract few visitors. There is, however, a surviving crafts heritage, in the shape of two elderly female potters turning out an assortment of practical and kitsch wares and the privately run **Pivlakion Museum** (daily 9am–noon & 2–5pm; donation). This is run by Theofanis Pivlakis, who personally escorts visitors through his collection of rural oddments while talking the hind legs off a donkey for up to two hours – you have been warned. Though enormous *pithária* (olive-oil jars) are no longer made commercially here, a number of older specimens, with date stamps just above their middle, are on view. Fashioned by a wheel-less method, they were built upwards from a knob at the base, like a swallow's nest. The only other local "sight" is the **Handára** (Chantara) **waterfall**, 2km uphill along a dirt track; follow signs towards the trout farm.

Finí's **restaurants** are, on the whole, better than those in Plátres. Slightly dull but reliable, *A Taste of Village* – *Phini Tavern* (☎25421828; closed Sun eve & all day Mon) is a wild misnomer; what's actually served is reasonably priced if rather retro European food, particularly fish (especially trout) and steaks ("Tournedos" and "Diane" for the 1970s time-warped); reservations in high season are all but mandatory. Just up the street, the locals frequent *To Iliovasilema*, which does all the standard grills nicely; there's limited outdoor seating, plus an indoor area, both looking towards the sunset of the name. Adjacent is a producer of *loukoúmi* or "Cypriot" delight, said to be the best in the South and flavoured with *mehlebí* (ground cherry stones). Finally, the *Neraïdha* (☎25421680; lunch only except Fri & Sat, closed all day Wed, closed low season except weekends), on the west side of town, right by the river draining from the waterfall, is a reliable purveyor of Cypriot and "continental" food; it gets periodic coach tours, so you might want to reserve.

## Áyii Anáryiri and Elía bridge

Some 2km west of Finí on the narrow paved road to Paleómylos, a sign by a small cement wayside shrine points down a dirt track towards **Áyii Anáryiri**, a fifteenth-century monastic church, in a lovely setting surrounded by orchards. An eerie legend attaches to the place, specifically that on Saturday at dusk a ghostly horseman emerges through the dog-toothed west portal, the oldest surviving portion of the building. A new, locking door has been fitted, presumably resistant to spectral dashes, yet Áyii Anáryiri seems an altogether unlikely spot for hauntings. It is probably not worth hunting down the key to glimpse the few surviving, late-medieval frescoes within.

Just past the Áyii Anáryiri wayside shrine, bear left (west) onto a rough but passable dirt track; after 7.5km, you'll reach another junction on the paved Kaminária–Kélefos road. Very nearby stands the single-arched **Elía bridge** (signposted as "Gefyri tis Elias"), the easterly link in the Venetian caravan route (see p.220). Though smaller and less impressive than the Kélefos and Roúdhias bridges to the west, the little bridge enjoys a fine position amid dense forest, with a perennial brook flowing underneath.

## Kaminária: the chapel of Panayía

From the Elía bridge, a broad paved road leads west towards Kélefos and Áyios Nikólaos village (see p.223); going north, the road – still paved but narrower – reaches within 5km the friendly, surprisingly large village of **KAMINÁRIA**. On a knoll west of the village is the early sixteenth-century **chapel of Panayía**, with frescoes from the same era. Ask at the central *kafenío* for the priest-with-key, and expect to return here for a post-viewing coffee.

Although it cannot compare with the first-division painted churches of the Tróödhos, Panayía is compelling enough in its own right. The most interesting surviving paintings include, on the north wall, the donor family in French-influenced period dress; the *Sacrifice of Isaac* inside the *ierón*; Saint Mamas on his lion on the west wall; and, as part of the *Crucifixion*, a weeping, crouching Virgin, with two friends standing behind – entirely western imagery imported into late-Byzantine iconography.

## Pródhromos

Along with Páno Amíandos, **PRÓDHROMOS** (Prodromos) is the highest true village in the country at 1400m elevation. It's also noted for its apples and cherries, the trees ablaze with blossom in spring, but they are being uprooted and replaced (lower down the mountain) with olives, a move subsidized by the government in its desire to fall in line with EU policy, with the result that Cyprus has to import apples now. The most interesting item here is the rambling, hilltop, chateau-like **Hotel Berengaria**, built as one of the first "modern" Cypriot lodgings during the 1920s but abandoned in 1980 – it couldn't compete with the luxurious *Churchill Pinewood Valley*, just downhill to the north. A foreign consortium intends to convert it to a casino, but has accomplished little other than repeatedly reroofing it after arsonists set fires; the general dereliction of the place, now close to write-off status, makes it an oddly haunting relic of the British empire.

The village itself is fairly desolate, with just one or two shops and a petrol pump (no unleaded) at its top end. Its other hotel has also closed down and anyone staying in the immediate area does so at the 1994-remodelled, family-orientated three-star *Churchill Pinewood Valley* (☎22952211, ⓔpinewood@churchill.com.cy; ➎), 3km north towards Pedhoulás, an isolated and thus self-sufficient chalet-hotel available through virtually every tour operator. However, we've received complaints about smoke-permeated rooms and poor choice in the restaurant. Independent **eating** opportunities in the area are a bit better; there are a handful of carniverous *exokhiká kéndra* near the main ridgetop crossroads, strategically placed to cater for pilgrims to Kýkko.

# Marathássa

Directly north over the ridge from Pródhromos yawns the valley of **Marathássa** (Marathasa), a deep, introspective canyon of Asiatic grandeur. Like most watercourses on the north side of the Tróödhos, the Setrákhos stream draining it runs into North Cyprus, and a dam has been built to rescue the water that would otherwise go unharnessed into "enemy" territory. Marathássa is famous for its cherry orchards, from which it makes a partial living (though as noted above, their days may be numbered); tourism, while catered to, is not the be-all and end-all that it is at Plátres. The valley can boast a respectable concentration of frescoed churches, and though not strictly speaking within Marathássa, the prestigious **monastery of Kýkko** is easiest reached from here.

## Pedhoulás

At the top of the Marathássa valley, 1100m up, compact **PEDHOULÁS** (Pedoulas) is amphitheatrically laid out in tiers, though close up most of the buildings are not so attractive. Somewhat unusually for a Tróödhos village, it has an unobstructed view of the sea to the north on clear days. As a base it's a viable alternative to Plátres, both for convenience to Marathassan sights and for the range of choice in eating and sleeping.

### Arkhángelos Mihaïl church and Byzantine Museum

The main sight, and quite possibly your first frescoed church of the Tróödhos, is **Arkhángelos Mihaïl** (Archangelos Michail), well signposted in the lower quarter of the village. The core of the church dates from 1474, so the images (cleaned in 1980) depart from the austerity of earlier work in favour of the naturalism of the post-Byzantine revival. The archangel Michael himself looms left (north) of the minimalist *témblon*; inside the *ierón* is the *Sacrifice of Abraham*, with the principals of the potentially gruesome drama radiating a hieratic serenity.

Starting on the south wall, there's a clockwise life-cycle of the Virgin and Christ. The *Baptism* features the River Jordan stylized like a throw-rug with fish embedded in it; in the *Betrayal* a miniature Peter lops off the ear of the high priest's servant, here in Crusader dress, while two apostles cense the Virgin's bier in the *Assumption*. Over the north door, donor Basil Khamadhes and his family, in noble costume of the period, hand a model of the church to the archangel, who emerges from a curtain-like fold of cloud next to the dedicatory inscription. Above the *Virgin Orans* in the apse looms a smudged *Ascension*, in lieu of the usual *Pandokrátor*.

Admission to the church is courtesy of the warden of the **Byzantine Museum** just opposite (daily: April–Oct 9.30am–1pm & 2–6pm; Nov–March closes 5pm; C£1), which contains a fine collection of local icons and ecclesiastical artefacts.

### Practicalities

The only reasonable **hotel** in the village centre is the one-star *Christy's Hotel* (T22952655, ❸); the spartan but salubrious rooms were lightly renovated in 1995, with heating permitting all-year operation. Other central, inexpensive options on the main through road – all well received by readers – include the *Pension Mountain Rose* (T22952727, F22952555; ❸) and the *Two Flowers* (T22952372, F22952235; ❸), more or less opposite *Christy's Palace*.

However, when **eating out**, it's best to avoid the unseemly lunchtime scrums of the coach-tour and jeep-safari groups at *Mountain Rose* and *Two Flowers*, where microwaving or serving independent travellers the leftovers are common ploys. The food tends to be better at the attached diner at *Christy's Palace*, which doesn't accept coach tours. But top choice, at midday at least, is sixty-year-old *To Vrysi* (alias *Harry's*), a shady and authentic *exokhikó kéndro* on a minor road up to the main highway, open daily most of the year. This features Arsos red wine, home-style dishes such as pickled wild mushrooms, occasional white-fleshed wild trout (as opposed to the pink farmed variety) and a full spectrum of candied fruits and vegetables. It's not rock-bottom cheap, but portions are generous, so show up hungry. "Harry" also sells canned and bottled products to take away, including his own cherry brandy.

Rounding out the list of amenities are two **banks** (but no ATMs) and a minuscule **post office** (Mon–Fri 3–5pm). The once-daily market **bus** on the Nicosia–Plátres line passes through here very early in the morning heading downhill, returning at lunchtime.

## Kýkko monastery and around

Nineteen paved but twisty kilometres west of Pedhoulás sits the enormous, fabulously wealthy **monastery of Kýkko** (Panagia tis Kykkou, *Tchýkou* in dialect), one of the most celebrated in the Orthodox world. Here Michael Mouskos, better known as Makarios III, began his secondary education, and later served as a novice monk, prior to using the monastery as a hideout during his EOKA days (when Grivas's headquarters were nearby). Thus Kýkko is inextricably linked with the Cypriot nationalist struggle.

## Frescoed churches of the Tróödhos

Indisputably the most remarkable monuments in the Tróödhos, if not the whole island, are a group of lavishly **frescoed Byzantine churches**, predominantly on the north slopes of the range. **Architecturally**, the majority of these country churches were originally simple rectangular structures about the size of a small barn; later they often grew domes, less frequently narthexes. If it didn't originally exist, an all-encompassing, drastically pitched roof would be added at some point to shed dangerously heavy snow, with ample allowance for protruding domes if necessary. Most importantly, by extending down to the ground on one or both sides, they enclosed L- or U-shaped spaces which *de facto* served as narthexes, so that many frescoed exterior walls were now afforded some protection. Almost every Tróödhos village has such a pitched-roof church – but only a very few are still painted inside.

Strictly speaking, few of the **paintings** actually employ the fresco technique (in which the pigment is applied while the plaster is still wet), so they should more accurately be termed wall paintings or murals; however, with this understood, this guide refers to them as frescoes for convenience. The earliest date from the eleventh century, with construction continuing until the early 1500s; murals were applied sporadically over the whole period, so that they serve as a chronicle of changing dress styles and artistic tastes, often juxtaposed in the same building. The oldest were executed in what is termed the **hieratic or monastic style**, with roots in Syria and Cappadocia; later Byzantine work reflected the arrival of artisans from Constantinople in the twelfth and thirteenth centuries. As Lusignan rule advanced, the building and decorating of these chapels became of necessity a provincial, rearguard action, since the Orthodox were effectively banished from the larger towns. The so-called **post-Byzantine revival style** of the fifteenth and sixteenth centuries is at once more naive and naturalistic, with fascinating period details, humanistic liberties taken with Orthodox iconographic conventions and, in general, echoes of Renaissance art.

Certain departures from the usual **iconography** were caused by the many pitched, domeless roofs; there were often no cupola, pendentives or vaults for the usual hierarchical placement of the *Pandokrátor* (Christ in Majesty), cherubim, evangelists and so on. However, the cartoon-strip story-telling format, chosen to teach the Gospel to largely illiterate parishioners, was enhanced in small rectangular churches. The usual arrangement is a fairly complete life-cycle of the Virgin and Jesus on the south and north upper walls, with emphasis on the crucial dedications to God of both and various miracles and events of Christ's ministry. Over the west door, the donor/builder usually appears in a portrait, presenting the church in miniature to Christ or the Virgin, below an inscribed request for mercy at the Last Judgement.

Despite these hallowed associations, the place is of negligible artistic or architectural interest; repeated fires since Kýkko's twelfth-century foundation by the hermit Isaiah have left nothing older than 1831, and the garish mosaics and frescoes lining every corridor and the *katholikón*, however well intentioned, are workmanlike and of recent vintage, some as new as 1987. Isaiah had been given an **icon** of the Panayía Eleoússa, the Most Merciful Virgin, by the Byzantine emperor Alexios Komnenos in gratitude for curing the latter's daughter. The monastery grew up around this relic, claimed to have been painted by Luke the Evangelist, which now has pride of place in a rather gaudy shrine in front of the *témblon* or altar screen. Considered too holy for the casual glances of the possibly impious and unworthy, who would run the risk of a most unmerciful instantaneous blinding, the original image has been encased in silver for almost four centuries now. Nearby in the *katholikón* is a brass arm, said to be that of a blasphemous Turk who had it so rendered by

Variations on the pattern – details such as shepherds playing rustic instruments of the time, period costumes and humorous touches – are what make each church interesting. Selected Old Testament personalities or episodes, rarely seen in Cyprus outside the Tróödhos, such as the *Sacrifice of Abraham*, recur particularly in late fifteenth-century churches, and act as the signature of a certain **Philip Goul**, presumably a Latinized Greek, or one of his apprentices.

The way to most of these churches is well signposted from the main roads, and many are proudly proclaimed on their identifying plaques as being listed on the UNESCO World Cultural Heritage roster, and kept firmly **locked**. Thus hunting down the key is an integral part of your visit; usually the contact name and number for the key-keeper and permissible visiting hours are posted (and repeated in this guide). Sometimes the **caretaker** is a layman who lives nearby, otherwise a peripatetic priest who might not show up until the next day, as he could be responsible for conducting liturgies at several neighbourhood churches. A few of the most noteworthy churches now have set hours during which they are supposed to be open. Caretakers vary in terms of knowledgeability (none is a trained guide, though if you understand Greek they can convey a basic summary of the images) and cordiality, the latter not surprisingly often a function of how many importunate foreigners they have to escort. While there is usually no set admission fee, a **donation** is expected, especially in cases where you've taken the key-keeper miles out of his daily routine. Usually a box is provided in the church; otherwise you should tip the responsible person at the conclusion of your visit. Fifty to seventy-five cents per person is sufficient for a small church where the guard lives next door; a pound or C£1.50 for a large monument off in the woods. In most of the churches **photography** of any sort is strictly forbidden, though enforcement of this rule varies – videoing tends to be looked on with more favour than still cameras with flash, which degrades the pigments.

Binding **recommendations** would be subjective; if you're keen, you can see all of the churches in a few days. If your interest is more casual, three or four will be enough – the most important are reckoned to be Asínou, Áyios Ioánnis Lambadhistís, Áyios Nikólaos tís Stéyis, Panayía toú Araká and Stavrós toú Ayiasmáti. A whirlwind taxi trip taking in Asínou, Araká and Ayiasmáti would occupy between five and six hours and cost about C£35, not including tips – and not overly onerous if shared among four passengers. If you develop a compulsive interest in the subject, a recommended specialist guide is *The Painted Churches of Cyprus*, by Andreas and Judith Stylianou. Reprinted in 1998 by the A G Leventis Foundation, it has gone out of print again but is shortly to be reissued; Moufflon Books in Nicosia (see p.295) has the most current information.

the icon's power, when sacrilegiously attempting to light his cigarette from a lamp in the sanctuary.

On weekends Kýkko is to be avoided (or gravitated towards, according to your temperament), when thousands of Cypriots descend upon the place. A ban on photos or videoing inside, enforced against the heterodox, is cheerfully ignored by proud relatives snapping the relay baptisms which dominate Saturdays and Sundays; lottery ticket-sellers circulate out in the courtyard as howling babies are plunged one after another into the steaming font. Monks at more austere monasteries ridicule the practice – what's the matter with one's local parish church for christening your child, they say – but this ignores the tremendous prestige of Kýkko, and the ease of access from Nicosia.

Besides the pilgrimage activities, there's a worthwhile **museum** of ecclesiastical treasures adjoining the inner courtyard (daily: Nov–May 10am–4pm; June–Oct 10am–6pm; C£1.50). At Room 13, to the right of the main gate

△ Courtyard of Kýkko monastery

of the outer courtyard, you can request a room in the enormous *xenónas* or **guest quarters** if you're Orthodox Christian. The overpriced, listless fare in the "tourist restaurant" in the adjacent arcade of shops is eminently avoidable; eat in a mountain village en route, or bring your own snack.

## The EOKA hideouts

About 3km before arrival at Kýkko, a small brown-and-white sign by the roadside points right (north) to "EOKA hideouts, 2km". A curvy, one-lane track – just negotiable in a saloon car – leads to a clearing where some of the EOKA bunkers have been preserved, more or less in their original state. Still further uphill is the main HQ, reached by a steep path with a loose shale surface – take care on the descent in particular. All this glorification of EOKA and its doings is part and parcel of the tide of Hellenic nationalism which has engulfed the South since the early 1990s.

## Throní

The longish, scenic trip in from Pedhoulás is much of the attraction; it can be prolonged by another 2km to a final car park below **Throní**, the hill atop which stands the **tomb of Makarios**. This is a bunker-like capsule, with the main opening to the west and a National Guardsman keeping a permanent vigil. A modern **shrine** just south adorns the true summit, which allows comprehensive views of the empty Tillyrian hills to the west, and Mount Olympus to the east; in many ways it's a better vantage point than the latter. On the yearly festival (Sept 7–8) the numinous icon of Kýkko is paraded to the shrine and back amid prayers for a rainy winter. The stark concrete design of the chapel is further offset by a **wish-tree** (more accurately, wish-bush) on which the faithful have tied votive hankies, tissues and streamers as petitions for more personal favours from the Virgin.

## Kámbos, Chakístra and the road to Pólis

Just before Kýkko, where the E912 peels off to the north, signs beg you to head north 9km to visit **KÁMBOS** (Kampos), the only substantial habitation in Tillyría, poised in isolation about halfway down the slope towards the Attila Line. It's a scenic, untouristed spot, with the locals fairly unused to foreign visitors – you'll have celebrity value. There's even a **guest house**, the unlicensed *Kambos* (☏22942320; ❷), where meals are also offered; enquire at the café on left, just over the river bridge going downhill. The taverna in the middle of the vast square is presently closed but may of course reopen in the future. Families might prefer to call in at **CHAKÍSTRA** (Tsakistra), 2km before, where *To Spiti tis Christinas* (☏22316514 or 99476514, ℱ22316889; ❸ for 4 persons) is the local agrotourism option; it's a pleasantly restored two-bedroom house, though right on the road. Chakístra lives primarily from its sawmills, while in spring the valley floor here is a mass of white cherry blossom.

Between the junction and Chakístra, about 3km below the farm, there's another prominently signposted forking for the paved **road west**, then north, towards various attractions in Tillyría. As per the placard, it's 10km to the Cedar Valley, 22km to Stavrós tís Psókas, 52km to Káto Pýrgos, and 56km to Pólis. But don't let the asphalt and nominal distances lull you into taking the drive lightly; the forestry department forbade straightening of the bends when the road (still subject to rockfalls) was surfaced, and howling wilderness prevails between the destinations cited, so be prepared for up to two hours of fairly strenuous driving.

### South to Milikoúri and the Eliá/Kélefos bridges

If you're based at Plátres, much the most enjoyable return from the Kýkko area is via the remote village of **Milikoúri** (Mylikouri; no facilities), near the head of the beautiful Platýs valley. One of the wildest in the Tróödhos, alive with springs and rivulets (a picnic area takes advantage of these), the valley has been saved from a proposed dam but is now threated by a planned E-standard road up from Áyios Nikólaos in Páfos district, as this is the most likely route. After about 14km of fairly easy driving, you emerge on the paved road between the two historic bridges of Eliá and Kélefos, a bit closer to the latter.

## Moutoullás: Panayía toú Moutoullá

The earliest surviving example of the Tróödhos pitched-roof church, **Panayía (Panagia) toú Moutoullá** (1280), stands next to the cemetery at the highest point of **MOUTOULLÁS** village, 3km below Pedhoulás. A set of steps leads up from the marked side road, above the sharp turn in the ravine, to the house of a somewhat crotchety caretaker, just below the church.

You enter via two sets of doors, the outer pair piercing the protective structure grown up around the original church, the inner ones (and the altar screen) very fine, carved antique pieces. The village is still renowned for its carved feed-troughs and other utilitarian objects, as well as its spring water, bottled way down in the canyon.

On the original exterior wall of the church, now enclosed by the L-shaped "narthex", Christ is enthroned over the inner doors, flanked by Adam and Eve, Hell and Paradise (with the saints marching into the latter). Inside, the cycle of events is similar to that of Arkhángelos Míhaïl in Pedhoulás, but less complete, and stopping with the *Assumption* rather than the *Ascension*; the caretaker claims that the British, while engaged in an anti-EOKA raid, damaged many scenes. An unusual *Nativity* on the south wall shows the Virgin rocking the Christ Child in his cradle (she's usually still reclining after having given birth), while Joseph sits on a wooden donkey saddle much like ones that were formerly produced in the village. An equally rare martial Áyios Khristóforos (Saint Christopher) stands opposite Áyios Yeóryios (Saint George) on the north wall, slaying a dragon with the crowned head of a woman. On the west wall, the *Raising of Lazarus* includes the obligatory spectator holding his nose against the reek of the tomb; on the north wall, there's a rather stiff portrait of donor Ioannis Moutoullas and his wife. Overall, the images don't rank among the most expressive or striking in the Tróödhos, but are the earliest, unretouched frescoes in any of the churches.

### Kalopanayiótis and around

Just over 1km further down the Setrákhos valley from Moutoullás, **KALOPANAYIÓTIS** (Kalopanagiotis) seems a bit less concrete than Pedhoulás, more geared to tourists than facility-less Moutoullás and the most compact of the three villages – though it has a suburb hamlet, Íkos (alias Níkos, officially Oikos), downstream and across the river. Many old handsome houses have retained their tiled roofs, and there are fine views up-valley to Pedhoulás. The village is thought to be the descendant of ancient Lampadhou, which produced the saints Iraklidhios and Ioannis (see below). There are also two fine old **bridges** in the area: one next to the local sulphur springs, the other just upstream from the local reservoir and below Íkos, still serving a little-used medieval trail descending from Íkos to the west bank of the valley. There is now a marked trail leading within thirty minutes from the monastic church (see below) to Íkos, making a loop-hike possible. Some 4km west of Íkos and Kalopanayiótis lies **YERAKIÉS** (Gerakies), a quiet, traditional village with two authentic **kafenío-restaurants** in the centre, and a short-loop (2-hr) **nature trail**, the "Ariadni", taking off just west from the brow of a ridge.

Of the three no-star **hotels** here, all on the through road and all seemingly geared to the domestic spa trade, the sprucest is the 1997-renovated *Heliopoulis* (T 22952451; ❸) at the south end of Kalopanayiótis. Slightly pricier – and more unusual – is an agrotourism offering, *Olga's Katoi* (T 22952432 or 22350283; ❸), a village-centre complex with the original main house providing the lounge and self-catering facilities for the annexe rooms. For **meals**, you're restricted to the hotel's diner or two kebab houses.

### The monastery of Áyios Ioánnis Lambadhistís

Plainly visible from Kalopanayiótis across the river, and accessible by a one-kilometre side road or a more direct footbridge (or by dirt track from Íkos), the rambling **monastery of Áyios Ioánnis Lambadhistís** (Agios Ioannis Lampadistis; May–Sept daily 8am–1pm & 2–6pm, pm hours unreliable) is probably the successor to a pagan shrine, owing its foundation to some cold sulphur springs just upstream. The saint in question is not John the Evangelist, but a local ascetic who died young, and to whose tomb were ascribed healing powers. This is one of the few early Tróodhos monasteries to have survived relatively intact from foundation days – many of the painted churches are lonely *katholiká* bereft of long-vanished cloisters, and those monasteries that still exist have been renovated beyond recognition over the centuries. If the courtyard and church doors are not open during the posted hours, enquire at the café adjacent for the (none too friendly or patient) caretaker-priest. From October to April, the café will probably not be operating, and you may have to fetch the priest from his house in the village, on the east side of the through road, north of Ayía Marína church. The local **festival** takes place on October 3–4.

Huddled together under a single, huge, pitched roof are three **churches** built to an odd plan, their aggregate south-to-north width much greater than their lengths. The double main nave, one part dedicated to Iraklidhios during the eleventh century, the other to Ioannis a hundred years later (though redone in the mid-1700s), is entered from the south side; other doors lead to a later narthex and a Latin chapel added towards the end of the fifteenth century.

By virtue of the building's sheer size, there is room for nearly complete coverage of the synoptic gospels, including a number of duplications as a result of the **frescoes** having been added in stages between the thirteenth and fifteenth centuries. The *Pandokrátor* in the dome of the nave dedicated to Iraklidhios, and panels over the side entrance, are the oldest frescoes.

The earlier subjects are the usual locally favoured ones, with slight variations: in the *Resurrection*, Christ only lifts Adam, and not Eve, from Hell, and the *Sacrifice of Abraham* is idiosyncratic in its position on the south wall rather than in the *ierón*. There are several versions of *Christ before Pilate*, and two *Raisings of Lazarus* from obviously different eras, both on the south side of the nave. As so frequently in Tróodhos frescoes, children – here wearing black gloves – shimmy up a date palm for a better view of the *Vaïofóros* or *Entry into Jerusalem*, where Christ rides side-saddle on a rather grouchy-looking ass.

The later frescoes of the northerly Latin chapel constitute the most complete Italo-Byzantine series on the island, and it seems almost certain that the native Cypriot painter had stayed for some time in Italy. Most panels take as their theme the *Akathistos* hymn in praise of the Virgin, with 24 stanzas (and thus 24 scenes) beginning each with a letter of the Greek alphabet. By the small apse, a naturalized *Arrival of the Magi* shows the backs of all three galloping off, on horses turned to face you, as if part of the background to a Renaissance canvas, not the main subject. The Roman soldiery in several panels not only wear Crusader armour, but fly pennants with a red crescent, apparently a Roman symbol, and then a Byzantine one, before being adopted by the Turks. In the *Hospitality of Abraham*, one of a few exceptions here to the *Akathistos* theme, the patriarch washes the feet of three decidedly Florentine angels prior to serving them at table.

Also in the grounds of the monastery is a **Byzantine Museum** (daily: Oct–April 9am–5pm; May–Sept 9am–6pm, but subject to priestly whim; free), containing many rare and high-quality icons.

# Soléa

The region of **Soléa**, centred on the Karyótis stream valley, was the most important late-Byzantine stronghold in the Tróödhos, as witnessed by its large concentration of churches. The terrain is much less precipitous than adjacent Marathássa on the west, from which Soléa is accessible by a steep but completely paved road, taking off from just above the *Churchill Pinewood Valley* resort between Pródhromos and Pedhoulás. **Kakopetriá** is Soléa's chief village and showcase, conveniently close to several frescoed churches, but nearly half a dozen small hamlets, in varying states of preservation, are scattered downstream and worth a visit, ideally on a bicycle.

## Kakopetriá

**KAKOPETRIÁ**, "Wicked Rock-Pile", takes its name from a rash of boulders which originally studded the ridge on which the village was first built. Most were removed, but some had to stay, including the **Pétra toú Andhroyínou** (Couple's Rock), a particular outcrop on which newly-weds used to clamber for good luck – until one day the monolith heaved itself up and crushed an unlucky pair to death.

Low enough at 660m elevation to be very warm in the summer, Kakopetriá was formerly a wine- and silk-production centre, but is now a busy, trendy resort, the closest Tróödhos watering-hole to Nicosia. The village straddles the river, which lends some character, as does the officially protected (and not yet too twee) old quarter. This was built on a long ridge splitting the stream in two; a preservation order was slapped on it in 1976, but a few new buildings apparently got in after it went into effect. Derelict traditional dwellings were salvaged by the Department of Antiquities between 1979 and 1986, and subsequently bought up at premium prices and further done up by Nicosians and foreigners, a process continuing briskly today.

Down in the western stream, across a medieval bridge, hides an old water-powered grain mill, also refurbished, and bird houses for the ducks and pigeons that frequent the place. An adjacent drink stall has seats at the base of the towering *Mill Hotel* (see below).

### Practicalities

Regular **buses** ply between here and the Constanza bastion terminal in Nicosia. Other Kakopetriá amenities include **banks** (two with ATMs), a **post office** (Mon–Fri 9.30am–1.30pm & Thurs 3–6pm) and a 24-hour **petrol pump**.

A half-dozen ordinary **hotels** are grouped around the telecommunications tower east of the river on Gríva Dhiyení and Ayíou Mámmandos, but they are relatively poor value and have little character compared to certain unlicensed establishments lining the river, some of which have waterfront balconies. Two very central such choices include the *Romios* (℡22922456; ❶), with a decent attached restaurant, and the adjacent *Zoumos* (℡22922154; ❶). Down past the bridge on the old road to Galáta – in fact near the edge of the latter – is another place renting **rooms**: *Kendro Dhilinia* (℡22922455; ❶), surprisingly comfortable for the price, with attached bathrooms. More rooms are available at *Dimos* (℡22922343; ❷), up past the old quarter on the minor road to Áyios Nikólaos tís Stéyis (see below). In the old quarter proper, with its single "high-street" lane, the only rooms are those under the *Kafenio Serenity*, most of which overlook the stream ravine (℡22922602 or 22922810; ❷).

If money's no object, however, much the best choice in town is Stelios Alkiviades and Katia Karekla's twenty-unit *Linos Inn*, at the heart of the old quarter (℡22923161, ⓦwww.linos-inn.com.cy; B&B rooms ❹, suites ❺; credit card required for mandatory reservations weekends and summer). Opened in 1997, this rambling restoration complex of knocked-together houses comprises a mix of different-sized rooms, some self-catering, all with antique furnishings, plus mod cons such as jacuzzis (there's also a communal sauna). The five newest units occupy a restored annexe a few paces towards the river and are probably the best-appointed on the island, with original architectural features preserved where possible. There's a pleasant bar-café (noon until late) between the two lodging units, while the in-house **restaurant** is massively popular at weekends, when diners spill out onto the garden terrace. However, it's been somewhat eclipsed by the affiliated *Mesostrato* (closed Tues), just up the lane at no. 47, a 2004-opened *mezé* house with excellent fare (home-made sausages, *kolokýthia me avgá*, ravioli) on à la carte or set-price basis, and a welcome fire during winter.

The only local rival is the 2001-inaugurated *Mill Hotel* (℡22922536, Ⓕ22922757, ⓦwww.cymillhotel.com; closed mid-Nov to mid-Dec; ❺–❻), an enormous, mock-trad multi-storey building across the river. A lift whisks you from the riverbank to the three grades of lodging; accommodation consists of either standard rooms, "large" rooms or suites, the latter two generous-sized and suitable for three or four, with balconies and tasteful furnishings running to terracotta tiles and marble trim. The in-house restaurant, *The Mill* (closed Wed & mid-Nov to mid-Dec) can't really compare to *Mesostrato* (too many coach tours), and other restaurant options in Kakopetriá are limited and fairly undistinguished.

## Áyios Nikólaos tís Stéyis

The engaging church of **Áyios Nikólaos tís Stéyis** (Agios Nikolaos tis Stegis) stands 3km above Kakopetriá, just off the paved road over to Marathássa. Once part of a monastery, it is now isolated at the edge of the archdiocese's YMCA-type camp and recreation centre. You cannot drive up to it, but must walk through a gate and turnstile, then along a path skirting the playing pitch. When the church is open (Tues–Sat 9am–4pm, Sun 11am–4pm; donation), the charming, English-speaking warden, Spyridhoula, will give a lucid, informative tour.

The core of the church, with some of the oldest frescoes in the Tróödhos, dates from the eleventh century. A dome and narthex were added a hundred years later, and during the fifteenth century an unusually extravagant protective roof (hence the name, *tís Stéyis* meaning "of the Roof") was superimposed on the earlier domed cross-in-square plan. As so often, the frescoes are attributable to a sequence of periods, from the eleventh century to (in the south transept) the fourteenth and fifteenth, thereby spanning all schools from the traditional to post-Byzantine revival.

The most unusual, later images are found in the transept: the north side has a *Crucifixion* with a personified sun and moon weeping, and an unusual *Myrrofóri* (spice-bearers at the sepulchre), with the angel sitting atop Christ's empty tomb, proclaiming Christ's resurrection to the two Marys (Magdalene and the mother of James) and Martha.

The *Nativity* in the south transept vault shows the Virgin breast-feeding the Child with a symbolic, anatomically incorrect teat – icons of the subject (*Panayía Galaktotrofoússa*) abound but frescoes are rare, mostly confined to Coptic Egypt. Around her goats gambol and shepherds play bagpipe and flute, while a precociously wizened duplicate infant Jesus is given a bath by two serving-maids. Similarly unusual is the *Archangel Holding the Child* in the same corner.

Opposite the *Nativity* unfolds the locally more favoured ordeal of the *Forty Holy Martyrs*, Christian soldiers in the Roman army tortured by immersion in a freezing lake at Anatolian Sebastaea. One, weakening in resolve, heads for the shore, but a Roman guard, overcome with admiration for the Christians, is seen shedding his tunic to join them. At the top of the image are rows of martyrs' crowns, descending from heaven as a reward to the condemned. The tale of the Forty Martyrs, with its moral of solidarity, constancy and endurance of pain, was a favourite among the officers of the Byzantine army. The warrior saints Yeóryios and Theódhoros (George and Theodore), in Crusader dress, brandish their panoply of arms on one column of the nave.

On the ceiling of the main vault, the *Transfiguration* is juxtaposed with the *Raising of Lazarus* on a single panel; in the former, three disciples cower in fear at the base of strange mountains reminiscent of volcanic Cappadocia, while in the latter scene Mary, the sister of Lazarus, is clutching Christ's foot, as told in John 11:32.

## Galáta

Around 1500m north of Kakopetriá, **GALÁTA** is a far more aesthetic village, the through road lined with handsome old buildings sporting second-storey balustrades. Just 2km further down the valley, the best example of these is an old **kháni** or wayfarers' inn, between the turnings for Kaliána and Temvriá. Keep an eye peeled for a modern *kafenío*; the old inn is three buildings beyond, on the same side of the road.

Galáta's notable **churches** are numerous, scattered and – as usual – locked. You'll need a vehicle to chauffeur around yourself and the current key-keeper, Kyriakos Haralambidhes, a gentleman in his late seventies who speaks some English. If he's not at home (☎22922245), he can usually be found at the postal agency-cum-coffee-house on the west side of the bridge; designated touring hours are 9.30am to 1pm and 2 to 5pm.

### Arkhángelos and Panayía tís Podhíthou

The road from the east side of the bridge leads north about a kilometre to the adjacent sixteenth-century churches of Panayía tís Podhíthou and Arkhángelos, the most notable of several in and around Galáta. The former was once part of a monastery, but today both stand alone, awash in springtime beanfields, on the east bank of the river.

Dating from 1514, **Arkhángelos** (Archangelos), the first and smaller church, is also known as Panayía Theotókou, but described as such to avoid confusion with a nearby namesake church (see below). The interior adheres to local conventions as to style and choice of episodes, featuring an unusually complete life of Christ, with such scenes as the *Agony in Gethsemane*, the *Washing of the Disciples' Feet* and *Peter's Denial*, with crowing cock; fish peer out of the River Jordan in the *Baptism*. The chronological sequence begins with the *Prayer of Joachim* (the Virgin's father) near the door, finishing with the *Redemption of Adam*. Most unusually there's the signature of the painter, Simeon Axenti, in the panel depicting the donor Zacharia family, who were of Hellenized Venetian and Lusignan background, the women following the Catholic rite, the men adhering to Orthodoxy. Such arrangements were not uncommon in formerly Byzantine territories captured by the West.

The unusual shape of **Panayía tís Podhíthou** (Panagia tis Podythou), built in 1502, dictates an equally unconventional arrangement of the cartoon-like panels. Abbreviated lives of the Virgin and Christ are relegated to the *ierón* (the area beyond the altar screen). In the apse, Solomon and David stand to either side of the Italo-Byzantine *Communion of the Apostles*; at the top of the pediment formed by the roofline, the Burning Bush is revealed to Moses. The walnut *témblon* itself, complete with gargoyles from which lamps are hung, is magnificent despite its icons having been variously stolen or taken to Nicosia for restoration.

Above the west entry door, its favoured position, there's a very detailed, Italianate *Crucifixion*, complete with the two thieves, the Virgin fainting, Mary Magdalene with loose hair at the foot of the Cross and the soldier about to pierce Christ's side. Indeed the sense of tumult and vulgar spectacle is totally un-Byzantine; onlookers' dress, demeanour and facial features are highly differentiated, and approach caricature at times (for similar treatment, see the same in the church at Vyzakiá, p.255). Out in the U-shaped "narthex", created by the later addition of the peaked roof, the donor Dhimitrios de Coron and his wife appear on the left of the *Redemption*; above this the *Virgin Enthroned* appears in the company of various Old Testament prophets, rather than with the usual Fathers of the Church as at neighbouring Arkhángelos.

### Áyios Sozómenos

If you wish, the same key-keeper will accompany you to **Áyios (Agios) Sozómenos**, 50m behind and uphill from Galáta's big modern church. Its iconography is very similar to that of Arkhángelos – hardly surprising since the artist (Axenti) and construction date are identical. The frescoes are numerous but relatively crude, and can't compare with those at Podhíthou or Arkhángelos.

However, there are some wonderful touches: in the lower echelons of saints on the north wall, the dragon coils his tail around the hind legs of Saint George's charger as he's dispatched; a maiden chained at the lower right demonstrates how the tale is a reworking of the Perseus and Andromeda myth. On the south wall, Saint Mamas holds his lamb as he rides an anthropomorphized lion (see p.262 for an explanation). Overhead, the original painted wooden struts are still intact (they've rotted away in most other churches); behind the *témblon* is a *Pentecost* on the left, in addition to the typical episodes of Abraham's life to either side of the apse. Out in the U-shaped narthex, there's a damaged *Apocalypse* left of the door, while various ecumenical councils (complete with heretics being banished) meet on the other side.

### Panayía Theotókou and Ayía Paraskeví

Two more churches, one of essentially specialist interest, flank the road up to Kakopetriá. The early sixteenth-century **Panayía (Panagia) Theotókou** is next to a petrol station, where the key is kept; the interior preserves an unusually large panel of the *Assumption*, with Christ holding the Virgin's infant soul, plus a *Pentecost* and a fine *Angel at the Sepulchre*. Behind the handsome *témblon*, the *Hospitality of Abraham* is offered on the right, with his vivid attempted *Sacrifice* opposite. In the apse conch, the *Virgin Enthroned* reigns over the six *Ierárkhi* (Fathers of the Church) below, while over the entrance, the donors, Leontios and Loukretia, huddle with a half-dozen others.

**Ayía (Agia) Paraskeví**, contemporary with Áyios Sozómenos and Arkhánge-los, is a bit downhill on the opposite side of the pavement, next to a playground, but it's not worth the bother to fetch the key opposite, as there's nothing inside but some fresco fragments in the apse and a faded painted *témblon*.

## Asínou (Panayía Forviótissa)

Arguably the finest of the Tróödhos churches, **Asínou** (Panayía Forviótissa) lies out in the middle of nowhere, but emphatically justifies the detour off the B9 Kakopetriá–Nicosia road. Unless you have a 4WD vehicle, don't be tempted by the twelve-kilometre "shortcut" from Áyios Theódhoros village to Asínou – this forest track is pretty rough, and you won't save much time in any case. The key-priest Father Kirykos lives in the nearby village of **NIKITÁRI**, reached via Koutrafás or Vyzakiá; you can ring him on ☎22852922 or 99689327, or call in at Nikitári's central *kafenío*, though he will probably be at the **church**, 4km above Nikitári, during its formal opening hours (Mon–Sat: March–Dec 9am–1pm, Jan & Feb 9.30am–1pm; also Nov–Feb 2–4pm, March & April 2–4.30pm, May & June 2–5.30pm, July & Aug 2–6pm, Sept & Oct 2–5pm; plus all year Sun 10am–1pm & 2–4pm; donation).

The popular, less formal name of the church stems from the ancient town of Asinou, founded by Greeks from Argolid Asine but long since vanished; the same fate has befallen any monastery which was once here, leaving only a half-dozen *exokhiká kéndra* in the immediate vicinity – surely surplus to requirements, though the beautiful countryside does make for an ideal Sunday outing. *Panayía Forviótissa* may mean "Our Lady of the Pastures", though only the church-crowned hilltop is treeless, with forested river valley all around; another derivation has it as "Our Lady of the Milkwort", and it must be said that botanical epithets of the Virgin are common on Cyprus. A barrel-vaulted nave, remodelled during the fourteenth century, dates originally from 1105; an unusual narthex with dome and two bays was added a century later, giving the church a "backwards" orientation from the norm. Panayía Forviótissa's frescoes span several centuries from 1105–06 to the early 1500s, and were cleaned between 1965 and 1967.

### The interior

Many of the myriad **panels** in the nave were skilfully redone in the four-teenth or fifteenth century. The vaulted **ceiling** of the nave is segmented into recesses by two arches: one at the apse, the other about two-thirds of the way west towards the narthex door. In the westernmost recess, the *Forty Martyrs of Sebastaea* on the north curve seem more natural than those at Áyios Nikólaos tís Stéyis, despite their crowns floating down from Heaven; the Holy Spirit also descends at the *Pentecost* overhead, and Lazarus is raised on the south of the same curve. In the middle recess, the life of Christ from the Nativity to the Resur-rection is related; here the *Crucifixion* is treated as just one panel of many, not as in higher, barn-like churches where it often dominates the triangular pedi-ment over the door. Generally, the fresco style is highly sophisticated and vivid: Saint Tryphon on one arch could be a portrait from life of a local shepherd, while the three *Myrrofóri* (spice-bearing women at the sepulchre) in the north recess recoil in visible alarm from the admonishing angel. In the apse, an almost imploring twelfth-century Virgin raises her hands in benediction, flanked by the two archangels, while to either side Christ offers the wine in the *Communion of the Apostles* (save for Judas, who slinks away). Over the south door, the builder Nikíforos Mayístros presents a model of the church to Christ in a panel dated 1105 by its dedicatory inscription, while a fine *Dormition of the Virgin* hovers over the west door of the nave.

The **narthex frescoes** are of the fourteenth century, with wonderful whimsical touches. On the arch of the door to the nave, a pair of hunting hounds tied to a stake and their moufflon quarry make an appearance, heralds of the Renaissance as Byzantine iconography has no place for dogs. In the shell of the north bay, Earth (riding on a lion) and Sea (upon a water monster) are personified; in the opposite bay, the donors appear again, praying in period dress before a naturalistic Virgin and Child, above an equestrian Saint George and the lion-mounted Saint Mamas. Below the Earth and the Sea, Saint Peter advances to open the Gates of Paradise, while the patriarchs Abraham, Isaac and Jacob wait to one side. In the cupola the *Pandokrátor* presides over the Twelve Apostles, with the Blessed and the Damned depicted on arches to either side.

## Vyzakiá: Arkhángelos Mikhaïl

It's well worth continuing down-valley to **VYZAKIÁ**, 6.5km away in total via Nikitári, to see the crude but vividly unique images in the little post-Byzantine church of **Arkhángelos Mikhaïl**. This stands just west of the stream running past the village, on the north side of the road, but you'll have to go into the centre for the key from the priest Papa Savvas, who lives in the house right opposite the modern church of Ayía Ekateríni.

Both church and frescoes date from the early sixteenth century, with the latter exhibiting pronounced Venetian influence despite their rustic, even deformed execution. On the upper zone of the south wall, from east to west, a squat, stubby angel figures in the *Annunciation*; in the *Nativity*, one shepherd plays a shawm, and another, wearing an extraordinary patchwork sheepskin, converses with Joseph; while the personified river god lolling about in the *Baptism* is so distorted as to appear club-footed. On the same level of the west wall, the food in the *Last Supper* (with multiple fish, not just one as customarily) is being consumed with two-pronged wooden forks, a habit introduced by the Venetians and found in no other Cypriot depiction of the scene; in the *Betrayal*, the massed Roman soldiery are all hooded, undifferentiated grotesques with beaky noses, and in the *Deposition* the dead Christ is almost floppy in the Virgin's arms. Above these scenes, in the west pediment, is a remarkable *Crucifixion*, where a youth in Venetian carnival dress is lancing Christ's side, while on the right of the cross, another youth in noble attire proffers the sponge with vinegar on a spiral wand.

# Pitsyliá

Southeast and uphill from the Soléa valleys, the region of **Pitsyliá** is a jumble of bare ridges and precipitous valleys forming the east end of the Tróödhos range. Instead of forests, groves of hazelnut and almonds grow, though there are pines on the north slopes. Grapevines flourish, too, but for local use, not the vintners' co-ops; in some villages they're guided on elaborate trellises over streets and houses.

Pitsyliá is noticeably less prosperous and less frequented than Marathássa or Soléa, though three surprisingly large villages – almost small towns – are strung along near the ridge line: **Kyperoúnda**, **Agrós** and **Palekhóri**, the latter with its worthwhile church of **Metamórfosis toú Sotírou**. Kyperoúnda and Agrós, while excellent start-points for hikes, have no painted churches of their own; the closest are below Agrós, at **Peléndhri** (**Stavrós**) and **Louvarás** (**Áyios Mámas**). Roads, though improved on the main trunk routes, are still challenging and slow-going for the most part.

The easiest roads into Pitsyliá head east from Tróödhos resort (the B8) or southeast from Kakopetriá (the B9), converging at the junction known as the Karvounás crossroads 1200m above sea level (just south of which, on the E801, is a 24-hr automat petrol station). From there you are within easy reach of Kyperoúnda and the several walks above and west of it, or the vast church of **Kímisis tís Panayías** at **Koúrdhali**, actually a short way off the road up from Kakopetriá.

From Vyzakiá, the F929 heads up the Kannávia valley past Ayía Iríni (with its diminutive church of **Tímios Stavrós**) and Spília, emerging on the B9 just downhill from the strategic Karvounás junction in the central Tróödhos. However, about 3km above Vyzakiá, a minor paved road veers east to Ayía Marína (Agia Marina) village, just off the E907, which gives direct access to the two of the finest churches in Pitsyliá: **Panayía tou Araká** in Lagoudherá village, and **Stavrós toú Ayiasmáti** outside Platanistássa.

## Xyliátos reservoir

About halfway along this scenic, forested canyon you pass the pine-set **Xyliátos reservoir**, the last known habitat of the aquatic "grass" snake, which is endangered by the practice of stocking the water here with trout (the fish eat the juvenile snakes). "Snake George" (see p.191) charges that a combination of bowing to pressure from the anglers' lobby, and several dry years before the millennium which devastated the lakeshore vegetation, will ensure the snake's extinction in the near future; hopefully several rainy winters since have benefited the species.

Just above the reservoir, at the start of a minor but marked jeep track to Stavrós toú Ayiasmáti, another Venetian-era **caravan bridge** (see p.220) is prominently signposted.

## Panayía toú Araká

The large, single-aisled church of **Panayía toú Araká** ("Our Lady of the Pea") enjoys a wonderful setting amid trees – and the wild peas of the name – on a terrace 500m northwest of the village of **LAGOUDHERÁ** (Lagoudera), about halfway to Sarándi village (both villages have tavernas, the closest about 200m from the church). The caretaker priest Stylianos, a refugee from Mórfou in the North, lives in the large adjacent building, possibly a surviving portion of the monastery which was once attached; he will expect the usual donation for visiting the church, but resist blandishments to buy overpriced souvenir guidebooks and postcards. The local **festival** on September 7–8 celebrates the birth of the Virgin.

The **interior frescoes** of 1192 are not as numerous as they might be, since the original west wall, presumably with a *Crucifixion* and/or *Apocalypse*, was removed when the existing narthex was built late in the seventeenth century. They are exceptionally clear, however, having been cleaned between 1968 and 1973, and include, unique in the Tróödhos, an undamaged *Pandokrátor* in the dome (which protrudes partially through the pitched roof). Below Christ, his eyes averted in the manner of Hellenistic portraits, Old Testament prophets, rather than the usual apostles, alternate with the twelve dome windows, each clutching a scroll with his prophecy anticipating the Saviour. Lower down, the Archangel Gabriel, wings and robes swept back by the force of his rapid descent, approaches the Virgin opposite for the *Annunciation*.

Above the *Virgin Enthroned* in the apse, strangely averting her eyes to the right, Christ ascends to heaven in a bull's-eye mandorla, attended by four acrobatic angels. The *témblon* is intact, its Holy Gates (for the mysterious entries and exits of the priest during the liturgy) still in place. Instead of a true transept, there are two pairs of painted recesses on each of the side walls. Flanking the south door, Zozimadhon spoon-feeds Osia Maria (Mary the Beatified) of Egypt; Mary was an Alexandrian courtesan who, repenting of her ways, retired to the desert to perform austere penances for forty years and was found, a withered crone on the point of death, by Zozimadhon, abbot of St Paul's monastery near the Red Sea. Above them there's a fine *Nativity*, with, as ever, a preternaturally aged Infant being bathed, while on the right the angel gives the good news to the shepherds, one of whom plays a pipe. In the north recess nearest the apse, reflecting the episode described in Luke 2:28, Simeon lovingly holds Christ for his Presentation in the Temple, the child wearing a single earring in his left ear, as was the Byzantine custom for infant sons. The *Panayía Arakiotissa*, in the opposite south-wall recess, is conceptually linked with the Presentation; having received back her son, the Virgin's expression is sorrowful in the knowledge of her son's eventual fate, as indicated by the two flanking angels proffering the instruments of the Passion.

## Stavrós toú Ayiasmáti

In the next valley east of Lagoudherá, **Stavrós toú Ayiasmáti** (Stavros tou Agiasmati) is an attractive basilica-church, again once part of a monastery. You need to stop first in the village of **Platanistássa** (Platanistasa), where the key-keeper Vassilis Hadjiyeoryiou lives – he is most easily found by enquiring at Makis' café, or ring in advance (he speaks some English) on ☎ 22652562. The church itself, whose **festival** is on September 13–14, is located 7km to the north: 3km down-valley on tarmac, the rest on a paved side road. The setting is even better than at Panayía toú Araká, in an almond grove at the margin of the forest, with a patch of the Mesaoría visible to the northeast. If it weren't for the fact that you have to shuttle Vassilis back to the village, you could explore the marked trail which links the church here with the one at Lagoudherá; this takes two-and-a-half hours each way.

### The church
The church is filled with late fifteenth-century **frescoes** by Philip Goul (cleaned in the 1980s); an inscription over the south door records both his artistry and the patronage of the priest Petros Peratis. The highlight is a **painted cross** in a niche on the north wall (the name *Stavrós* means "Holy Cross"), surrounded by small panels of episodes relating, however tenuously, to its power, sanctification and rediscovery, such as the Hebrews petitioning Pharaoh (top), or the vision of St Constantine in 312 AD (left).

Behind the *témblon*, and above an interesting Holy Table (for celebrating the Orthodox liturgy), the Virgin and Child both raise hands in blessing in the apse, flanked by archangels, and the Old Testament prophets David, Daniel, Solomon and Isaiah; nearby the *Communion of the Apostles* has a single figure of Christ (usually there were two) offering the Eucharist to six with his right hand, and the Communion wine to the other half-dozen with his left. The four Evangelists are arranged in pairs to either side of the altar screen; the archangel Michael, in the arched recess to the right of the *témblon*, holds not the usual opaque orb but a transparent "crystal ball" containing the Christ child.

Elsewhere along the vaults and walls of the nave there's a complete gospel cycle, including such arcane details as apostles with their backs to the viewer in the *Last Supper*, Pilate washing his hands, trumpeters in the panel of the *Mocking* and Doubting Thomas probing Christ's lance wound. The crowing rooster in *Peter's Denial* is larger than any of the human figures. In the otherwise serene *Assumption of the Virgin*, a miniature angel strikes off the hands of an impious Jew who attempted to knock over the Virgin's bier. On the pediment of the west wall, the Ancient of Days presides over the descent of the Holy Spirit above the *Crucifixion*; Christ's blood drips down into Adam's skull below, the key-warden will tell you, in order to revivify it for the *Redemption*, shown outside in a niche of the uncleaned narthex.

This and other exterior frescoes are thought not to be by Goul, and were repainted last century to detrimental effect. Right of the *Redemption* unfolds the *Last Judgement*, while on the left stand the three patriarchs Abraham, Isaac and Jacob. The U-shaped narthex, extending around the north and south sides of the church, was used by local shepherds as a sheep pen before the monument's importance was recognized.

## Walks around Madhári ridge

From either Lagoudherá or Platanistássa paved roads complete the climb to the Tróodhos summit ridge, where the vine-draped villages of Álona and Polýstipos huddle just under 1100 metres. **POLÝSTIPOS** (Polystypos) can offer a single agrotourism facility, *Evridiki's House* (☎22652216 or 22750509; 2-bedroom unit ❹), with balconied upstairs rooms and a coffee-shop on the ground floor. The watershed is crossed a little higher, with a well-marked side road to the CYTA transmission station on the sides of 1612-metre **Mount Adhélfi**.

If you're interested in walking the **nature trail on Madhári ridge**, this is one possible starting point. Near the end of this side road, which is also signposted for the nature-trail system, park opposite the CYTA towers, next to an abandoned military guard house. Here a standard-issue wooden sign announces "Circular Nature Trail Teisia tis Madharis 3½ km". The path begins right behind the guardhouse, heading northwest on a course that roughly follows the contour through midget golden oaks and weird rock formations. After 45 minutes of roller-coastering along the north flank of Adhélfi peak, you'll emerge right under the fire tower capping Point 1612, having linked up with the longer, point-to-point trail from Kyperoúnda (see below). From this point it's less than fifteen minutes back east along the road to the old guardhouse.

On balance, this not-quite-circular walk is best viewed as an extension to the basic Madhári ridge walk, more usually begun **from Kyperoúnda**, some 7km west via Khandhriá. At the western edge of Kyperoúnda, just beyond the summit pass on the bypass road, a paved side road signposted for Spília and Kannávia heads north for 1800m to the saddle at 1335m elevation. Just to one side stands the familiar wooden paraphernalia marking the start of such trails, with a sign proclaiming "Glory be to God" in New Testament Greek (*Doxa Si O Theos*) – plus a wooden plaque with the precise distance to be covered (3.75km). Except for some clumps of man-high golden oak (*Quercus alnifolia*), there's little but low scrub en route, so the exposed ridge is best traversed early or late in the day during summer. Views of virtually half the island, from the Kyrenia hills to the Akrotíri salt lake, are the thing: you gaze over nearer valleys and villages both north and south of the ridge, with the sea on three sides of Cyprus visible in favourable conditions.

After some initial tangling with a more recently cleared firebreak track, the path settles into a rhythm of wobbling either side of the watershed (also the boundary between Limassol and Nicosia districts) as it meanders through scrub and thin forest. Some 45 minutes along, you reach the 1500-metre saddle between Madhári ridge and Adhélfi peak, with another half-hour's hiking bringing you to the fire tower atop Point 1612 – a bit more if you detour to the modestly described "Excellent Viewpoint" partway.

It is possible to leave a car at either end of the ridge and execute a larger **loop route** totalling 13km, as traced on our chapter map; local paths designated as nos. 2, 3, 4 and 5 are combinable, taking you not only along the ridge but down into the valleys north of the watershed and then back up. Allow a good five hours for the outing.

## Minor churches: Tímios Stavrós and Kímisis tís Panayías

Immediately north of Madhári ridge, in the vicinity of Spília village (see next section), nestle two relatively minor but enjoyable painted churches, both dating from the first quarter of the sixteenth century. The road to the western trailhead of the Madhári nature path continues 2km to a junction: left leads within 500m to Spília and thence Koúrdhali hamlet; straight descends 2km in tight curves to Ayía Iríni village, just before Kannávia.

### Tímios Stavrós

The diminutive church of **Tímios Stavrós** at **AYÍA IRÍNI**, just north of and above the village on a hillock, had its frescoes cleaned and masonry consolidated throughout 1995; the current key-custodian lives in the last village house on the right along the road, going downhill. Once inside, you'll see a rustic *Nativity* over the south door, with the *Convention of the Archangels* just east. The conch of the apse is devoted to the iconographic convention known as the *Deisis*, the only such depiction on Cyprus: the Virgin and John the Baptist flank a seated Christ, who proffers with his left hand a text proclaiming him to be the prophesied Christ and Judge of the Last Day. To the left of the apse, an angel lifts Christ from the sepulchre, an artistic convention combining the so-called "Utter Humiliation" variation of the Byzantine *Deposition* and the western *Pietà*. In the triangular pediment above the apsidal vault, there's an unusual, Westernized Holy Trinity, with the enthroned Father upholding the crucified Son, appropriately enough for a shrine of the Holy Cross (*Tímios Stavrós* in Greek).

### Koúrdhali: Kímisis tís Panayías

The three-aisled basilica of **Kímisis tís Panayías** (Koimisis tis Panagias) in **KOÚRDHALI** (Kourdali), currently signposted as "*Khrysokourdhaliótissa*", lies just under 2km below the central junction in Spília, on the bank of a stream crossed by a tiny humpback bridge built entirely of roof-tiles. It was founded in the sixteenth century as the *katholikón* of a (long-vanished) monastery by the deacon Kourdhalis, for whom the hamlet is named. The bulk of the surviving frescoes are on the west wall, surmounted by a naturalistic, Italo-Byzantine *Crucifixion* featuring, as to be expected from a sixteenth-century church, notables in Venetian apparel – including a rather scandalously attired Virgin in a low-cut dress, fainting into the arms of her friends. Subsequent episodes include a dramatic *Doubting Thomas*, at the far upper right of the panels here, with Christ all but daring the apostle to touch his wound. Right of the west door, in the *Dormition of the Virgin* above the donor portraits, a rather piratical-looking, long-fingered St Paul crouches at the foot of the bier. The eastern apse is taken up by a fine *Virgin Orans*, attended by archangels in Byzantine noble costume.

The guardian at present is a young, friendly nun, Sister Isidhora, who stays on-site except for a variable lunch hour. Otherwise, the key is sometimes left in the door, but the light switches inside are hard to find without a torch. The local festival is August 14–15.

## Spília

SPÍLIA village, like many of the more isolated Tróödhos settlements, was an EOKA stronghold; four statues in the plaza commemorate EOKA activists who managed to blow themselves up in a bomb-making safehouse nearby in Koúrdhali. Today, however, it's a resolutely peaceful place, with a recommended small **hotel-restaurant** in the centre: Jerey and Eleni Ashcroft's *Marjay Inn* (℡22922208, Ⓦwww.marjay.com; ❸). The rooms, of two to four beds with blonde-pine furniture, are comfortable and squeaky clean, all with showers (not bathtubs) and balconies facing the river. The inn is geared towards activity holidays – mountain biking, jeep safaris and hiking – and reservations are required much of the year, as capacity is limited. The ground-floor restaurant operates on a *table d'hôte* basis, with guests pre-ordering supper in the morning so that only fresh ingredients are sourced.

## Agrós

Besides Spília and the agrotourism inns in Polýstipos and Askás, the only other feasible overnight option in Pitsyliá is **AGRÓS**, a large village more or less at the top (920m elevation) of Limassol district's commercial wine-grape region. Also known for its sausages, ham and rosewater, Agrós won't win many beauty contests but it's well placed for two days' forays to nearby sights, as it lies roughly equidistant from several post-Byzantine frescoed churches. Being less frequented than the monuments of Marathássa and Soléa, these give more sense of personal discovery, and their surrounding villages deserve a brief stroll-through as well. In Agrós proper, there are no historic churches, despite its role as refuge for two venerable twelfth-century icons of Christ and the Virgin; the villagers themselves pulled down the 800-year-old, frescoed monastery housing them in 1894, during a protracted land-ownership dispute with the local bishop.

The early-1990s appearance of Agrós on the tourism map was due almost entirely to the efforts of Lefkos Christodoulou, enthusiastic booster of the area's merits and manager of the enormous, communally-owned **hotel**, the three-star *Rodon*, 1km south of the village on the Potamítissa road (℡25521201, Ⓦwww.swaypage.com/rodon; ❾). Substantial discounts apply off-season, and also to bookings through the several UK package companies which represent it. The hotel has a well-regarded restaurant – a reliable lunch venue in a region rather deprived of such, plus excellent C£8-a-head dinner buffets – two pools, children's facilities and a tennis court. Lefkos has been instrumental in rehabilitating some of the area's forgotten footpaths, and hands out a 1:25,000 photostat map detailing various **walks around Agrós**; he also arranges organized treks with transfers to your start point, the best and most demanding of these being the six-hour traverse from Stavrós toú Ayiasmáti via Lagoudherá and Madhári ridge to Agrós.

In the village itself, the one-star *Vlachos Hotel* (℡25521330, ℻25521890; half-board ❸), despite an indifferent position on the high street, represents excellent value, with supper a groaning *table d'hôte*. Otherwise *Iy Kiladha*, a taverna just north of the *Vlachos* in a tree-shaded kink of the through road, offers some vegetarian fare. Agrós also has two **banks**, and the only **petrol** for some way around (diesel from a pump, unleaded from 25-litre jerry-cans), so fill up before a day's touring.

## Peléndhri: Stavrós church

Of the villages with frescoed churches around Agrós, **PELÉNDHRI** (officially Pelendri, also sometimes rendered "Peléndhria") is the easiest to reach being accessed initially on the direct, paved Agrós–Potamítissa road, which as yet does not appear accurately on any commercial map (though it is shown on the CTO "Troodos Area" sheet). The main attraction here is the fourteenth-century painted **church of Stavrós**, isolated at the south edge of Peléndhri, overlooking a reservoir; the friendly key-keeping priest lives 200m up the road towards Káto Amíandos, though during 2003–04 the church was undergoing extensive renovation, and may yet be closed for some time. A square ground plan divided into three aisles, unique in Cyprus, is capped by a very narrow, high dome supported by four columns; for once there is no narthex.

On your right as you enter, there's a *Tree of Jesse*, showing the genealogy of Jesus. Straight ahead on a column, the two donors of the church are shown below Doubting Thomas; just to the left is a Lusignan coat-of-arms. At the rear of the central aisle, above the wooden lattice of the deacon's pulpit, are scenes from the life of the Virgin, the best-preserved (or at least the cleanest) frescoes in the entire building. Opposite this, the *Nativity* tells much about Lusignan domestic life, while Joachim and Anna present the infant Mary for blessing by the high priests, the most vivid of fourteen panels on the life of the Virgin. A multi-coloured *témblon* is in good condition, and to its left the enshrined cross for which the church is named stands encased in silver near a representation of the *Epitáfios* (the Dead Christ), next to a fresco of three *Ierárkhi* (Fathers of the Church) in the left-hand apse.

Peléndhri can also offer one of the best micro-wineries in the Tróodhos: the **Tsiakkas Pitsilia Winery**, run by Kostas and Marina Tsiakkas. They produce a full range of wines from both traditional native grapes like Xynis-teri and imported varieties such as Mataro and Cabernet. Visits are generally by appointment (℡25991080), as they're a bit tricky to find; if you want to chance dropping by on spec, head about 2km southwest of Peléndhri on the Trimíklini road, then bear right 700m on a dirt track seemingly headed for the middle of nowhere; the winery buildings are perched right above the vineyards amidst pine forest.

## Louvarás: the chapel of Áyios Mámas

The main Limassol-bound E110 road from Agrós via Káto Mýlos descends to Péfkos junction above **KALOKHORIÓ** (Kalo Chorio), where there's the only food and petrol for quite some distance around. Meals can be had from the **café** on the south side of the crossroads, and the **fuel** is sold from jerry-cans at the postal agency across from the irrigation pool in the village centre.

## Saint Mamas and his lion

Prominent on the north wall of the Louvarás church is a panel of the church's dedicatory saint, **Mamas**, cradling a lamb as he rides a rather bemused, anthropomorphized lion. The legend behind this peculiar iconography, found in many Cypriot churches, runs as follows: Mamas was a devout Byzantine hermit in the Paphlagonia district of Anatolia who refused to pay income tax since, as he logically pointed out, he had no income other than alms. The local governor ordered him arrested, but as he was being escorted into custody a lion – unknown in the region – leapt from a roadside bush onto a lamb grazing peacefully nearby. The saint commanded the lion to stop his attack, picked up the lamb and completed his journey into the capital riding on the chastened lion. Sufficiently impressed, the governor exempted Mamas from taxes thereafter, and ever since the saint has enjoyed fervent worship as the patron of tax-evaders (a massively popular cult in the Hellenic world) as well as herdsmen.

A four-kilometre side road takes off southeast from the crossroads, ending at **LOUVARÁS**, whose dishearteningly modern outskirts give no hint of the traditional village core to the east, nor of the tiny but exquisitely painted **chapel of Áyios Mámas** (signposted as "Ayios Mamantos"), hidden on the edge of the old quarter, at the very end of the paved road in. Don't confuse it with the bigger, newer church of Pródhromos nearby, across from which lives Grigoris Stavrinou the key-keeper, in the house with a front garden. He speaks some English, learned (he claims) during five years as an aide to General Montgomery, and is unusually enthusiastic about his vocation; after visiting the church, you'll probably be invited for coffee and the viewing of massive photo-albums with snaps sent by guests the world over. Photos of the church (without flash) are allowed, within reason.

The little chapel, with frescoes dating from 1495, features Philip Goul at perhaps his most idiosyncratic. On the south wall, Christ heals the paralytic and the blind man, teaches and meets the Samaritan woman at the well; the three sleeping guards at the *Resurrection* wear Lusignan armour. Also on the south wall, closer to the *témblon*, is an exceptionally expressive John the Baptist, clutching a staff which ends in a cross-and-anchor motif. Beside the west door, Christ casts out the demons from two visibly grateful lads, with one of the Gadarene swine lurking behind, ready to take the little devils over the brink; just below this in the *Last Supper*, Christ does not (as in other local murals) attempt to prevent Judas from reaching for the fish. Over the door appear the donors of the church, two couples in late Lusignan dress, while above this soldiers in late medieval armour seize Christ in the *Betrayal*. At the very top of the apsidal pediment on the east side, the Ancient of Days hovers over the *Annunciation* – these images may be by a hand other than Goul's, since the episode is repeated on the south wall.

## Palekhóri: Metamórfosis toú Sotírou

From Agrós (or from Peléndhri), the quickest route to Palekhóri, 13km away, is eastward along the E903 ridge route; from Louvarás and Péfkos junction, you can link up with this via Áyios Theodhóros.

However you arrive, **PALEKHÓRI** (Palaichori) proves to be a sprawling, friendly, workaday place hidden in a gulch at the headwaters of the Peristeróna River – there are a few *kafenía* down by the stream, but no other concessions to tourism. (There is, however, an agrotourism **inn** 2km northeast at

**ASKÁS**, *Evgenia's House*, comprising four large studios accommodating families (☎22642644 or 22642344, ⑤22643122; ❷).

The small fifteenth-to-sixteenth-century chapel of **Metamórfosis toú Sotírou**, signposted from the main bypass road, perches at the east edge of the old quarter, atop the slope up from the river. The very engaging key-keeping priest lives in the apartment building two doors north, beside which you should park, but in the evening (a likely arrival time if you've been touring all day) he may be conducting the liturgy down at Panayía Khrysopantánassa, which, though contemporaneous, has few surviving frescoes.

The frescoes of Metamórfosis toú Sotírou were painted by an unknown artist, sometime between Philip Goul's heyday and that of Simeon Axenti. They rival those in Áyios Mámas at Louvarás for whimsy, with lions and rivers the main themes. Saint Mamas appears again, riding a particularly elongated feline; on the south wall, another lion approaches, as tradition holds, to bury Osia Maria (Mary the Beatified of Egypt) with his paw, while opposite her Daniel braves the lions in their den. To Daniel's left is portrayed a miracle whereby the angelic diversion of a river saves a monastery; in the *Baptism of Christ*, a crowned-and-sceptred water sprite – personification of the river, derived from pagan portrayals of river-gods – rides a fish in the Jordan. As befits a church dedicated to the Transfiguration (*Metamórfosis* in Greek), the panel of that episode on the south wall is particularly vivid, with two disciples cowering on the ground in fear and awe. Scenes from the life of the Virgin are completely absent, though the apse features an elegant *Virgin as Mistress of Angels*. Below her to the left, a cow suckling her calf lends an engaging touch to the *Hospitality of Abraham*. In a nearby recess, Saint George lays a fraternal hand on the shoulder of Saint Demetrios with whom he rides; their equestrian pairing, common on Crete but unique here on Cyprus, shows these warrior saints' evolution from the ancient Dioscuri, Castor and Pollux, ever ready to rush to the aid of supplicants.

The other two churches visible in the western part of Palekhóri contain nothing especially compelling inside; the priest may, however, volunteer to escort you to another pair of local monuments east of the village in an orchard-cloaked valley, including the frescoed sixteenth-century church of **Áyii Anáryiri**, signposted off the road to Aplíki.

## Mountain villages en route to Makherás

At Aplíki junction, you can turn up towards Farmakás onto a narrow but paved road around a large reservoir. **Farmakás** and its neighbour **Kambí** (Kampi) are both spectacularly set overlooking the top of the valley draining to the dam, but, as with so many communities in rural Cyprus where inhabitants have (to some extent) made good and/or stayed put, the visual appeal diminishes on close examination, compromised by tin roofs and shabby brick walls. The two local showcase villages lie a few kilometres northeast along an improved road, better than maps imply, beyond Goúrri.

At **FIKÁRDHOU** (Fikardou) the vernacular architecture of stone, mud-straw bricks and tiled roofs is preserved – or rather embalmed – in the forty or so houses of this museum-village; the permanent population has dwindled to three. Two of the dwellings are now a house museum (summer Tues–Fri 9.30am–4.30pm, Sat 9.30am–4pm, Sun 10am–1.30pm; winter Tues–Fri 9am–4pm, Sat 9am–3.30pm, Sun 10.30am–2pm; C£0.75), with plans, photos and text in the ticket office giving a full explanation of the project's aims. The house of Akhilleas Dhimitri, with its loom and period furnishings, is not too cluttered as ethnographic collections go, since it's the occasional residence of the project's supervising archeologist. The Katsinioros house has an olive press, *zivanía* stills and storage urns in its basement, and traditional women's implements such as a spinning wheel and loom in the peaked-roof upper storey.

All in all it's a conscientious restoration job, but ultimately with an obscure purpose – the effect seems a bit lifeless without even the animation of a weekend population (though some of the buildings are reportedly for sale). The only other tourist amenity thus far is the *Yiannakos Kafenio*, serving drinks and light meals.

**LAZANIÁS**, 5km south on the way to Makherás monastery, is more of a going concern, and therefore less twee and perhaps more representative of such hill-villages.

## Makherás monastery

The **monastery of Makherás** (Machairas) just east of Lazaniás is distinguished by its setting on the north slope of Mount Kiónia, near the headwaters of the Pedhiéos River, and by its associations with **Grigorios Afxentiou**, second in command of EOKA after George "Dhiyenis" Grivas, and by all accounts a more sympathetic figure.

The monastery was established by two hermits in 1148, who arrived from Palestine and, guided by the usual preternatural glow, found an icon of the Virgin attributed to the hand of Luke the Evangelist. Makherás ("The Cutler") is taken variously to mean the sharp-edged, thousand-metre ridge overhead, the biting wind swooping down from it in winter or the point in the foundation legend when a knife supernaturally materialized and a "voice not of earth" instructed the hermits to use it to free the icon from the underbrush. Soon the community had the support of the Byzantine emperor Manuel Komnenos, and it even enjoyed the subsequent patronage of Lusignan rulers – one of whom, Queen Alix d'Ibelin, was rendered mute for three years after sacrilegiously insisting on entering the *ierón* or priestly chambers behind the altar screen. Makherás claims five martyrs (six, counting Afxentiou), commemorated on plaques in the courtyard.

It has also suffered two comprehensive fires (in 1530 and 1892), though the resulting bleak, echoing stone compound of minimal architectural interest was comprehensively and admirably restored during 1997–98 by the Levendis Foundation; the icon miraculously escaped the blazes and is the glory of the *katholikón*. There is also a one-room **museum**, with labelling only in Greek, featuring photos of EOKA hero Grigorios Afxentiou disguised as a monk – and of his charred remains after the British Army had finished with him (see below). Like several Cypriot monasteries of late, access to non-Orthodox is restricted to **group visits** (Mon, Tues & Thurs only 9am–noon), and no photos are allowed; an adjacent *xenónas* or pilgrims' inn, constructed in tandem with the restoration, fills up around the November 20–21 and August 14–15 **festivals**.

### Krysfíyeto toú Afxentíou

When he was not in monk's garb, the brothers of Makherás continued to feed Afxentiou in his hideout, the **Krysfíyeto toú Afxentíou**, 1km below the monastery; a Greek flag, sign and memorial plaque point you down to the (much repaired) bunker in which he met his end on March 3, 1957. Tipped off by a shepherd, British forces surrounded the dugout and called on the occupants to surrender – EOKA members were usually happy to comply in hopeless situations. All of them did except Afxentiou, who, despite being wounded, held off a platoon of sixty for ten hours before being dispatched with a petrol bomb and high explosives.

Approaching the *krysfíyeto* (hideout), you pass a huge **statue**, erected just below the monastery at the expense of the diocese, showing a quadruple-life-size Afxentiou standing arms akimbo, guarded by an eagle (his *nom de guerre* was Stavraetos or "golden eagle"). The actual **hideout** is maintained as a shrine, with a photo of the man and regular floral offerings; if you visit soon after the death anniversary, you'll find dozens of laurel wreaths propped by the entrance, left by relatives, school groups and military organizations. The actual ceremony is held on the Sunday closest to 3 March, when the British are explicitly not welcome.

## Onward routes from Makherás

From Makherás your most obvious course is north down **to Nicosia**, 43km distant via the inviting, piny picnic grounds of Mándhra toú Kambioú and the adjacent sites of ancient Tamassos and Áyios Iraklídhios monastery (see p.298). **Towards Larnaca district**, a somewhat rough dirt road heads due south through forest and past another picnic ground beside 1423-metre Kiónia peak, last outrider of the Tróödhos range. Áyii Vavatsiniás marks the start of the improved road surface down **to Khirokitia**, 33km distant from the monastery (see p.109). Alternatively, you can choose Vavatsiniá as your interim destination (16km), from where it's 10km more on paved road **to Páno Léfkara** (see p.111). Finally, heading east, you can brave about 8km of dirt track before emerging at **LYTHRODHÓNDA** (Lythrodontas), at the end of the E103, with its historic *Avli Georgallidi* (☎99655100, ℗22510061, Ⓔmotorama@cytanet.com.cy; ❸), three old houses joined together to make a five-room inn around a courtyard, with airy and extensive common areas and meals available; reservations are suggested owing to its proximity to Nicosia.

# Travel details

### Buses

**Agrós** to: Limassol on Agros bus (Mon–Sat 1 daily, at about 7am; 1hr 30min).

**Kakopetriá** to: Nicosia on Clarios bus (July/Aug Mon–Sat 11 daily, Sun 2; 1hr 20min).

**Plátres** to: Limassol on PEAL bus (daily at 8am; 1hr 15min); Nicosia via Pedhoulás and Kalopanayiótis on Clarios bus (Mon–Sat 1 daily, at 5.50am; 2hr 30min).

**Peléndhri** to: Limassol (up to 6 daily, but mostly for schoolchildren and local commuters; 1hr 30min).

**Tróödhos** to: Limassol on PEAL bus (1 daily at about 3pm; 1hr 30min); Nicosia on Clarios bus (Mon–Sat 1 daily, at 7am; 2hr).

## Greek place names

| Old system | New system | Greek lettering |
|---|---|---|
| Adhélfi | Adelfi | ΑΔΕΛΦΙ |
| Agrós | Agros | ΑΓΡΟΣ |
| Amíandos | Amiantos | ΑΜΙΑΝΤΟΣ |
| Arkhángelos Mikhaïl | Archangelos Michail | ΑΡΧΑΓΓΕΛΟΣ ΜΙΧΑΗΛ |
| Asínou | Asinou | ΑΣΙΝΟΥ |
| Ayía Iríni | Agia Eirini | ΑΓΙΑ ΕΙΡΗΝΗ |
| Áyii Anáryiri | Agioi Anargyroi | ΑΓΙΟΙ ΑΝΑΡΓΥΡΟΙ |
| Áyios Ioánnis | Agios Ioannis | ΑΓΙΟΣ ΙΟΑΝΝΗΣ |
| Lambadhistís | Lampadistis | ΛΑΜΠΑΔΙΣΤΗΣ |
| Áyios Mámas | Agios Mamantos | ΑΓΙΟΣ ΜΑΜΑΣ |
| Áyios Nikólaos tís Stéyis | Agios Nikolaos tis Stegis | ΑΓΙΟΣ ΝΙΚΟΛΑΟΣ |
| Áyios Sozómenos | Agios Sozomenos | ΑΓΙΟΣ ΣΩΖΟΜΕΝΟΣ |
| Chakístra | Tsakistra | ΤΣΑΚΙΣΤΡΑ |
| Elía | El(a)ia | ΕΛΗΑ |
| Farmakás | Farmakas | ΦΑΡΜΑΚΑΣ |
| Finí | Foini | ΦΟΙΝΙ |
| Fikárdhou | Fikardou | ΦΙΚΑΡΔΟΥ |
| Galáta | Galata | ΓΑΛΑΤΑ |
| Íkos | Oikos | ΟΙΚΟΣ |
| Kakopetriá | Kakopetria | ΚΑΚΟΠΕΤΡΙΑ |
| Kaliána | Kaliana | ΚΑΛΙΑΝΑ |
| Kalokhorió | Kalo(n) Chorio(n) | ΚΑΛΟ ΧΩΡΙΟ |
| Kalopanayiótis | Kalopanagiotis | ΚΑΛΟΠΑΝΑΓΙΟΤΗΣ |
| Kambí | Kampi | ΚΑΜΠΙ |
| Kámbos | Kampos | ΚΑΜΠΟΣ |
| Kaminária | Kaminaria | ΚΑΜΙΝΑΡΙΑ |
| Kannávia | Kannavia | ΚΑΝΝΑΒΙΑ |
| Khandhriá | Chandria | ΧΑΝΔΡΙΑ |
| Khionístra | Chionistra | ΧΙΟΝΙΣΤΡΑ |
| Kímisis tís | Koimisis tis | ΚΟΙΜΗΣΙΣ ΤΗΣ |
| Panayías | Panagias | ΠΑΝΑΓΙΑΣ |
| Koúrdhali | Kourdali | ΚΟΥΡΔΑΛΙ |
| Kýkko | Panagia tis Kykkou | ΠΑΝΑΓΙΑ ΤΗΣ ΚΥΚΚΟΥ |
| Kyperoúnda | Kyperounta | ΚΥΠΕΡΟΥΝΤΑ |
| Lagoudherá | Lagoudera | ΛΑΓΟΥΔΕΡΑ |

| | | |
|---|---|---|
| Lazaniás | Lazanias | ΛΑΖΑΝΙΑΣ |
| Louvarás | Louvaras | ΛΟΥΒΑΡΑΣ |
| Lythrodhónda | Lythrodontas | ΛΥΘΡΟΔΟΝΤΑΣ |
| Madhári | Madari | ΜΑΔΑΡΙ |
| Makherás | Machairas | ΜΑΧΑΙΡΑΣ |
| Makriá Kondárka | Makrya Kontarka | ΜΑΚΡΙΑ ΚΟΝΤΑΡΚΑ |
| Marathássa | Marathasa | ΜΑΡΑΘΑΣΑ |
| Mesapótamos | Mesopotamos | ΜΕΣΟΠΟΤΑΜΟΣ |
| Metamórfosis toú Sotírou | Metamorfosis tou Sotirou | ΜΕΤΑΜΟΦΩΣΙΣ ΤΟΥ ΣΩΤΗΡΟΥ |
| Milikoúri | Mylikouri | ΜΥΛΙΚΟΥΡΙ |
| Moutoullás | Moutoullas | ΜΟΥΤΟΥΛΛΑΣ |
| Nikitári | Nikitari | ΝΙΚΙΤΑΡΙ |
| Palekhóri | Palaichori | ΠΑΛΑΙΧΩΡΙ |
| Panayía tís Podhíthou | Panagia tis Podythou | ΠΑΝΑΓΙΑ ΤΗΣ ΠΟΔΥΘΟΥ |
| Panayía Theotókou | Panagia Theotokou | ΠΑΝΑΓΙΑ ΘΕΟΤΟΚΟΥ |
| Panayía toú Araká | Panagia tou Araka | ΠΑΝΑΓΙΑ ΤΟΥ ΑΡΑΚΑ |
| Panayía tou Moutoullá | Panagia tou Moutoulla | ΠΑΝΑΓΙΑ ΤΟΥ ΜΟΥΤΟΥΛΛΑ |
| Pedhoulás | Pedoulas | ΠΕΔΟΥΛΑΣ |
| Peléndhri | Pelendri | ΠΕΛΕΝΔΡΙ |
| Pitsyliá, Pitsiliá | Pitsylia | ΠΙΤΣΥΛΙΑ |
| Platanistássa | Platanistasa | ΠΛΑΤΑΝΙΣΤΑΣΑ |
| Plátres | Platres | ΠΛΑΤΡΕΣ |
| Polýstipos | Polystypos | ΠΟΛΥΣΤΥΠΟΣ |
| Pródhromos | Prodromos | ΠΡΟΔΡΟΜΟΣ |
| Soléa | Solea | ΣΟΛΕΑ |
| Spília | Spilia | ΣΠΗΛΙΑ |
| Stavrós | Stavros | ΣΤΑΥΡΟΣ |
| Stavrós toú Ayiasmáti | Stavros tou Agiasmati | ΣΤΑΥΡΟΣ ΤΟΥ ΑΓΙΑΣΜΑΤΙ |
| Throní | Throni | ΘΡΟΝΟΙ |
| Troödhítissa | Panagia tis Trooditissas | ΠΑΝΑΓΙΑ ΤΗΣ ΤΡΟΟΔΙΤΙΣΣΑΣ |
| Tróödhos | Troodos | ΤΡΟΟΔΟΣ |
| Yerakiés | Gerakies | ΓΕΡΑΚΙΕΣ |

# 5

# South Nicosia
# and around

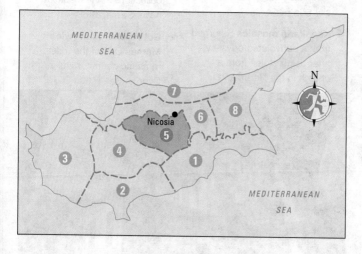

CHAPTER 5 # Highlights

* **The Green Line and "dead zone"** While they endure, these exercise a baleful fascination as the last no-go barriers in an increasingly integrated world. See p.273

* **Famagusta Gate** Now refurbished as a cultural and events centre, this is the culmination of Nicosia's sixteenth-century Venetian ramparts, which completely surround the old city See p.281

* **Kanakariá mosaics** Returned from a convoluted odyssey after being stolen from a church in the North, and now the star exhibits of the Makarios Cultural Centre. See p.286

* **Khrysaliniótissa district** Lovely vernacular houses in this neighbourhood have been refurbished as part of the UN/EU-funded Nicosia Master Plan. See p.287

* **Cyprus Museum** Simply one of the best archeological collections in the Mediterranean. See p.288

* **Gothic church of Áyios Mámas** One of the most romantic country ruins in Cyprus. See p.300

△ Restored house, Nicosia

# 5

# South Nicosia and around

The southern sector of divided Nicosia (*Lefkosía* in Greek, pronounced "Lefkosha" in dialect) is the capital and largest town of the internationally recognized Republic of Cyprus. Prosaically set and somewhat gritty, it is visited by few package tourists apart from groups coached in to visit the Cyprus Museum, indisputably one of the best archeological collections in the Middle East, and required viewing. A relative lack of the rampant commercialism found on the coast is refreshing, as is the surviving Gothic and Ottoman domestic and religious architecture of the medieval town. And if you're interested in getting to grips with what contemporary Cyprus is about, then crossing back and forth between the two sectors of the city (see Chapter 6) is an essential exercise, and infinitely easier than it once was.

By comparison, there is little of note in the surrounding countryside under Greek-Cypriot control, part of the vast **Mesaoría** ("Between the Mountains"). This is not so much a plain between the Tróödhos range and Kyrenia hills as undulating terrain, patchworked with green or yellow grain according to season and dotted with large villages which have become dormitories for the capital in recent years. Here you become acutely aware of the island's division: roads close to the boundary – except for the permitted crossings shown on the map – are diverted or barred suddenly, and watchtowers dot the horizon. Amid this bleakness, just a few isolated spots really appeal, and then only if you have time (and a car) on your hands: the ruins of **Tamassos** and the adjacent nunnery of **Áyios Iraklídhios**, a fine church-and-mosque duo at **Peristeróna,** another minor church at **Perakhorió**, paired with the scanty nearby remains of ancient **Idalion,** and an exquisite Gothic ruin nearby at **Áyios Sozómenos**.

## South Nicosia

Great is the contrast between the town and its surroundings, and greater still between the objects within the city. There are Venetian fortifications by the side of Gothic edifices surmounted by the Crescent, on antique Classic soil. Turks, Greeks and Armenians dwell intermingled, bitter enemies at heart, and united solely by their love for the land of their birth.

Archduke Louis Salvator of Austria, 1873

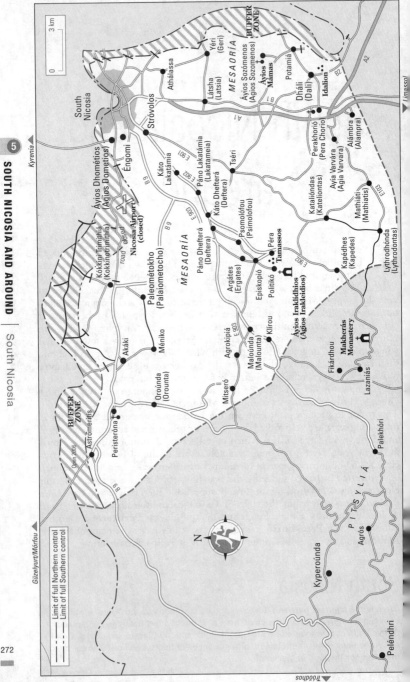

Larnaca ▲

BUFFER ZONE

MESAORÍA

Yéri (Geri)

Athálassa

Látsha (Latsia)

Áyios Sozómenos (Agios Sozomenos)

Áyios Mámas

Potamiá

Dháli (Dali)

Idálion

B2

B1

A2

South Nicosia

Stróvolos

A1

Perakhorió (Pera Chorio)

Alámbra (Alampra)

Áyios Dhométios (Agios Dometios)

Éngomi

Ayía Varvára (Agia Varvara)

E901

Káto Lakatámia

Páno Lakatámia (Lakatameia)

E902

Tséri

Katalióndas (Kateliontas)

Mathiáti (Mathiatis)

E103

Kyrenia ▲

Kókkini Trimithiá (Kokkinotrimithia)

old road

B9

Nicosia Airport (closed)

E903

B9

Káto Dhefterá (Deftera)

Psomolófou (Psimolofou)

Kapédhes (Kapedes)

Paleométokho (Palaiometocho)

MESAORÍA

Páno Dhefterá (Deftera)

Péra

Tamassos

Lythrodhónda (Lythrodontas)

Akáki

Méniko

Argátes (Ergates)

Episkopió

Politikó

Áyios Iraklídhios (Agios Irakleidios)

E902

Giizelyurt/Mórfou ▲

Oroúnda (Orounta)

Agrokipiá

E903

Kliroú

Maloúnda (Malounta)

Fikárdhou

Makherás Monastery

Kapédhes

Astromeritis

BUFFER ZONE

Open 2005

Peristeróna

Mitseró

B9

Lazaniás

Palekhóri

P I T S Y L I Á

Agrós

Kyperoúnda

Peléndhri

N

0    3 km

Límassol ▼

Lythrodhónda

Tróodhos ▼

**SOUTH NICOSIA**, depending on whom you ask and how many incorporated suburbs you include, today has between 190,000 and 270,000 inhabitants. Despite the relatively small population, it's a sprawling, amorphous, modern city that makes a poor first impression. The dust and heat – on average 2°C higher than on the coast – beginning in April and lasting until October, are prostrating, grit coming in equal measure from the prevailing winds and nearby building sites. Nicosia's inland setting, near the western extreme of the Mesaoría, is prone to earthquakes and flash-flooding from the river Pedhiéos, and it is otherwise not naturally favoured except in its near-equidistance from the important coastal towns. Since early Byzantine times every ruler has designated the place capital virtually by default, because the island's shore defences were poor, its harbours exposed to attack.

Medieval Nicosia's profile is owed in varying proportions to the Lusignans, Ottomans and Venetians; the latter endowed the old town with a five-kilometre circuit of walls which largely survives. The map outline of the medieval quarter,

## The divided city

The Green Line, as the ceasefire line is known within the city limits, has existed in some form since the communal troubles of winter 1963–64: first as impromptu barricades of bed-frames, upturned cars and other domestic debris, later more sturdily fashioned out of oil drums, barbed wire, sandbags and sheet metal. Despite the recent thaw, Nicosia is – as the authorities still remind you on wall signs and in tourist literature – the last divided city, now that arrangements of one sort or another have been reached in Berlin, Jerusalem and Beirut.

As such, the barrier exercises a morbid fascination on visitors as well as locals. You find yourself drifting towards it again and again, trying to follow its length, peering through chinks when out of sight of the Greek, Turkish or UN checkpoints. Beyond the boundary stretches the "dead zone", here just a twenty-to-fifty-metre-wide stretch of derelict, rat- and snake-infested houses – and a showroom full of dust-covered Toyotas and Datsuns, rushed in from the Famagusta docks on the day of the invasion to prevent their destruction, which have been irretrievably trapped here ever since. Before the "border" opened in April 2003, the very existence of the Attila Line (the limit of Turkish army advance) constituted a provocation, to which a steady trickle of Greek Cypriots responded. Periodically, refugee groups staged protest marches towards their home villages in the North, putting their own National Guard in the embarrassing role of trying to prevent them crossing the Attila Line (often they got several hundred metres, or even further, inside northern Cyprus); men alone or in some numbers crashed the barriers on foot or in vehicles, only to be imprisoned by the Turks, with attempts every several months on average. A slogan overhead at one Greek checkpoint – "Our frontiers are not these, but the shores of Kyrenia" – hardly argued for self-restraint.

All that is now (not very ancient) history, and despite what you may still be told at your coastal resort or your car-rental outlet, the Line is more porous than the average recognized border between an EU and contiguous non-EU country. The main catch concerning the Green Line within Nicosia (see p.291) is that only pedestrians are allowed across at the moment.

Nonetheless, the rift (while it endures) remains the essence of Nicosia and, by extension, of the island. The Greek area of the city is, indeed, mostly Greek in its monumental architecture, the Turkish zone largely Turkish and Gothic, but in the midst of each are marooned traces of the other element: mosques and houses emblazoned with a star and crescent in the south, belfried churches and dwellings with Greek Ottoman inscriptions in the north, reminders of the pre-1974 heterogeneity of Cyprus.

still the core of the city, has been variously compared to a star, a snowflake or a sectioned orange, but in the troubled circumstances prevailing since the 1950s a better analogy might be a floating mine, the knobbly silhouettes of its eleven bastions the detonators.

Old Nicosia began to outgrow its confines during the 1930s; the British answered this problem with post-war cantonment-style development just outside the walls, while the post-independence response was to throw up generic modern-Middle-Eastern suburbs beyond, dotted with high-rises. The British as well as the Cypriots are to blame for the neglect and even desecration of much in the old city; many monuments, including a Lusignan palace, were senselessly pulled down at the end of the nineteenth century, and the Venetian ramparts first pierced by viaducts and later allowed to crumble at the edges. Most streets inside the walls are no longer architecturally homogeneous, defaced by thoughtless concrete construction of recent decades.

So the romantic orientalist's town, which the Archduke admired on the eve of British rule, has vanished forever. Indeed, Nicosia is not an immediately likeable city: especially around the Páfos Gate, the old town can be depressing and claustrophobic, qualities made worse by the presence of the Green Line, tensely palpable even when out of sight. Profuse wall graffiti in Hellenic blue are concerned exclusively with what is delicately termed the Cyprus Question, the search for a solution to the island's de facto partition. The "Attilas Out" (or the more racist "Mongols Out"), and "Federation = Turkification" of past years have been replaced by commentary on the ill-fated Annan Plan: a terse "No" (often painted over a diffident "Yes"), the inflammatory "Want to Wear a Fez? Then You Want the Annan Plan" or the witty "AMAN ANNAN AN-ATHEMA-N". Absent is the Levantine ease of the coastal towns: clusters of men stand or sit about Platía Eleftherías expectantly, and by Cyprus standards there is considerable hustle from shop and restaurant proprietors. As in Limassol, an entire neighbourhood is given over to obvious girlie bars and cabarets; the only other significant industries inside the Venetian fortifications appear to be cabinet-making, chair-making, metal-working and offset printing.

Lawrence Durrell bemoaned Nicosia's lack of sophistication and infrastructure in the mid-1950s; it's come a long way since then, with trendy boutiques peddling the latest fashions, and some excellent restaurants which only Limassol can rival. A small capital that might be expected to be provincial supports a cosmopolitan population that includes Lebanese, Iranians, Syrians and east Europeans, studying or surviving as refugees. Among the Europeans are, or have been, Serbian draft-dodgers, Russian businessmen laundering money and Romanian, Moldovan or Russian women swelling the ranks of the prostitutes – unforeseen legacies of non-aligned 1960s Cyprus's diligent cultivation of ties all round. You will also come across journalists monitoring the Middle East from a relatively safe haven, and delegates to the numerous conferences which are a feature of Nicosia's winter calendar; less obvious will be the legions of spies and undercover agents which the city is famous for, another holdover of Cyprus's role as a pivotal point in the Cold War, though now they may just as likely be Syrian, Kurdish, Iranian, Israeli or even Turkish, pursuing their own agenda.

## Some history

Most authorities believe that present-day Nicosia lies on or just north of the site of a Neolithic settlement, subsequently the Archaic town of Ledra. But the city only became prominent in Byzantine times, eclipsing Constantia (Salamis) after the disastrous seventh century AD, and embarking on a golden age with the arrival of the **Lusignan kings**. Particularly during the fourteenth century, they endowed the place with over eleven kilometres of fortifications, plus the palaces, churches and monasteries appropriate to a court of chivalry. Their surviving monuments constitute much of Nicosia's appeal; nowhere else on Cyprus except at Famagusta can you take in the spectacle of Latin-Gothic architecture transplanted to the subtropical Levant. The underpinnings of such a hothouse fantasy were by their very nature transient: the Genoese raided Nicosia in 1373, and the Mamelukes sacked the city again in 1426. Following **Venetian** assumption of direct rule in 1489, Nicosia became even more of a stronghold. With an eye to the growing Ottoman threat, the Lusignan circuit of walls shrank between 1567 and 1570 to a more compact, antiballistic rampart system designed by the best engineers of the age. Monuments falling outside the new walls were demolished in the interest of a free field of fire. But it was all to no avail, as the Turks took the city on September 9, 1570 after a seven-week siege, swarming over the Podocataro and Constanza bastions. In a paroxysm of rape, plunder and slaughter graphically described by survivors, the victors dispatched nearly half the 50,000 inhabitants and defenders.

Under **Ottoman rule** the city stagnated, albeit picturesquely, not to regain such a population level until the 1940s. The three centuries passed quietly, except for riots in 1764, in which a particularly unpleasant governor was killed, and mass executions of prominent Greek Cypriots (including the island's four bishops) in 1821, to preclude imitation of the Greek peninsular uprising. The **British** raised the Union Jack over the town in 1878, but saw their wooden Government House burnt down in the pro-*énosis* riots of 1931.

Colonial authorities moved the administrative apparatus outside the walls in 1946, paralleling the growth of the city. But during the 1950s and 1960s the capital was wracked, first by the EOKA struggle and later by violence between the Orthodox Christian and Muslim communities. After the events of December 1963 (see "History" in *Contexts*), **factional polarization** proceeded apace: Greeks and Armenians were expelled or fled from mixed neighbourhoods in the north of the city, and any remaining Turks deserted the south, so that Nicosia was already all but partitioned when the Turkish army reached the northwestern suburbs, and then penetrated the Turkish quarter of the old town, on July 22, 1974.

Since then, the runaway growth of the new southern boroughs has been spurred by the necessity of quickly providing housing for tens of thousands of Greek refugees from North Cyprus. By contrast old Nicosia has suffered even where not explicitly damaged by warfare, as shopkeepers and residents close to the Line deserted their premises, leaving often exquisite buildings to decay. Only since the late 1980s has the trend of neglect been reversed, under the aegis of the **Nicosia Master Plan**, funded by the United Nations Development Programme and the EU. Tentative co-operation between urban planners in the Greek and Turkish sectors, based on the assumption of a reunited city in the future, has resulted in co-ordinated restoration and pedestrianization of the most attractive neighbourhoods on both sides of the Green Line, and even (in 1979) the mundane but necessary completion of a joint sewage plant, left stranded in the Turkish zone after 1974. The population of "Nicosia within the walls" seems to have stabilized, and (especially in the event of a final political settlement) it may have some future other than as a depressed, traumatized backwater. As of writing, the historic residential neighbourhoods east of Sólonos have been fairly comprehensively refurbished, with concentrations of quite striking old houses getting denser as you approach the Famagusta Gate.

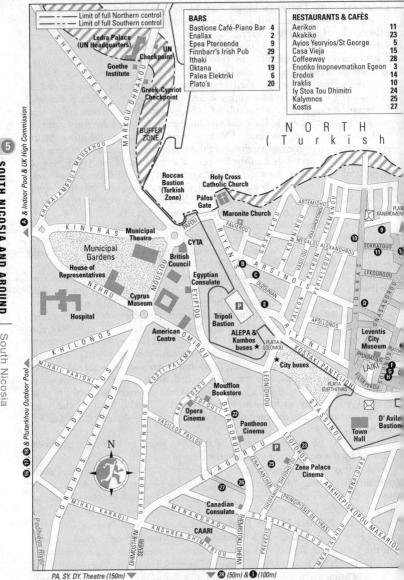

| BARS | |
|---|---|
| Bastione Café-Piano Bar | 4 |
| Enallax | 2 |
| Epea Pteroenda | 9 |
| Finnbarr's Irish Pub | 29 |
| Ithaki | 7 |
| Oktana | 19 |
| Palea Elektriki | 6 |
| Plato's | 20 |

| RESTAURANTS & CAFÉS | |
|---|---|
| Aerikon | 11 |
| Akakiko | 23 |
| Ayios Yeoryios/St George | 5 |
| Casa Vieja | 15 |
| Coffeeway | 28 |
| Enotiko Inopnevmatikon Egeon | 3 |
| Erodos | 14 |
| Iraklis | 10 |
| Iy Stoa Tou Dhimitri | 24 |
| Kalymnos | 25 |
| Kostis | 27 |

# Arrival, orientation, transport and information

Whether you approach from the south along the motorway from Larnaca or Limassol, or in a more leisurely fashion from the Tróödhos foothills, arrival in Nicosia is not a thrilling prospect (the international **airport** has languished in the

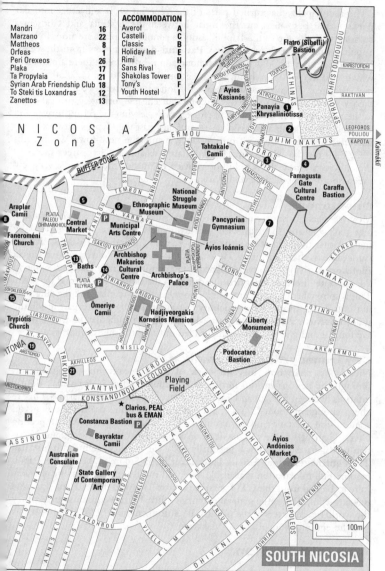

Mandri 16
Marzano 22
Mattheos 8
Orfeas 1
Peri Orexeos 26
Plaka 17
Ta Propylaia 21
Syrian Arab Friendship Club 18
To Steki tis Loxandras 12
Zanettos 13

**ACCOMMODATION**
Averof A
Castelli C
Classic B
Holiday Inn E
Rimi H
Sans Rival G
Shakolas Tower D
Tony's F
Youth Hostel I

NICOSIA
Zone)

Flatro (Sibelli) Bastion

Kaïmaklí

SOUTH NICOSIA

0        100m

Cyprus Airways & British Airways

dead zone, used as UNFICYP headquarters since 1974, its ultimate fate subject to a final peace settlement). You negotiate seemingly interminable suburbs indistinguishable from those of any other Mediterranean or Middle Eastern city, until suddenly thrust into the ring system of streets mirroring the Venetian bulwarks. Most of the **bus terminals** are a short distance from the ramparts, or even on them; see "Listings" on p.295, and our map, for precise locations.

The municipality has turned parts of the Venetian walls and moat into **car parks** – the best areas are the moat between the D'Avila and Constanza bastions, with the top of the Tripoli bastion a runner-up; plans are afoot to build a multi-storey car park in the moat. **Pay-and-display** tickets from the vending machine start at C£0.50 for two hours; on nearby streets there are **meters** which cost C£0.20 per hour, but occasionally C£0.40 or C£0.50 in very high-use areas. Regulations are enforced Monday to Saturday, 7am to 7pm, in theory. Alternatively, you can use remoter, but cheaper, privately run car parks in the new city away from the walls; for example, leaving the A1 motorway and entering the built-up area, keep an eye out, just past the Cyprus Airways headquarters, for a large car park on the right, before the new-town Woolworths – C£0.60 for the whole day. The only fairly reliable fee-free street spaces in the old city are near the Archbishop's Palace, or outside the walls in a very few streets south of the Constanza bastion.

## Orientation

Most of what a visitor will want to see in south Nicosia lies within the old city walls. Getting to grips with the main streets there is made difficult by the fact that the longest one, the ring boulevard linking the bastions, changes names no less than four times. The busiest entrance to the old town is at **Platía Eleftherías**, giving onto pedestrianized and commercialized **Lídhras**, while in the opposite direction **Evagórou** leads out to the **new town** beyond the walls. This is somewhat more orderly but by no means grid-regular, and the ring road just outside the moat changes identity just as often as its counterpart inside the walls; **Leofóros Arkhiepiskópou Makaríou**, perpendicular to Evagórou, is the longest and glitziest boulevard, headed out towards the A1 motorway.

## City transport and information

Nicosia has an **urban bus network** of about twenty lines, straggling off through the new town into further-flung suburbs; services run at half-hourly intervals between 5.30am and 7 or 8pm, twice as often at peak periods. They're cheap enough at about C£0.40, but you probably won't use them unless you want to visit a distant embassy or cultural centre. Bluntly put, no self-respecting Greek Cypriot will be caught dead on a bus or (worse) walking, and Nicosian teenagers more or less obligatorily get a car for their eighteenth birthday. The **central terminal** for city buses is on Platía Solomoú, beside the Tripoli bastion. Full information is available here, and route and city maps are sporadically to be had from the **CTO** at Aristokýprou 11 (Mon–Fri 8.30am–4pm, Sat 8.30am–2pm). This is the general enquiries office; for more unusual requests try the world headquarters of the CTO at Leofóros Lemesoú 19 (☎22331644), just past the end of Arkhiepiskópou Makaríou.

## Accommodation

Unless some international conference is being held – most take place between September and April – finding a bed in Nicosia shouldn't be too difficult; hotels welcome walk-in trade, as there's not much of a package industry inland. Getting something salubrious and good value, however, presents a bit of a challenge, since many establishments that seem promisingly located at the edge of the medieval town fall inside the main **red-light district**, a roughly triangular area bounded by Riyénis, Lídhras and Arsinöis streets. Some hotels here are acceptable, and indicated in the listings below, but even at the better hotels "short stay" or "rooms by the hour" are a fact of life.

Just east of Lídhras, the **Laïkí Yitoniá**, formerly an annexe of the disreputable zone, has been rehabilitated as a tourist-oriented pedestrian area. There are a handful of passable guest houses and small hotels here, particularly on or near Sólonos, though some are mosquito- and noise-plagued, the commotion starting at about 6.30am and not letting up until midnight. Budget or mid-range hotels in the new town are almost non-existent, though again one noteworthy exception is given below.

Unless otherwise noted, all rooms have en-suite facilities, and breakfast is included in the rates. However, summer water shortages can mean that bathing is out of the question for much of the day in the least expensive hotels.

**Averof** Avérof 19, 700m across the Pedhiéos River, accessible via bus #23 ☎22773447, ⊛www .averof.com.cy. Old-fashioned but good-value two-star on a very quiet street, with restaurant (table d'hôte meals on request) and bar; managed by a pleasant young Anglo-Cypriot couple who thoroughly updated the balconied rooms – biggish doubles with full bathtubs, also some family suites – in 1999. No "short stay" clientele allowed. The public pool (May–Sept) is a 15min walk away on Ploutárkhou, and the hotel has some limited off-street parking. ③

**Castelli** Ouzoúnian 38 ☎22712812, ℱ22673337, ℮hinnicres@cytanet.com.cy. Probably the best-value three-star in town, thoroughly renovated in October 2000, its medium-sized balconied rooms come complete with ISDN data ports; common areas include a gym, sauna and Polynesian-themed restaurant. Private parking is a big plus; discount rates often available. ⑦

**Classic** Riyénis 94 ☎22664006, ⊛www.classic .com.cy. The modest exterior and slightly dingy corridors of this three-star belie the pleasant ground-floor bar/restaurant and the rooms, all redone in 1999–2001 with simple but tasteful furnishing, wood parquet floors, air con, double glazing and (sometimes) balconies. ⑥

**Holiday Inn** Riyénis 70 ☎22712712, ℱ22673337, ℮hinnicres@cytanet.com.cy. Four-star, mid-1990s renovation with large rooms, indoor and outdoor pool, fitness centre, conference facilities and ample public parking opposite. Japanese restaurant on-site; most rooms are non-smoking. ⑨

**Rimi** Sólonos 5 ☎22680101, ℱ22660816, ℮rimi@cylink.com.cy. The most comfortable and savoury hotel in Laïkí Yitoniá, renovated in 1996–97 and now boasting two stars; all rooms have heating/air con, TV and bathtubs, plus there's a restaurant (touting somewhat assiduously) on the ground floor. ⑤

**Sans Rival** Sólonos 7-G ☎22669383. Painfully plain but adequate rooms in this, one of only two surviving budget pensions in Laïkí Yitoniá. ②

**Tony's Bed & Breakfast** Sólonos 13, corner of Ippokrátous ☎22666752, ℱ22662225. Laïkí Yitoniá's other licensed pension, mostly en suite, in startlingly authentic London B&B style, friendly and with an unbeatable roof terrace where full English breakfast is served. Exact rates depend on location in the building and plumbing arrangements. ②

**Youth Hostel** Ioánni Hadjidháki 5, near Themistoklí Dherví, 700m southwest of Platía Eleftherías ☎22674808. C£5 per person, plus C£1 sheet fee.

# The City

The city's old quarter is often termed "Nicosia within the walls", and almost all historic monuments lie within, on or just outside its formidable Venetian ramparts. Since their circuit (within the South's territory) is a shade over 2km in circumference, the highlights can be toured on foot in a fairly leisurely two days. After dark the labyrinthine old town (except for the lively Famagusta Gate area, and a few nightspots around Faneroménis and Trypiótis churches) is essentially deserted, even eerie, and most life shifts outside the walls.

## The Venetian walls

Nicosia's **Venetian fortifications** are its most obvious feature, and a good place to start your wanderings. Of the eleven bastions, named after Venetian personalities, five fall into the Greek zone and five, now confusingly renamed, into the Turkish zone; the Flatro bastion, in the no-man's-land between the zones, is under UN control. Three surviving gates, called Páfos, Kyrenia and Famagusta after the towns which they face, breach the walls roughly 120 degrees apart. The Venetians engaged the military engineers Ascanio Savorgnano and Francesco Barbaro to design the ramparts between 1567 and 1570. At the foot of the fortifications they appended a moat, which was never intended to carry water – though the Pedhiéos River, later diverted, managed to fill it sporadically. It was not the fault of the walls themselves that Nicosia failed to withstand the siege of 1570; the Turks took the city mainly because of the incompetence of the pusillanimous commander Nicolo Dandolo and the exhaustion of the defenders. The Ottomans maintained the ramparts, which were captured more or less intact; it is only since 1878 that substantial alterations have been made. Most of the following monuments are atop, or an integral part of, the bastions which form the most obvious bits of the ramparts. Otherwise it's easy to tread the course of the walls without realizing it, a testimony to how domesticated they've become.

## The Páfos Gate area

If you come from the Tróödhos by car, the **Páfos Gate** will probably be your somewhat grim introduction to the old city. Poised between the Greek and Turkish zones of the town, it's been a trouble spot since 1963. The flags of the South and the North, plus those of Greece and Turkey, oppose each other here across a ten-metre space, and signs on the Turkish-held Roccas bastion, now transformed controversially into a park (see p.327), warn off "trespassers". Originally this gate was called Porta San Domenico, after a Lusignan abbey just outside, which the Venetians demolished in 1567 when they contracted the circumference of the walls. The Ottomans had a large barracks and arsenal in and on it; the British made the internal chambers their police headquarters.

Just inside the gate stands one of the many anomalies of the post-1974 situation: the **Holy Cross Catholic church** and papal nuncio's residence, though squarely in the dead zone with its rear in Turkish-occupied territory, was allowed to reopen for business in 1976 on condition that the back door was sealed. The Maronites (see box on p.362) also have a church, school and clubhouse around the corner, though their main place of worship is now out in Lakatámia suburb.

Moving anti-clockwise, the moats and next two bastions have been put to use as dusty parkland, playing fields, bus terminals or car parks, with the **D'Avila bastion** also supporting a small cluster of public buildings. Three viaducts now compromise the walls and moat, the largest, **Platía Eleftherías**, having undergone a face-lift under the Nicosia Master Plan.

## Bayraktar Camii and the Liberty Monument

The small **Bayraktar Camii** (Mosque of the Standard-Bearer), standing in a well-landscaped area beyond the bus stations on the **Constanza bastion**, marks the spot where the Ottoman flag-carrier first scaled the walls in the 1570 siege. Vulnerable as such individuals always were – it was essentially a suicide mission – he was cut down immediately by the defenders, and buried on the subsequently revered site. It was long commonly believed that EOKA activists had bombed the mosque and tomb twice in 1962 and 1963, toppling the minaret the second time, but it is now certain that both incidents were actually the work of TMT provocateurs; the damage has been repaired and the mosque grounds are now kept locked to prevent recurrences. A sign up front, in Turkish and Greek, informs passers-by that while the Greek Cypriots respect the remaining Islamic holy places in the South, the Turks have not reciprocated in the matter of churches in the North.

A haven of parkland also surrounds the **Liberty Monument** sculpture, on the **Podocataro bastion**, consisting of fourteen representative Greek-Cypriot figures in bronze being released from a white marble jail by two soldiers, the whole scene presided over by a female personification of Liberty. Commissioned and opened to great hoo-hah in 1973 (ironically enough), the monument is now presumably such an embarrassing obstacle to communal reconciliation that it is absent even from most official tourist literature and maps.

## The Famagusta Gate

Tucked into an angle of the Caraffa bastion, the **Famagusta Gate** (Mon–Fri 9am–1pm & 4–7pm; free, plus special evening events) is the most elaborate and best preserved of Nicosia's three gates. Designed by Giulio Savorgnano (brother of Ascanio) as a copy of another such Venetian structure in Iráklion, Crete, and thus long known as the Porta Giuliana, the gate is essentially a tunnel through the walls; the inner facade, with its six coats-of-arms and original wooden doors, is far more aesthetic than the mean outer portal. After more than a century of neglect, the great domed chamber that opens out at the centre of the tunnel was refurbished in 1981 as an **exhibition and concert venue**; the heart of the latter is an acoustically marvellous, gently inclined tunnel surmounted by a dome like a miniature Parisian Pantheon. A side chamber, once either the Ottoman powder magazine or guard house, is now the exhibition hall. Beyond the outer portal stretches a small open-air amphitheatre used during the Nicosia September festival.

## The traditional commercial centre

Using Platía Eleftherías as a gateway, you're set at the Y-junction of **Lídhras** and **Onasagórou** streets to explore the time-honoured city centre of Nicosia. A graceless architectural mix of British Raj, Greek Neoclassical and ugly 1950s and 1960s buildings lines these two main shopping streets, which were pedestrianized during the 1980s as part of the Master Plan. On the eleventh floor of the Woolworth's skyscraper on Lídhras, now known as the **Shakolas Tower**, there's an air-conditioned **observatory** (May–Sept Mon–Sat 10am–8pm, Sun 10am–6pm; Oct–April Mon–Sat 9.30am–5pm; C£0.50) with sweeping views of both south and north Nicosia, plus audiovisual guides to what you're looking at.

The Greek-Cypriot barricade at the north end of Lídhras, with its little shrine to the lost homelands and "informative" displays to one side, is the only point on the Green Line you may (usually) photograph; you're supposed to stay a healthy ten metres away from other checkpoints aside from the Ledra Palace crossing. Businesses, in any case, peter out upon reaching the last three or four premises away from the Line – the uncertainty (and in former years, proclamation battles by the opposing sides using loudhailers) was too nerve-wracking. There was a wave of purchases of these buildings in 1992–93, when a settlement last seemed imminent; they have since plummeted in value, but the buyers may yet have the last laugh if post-Annan negotiations are fruitful. It is not the first time the street has been embattled; during the late 1950s Lídhras was dubbed "Murder Mile" after EOKA's habit of gunning down its opponents here.

## Platía Faneroménis

The north end of Onasagórou gives onto **Platía Faneroménis**, tipped to replace Eleftherías as the official city centre and named after the huge **church** that dominates the square. A hotchpotch of Neoclassical, Byzantine and Latin styles, this was erected during the final Ottoman years to replace a derelict medieval basilica. Inside the present structure are the remains of the four clerics murdered by the Ottoman governor in 1821. Behind the apse stands the Neoclassical Girls' Gymnasium, counterpart to the Pancyprian Gymnasium (see p.284).

More compelling than the Faneroméni church, and effectively filling the adjacent tiny Platía Ikostiogdhóïs Oktovríou, the **Araplar Camii**, originally the sixteenth-century church of Stavrós toú Missirikoú, is a good example of the mixed Byzantine-Gothic style particular to Lusignan times. Should you gain admission to the mosque (most unlikely), you'll be able to admire the octagonal-drummed dome, supported on magnificent columned arches. Taking advantage of the setting with outdoor seating is the recommended *Mattheos* taverna (see "Eating", p.292).

## Laïkí Yitoniá and around

Just east of the Lídhras pedestrianization, the so-called **Laïkí Yitoniá** or "Folk Neighbourhood" forms a showcase district reclaimed from the sin merchants in the late 1980s, with restored premises made available to half a dozen indifferent restaurants and numbers of souvenir shops. Almost the lone exception to the prevailing schlock here is Gallery Dhiakhroniki, Aristokýprou 2B (see "Shopping" for a full description).

The south Nicosia municipality is also extremely proud of the nearby **Leventis City Museum** at Ippokrátous 17 (Tues–Sun 10am–4.30pm; donation requested), which won the European Museum of the Year award in 1991. This folk-cum-historical collection occupies three floors of a restored mansion, and the collection is arranged thematically as well as chronologically from prehistoric to British eras, with much-improved labelling of late. Exhibits include traditional dress, household implements, rare books and prints, with scattered precious metalware and archeological treasures. The best sections are those devoted to the Venetian and Ottoman periods, as well as postcard collections (mostly by Armenian photographers) on the first floor. However, there's little on the history of individual monuments, and nothing yet on how the two zones of the city function together now, nor any background on the Laïkí Yitoniá or Khrysaliniótissa renewal projects

Around the corner on Sólonos, the **Trypiótis church** (open all day except for variable lunch hour), dedicated to the Archangel Michael, is the most beautiful of the old town's surviving medieval churches. On the south side, a glassed porch protects a pair of Gothic-arched windows. Over the door between, a fourteenth-century relief shows two lions being subdued by a being sprouting from leafy tracery, clutching hoops; to either side, mermaids and sea monsters gambol. Inside, the brown sandstone masonry has been left unpainted, as has the fine wooden *yinaikonítis* – indeed the whole interior is relatively restrained for a Cypriot church.

### The Ömeriye Camii

Variously spelled Omerieh, Omerye, Omergé (the phonetic, dialect pronunciation) and Omeriyeh, the **Ömeriye Camii** on Platía Tillyrías is the only Gothic house of worship converted into a mosque in the Greek zone of Nicosia. Originally it was a church of Saint Mary, part of a fourteenth-century Augustinian monastery largely destroyed by the Ottoman bombardment in 1570. Many Lusignan nobles were buried here, but as in the case of the Ayía Sofía cathedral in north Nicosia, the victors sacrilegiously "recycled" their tombstones to refloor the mosque during reconstruction. The Ottoman conqueror of Cyprus, Lala Mustafa Paşa, got it into his head that the caliph Omar had rested here during the seventh-century Arab raids on Cyprus – hence the name. Today it serves the needs of the city's Arab, Pakistani and Bangladeshi population; you are welcome to shed your shoes inside the ornate west portal and visit the simple, barn-like **interior** (Mon–Sat 10am–12.30pm & 1.30–3.30pm) with its shallow pitched roof and succession of rib vaults supporting this. You can also climb the minaret for the fine view, but it's probably best to stash spare footwear in a daypack, as the top dozen or so steps are caked in a thick layer of pigeon-shit. Be sure also to follow the indicated walkway around the apse for a flattering view of the church from the south, with flying buttresses. At dusk, the Arabic-speaking muezzin here vies with the Turkish tropes emanating from the minarets of the Selimiye Camii in north Nicosia, their unsynchronized calls to prayer stirring up formations of swallows.

The late sixteenth-century namesake **baths** across the square functioned as such until 2002, well attended by the prostitutes from three adjacent bordellos (now closed), but thereafter the baths were meticulously restored as part of the Master Plan. As of late 2004, however, they were tightly shut except for special events, and it seems unlikely that they'll work regularly as a *hamam* in the future. **Platía Tillyrías** itself is a rather busy street and car park, but there are a few cafés to one side from where you can admire the mosque.

## The Hadjiyeorgakis Kornesios Mansion

A few steps down Patriárkhou Grigoríou from the Ömeriye mosque, the delightful fifteenth-to-eighteenth-century **Hadjiyeorgakis Kornesios Mansion** (Mon–Fri 8.30am–3.30pm; C£0.75) is a hybrid of Venetian and Ottoman forms – a wooden Turkish lattice balcony perches over a relief coat-of-arms at the front door – that easily overshadows any of its contents. Supposedly home to the Cyprus Ethnological Museum, only a single room at the back is an authentic re-creation of the house in its heyday; most of the others serve as a contemporary antique gallery, rather than featuring medieval furnishings, though several rooms do exhibit assorted metal, glass and ceramic items from various eras.

The house takes its name from one **Hadjiyeorgakis Kornesios**, a native of Krítou Térra in Páfos district, who served as the dragoman (multi-lingual liaison between the Ottoman authorities and the Orthodox Christians) of Cyprus from 1779 until 1809. With a fortune accumulated from his vast estates and tax exemption, he was the most wealthy and powerful man on the island, but he met the usual end of Ottoman officials who became too prominent. A peasant revolt of 1804 was aimed at him and the Greek clerics, as much as at the Muslim ruling class; fleeing to İstanbul, he managed to stay alive and nominally keep office by seeking asylum in sympathetic foreign embassies, until he was beheaded in 1809 as part of the intrigues surrounding the consecutive depositions of the sultans Selim III and Mustafa IV.

## Around the archbishop's palace

An alarming concentration of coffin-makers lines the street leading from the Hadjiyeorgakis Kornesios mansion to **Platía Arkhiepiskópou Kypriánou**, which is flanked by a cluster of buildings including the city's diminutive de jure cathedral and three museums. The **Archbishop's Palace** is the most immediately obvious monument, a grandiose pastiche built during the 1980s to replace its 1950s predecessor, shelled and gutted by EOKA-B in their July 15, 1974 attempt to kill Archbishop Makarios. Except for the "Cultural Centre" wing (see below), it is not open to the public. At the southeast corner of the palace precinct, a controversial, not to say downright hideous, **statue of Makarios** looks (below the waist especially) more like Lot's petrified wife than a cleric, as he stares down Koräï street towards the Liberty Monument. This was the first, and probably the worst, of a growing contingent of similar ones inflicted on the city ever since.

Travelling about in the South, you can't help noticing that practically every town has a Gríva Dhiyení avenue, sometimes even two. They honour a man as controversial as Makarios – and who, particularly since independence, brought considerable misery, directly or indirectly, to both Greek and Turkish Cypriots.

Born on May 23, 1898, a native of Tríkomo (now renamed İskele) in the North, **George Grivas** attended Nicosia's Pancyprian Gymnasium before enrolling in the officers' academy in Athens. He graduated just in time to see several years' service in Greece's disastrous Asia Minor campaign – which doubtless fuelled his lifelong aversion to Turkey and Turks.

Grivas remained in Greece after the loss of Asia Minor, taking part under General Papagos in the repulsion of the Italians on the Epirot front during the winter of 1940–41. Having idly sat out most of the German occupation of his adopted home-land, in 1944 he formed a far-right-wing guerrilla band of royalist officers known as **Khi** – written "X" in the Greek alphabet – which by all accounts was collaborationist, devoting most of its time to exterminating left-wing bands and leaving the departing Germans alone. When full-scale civil war broke out in 1946, he emerged from retire-ment as a lieutenant-colonel to help crush the communist-inspired rebellion, again with Papagos as his superior.

A semblance of normal life and elections returned to Greece in 1951. Grivas ran under the banner of Papagos's party but failed to secure office – his forbidding, abstemious personality, appropriate to the battlefield, did not strike a chord with the Greek electorate. Disgusted, Grivas swore off electoral politics for good, and returned to Cyprus the same year to test the possibility of an uprising here to throw off British rule. It was then that he met Makarios, whom he tried to convince of the necessity of some sort of rebellion. Neither Makarios nor Grivas's Greek sponsors were persuaded until an Athens meeting in early 1953, when Makarios, Grivas and ten others resolved to fight for énosis or union with Greece, founding **EOKA**, the *Ethnikí Orgánosis Kypríon Agonistón* or "National Organization of Cypriot Fighters".

At this point Makarios would only assent to violence against property, but during 1954 two caïques loaded with explosives and weapons made their clandestine way from Rhodes to Cyprus, landing on the then-deserted Páfos coast (see p.187). Most of the year was taken up establishing EOKA in Cyprus, with recruits taking oaths of secrecy, obedience and endurance till victory, similar to those of the IRA.

Makarios gave the final go-ahead for the insurrection in March 1955; EOKA made its spectacular public debut on April 1 with bomb explosions across the island. Self-introductory leaflets were signed **"Dhiyenis"**, Grivas's chosen *nom de guerre,* after Dhiyenis Akritas, folk hero of a tenth-century Byzantine epic.

The revolt gathered momentum throughout 1955 and early 1956, when Grivas halted a promising round of negotiations between Makarios and Governor Harding with timely explosions which also provoked Makarios's deportation. Thereafter Grivas

---

Across the way sprawls the imposing Neoclassical façade of the **Pancyprian Gymnasium**, one of the more prestigious secondary academies for Greek Cypriots since the 1880s. In *Bitter Lemons* Lawrence Durrell described his experiences teaching here in the mid-1950s, when it became a hotbed of pro-énosis sentiment.

### The church of Áyios Ioánnis

Between the Gymnasium and the palace sits the seventeenth-century **church of Áyios Ioánnis** (St John; Mon–Fri 8am–noon & 2–4pm, Sat 8am–noon), which gets some prizes for the quantity (if not always the quality) of its eighteenth-century interior **frescoes** by a certain Filaretos, whose work can also be seen

and EOKA included murder in the scope of their operations, targeting British service-men, leftist or pro-British Greeks and occasionally Turkish Cypriots as victims. From his movable headquarters in the Tróödhos – at or near Kýkko monastery – Grivas mocked the British with a steady barrage of communiqués and ultimatums. To the British, at their wits' end, he was not "Dhiyenis" but "Egregious" Grivas; numerous search and/or entrapment missions were mounted in the hills, at least one involving MI6, and nearly succeeded in catching the wily guerrilla leader in 1956 and again in 1959, the latter hunt aborted by higher-ups for political reasons.

When Makarios returned to Cyprus in 1959, he found himself estranged from Grivas who, furious at the archbishop's acceptance of independence rather than *énosis*, stalked off to self-exile in Greece and a hero's welcome, including promotion to the rank of lieutenant-general. This all apparently went to Grivas's head, and his subsequent paranoid public utterances were deeply embarrassing to all concerned, earning him denunciation by the Greek government.

By 1964, however, Greece, Makarios and Grivas had patched things up to the extent that the Athens government sent Grivas back to Cyprus, ostensibly to impose discipline on irregulars of Greek nationality who had smuggled themselves onto the island. This he did, but he also assumed command of Makarios's new **National Guard** and led several attacks on Turkish enclaves, most notably at Kókkina in 1964 and Kofínou in 1967, pushing Greece, Turkey and Cyprus to the brink of war each time. After the 1967 episode, American diplomacy secured what was hoped would be his permanent removal from the island.

But the 1967–74 Greek junta, in its obsessive machinations to oust Makarios from office, found Grivas useful once again: in 1971 he secretly entered Cyprus disguised as a priest to organize **EOKA-B**, literally "The Second EOKA", whose express intent was the elimination of all enemies of Hellenism – and of the colonels – on the island. This came to include virtually anyone who stood in the junta's way: communists, socialists, centrists, Turkish Cypriots and eventually Makarios himself. Whether Grivas subscribed to all of this as the junta's willing patsy, or as a royalist shared some of Makarios's disdain for the colonels and remained opposed to any *"énosis"* that would invite the Turks in for a chunk of the island, will never be known; he died in January 1974, still in hiding. Yet had he not left the scene when he did, it is possible to imagine Grivas being persuaded to lead the July 1974 coup against his erstwhile comrade-in-arms, Makarios. Those who knew him personally assert that his over-riding qualities were impulsive chivalrousness – he was known to pay benefits to widows of his fighters out of his own pocket – murderousness (he or bands under his direct command killed nearly three hundred mostly leftist Greeks, far more than the British) and complete inability to consider the eventual consequences of his actions. With hindsight, it is possible to respect Grivas for his obvious dedication and skill as a guerrilla – but for little else.

at Monágri. Among recognizable scenes are the *Last Judgement* and the *Creation* over the south and north doors respectively, and on the south wall a sequence on the rediscovery of the Apostle Barnabas's relics. Despite its small size (compared to Faneroméni, for instance), Áyios Ioánnis is the official cathedral of the city; here the archbishops of Nicosia are still consecrated, standing on the floor medallion featuring a Byzantine double-headed eagle.

## The Ethnographic Museum

Just north, the **Ethnographic Museum** (and "Society for Cypriot Studies"; Mon–Fri 9am–2pm; C£1) occupies the surviving wing of a fourteenth-century Benedictine monastery, handed over to the Orthodox and done up as the old archbishop's residence after Latin rule ended. It reopened in 1997 after a lengthy period of closure during which the collection of nineteenth- and twentieth-century ceramics, woodcarving and household implements was reshuffled, but there is still, regrettably, no interpretation or discussion of the various crafts. One, perhaps unintended, effect of a visit will be to make you *not* want to buy any contemporary souvenirs, as the quality of the small objects – *lefkarítika* (linen and silk work from Léfkara), *kolótzi* or engraved gourds, musical instruments, Nicosian silver filigree work – is so manifestly superior to modern work. But the plurality of the exhibits are carved and (usually) painted wood: magnificent chests, doors, cornices, chunks of wooden water-wheel in the exterior portico.

## The Makarios Cultural Centre and Kanakariá mosaics

Within sight of both Áyios Ioánnis and the Ethnographic Museum is the entrance to the **Archbishop Makarios Cultural Centre** (Mon–Fri 9am–4.30pm, Sat 9am–1pm; C£1), which owes its grandiose name to the presence of several research libraries and a very audible school of ecclesiastical music, where laymen learn to be *psáltes* or chanters for Orthodox church services. On the upper floor, lit and opened only on request, resides Makarios's private collection of kitschy religious canvases with doubtful attributions, assembled for him by a French-educated Cypriot, Nikolaos Dikeos. The ground floor, however, is another matter, and for most visitors a tour of the **Byzantine galleries** here (same hours as above, but may close at lunchtime) will be one of the highlights of a day in Nicosia.

Pride of place, and deservedly so, is given to the recovered **Kanakariá mosaics**, stolen from a church in North Cyprus in the late 1970s but returned to Nicosia in 1991 after a lengthy court battle (see p.406 for more details). Since late 1992 they have been displayed in the purpose-built, right-rear wing, though their layout here – an artificially flat surface – does not recreate their former position in Panayía Kanakariá church, in a curved apse, viewed from below. Originally, the Virgin Enthroned sat between the two archangels, with a band above containing the busts of the apostles. The most famous image is that of Christ clutching a scroll, looking like a young pagan god and adhering to Hellenistic, rather than later, iconographic conventions. Only one archangel, Gabriel, survived into modern times; his eyes, which look strangely averted in the mosaics' present position, would originally have been gazing at the Virgin. The apostles Matthew, James and Bartholomew were recovered more or less intact; all are distinguished by preternaturally large, asymmetrical eyes. Stylistically, all the figures show the marked Hellenistic traits typical for such early Christian mosaics of the sixth century. In 1997 images of saints Thomas and Thaddeus were recovered, and you can expect these to join their fellows at the exhibit here in the near future.

The mosaics are a hard act to follow, but the **icons** in the adjacent gallery, about 150 in all retrieved from various Cypriot churches, along with a reconstructed apse full of fourteenth-century frescoes rescued from Áyios Nikólaos tís Stéyis in the High Tróödhos, acquit themselves commendably. Even when the exhibits are not of the highest artistic standard, they mostly prove unusual in some respect; under the influence of the Lusignans, artists often made astonishingly free with the usual iconographic rules, especially in the variations of the Virgin and Child from the sixteenth century.

To the right, just inside the main door, stands a familiar portrayal of the Prophet Elijah from the thirteenth century, being fed in the wilderness by the raven, symbol of God's providence; adjacent, an earlier, pensive Saint John the

Baptist is rather more spruced up than his usual shaggy norm. Rarely seen topics include Saint Anne holding the Virgin and Child; the Burning Bush, as a herald of Christ; and a *Threnos*, similar to a Latinate *Pietà* with just the dead Christ and the Virgin, whereas Orthodox portrayals of the *Deposition* are usually group scenes. At the rear of the main gallery, a sixteenth-century icon of the *Adoration of the Magi* turns out in practice to be a Renaissance-style family portrait; a *Virgin Orans* of the same period shows the donor family kneeling to either side. Their costumes, and those of other figures, were invaluable in dating these works, and offer an absorbing insight into medieval Cypriot life. Unfortunately, the souvenir stall by the ticket booth disagrees with these assessments, and the postcards and books on offer are generally disappointing.

## The National Struggle Museum

Just north of the Ethnographic Museum stands the purpose-built **National Struggle Museum** (*Mouseio Agonos*; Mon–Fri 8am–2pm, also Sept–June Thurs 3–5.30pm; free), completed in 2001 to replace a far smaller facility, and representative of the prevalent trend to glorify EOKA and its works. Housed on several levels joined by ramps, it's an overwhelming accumulation of memorabilia, mostly photo-archival, on EOKA's 1950s anti-colonial campaign of demonstrations, sabotage and murder. Exhibits include cartoons, graffiti (first prize to "When the English were living in huts, the Greeks were building Parthenons") and press comment of the time documenting British reprisals, searches, tortures and detention camps; the personal belongings of fighters (including Grivas); plus arrays of weapons and gruesomely ingenious bombs. The centrepiece of the displays is a memorial to EOKA's martyrs, plus a mock-up gallows commemorating the nine hanged at the city's Central Prison by the British in 1956 – along with their last letters from the death cells. Labelling, though now partly in English, remains minimal; the propaganda impact is visual, and primarily intended for Greek-Cypriot schoolchildren. Interestingly, the main emphasis is on opposition to (and from) the British, with little about adverse Turkish-Cypriot reaction (though there is a table of victims of the TMT) – or the vast number of leftist Greek-Cypriots and British troops killed by EOKA.

## Municipal Arts Centre

About 150m west of the Makarios Centre along Apostólou Varnáva, the **Municipal Arts Centre** (Tues–Sat 10am–3pm & 5–11pm, Sun 10am–4pm; free), housed in a former generating plant, is the city's main venue for changing exhibits of avant-garde art. There's a gift shop selling books, cards, posters and other souvenirs, as well as a posh attached restaurant/coffee bar, *Iy Palea Elektriki*, serving Mediterranean-cum-Cypriot fare (℡22432559 for reservations; only operates when an exhibition is on).

## Tahtakale and Khrysaliniótissa districts

Heading north from Platía Kypriánou on pedestrianized Ayíou Ioánnou, you shortly reach the small **Tahtakale (Taht-el-Kala) Camii**, the homely focus of the eponymous neighbourhood. Here the Master Plan has borne the most fruit, as dozens of old houses have been renovated for occupation by young families in an effort to revitalize the area. But for a taste of the exotic Ottoman town of the nineteenth century, accented with palm trees, arched mud-brick houses and domes, you really need to continue across Ermoú into the **Khrysaliniótissa district**, strolling along Axiothéas, Ayíou Yeoryíou and Avtokratóras Theodhóras streets in particular.

This area is anchored by the namesake church of **Panayía Khrysaliniótissa** (Panagia Chrysaliniotissa), a rambling L-shaped building with fine relief carving on its exterior, arches under the two domes, and (formerly) an overwhelming collection of icons inside, many of which have found their way into the Makarios Cultural Centre. Construction was begun in 1450 by Helena Paleologina, the Greek wife of Lusignan King John II; the name, "Our Lady of the Golden Linen", is supposed to derive from its vanished original icon's having been found in a flax field.

Perhaps on the heels of the rehabilitation efforts, businesses and residences are used right up to the barriers here, in contrast to elsewhere in town; the dead zone also seems narrower, with North-Cypriot/Turkish flags plainly visible over the housetops. But of the 23 types of exotic bazaars catalogued by Louis Salvator, effectively bisecting the town between the Famagusta and Páfos gates, only traces of the cabinet-making, tin-smithing, cloth and candle-dipping industries remain in the Greek zone, mostly on the few commercial streets between Tahtakale and Khrysaliniótissa.

## The Cyprus Museum

Founded early in the British tenure, the **Cyprus Museum** (Mon–Sat 9am–5pm, Sun 10am–1pm; C£1.50) is easily the best assemblage of archeological artefacts on the island. It stands between the Tripoli bastion and the pleasant **municipal gardens**, Nicosia's largest green space and, with its outdoor café, is a worthwhile adjunct to any visit; on Sundays there's an outdoor market here, run by and for the large Sri Lankan immigrant community.

You should tour the galleries anti-clockwise from the ticket booth for rough chronological order, but the museum is organized thematically as well. Typically for Cyprus, the pre-Classical displays are the most compelling, though every period from Stone Age to early Byzantine is represented. All told, it's an absorbing medium-sized collection that requires at least two hours for a once-over. Individual labelling is often mercifully replaced with hall-by-hall or glass-case explanatory plaques placing the objects in context. The museum is frankly overstuffed, with many exhibit-worthy items in storage; ground is to be broken for a large museum if and when a final peace settlement occurs.

### Highlights of the collection

**Room 1** is devoted to Neolithic items, in particular andesite ware and shell jewellery from Khirokitiá, and a case of Chalcolithic fertility idols. **Room 2**, the Early Bronze Age gallery, features fantastically zoomorphic or beak-spouted composite red-clay pottery from the Kyrenia coast. The central exhibits illustrate aspects of a pervasive early Cypriot cult: two pairs of ploughing bulls, a rite conducted by priests (wearing bull masks) in a sacred enclosure, and a model sanctuary crowned with bulls' heads.

The pottery of **Room 3** presents the best pictorial evidence of Mycenaean influence in Late Bronze Age Cyprus. A gold inlaid bowl from Enkomi and a faience rhyton from Kition are the richest specimens here, though decorated *krater*s (wine-mixing bowls) are more revealing in their portrayal of stylized humans in chariots being drawn by equally fantastic horses. Recurrent left- and right-handed swastikas obviously predate any Nazi associations, and merely indicate Asian contacts.

**Room 4** is dominated by its startling corner display, a panoply of seventh- and sixth-century votive figurines from a **sanctuary at Ayía Iríni** near Cape Kormakíti, excavated in 1929. The shrine was active after 1200 BC as the focus

289

△ Aphrodite of Soli, Cyprus Museum

of a fertility cult, yet few of the two thousand figurines discovered were female. Most of the terracotta men of various sizes are helmeted, prompting speculation that the deity was also one of war.

A limestone **Zeus Keraunios** ("Thunderer") from Kition, familiar from the C£10 note, hurls a missing lightning-bolt in **Room 5**. This and other Greek/Hellenistic statues show marked Assyrian influence in beard, hairdo and dress; an Oriental voluptuousness in male or female facial expression decreases as the Hellenistic period is reached, but never entirely vanishes. Among several renderings of the goddess is a first-century AD Roman statuette of **Aphrodite of Soli** – an image reproduced ad infinitum across Cyprus in tourist literature proclaiming it "her" island, as well as on the Cypriot five-pound banknote.

A cast-bronze, large-than-life-size nude of the second-century Roman emperor **Septimius Severus**, unearthed at Kythrea in 1928, forms the centrepiece of **Room 6**. **Room 7A** showcases an intricate **wheeled stand** for a bowl, ranks of animal figures rampant on its four sides, with an account of its rescue by the Cyprus government from Turkish thieves (pre-1974) and German art dealers. Ancient Enkomi, near Famagusta, yielded this and other twelfth-century BC finds like the famous bronze "**Horned God**", one hand downturned in benediction.

Subterranean **Room 8** demonstrates the progression from simple pit-tombs under dwellings, as at Khirokitiá, to rock-cut chamber-tombs, accessed by a *dromos* or "passage". Other steps lead to **Room 11**, the royal Salamis tomb room. Trappings from a hearse, and chariot traces for the horses sacrificed in the *dromos* (see p.398), are overshadowed by the famous **bronze cauldron** on a tripod, with griffon and sphinx heads welded onto its edge. A metal throne was found together with an Egyptian-influenced, finely crafted bed and a throne or chair of wood and ivory.

**Room 7B** offers a miscellany of objects from around the island, including the famous original mosaic of Leda and the Swan from Palea Paphos. Gold specimens include that portion of the Byzantine Lambousa Treasure which escaped the attentions of plunderers and smugglers in the nineteenth century (most of the hoard went to US museums, particularly the Metropolitan Museum in New York).

The exhibits are rounded off with **Room 14**'s terracotta figurines from all eras. Among the more whimsical are three humans and a dog in a boat, and a thirteenth-century BC side-saddle rider, recovered from thieves in the 1980s. *Ex votos* of expectant mothers depict midwives delivering babies, and strange bird-headed and earringed women fondling their own breasts. From the Meniko sanctuary dedicated to the Phoenician god Baal Hamman, an outsize, unsettling figure of a bull being led to sacrifice completes a spectrum of taurean worship begun in Room 2.

## State Gallery of Contemporary Art

Housed in a magnificent building just south of the Constanza bastion, the **State Gallery of Contemporary Art** (Mon–Fri 10am–5pm, Sat 10am–1pm; free) at Stassínou 24 is the only other significant museum in the new town. It highlights the best Cypriot painting and sculpture from the twentieth century; the sumptuous catalogue is yours to buy, either here or at Moufflon Books (see "Listings"). Rather tellingly, there are almost no Turkish-Cypriot artists.

### Kaïmaklí

Nearly 2km northeast of the UN-controlled Flatro bastion, the suburb of **Kaïmaklí** – until 1968 a separate village – boasts the finest domestic architecture outside the city walls. Local Greek Orthodox architects and stonemasons first came to prominence during the Lusignan period, when the Latin rulers trained and used this workforce in the construction of the massive Gothic monuments of the city centre. Their skills persisted through subsequent changes of regime, and during the late Ottoman years the master masons would often travel abroad for commissions.

With the coming of the British, there was no longer a need to conceal wealth from the powers that were, and the former simple but functional mud-brick houses, with perhaps just a pair of sandstone arches or a lintel, were joined by grandiose stone churches and dwellings sporting pillars, balcony grillwork, and other architectural follies. More recent Kaïmaklí history has not been happy. As a mixed district, it was the scene of bitter fighting and EOKA atrocities during December 1963, particularly in the Omórfita neighbourhood (Küçük Kaymaklı to the Turkish Cypriots); this, like much of Kaïmaklí proper, now lies in the Turkish zone.

Every Monday the south Nicosia municipality lays on a bus and walking **tour** of Kaïmaklí; just show up at 10am at the Laïkí Yitoniá CTO office (Aristokýprou 11). The two-hour outing, which involves a coach transfer along the Green Line in addition to the foot itinerary, is free, but patrons are "encouraged" to buy things at points of interest along the way. If you'd rather go by yourself, **bus** lines #46 and #48 serve Kaïmaklí.

## Ledra Palace checkpoint: pedestrian access to the North

From the Páfos Gate area, Márkou Dhrákou winds north towards the Green Line and the UN headquarters in the former Ledra Palace hotel. As you approach, opportunistic commerce makes itself felt: one or two souvenir stalls print commemorative T-shirts for UN forces (as well as archeological excavation teams), who hang their shirts out to dry from balconies of the **Ledra Palace**; estate-agent signs pitch abandoned or under-used properties in the area. Among these (though not for sale) is the former Greek embassy (now merely the chancery), which had to move to less precarious quarters down the road, past the Cyprus Museum – a fitting denouement, perhaps, for all its pre-1974 intrigues. If you approach by car, you'll have to leave it behind, either in one of the fee lots or legal kerbside spaces west of Márkou Dhrákou.

There are two separate halts at the Ledra Palace **pedestrian crossing**: at the Greek-Cypriot and Turkish-Cypriot posts respectively (the sporadically manned UN booth in between no longer vets anybody). The crossing is open 24 hours, and heading **from south to north** there are no formalities for EU nationals at the Greek-Cypriot booth, across from the Goethe Institute. (Non-EU nationals should get themselves stamped out – read on for why.) When you reach the Turkish-Cypriot booth, travellers of all nationalities present their passport and receive in return a free "visa" on a loose sheet of paper – make sure *not* to have your passport itself stamped, as this may cause difficulties when re-entering southern Nicosia.

Beyond the Turkish-Cypriot checkpoint, the money-changers, souvenir stalls and taxi drivers of yore are reduced to almost nil, since the Cypriot pound is widely used in the North and anybody who wishes to do so can bring a vehicle through the Áyios Dhométios crossing-point further west. It's best, therefore, to regard this crossing as a way of visiting the monumental district of North Nicosia, for coverage of which see p.313.

Returning **from north to south**, you should surrender your loose visa at the Turkish-Cypriot booth and then proceed to the Greek-Cypriot post, where in contrast to an outbound trip one's passport will be scrutinized. EU nationals are automatically let in, but non-EU nationals will be quizzed and may have to demonstrate that they did not enter the island via the North in the first instance (this is where your exit stamp, as noted above, is crucial). You should also not bring noticeable quantities of shopping from the North, especially liquor or cigarettes, as this will be confiscated. (The Cypriots themselves, however, assiduously practise cross-"border" retail therapy – Turkish-Cypriots bringing back luxury goods not yet available in the North, Greek-Cypriots smuggling in Oriental sweetmeats regarded as better than those available in the South.)

## Eating

Nicosia has vast numbers of decent, authentic places at which to eat, but they are fairly well hidden – and are most emphatically not to be found in the much-touted Laïkí Yitoniá, a twee tourist trap whose nature will be familiar to anyone who's visited the Plaka in Athens or Paris's Quartier Latin. The better tavernas and less pretentious *ouzerí*s are in fact scattered fairly evenly across the old town, mostly within brisk walking distance of the walls. As elsewhere in the South, there's been a sharp rise, since the turn of the millennium, in the popularity of metropolitan Greek cuisine, as well as exotic cuisines such as Japanese, Italian and Arabic. Western-style coffee bars are a big hit too, with Greek chains like *Coffeeway* and American ones like *Starbucks* staking their claims.

### Within the walls

**Aerikon** Onasagóras 86–90, entrance (inconspicuous) on Sokrátous. Up on the second floor over the Bank of Cyprus HQ, this lives up to its name ("aerial") with a view terrace; the food's fusion Balkan/Cypriot, with plenty for vegetarians. Lunch only.

**Ayios Yeoryios** Platía Paleoú Dhimarhíou 27. Old Nicosia's favourite taverna, especially at lunch (even ex-President Clerides has dined here). Punters come for excellent, mid-priced home-style fare, including *agrélia me avgá* (asparagus with eggs), *óspria*, stews, artichokes and the like, washed down with choices from an excellent wine list. Sit inside or out on the little terrace, surrounded by potted plants and latticework.

**Casa Vieja** Arkhangélou Mikhaïl 3. Though Cypriot-run, a fairly authentic Spanish *tapas* bar lodged in a lovely old house, with most platters in the C£2–3 range. Dinner only, from 7.30pm.

**Enotiko Inopnevmatikon Egeon** Éktoros 40 ☏ 22433297. An oddball multi-purpose centre, combining bookshop, "culture club" and taverna. Run by a one-time anarchist, now belatedly (and fanatically) converted to the cause of *énosis*; his cuisine is more digestible than his politics, successfully combining metropolitan-Greek and island dishes – allow C£13 each with house wine. Seating is in the courtyard, or the revamped indoor *sála*. Dinner only. Credit cards accepted, reservations suggested.

**Erodos** Patriárkhou Grigoríou 1, corner Platía Tillyrías. Traditional Cypriot/metropolitan Greek dishes with an upmarket twist make this popular with a younger crowd.

**Iraklis** Lídhras 110. Best of several *gelaterie* on this stretch, with locally produced, quality ice cream; always has customers queuing out the front for takeaway, whatever the hour, and there's a pleasant sit-down snack-café attached.

**Mattheos** Platía Ikostiogdhóïs Oktovríou, beside the Araplar mosque. One of the best spots for lunch inside the walls, with pleasant management, summer outdoor seating and a wide-ranging, seasonally changing menu – quails, octopus, rabbit, *óspria*, artichokes with *goutsiá*, lamb and spinach, and mixed vegetables, with puddings, *shamísi* and walnut cake to finish up. Closes 4pm, and all Sun.

**Orfeas** Athinás 20. A good venue for kebabs, in an area currently suffering from a deficit in straight-ahead eateries and a surfeit of night-spots.

**Ta Propylaia** Trikoúpi 15–17. A traditional lunch-only tradesmen's greasy spoon, with a rather lurid decor of past-it electrical goods in glass cases. There's a broad selection of excellent-value ready-cooked dishes, especially *óspria*.

**To Steki tis Loxandras** Faneroménis 67, corner Sokrátous ☏ 22675757. Simple presentation and high-quality ingredients for Asia Minor/metropolitan Greek *mezédhes* and grills make this a sure-fire hit; reservations advised. Outdoor tables in summer. Dinner only; closed Sun.

**Zanettos** Trikoúpi 65. Long-running hole-in-the-wall that's been tarted up a bit under new management. There's a C£8 *mezé*, and snails in season; otherwise more ordinary fare, some of which (*revýthia*, black-eyed peas, white-bean salad) may be "off-menu". Dinner only.

### The new town

**Akakiko** Arkhiepiskópou Makaríou 9A. Excellent, convenient and affordable Japanese food, encompassing sushi, teppanyaki dishes and soups.

**Coffeeway** Themistoklí Dherví 27. An arm of the metropolitan Greek chain, this is just the place when you're craving a properly brewed western coffee or tea.

**Kostis** Ground floor Megaro Irini, in pedestrian lane off Evagórou 31 ☎ 22670904. Primarily seafood *mezé* restaurant (though there's also a meat option) that's busiest at lunchtime in the summer, when seating spills out into the lane. Some of the (clearly frozen) seafood platters might not quite pass muster in the proprietor's native Greece, but overall it's pretty good, abundant and affordable.

**Kalymnos** Zénas Kánther 11, beside a car park behind Zena Palace cinema. Reckoned the best place for seafood meals in Nicosia, and priced accordingly – reckon on C£9 for your fish and nearly as much again for the trimmings.

**Marzano** Dhiagórou 27. Upmarket, but not intimidatingly so, general Italian eatery, with affordable pasta dishes, salads, grills and pizzas.

**Peri Orexeos** Themistoklí Dherví 4–6 ☎ 22680608. Superb mainland-Greek cuisine with lots of vegetarian *mezédhes* and savoury dips: *fáva*, artichokes *ála políta*, courgettes with eggs, sausages, etc, as well as roasted main dishes. Portions are on the small side, and not bargain-basement at C£8–13 for two to three platters per person, booze extra, but well worth it; booking recommended.

**Plaka** Stylianoú Lénas 8, corner Platia Arkhiepiskópou Makaríou, Éngomi, 3.5km west of the old town ☎ 22446498. A good, moderately expensive *mezé* house out in the suburbs, where you're advised to fast before indulging. Closed Sun; dinner reservations advisable.

**Iy Stoa tou Dhimitri** Arcade in the Áyios Andónios market. A classic for affordable *óspria* and Cypriot casserole dishes; lunchtime only, indoor seating only.

**Syrian Arab Friendship Club** Vassilíssis Amalías 17, Áyios Dhométios, 1.5km west of the Tripoli bastion, en route to the US Embassy ☎ 22776246. What started out as a three-to-four-table café for (allegedly) Syrian secret-services personnel to smoke their hubble-bubbles has grown into an ample garden restaurant, with seating under three parallel tents or marquees (kept well heated in winter). The C£8-per-head *mezé* will have you begging for mercy, and it's very good indeed – much the best of several Middle Eastern outlets in town – though strict veggies should order à la carte. Wash it all down with a little bottle of *zivanía*, and you don't have to be a Syrian spy to enjoy the hubble-bubbles, still there in all their glory. Dinner only, from 7pm; large parties should book.

## Drinking and nightlife

There's actually a bit more nightlife in south Nicosia than the naff or dubious pubs in and around Laïkí Yitoniá would suggest, but much of it is out in the suburbs, and you'll need both a car and local contacts to find it. Exceptions, many of them in or near the trendy Famagusta Gate area, are listed below. The best strategy for old Nicosia in general is to stroll by and see what's happening, as new openings and changes of format are frequent.

**Bastione Café-Piano Bar** Athinás 6. Pretty much exactly as described, sheltered under medieval vaulting.

**Enallax** Athinás 16–17. Long-running lodestar of the Famagusta Gate area, with live gigs (rock or Greek pop) several nights weekly.

**Epea Pteroenda** Nikokléous 19, Stoa Papadhopoulou ☎ 99454896 for programme. Also known as Tou Simi after the owner, this is currently the best place in Nicosia to hear authentic Greek music in a variety of styles on acoustic instruments, played by Epea Pteroenda (also the name of the five-member band). Events start Fri & Sat after 10.30pm; moderate cover and drinks (C£25 or so for 2), reservations essential as only 45–50 seats. At other times, Simi and staff can be found next door at Kala Kathoumena, an alternative coffee-house, with herbal teas and backgammon on equal footing with inexpensive Middle Eastern coffees.

**Finnbarr's Irish Pub** Arkhiepiskópou Makaríou 52B. A decidedly Cypriot clientele comes for real ale and stout, Irish coffee and nibbles; happy hour most days.

**Ithaki** Nikifórou Foká 33. Large, indoor-outdoor music bar (live rock), at its best in summer.

Oktana Aristídhou 6. Multi-functional coffee-house that also does drinks and snacks (plus hubble-bubbles), as well as stocking an impressive range of books in Greek and English; open 4pm–2am. In the basement of the same premises is a very quiet, chill-out hard-liquor adjunct, called UQ Bar.

Palea Elektriki/Power House Municipal Arts Centre, Apostólou Varnáva 19. There's a piano bar here, as an adjunct to the restaurant, though it tends to be closed between exhibits.

Plato's Plátonos 8. Very congenial pub installed in an old arcaded house, with an improbably long list of drinks, good grub (especially chicken kebabs), and classic rock, jazz and blues out of the speakers.

# Theatre, music and film

For theatre and musical events, south Nicosia has four medium-sized indoor venues: the **Famagusta Gate Centre**, with good acoustics for chamber concerts in its small hall; the 1200-seat **Municipal Theatre** (℡22463028) across from the British Council and Cyprus Museum at the edge of the Municipal Gardens; **Theatro Ena** at Athinás 4 (℡22348203), though most performances are in Greek; and the **PA.SY.DY Theatre**, for orchestral works, at Dhimosthéni Sevéri 3, the continuation of Leofóros Evagórou.

**Film** hounds are catered to by numerous commercial cinemas, which include the Zena Palace at Theofánous Theodhótou 18 (℡22674128); the Opera 1 & 2 on the corner of Sofoúlis and Khrístou Sózou (℡22665305); Pantheon 1, 2 & 3 just above Evagórou on Dhiagóra 29 (℡22475787); and last but by no means least the plush K-Cineplex at Makedhonitíssis 15 (℡22355824), with six screens and flawless sound system. For art-house fare, the British Council and French Cultural Centre host films (and sometimes theatrical events) once or twice a month; for these addresses, see the "Listings" below. Other cinematheques include *The Weaving Mill/To Ifandouryio* at Léfkonos 67–71 (℡22762275), with screenings of cutting-edge films Monday, Wednesday and Friday at 9pm (though open all day for coffee or a glass of wine), and the Friends of the Cinema Society, operating once weekly out of the Opera 2.

For **current schedules** of all events consult the (fairly) useful pamphlet *Nicosia This Month*, published by the municipality and available at the CTO; the pull-out section of the *Cyprus Weekly*; or the Sunday *Cyprus Mail*. More authoritative than any of these is the monthly listings mag *Time Out Cyprus*, though this is in Greek only.

# Shopping

In general, shopping opportunities in south Nicosia are overrated; only optical goods are inexpensive compared to northern Europe, though savings have been eroded considerably since the introduction of VAT and entry to the EU. Shoes are good quality and reasonably priced, clothes somewhat less so. The focus for all these types of merchandise is pedestrianized Lídhras, and to a lesser extent Onasagórou. In the new town, most department stores and fashionable boutiques are found along, or just off, the initial reaches of Arkhiepiskópou Makaríou, especially a block southwest on ultra-trendy Stasikrátous. For arts and crafts, and more specifically tourist-orientated items, the following shops, all within the walls unless otherwise specified, are worth visiting.

Andhreas Haralambous Koráï 9, near the Archbishop's Palace. This artist's paintings and models of his theatre sets fill several lofty rooms in a slightly down-at-heel building. Open 11am–1pm & 6–11pm; ring ℡22457280 to confirm days.

Chrysaliniotissa Multicraft Centre Dhimonáktos 2. Part of the revitalization of the eponymous district, this comprises eight traditional crafts shops arrayed around a courtyard – and with a handy coffeeshop included. Open 10am–1pm & 3–6pm.

Cyprus Handicraft Service Athálassas 186, in the new town. Textiles, lace, wall hangings, reed mats and other characteristic Cypriot crafts items. Open Mon–Fri 7.30am–2.30pm, plus Thurs 3–6pm.

Gallery Dhiakhroniki Aristokýprou 2B. Dwindling stock of antiquarian engravings and woodcuts from Cyprus, the Middle East and Europe (there are more facsimiles now); icons by modern master Christos Christides; and original art and postcards by top contemporary Cypriot artists and foreign painters. Engravings are partially mounted, and reasonably priced (discount on multiple purchases). If you don't find it here, there are two nearby annexe premises with more stock, as well as a reasonable in-house framing service.

Horis Synora/Sans Frontières Akhéon 6–8, about 600m west of the Cyprus Museum. Small gallery selling hand-made jewellery and other craft objects, as well as hosting art exhibitions. Hours generally 9.30am–12.30pm and 4.30–9.30pm, but ring ☏ 22369435 to confirm.

Leventis City Museum Giftshop Ippokrátous 17. Specializes in reproduction Byzantine silverware.

# Listings

Airlines First Choice Airways (ex-Air 2000), c/o Amathus Navigation, Omírou 17 ☏ 22716500; British Airways, Arkhiepiskópou Makaríou 52A ☏ 22761166; Cyprus Airways, Arkhiepiskópou Makaríou 50 ☏ 22751996 or toll-free 80000008; Egyptair, c/o Mantovani Travel, Agapínoros 2E ☏ 22763777; Emirates, Arkhiepiskópou Makaríou 66E ☏ 22374010; Gulf Air, c/o R. A. Travelmasters, Arkhiepiskópou Makaríou 82A ☏ 22374064; KLM, Zínas Kánther 12, 3rd floor ☏ 22671616; Lufthansa, Arkhiepiskópou Makaríou cnr Evagórou, Capital Centre, 6th Floor ☏ 22873330; Malev, Dheliyórgi 5, Lapithio Megaro ☏ 22680980; Olympic Airways, c/o Amathus Navigation, Omírou 17 ☏ 22716500; Royal Jordanian, Arkhiepiskópou Makaríou 66, Kronos Court ☏ 22375360.

Banks and exchange Most banks, all with ATMs, cluster around Platía Eleftherías and along the start of Arkhiepiskópou Makaríou.

Bookshops Moufflon, Sofoúli 1, opposite Chanteclair House, 150m southwest of Platía Solomoú, is perhaps the best bookshop in the Middle East, with an extensive stock of new and used (displayed across the street) art, literature and general archeology as well as material specific to Cyprus and the Middle East. They post material abroad and conduct searches for rare material; catalogue available, (F) 22668703, (E) bookshop@moufflon. com.cy. It's unlikely you'll need to go elsewhere, but for the record there's Kokhlias at Avónos 9, near Cyprus Airways, with a mixed stock of Greek and foreign-language titles and Soloneion Book Centre, out in Stróvolos suburb at Vyzandíou 24.

Bus terminals ALEPA, on the Trípoli bastion, near Platía Solomoú, for Páfos and Limassol; EMAN, from the Constanza bastion, for Ayía Nápa; Intercity, on Platía Solomoú, for Larnaca; Clarios, on the Constanza bastion, for Kakopetriá, Plátres and Tróödhos resort; Kambos Buses, Tripoli bastion, for Kambos.

Car rental ASG/Europcar, Armenías 11 ☏ 22338226; Avis, Výronos 2 ☏ 22713333; Astra/National-Alamo, Iróön 2–4, Áyios Andhréas ☏ 22775800; Petsas, Kostáki Pantelídhi 24A ☏ 22662650; Hertz, Salamínos 4, Éngomi ☏ 22777411; Sixt, Lemessoú 46D, Stróvolos ☏ 22333841.

Cultural centres American Centre, Omírou 33B; British Council, Mousíou 3, by the Cyprus Museum; French Cultural Centre, Jean Moreas 3–5 ☏ 22317771; Goethe Institute, on Márkou Dhrákou across from the Greek-Cypriot checkpoint; Russian Cultural Centre, Alassías 16, Áyii Omoloyíti ☏ 22761607 (bus #13 or #57). Most have morning and late-afternoon split shifts, with special events in the evening. The Cyprus-American Archeological Research Institute (CAARI), at Andhréa Dhimitríou 11, just off Themistóklí Dherví ☏ 22670832, has a limited number of publications and a newsletter for sale, stages lectures and has a library available to specialists.

Embassies/high commissions/consulates Australia, Ánnis Komnínis 4, corner Stassínou ☏ 22753001; UK, Alexándhrou Pálli, northwest of the old town by the Green Line ☏ 22861100; USA, corner Metokhíou and Ploutárkhou, Éngomi ☏ 22776400. Other consulates important for procuring visas include Egypt, Éyíptou 3 (near CYTA) ☏ 22680650, and Syria, Nikodhímou Myloná 24 ☏ 22764481.

Fruit and vegetable markets The old central market, best on Friday and Saturday, is up on Platía Paleoú Dhimarkhíou, at the end of Trikoúpi by the Green Line; two others are the Wednesdays-only street bazaar on the Constanza bastion, and the daily Áyios Andónios market at the corner of Dhiyení Akritá and Evyenías Theodhótou.

Internet Internet Café, Lemessoú 17A (noon–2am); IntenCity Media, 1st Floor, Capital Centre, Stassínou 15, Engomí (24hr).

Post offices The main branch (open standard morning hours, plus Mon, Tues, Thurs & Fri 3–6pm,

In the wake of the communal disturbances of December 1963, the British (as guar-antors of the 1959 settlement) announced themselves unable single-handedly to maintain civil peace on Cyprus, and the crisis was referred to the United Nations. A Security Council resolution of March 1964 mandated the dispatch of a 6000-strong UN peacekeeping force, henceforth known as **UNFICYP**. This originally drew its blue-bereted ranks from the armies of the UK, Canada, Austria, Finland, Sweden, Denmark, Australia and Ireland. The initially authorized period was six months, but this has been renewed more or less automatically ever since. What was intended at the outset as a stopgap measure pending a durable solution to Cyprus's ethnic problems showed signs over the years of becoming an apparently permanent island institution.

UNFICYP's brief has always been narrowly defined: to keep physically separate hostile communal factions; to discourage atrocities by their mere presence; and, in their capacity as potential witnesses, to verify the facts of such incidents. However, UN troops have limited means of imposing calm; they cannot launch a pre-emptive strike to nip factional violence in the bud, but are only allowed to return fire if attacked. Nonetheless, UNFICYP were arguably successful in preventing more casu-alties than actually did occur from 1964 to 1974. Detractors have, however, pointed out that by "stabilizing" the newly formed Turkish Cypriot enclaves, UNFICYP acted, unwittingly or otherwise, to accelerate the process of partition.

Since the events of summer 1974 the deployment (if not the role) of UNFICYP changed radically. Instead of policing the boundaries of a number of scattered Turk-ish-Cypriot enclaves, troops now patrol the single, 180-kilometre-long ceasefire line and the buffer zone of varying width straddling it, where 150 watchtowers constitute landmarks. Duties include maintaining utility lines crossing the zone, and ensuring the safety of farmers wishing to cultivate their fields right up to the boundary. UNFICYP has been instrumental in defusing sensitive spots – especially in and around Nicosia where opposing Greek and Turkish troops are close enough to abuse each other verbally. Until the "borders" opened in April 2003, they also provided humanitarian aid to the remain-ing Greek Cypriots and Maronites in the North, as well as helping to settle disputes between Greek and Turkish Cypriots in the two remaining mixed villages of the South.

Amazingly the ceasefire of August 1974 has substantially held since then, with only the very occasional (sometimes fatal) potshot in or across the buffer zone – though

or 4–7pm in July/Aug, and Sat 8.30–10.30am), sits atop D'Avila bastion, entrance from Konstand-ínou Paleológou – poste restante service here. A secondary branch, with standard morning-shift-only hours, is at Lídhras 67.

Service taxis Travel and Express, Tagmatárkhou Poulíou 18, in Áyios Dhométios ☎ 22730888, about 1200m west-southwest of the Páfos Gate.

Swimming pools The largest and most central indoor public one is on Loúki Akritá, just off this book's map, due west of the old city, across the Pedhiéos riverbed; the most convenient outdoor

one is on Ploutárkhou, also west of the Pedhiéos in Éngomi.

Travel agencies Elijela Travel at Íon 1, Éngomi ☎ 22664164, is the local booking rep for most of the agrotourism properties. Anthology Travel & Tours, Stassándhrou 7, Suite 101 ☎ 22757763, organizes trekking tours in Páfos district and the Tróödhos. Top Kinisis, at Themistoklí Dherví 20, Flat 201 ☎ 22681832, and at Leonídhou 2, corner Akropóleos in Akropolis district ☎ 22869999, are designated agents for Continental Airlines, and thus should be able to get you good fares to North America from their European hubs.

# Around south Nicosia

The hummocky expanses around the capital hold little of compelling inter-est for a traveller, and access to many sites is complicated by the presence of

Greek-Cypriot civilian demonstrations near Dherínia in August 1996 met with a lethal Turkish-Cypriot response in two cases, with two Turkish-Cypriot soldiers shot by Greek Cypriots firing from the Dhekélia base a few weeks later. Northern officialdom and the Turkish army have repeatedly accused UN personnel of leaking strategic information to the Greek Cypriots, with resultant restrictions on UNFICYP movements in North Cyprus, and signs forbidding passage of UN vehicles near sensitive military sites.

However tolerated UN personnel may be individually, many feel that their continued presence merely delays the day of reckoning – hopefully non-violent– between the two Cypriot communities, and that the islanders should sooner rather than later be left to their own devices. Such sentiments are increasingly endorsed at the UN Command, no doubt enhanced by the arrears in maintenance payments to the UN running to hundreds of millions of dollars. Until now the troop-contributing countries themselves have been footing most of the bill, which runs to $25 million yearly. The Swedes left Cyprus in 1988, saying they would not serve indefinitely without tangible progress towards a settlement. Denmark withdrew its troops in December 1992, and the Canadian contingent followed in June 1993, leaving the UK with the main burden of peacekeeping in the central Sectors II and III, to either side of Nicosia – essentially a reversion to pre-1964 conditions. Somewhat ironically, Britain's Falklands adversaries, the Argentines, have (along with some Bolivians) replaced the Danes and Canadians in Sector I (the westernmost zone), while in Sector IV, around Famagusta, Slovakian, Uruguayan and Chilean troops predominate. There is also a corps of civilian UN police, at the moment mostly Australians, joined by a smaller contingent of Hungarians, Dutch and a dwindling Irish presence – altogether a force barely 900 strong, now rather outnumbered by civilian employees of service contractors.

These departures and reductions make it less probable that a fair system of assessing contributions from UN member states will be devised, an increasingly pressing need in light of the multiplying number of UN expeditions elsewhere since 1992. Yet UNFICYP will continue to be a Cyprus player as long as no definitive political settlement is reached, and probably for some time thereafter – the failed Annan Plan envisaged UN forces as one of the components guaranteeing its peaceful implementation.

the Attila Line. Still, certain highlights can be easily taken in while in transit between Nicosia and either the Tróödhos or the coast, and as such make worthwhile stops.

## Peristeróna

Heading west from Nicosía towards the Soléa or Marathássa districts of the Tróödhos, you've a long diversion around the disused airport in UNFICYP territory; 34km along, the village of **PERISTERÓNA** straddles a usually dry stream. The five-domed, tenth-century **church of Áyii Varnávas and Hilárion** on the riverbank is very handsome even just from the outside, but hang about purposefully and the café proprietor next door will appear with the key. The architecture inside is imposing, with its pair of apsed aisles separated from the nave by arches, though there's not much else to see: a surviving sixteenth-century wall painting of King David, another twelfth-century one of the Virgin and Child, the huge contemporary *témblon* and an antique chest of uncertain date in the narthex depicting the siege of a castle.

The CTO makes much of the church's juxtaposition with a **mosque** a couple of hundred metres southwest, one of Cyprus's oldest and finest, as a token of the supposedly long, peaceful co-existence of the two main island communities. Perhaps ironically, then, the Turkish Cypriots accused vengeful Greek Cypriots of setting fire to it in April 1976, though any damage seems to have since been patched up. The square groundplan with its high superstructure and arched, tracery-laden windows is decidedly Lusignan – prompting suspicions that this is in fact a converted church. The grounds are locked and fenced to prevent vandalism (though the minaret is infested with pigeons), but the front door may be ajar for peeks into the vaulted interior.

## Tamassos and Áyios Iraklídhios

Ancient Tamassos and Áyios Iraklídhios convent, some 22km southwest of Nicosia, can easily be combined with a day-visit to the monastery of Makherás (see p.264), or longer forays into Pitsyliá (see p.255). From central Nicosia, the route out passes through the suburb of Stróvolos, and then the village of Káto Dhefterá.

### Tamassos

One of the oldest-known Cypriot settlements, **Tamassos** owed its existence to extensive local deposits of copper, first exploited in the Early Bronze Age. In Homer's *Odyssey*, Athena went to "Temese" to trade iron for copper; later the revenues from the local mines accrued to the Phoenicians, the kings of Salamis and the biblical Herod, though these beneficiaries fail to give a clear idea of who was actually living, working or ruling at Tamassos itself. Excavations since 1975 have revealed the foundations of a Classical temple of Aphrodite/Astarte with traces of copper on the floor, implying, as at Kition, that metallurgy was considered sacred and that the priests controlled the deposits. Continuing the metallic and mercenary theme, local farmers dug up a life-size bronze statue of Apollo in 1836 – and hacked it apart, selling the bits to a scrap dealer. The head was salvaged and eventually found its way into the British Museum, though again it tells us little about Tamassan culture since it was made in Athens during the fifth century.

The **site** (Tues–Fri 9am–3pm, Sat & Sun 10am–3pm; C£0.75) exposed to date consists of about half an acre of jumbled foundations, on a slight slope overlooking grain fields at the northeast edge of the modern village of Politikó. The most interesting items are two sixth-century BC **subterranean tombs**, excavated in the 1890s but partially looted before then; the pitched roof of the larger, double-chambered tomb still shows a hole made by the thieves. The sandstone masonry has been cleverly carved in places to imitate wood and bolts appropriate to wooden doors, a style reminiscent of the "house tombs" of Anatolian Lycia.

### Áyios Iraklídhios convent

The **convent of Áyios Iraklídhios** (Agios Irakleidios), near Tamassos, honours Cyprus's first bishop-saint, a native of the region, who guided the apostles Paul and Barnabas from Larnaca to Tamassos during their missionary journey across Cyprus. They subsequently ordained Iraklidhios (Heracleidius) first bishop of Tamassos, and legend has it he was martyred on this spot at the age of sixty. By 400 AD a commemorative monastery of some sort had been established here, to be destroyed and rebuilt a number of times; the last reconstruction took place in 1773, though the present *katholikón* is three centuries older. After twice housing monks, it was taken over as a ruin in 1963 by an order of nuns, who transformed it as you see today; this was in fact the only convent on the island during Makarios's time.

To find the convent, drive through Politikó village until you see the obvious compound on a slight rise to the south. Inside (group visits only Mon, Tues & Thurs 9am–noon), it's a peaceful, domestic, ship-shape world, alive with birdsong: canaries from the aviary are for sale, along with pickled capers. A dozen or so sisters read missals, water the well-tended flowerbeds or doze near sheets of newspaper laid down to catch droppings from the nesting swallows. In the *katholikón*, you'll be shown a smudged fresco of the two apostles baptizing Iraklidhios; **reliquaries** containing his purported forearm and skull; some icons; and the sole exposed portion of an old **mosaic floor** regrettably covered over by modern tiling. From the side chapel to the south, a narrow stairway descends to a small **catacomb** where it is said the saint lived his last years and was buried.

## Perakhorió, Dháli and around

Heading south of the capital towards either Larnaca or Limassol, monuments near the two adjacent villages of Perakhorió and Dháli are worth a short halt if you've time. You wouldn't, however, make a special trip, and both places lie out of reach of the Nicosia urban bus system.

### Perakhorió

**PERAKHORIÓ** (Pera Chorio) is visited mainly for the sake of the twelfth-century church of **Áyii Apóstoli**, perched evocatively on a hill to the west, surrounded by the village churchyard (the key tends to be in the door). Inside, the contemporaneous **frescoes** are disappointing – surviving fragments appear to be of the same style as the work at Asínou, and if you've toured the Tróödhos you needn't feel guilty about missing them. Highlights include two from among a troupe of angels lining the drumless dome, just below a badly damaged *Pandokrátor*; two shepherds conversing, their shoulder bags hanging from a nearby tree, while the infant Jesus is bathed in a rather rustic *Nativity*; and a somewhat smudged Virgin in the conch of the apse, flanked by Peter and Paul. If you need a meal, the *Peristeri* taverna comes recommended.

### Dháli and ancient Idalion

Four kilometres east, **DHÁLI** (Dali) is an altogether busier place, a formerly mixed village perilously close to the Attila Line. (Potamiá, 3km down the valley beside the buffer zone, remains bi-communal, though there are just a few dozen Turkish Cypriots left – among them Fatma Mehmet, another "star" of the recommended film *Our Wall* – as against their former three-to-two predominance.) On the main thoroughfare into the village the *Kendron Iy Myli* rates highly for a night out. Nearby, in an annexe of Gallery Dhiakhroniki in Nicosia, there's a permanent exhibition entitled "Cyprus Yesterday and Today, Through Arts and Crafts".

The main local interest, however, is not in the village, but a few hundred metres outside, to the south. Here the fortified hillside site of **ancient Idalion** is fairly obvious, though the place is still under excavation, with portions periodically closed to the public. Deep pits and courses of masoned wall in various states of exposure are of essentially specialist interest, but 1990s digs uncovered several giant *pithária* (urns) which, after cleaning and repair, are supposed to be reinstalled where found, under protective canopies.

The small city here dated from the Bronze Age and survived almost until the Roman era. American consul-turned-antiquarian Luigi Palma di Cesnola spent several summers here, plundering (according to his boast) 10,000 tombs; yet

## Greek place names

| Old system | New system | Greek lettering |
|---|---|---|
| Áyii Omoloyíti | Agioi Omologitoi | ΑΓΙΟΙ ΟΜΟΛΟΓΙΤΟΙ |
| Áyios Dhométios | Agios Dometios | ΑΓΙΟΣ ΔΟΜΕΤΙΟΣ |
| Áyios Iraklídhios | Agios Irakleidios | ΑΓΙΟΣ ΗΡΑΚΛΕΙΔΙΟΣ |
| Áyios Sozómenos | Agios Sozomenos | ΑΓΙΟΣ ΣΩΖΟΜΕΝΟΣ |
| Dháli | Dali | ΔΑΛΙ |
| Éngomi | Egkomi | ΕΓΚΩΜΗ |
| Idhálion | Idalion | ΙΔΑΛΙΟΝ |
| Kaïmaklí | Kaïmakli | ΚΑΪΜΑΚΛΙ |
| Laïkí Yitoniá | Laïki Geitonia | ΛΑΪΚΗ ΓΕΙΤΟΝΙΑ |
| Nicosia | Lefkosía | ΛΕΥΚΩΣΙΑ |
| Panayía Khrysaliniótissa | Panagia Chrysaliniotissa | ΠΑΝΑΓΙΑ ΧΡΥΣΑΛΙΝΙΟΤΙΣΣΑ |
| Pedhiéos | Pediaios | ΠΕΔΙΑΙΟΣ |
| Perakhorió | Pera Chorio | ΠΕΡΑΧΩΡΙΟ |
| Peristeróna | Peristerona | ΠΕΡΙΣΤΕΡΩΝΑ |
| Potamiá | Potamia | ΠΟΤΑΜΙΑ |
| Stróvolos | Strovolos | ΣΤΡΟΒΟΛΟΣ |
| Tamassós | Tamassos | ΤΑΜΑΣΣΟΣ |

such was the archeological richness of the area that local farmers subsequently ploughed up many painted votive figurines of Aphrodite, the most important local deity, and an American team continues digging. Legend places the killing of Aphrodite's lover Adonis by a wild boar in the area, and in early spring you can still see red anemones, which supposedly sprang from his blood, poking out among the rocks here.

### Áyios Sozómenos: Áyios Mámas church

If you've come this far, it's eminently worthwhile pressing on to see one of the most evocative minor Gothic ruins in Cyprus, near Potamiá. Unless you're already at Dháli, leave the A1 motorway at Exit 6 (posted for Potamiá) for some contrastingly unromantic Mesaória scenery during the approach from the northeast: a vast industrial estate just east of the highway, then stinking cattle ranches. About 2km before Potamiá, bear north onto a minor but paved road, following a sign in the standard monument convention announcing "Áyios Sozómenos"; this immediately crosses the Yialiás stream, with hay fields and orientalist palm trees heralding your arrival at the ruined, mud-brick village of **Áyios Sozómenos**, sheltered under a low palisade.

The romantic, triple-apsed ruined church, apparently (despite the road-sign) dedicated to **Áyios Mámas**, sits on high ground at the southwest edge of the village; dating from the early 1500s, it was built in a retrograde Lusignan style of a century or two earlier, and possibly never finished. The site is kept fenced and securely locked, but you can easily admire the delicate arcades dividing the nave from the two aisles, and the monumental west door flanked by colonnettes with elaborate capitals. The two south portals were unhappily bricked up at some later date.

Áyios Sozómenos itself has lain abandoned since some February 1964 inter-communal incidents, in which local cadres of TMT killed two Potamiá Greek-Cypriots, while the next day Greek-Cypriot police took revenge by attacking the place, with more heavy casualties on both sides.

# Travel details

## Buses

Nicosia to: Ayía Nápa (Mon–Sat 1 daily, on EMAN; 1hr 20min); Kakopetriá (Mon–Sat 11 daily, plus 2 on Sun in July/Aug, on Clarios; 1hr 20min); Kámbos via Kýkko monastery (Mon–Sat 1 daily at noon, on Kambos Bus; 2hr 30min); Larnaca (Mon–Fri 6 daily, Sat 3, on Intercity; 40min); Limassol (Mon–Fri 10 daily, Sat & Sun 4, on LLL, plus Mon–Sat 1 daily on ALEPA; 1hr); Páfos (Mon–Sat 1 daily, via Limassol, on ALEPA; 2hr); Plátres (Mon–Sat 1 daily at 12.30pm, on Clarios, via the Marathássa valley; 2hr 30min); Protarás (1 daily at 3pm on PEAL; 1hr 20min); Tróödhos (Mon–Sat 1 daily, on Clarios; 2hr).

# The North

# The North

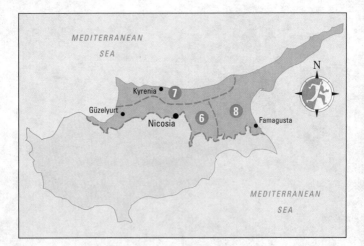

# Introduction

The Turkish Republic of Northern Cyprus (TRNC) came violently into existence in August 1974 as a refuge for beleaguered Turkish Cypriots: first as the zone occupied by the Turkish army, later as the interim Turkish Federated State of Cyprus, and finally, by a unilateral declaration of independence in 1983, as the TRNC. Recognized diplomatically by no state except Turkey, its creator and main sponsor, North Cyprus possesses at first glance a Ruritanian charm. Dwindling fleets of antique Hillmans, Triumphs and Austins tool about (or moulder abandoned in fields); policemen in grey imperial summer twill control intersections. During the mid-to-late-1990s signs of prosperity – often from dubious sources – appeared: fleets of recent-model cars, representatives for most European brands of consumer durables, cash dispensers with queues of locals. But the collapse of the mainland Turkish economy in early 2000 dragged the North along with it, and the place spent two-plus years in its worst crisis since 1974 – which has served, from the Turkish-Cypriot point of view anyway, as a spur to finding a final, equitable solution of the island's division.

## Public relations problems

While travelling around you'll see a number of conditions contributing to the North's image as a pariah state, and some obvious results of that status. The ubiquitousness of the **Turkish army** is immediately off-putting: although there are now fewer no-go areas than before, barbed-wire-fenced camps and unaesthetic military memorials abound, and an estimated 30,000 mainland conscripts still lend a barracks air to Kyrenia and north Nicosia in particular – even if they're now allowed to circulate in "civvies" while off-duty.

Although nearly 20,000 Greek Cypriots chose to stay in the Karpaz (Kárpas) peninsula and around Kyrenia in 1974, and approximately 1000 Maronites on the Koruçam (Kormak'ti) peninsula, **systematic harassment** by the army and the civil authorities has reduced those numbers to roughly 400 and 140 respectively. Since the "border" became porous in April 2003, their lot – and future prospects – have improved no end, but there is still a long way to go before their treatment meets the standards expected of an EU-candidate territory.

The much-publicized **desecration** of Greek churches and graveyards is largely true, though Southern Cypriot public relations artists occasionally overstate their case: the Byzantine monastery of Akhiropi'tos near Kyrenia and the monastery of Khrysóstomos near Nicosia, both now occupied by the Turkish army, had already been partly deconsecrated and used by the Cypriot National Guard before 1974. Greek Cypriots tend to attribute the blame for desecration where it usually belongs – with the invading mainland army or settlers – since for many of the Turkish Cypriots, Orthodox shrines, monasteries and catacombs had also been sacred. An outstanding example is Áyios Mámas in Güzelyurt (Mórfou), which was kept in good repair, unlooted, for three decades before being returned to Orthodox use in September 2004. But there have been instances of native Turkish Cypriots applying axes or sledgehammers to abandoned church interiors and cemeteries, and little evidence of repair or security for such premises.

## Arrested development

Overall there's a feeling of grass growing between the cracks, often literally – this atmosphere of **dereliction** can be attributed partly to the fact that the Turkish army in 1974 bit off rather more than the 120,000 Turkish Cypriots then resident on the island could themselves chew. Much of the North is under-utilized, its rural villages half-empty: citrus orchards a couple of kilometres from Kyrenia or Güzelyurt die of neglect despite often abundant supplies of water to irrigate them. Ironic, this, in light of how *Yeşilada* (Green Isle) was the traditional Ottoman epithet for Cyprus, a tribute to the groves and orchards which dotted the island until the eighteenth century. The public **infrastructure**, too, is starved of improvement funds, one result of keeping the civil service rolls artificially swollen – the bill footed mostly by Turkey – to stem a brain drain. Major facilities, save for Ercan airport and Kyrenia's commercial harbour, are kept ticking over, but no more; improved, enlarged roads are limited to a single strip west of Kyrenia, another between Nicosia and Güzelyurt (Mórfou) and the vital Nicosia–Famagusta–Kyrenia highway. Except for some Saudi investment, most post-1974 international aid is shunted to the South; there's diminishing support from Turkey, which lately has had other, more pressing problems. Chronic water shortages are supposed to be alleviated by a submarine pipeline from the abundant waterfalls of Manavgat on Turkey's south coast, though it won't be completed before 2007 at the earliest. Meanwhile small dams (as in the South) have appeared everywhere, and giant balloons full of fresh water have occasionally been floated across from Anatolia, despite a tendency to lose most of the contents through leakage.

It was widely assumed that sufficient aid would materialize, and the place would really take off, following **international recognition**, so far withheld. At various times since 1974 certain pro-Turkish and/or Muslim nations like South Korea, Azerbaijan, Bangladesh and Pakistan, with turbulent origins or ethnic conflicts similar to North Cyprus, have considered extending recognition – but always backed down in the face of Greek or Greek-Cypriot threats in the international arena. In 1994 the Greek Cypriots intensified their pressure campaign by convincing the European Court of Justice to ban any agricultural produce or clothing originating in the North, which now must be sneaked into Europe under the Turkish quota. This has effectively brought the Northern economy to its knees by limiting exports to about $60 million annually, and forced it to rely on other, less traditional foreign-currency earners. For much of the mid-1990s the TRNC was heavily dependent on casino and sex tourism from Turkey, but this inevitably entailed progressive penetration of the economy by mainland Turkish gangsters, with the acquiescence of the relevant authorities.

The North has also pinned its hopes on matriculation fees at its various **universities**. At last count there were eight of them, attended by over 20,000 students (more than ten percent of the population); the language of instruction is English, a choice designed to attract students from the Gulf States, the Indian subcontinent and Africa. Most of these institutions, it must be said, are little more than glorified crammers or miniature old-style UK polytechnics, with (often) fifth-rate instructors who wouldn't even get an interview elsewhere, though the Eastern Mediterranean University in Famagusta has a solid reputation – and (tellingly) was recently rated among the "top ten universities in Turkey (sic)".

Owing to the Greek-Cypriot orchestrated embargo of the stigmatized North, and overpriced, artificially long air links from northern Europe, conventional, family **tourism** is hardly more developed than in 1974. The trans-island freedom of movement since 2003 has inevitably brought changes, most obviously vast numbers of trippers (and overnighters) from the South, but especially off-season you can still enjoy the TRNC's sandy beaches, Crusader monuments and often excellent food in relative solitude, at a leisurely pace so in contrast to that of the busy South. Especially off the beaten track, people's helpfulness and hospitality is also reminiscent of the Mediterranean of the 1960s and 1970s.

## Native islanders vs Anatolians

The best lands and houses were **allotted** in 1975 to refugees from the South according to a complex point system; people were credited points for both commercial and residential property according to the value and type of such assets left behind. This government scheme was, not surprisingly, prone to abuse so that inequities in the distribution of real estate were widespread.

Poorer, isolated spots – fit mainly for goat-grazing – were assigned to **settlers** from Anatolia. Turkey, especially between 1975 and 1977, treated the North as a transportation colony (as indeed it had after the 1570 conquest), off-loading families of 1974 campaign veterans, surplus urban underclass, landless peasants, and even low-grade criminals and psychiatric cases, until the native islanders mobilized to oppose the process, and sent the worst elements packing. As no accurate census has been conducted on Cyprus since 1973, estimating current immigrant numbers is an inexact science, with guesses ranging from 50,000 to 100,000 (80,000 seems most probable). Their fate remains a big sticking point in any potential peace agreement, and their presence has caused chronic tension between native Turkish Cypriots and Turks, with the former considering them-selves to have a higher standard of living and education. Relatively few of the settlers participated in the conspicuous consumption of the late 1990s, and their villages are unmistakably backward, dusty places reverted fifty years in time. The islanders pejoratively dub mainlanders *karasakal* or "black beard"; Turkey returns the compliment in a long-standing, patronizing quip characterizing Anatolia as *anavatan* (mother homeland) and North Cyprus as *yavru vatan* (baby homeland).

Starting in the early 1990s, a second wave of quasi-settlers came to the island, semi-legal migrant workers who have even lower status and less job or residence security than the original colonists; concentrated in Nicosia's old town, they are blamed for such crime as northern Cyprus has. The only other significant emigrant community is of Pakistanis, apparently all from a handful of clans in the Punjab; as Muslims from a state generally supportive of the TRNC, with valuable English skills, they are easily granted residence/citizenship rights.

Since 1974 the Turkish army and nationalist ideologues in local government have acted to dilute the British-ness and Cyprus-ness of the North, not only with settlement programmes, but also by erecting myriad busts of Atatürk and stark monuments commemorating the events of 1974. But a fair amount of pre-1974 *Kıbrıs Türktür* (Cyprus is Turkish) graffiti, scrawled by the TMT, the 1950s-to-1970s Turkish-nationalist action group, suggests that such sentiments are not completely new; accordingly, the North has indeed been subject to a campaign of **creeping annexation by Turkey**. First, the Cypriot pound was replaced by the unstable old Turkish lira; next, branches or affiliates of Turkish banks replaced many island ones; then, telephones were completely integrated into the Turkish system; and finally (as in the South), metric measurements were applied to motoring. Northerners have successfully resisted giving up left-hand driving, the most conspicuous remaining token of their separate identity. Those who object to the process say all this is only to be expected, pointing out that, after all, "Mersin 10" – the special post code used to circumvent the Interna-tional Postal Union's boycott of the North – just means the tenth county of Mersin province, in Turkey.

## Obstacles to reconciliation

Until the barriers came down in April 2003, many adults in the North, not having spoken to a Greek Cypriot in three decades, found it hard to believe that *énosis* has almost no support in the South now. On a human level, they felt sorry for the northern Greeks who were forced from their homes, but considered the Attila Line, guarded by mainland Turks, as the best guarantee of personal safety. Those born since 1970 or so were indoctrinated in school to believe that EOKA activists will make kebab out of them should the existing barriers fall. When they did in fact come down on April 23, 2003, the fear-mongers were proven wrong, as since that date most people's behaviour has been exemplary and there have been fewer "incidents" than you might expect at the average UK football match.

But new, or renewed, friendships and general person-to-person civility won't be a substitute for the hard graft of constructing a polity that functions. The position of more accommodating Turkish Cypriots has always been that the South must decisively renounce the ideal of *énosis* and make the most of an independent, federal republic. Conciliatory Turkish Cypriots want to see veteran EOKA figures purged from positions of high responsibility in the South. What happened instead was (in 1992) the early release from prison of 1974 coup protagonist Nikos Sampson, and in 1995 the rehabilitation of 62 coup-supporting civil servants, both actions causing enormous offence in the TRNC. Subsequent policies promulgated by the South, from the new transliteration scheme to accelerated rearmament, plus continued adversarial actions in the international arena, have compounded the damage. Such examples of continuing EOKA influence are considered as further evidence of an underlying, unreconstructed Greek-Cypriot attitude, summarizable as "You (Turkish Cypriots) are just 400-year squatters. Now get lost." At one point the Makarios government offered money and a one-way plane ticket to any Turkish Cypriot willing to resettle overseas, while the Orthodox Church encouraged Greek-Cypriot purchase of Turkish-Cypriot property at double its value, before the violent **coercion** of EOKA spawned open hatred and, ultimately, partition.

Not that the North was slow to devise provocations of its own on an official or semi-official level. From 1999 to early 2004, in response to growing unrest and opposition, the Denktaş regime or its extension, the UHH – essentially a resurrection of the TMT – stepped up **harassment of reconciliationists** in the North: hounding independent newspapers and websites, physically attacking demonstrators and journalists, prosecuting trade unionists and opposition politicans, and interfering with intercommunal meetings in the buffer zone.

All of this acted to continually replenish the large **exile** community: while about 75,000 native Turkish Cypriots still reside on the island, easily three times that figure live overseas, mostly in Turkey, Britain, Australia and North America. (Proportionately, there has not been such a diaspora from the Greek side.) Since 1974, not enough Turkish Cypriots abroad have responded to their government's pleas to return and "rebuild the homeland"; instead there's been a slow leak outwards of those fed up with the settlers and political and economic stagnation – and of military-age lads fearful of two years' compulsory service under the harsh supervision of mainland Turkish officers. It now seems certain that, in a population of about 200,000 (including the more or less permanent figure of 30,000 soldiers and 20,000 students), the number of mainland settlers exceeds the level of native islanders. Amongst the remaining Turkish Cypriots, rentier status – holding down a civil service post or being a landlord – seems to be the prime ambition, leaving the grunt work in hotels, kitchens and building sites to mainlanders, Pakistanis and even a few Brits. Failing that, many local and overseas Turkish Cypriots have opted for cashing in on their post-1974 property titles by selling up to developers before any settlement renders them worthless – and thus creating more inconvenient "facts on the ground" for intercommunal negotiators.

## Economic and infrastructure interdependence

Cyprus is simply too small ever to be hermetically divided: its regional economies, if not always its peoples, were too **interknit** under past unitary administrations. Until the 1950s, intermarriage (or clandestine sexual relations) between the two communities – and attendant religous apostasy in either direction – were far more common than generally admitted, and numbers of relationships have blossomed since the barriers came down. At present about 10,000 Turkish Cypriots work in the South, most of them commuting daily; these numbers are up more than threefold since April 2003.

Huge flocks of sheep graze the grain-stubble of the central plain, the Mesarya; even before the events of April 2003, a steady supply of them – along with market-garden produce – headed clandestinely south across the supposedly impervious Attila Line, in exchange for tractors and other manufactured goods **smuggled** in the opposite direction. "Black" money from the South's large contingent of illegal immigrant workers, many in the sex industry, heads North for wiring home to central Europe or Asia via the less regulated banking system of the TRNC. Cheap Turkish cigarettes and booze are exchanged across the Line for cash or the much-prized Greek-Cypriot brandy to such an extent that both sides feel obliged to enforce customs limits. However, "**legitimate**" **trade** is growing by leaps and bounds in accord with the so-called Green Line Agreements promulgated in August 2004 by the EU.

Not many people know that the Turkish-Cypriot *Vakıf*, or Islamic benevolent fund, has a substantial interest in Cyprus Airways, the Greek-Cypriot airline; the proportion's been reduced since shares were split, but the Vakıf is not about to sell up. Until the North's own dynamo came on-line in 1995, the South provided the North with electricity from its plant at Dhekélia, as a "humanitarian" gesture (but also to ensure that Nicosia's joint sewage system, based in the North, was not interfered with).

## Momentum towards a solution: a change of heart

Despite their overwhelming economic and diplomatic advantages, it was the Greek Cypriots who historically pressed the hardest for a **resolution** of the island's division, whether prior to or part of an EU-accession deal. The Northerners always felt that they had more to gain than lose from persistence of the status quo; their "enclave" was more comfortable than the besieged ones of 1963–74, with more ways out.

But with the local economy in free-fall after 1999, and the ruling elite responding increasingly harshly to dissent, the pendulum of initiative swung decisively to the North, even as pro-settlement sentiment stagnated or cooled in the South. Beginning in late 2001 and continuing into early 2003, periodic, massive **street demonstrations** in Nicosia – occasionally comprising nearly half the civilian population of the North – put increasing pressure on hardliners in the government. These gatherings, a new civilian government in Turkey and yet another UN censure of northern leader Rauf Denktaş for intransigence directly influenced the latter's decision to **open the barriers of the Green/ Attila Line** to free movement on April 23.

The opposition political parties and NGOs backing the demonstrations were also instrumental, in the face of continued threats and dire predictions by the northern government, in mobilizing the population in favour of both **EU membership** – whether or not Turkey ever joins – and a "yes" vote to the UN-promulgated **Annan Plan** for a solution to the island's partition. On the day (April 24, 2004), the two linked concepts carried in the North by a margin of 65:35, but unfortunately this was not matched by approval in the South. Reunification advocates confessed that they felt severely let down by their Greek-Cypriot counterparts, and to date not enough benefits of EU membership have accrued to northerners (unless they have secured Republic of Cyprus passports). But generally the reconciliationists are on the ascendant, and hopeful of a final breakthrough once Denktaş leaves office in April 2005.

# 6

# North Nicosia and around

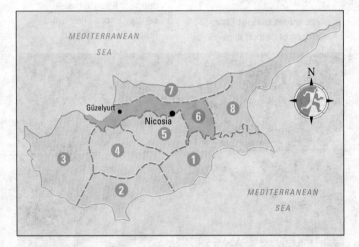

CHAPTER 6 # Highlights

✳ **Büyük Han** This court-yarded inn, restored over a decade to its former glory, is the most impressive of Cyprus's purpose-built Ottoman Turkish architecture. See p.323

✳ **Selimiye Camii and Bedesten** Once the churches of Ayía Sofía and St Nicholas respectively and boasting fine Gothic vaulting and portal relief carving. See p.324

✳ **Arabahmet district** Entire terraces of colourful, over-hanging plaster and stone houses, like their slightly less grand counterparts in the south of the city, have been skilfully restored. See p.327

✳ **Ancient Soli** Excellent mosaics are protected by an unsightly if necessary shelter. See p.334

✳ **Palace of Vouni** Perched high above the sea, this mysterious palace was used for less than a century in pre-Hellenistic times. See p.335

△ Büyük Han

# 6

# North Nicosia
# and around

Although most visitors to North Cyprus, as with the South, will be interested in reaching the coastal resort of their choice as quickly as possible, it's worth remembering that **north Nicosia** and its suburb villages *are* to a great extent North Cyprus, with nearly a third of its population. The events of 1974 and North Cyprus's UDI of 1983 resulted in the city becoming the capital of a never-recognized (and now very probably provisional) state. What the relatively few day-visitors to north Nicosia are after, though, is its concentration of Gothic and Ottoman monuments; there's little else available for the casual tourist. Excursions elsewhere in North Cyprus's patch of Nicosia district head exclusively west past the agricultural centre of **Güzelyurt**, with a museum and newly reconsecrated monastery, to the intriguing ancient sites of **Soli** and **Vouni** on the coast. Inland from these, the foothill oasis of **Lefke** makes a relaxing destination, though again with few specific attractions.

## North Nicosia

**NORTH NICOSIA** (*Lefkoşa* in Turkish, but actually a fairly accurate rendition of the Greek-Cypriot dialect pronunciation of *Lefkosía*) is a much sleepier place than the southern portion of the city, with about a quarter as many inhabitants (barely 60,000, including the satellite villages of Ortaköy and Gönyeli). Obviously the history of the two sectors, enclosed at their core by the same Venetian wall, was largely shared until 1974; the approaching Turkish army quite deliberately ensured that all traditionally Turkish districts in the northwest of the city fell under their control.

The justification for north Nicosia's emergence as capital of the North, and indefinite continuance in that role, is epitomized by the story behind the huge Turkish-Cypriot flag picked out in white- and red-painted rocks on the foothills of the Kyrenia range, just north of town, placed for maximum provocative effect on south Nicosia. The current inhabitants of the nearest village, Taşkent (Vounó), all came from Tókhni (near Khirokitía) in the South; on August 15, 1974 most of that village's Turkish-Cypriot men of military age were massacred

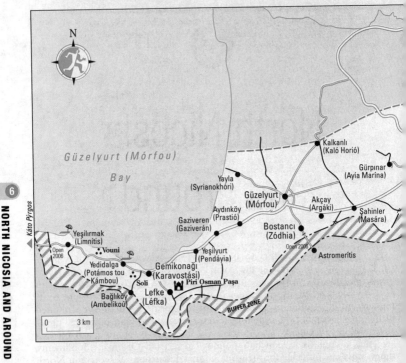

there by an EOKA-B contingent. For the widows, orphans and very few survivors, responsible for the rock-flag, the continued existence of North Cyprus is insurance against a recurrence of such nightmares. A further reminder of the past is Lefkoşa's Küçük Kaymaklı district (formerly Omórfita suburb), a vast area of desolate houses, devastated between December 22 and 25, 1963 by Nikos Sampson and his EOKA irregulars (see p.439). A cenotaph honours the many casualties, as does a new (seldom-used) mosque, and the ruins have been left untouched as a memorial, shown (until very recently at least) to schoolchildren to keep fear and hatred of the Greek Cypriots alive.

Much more than in south Nicosia, the reality of remoter corners in the old town is desolation: especially in the eastern half of the Turkish sector, dust-devils eddy on the battered streets, windows are broken even on used buildings, and fine domestic and monumental architecture seems preserved more through inertia than any conscious effort. Outside the walls there is little of interest, with colonial-era brownstones being outstripped by the tatty modern constructions that increasingly disfigure the whole island. Within the walls live the most impoverished Anatolian settlers, principally ethnic Arabs and Kurds from Turkey's Hatay district, enhancing the Anatolian-villagey atmosphere; native Turkish Cypriots have almost without exception fled to the roomier, more desirable suburbs.

## Points of arrival

The small size of north Nicosia makes arrival relatively painless; junctions are fairly well signed, though when driving it's easy to get trapped in one-way

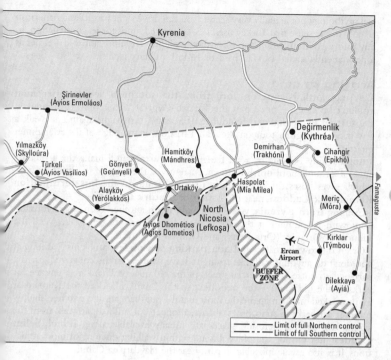

systems, or to leave roundabouts at the wrong exit. The way to individual attractions is not well marked, though once you've found them, they do have bilingual identification placards.

### Arriving by air

**Ercan airport** lies southeast of town, around 20km by road (off the dual carriageway towards Famagusta) and rather abruptly signed, with little advance warning. It got a thorough overhaul in 2002–2003, but still has few amenities: no bank ATMs, money-exchange bureaux or car rental booths, just a second baggage carousel and a tourist information post (open for arriving flights) to show for two years of hard labour. There's also no public bus service for the airport; if you arrive as part of a package, you'll meet a courier who bundles you into a tour-agency **minibus** for transfer to your resort, or hands over your pre-reserved car. Otherwise, a **taxi** transfer to Kyrenia will cost £15–20, to Famagusta £20–25 and to north Nicosia about £5 (sterling notes gladly accepted, change given in Turkish lira). Journey time to central Kyrenia is about forty minutes. Given the total lack of banking facilities here, you should come prepared with some £5 and £10 sterling notes handy for taxi-drivers. (Neither is there a restaurant in the departures area, just two small cafés and a clutch of duty-free stalls where you can spend your last lira on booze, perfume and tobacco, though it's best to wait till the mandatory layover in Turkey, where you'll have a better choice of goods).

Whenever Ercan is shut for any upgrade, flights are diverted to a predominantly military airport, 3km south of **Geçitkale** (Lefkóniko, Lefkonuk), nearer to the Famagusta resort area. This is the so-called "secret American base" of conspiratorial mythology, not actually very secret (you can drive right past it) and American mainly in the sense that Turkey used US-originated funds for its construction. In any future political settlement, this facility will play an important role – either as a permanently staffed NATO base, or Turkish military facility.

### Arriving by land

Entering north Nicosia **on foot from the southern sector**, orientation couldn't be easier – once past the Turkish-Cypriot checkpoint, turn right at the first set of stoplights (Memduh Asaf Sokağı), turn right again and walk a few paces to begin a tour on the Zahra bastion, at the edge of the Arabahmet quarter.

Approaching Nicosia by road **from Famagusta**, you'll make the acquaintance of a roundabout north of town, currently at the edge of the built-up area, which gives buses the opportunity to barrel south to the **bus terminal** on Kemal Aşık Caddesi, near the corner of **Atatürk Caddesi**.

Coming **from Kyrenia**, you'll be caught up in another, even larger, roundabout-with-monument at the northwest edge of the city, poised between the suburbs of Ortaköy (Orta Keuy) and Gönyeli (Geunyeli).

Given the town's small population, **parking** presents few problems – as long as you don't do anything rash like trying to leave your car in the congested, narrow, part-pedestrianized commercial streets of the old quarter. There are a few fee car parks in the old town – the ones next to the Büyük Han and the Kumarcılar Hanı, marked on the map, are the most useful – but there are also two free, slightly remoter car parks in Arabahmet district, a longer but still feasible walk from the sights. Unrestricted kerbside spaces are usually available along İkinci Selim Caddesi, just outside the old walls and within walking distance of most attractions. It is also usually possible to park near the Haydarpaşa Camii.

## Orientation, information and accommodation

The northwestern roundabout shunts traffic in every direction, particularly southeast along the road which eventually splits into **Mehmet Akif Caddesi** (universally known as **Dereboyu** after the neighbourhood it threads through) and **Bedreddin Demirel Caddesi**. Bedreddin Demirel and Kemal Aşık come very close to meeting at the **Kyrenia Gate**, the most historic entrance to north Nicosia's bit of the old town; just inside it, **İnönü Meydanı** marks the north end of **Girne Caddesi**, the main commercial thoroughfare and continuation of Lídhras on the Greek side. Partway along its length is the swelling known as **Atatürk Meydanı**, effectively the city centre.

Like the rest of the town's tourist infrastructure, provision of information tends to be haphazard. A **tourist information** booth stands just past the Turkish-Cypriot checkpoint near the Ledra Palace crossing, at the disposal of those crossing on foot from the South. The main office is upstairs in the Ministry of Culture complex immediately opposite the Haydarpaşa Camii (Mon–Fri 9am–3pm).

North Nicosia has almost no international-standard tourist facilities, since few foreigners stay the night. There are just two government-approved **hotels**: the overpriced, 1962-vintage *Saray* at Sarayönü (☎228 31 15, ℱ228 48 08; ❹), the tallest, and arguably ugliest, building in the old quarter – though the rooftop restaurant (£1 admission, includes a drink) is well worth a visit for its superb views – and the smaller, more up-to-date *Royal-Germania* (☎228 76 21, Ⓦwww.city-royal.com; ❸), near the bus terminal at Kemal Aşık Cad 19. It's reasonably comfortable, with an indoor swimming pool and *hamam*.

# The City

North Nicosia's sights can be seen in a single longish day; as on the other side of the Green Line, you won't need to learn bus routes but should rely on good shoes. Wander the back streets the least bit away from the standard tourist circuit and you're an instant celebrity; stray too far off the main thoroughfares or get too close to the Line, though, and members of the Turkish armed forces may shadow (or even stop) you, particularly if you're carrying a camera.

Urban renewal, in accordance with the Master Plan (see p.275), has so far been limited to the pedestrianization of the bazaar and Arabahmet district, near the Green Line, the restoration of the Büyük Han, and ongoing restoration of some stately houses also in Arabahmet; you're made painfully aware of what a judicious influx of funding can accomplish.

## The ramparts

The five bastions lying wholly within the Turkish zone are not, with one exception (see below), put to as much use as on the Greek side, though the moats are nominally parkland. What used to be the vice-presidential residence in unitary republican days, on the Cephane (Quirini) bastion, is now the North Cypriot presidential palace – and a new grandiose structure was added beside the old in 2000. On the Musalla (Barbaro) bastion the army has erected a **National Struggle Museum** (daily: summer 9am–2pm; winter 9am–1pm & 2–4.45pm, but subject to arbitrary closure; £1), a predictable propaganda excercise in response to the one in south Nicosia.

Between these two ramparts stands the **Kyrenia Gate**, once the classic entry into the Turkish quarter, now stranded uselessly in the middle of Inönü Meydanı. In 1931, broad swathes were cut through the walls to either side of the gate to allow the passage of motor traffic, isolating it as a sort of pillbox-cum-guard house. The Venetians knew it as the Porta de la Proveditore, or "Gate of the Military Governor", and fitted it with a portcullis and still-visible lion of Saint Mark; after their victory, the Ottomans added an inscription lauding Allah as the "Opener of Gates".

## The Mevlevî tekke (Ethnography Museum)

Once inside the gate, almost the first thing on your left is the former Mevlevî dervish *tekke*, now home to a small **Ethnography Museum** (Mon–Fri: summer

### The teachings of the Mevlevî order

A *tekke* is the ceremonial hall of any Islamic mystical *tarikat* or order; the Mevlevî *tarikat* is the outgrowth of the teachings of Celaleddin Rumi, later known as the Mevlâna, whose life spanned most of the thirteenth century and took him from Balkh in Central Asia to Konya in Anatolia. He is most esteemed for the *Mathnawi*, a long devotional poem summarizing his teachings, which emphasized the individual soul's separation from God during earthly existence, and the power of Divine Love to draw it back to the Infinite. Quite scandalously to orthodox Muslims of the time, Rumi stressed music and dance as an expression of this mutual love and yearning, and the Mevlevî order became famous over the centuries for its *sema* or "whirling" ceremony. Musical accompaniment always included at least one *ney* or reed flute, whose plaintive tones have approximately the same range as the human voice. As the *Mathnawi* explains in metaphor, the lonely reed of the instrument has been uprooted from its reedbed as the soul has been separated from the Godhead, and its voice is like the lament of the human soul for reunion with the Infinite.

▲ Kyrenia & KTHY office

# NORTH NICOSIA (LEFKOŞA)

Yenişehir Mosque

Parcels ✉

Onur Air (TWI Travel)

**RESTAURANTS, CAFÉS & BARS**

| | |
|---|---|
| Amasyalı | 8 |
| Anibal | 5 |
| Avcılar | 1 |
| Bizim Ahır | 2 |
| Boghjalian Konak | 13 |
| Californian Bar & Grill | 3 |
| Hamur | 9 |
| Londra Pastanesi | 6 |
| El Sabor Latino | 11 |
| Sedir Café | 14 |
| Sila 4 | 12 |
| Umutlar | 10 |
| X-Mek | 4 |
| Yahya Usta | 7 |
| Yusuf Usta | 15 |

Australian Representative

British Council

Cephan (Quirin Bastio

Turkish-Cypriot Checkpoint

Zahra (Mula) Octagonal Bastion Fountain

NUR EFENDI SO

Arabahmet Camii

MUFT

Ledra Palace Hotel (UN Headquarters)

Derviş Paşa Kon

**ACCOMMODATION**

| | |
|---|---|
| Royal-Germania | A |
| Saray | B |

Armer Chur

SOUTH NICOSIA (Greek-Cypriot)

0     400m

Yiğitler Park

Kaytazağa (Roccas) Bastion

—·—·— Limit of full Northern control
——— Limit of full Southern control

9am–2pm; winter 9am–1pm & 2–4.45pm; £1.50). The Mevlevî order survived here as a vital *tarikat* until 1954, long after their proscription in Republican Turkey. As so often in Cyprus, the building, dating from the early seventeenth century, matches or exceeds the exhibits for interest. Focus of the interior is a fine pine-wood turning floor, just big enough for perhaps ten devotees; the former musicians' gallery is perched overhead. An archival photo shows one of the last

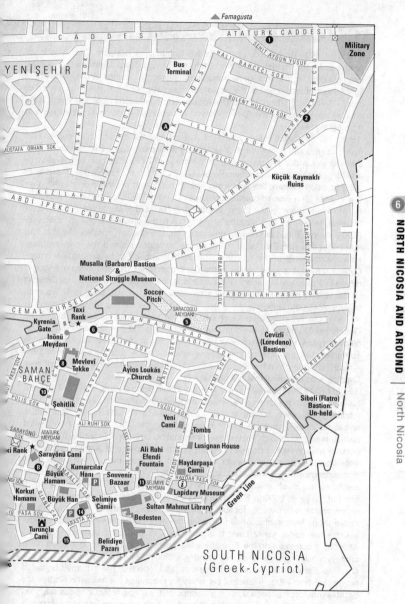

ceremonies: the *şeyh* or head of the order watches over six dervishes revolving in the confined space, while above in the gallery sit the players of a *ney* (reed flute), *oud* (Levantine lute) and *kudum* (paired drums), the instruments inextricably linked with Mevlevî observance. Today the same instruments occupy glass cases (with mannequins holding them); other displays include more archival photos, and – in a room to the side – a mock-up of the dervishes' refectory (communal

President, until April 2005, of the Turkish Republic of Northern Cyprus (and its predecessor the Turkish Federated State of Cyprus), **Rauf Denktaş** is a classic example of a big fish in a small pond, long enjoying a position in the world spotlight far out of proportion to the size of his realm. His non-recognition as a head of state – Denktaş's official title at UN-sponsored negotiations from 1974 until 2004 was "representative of the Turkish-Cypriot community" – has never prevented him from acting like one.

Born in the Soléa valley village of Áyios Epifánios (though his mother was from Loukrounoú, a now-derelict village in Páfos province), Denktaş trained as a barrister in London before serving as a protégé of Dr Fazil Küçük, later first vice-president of the unitary republic. Probably with the latter's knowledge, Denktaş in 1957 founded **Volkan**, the right-wing Turkish nationalist organization modelled on the lines of Sinn Fein to counter the Greek Cypriots' EOKA. This was succeeded by the even more militant and reactionary **TMT** (*Türk Mukavemet Teskilati* or "Turkish Resistance Organization"), analogous to the provisional IRA, banned (like EOKA) by the British but revived soon after independence. Officially, Denktaş had no connection with TMT after 1960, having accepted instead the more respectable chairmanship of the Turkish Communal Chamber. But he was expelled from Cyprus for indirect involvement in the December 1963 disturbances, and sought refuge in Turkey (ex-President Glafkos Clerides has since claimed he took Denktaş to the airport himself, at the latter's request). Denktaş was summarily returned to Anatolia upon being caught trying to land on the Karpaz (Kárpas) Peninsula in 1966, but returned under amnesty in 1968 to resume his leadership of the Communal Chamber. As the dominant personality in the Turkish community, soon elbowing aside even his mentor Dr Küçük, he acted as the regular negotiator in the sporadic intercommunal negotiations which took place until the summer of 1974 – a strange role given his life-long conviction that living side by side with Greek Cypriots was undesirable if not impossible.

Even before the establishment of a mono-ethnic North Cyprus in 1974–75, Denktaş was never squeamish about rough-and-tumble politics and (when necessary) resorting to pressure tactics. In 1963 he managed to get Emil Dirvana, the Turkish ambassador to Cyprus, recalled for condemning the TMT murder of two leftist barristers who favoured greater intercommunal co-operation. From 1970 onwards, outspoken domestic opponents, such as Özker Özgür and Ahmet Berberoğlu, were intimidated or placed under house arrest; Denktaş, through TMT, effectively pressurized Dr Küçük into early retirement in 1973, on the grounds that the latter displayed too much spine in his dealings with the mainland Turks. Denktaş spent most of the years 2000 to 2003 harassing the lively opposition newspaper *Avrupa*, either directly with lawsuits for libel and criminal prosecutions, or indirectly through rent-a-thugs firebombing or sequestering the paper's premises (the paper, under courageous editor şener Levent, is now back in business, pointedly renamed *Afrika* as a comment on the Zimbabwe-like politics of the North). Denktaş's chutzpah typically extends to all and sundry, including his dealings with the Greek Cypriots. Early in the 1980s he demanded, and received, the exhumed bones of his mother from Páfos municipal cemetery for reburial in the hallowed North – the South's meek compliance was roundly criticized, especially by Orthodox refugees from the North denied the privilege of tending their ancestors' graves (assuming they hadn't been thoroughly desecrated).

Denktaş's political machine, the **UBP** (*Ulusal Birlik Partisi* or "National Union Party"), held civilian power uninterruptedly in North Cyprus from 1975 until late 1993, and while, as president, Denktaş was officially non-partisan, the UBP was still very much his creature. Little tolerance was exhibited within the party apparatus towards those who disagreed with him; his feud with Dervis Eroğlu, a former UBP prime minister, considered even more hard-line than Denktaş on the question of a possible settlement, provoked the splitting-off of the Denktaş-loyalist **DP** (Democratic Party) in 1992. Government jobs have historically been much easier to get with UBP or DP membership, and once employed, civil servants were "encouraged" in various ways to vote for these parties. Denktaş periodically (and tactically, as he always changed his mind) announced his intention to resign from all public offices, news greeted with relief by those fed up with his autocratic manner. The last exercise of this ploy was in 2004, when he threatened to resign if the Annan Plan was approved by referendum; in the event he wiggled out of his promise by pointing out that, while the Turkish-Cypriots may have voted yes to the plan, the Greek-Cypriots hadn't. His 2000–2005 presidential term, won against Eroğlu in a hard-fought – if bizarrely concluded (see p.451) – election is almost certainly the last, as 81-year-old Denktaş has been in frail health since late 2002, with three artificial heart valves.

Despite (or because of) the unilateral declaration of independence in 1983, more communally conciliatory elements in North Cypriot public life always regarded him as a mere cat's-paw of mainland Turkish policy, not acting (in contrast to Küçük) in the long-term interest of the Turkish-Cypriot community. Denkaş attracted some grudging admiration for a lifetime as a wily, tenacious and even charming **negotiator**, but over time most observers came to the conclusion that his consistent strategy of teasing the Greek Cypriots with proposals not really made in earnest, together with moving the goalposts when matters look hopeful, was merely a cover for incorrigible intransigence. Thus, until the April 2004 referendum at any rate, he was long reckoned the chief obstacle to any federal settlement of the Cyprus issue – sentiments officially reflected in UN Security Council resolutions of November 1992 and April 2003, and by Richard Holbrooke's statement of May 1998.

In 2001, however, the international (and domestic) ground began to shift beneath his feet, and impending mortality – his own as well as that of long-time sparring partner Glafkos Clerides – began to bite. The **EU** made it clear that a decision on Cyprus's accession to an enlarged Europe would be made sometime in mid-2002, with or without the North's participation, and with this concentrating minds – and possibly a mutual desire to make as statesman-like an exit from public life as possible – contacts between Denktaş and Clerides were renewed in December 2001. Unfortunately, negotiations bore little tangible fruit before Clerides left office in early 2003, replaced by the more hard-line Tassos Papadopoulos.

Although the President's disrespectful nickname in the North was (and remains) *Kel* ("baldie" in Turkish), and he was increasingly dismissed as a Cold-War relic for his knee-jerk right-wing politics, no successor of comparable (inter)national stature was ever allowed to emerge – his surviving son in particular, now head of the DP, is dismissed with the tag "Junior". But as the elder Denktaş's various defects became apparent even to those who formerly supported him, the northern public viewed the approaching end of the Denktaş era as an opportunity (perhaps the last) for improvements. The serious civil unrest and demonstrations of 2000–2004, and the fact that the North's judiciary managed to maintain its independence, had their effect. In contrast to prior style, where Denktaş circulated informally and with a minimum of security, confident in the knowledge that no one would hasten the impending succession crisis by attempting to assassinate him, the President of the North spent the end of his era with a retinue of armed, frowning guards, just like any Third-World caudillo.

meals and food preparation also being an integral part of life in most dervish orders). In a multiple-domed side hall, whose outline is so distinctive seen from the street, are serried tombs of sixteen people associated with the *tekke*, including founder Arab Ahmet and the last *şeyh* Selim Dede, who died in 1953.

## Along Girne Caddesi to Atatürk Meydanı (Sarayönü)

Tucked into a side street south of the *tekke* are more graves – this time arranged as a **Şehitlik** or Martyrs' Memorial created in 1963, and representative of many such in the North. A trilingual sign extolling the hundred-plus "unarmed and defenceless [civilian] victims of Greek thugs" is somewhat undercut by the presence of dozens of headstones for mainland Turkish soldiers who died in the opening days of the July 1974 campaign. In fact more than 1500 casualties were buried here in mass graves between July 24 and 28, often eight bodies to a hole, first by press-ganged local teenagers, later with a captured Greek-Cypriot bulldozer. However, the bones were exhumed three years later, and the current, entirely symbolic grave markers installed.

Immediately west of the Şehitlik, on the far side of Girne Caddesi, stands an altogether more cheerful sight, reflecting the benevolent side of Islam: the **Samanbahçe** neighbourhood, a social housing project dating from the early 1900s and funded by the Cypriot *vakıf* or religious trust. Its most striking feature is a roundabout plaza, ringed by concave-fronted houses, with a round *sarnıç* or water cistern (still working) in the middle – an aesthetically pleasing ensemble, despite the evident humbleness of the dwellings.

The commercial aspect of Girne Caddesi and the streets immediately around Atatürk Meydanı seems a faint echo of southern Nicosia, and is pitched primarily at soldiers and settlers from Turkey taking advantage of cheaper North Cyprus clothing prices. In certain photo shops you see a popular ready-frame – intended for mainland conscripts writing home – in which aeroplanes, paratroopers and artillery pieces swirl around a blank spot for sticking one's mugshot, with overhead the motto *Barış için Savaş* ("War for Peace"). The 1974 Turkish intervention is universally proclaimed the "Peace Action" in North Cyprus, a nice Orwellian conceit.

**Atatürk Meydanı** itself has been the hub of Turkish life in Nicosia since the Ottoman conquest, and is still surrounded by the British-built post office, a rambling, colonial-standard-issue police station, law courts and a considerable number of banks with ATMs. In Ottoman days it was called Konak Meydanı, after the governor's mansion (*konak*), more popularly known as the *Saray* (palace), which stood to the southwest. Formerly a Lusignan/Venetian palace, it was destroyed by the British at the beginning of the twentieth century; the name only lives on in the shape of the modern *Saray Hotel*, and the mock-Moorish pastiche of the little-used Sarayönü Cami, which has lent its name to the popular term for the area – **Sarayönü** (nobody actually says Atatürk Meydanı). In the centre of the roundabout, a grey **granite column** from Salamis, stuck here by the Venetians after 1489 and so erroneously attributed to them, was once surmounted by their symbol, the lion of Saint Mark. The Ottomans did away with the lion and toppled the column in 1570, which remained prone until 1915 when the British re-erected it, capping it with a neutral metal globe.

### The hamams

From Atatürk Meydanı, Asmaaltı Sokağı leads southeast towards the bazaar and the main monumental zone. The **Büyük Hamam**, on a short street of the same name bearing off Asmaaltı, was once part of a fourteenth-century church (St George of the Latins), of which only the portal remains, slightly below ground level. It's now north Nicosia's largest **public bath** (daily 8am–10pm), plain but passably clean, serving men and women at separate hours. Another, less distinctive steambath, the **Korkut Hamamı** (daily 8am–10pm), stands nearby on Beliğ Paşa Sokağı.

## The Kumarcılar Hani and the Büyük Han

A *han* in medieval Turkey was an inn providing an overnight stop for both travelling merchants and their horses. Such inns were once common across the island, but those in the South have been bulldozed or altered beyond recognition, so the following two sites are your best chance to see such buildings in Cyprus.

Within sight of the Büyük Hamam is the seventeenth-century **Kumarcılar Hanı** or "Gamblers' Inn" (closed for works), with shops, including a popular tea-house, occupying its outer perimeter. Inside the grassy courtyard (still visible through the gate), pointed arches on the lower arcade level and square-capitalled columns on the upper one demonstrate Cypriot vernacular architectural influence.

This isn't true of the altogether grander **Büyük Han** (Mon–Wed 8am–9pm, Thurs–Fri 8am–midnight, Sat 8am–4pm; free), nearby at the corner of Asmaaltı and Kurtbaba, which having spent the period 1992–2002 being restored has finally taken its rightful place among the island's finest buildings. The "Great Inn" was among the earliest (1572) Ottoman public works following the conquest; it became the first city prison under British administration, but reverted in 1893 to a hostel for destitute families, something more like its original role. Each of the guest rooms in the upper arcade, now (like the lower ones) partly occupied by various artisans' shops, was originally heated by fireplaces. A little *mescit* (the Islamic equivalent of a chapel; visitable) balances on six columns over its own *şadırvan* or ablutions fountain, a design seen elsewhere only in Turkey at the Koza Hanı in Bursa, and the Sultanhanı near Aksaray. In the southwest corner a snack-bar/café operates, and there are plans for an adjacent wine bar (see below).

## The bazaars

If you follow Girne Caddesi from Sarayönü towards the Green Line, you intersect pedestrianized Arasta Sokağı, the heart of north Nicosia's **main shopping district**. Cloth and clothing, especially cheap jeans, predominate, with machinists and junk metal depots in surrounding streets, but it's a far cry from the 26 different bazaars the city had towards the end of the nineteenth century. A section of Girne Caddesi is still called the *Eski Kadınlar Pazarı* or "Former Women's Bazaar", where female vendors hawked a variety of textiles and household items of interest to other women. *Arasta* means a bazaar either physically built into the ground floor of a mosque, or if separate, one whose revenues go to the upkeep of a religious foundation. In this case the foundation concerned was probably the Selimiye Camii (see below), reached by following Arasta Sokağı east until you emerge in front of the covered bazaar and the Bedesten.

The **Belediye Pazarı**, or covered municipal market (Mon–Fri 6am–3pm, Sat 6am–1pm), is popularly known as the **Bandabulya** (a corruption of the Cypriot Greek *bandobolío* or "general store"). Like its counterpart in south Nicosia, this was erected during British rule; most of the stalls are devoted to fresh produce and meat, though there is a concentration of luridly lit "Cyprus

Delight", or *lokma* in proper Turkish. Antique and craft stalls of more obvious interest to tourists have all moved to a designated row shown on our map ("Souvenir Bazaar"), immediately north of the Selimiye Camii.

## The Bedesten

The **Bedesten**, squatting between the Selimiye Camii and the covered market hall, was originally a sixth-century Byzantine church which eight hundred years later had the Roman Catholic Saint Nicholas church of the English grafted onto it, the whole being made the Greek Orthodox cathedral during the Venetian period. Under the Ottomans it served for a while as a grain store and cloth market (though strictly speaking *bedesten* means a lockable bazaar for precious metals or jewellery), but was later allowed to deteriorate so that only the north vaulting remains intact. Today the building is kept off-limits to protect the collection of medieval tombstones stored here; even from outside the ground plans of two separate churches are apparent, though UN-sponsored restoration has begun and more of the complex should become evident as time passes. The magnificent north portal, with six coats-of-arms above, is a lesser version of the fine Gothic arches of the Selimiye Camii's narthex.

At the northeast corner of the Bedesten, a late medieval, two-roomed structure once served as the local *imam*'s residence; today it serves as a warehouse of medieval stonework, including tombstones and coats-of-arms gathered from various places around the island, but is at present closed to the public.

## The Selimiye Camii (Ayía Sofía)

The **Selimiye Camii**, originally the Roman Catholic cathedral of Ayía Sofía, is the oldest and one of the finest examples of Gothic art in Cyprus, the work of French masons who accompanied the Crusades. Construction began in 1209 during the reign of Lusignan King Henry I and lasted 150 years; it was consecrated in 1326 while still incomplete, and the blunt-roofed bell-towers were never finished. The intricate west façade, with its triple, sculpted portal and giant window above, seems transplanted directly from the Île de France. Within, Lusignan princes were crowned kings of Cyprus before proceeding to Famagusta for a second, essentially honorary coronation as king of Jerusalem.

When the Ottomans took the city in 1570, they reserved their special fury for the cathedral, chopping up the pulpit and pews for firewood and opening the tombs, scattering the bones within and using the tombstones as flooring; just a few of the stones escaped such treatment, and can be seen stacked in a former side-chapel, as well as in the now-shut warehouse at the Bedesten (see above). The pair of incongruous, fifty-metre-high minarets, which constitute an unmissable landmark almost at the exact centre of the old city, were added immediately, as was the ablutions courtyard fountain with trefoil-arched niches, but the building was only officially renamed the Selimiye Camii in 1954. You may be able to "tip" the custodian for the privilege of climbing the minarets for unrivalled views over the town.

Since the mosque still serves as a house of worship, there are no set visiting hours; try to coincide with the five prayer times, when you are allowed in shoeless, modestly attired and silent. The sense of internal space is as expected from such a soaring Gothic structure; abominating as good Muslims did all figurative representation, the Turks whitewashed the entire interior as part of their conversion process, so that the Selimiye presents a good example of clutter-free Gothic. But unhappily most of the original window tracery has disappeared over the centuries, replaced by tasteless modern concrete grilles. Other significant adaptations for Muslim worship include a *mihrab* (a niche indicating the direction of

△ Gothic vaulting, portico, Selimiye Camii (Ayía Sofía)

Mecca) and *mimber* (a pulpit from where the congregation leader may speak) set into the south transept, plus a women's gallery in the north transept. Outside, high up on the second, southeast flying buttress, hangs a small sundial; the *imam* resident next door could consult it from his doorway to determine the proper hours for prayer. Stroll a little further along this side of the building and you'll find a peaceful café with outdoor seating, based in the former chapter house, where you can order a drink and contemplate the cathdral exterior at leisure.

## Other central monuments

Just north of the Selimiye Camii, at the bend in İdadi Sokağı, stands the **cistern-fountain** of Ali Ruhi Efendi, built in 1829 by the eponymous governor, with an Ottoman Turkish inscription inside a handsome pointed-arch recess. This was one of nearly a dozen such built inside the walled town by the Ottomans to provide drinking and gardening water for householders – and which functioned until quite recently.

Directly behind the apse of the Selimiye Camii, the diminutive **Sultan Mahmut Library** (summer Mon–Fri 9am–2pm, winter Mon–Fri 9am–1pm & 2–4.45pm; £1.25) was founded by the Ottoman Governor Ali Ruhi in 1829 on behalf of the reforming Sultan Mahmut II. The appealing octagonal, domed building, which doubled as a *medrese* or religious academy, houses an array of precious manuscripts and leather-bound books.

### The Lapidary Museum

Directly across from the Selimiye Meydanı stands the **Lapidary Museum** (summer Mon–Fri 9am–2pm, winter Mon–Fri 9am–1pm & 2–4.45pm; £1.25), which occupies a Lusignan-era pilgrims' guesthouse formerly known as the Jeffrey Museum, after the colonial official in charge of antiquities early in the last century. A jumble of unsorted stone relief-work in the building and the garden behind includes a Lusignan sarcophagus, a Venetian lion of Saint Mark, lintels with coats-of-arms, column capitals, Islamic headstones and gargoyles. But more compelling than any of these, and the first thing you see upon entering, is the delicate Gothic tracery window fitted into the north wall, all that was rescued from the Lusignan gatehouse which stood west of Atatürk Meydanı until being demolished under British rule.

### The Haydarpasa Camii

Walking up Kırlızade Sokağı from Selimiye Meydanı, you can't miss the **Haydarpaşa Camii**. Once the late fourteenth-century Lusignan church of Saint Catherine, and restored in 1994 as an art gallery (Mon–Fri 9am–1pm & 2–5pm, Sat 9am–1pm; free), it is the most substantial Gothic monument in Nicosia after the Selimiye Camii. Great buttresses arc up to flank its high, slender windows, the roofline rimmed with gargoyles. Over the south door sprouts an ornamental poppy or acanthus bud; the west façade is adorned with (appropriately) a Catherine window, shaped like the wheel of the saint's martyrdom. A purpose-built minaret was tacked awkwardly onto the southwest corner of the structure, rather than adapting the square, keep-like sacristy northeast of the apse. The glorious, airy interior, scarcely altered during the Ottoman centuries, features three ceiling bosses from which sprout fan vaulting, joining eight wall columns.

### Lusignan House and Yeni Cami

Continuing north along Kırlızade Sokağı, you pass the so-called **Lusignan House** (summer Mon–Fri 9am–2pm, winter Mon–Fri 9am–1pm & 2–4.45pm; £1.25), a fifteenth-century mansion (restored in 2002) which, while impressive enough, has very little in it at present. Shortly after you reach the **Yeni Cami** or "New Mosque", the eighteenth-century replacement for a previous one destroyed by a rapacious pasha in his dream-inspired conviction that treasure was concealed underneath. The townspeople complained to the sultan, who executed the impious malefactor, presumably confiscating his assets to build the new mosque. Just the minaret and a Gothic arch of the original building, which must have once been a church, remain marooned in what is now a schoolyard; the successor stands to one side, next to the tomb of the disgraced pasha. There are two more domed tombs across the narrow street.

## Áyios Loukás

A final item of interest east of Girne Caddesi is the former eighteenth-century church of **Áyios Loukás** near Alsancak Sokağı; Greeks hailing from this formerly mixed district claim it was completely wrecked during the disturbances of 1963–64, but since then the church has been meticulously restored to house the municipality's Popular Art Association, with occasional exhibits.

## The Arabahmet district

West of Girne Caddesi, the **Arabahmet district** is the counterpart to south Nicosia's Khrysaliniótissa neighbourhood, with imposing Ottoman houses on Zahra, Tanzimat and Salahi şevket streets. Since 1995, as part of the Master Plan, many fine buildings on the parallel, narrow lanes between Tanzimat and Salahi şevket have been renovated and rented out to various cultural and commercial organizations, though as yet there are scarcely any restaurants or nightlife venues on a par with those around south Nicosia's Famagusta Gate. The Green Line is less obtrusive here, so many other houses are still inhabited despite their semi-dereliction. Also forlorn is the elaborate, octagonal **Ottoman fountain** at the Y-junction of Zahra and Tanzimat, which was allowed to run dry some years ago.

Arabahmet was, until the troubles, the **Armenian quarter**, and had been so since the tenth century (though most of Cyprus's Armenians are much more recent arrivals from Anatolian Silicia). Salahi şevket was, in British times and for a while after, Victoria Street, and you can still find plenty of ornate mansions with ironwork and Armenian (sometimes Greek) inscriptions over the doorways. The spire of the Roman Catholic church, straddling the Green Line, punctuates the south end of Salahi şevket Sokağı; east of it, and now visitable, stands the fourteenth-century Armenian **church of the Virgin**, originally a Benedictine monastery but handed over to the Armenians as a reward for siding with the Ottoman invaders. Ironically, the Armenian community was expelled from this area at the end of 1963 by the TMT, on the grounds that they had allied themselves with the Greek Cypriots. The church is now, unsurprisingly, fairly comprehensively trashed, with an unfinished cloister on the north side held up by scaffolding. Inside, you can still admire fine vaulting and a wooden altar canopy and a *yinaikonítis* which have miraculously survived.

Immediately west of the church sprawls the **Kaytazağı Burçu (Roccas Bastion)**, the point of closest contact to the South in all of North Cyprus – the buffer zone dwindles to nothing here. It was opened as the Yiğitler Park in the late 1990s, to the profound consternation of the Greek Cypriots, who claimed it would make a perfect platform for spying. From the edge of the landscaped area, you can indeed take in the CYTA building, the municipal theatre and municipal gardens of South Nicosia, and (were you so inclined) easily converse with pedestrians on the sidewalk thirty feet below, at the base of the sloping fortification. With the unrestricted opening of the Ledra Palace crossing, the park's novelty value has waned, but the use of cameras here is still strictly banned.

## The Arabahmet Camii

The attractive eighteenth-century **Arabahmet Camii**, named after one of the commanders of the 1570–71 expedition, serves as the fulcrum of the district; it was restored in 1845 and again, to good effect, during the 1990s. This mosque is only one of two examples of the Anatolian dome-on-square plan on Cyprus (the other is in Lapta), a convention based partly on Byzantine prototypes. A hair of the Prophet's beard is said to be kept inside and shown to the faithful once a year; Archduke Salvator saw instead an ostrich egg suspended before the *mihrab*. As at the Selimiye Camii, the floor is paved partly with Lusignan tombstones taken from a church formerly on this site; it also shelters the more venerated tomb of Kâmil Paşa, briefly grand vizier of the Ottoman empire towards the end of the nineteenth century and the only Cypriot ever so honoured.

## The Derviş Paşa Konağı

The first main street north of the Line on which you can head east without obstruction is Beliğ Paşa Sokağı, with its **Derviş Paşa Konağı** (daily: summer 9am–7pm; winter 8am–1pm & 2–4.45pm; £1.75), an ethnographic collection that's the North's version of the Hadjiyeorgakis Kornesios house in south Nicosia. Once again, the well-restored nineteenth-century building proves at least as interesting as the embroidery, copperware and basketry adorning the room mock-ups. The original builder and owner Derviş Paşa was the publisher of Cyprus's first Turkish newspaper, archival copies of which are also displayed. In the courtyard a bar sporadically functions, and behind it are certainly the cleanest toilets in the city.

# Eating and drinking

The choice of **restaurants** in North Nicosia is certainly an improvement on the Famagusta area, though in the town centre there's a preponderance of continental-Turkish soup and kebab kitchens popular with settlers and soldiers. With the advent of cross-"border" tourism and more disposable income for wealthier Turkish-Cypriots, there is now also a number of more exotic, cutting-edge alternatives.

The Lefkoşa area specializes in after-dark **meyhanes**, the Turkish-Cypriot answer to the *mezé* house of the South, and lately – it must be said – superior and more genuine in execution. There are claimed to be over half a dozen in the city and in nearby villages of the district, none of the latter more than a twenty-minute drive away (if you don't get lost). The four most durable and reliable are listed below. Unlike in continental Turkey, all of them welcome women, though it's best to go in a mixed-gender group. We give phone numbers where known, as by their nature *meyhane*s are whimsical – check before driving out for nothing.

## Restaurants, café-bars and desserts

**Amasyalı** Girne Cad 174. Reliable and inexpensive spot for *döner* and *iskender kebap*, as well as soups and the casserole stews known as *sulu yemek*. Best (and busiest) at lunchtime.

**Anibal** Saraçoğlu Meydanı. Classic kebab-and-*meze* restaurant that's been going for decades, with consistent quality. Closed Sun.

**Boghjalian Konak Restaurant** Boghjalian Konak Restaurant Salahi Şevket Sok 53. The main attraction here is the setting – a well-adapted Armenian mansion – rather than the kebab-and-*meze* fare, which seems pitched largely at visiting Greek Cypriots. That said, not too overpriced.

**Californian Bar & Grill** Mehmet Akif (Dereboyu) Cad 74. A more-or-less-as-described diner-with-booze that's caused a sensation amongst trendier Lefkoshans since opening in 2000. The menu is wide-ranging – own-farmed chicken, Mexican snacks, burgers, fish and chips, all-American desserts and North American beers – and extremely reasonable at £5–6 for two or three courses. Closed Sun lunchtime.

**Hamur** İkinci Selim Cad 46. *Hamur* means "dough" in Turkish, and that's the staple ingredient of the excellent, inexpensive *mantı*, *pirohu* and vegetarian *börek* purveyed at this lovely 1930s house where fireplaces roar in the cooler months. Closed Sun.

**Londra Pastanesi** İnönü Meydanı. Dishes up *dondurma* (Turkish ice cream) and pastries in fairly pleasant surroundings.

**El Sabor Latino** Selimiye Meydanı. Indisputably the old town's sleekest premises – incongruously so – though somewhat misnamed as the fare's mostly generic Mediterranean and Italian. Between meal times, enjoy properly executed cappuccino or espresso. Open all day, continuously.

**Sedir Café** Inside Büyük Han, ground level. The quality and portion size of a two-course meal here – *helim böreği*, spinach with meat and rice – could both do with some bumping up, especially at about £5.50; however the setting for just a drink (normal resort prices) is unbeatable.

**Sıla 4** Zahra Sok, corner Tanzimat Sok. The first proper bar-with-taped-music to open in Arabahmet, catering to both locals and foreigners.

**Umutlar** Girne Cad 51. Excels in the traditional Cypriot *şşeftali kebap* (sheftaliés to Greek-Cypriots and London diners) as well as soups.

**X-Mek** Osman Paşa Cad 28. Newish (2004-opened), with attention to detail and a wide-ranging fusion menu (including sushi); it's okay to just pop in for an excellent western coffee. Closed Sun lunch.

**Yahya Usta** İkinci Selim Cad, by Quirini Bastion. Zero atmosphere in this cavernous place, with the TV often going, but reckoned by many to have some of the best kebabs in the city.

**Yusuf Usta** Green Line end of Girne Cad, near corner of Baf Cad. Attractive open-air bazaar eatery with tables out on the pedestrian zone. Standard Turkish fare, particularly meat. Open most of the day; closed Dec–March.

### Meyhanes

**Avcılar** Atatürk Cad 130 (may be no sign out). As the name ("Hunters") implies, game and sometimes wild mushrooms in season, but the usual starters are wild *gömeç* (mallow) greens, *piyaz* (white beans), *eşeksiksin* humus, *çakistes*

olives, grilled rabbit chunks, and *bakla* beans. Home-made *makarna* (pasta) with grated cheese as a second course precedes kebab mains, with fruit as dessert. Ten tables are distributed across three rooms, packed out with political, trade-union and mafia personalities of every stripe – a measure of the traditional Cypriot social tolerance which still exists. The main wall decor consists of ranks of bottles – some, disguised as Napoleon brandy, really smuggled-in Peristiany 31, the favourite Turkish-Cypriot tipple; beer, *rakı* and wine are also on offer. Budget £18 for four persons, drink extra.

**Bizim Ahır/To Ahouri Mas** Kahramanlar Cad, near cnr Bülent Hüseyin Sok ☎227 71 33 (not well marked; look for the more prominent sign saying "*Bizim Ahır'da fırın kebap ve kelle*" – "at Bizim Ahır there's fırın kebap and cooked (sheep's) head"). The name ("Our Barn") records the fact that the premises were once an abandoned house used as a sheep pen. The platters – everything from mushrooms to *kağıt kebap* (paper-roasted meat) – are excellent, if a bit pricier than at *Avcılar*, and the colourful proprietor Kemal – a former smuggler into the enclaves, jailed by the Greek Cypriots – can sometimes be persuaded to converse in English.

**Dilekkaya Restaurant (Ahmet'in Yeri)** Centre of Dilekkaya (Ayiá) ☎239 23 12 or 0542/851 77 72. To get here, go to the airport, then veer around it onto the old Famagusta road until you see signs to the village. Typical fare here includes *nor* cheese, chunky *humus*, eggs with *kaymak yağı* (an extra-rich butter), seasonal wild vegetables, quails' eggs, and stellar meat mains. Wine available, as well as the usual *rakı*, budget around £10 for two, plus drink. Roof terrace in summer, overlooking the little square.

**Pilli Kebab** Centre of Şirinevler village (Áyios Ermoláos, still called Ayaermola by Turkish Cypriots) ☎241 20 25 or 0533/860 90 12. As the name suggests, another popular meat-oriented *meyhane*, housed in an old double-arched building (summer seating outside on the *meydan*). Maybe not as cutting-edge as Dilekkaya, but a tad cheaper at £12 for two, including drink and post-prandial coffee. Closed every fourth night when the proprietor moonlights at the airport, so ring to make sure it's open.

# Listings

**Airlines** Cyprus Turkish Airlines, Bedreddin Demirel Cad ☎227 38 20; Turkish Airlines, Mehmet Akif (Dereboyu) Cad 52 ☎227 10 61 or 227 13 82; TWI Flights (Onur Air), Şehit Cevdet Yusuf Cad 30, Yenişehir ☎220 01 20.

**Airport information** Flight schedule confirmation: Turkish Airlines ☎231 47 90; Cyprus Turkish Airlines ☎231 46 39.

**Banks and exchange** Numerous banks around Sarayönü and on Girne Cad have ATMs. Otherwise, try Sun Car Rental at Abdi İpekçi Cad 10, also a currency exchange house; Alav, Girne Cad 89/D; or Denizatı, ground floor of *Saray Hotel*.

Books Kemal Rüstem, Girne Cad 26, opposite the *Saray Hotel*, has a decent stock of Turkish-English dictionaries, books on the North, and used English paperbacks.

Cultural centres/cultural interest offices Because of North Cyprus's international non-recognition, none of the foreign institutions here officially has consulate or embassy status, despite depiction/description as such on tourist maps and literature. They exist primarily for cultural outreach to the Turkish Cypriots, provision of libraries and events for expatriates and assistance in dire emergencies for travellers. They are: the American Centre & Liaison Office, Saran Sok 6, Küçük Kaymaklı, off map ☎ 225 24 40 (Mon–Fri 8am–5pm); the Australian Representation Division, Güner Türkmen Sok 20 ☎ 227 73 32 (Tues/Thurs 9am–12.30pm), in Köşklü Çiftlik district, northeast of the walled precinct; the British Council housed in the former embassy chancellery of the old unified republic, near the Green Line, at Mehmet Akif (Dereboyu) Cad 23 ☎ 228 70 51 (summer Mon–Fri 7.30am–1.30pm & 3.30–6.30pm; no afternoon hours Wed & in Aug; earlier afternoon hours in

winter); and the German Cultural Centre, Yirmisekiz Kasim Sok 15 ☎ 227 51 61. Each publishes lists of forthcoming events.

Internet The rather ominously named Virus, on Osman Paşa Cad, corner Mehmet Akif (Dereboyu), is claimed to be open 24hr.

Mobile phones Sales and repairs (including unblocking "locked" phones to swap SIM cards) at Çuvalcıoğlu & Sons, Girne Cad 154.

Post offices Central branch on Sarayönü Sok, just off Atatürk Meydanı (Mon–Fri 8am–1pm & 2–5pm, Sat 8.30am–12.30pm); parcels at the Yenişehir branch, Atatürk Cad 6–9, corner Cevdet Yusuf Cad.

Public toilets Near the Büyük Hamam, and on the ramparts east of the Kyrenia Gate (middling cleanliness).

Travel agencies A very helpful one with fluent English-speaking management is Birinci Turizm, in Kumsal district at Bedreddin Demirel Caddesi, 7Arabacıoğlu Apt, Ground Floor ☎ 228 32 00, (ⓦ www.birinciturizm.com), which can arrange hotels, air tickets, ferries to Turkey and competitive car rental, as well as currency exchange. They have proven quite useful for North Americans especially, who have few other ways of making travel arrangements in North Cyprus.

# Around North Nicosia

It is actually somewhat easier to approach the western salient of North Cyprus from Kyrenia, but since the end of Ottoman rule the attractions in this section have always been part of Nicosia district. With an early start, all the following sites can be toured in a single day from either Nicosia or Kyrenia. Given the orientation of the Attila Line, use of the pre-1974 main road from Nicosia through Alaykoy (Yerólakkos) and points west is not possible; from the north-western roundabout between Ortaköy and Gönyeli, traffic heads first to Yılmaz-köy (Skyllóura) and then along an upgraded secondary road to Güzelyurt.

## Güzelyurt (Mórfou)

Mention **GÜZELYURT** (Mórfou, Omorfo) to even the more accommodating among the Greek- or Turkish-Cypriot communities, and you'll quickly learn just how far apart are their negotiating positions on acceptable minimums for an island-wide solution. Besides the loss of the tourist infrastructure and the port of Famagusta, the abandonment of the Mórfou plain, with its burgeoning citrus orchards, melon patches and strawberry fields irrigated by vast underground water reserves, was a crushing blow to Greek-Cypriot enterprise. Not surprisingly, the South has always insisted on the return of some – preferably all – of the basin as part of any settlement; North Cyprus, with more than ten percent of its population now settled around here, has always balked at this. The unsuccessful Annan Plan indeed envisioned the return of the town, plus most of the surrounding villages, to Greek-Cypriot control; perhaps surprisingly, Turkish

Cypriots locally resettled voted overwhelmingly in favour of consenting to be refugees once again. They have in fact for some time been resigned to moving elsewhere, which accounts in part for the scruffy, down-at-heel appearance of what was once a prosperous market town.

Although the local Sunzest citrus export co-op has fallen on hard times, an increased acreage of citrus under cultivation since 1974, plus inefficient irrigation methods overdrawing the local water table, have caused the nearby sea to contaminate it. Turkish aid has allowed the Northern administration to improve existing reservoirs east and north of Güzelyurt to recharge aquifers, but progressive salinization of well-water remains a major potential threat, and only the advent of the Manavgat pipeline (now delayed to 2007 at the earliest) will alleviate the problem.

Today, as in the past, Güzelyurt serves as the entrepot for the plain around, with little to detain casual tourists; it does, however, have an excellent **restaurant**. The *Niyazi Şah Aile Gazinosu* (☎714 30 64), just south of the northerly roundabout, on the west side of the road (open daily, live music Fri/Sat eve when you should reserve), offers a fine six-platter *meze* (£6), including quail and a beer; it's possible to spend far more on the allegedly 42-platter seafood *meze*.

Approaching Güzelyurt from Kyrenia, railway buffs should keep an eye peeled for an isolated section of track east of the road supporting a **Baldwin locomotive** made in Philadelphia in 1924. This is one of two surviving relics (the other is in Famagusta) of the vanished railway across the Mesaoría, which ceased operating in 1951 after over half a century of transporting goods (and until the 1930s, passengers) between Famagusta and Gemikonağı (Karavostási).

## The Archeological and Natural History Museum

Towards the west end of town, past a nineteenth-century church with its belfry-top shot off, and the double minarets of an enormous, Saudi-financed modern mosque, you'll find the local **Archeological and Natural History Museum** (daily: summer 9am–7pm, winter 9am–1pm & 2–4.45pm; £2.25). Exhibits from the stuffed-animal collection, including two-headed and eight-legged lambs, are a bit bedraggled, but perusing the bird section is a good way to learn their Turkish names. Upstairs, several galleries contain clay objects from all periods, including one wing devoted to the nearby Late Bronze Age site of Toúmba toú Skoúrou, but it can't compare with any collection in the South. On the roundabout behind the museum, an exceptionally large **monument** honours Turkish Cypriots killed by EOKA in the South between 1950 and 1974 – plus a more recent casualty in 1980.

## The church of Áyios Mámas

On September 1, 2004, after months (if not years) of discreet negotiations, and a thirty-year gap in observance, the progressive bishop of Morphou, Neophytos, celebrated a proper liturgy in the adjacent **church of Áyios Mámas**, long the cult focus of Cyprus's most beloved saint. This has now become an established Sunday feature, and looks set to continue unless there's a drastic reversal in the North-South thaw. The resident warden of the museum used to have the keys to the church, but this may no longer be true, in which case you'll have to attend Sunday service to see any of the following.

Originally built in Byzantine times on the site of a pagan temple, the church acquired Gothic embellishments in the fifteenth century and had a dome added three hundred years later. The interior is in reasonable condition, considering the three decades of disuse, during which it functioned as a warehouse for icons rescued from around the district. A magnificent *témblon*, where lamps dangle from gargoyles, is the equal of massive columns and imposing masonry; you must stoop under arches to reach the seats of the upstairs *yinaikonítis*, evidence that it was added long after the original construction.

But you have come mainly to admire the purported **tomb of Mamas**, on the left as you enter the north door; above the undeniably ancient marble sarcophagus, a dangling curtain is festooned with votive offerings in the shape of ears – a strange image in view of the fact that the saint principally warded off tax collectors. But the story runs that early during Ottoman rule, Turks, convinced that there was treasure hidden in the coffin, bored holes in its side, at which a sort of nectar oozed out, terrifying the desecrators into desisting. The stuff, which appeared thereafter at unpredictable intervals, was claimed sovereign against earache, and additionally had the property of calming a stormy sea if poured on the waves. On the exterior west wall, there's a naive relief of Mamas on his lion (for the legend behind this iconography, see p.262).

## Gemikonağı

Soon after Güzelyurt you emerge on the namesake bay, initially a shingled, windswept coast that's unlikely to tempt you in for a swim, but improving further along. **GEMİKONAĞI** (Karavostási), 17km west, was for decades the roisterous port for the busy mines just inland; the 1974 war largely separated the two, but by then most of the open-cast pits inland were worked out anyway. Until the 1980s, pyrites for shipment to Turkey were still loaded from one of two conveyor-belted jetties here, but even this activity has ceased. The jetty could easily be adapted for loading such Güzelyurt citrus fruits as are still harvested, but Famagusta-based civil servants have apparently obstructed this strategy, so any fruit continues to be trucked at considerable extra cost to the latter port.

A strong local tradition of cabarets and girlie-bars continued under the tenure of free-spending Danish UN troops stationed locally, but with the post-1992 advent of the penurious Argentines (UN troops are always paid at "home" rates), the local sin industry went the way of the mines. Now that Greek-Cypriots are permitted nocturnal forays hereabouts, there's been a modest revival, with two "night clubs" opening, plus a smattering of restaurants and cafés. Indeed, apart from Lefke (see below), Gemikonağı is the hub of such tourism as exists west of Nicosia. However, the *Soli Inn*, built on the site of a former Ottoman *kervansaray* (☏727 75 75, ℻727 82 10, ✉soliinnhotel@kibrisbee.com; ❸), faces an uncertain future as its proprietor is gravely ill and the premises currently spend much of the year as long-term student accommodation.

**Restaurant** choices include the *Mardin Restaurant*, a bit west of the *Soli Inn*, whose *meze* and good fish are fairly pricey but have begun to attract a Greek-Cypriot clientele, for whose benefit the old site-name (Kalamiés) is signed. There's seaview terrace seating, plus a small artificially strewn beach at the edge of the premises. East of the inn, the characterful waterside *Karyağdı Hotel Bar* contains two yellow fridges for beer, a half-dozen shelves of booze and an antique collection the envy of many an official ethnographic museum, all presided over by Mehmet Karyağdı, a former miners' union organizer. Finally, at the very base of the easterly conveyor-jetty, the *Liman/CMC Bar* serves amazingly authentic fish and chips (dished out by Cemal, a returned Australian Cypriot), as well as functioning as another de facto museum of the old mining days.

# Lefke

To reach Lefke, turn inland at Gemıkonağı, bumping over the level crossing of a rare surviving section of the Cyprus railway. **LEFKE** (Léfka) itself sent three hundred Catholics to Nicosia in a futile attempt to help lift the Ottoman siege of 1570, but thereafter was always a staunchly Turkish–Muslim stronghold at the base of the Tróödhos foothills, and is set to stay that way under any comprehensive settlement. Formerly abundant water has fostered lush orchards, forming a stark contrast to the naked hills and slag heaps all around. *Léfka* means "poplar" in Greek but it's predominantly a date-palm and citrus oasis, claiming to have the best oranges on Cyprus, with apricots and plums thrown in for good measure. The Lefkans are traditionally proud farmers, known for not selling their land to any outsiders, but with the current water shortage, resistance to parting with real estate is crumbling. A single open-cast mine in northern territory worked until the late 1980s, but after the erection of the Attila Line and severance of any connection with the main mines further inland at Skouriótissa, the population fell from over 5000 to under 3000. Of late there's been a modest influx of foreigners: instructors and exchange students (from the University of

## Kıbrıslı Şeyh Nazim

Since the early 1980s, Lefke has acquired some fame (or notoriety) as the power base of the Naqshbandi Sufi leader **Kıbrıslı Şeyh Nazim** (or Nazem Rabban Haqani Al-Kobrossi to his many Arabic-speaking followers). The Naqshbandi order of Sufism, active mainly in Turkey and Bulgaria, plus (formerly) Yugoslavia, emphasizes the personal authority of the *murshid* or spiritual leader, with teachings that tend towards the reactionary. A trained engineer speaking smatterings of half-a-dozen languages (with a heavy, almost incomprehensible accent), şeyh Nazim is a charismatic figure, considered by many to be dangerously persuasive; Dr Küçük, the secularist vice-president under the old republic, saw fit to jail, then exile him to Lebanon. In 1974 he returned and set up the Turkish-Cypriot Islamic Society, ostensibly to promote greater piety in the notoriously lax religious environment of the North; this is one of several such groups here, whose membership does not much surpass a thousand. Both the late Turkish president Özal and North Cypriot leader Denktaş, who grew up in the same neighbourhood of Nicosia as the *şeyh* (and arranged his return to the island), have ranked among his adherents – as well as large numbers of Westerners, including (briefly resident in 1988) pop singer Cat Stevens, or Yusuf Islam as he is now known, and more recently Bob (Mahmut) Geldof.

That said, Nazim is far from universally popular in the North itself, and local opinions ventured on the man range from the dismissive to the unprintable. It is particularly galling to the *şeyh* – and a source of pride for the townspeople – that in all his years of residence he has not made one firm convert from Lefke itself. Instead, he seems to have accrued all the requisite trappings – an admiring international coterie of groupies (there are currently no resident Cypriot devotees at all), shenanigans concerning financial "donations", a hash bust during the 1990s on the premises (though he himself was not present) – of a cut-rate, Rajneesh-type guru.

Should you desire an audience with the great man, şeyh Nazim is fairly accessible, provided he's not at one of his several residences abroad; just ask to be pointed towards the house near the Mahkeme Mescidi, at the northern edge of the town, though his followers may want to "vet" you. If you have to wait around, the order keeps a rather squalid free hostel for impecunious believers. Of late şeyh Nazim spends considerable time in London, either at the Southwark mosque – where followers sleep on the premises just to be near their spiritual leader – or at another mosque on Queen Anne Avenue in Haringey.

Sussex at Brighton) at the Lefke European University, and disciples of a charismatic religious leader (see box), who in their outlandish Muslim-fancy-dress stick out a mile on the streets of conservative Lefke.

Drive through the town to catch a glimpse of the unremarkable but pleasing **Piri Osman Paşa mosque** at the edge of the oasis, flanked by palm trees and with the sere mountains as a backdrop. In the courtyard of the little mosque, which is usually locked, stands the ornate marble tomb of Osman Paşa, an Ottoman vizier supposedly poisoned as part of a political intrigue and buried here in 1820.

Back in Lefke proper, rambling old houses, many badly neglected, are scattered among the aqueduct-webbed greenery; up on the main road you'll see some British imperial architecture, the small university campus and a trilingual plaque marking the graves of the **Gaziveren incident** victims. In 1964 hundreds of EOKA activists attacked the enclave village of Gaziveren, near Yeşilyurt, whose inhabitants held them off with a dozen hunting rifles, at the cost of these casualties, until Turkey threatened action and a ceasefire was negotiated. On the roundabout just below is a more-extreme-than-usual equestrian statue of Atatürk on a prancing stallion.

For **accommodation**, there's the *Lefke Gardens Hotel* in the town centre at Fadil Nakipzade Sok 22 (☎728 82 23, ⓦwww.lefkegardens.com; ❷), where your cultured hosts are Ergun and Gönül. In 2000 they completed renovating a former nineteenth-century inn, and added a new wing in traditional style to enclose a courtyard with a small pool; rooms – including some three- or four-bed family units – all have air con and satellite TV, and most have wooden balconies. The ground-floor **café-restaurant** is open to non-guests, and is much the most reliable option in the area; there's also a separate bar, the area's most consistent nightlife option, popular with local students (who co-exist with green-turbaned devotees of the *şeyh*, sipping abstemious coffees out in the courtyard).

## Soli

About 1km west of the *Soli Inn* in Gemikonağı, the partly enclosed ruins of ancient **Soli** (daily: summer 9am–7pm; winter 9am–1pm & 2–4.45pm; £2.50 when warden present) are marked inconspicuously on the seaward side of the road – stay alert, as it's easy to miss the white-on-blue "Soli Harabeleri" or black-on-yellow "Soli" signs, both pointing inland, though nearly impossible to miss the huge protective roof (see below).

Soli was one of the ten ancient city-kingdoms of Cyprus, legendarily founded early in the sixth century BC when the Athenian lawgiver Solon, who supposedly lived here for a while, persuaded King Philocyprus to move the city down from a bluff overhead to its present site. But like Leonardo da Vinci's purported visit to Léfkara in the South, this probably never happened, and there appears to have been a town at this location since the Late Bronze Age, its name more likely a corruption of the Hittite word *Sillu*. Whatever its origins, it became a hotbed of pro-Hellenic sentiment, and was the last holdout against the Persians in 498 BC. The name in turn engendered that of Soléa, the Tróödhos foothill region inland, whose copper mines near present-day Skouriótissa spurred the growth of Soli, especially during Roman times, from which period most of the surviving ruins date. A Swedish expedition, funded by the archeology-loving crown prince of Sweden, excavated the site of the theatre between 1928 and 1930, while the post-independence government restored it badly with modern materials in 1963 (the original masonry now lines the Suez Canal and the quays of Port Said). A Canadian team uncovered the basilica and part of the agora after 1964.

### The site

The ugly concrete **theatre**, on its original location from the second century AD, looks out over the narrow but lush coastal plain, watered by the streams draining from Lefke. Lower down by the car park are foundations of a large fifth-century basilica, covered since the late 1990s by a hideous shed-roof resembling the ceiling of Stansted airport's concourse; some sort of structure (but not necessarily this one) was arguably necessary to protect the fine floor mosaics below, both geometric and animal. The most intact and famous of these, though now difficult to make out except on bright days, show waterfowl flanked by dolphins, and a magnificent swan enclosed in a circular medallion surrounded by floral patterns. The five-aisled basilica was destroyed in the seventh century, and some of the mosaics were built over during construction of a smaller, later church closer to the apse, where a mosaic inscription has been partly obliterated. During the Lusignan period, Soli was apparently the see of the banished Orthodox bishop of Nicosia, who would have mulled over the vagaries of fate amid little but rubble.

Canadian excavations in the **agora**, west of the custodian's hut and below the amphitheatre, were suspended after 1974 (as was all work in the North) and it is now fenced off, but before then a colonnaded paved street leading through the market to a nymphaeum (fountain shrine) had already been uncovered, as had the famous Aphrodite statuette and the bronze boy's head, both now in the Cyprus Museum in south Nicosia.

## Yedidalga and Yeğilırmak

Around 1500m northwest of Soli, at **YEDİDALGA** (Potamós toú Kámbou), acceptable **beaches** finally appear; the shore is pebbly but the warm sea shelves gently over a sand bottom, fine for pre- or post-ruin dips. It's probably worth continuing the 6km past Soli to **Yeşilırmak** (Limnítis), where there is a final cove, coarse shingle on shore but with a sand base once you're in the water. Despite the rather modest natural endowment of the bay, it's a popular place with no less than five **restaurants**, which however only operate during school holidays as their proprietors all live in the UK. The westernmost in line is the *Asmalı Plaj* with its "Guinness World Record" jumbo vine (*asma* in Turkish), planted in 1947. The easterly establishment is *Green River*, not surprisingly bounded on one side by the river draining this fertile valley with the taro (*kolokas*) plantations for which it's famous.

## Palace of Vouni

The mysterious hilltop **Palace of Vouni**, 3.5 twisty kilometres west of Soli, occupies a most spectacular setting, with views both over the sea and inland to the Tillyrian ridges. Watch for a "Vuni Sarayı" sign pointing right a kilometre or so after the main road veers inland. Along the paved, 800-metre side road, you may notice a few charcoal burners' pyramids, especially vital since wood-burning bread ovens were banned in the interest of air quality and tree preservation.

Vouni's history is controversial and obscure; even the original name is unknown, the modern one merely meaning "mountain" in Greek. It seems probable that the palace was first built around 480 BC by a pro-Persian king of Marion as an outpost to intimidate pro-Athenian Soli in the wake of a failed revolt; a few decades later another insurrection established a pro-Hellenic dynasty, which redesigned the premises. All sources agree that some time after 400 BC the palace was destroyed by agents unknown upon re-establishment of Persian dominion.

### The palace site

The site itself is just partially enclosed, though there are nominal **opening hours** (daily: summer 10am–5pm; winter 9am–1pm & 2–4.45pm) and a fee (£1.75) charged when the warden is present, in his hut next to the car park at the road's end.

The focus of the palace is a monumental seven-stepped stairway leading down into a courtyard, where a guitar-shaped *stele*, slotted at the top for a windlass, is propped on end before a deep cistern. This is one of several collection basins on the bluff top, as water supply was a problem – and a priority, as suggested by the sophisticated bathing and drainage facilities of the luxury-loving ruling caste in the northwest corner of the palace. At the centre of the *stele* is an unfinished carved face, thought to be that of a goddess.

The original **Persian entry** to the royal apartments, along a natural stone ramp at the southwest corner of the precinct, is marked by a metal sign; it was later closed off after the change of rulers and the entry moved to the north side of the central court, the residential quarters subsequently arrayed around this in the Mycenaean style. In the wake of the remodelling, the palace is thought to have grown to 137 rooms on two floors, the upper storey fashioned of mud bricks and thus long vanished.

Between the palace and the access road on its north flank is what appears to be a temple with remains of an obvious **altar** at the centre. On the opposite side of the site, beyond the car park and just below the modern trigonometric point, are the scarcely more articulate traces of a late fifth-century BC Athena temple, all but merging into the exposed rock strata here. Yet it must have been popular and revered in its day, for a large cache of votive offerings (now in south Nicosia's Cyprus Museum) was found here.

# Travel details

## Buses

**Güzelyurt** to: Lefke (every 30min; 30min).

**Nicosia** to: Famagusta (every 20min; 1hr); Kyrenia (several hourly, departing when full; 30min); Güzelyurt (every 30min; 45min); İskele (5–6 daily; 50min).

**7**

# Kyrenia and the north coast

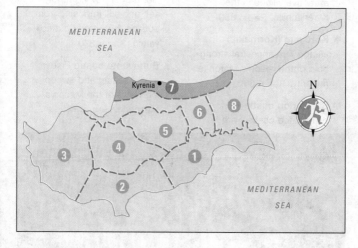

CHAPTER 7    # Highlights

* **Kyrenia castle** Houses a variety of small exhibits, best of these a Hellenistic shipwreck recovered from a hundred feet down. See p.345

* **Kyrenia harbour** Some tourists never shake themselves free from the achingly picturesque old harbour. See p.348

* **Lapta (Lápithos)** The most attractive village in the Kyrenia hills. See p.359

* **Koruçam (Kormakíti) village** The ancestral stronghold of the island's Maronite minority. See p.362

* **St Hilarion castle** This dilapidated castle, with its bird's-eye view of Kyrenia, was in use militarily until recently – and it's easy to see why. See p.366

* **Béllapais abbey** The last surviving, postcard-perfect monastery from the Lusignan era. See p.368

* **Monastery of Panayía Absinthiótissa** Typical of remote churches in the North post-1974: grandly set, and still imposing from outside, but utterly gutted within. See p.370

* **Buffavento castle** Enjoys a wild setting and sweeping views of the Mesarya/ Mesaoría. See p.371

△ St Hilarion castle

# Kyrenia and the north coast

Kyrenia and its environs have long been considered the most beautiful landscape on Cyprus, thanks to the imposing line of high hills to the south which temper the climate and separate the area from the rest of the island. More than one writer has characterized the Kyrenia mountains as the quintessential Gothic range; the limestone crags seem to not only mimic the handful of castles which stud them, but also suggest the delicate tracery of the Lusignan cathedrals in Nicosia and Famagusta, towns clearly visible from the heights, and the pointed arches of the contemporary abbey at Béllapais, in the foothills. The ridge appears remarkably two-dimensional, rising to over a thousand metres from a very narrow coastal plain and running for some 70km roughly east to west, but plunging equally swiftly down to the Mesarya (Mesaoría) plain to form a veritable wall. In particular it acts as an efficient barrier to moisture-laden cloud, with rainfall on the north flank a good fifty percent higher than on the inland side. Springs erupt suddenly partway down the grade on the seaward slopes, keeping things relatively green and cool even in high summer and permitting the irrigation of various orchard and market-garden crops. Under exceptional conditions, Anatolia's Toros mountains are clearly visible across the Karamanian Straits.

**Kyrenia**, capital of the namesake district, is also the linchpin of tourism here with its compact old quarter arrayed around a nearly circular harbour. When the distractions of the town pall – within a day or two for most – **Karaman**, **Alsancak** and **Lapta**, spectacularly set foothill villages in what was once the most forested part of the barrier range, beckon to the west. A mixture of Turkish military facilities and hotels co-exist uneasily along the shore below, with the fishing anchorage of **Güzelyalı** marking the end of the strip developed for tourism and real estate development. Beyond, the thinly populated **Koruçam** (Kormakíti) peninsula, with its small Maronite population, makes a good destination for a day's drive, and you can return via the southwestern slopes of the Kyrenia hills on scenic, if little-travelled, back roads.

Southeast of Kyrenia, the Lusignan abbey of **Béllapais** very much tops the list of things to see, despite its relative commercialization; the surrounding village of **Beylerbeyi** and its neighbours **Ozanköy** and **Çatalköy** have always been sought-after dormitory annexes of Kyrenia, even before the current building boom. The **Kyrenia hills** themselves offer satisfying destinations for a few

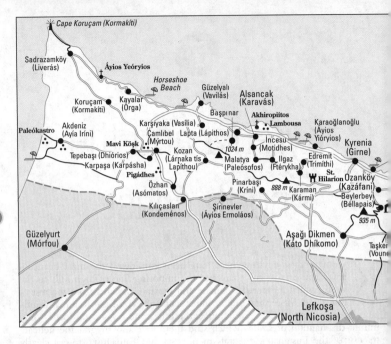

day-outings: the celebrated castles of **St Hilarion** and **Buffavento** and the remote, abandoned monasteries of **Absinthiótissa** and **Antifonítis**. Down on the coast, a succession of excellent **beaches** – in particular Lara, Alagadi and Onüçüncü Mil – remain as yet almost undeveloped.

# Kyrenia (Girne)

Despite unsightly expansion since 1974, **KYRENIA** (Girne, *Kerýnia* in Greek) – or more precisely its old quarter – can still easily lay claim to being Cyprus's most attractive coastal town, and the one with the most resonant reputation in foreign circles – helped along by Lawrence Durrell, plus scores of other eulogizing and expatriate Brits. It's certainly the only resort on the island that has anything of the feel of the central Mediterranean; down at the ruthlessly picturesque harbour, the Turkish Cypriots have no qualms about playing "Zorba's Dance" on endless loop tapes to impart Aegean "atmosphere", and of late even have Greek-Cypriot listeners.

Kyrenia's highlights – the harbour and its guardian castle, plus a trio of decidedly minor museums – can easily be seen on foot in a day. Move away from the kernel of the old town, however, and you enter what's in effect a vast building site, outpacing anything in coastal Turkey, southern Cyprus or in fact anywhere in the Mediterranean. Construction of villas and apartments has increased ten-fold since 2002, with over fifty estate agents in town to sell them, and a specialized commercial entourage – antique dealers, plant nurseries, building supplies, contractors' offices – to service them, largely displacing

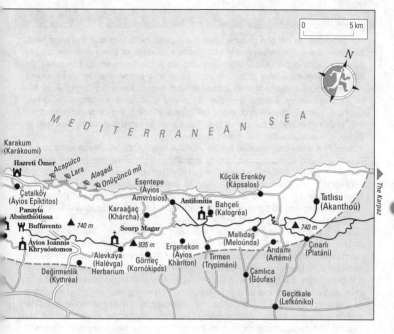

the former shops serving local needs. Traffic is almost non-stop even in the off-season, and gridlock is guaranteed at peak hours. A new bypass road is being built southwest of town, as the old one is now well inside the mess of three-to-four-storey blocks, a skyline redeemed only by the magnificent backdrop of the Kyrenia range.

## Some history

Kyrenia was founded by refugees from the Greek mainland in the tenth century BC, and figured among the ten city-kingdoms of Classical Cyprus. The chosen site, well to the east of the present castle, was conveniently near a source of suitable building stone at what's now called Khrysokava. The quarry doubled as a cemetery, and another necropolis was soon installed on the west. By the third century AD, Christians were living troglodytically and discreetly in the Khrysokava catacombs, prior to the establishment of Christianity as the Roman state religion. After the Arab raids of the seventh century contemptuously swept through the town's rickety outer walls, the castle was built; thereafter the history of the place more or less parallels that of its castle (see p.345).

Indeed, by 1300 the focus of Kyrenia had shifted northwest to within the present confines of the old town, though the eastern port was still in use, protected by a surviving Roman breakwater, and Khrysokava continued to supply building stone. The moat around the castle held water, and a chain across the entrance of the medieval port permitted its closure in troubled times. But by 1600, the town was in relative decline, its defences slighted by the Ottomans, and the moat now dry. Like the other ports on the island, Kyrenia only began to revive after the start of British administration, following the construction of roads to the interior and improvements to the harbour.

For three days at the end of June 1995, the Kyrenia region suffered the worst bush fire in living memory, when nearly 180 square kilometres of forest and olive groves between Lapta in the west and Beşparmak peak to the east went up in smoke. The blaze, set simultaneously at several points late on a windy afternoon, was almost certainly arson, intended to strike a blow at North Cyprus tourism, though the identity of the perpetrators remains a mystery. Paranoid speculation encompassed Greek Cypriots, Greeks, Israelis and, more likely, PKK (Kurdish separatist) activists from the Turkish mainland; a number of individuals were arrested and swiftly deported to Turkey in a suspiciously hush-hush operation.

Nearly an entire day elapsed before effective fire-fighting measures were undertaken, highlighting glaring deficiencies in staffing, equipment and general funding of North Cyprus's forestry division. The Turkish Cypriots turned down an offer of fire engines from the South, preferring to wait for Turkish helicopters dumping 1000-litre tubs, donated by one of the British Sovereign Bases, filled with seawater. Damage to real estate came to £3.5 million sterling, with the total value of destroyed wood and crops estimated at roughly £43 million.

Among inland holiday complexes, only two sustained any structural damage (swiftly repaired), but several other hillside outfits lost the lush environment and landscaping which had made them so appealing. In addition, the wood-and-plaster sections of St Hilarion castle, including the café, were completely gutted.

Subsequently, the burn zone was clear-cut by Anatolian woodcutters and the logs shipped by barge to paper mills in Turkey, prior to terracing, reseeding and replanting of young trees. Despite the amount of money raised by the sale of timber, logistical and budgetary problems sharply scaled back this programme as well, with a fair quantity of fast-growing mimosa – not part of the original native vegetation – mixed in with baby pines and cypresses (three varieties each). This type of Mediterranean forest takes over fifty years to attain any semblance of maturity – in the case of the olive groves, several hundred years – and given the spate of dry winters in the four years after the fire, which impeded natural resprouting, the seemingly endless bare hillsides, extending from just above sea level to the watershed of the Beşparmak (Pendadháktylos) barrier range, must now be reckoned a permanent feature of the Kyrenia landscape. Ironically, many of the olive groves which survived nearer the flatlands are now being assiduously grubbed out by developers,

As the British empire imploded after World War II, and redundant or retired colonial civil servants and army officers drifted homewards from less pleasant postings via Cyprus, many got no further than Kyrenia and its stage-set harbour. Those in particular without family ties reckoned correctly that "home" had uncongenially changed beyond recognition, and even after Cypriot independence British expats made up a substantial fraction of the town's population, with hundreds more in the surrounding villages. Foreign numbers plummeted after the events of 1974, as a result of confiscations by the early Turkish administration, and only during the late 1980s did they again attain three figures, against the town's current population of perhaps 16,000, many of whom are originally from Limassol. Since the millennium, however, expat numbers – even if resident only part of the year – have soared.

## Arrival, orientation and information

Visitors arriving **by plane** will be met by taxis and shuttle coaches, which take the main road from Ercan airport to Kyrenia (41km in total) via the northern edge of Nicosia; this (mostly dual carriageway up to here) becomes Ecevit

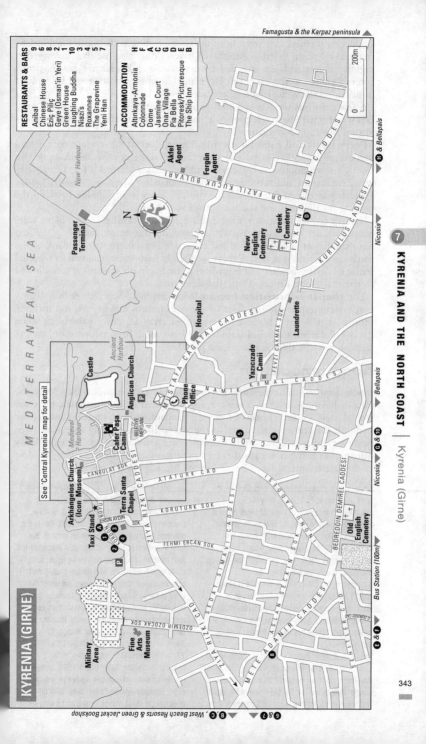

**KYRENIA (GIRNE)**

*Famagusta & the Karpaz peninsula* ▲

**RESTAURANTS & BARS**
| | |
|---|---|
| Anibal | 9 |
| Chinese House | 6 |
| Ezic Piliç | 8 |
| Geye (Osman'in Yeri) | 2 |
| Green House | 1 |
| Laughing Buddha | 10 |
| Niazi's | 3 |
| Roxannes | 4 |
| The Grapevine | 5 |
| Yeni Han | 7 |

**ACCOMMODATION**
| | |
|---|---|
| Altınkaya-Armonia | H |
| Colonnade | F |
| Dome | A |
| Jasmine Court | C |
| Onar Village | G |
| Pia Bella | D |
| Pitoresk/Picturesque | E |
| The Ship Inn | B |

*MEDITERRANEAN SEA*

New Harbour

Passenger Terminal

N

Akfel Agent

Fergün Agent

DR FAZIL KUCUK BULVARI

İSKENDERUN CADDESI

KURTULUS CADDESI

► **H** & Bellapais

► Nicosia

Greek Cemetery

New English Cemetery

**D**

Castle

Ancient Harbour

Anglican Church

Medieval Harbour

Arkhángelos Church (Icon Museum)

Cafer Paşa Camii

BELEDIYE MEYDANI

Phone Office

P

Hospital

MUSTAFA ÇAĞATAY CADDESI

MERSIN CAD

NAMIK KEMAL CADDESI

FEVZI ÇAKMAK SOK

Laundrette

Yazıcızade Camii

► Bellapais

See 'Central Kyrenia' map for detail

CANBULAT SOK

Terra Santa Chapel

ERBOYU

ERSIN AYDIN SOK

Taxi Stand

**A**

1 4
2 3

P

ATATURK CAD

ECEVIT CADDESI

5

6

ISMET CADDESI

► Nicosia, **G** & **10**

ZIYA RIZKI CADDESI

KORUTURK SOK

FEHMI ERCAN SOK

SEDAT STMAVI CADDESI

NON CADDESI

BEDREDDIN DEMIREL CADDESI

Old English Cemetery

Military Area

Fine Arts Museum

ÖZDEMIR ÖZÇAK SOK

ZIYA RIZKI CAD

SEDAT SIMAVI CADDESI

SELÇUK SOK

METE ADANIR CADDESI

SEHITLER CAD

**8**

► **E** & **F**

► Bus Station (100m)

0    200m

▼ **6** & **7**

▲ **B, G, C** , West Beach Resorts & Green Jacket Bookshop

**7**

**KYRENIA AND THE NORTH COAST** | Kyrenia (Girne)

343

Caddesi as it enters city limits from the south, ending at the mostly pedestrianized central plaza, Belediye Meydanı. Drivers could also use the narrower but slightly shorter and less crowded bypass road over Beşparmak saddle, which enters Kyrenia on the east from Değirmenlik – however it should be avoided until mid-2006, while it's being regraded.

A few **minibus** services still end within sight of Belediye Meydanı, but most **bus** services have been relegated to a newer station in the far southwest of town, just off our main Kyrenia map.

**Ferry boats and catamarans** from Turkey dock at the modern commercial harbour, about 1500m east of the town centre. The main west–east thoroughfare through town doubles as the coast road and changes names a few times: one-way Ziya Rızkı Caddesi on the west side of Belediye Meydanı, Mustafa Çağatay Caddesi just east of Ecevit, and then finally İskenderun Caddesi between the turning for Béllapais and the access road to the port.

Kyrenia is beginning to sprawl dauntingly, and **parking** is a problem year-round; besides the central fee lots (shown on our maps; roughly £0.20), a limited number of uncontrolled spaces lie along two narrow streets flanking the castle on its south and west. Except for the old harbour area, closed to wheeled traffic all day in summer and from 5pm to midnight off-season, cars are allowed to circulate along Kordon Boyu, the shore road.

The **tourist information bureau** (Mon–Fri 9am–5pm, Sat & Sun 10am–6pm) occupies the ground floor of the old customs building on the harbour, though it does little beyond dispensing an array of glossy pamphlets; when it's closed, the notice board outside may have some basic information, such as current museum opening hours and the like.

## Accommodation

If you want to savour the atmosphere of the old quarter and aren't sold on the idea of basing yourself in a remote, self-contained holiday complex, there are several small, en-suite **hotels** of varying standard within a short distance of the harbour, sometimes with views of the water. If you can pay three-star rates, however, and are willing to rent a car, there are a number of small-scale **holiday complexes** with pools and other facilities towards or at the edge of town. Most of the establishments listed below include breakfast in the price.

**Altınkaya-Armonia** Béllapais road, 2km south-west of centre ☎815 50 01, ⊛www .altinkaya-cyprus.com. Somewhat bleak grounds, and 1980s-vintage galleried one-bedroom units, but the location – just about walkable to the harbour – a fully equipped fitness centre with indoor pool, decent on-site restaurant and friendly managing family are big pluses. ➍

**Atlantis Hotel** Eftal Akça Sok 4, Old Harbour ☎815 22 42, ⊛www.atlantis.northcyprus .com. Well-worn but serviceable 1970s-vintage budget hotel in a good location; most en-suite rooms have partial bay views, limited parking out front. ➋

**Colonnade Hotel** Near top of Orhan Durusoy Cad ☎815 89 80, ⊛www.cypruscolonnade.com. Small (ten-room) boutique hotel run by a sympathetic couple. Rooms are tasteful but much of the charm resides in mock-antique-furnished common areas

and pool terrace. An extension of sixteen units is planned, as demand is high all year. ➍

**The Colony** Ecevit Cad ☎815 15 18, ⊛www. thecolonycyprus.com. Opened in 2003, this is the only real luxury hotel in Kyrenia (at least as the term is understood internationally). A less-than-brilliant location is compensated for by large, sumptuously appointed rooms with double glazing and internet socket, though the suites are worth the extra expense for superior baths. Common areas include the inevitable casino, several bars and restaurants, spa and fitness centre, plus the *pièce de résistance*, the rooftop pool terrace. ➏

**Dome Hotel** Kordon Boyu ☎815 24 53, ☏815 27 72, ✉thedome@kktc.net. Thanks to its colonial-institution status (since 1930) and Durrellian associations, this figures prominently in every package operator's brochure. With all-year operation, a small fitness centre and a long-term, loyal staff, it is also a businessmen's favourite. Most rooms – and the imposing common areas, including the pleasant sea-view bar – were thoroughly renovated in 1998, thus going some way to justifying the price tag; a fresh-water pool now accompanies the famous sea-water pool carved into living rock. **⑤**

**Harbour Lodge Motel** Kordon Boyu 22 ☏815 73 92, ☏815 37 44. An early twentieth-century refurbished building right at the edge of the unrestricted traffic pattern, so somewhat noisy. Just a few fairly large rooms, but no heating, air con, balconies or bar/restaurant – so pretty much a backpacker's fallback. **②**

**Jasmine Court Hotel** Western edge of town ☏815 14 50, ☖www.jasminecourthotel.com. The buildings look grim from outside, and the casino is diligently marketed, but the 14-acre site is a big plus, with a series of outdoor pool, lawns and lidos descending to the sea (there's no real beach). All units are suite format; good children's programme, two on-site restaurants. **⑥**

**Nostalgia Hotel** Çafer Paşa Sok, near the Round Tower and Central Market ☏815 30 79, ☖www .nostalgiahotel.com. Another "boutique" hotel complex spread over two adjacent buildings. The original, restored premises, with antique-furnished rooms, retains some of the feel of a French country inn, right down to the basic bathrooms; the superior *Nostalgia Court* annexe, purpose-built around a plunge-pool, is probably worth the extra for larger rooms and better baths. Both wings have their own attached restaurant, and in-house car rental. **③**, superior annexe **④**, half-board **④**

**Onar Village** Out of town on the main road to Nicosia ☏815 58 50, ☖www.onarvillage.com. Not the most verdant setting since the 1995 fire – though the gardeners are trying valiantly – but good standards in its two wings of hotel rooms, and villas. All are enormous for their type, while the latter have full kitchens (with ovens), baths and individual water heaters – thus suitable for winter-long stays. The 2002-built new hotel wing, arrayed around an indoor pool, Turkish bath, gym and massage facilities, has better bathrooms but also much more road noise. On-site restaurant, large outdoor pool and stunning views. Clientele tends to be mostly British, family and repeat. **④**

**Pia Bella** İkenderun Cad ☏815 53 21, ☖www .piabella.com. The main building is somewhat grim seen from the street, but the rooms are fairly large and carpeted, and many face the pool garden where the restaurant operates in summer. Annexe rooms, with mountain-view balconies round the back in a citrus grove, are superior in quality and worth insisting on (open only April–Oct & New Year's). Friendly, attentive staff. **③**

**Pitoresk/Picturesque Holiday Village** Top of Orhan Durusoy Cad ☏815 62 22, ☖www.pitoresk .com. Nicely set villa complex, enlarged in 2002, with sea views in a former olive grove, alive with cats and caged birds. Choose between self-catering one-bedroom units, or B&B-basis standard rooms, both in split level cottages. There can, however, be noise from adjoining units – most interconnect – and the new bypass road is set to go just downhill. Medium-sized pool, appealing mock-traditional architecture designed by German architects, and full-service bar/restaurant. **③** self-catering, **④** B&B

**The Ship Inn** 1.5km west of town, south side of the road ☏815 67 01, ☖www.theshipinn.com. Not the most inspired location, but once inside this is a pleasant development of one- and two-bedroom family villas arrayed around a pool and including tennis/squash courts. A newer, larger conventional hotel-room wing contains a small fitness centre, indoor pool and sauna; the bright if bland-decor rooms themselves have tubs in the baths and a mix of inland and partial sea views. Returned Anglo-Cypriot management keeps a "pub" corner-bar (thus the mock half-timbering) and adjoining, open-plan restaurant. Bookable direct by the week in the UK through T. Özdemir, 10–14 Leopold Rd, London SW19 7BD ☏020/8947 9110, ✉taner@ozdemirt. freeserve.co.uk. **④**

## Kyrenia castle

An amalgam of different periods and thus irregularly shaped, **Kyrenia castle** (daily: summer 9am–7pm; winter 9am–1pm & 2–4.45pm; £3.50) is only rivalled by the citadel of Famagusta for castellated interest on the island. The present Venetian structure is an adaptation of previous Byzantine and Lusignan fortresses: much of the walls' present thickness was achieved by simply filling the space between the compact Byzantine and overextended Lusignan fortifications with rubble. You can still see a now-superfluous round tower stump up on Hürriyet Caddesi, near Belediye Meydanı, and another remnant – possibly the base of a medieval lighthouse – out in the middle of the old port.

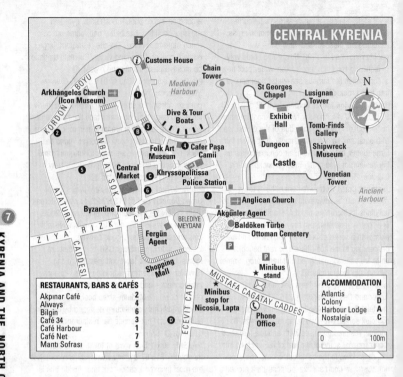

CENTRAL KYRENIA

Customs House
Chain Tower
Medieval Harbour
Arkhángelos Church (Icon Museum)
Dive & Tour Boats
St Georges Chapel
Lusignan Tower
Exhibit Hall
Tomb-Finds Gallery
Dungeon
Shipwreck Museum
Castle
Venetian Tower
Ancient Harbour
Folk Art Museum
Cafer Paşa Camii
Central Market
Khryssopolitissa
Police Station
Byzantine Tower
Anglican Church
Akgünler Agent
BELEDIYE MEYDANI
Baldöken Türbe
Ottoman Cemetery
Fergün Agent
Shopping Mall
Minibus stand
Minibus stop for Nicosia, Lapta
MUSTAFA CAGATAY CADDESI
Phone Office
KORDON BOYU
CANBULAT SOK
ATATURK
ZIYA RIZKI CAD
CADDESI
ECEVIT CAD

**RESTAURANTS, BARS & CAFÉS**

| | |
|---|---|
| Akpınar Café | 2 |
| Always | 4 |
| Bilgin | 6 |
| Café 34 | 3 |
| Café Harbour | 1 |
| Café Net | 7 |
| Mantı Sofrası | 5 |

**ACCOMMODATION**

| | |
|---|---|
| Atlantis | B |
| Colony | D |
| Harbour Lodge | A |
| Nostalgia | C |

0       100m

## Some history

The Byzantines probably built atop the site of a Roman fort; Guy de Lusignan seized the castle in 1191, finding the Armenian wife and daughter of Isaac Komnenos hiding inside. It subsequently served as a funk-hole during turbulent periods, as in 1426 when the Mamelukes overran the island, and again between 1460 and 1464 by Queen Charlotte, until her deposition by half-brother James. Rebels and disgraced personalities were also incarcerated here throughout the Lusignan period, including the rebellious Ibelin lords during Henry II's rule, and Peter I's mistress Joanna d'Aleman, immured briefly by his wife before Joanna gave birth to the king's bastard and was then bundled off to a convent.

The castle was never taken by force, repelling a fierce Genoese attack in 1374; its defenders always starved under siege or surrendered, as in 1570 when the Ottomans induced the defenders to capitulate by sending as a threat the severed heads of the Venetian commanders of fallen Nicosia. Thus the massive southeast, southwest and northwest towers – all constructed to slightly different specifications by the Venetians according to their military application – were not put to the test as at Famagusta. As elsewhere in the Ottoman empire, non-Muslims were forbidden access to the citadel after dark, when the ruling caste would retire there for the night. The British used it as a prison early in their administration, and again between 1954 and 1960 for EOKA captives.

## A tour of the walls

Today you enter the castle from the northwest via a bridge over the former moat. The first passage on the left leads to the small but perfectly formed

Byzantine **chapel of St George**, its four columns topped with Corinthian capitals; it stood outside the perimeter walls until the Venetians incorporated it into their circuit. A bit further along on the right, it's worth pausing in a vaulted chamber for "A Visual Introduction to Girne and its Castle", essentially a series of watercolours by long-time resident Kyreno-phile William Dreghorn (who died in 2001, in self-imposed "exile" at Famagusta), showing the evolution of the town and its fortifications from Roman times until the colonial era. Immediately opposite this, a ramp originally used for wheeling cannon heads up to the round northwest tower, and the start of a complete **circuit of the walls** (well supplied with guard-rails). The expected views of the harbour are at your feet, and you can make out St Hilarion castle up on its peak; continuing towards the northeast tower, you can detour briefly down to the exhibition/events hall, graced by more of Dreghorn's watercolours.

The **northeast bastion** is home to a permanent display of military history; in both the lower and upper chambers, mannequins pose with the armour or uniforms, and arms, of each historical period in the castle's life, from Byzantine to British. In the southeastern tower, a long gallery leads to its foundations where there's another mock-up of a Venetian cannon crew in action.

A complete clockwise circuit finishes at the original Byzantine **west wall**, in which the remains of Lusignan apartments (locked) and a chapel are also visible, but signs direct you to the Lusignan dungeon, a somewhat tasteless re-creation, complete with nude, anatomically correct mannequins of torture victims and prisoners (including Joanna d'Aleman) languishing at the bottom of oubliettes. Between this and the tree-shaded **café** in the northeast corner of the broad courtyard is a subterranean, vaulted cistern, still with a fair bit of water inside.

## The Tomb-Finds Gallery and Shipwreck Museum

Flanking the courtyard on its east are two superb archeological exhibits. The first is the **Tomb-Finds Gallery**, comprising three major exhibits spanning the Neolithic, Bronze Age and Hellenistic-to-Byzantine periods. In the main wing there's a reconstruction of a late Neolithic dwelling (c. 4100 BC), one of seventeen such located at Vrysi-Áyios Epíktitos near Çatalköy, sunk slightly below ground level for protection. The diorama suggests a harsh, utilitarian life, with only a few bone-segment necklaces as a concession to "luxury". In the adjacent hall an early Bronze Age (2075–1725 BC) tomb at Krini (modern Pınarbaşı) has been recreated with large numbers of clay funerary-gift vessels, many imported from overseas. The upstairs gallery is dedicated to finds from the ancient town at Akdeniz (Ayía Iríni); though the most spectacular, Archaic-age objects are at the Cyprus Museum, many Hellenistic and early Byzantine finds from the Paleokastro tomb complex are presented here, along with a mock-up of a catacomb: glass and terracotta, large hoards of coins, oil lamps and a pyramidal display case of gold jewellery recovered from nearby villagers or the result of internationally unrecognized excavations in 1986.

Next door, the **Shipwreck Museum** displays a cargo boat which sank just off Kyrenia some 2300 years ago, discovered over thirty metres down by a local diver in 1967. It is the oldest shipwreck known, and carbon-14 dating indicates it had been in service for nearly eighty years and much repaired when it foundered. The boat had just plied the coast of Anatolia, judging by freight from Samos, Kos and Rhodes – most of it stone grain-grinders which could double as ballast, and nearly four hundred amphorae of wine. A four- or five-man crew subsisted mainly on almonds, large quantities of which were found intact, and such fish as they managed to catch.

The upper levels of the exhibit halls show photos of the archeological dive, and lead to the viewing platform over the wreck itself, soaked in preservative and kept in a cool, dry, dimly lit environment now that it's out of protecting seabed mud. Curiously, the ship was built using the reverse of modern techniques: the lengthwise planks of Aleppo pine were laid down first, the cross-ribbing later.

## Around the old harbour

Although the British closed off its former, exposed north entrance and constructed the long breakwater east past the castle after World War II, Kyrenia's little **harbour** had ceased to be a working one even before 1974, despite being by far the safest anchorage on the north coast. Traces of its age-old importance remain in the medieval wall between some bait/dive-gear shops and the *Corner* restaurant, where a pair of stone lugs pierced with holes were used as fastening points for mooring ropes. In 1914, the British were persuaded to preserve the derelict western chain tower by elaborating it into the sturdy customs house visible today, with some of the original fortification features still visible. The port is now devoted entirely to pleasure craft touting all-day tours along the coast, the rental of speedboats, scuba-dive operations and berths for a score or so of yachts. A day out on an **excursion boat**, leaving at 10.30am and returning at 5pm, should cost £15–20 depending on the number of passengers, and should include *meze* barbecued on board, as well as several stops for snorkelling and swimming.

### Museums

The former church of Arkhángelos (the Archangel Michael), whose belfry provides a prominent landmark on the rise west of the water, now houses the **Icon Museum** (daily: summer 9am–5.45pm; winter 9am–1pm & 2–4.45pm; £1.25). The large collection on three levels (including the former women's gallery) offers an assortment of folksy seventeenth-to-nineteenth-century examples, rescued from unspecified churches in the district. The most unusual or artistically noteworthy include a *Beheading of John the Baptist*, with Herod's feast in full swing just above; Saint Luke with his emblematic ox; and three versions of the "Utter Humiliation", equivalent to a Western *Deposition* without spectators. Unfortunately, a rare icon of the ecumenical council of 843, which restored icon worship after the Iconoclastic period, has been either stolen or withdrawn from display.

By contrast to the Icon Museum, the **Folk Art Museum**, midway along the quay, contains traditional rural implements and dress in a Venetian-era house (summer Mon–Fri 9am–2pm; winter Mon–Fri 9am–1pm & 2–4.45pm; £1); the best single exhibit is the olive-wood olive press on the ground floor, made partly from unpruned trunks, but it's hardly a compelling display, with the house bidding to overshadow the collection.

Much the same can be said for the strictly time-filling **Fine Arts Museum** (daily: summer 9am–7pm; winter 9am–1pm & 2–4.45pm; £1.25), installed in a 1930s villa out at the west edge of town on Özdemir Özocak Sokağı, near the military hospital. Its expat builder obviously had Hearst-Castle-type ambitions, if not a Hearst wallet; the fake-baronial interior features grandiosely named kitsch fireplaces in every room. Neither is there anything Cypriot in the collection, which resembles a downmarket auctioneer's sales lot of Asian porcelain and painted screens, and ghastly, unattributed eighteenth- and nineteenth-century oil paintings.

## Houses of worship

More specifically Ottoman and Cypriot, the chunky **Cafer Paşa Camii** has stood one street back from the water at least since 1589, though one source plausibly claims the building is a converted Lusignan warehouse; sometimes you can't get in because of a funeral, when the municipality lays on a hearse inscribed in Turkish "Only God is Immortal". Just west stands the rather battered Lusignan **church of Khryssopolítissa** from the early fourteenth century, whose dilapidation has accelerated post-1974, though there are some interesting relief carvings on the exterior, especially around the blocked-up north portal.

A block inland from the *Dome Hotel*, on its own plot of land off quiet Ersin Aydın Sokağı, the **Terra Santa Catholic Chapel** is another undesecrated, late-medieval structure that still sees occasional use (Mass 1st & 3rd Sun of the month) in the tourist season. The only other functioning church in town is the Anglican **St Andrew's**, erected on English-owned land in 1913; immediately south and uphill from this is a remnant of the once-vast Ottoman cemetery, now edged by the town's main car park, with the **Baldöken (Fakizade) Türbe** (free-standing tomb with a sheltering gazebo) as a focus.

## Eating and drinking

It's difficult to resist eating or just having a drink in the old port at least once, where over a dozen restaurants and bars shamelessly exploit their position. Prices aren't usually any lower inland, or further west along Kordon Boyu, but food variety and quality – plus atmosphere – are occasionally superior. If you have your own transport, consider driving out to Karaoğlanoğlu, just to the west of town, with its clutch of fine restaurants.

### The seafront

**Akpınar Café** Kordon Boyu, 200m east of the *Dome Hotel*. Sticky cakes, *firin sütlaç, aşure* (during Ramazan), juices, coffees, flavoured herbal teas, continental pastries and breakfast, served in pleasant surroundings with a view of the sea across the road; indoor and outdoor seating.

**Always** Old Harbour. Good-value seafood-based *meze* at £10 per person, booze extra, served in an arched upstairs gallery (or, in summer, outside).

**Geye (Osman'in Yeri)** Kordon Boyu, between *Rocks Hotel* and *Green House*. The only Cyprus branch of the famous Bursa *dondurma* (Turkish ice cream) confectioners, founded in 1927. Just half a dozen flavours, plus a few cakes, but the best in town.

**Green House** Kordon Boyu. Popular youth hangout, with a menu divided between pizza, pasta and Tex-Mex specialties. Pleasant seaside terrace seating during warmer months.

**Niazi's** Kordon Boyu, opposite the west wing of the *Dome Hotel*. Long-established mecca for carnivores, featuring grills prepared on a central hooded fire. The full kebab at £6.80, plus £1.30 for the run of the sweet trolley (reckoned the best in the North), represents excellent value, and quality is consistent – as attested by hordes of locals in here at weekends.

### Inland

**Anibal** Ecevit Cad 39. An offshoot of the Lefkoşa *Anibal*, this ultra-hygienic, airy, 2003-founded outfit does excellent full kebab with unusually salubrious *meze*-trimmings like mint leaves, spring onions, *sumac*, and cabbage/celery *tursi*; under £6 for the works (no booze served).

**Bilgin Simit ve Fırın Börek stall** Behind the Belediye Pazarı, next to Aladdin's craft shop. The best breakfast-on-the-hoof in Kyrenia: spinach, cheese or mince *börek* to take away only. They'll have run out, and closed up, by noon.

**Chinese House** 1.5km west of Kyrenia, diagonally opposite the *Ship Inn*. Reckoned tops on the island – North or South – for Cantonese, courtesy of Chinese chefs (but local management). The haunt of the great and good, but despite an expensive 2002 refit the prices are definitely folksy at £8.50 per person for the set menu, which includes soup or spring roll plus three more courses, with few excluded items. Drink, including Chinese beer, extra; well-kept summer garden out front, ramps for the disabled. Dinner only.

**Eziç Piliç** Mete Adanir Cad, opposite Tempo Market. Roast chicken and very little else at this very popular spot on the old bypass road, both eat-in and take-away. Open noon to very late.

**The Grapevine** Ecevit Cad, next to the upper *Petrol Ofisi* filling station (the logo is a fire-breathing monster). A pre-1974 institution, now run by Kutlay "Jimmy" Keço and Arif Ahmet, offering *objet-trouvé* decor and generously portioned international/pub-style cuisine to a varying clientele; they're famous for own-raised duck and good steaks. Some evenings it's the "expats' club", but then again Rauf Denktaş chose to have his 74th birthday party here.... "Jimmy" and Arif are fascinating company, and the former will tell you anything you care to know about SPOT, the local turtle conservation project (see p.377), which he helped start. About £11 for a meal, booze (including a well-chosen wine list) extra; closed Sun.

**Laughing Buddha** 1km up the main Nicosia road from the big roundabout, just below *Onar Village*. Kyrenia's second-best Chinese restaurant, installed in a characterful old house and purvey-ing competent Cantonese food (MSG-free but a bit corn-starchy). Good set meals at £7.50 apiece for two; going à la carte gives you access to duck and fancy seafood dishes. Sometimes closed Sun off-season.

**Mantı Sofrası** Göksu Sok. Traditional Turkish snacks, such as *mantı* (central Asian ravioli), *gözleme* and *çiğ böreği*, available at seating inside or on the terraces. Serves all day continuously until early evening.

**Yeni Han** 1.6km west of Kyrenia, north side of the road, near *Chinese House*. Pide, soups, kebabs and a few more elaborate baked or veggie dishes, all (except perhaps for the sheep's head) appetizing and inexpensive. The sort of place locals love for breaking the Ramazan fast; indoor/outdoor seating. Open approximately 10.30am–11.30pm.

# Nightlife and entertainment

Organized **nightlife** – or rather the lack of it – mostly conforms to the tenor of forty-to-sixty-something tourism and part-time residence hereabouts. Even with a large student contingent, few music clubs or discos survive more than a year at a time. More sedentary, low-key **bars**, especially by the sea, have a longer shelf-life, and we list some of the more durable below. Out on the coast road well west of Kyrenia, a few "nightclubs" (*gece külübleri*), such as the *Zakkum* and *Sarıtaşlar*, contain a fair number of the area's hookers; most of those in the North are now in various cabarets lining the northern and western approaches to Lefkoşa, sited for the maximum convenience of Greek-Cypriot customers.

**Casinos**, which once totalled eighteen in North Cyprus, but have now dropped to about a dozen outfits, remain a distinctive feature of the landscape; with the ongoing economic crisis in both Turkey and North Cyprus, most of the punters are Greek Cypriot of late. All of the larger seafront hotels and resorts in the Kyrenia area – the *Dome, Oscar's, Jasmine Court, LA Hotel, Club Lapethos, Deniz Kızı, Merit Crystal Cove, Acapulco* and *Celebrity* – and many small inland resorts have one, mostly equipped with fruit machines but also with a few hard-currency-only roulette tables. The casino at *Jasmine Court*, open 24 hours, is claimed to be the largest in Europe or indeed in the Mediterranean. North Cypriots and resident students are theoretically banned from their premises, but in practice the restriction is a farce, with both students and Cypriots to be seen playing by the hour on quieter weekday nights; alarm systems warn of impend-ing Keystone-Koppish raids, giving the punters time to scarper.

In terms of more high-brow organized entertainment, there's a popular and well-regarded late-spring **music festival**, held in the atmospheric surroundings of the Béllapais abbey refectory. There are three **cinemas** in the Kyrenia area, by far the best being the Lemar Cineplex 2, in the basement of the eponymous supermarket, just west of town. At least one of the two films will be foreign, first-run fare, in the original soundtrack. Also worth a mention is the *Semel Cinema Club*, also in the west of town.

Café 34 (Angels) Old Harbour, next to *Canlı Balık Restaurant*. Most established of several bars and cafés clustered here, but talk still predominates over the taped music; mixed crowd of locals and tourists, with indoor/outdoor seating.

Café Harbour Old Harbour. Probably the busiest of the bars in the old harbour area, with live music some nights.

Roxannes Kordon Boyu, next to *Rocks Hotel*. TGIF-type place that's renowned for strong cocktails and a decent buzz. Also light snacks and burgers.

## Listings

Airline Cyprus Turkish Airlines, Philecia Court, Suite 3, Kordon Boyu ☎815 25 13.

Banks and exchange ATMs of the Kıbrıs Türk Kooperatif Merkez Bankası on Belediye Meydanı, the İş Bankası on the corner of Hürriyet and Atatürk, and the Türk Ziraat Bankası or the standalone HSBS booth on the front near the *Dome Hotel* are four that accept foreign plastic, with screen instructions in English. Otherwise, numerous *döviz buroları* (foreign exchange agencies) swap foreign currency notes instantly, travellers' cheques with a bit more bother (and a marginally lower rate).

Bookshop Green Jacket Bookshop, Yirmi Temmuz Cad, at the extreme west end of Kyrenia (Mon–Fri 9am–1pm & 3–6pm or 2–5pm depending on season, Sat 9am–1pm). Friendly English-speaking staff and a large stock of Cyprus-related books and maps, many difficult to get elsewhere. Also quality cards, gift stationery and a small art gallery next door.

Car rental Long-lived and reliable operators include Abant, İskenderun Cad 12, near the *Pia Bella Hotel* ☎815 45 24, ☎815 72 09; Arizona, Vakıflar Çarşısı B/11, Ecevit Cad ☎815 13 55, ☎815 13 56; Atlantic, in the *Dome Hotel* ☎815 30 53, ☎815 56 73; Başpınar, on Yirmi Temmuz Cad, opposite the Zeytinlik road ☎ & ☎815 71 06, ☎www.baspinar-rentals.com; Oscar, Kordon Boyu opposite the *Dome*, also branch next to the *Pia Bella Hotel* ☎815 56 70, ☎815 38 58; Pacific, Ecevit Cad 23 ☎815 25 08, ☎815 55 70; Sun, Kordon Boyu ☎815 44 79, ☎www.sunrentacar.com.

Expeditions Follow Me Forest Tracking, Orhan Durusoy Cad, Palidama Apt B1, en route to *Pitoresk Holiday Village* ☎815 38 03 or 0542/851 66 70, ☎www.cyprustrekking.com, is run by Yücel Aşan, a retired forester with over two decades of experience in the Kyrenia hills. He offers van- or Landrover-assisted one-day outings involving several hours of walking, for about £30 per person, lunch included.

Ferry boat/catamaran agents Fergün, main office on the new harbour access road ☎815 17 70, or in the passenger terminal at the harbour before departure ☎815 49 93; Akfer, also on the new harbour access road ☎815 16 92, or in the passenger terminal at the harbour before departure ☎815 60 02.

Internet Most central and reliable is Café Net on Efeler Sok, just west of the Anglican church; several terminals, about £1/hr. Mavi Net, near the junction of İkenderun Cad and Kurtuluş Cad, and Izzy Net, just west of the *Pia Bella Hotel*, are easier to park by.

Laundry Wash and Go, 200m west of the *Pia Bella Hotel* on Mustafa Cağatay Cad; service wash, not self-service.

Paragliding Operating from a small office at mid-quay on the harbour, the multinational staff at Highline Air Tours ☎0542/855 56 72, ☎www.highlineparagliding.com, offer tandem flights up to four times daily in season (once in winter) from a launch point near St Hilarion castle. Conditions are generally excellent, with 45-min soars the norm; £49–55 per flight.

Post office Just off Belediye Meydanı (Mon–Fri 8am–1pm & 2–5pm, Sat 8.30am–12.30pm); parcel post in the basement (Mon, Wed & Fri 9–11.30am).

Scuba diving Blue Dolphin ☎0542/851 51 13, ☎www.bluedolphin.4mg.com is about the best equipped school, with two "rib" boats; currently they operate out of the *Jasmine Court* and *Merit Crystal Cove* hotels, though they plan to build their own centre in 2006. Longest running, based at "Escape" Beach in Alsancak, is PADI/BSAC-certified Amphora ☎0542/851 49 24, ☎www.amphoradiving.com. The newest entrant is Funky Fish ☎0533/845 88 63 or 0533/845 88 69, ☎www.lakeside-diving. com, which runs out of the *Dome*, *Mare Monte* and *Acapulco* resorts. "Try dives" for novices or single dives for qualified persons both run at about £20, with all gear supplied; a PADI five-day Open Water or BSAC Ocean Diver certification course costs £200, Advanced Open Water certifications £125. (See p.358 for general information on diving in North Cyprus.)

Taxis Most central rank, 24-hr, is Dome Taxi ☎815 23 76, by the eponymous hotel.

Telephones There are half-a-dozen grey cardphones in a row, next to the post office; cards are sold opposite.

Traffic tickets Pay your "tolls" for the notorious west-of-Kyrenia radar trap at the police station shown on the central Kyrenia town plan – read the text in *Basics*, p.49, before binning tickets.

# West of Kyrenia

The stretch of coast west of Kyrenia comprises the district's main hotel strip, with a good two-thirds of the North's tourism facilities either on the sea or just inland. Beaches are not brilliant, often merely functional, but the character of the foothill villages with their eyrie-like situations compensates.

## Karaoğlanoğlu (Áyios Yeóryios)

The first distinct community west of Kyrenia on the coast, **KARAOĞLA-NOĞLU** (Áyios Yeóryios) is remarkable only as the site of the Turkish landing at dawn on July 20, 1974; the village has been renamed in honour of a Turkish officer who was killed as he came ashore. A higher density than usual of grotesque monuments, including a cement abstract vaguely suggestive of an artillery piece (dubbed the "Turkish erection" by many local residents, as it's complete with wedge-shaped testicles), marks the spot some 8km west of Kyrenia. There's also a "Peace and Freedom Museum" consisting mostly of disabled Greek-Cypriot military vehicles in an open-air display, a chronicle of EOKA atrocities against Turkish Cypriots and general glorification of the Turkish intervention.

The small **beach** itself, the first decent strand this side of Kyrenia and sheltered by a large offshore rock, was "Five-Mile Beach" in British times, but is now officially Yavuz Çıkartma ("Resolute Outbreak" in Turkish) or Altınkaya, after the rock and a recommended namesake restaurant which overlooks it – though **Beşinci** Mil (Fifth Mile) is still widely understood, and the Greek "Pénde Míli" is beginning to reappear on private signage. Unfortunately a private beach-bar and Amphora Diving facilities monopolize most of the bay.

### Accommodation

The Karaoğlanoğlu area has a couple of modest **accommodation** options with beachfront settings. The *Top Set Hotel and Bungalows* (℡822 22 04, Ⓦwww .topsethotel.com; ❸), while probably overrated at three-star, has a well-kept, lush garden setting, with a large swimming pool (appreciated as there's some reef offshore), and a second sauna under construction. Off-season, the place tends to be taken over by German special-interest groups, who do yoga, Tibetan meditation, etc on the lawn. Two post-1998 wings, either the "Emir" standard hotel rooms or galleried self-catering bungalows taking up to four people, are preferable to the original studio units.

The nearby *Riviera Beach Bungalows* (℡822 28 77, Ⓦwww.rivierahotel -northcyprus.com) are more rustic and appealingly landscaped, with a large novelty pool, though again there's plenty of rock offshore, with only lido access to the sea. Choose from among three types of wood-trimmed units (❷), including peculiar vaulted studio cottages or galleried one-bedroom flats (❸), with air con and central hot water.

### Eating

Karaoğlanoğlu has an ample choice of **restaurants**, from the most basic of Cypriot kebabs to affordable seafood in relatively elegant surroundings, often at a third less than the prices found at Kyrenia harbour.

**The Address** On the shore, well signposted from middle of village ℡822 35 37. This "restaurant and brasserie" is run by an ex-manager of *Niazi's* in Kyrenia, and nearly matches it in quality. Excellent-value full kebab with imaginative *meze* accompaniment for about £7; for £1.50 extra you can raid the very rich Western sweet trolley. There's also a respectable if pricey continental menu – budget

7

£22 for two, booze extra – plus fish or calamari for non-meat-eaters. Very tasteful environment, with a view of the breakers crashing just outside – but dress up in something better than beach wear, and book tables in peak season. May close lunch for part of the winter.

**Altınkaya I/Pende Mili** North side of highway, extreme west end of town. Taking its Greek alternative name from the nearby beach, these deceptively austere premises are well thought of by the partly local clientele. The excellent-value, consistent-quality set *meze* of *molehiya*, calamari rings and *tatar böreği*, plus fish main courses, costs about £8 per person, with drinks and service extra.

**The Ambiance** Paraşut Sok ☎ 822 28 49. An offshoot of almost adjacent *The Address*, this is the latest see-and-be-seen restaurant in the North. Unfortunately you pay – dearly at £16 each, including one bottle of wine – for the lovely sea/pool-side setting, and not for the overrated food (aubergine paté, fillet parcels, fish), which can be very hit-or-miss. Despite this, booking mandatory May–Oct.

**Dünya** 300m west of the Karaman junction, north side of the road. This shack-like *meyhane*, the only surviving one in the Kyrenia area, began as something of a lark in the early 1990s but has attained cult status since. The place is often known by its alias of *döşeme evi*, "upholstery house", after proprietor Hasan's (former) daytime profession. A set £10 *meze* includes drink (except *rakı*), but quality is uneven, and of late there are more expats (and Greek Cypriots) in attendance than locals; nice rear garden seating in summer though. Dinner only, until midnight.

**Jashan** East edge of Karaoğlanoğlu on inland side of main road, near turning for *Riviera Beach Bungalows* ☎ 822 20 27 or 0542/850 9500. North Cyprus's best and longest-established Indian restaurant, with pretty authentic Indian/Pakistani dishes, plus a token French and Italian menu. Budget £13 a head including modest drink.

**Sezai Yelken** Kervansaray district, overlooking the sea, well signposted from main road ☎ 822 2215. The best surviving local option for seafood with unusual starters.

**Stonegrill** Inland side of main highway, near Kervansaray turning ☎ 822 20 02. Local outlet of an Australian chain, where a fixed price is charged for a copious three courses, comprising soup, *meze*-lite, and a choice of mains (meat, seafood, combos) which you grill yourself at the table on a hot stone. Drinks and the sweet trolley are extra, bumping up the likely bill to £12.50 minimum – retro (eg Sinatra) soundtrack included. Dinner only.

**The Veranda** East edge of Karaoğlanoğlu, north of the through road ☎ 822 20 53. Recommended for a nightcap in congenial surroundings, or a good, relaxed bistro-style meal, with an enclosed sun-porch overlooking the sea, outside seating in summer and an open fire in winter. Bar drinks are normally priced, and you can just snack on soup and grilled *hellim*, though a three-course meal – mostly continental dishes with added Cypriot flair and good desserts – will set you back about £12, drink extra (best avoid the fish). Reservations advisable in season. Winter closed Mon and weekday lunchtimes.

# Karaman (Kármi)

With its whitewashed houses scattered along a web of arcaded, cobbled lanes, **KARAMAN** is superficially the most attractive of the Kyrenia hill villages. Still referred to, even by officialdom, by its Greek name Kármi, it has in recent decades acquired a reputation as an expats' Tunbridge-Wells-on-Med. After lying abandoned since 1974 (it was agriculturally too marginal to appeal to either Turkish Cypriots or Anatolians), the place was assigned a special development category in 1982. Only Europeans – except for two Turkish-Cypriot war heroes, one married to a foreigner – were allowed to renovate the hundred or so derelict properties on renewable 25-year leases; tenants bore all costs of restoration and continue to pay a yearly ground rent. As a social experiment and architectural showcase, it initially proved more successful than some; latterly, though, it became twee (lots of plaque-named cottages, and signs telling you when and where to put the rubbish) and increasingly ingrown. The British-controlled residents' council still excludes not only native Cypriots but gays (as an unfortunate same-sex couple who unwisely purchased a property were quick to learn), Jews and people of colour. Since the 1995 fire, Kármi's appeal has diminished, with many restaurants and shops operating fitfully and a fair

Travelling around North Cyprus, you'll certainly encounter traces of the former business holdings of **Asil Nadir**. This secretive entrepreneur made UK headlines in late 1990 when his vast financial empire crashed, sending shock waves across both the City of London and North Cyprus, and again in May 1993 when, facing multiple indictments for £155 million in fraudulent transactions, Nadir jumped bail and flew back to Cyprus, declaring that he had no chance of a fair trial.

Born in the traditional Turkish-Cypriot stronghold of Lefke (Léfka) and the son of a prominent businessman, Nadir studied briefly in İstanbul before moving to London in the early 1970s. Having made his first bundle in the East End clothing industry, he used it in 1980 to acquire a controlling interest in a small company called Polly Peck. It provided a handy umbrella when Nadir began diversifying into electronics (the Japanese brand Sansui and Turkish Vestel), fruit-packing (Del Monte of California, Sunzest Citrus and Unipac in North Cyprus), plus an array of newspapers and magazines in Turkey and North Cyprus. Large numbers of hotels were also purchased or constructed in Turkey and North Cyprus. His sister, Bilge Nevzat, was placed in charge of two London divisions devoted exclusively to tourism: Mosaic Holidays for packages to Turkey and North Cyprus, and Noble Air to fly the customers there. The name "Polly Peck" was seen only on the large fleet of cargo ships plying between Famagusta and northern Europe, trading North Cyprus's agricultural produce for manufactured goods. The Nadir family empire, worth £2 billion on paper, became – after the public sector – the largest single employer in the North, keeping nine thousand adults in work at its peak.

Despite occasional murmurs of discontent from lending agencies, everything seemed to go smoothly until September 1990, when a prejudicial Inland Revenue investigation, coupled with sudden, severe cash-flow problems at Polly Peck, triggered a sharp dive in its share value on the London stock market. Several subsidiaries ceased trading immediately, and by mid-1991 Nadir had been declared personally bankrupt, with debts of over £1.3 billion. Court-appointed administrators spent much of 1991 and 1992 filing civil suits on behalf of former shareholders to retrieve £378 million in funds improperly removed from Polly Peck and subsidiaries. Unfortunately many of the more valuable assets, such as hotels, warehouses and ships, lay out of reach in unrecognized North Cyprus, where court orders would have no effect; the selling off of more accessible holdings such as the Turkish media titles produced very little in the way of proceeds.

Following Serious Fraud Office investigations, multiple indictments were drawn up in 1991 charging Nadir with fraud, embezzlement and false accounting, and his two passports (he had British nationality as well) were confiscated. A friend, Ramadan Güney, and Nadir's ex-wife Ayşegül acted as partial sureties for his bail, set at £3.5 million; he repaid their trust, and outwitted the Home Office, by sneaking out of Britain on May 5, 1993 on a chartered private jet. The Serious Fraud Office, which had always urged that bail should not be granted to Nadir, was furious, but little could be done; there was (and still is) no extradition treaty between Britain and unrecognized North Cyprus, which claimed that he had broken no local laws. It has been suggested that the UK Conservative Party was secretly glad to have Nadir out of the way, since this would ensure a quiet trial rather than a boisterous and potentially embarrassing one (see below), now postponed indefinitely from its original September 1993 date.

The root causes of the crash were in part similar to the BCCI scandal: Nadir's pre-emptory and highly personalized management style relied heavily on largesse to friends and purchase of favours, preferably with other people's money. Recipients included the Conservative Party, as embarrassingly revealed by a letter, leaked in late 1990, of effusive gratitude for Nadir's generous contribution of £440,000, signed by then-Prime Minister Thatcher. By early 1995, the Conservatives were under strong pressure from the administrators to cough up this donation, convincingly shown to be part of the stolen funds. The "fraudulent accounting" portions of the various indictments stem from the Nadir practice of citing profits and assets based on the Turkish lira exchange rate at the beginning, rather than the end, of a statement period, which disregarded its dizzying devaluation; thus his various companies tended to be overvalued by as much as 35 percent. Many North Cypriots, aware of his dubious reputation all along, derived a grim told-you-so satisfaction out of the whole affair, noting that Nadir's backers were almost exclusively foreign and that few Turkish Cypriots had been gullible enough to invest in his various companies – or if they did, they wised up and sold up quickly. Nadir's hare-brained schemes have included bringing giant polythene sacks of water from Turkey by helicopter (actually done by the government, with poor results); drilling for oil at Alagadi Beach; and setting up three heavy industrial plants in the North.

After 1995, Nadir's luck on his own turf ran out; the government, tired of waiting for a huge back assessment of taxes and social security contributions, beat overseas investigators and administrators to the punch by seizing most of his hard assets in North Cyprus. The Sunzest Citrus processing plant at Güzelyurt was nationalized (and more or less ceased operating), all the Polly Peck freighters formerly based in Famagusta were sold to overseas buyers and Nadir's cherished resorts – the *Jasmine Court*, *The Olive Tree* and the half-finished *Crystal Cove* near Kyrenia, plus the *Palm Beach* at Famagusta – were expropriated and resold to the highest bidders. Only his media interests – the high-tech, four-colour newspaper *Kıbrıs*, long a mouthpiece of the UBP party but now more pro-federation, as well as the English-language *Cyprus Today* – escaped going under the hammer.

Despite all these woes, Nadir can probably live indefinitely on the more than £1 billion he is alleged to have spirited out of the UK in the years prior to 1993. After a brief spell in Turkey, spent investing unsuccessfully in the Turkic "Stan" republics of central Asia, he is back in Cyprus. Mostly he hides out in a villa at Lapta, venturing forth only in a cocoon of bodyguards brandishing submachine guns, as a precaution against being kidnapped by British agents, and travelling in one of two consecutive smoked-glass limos to confuse potential assassins. In September 2003 there was a flurry of interest in the UK press when it seemed that Nadir, sensing an imminent settlement which would permit his extradition, was on the point of flying back voluntarily to Britain to "face the music", but since then nothing more has been heard from him.

From the standpoint of civic health, the greatest cause for concern is not Asil Nadir's long-running financial antics but the near-identity between Polly Peck and the UBP (National Unity Party), which ruled the North uninterruptedly from 1975 to 1993. The Nadir-controlled local media were always completely at the disposal of the UBP regime, especially at polling time, and employees of Polly Peck and its subsidiaries were allegedly threatened with the sack during the hard-fought 1990 elections if they did not vote for UBP lists. In return, Rauf Denktaş – a personal friend of the Nadir family – ensured that no legal harm befell them during that period, at least within the confines of North Cyprus.

Despite his various crimes and misdemeanours, the "Prince of Thieves" is missed even by his many enemies, who admit that North Cyprus is a duller place without Nadir in full sail amidst his habitual bevy of stunning female escorts. Panache and style were evident in his resorts, the first in the North to approximate international luxury standards, in part because staff were well trained and paid theoretically generous salaries (in practice, seldom collected in full – non-payment of bills being a Nadir speciality). While it seems unlikely, in such a small society, that more than one such prodigy should emerge in a generation, it's discouraging that the most internationally famous Turkish Cypriot should have run the North for years almost as his private fiefdom.

...ion of the cottages up for grabs – at startlingly high prices considering
...short leases and general uncertainty surrounding titles in the North.

The "villagers", who at certain times have included such high-powered personalities as two former (now deceased) British Tory MPs, in general strongly support the North's position (the very act of settling here is a political statement), and consider that their predecessors got their just desserts. Greek-Cypriot Kármi was an EOKA-B stronghold, and thus was heavily damaged in the 1974 fighting; for many years any heavy rain would leach the blue paint of "ENOSIS" slogans through the covering of new whitewash. The foreign community always viewed the possibility of any peace settlement with considerable ambivalence, and predictably when the barriers came down in April 2003, some leaseholders behaved appallingly towards Greek Cypriots coming to visit their former homes.

If you're here on a Sunday between 11am and 1pm, it's worth stopping in at the old church by the central car-park to view the **icon screen** which residents have assembled (rather un-canonically) from other abandoned churches in the area, as well as a copy of the *firman* (concession) granted by the sultan in 1860 allowing the extension of the building. Rather churlishly (and typically), the locals are resisting its reconsecration, though the roof is badly in need of repair.

Just before the *Hilarion Village* complex, a small sign ("Bronze Age Cemetery") points towards some Bronze Age **chamber-tombs**, though they're hardly essential viewing. The most substantial of a dozen holes in the ground has a stone shelter built atop it, and incised slabs flanking the subterranean entry. In one of these tombs was found the so-called "Kármi Cup" (now in the Cyprus Museum in south Nicosia), a specimen of Minoan Kamares ware, important evidence of Middle Bronze Age contacts between Crete and Cyprus.

### Practicalities

Whatever their attitudes towards each other, prospective lease-holders, the Greek Cypriots or the Northern authorities, the "villagers" welcome short-term visitors, who might make their first stop at the *Crow's Nest Pub* (Tues–Sat noon–3pm & 7pm onwards, Sun noon–8pm), also offering a limited range of pub grub. For full-on **meals**, combining western and Cypriot tastes, your most reliable option is *Treasure* (in the old school outside the village, closed Wed), where about £8 will get you a hearty *molehiya*-based stew with trimmings, dessert and a beer; Turkish Cypriots feel comfortable coming here, a good sign. At *Halfway House*, that distance down the road to Edremit village, a mother-and-son team provide a copious *meze* (dinner only).

If you fancy **staying short-term** in the village, this needs to be arranged beforehand through the Karmi Service Center (☎ & ℻822 25 68; closed Nov–March), which manages 24 houses of various sizes (rates approximately £300 a week).

Otherwise, just east of and below Kármi is the small, well-vegetated *Hilarion Village* complex (☎822 27 72, ⊛www.hilarion.com) offering two types of bungalow: galleried studios (❸) with a small kitchen, bathtubs, water heaters, heating/air con, but no TV or phone, and two-bedroom villas (❹) suitable for a family of four. The management quotes advantageous weekly rates of £270 for the studios, £400 for the four-person villas; there's a small pool, now open to the public (read Kármi residents) for the price of a drink from the bar.

## Edremit (Trimíthi)

Going up to Kármi you'll pass through the much smaller village of **EDREMİT** (Trimíthi), 2km below, where you'll find an excellent basketry-wares specialist – the best in the North – across from the central church.

Just below, east off the through road, is *The Hideaway Club* (☎822 26 20, ⓦwww.hideawayclub.com; closed Jan to late-Feb), one of the more popular inland resorts. Choose between two grades of suite: mixed sea/garden view standards, (③), or superior "VIP Suites" (④–⑤), featuring exceptional decor – carpets, wrought-iron beds, fireplaces – and the ability to knock units together to form quads. Breakfast (included) is served by request on your own terrace during the warmer months, or at the decent poolside restaurant. The returned London-Cypriot hosts generally have a knack for knowing what clients want – bathtubs, CD players, complimentary robes, hammocks – and also quote weekly rates of £275–360.

Housed in the church of Panayía Khryssotrimithioússa just below the village, the **Levantine College of Art** holds courses throughout the year (though spring and autumn are their peak times), and rents limited studio space to established artists. For current information, contact Roger Anderson at the Levantine College of Art, PO Box 291, Girne, Mersin 10, Turkey (☎822 24 37, ⓦwww.lcanc.com). Upon booking of a course, the College is also able to arrange affordable local accommodation.

## Alsancak and around

Some 5km west of Karaoğlanoğlu, the main district of **ALSANCAK** (Karavás, Karava) runs along a single ravine, with runnels and aqueducts everywhere irrigating the lemon orchards. Fire-damaged olive groves and quicker-recovering carobs are interspersed with abandoned houses higher up the slopes. It was founded after the first Turkish conquest as an overflow of Lapta and most of its present inhabitants are refugees from Páfos, who have converted the huge church into a mosque; the carved *témblon* is still there, though the icons have vanished. Alsancak blends seamlessly with İncesu (Motídhes) just south, and the road out of the latter continues uphill to **MALATYA** (Paleósofos), visited primarily for its waterfall. Go through the village, then continue along a narrow paved lane about 350 metres to where the surface changes to dirt just past a little bridge. The dell in the rock cleft just upstream is watered by a ten-metre cascade surging from a lip of rock; obviously it's most impressive in spring, assuming a wet winter.

### Ancient Lambousa

Out on a promontory directly north of Alsancak, the twelfth-century **monastery of Akhiropiítos** (Acheiropoiitos) can only be glimpsed from a distance, as it falls squarely within a Turkish army camp, its buildings used as storage depots. The monastery takes its name ("Made Without Hands" in Greek) from a foundation legend asserting that the central church was teleported whole from Anatolia to save it from marauding infidels. Adjacent to seaward stands the emphatically made-with-hands chapel of **Áyios Evlámbios** (also off-limits), supposedly hewn from a single monolith. Both share the peninsula with the scant ruins of **ancient Lambousa**, of which the most famous evidence is the so-called "Lambousa Treasure", quantities of sixth-century Byzantine silver and gold items dug up beside Áyios Evlámbios in 1905 and presently distributed among the Cyprus Museum in south Nicosia, the Medieval Museum in Limassol, the Metropolitan Museum in New York and the British Museum in London.

The only portions of ancient Lambousa now open to the public lie on the east side of the promontory. To reach them, take the turning for the *Mare Monte* hotel, bear left onto a dirt track when you reach the resort gate, and continue around the perimeter fence towards the shore; 4WDs can get within

## Scuba diving in North Cyprus

Like the South, North Cyprus is an excellent place to learn to **dive** or just brush up on acquired skills. Dive sites comprise a mix of reefs, drop-offs and archeological relics, with plenty of marine life on view. The sea is at its warmest from May to November (21–28°C), with just a long-john suit feasible in July and August for shallower dives. You should, however, ask for hoods and gloves from November to March – the latter also necessary in any month for protection against the rather aggressive lahoz/lágos who have learned to cluster around you for hand-feedings. Visibility is generally good, exceptionally up to 25m.

There are nearly a score of dive sites to choose from around Kyrenia, ranging in depth from 10 to 45 metres. Even shallow day-divers will see huge groupers and enormous shoals of banded bream, with luckier sightings of scorpion fish, moray or even sea turtle. One popular outing near Kyrenia is to "Fred's Reef" near the new harbour, at about 21m depth, where fish appear for their rations of Spam or boiled egg. More advanced sites include the recovery site of the Kyrenia castle's shipwreck, at 30m, or the 38-metre plunge at Zephyros reef well west of Kyrenia. All-day trips to a modern wreck site off the Karpaz (Kárpas) peninsula may be undertaken during high season.

five minutes' walk of the site. The main things to see, just before the army-base barbed wire, are a series of **rectangular tanks** carved into the soft rock, the largest about the size of an Olympic swimming pool. These were fashioned by Roman-era fishermen to keep their catch alive prior to sale, and feature a pair of ingenious, diagonal sluices leading to the sea for water to flow in and out. Just inland, fairly obvious behind intermittent chains and stanchions, is a complex of similarly rock-cut **cliff tombs**.

### Practicalities

Most tourist facilities near Alsancak are on or north of the coast road, around the *Deniz Kızı Hotel*. Best **accommodation** by some way is the 2003-completed *Merit Crystal Cove* resort (☎821 23 45, ⓦwww.merithotels.com; ⓪), which actually, well, merits its five-star rating. About half the largish rooms (with good baths) look west over the cove of the name, open to the public and one of the best beaches on this coast.

More modest seaside alternatives include the *Green Coast Bungalows* (☎821 12 10, ⓕ821 12 13; ❷), offering a mix of simple but adequately equipped studios and galleried one-bedroom apartments (self-catering), as well as a large pool, an artificially supplemented sand beach and horse riding nearby. Also on the west side of Alsancak is *Citrus Tree Gardens* (☎821 28 72, ⓦwww.citrus.tree.com; ❷), a small-scale complex of galleried units, some appropriate for families; amenities are rather ordinary, and the place scores for the personal service, lending library and congenial proprietor.

Inland, the well-landscaped, four-star *Riverside Holiday Village*, at the east edge of town south of the main road, has indoor and outdoor pools, sauna, gym, kids' water-park and aviaries (☎821 89 06, ⓦwww.riversideholidayvillage.com; ❸–❺); however a casino has been installed by the indoor pool, and in the opinion of most, too many new "superior" units have been thrown up since 1997, adding to an air of impersonality. Their on-site **car-rental** outfit (same contacts) is one of the busiest in the North, and still offers good service (direct web bookings welcome). Their local rival is Green, out at the eponymous filling station on the main highway (☎821 88 37, ⓦwww.greenrentacar.com), honest and with good-condition cars (most with sound systems).

For **eating out** locally, the *St Tropez Restaurant*, roughly halfway between Karaoğlanoğlu and Alsancak (open Tues–Sat dinner, Mon too in summer, plus Sun lunch; ☎821 83 24), delivers three courses of very elegant Frenchified food smothered under rich sauces for about £16, with its exquisite and reasonable dessert menu a highlight. Don't dare ask for kebabs – the cream of North-Cypriot society (plus on occasion diplomatic personnel over from the South) will be watching you. Head chef and maître d' Hüseyin worked in London hotels for many years, still returns to the UK regularly for "further education", and prides himself on his extensive Turkish and French wine list (budget extra for this); reservations are usually necessary.

In Alsancak village centre, *Cenap* occupies a pleasant old house, with outdoor seating in summer; despite an increasingly commercial vibe, and gaffes such as serving meat and fish together, and tepid fruit, it's popular with locals and reasonable value at about £18 for two with a bottle of *rakı*.

## Lapta (Lápithos)

A sprawling community draped over several ridges separated by canyons, its dwellings scattered in spring-fed greenery or perched on bluffs, **LAPTA** (Lápithos) seems a more elaborate, shaggy version of Alsancak, largely unscathed by the 1995 fire and so your only chance to see what the Kyrenia escarpment once looked like. Its abundant water supply has attracted settlers since the twelfth century BC, though most of them lived down at Lambousa until the turbulence of the seventh century AD compelled them to retreat inland. Ancient Lapethos was one of the original city-kingdoms of Cyprus, and during the Roman era served as a regional capital.

Lapta was famous in former times for its silk, carved chests, potters and water-powered corn mills – and more recently for a strange snake-charmer who lived in a house full of serpents, some poisonous. He not only tamed them, but was apparently able to neutralize their venomous bites, and once appeared on Turkish TV to demonstrate his talents to 1980–84 junta leader Kenan Evren.

Lapta was originally a bicommunal village; the pair of mosques and seven churches and monasteries correspond to the nine separate historical districts, but the minaret of the seventeenth-century Mehmet Ağa Camii was severely damaged during the 1963–64 troubles and the Turkish Cypriots "persuaded" to leave. It's still mixed after a fashion: Turkish Cypriots, Anatolians and a burgeoning number of foreigners, who will soon be in the majority.

### Practicalities

The developed coastline below Lapta supports several large resort **hotels**, but most of these are dominated by casinos, weekenders from the mainland and (in certain cases) prostitution, and can no longer be unreservedly recommended for conventional tourism. The possible exception is the low-rise *LA Holiday Centre* (☎821 89 81, ⓦwww.la-hotel-cyprus.com; ❹), where a pedestrian underpass gives access to a fair-sized natural beach with summer watersports on offer. The complex, officially rated four-star, also has a tennis court and sauna.

For independent travellers, far more characterful accommodation is available in **upper Lapta**, at the *Aphrodite Antique Houses*, Anadolu Sok 2 (☎821 28 09 or 0542/852 67 39, ⓕ821 17 46). Doğan and Cemile Boransel have admirably restored five houses, successfully combining mod cons (even a jacuzzi in one) with quality building materials and heirloom furnishings – virtually the only such outfit in the North. The units vary in capacity from two to six persons, with prices accordingly ranging from £130 per week for two persons November

*Başpınar* restaurant marks the start of the most worthwhile waymarked local hike, largely on path surface, described as Walk No. 8 in the book of North Cyprus hikes (available from Green Jacket Bookshop in Kyrenia). It's a more pleasant experience during spring or autumn, with vivid foliage colours in November, though Sundays during the autumn hunting season are to be avoided. While it's waymarked with paint dots, much of the trail is rough and faint, unmaintained since the colonial era, and thus not really a stroll for beginners – you'll need proper boots, as well as adequate water for half a day.

Take the dirt track heading straight west from the taverna, ignoring the first trail which hairpins up and left (this soon ends at a barbed-wire fence). Fork left when the track system divides, and then, some 350m from the restaurant, take the hairpin-left path flanked by red or maroon paint splodges. Except for one brief downhill stretch, this trail zigzags up relentlessly through intact pine and juniper forest, heading east, then south. About 1hr 15min along, the path levels out and veers west, allowing a glimpse of the radio mast atop Selvili Dağ (Kyparissóvouno, 1024m); you pass an abandoned cottage, and the Assa shaft well (dry, and dangerously deep). Beyond these, you climb again in earnest towards the south, with the sea reappearing beyond the local meadows and low intervening ridges.

At 1hr 40min, you join the old ridge road beside a disused pre-1974 phone pylon; turn right, heading west and slightly downhill towards Kórnos peak (945m), which soon appears, framed by pines. You've 35min progress along this track, before hairpinning down and right onto a track flanked by blue dots. Walking along this is pleasant enough, as vehicles can no longer use it, and it becomes a path within fifteen more minutes, just above a dry fountain. Immediately adjacent is the shattered medieval church of **Panayía Kriniótissa** (Our Lady of the Spring); long bereft of frescoes, it probably dates from the fourteenth or fifteenth century, although there's no record of it in contemporary sources.

From this church you've half an hour's walk down to rejoin the track system; fork right at the outset (left heads towards the monastery of Sinai, for which see Karşıyaka account). Once on the track (turn right when you meet it), you're back in the fire zone, and until near the end there are no possible shortcuts to mitigate the 35min of obligatory track-tramping across bare hillside. This anticlimax aside, the loop walk is a pleasant three-and-a-half-hour trek (plus another half-hour for rests); probably the wisest strategy is to go just after breakfast or after lunch, arranging for a meal at *Başpınar* on your return.

to March in the *Cyprus House*; £200 per week at the *Mill House* (two separate units hosting up to four people each); on up to £320 per week for four persons, all year, in the luxurious *Blue Door House*. Of late the emphasis has shifted to longer-term occupation, with many of the units rented for six months to a year; Doğan is also your man if you've bought an old ruin needing loving restoration. The same, very welcoming family runs a beachfront restaurant in Lapta, the *Aphrodite*.

In the wake of several recent local closures, your only village-centre **dining** options are the *Lapta Belediye Restaurant* (summer only), with garden seating; or the well-signposted *Başpınar* ("Headspring") *Restaurant*, an appealing eyrie under plane trees at the very top of the village. Just adjacent, the fountain-water in question used to emerge from a tunnel after a long trip down the mountain, prior to entering a purportedly Roman aqueduct whose arcades partly support the restaurant; the massive recent growth in demand from the new villa projects has wrecked the water table and halted the flow. Despite this, the place remains a massively popular venue for Sunday lunch especially, when goat or lamb stew, and *küp kebap*, are available only by advance arrangement (℡821 86 61); on spec, fare will be rather more ordinary (chops with some *meze*) and quite pricey for the locale (£7, drinks extra).

## Karşıyaka (Vasília) and Güzelyalı (Vavilás)

Some 18km west of Kyrenia, you reach an unmarked crossroads, though on the seaward side of the road there's an Atatürk bust at the middle of a plaza ringed with coffee houses. The inland turning leads shortly to **KARŞIYAKA** (Vasília, Vasilya), whose gushing fountain contrasts with its barren, sunbaked setting near the western end of the Kyrenia range. The abundant water allows for the irrigation of farmland in the plain below, but the village is about as far west as expats – and more casual tourists – are inclined to venture, with villa construction down on the plain clearly more profitable now than farming. Above Karşıyaka stand the shattered remains of the **monastery of Sinai**, which like Panayía Kriniótissa (see hike box, p.360) appears in no historical annals.

If you instead follow restaurant signs to seaward from the plaza with the Atatürk bust, **GÜZELYALI** (Vavilás, Vavila) soon appears. Formerly a port for shipping carob pods, it still has three visible warehouses. Beautiful (*güzel* in Turkish) it ain't – nor are there any beaches worth mentioning – but it is an authentic outpost of Cypriot fishing culture. The *Şirinyalı* restaurant (closed Thurs) here, run by the Üçok family, is an inexpensive seafood place, one of the best in the North, with indoor and outdoor seating overlooking the water, and makes an excellent halt while touring.

A bit past the crossroads, the road meets the sea again near a defunct hotel. Opposite this is a tempting-looking **beach**, which up close proves to be heavily striated with reef – though there is one sandy corridor to get into the water, in front of a seasonal beach-bar.

# The Koruçam (Kormakíti) peninsula

The western reaches of Kyrenia district terminate in the **Kormakíti peninsula** (Koruçam Burnu to the Turks), a rolling expanse of farmland and sparsely vegetated hills. Like the Akámas and the Karpaz, the other great promontories of Cyprus, it has a back-of-beyond feel and an interesting demographic history, in this case as the last redoubt of the island's thousand-year-old Maronite community.

Once past the turnings for Güzelyalı and Karşıyaka, and the reefy beach noted above, the previously generous road dwindles somewhat as it bears inland on its long, indirect way towards Nicosia; the entire route is heavily militarized from here on, as it's the easiest way around the Kyrenia hills for potential invaders.

## Kayalar to the cape

Less than a kilometre inland, by an improbably located cluster of "nightclubs", a paved, narrow road heads west back towards the coast, and the village of **KAYALAR** (Órga), where mushrooming numbers of foreigners' villas perch incongruously above crumbling dwellings occupied by settlers from Turkey. Just before reaching Kayalar, a few coves look appealing from afar, but up close prove to be reefy and (usually) filthy; the exception is so-called "**Horseshoe Beach**", also the only one with facilities, in the form of a seasonal café-restaurant at the top of the drop to the shore.

Beyond the modern, undesecrated Maronite chapel and bay of Áyios Yeóryios, the next settlement, **SADRAZAMKÖY** (Liverás), is too poorly sited to have attracted more than a handful of Anatolian settlers – but has attracted another unlikely, and sizeable, villa-village close to the shore. You can bump further along dirt tracks to the unmanned gantry-mounted beacon out on bleak **Cape Koruçam** (Kormakíti) itself; this is Cyprus's nearest point to Turkey, some forty nautical miles from the promontory to Cape Anamur in Anatolia.

## Koruçam (Kormakíti)

The road hairpins on itself from Sadrazamköy to head back southeast, passing a tiny medieval chapel of the Virgin just before arriving at the once-prosperous Maronite "capital" of **KORUÇAM** (Kormakíti). Set amid gently inclined, piny uplands, the little town gazes towards the Gulf of Mórfou and the great coastal bight to the west. Its permanent population, about 1100 in 1960, has dwindled to 140 mostly elderly residents; just a bare handful of children, taught by two nuns from a small, well-kept convent in the village centre, keep the primary school going. A priest is still resident, with mass celebrated regularly in the enormous modern church of Áyios Yeóryios; you can visit the interior at other times by applying to the convent or the nearby municipal coffeehouse, where

### The Maronites of Kormakíti

The Maronites are an ancient Middle Eastern sect whose identity arose out of a seventh-century theological dispute between the Monophysites, who postulated a single, divine nature for Christ, and the mainstream Orthodox, who believed Christ was simultaneously God and Man. When asked their opinion by the Emperor Heraclius, the monks of the Monastery of St Maron in Syria proposed that Christ had a dual nature but a single divine will. For a time this was championed as an ideal compromise, but later the doctrine was deemed heretical and its adherents had to seek safety in the mountains of the Lebanon.

Supposedly, the Maronites first came to Cyprus in the twelfth century with the Crusaders, whom they had served in Palestine as archers and guides, settling primarily in the Karpaz and Kormakíti areas. A contending theory asserts that these merely supplemented an existing Maronite colony which had been on the island since the seventh century.

Although Uniate Christians – they acknowledge the supremacy of the pope, and still call themselves Katholikí (Catholics) – the Maronites have always been culturally similar to the Greek Orthodox majority, being bilingual in modern Greek as well as their own medieval Syriac, and using Greek personal names. The Karpaz community assimilated some time ago through intermarriage, and like the island's Latin Catholics, the Maronites have for some years observed Easter on the same date as the Orthodox, not least so that children at university can visit parents during a uniform week of holiday.

Despite all this, the Maronites attempted to remain neutral in the struggle between the Greek Orthodox and Turkish Muslim communities, taking no part in EOKA excesses either before or after independence. In their opinion the current situation in Cyprus is largely the result of pre-1974 government policy, and they bear little animosity towards Turkish Cypriots.

Accordingly, the Maronites of Kormakíti were among the enclave Christians theoretically allowed to remain in the North after 1974, though in practice Turkish military and civil administration was until 2003 very nearly as hard on them as on the Greeks of the Karpaz. Like the Greek Orthodox of the Karpaz peninsula (see p.410), they were issued with identity cards by the Northern authorities, but not allowed to vote.

Beirut football pennants hang near portraits of various Maronite patriarchs and civic leaders, while religious postcards and calendars flank mandatorily displayed images of Rauf Denktaş and Kemal Atatürk.

Notwithstanding recent hopeful developments (see box), the village only really comes to life at weekends, especially during hunting season when Maronites in the South come to visit. Their favourite target, opposite the church, is *Yorgo Kasap Restaurant,* where some of the spirit of the multi-ethnic Cyprus of old can be recaptured. Before April 2003, Turkish-Cypriots who came here for Sunday lunch were making something of a low-key political statement about the continued social segregation, and cocking a snook at the plainclothes policeman dining alone, keeping tabs on attendance. Yorgo's *meze* is not bargain-basement at £8 a head (including his own red wine), but it's great value and one of the most savoury on the island: *tahíni, talatoúra,* sheep's yogurt, pickled capers and cauliflower, succulent *kléftigo,* and to finish off, superb *köfter* – like the *soudzoúki* of the South, but without nuts.

## South and east from Koruçam

**Çamlıbel** (Mýrtou), near the high point of the road to Nicosia, has become a major Turkish army strongpoint, though the direct road between here and

Then there was the farce of the two *múkhtars* for the village, one appointed by the North, one by the South – each considered a spy of the "sponsoring" regime, and amidst a muddle of countermanded edicts, there was (and still is) no real authority in Koruçam. Most supplies and foodstuffs were brought in from the South, as the Maronites were, either by official choice or their own, not well integrated into the Northern economy.

Although there are no Turkish-mainland settlers in Koruçam village proper, nearby houses, public buildings and farmland (including rich citrus groves and corn fields) have been expropriated without compensation, and secondary schools shut down, making the continued existence of a viable community virtually impossible. By the mid-1990s, when the worst harassment eased up (and telephones arrived), almost everyone between the ages of 12 and 45 in the four traditional Maronite villages had elected to emigrate, either to the South or abroad: rarely to ancestral but troubled Lebanon, more usually to Italy and England, where intermarriage with other Catholics is common.

What's left of the Kormakíti Maronite community now lives in the eponymous village, officially renamed Koruçam. The three other traditional settlements, Karpaşa (Karpásha), Özhan (Asómatos) and Gürpınar (Ayía Marína), were completely devoid of Maronites by 1996, despite the fact that their main monastery, Profítis Ilías, was near Gürpınar. The remaining Maronites – average age 68 – were some of the few individuals allowed relatively free movement between the two sides of the island prior to 2003. This status made them useful business intermediaries – for instance in the smuggling back and forth of title deeds for Greek-Cypriot properties whose refugee owners, despairing of a settlement providing for the right of return, elected to sell land or ruins to foreigners.

In 2003, living conditions for the Kormakíti Maronites improved markedly. With the Vatican discreetly fronting the money, airtight titles for all their agricultural property – from both the northern and southern authorities – were "ransomed", and their use thereof guaranteed when the Turkish military was induced to withdraw from them. Houses are now well kept, and there are even some confident new-builds, with the freedom to cross the barriers making full-time residence theoretically possible.

Koruçam is unrestricted. There's a tourist attraction of sorts just west, the so-called **Mavi Köşk** or "Blue Villa". To reach it, head southwest on the bypass road towards Güzelyurt, passing various army-camp entrances shut to the public, then turn right at a minor road with a fruit stall at the junction – if you pass a filling station you've gone too far. This is the narrow but more direct road to Koruçam. A few hundred metres along, there's an unmanned checkpoint; turn right off the Koruçam-bound road, and at the next gate you will have to leave a passport. Enter the military zone and park right in front of the **villa** (daily 9am–5pm; guided tours only; £0.25); once inside you'll have to leave another piece of ID per group (a driving licence should do).

In unitary-Republic years the Mavi Köşk belonged to one **Pavlos Pavlides**, a lawyer, arms-dealer and associate of Archbishop Makarios, who stayed here on occasion. The villa and its past occupants are now firmly entrenched in the official demonology/mythology of the North, albeit in a slightly sanitized version as pattered forth by your (possibly English-speaking) guide. Tours consist of a visit to about half of the rooms (the rest is off-limits, residence of the local Turkish Army commander) and the gardens, including a breathtaking viewpoint above a bunker, from where Pavlides could supposedly watch for his gun-running ships in the Karamanian channel. The decadence of Pavlides and his guests is allegedly borne out by a tiled fountain where foreign actresses are said to have taken milk-baths in public view (though the fountain-basin is far too small). Another story goes that the jovial host would toss apples out of an upper-floor window to nubile young ladies bobbing in the courtyard pool and whoever caught the fruit would share his bed that night. The only slight problem with the latter anecdote is that Pavlides was decidedly gay, and the pool would have been full of hunky lads; the lucky winner could be smuggled into and out of Pavlides' bedroom by a secret tunnel (only a few yards long), which you're shown. Pavlides himself went into exile post-1974 and was shot dead by a Turk in 1986, in Italy.

This much is demonstrable; wilder speculation asserts, on the basis of a few zodiacal symbols in wrought-iron-outline on the walls, and a Bacchus-faced fountain-spout for wine (on the terrace by the refectory), that Pavlides and Makarios were satanists who conducted orgies here. In reality the villa is nothing more than a pastel-coloured kitsch 1960s period piece; some of the furnishings are original, though many have been looted since 1974.

From just south of Tepebaşı (Dhiórios), another road leads west towards **Akdeniz** (Ayía Iríni), near the important eponymous Late Bronze Age-to-Archaic site excavated in 1929; since the place yielded up its treasures, it's of strictly specialist interest, and anyway falls squarely within Turkish army territory, whose conscripts will insist on accompanying you around, if indeed they let you in at all. Closer to the sea, and likely to be firmly off-limits since it also falls within a military installation, is the clifftop site of **Paleókastro**.

Most visitors head this way for a patch of serviceable **beach** ceded by the military in 1994, and indeed the turning just south of Tepebaşı towards Akdeniz is helpfully signposted "Beach/Plaj". At the Akdeniz village mosque, 5km along, bear left, and then again onto a dirt track, following more "Beach/Plaj" signs. It's just over 7km in total to the beach, trash-strewn like the other public beaches around Kyrenia and equipped only with toilets, showers and a seasonal drinks stall. The shore itself is gravel on hard-packed sand, best for jogging on a calm day; dunes behind and the sweeping views along the arc of the bay lend what beauty there is.

You can also proceed unhindered a couple of kilometres south from Çamlıbel to **Karpaşa** (Karpásha), where the Maronite church at the east edge of the village stands, though it's been permanently locked since the last handful of elderly Maronites died or moved to Koruçam or the South in the late 1990s. Some hay in spring, barley in summer and pasture for a few sheep are all that the land here affords to the inhabitants.

## The Pigádhes sanctuary

Returning to the main road and heading towards north Nicosia, you sense the beginnings of the Mesarya; corn fields become increasingly common, and all open water disappears. Exactly 2km southeast of the junction at Çamlıbel, keep an eye out on the right for a narrow but paved track running between cypresses; the start is obliterated by a ditch, though a helpful sign has been erected. After about 250m, you end up at the fenced enclosure (unlocked gate) containing the Bronze Age shrine known as **Pigádhes**. The most prominent structure is a restored stepped altar of rough ashlar masonry, carved with geometrical reliefs and crowned by a pair of stone "horns of consecration" reminiscent of Creto-Minoan sacred art of the same period. Around this sprawl the foundations of the courtyard sanctuary, plus some more trees which make the site fairly easy to spot from the road. Though not dazzling in impact, it's an intriguing antiquity, well worth the short detour and the slight risk to your undercarriage involved in crossing the roadside ditch.

## An alternative return to Kyrenia

For an interesting return route to the Kyrenia coast, bear north at Kılıçaslan (Kondeménos) towards **Kozan** (Lárnaka tís Lapíthou), beautifully set on the southern slopes of Selvili Dağ (Kyparissóvouno), at 1024m the summit of the Kyrenia range. A few grapevines are coaxed from the sunny terraces here, but nothing like the profusion south of the Tróödhos. The main church here is now a mosque, though the monastery of Panayía tón Katháron visible to the west was thoroughly sacked after 1974.

The onward road over a 500-metre-high saddle in the ridge ahead is steep and single-lane, but also paved and scenic; near the top debouches the colonial dirt-track system that runs along the ridge. Blasted through in the early 1950s at a purported cost of £300 per mile, this can be followed (preferably with a 4WD or mountain bike) past the highest summits all the way to St Hilarion castle (see below). Beyond this junction the tarmac route descends to Karşıyaka to pick up the coastal highway.

# Inland from Kyrenia

Immediately **southeast of Kyrenia** cluster several inland villages which, perhaps even more than those to the west of town, have been particularly favoured by foreigners since the start of British administration. The coastal plain seems wider and more gently pitched; the hills are further in the background, permitting more winter sun than at Kármi or Lapta. Even the laziest visitor manages to make it up here, if only to see one of the crown jewels of North-Cypriot tourism, the romantically half-ruined **Béllapais abbey**.

Further inland, along the watershed of the Kyrenia hills are scattered a handful of castles and monasteries, evocatively set on rock spires or down in wooded valleys, and justifiably some of the biggest tourist attractions in the North. Sited to be in visual communication with each other, Kyrenia and Nicosia, the castles of **St Hilarion**, **Buffavento** and **Kantara** served as an early-warning system for pirate raids on the north coast. At the start of the Venetian era, they were all partially dismantled to prevent further mischievous use, though the development of artillery had effectively made them obsolete already. All of these sights, with the exception of Buffavento and Antifonitis, are served by roads of decent standard taking off from the two main Kyrenia–Nicosia routes.

## St Hilarion castle

Just west of the main Kyrenia–Nicosia highway, in the Kyrenia hills, **St Hilarion castle** (daily: summer 8am–4.30pm; winter 9am–1pm & 2–4pm; £2) is the westernmost and best preserved of the three redoubts built by the Byzantines and Crusaders. With walls and towers that appear to sprout out of the rocks almost at random, it's a fairy-tale sight living up to Rose Macaulay's much-quoted description – "a picture-book castle for elf-kings" – and the rumour that Walt Disney used it as a model for the castle in *Snow White and the Seven Dwarfs*. Local legend once credited St Hilarion with 101 rooms, of which 100 could easily be found; the last, an enchanted garden, contained a fabulous treasure belonging to an elusive "queen" of Cypriot folklore, probably a holdover of Aphrodite worship. Shepherds or hunters stumbling through the magic doorway of the treasury had a tendency to awaken years later, Rip Van Winkle-like, empty-handed among the bare rocks.

### Some history

The castle's verifiable history is almost as intricate as its battlements, with occasional valiant or grisly episodes belying its ethereal appearance. The saint of the name was a little-known hermit who fled Palestine during the seventh century to live and die up here, purging the mountain of still-lurking pagan demons; a Byzantine monastery, and later a fort, sprang up around his tomb.

Owing to its near impregnability, it was one of the last castles taken by the Crusaders in 1191. The Lusignans improved its fortifications throughout the early thirteenth century and knew Didhymi, the Greek name for the twin peaks overhead, as Dieu d'Amour. St Hilarion was the focus of a four-year struggle between Holy Roman Emperor Frederick II and regent John d'Ibelin for control of the island, won by John's forces at the battle of nearby Agírda (today Ağırdağ) in 1232. During the subsequent 140 years of peace, sumptuous royal apartments were added, so that the castle doubled as a summer palace and, during 1349–50, as a refuge from the plague.

In 1373, during the Genoese invasion, the castle again acquired military importance as the retreat of the under-age King Peter II. His uncle and regent John of Antioch, misled by his hostile sister-in-law Eleanor of Aragon into believing his bodyguard of Bulgarian mercenaries treasonous, had them thrown one at a time from the highest tower of the castle; the tale seems apocryphal, and probably only the senior officers were defenestrated, and the rest sent on their way. In any case, without his loyal retinue John – implicated in the murder of Eleanor's late husband, Peter I – was easy prey for the vengeful queen and her followers, who lured him to supper with Eleanor in Nicosia, where they stabbed him.

The Venetians rendered the castle useless, they thought, for modern warfare. But in 1964 the beleaguered Turkish Cypriots found the castle not so militarily obsolete after all, using it as headquarters of their main enclave which included several Turkish communities straddling the main Kyrenia–Nicosia road. A small garrison of teenage TMT activists was able to fend off EOKA attacks on the castle, and the Turks remained in control of the place thereafter

With passage on the traditional main highway prohibited to Greek vehicles, and possible only in slow, UN-escorted convoy, the central government was forced to construct a bypass via Beşparmak (Pendadháktylos). In 1974 St Hilarion and its surrounding enclave were a primary goal of Turkish paratroop landings early on July 20.

## The site

Although St Hilarion itself is now very much open for visits, the twisty but well-marked approach road from the highway still passes through a Turkish army base, with signs forbidding stopping or walking, let alone photography. It is also closed to civilian traffic just before sunset, so if you tarry too long you may be forced to leave the area via the tortuous, dirt ridge-track west to Karşıyaka. Partway along, the restricted zone ends just past a clearing where the Crusaders held their jousting tournaments, and suddenly the castle appears, draped over the bristling pinnacles before you.

Once arrived, you'll spend a good hour scrambling over the crags to see it all. It's hot work in summer: come early in the day, and bring stout shoes – beach- or pool-wear won't do on the often uneven ground.

First you cross the vast lower ward beyond the ticket booth, where medieval garrisons kept their horses; the wood-and-plaster work – scorched by the 1995 bush fire – of the lower towers must have appeared during the TMT occupation. Once through the hulking gatehouse and tunnel into the middle enceinte (the name given to the defended area enclosed by the castle walls), your first detour is to the half-intact Byzantine chapel, the earliest structure in the castle. You continue through a myriad rooms on a variety of levels; these include the monastic refectory, later the royal banqueting hall, up some stairs north of the chapel, and the handsome vaulted belvedere just beyond it.

Occasional modern roofing that survived the fire dates from the colonial era; almost everything else became a casualty of the blaze, including the drinks café with its unbeatable views over the Kyrenian coast, now relocated in a less exalted structure down by the car park.

An **arched gate** allows entry to the upper enceinte; you can scramble immediately up south to the highest towers (elevation 732m). The more outrageously placed, "Prince John's", is the purported venue for the massacre of his Bulgarian auxiliaries – not a spot for acrophobics to linger. Alternatively, climbing the stony stair-paths towards the west end of the complex, you'll pass the aqueduct and cistern (the latter now just a dangerously deep mud-puddle), which supplied the otherwise waterless garrisons here. Excursions end at the royal apartments, whose windows afforded the TMT garrison a good view of their mortal enemies in Kármi before 1974.

# Ozanköy (Kazáfani) and Çatalköy (Áyios Epíktitos)

East of Kyrenia, and reachable from the coastal highway by a secondary road, are two attractive settlements. **OZANKÖY** (Kazáfani, Kazafana) was, before the troubles began, a mixed village famous for its carob syrup and olive oil; at the Kaya Market in the very centre you can still buy a bottle of *harup pekmezi* (carob syrup) for about £1.50 – excellent over oatmeal or baked into muffins, reckoned a mild aphrodisiac and perhaps the most authentic North-Cypriot souvenir. In the faded-frescoed medieval church of Panayía Potamítissa, now the village mosque, a fourteenth-century tomb in one corner sports a bas-relief of the occupant in period dress. Ozanköy is also home to two of the more long-running village **restaurants** in the area. *Erol's* (dinner only; closed Sun; ☎815 91 36 or 0533/864 63 72), well signposted at the southeastern edge of Ozanköy, is slightly pricey for local cuisine (budget £8 per person), but the quality, especially of the meat, is high. For that amount you'll get home-made soup, chops, garnish and nibbles, plus a beer in winter, but their famous hot/cold *meze* in season, when more customers are about (and reservations are suggested). Just east of Kaya Market stands *Şenol's Old Mill* (daily except Wed, dinner only), a cheap-and-cheerful venue where the set meal (starter plate, three grilled items with rice, fruit platter) and two brandies (or a beer) will set you back perhaps £6. Portions aren't hugely generous, and the quality isn't four-star – this is somewhere to go when you want a quick feed with no fuss. The "mill" part in the back, with its rural knick-knacks, is appealing.

**ÇATALKÖY** (Áyios Epíktitos) is built atop a peculiar low escarpment riddled with caves; in one of these lived the hermit Epiktitos during the twelfth century. Above the village lies the *Dedeman Olive Tree* (☎824 42 00, ⓦwww .dedemanhotels.com; ⓢ), one of the more luxurious yet good-value **suite-hotel** complexes in the North and represented by most package companies. Arrayed around an enormous pool are three types of accommodation: a wing of very large hotel rooms with high-quality furnishings, a few three-bedroom bungalows sleeping five and (closest to the pool and thus popular) one-bedroom suites. Double-occupancy prices are the same throughout, and there's no true self-catering. With massive common areas, a casino and on-site restaurants, the management has set its cap at "conference and business tourism" (for which read Turkish mainlanders and the occasionally glimpsed hooker).

On the east side of the village stands *Anı*, one of the best and most reasonable fish **restaurants** in the North; their cold and hot *meze* are unusual and whole-somely fresh – all their vegetables are own-grown – and they're able to find fresh fish even in midsummer; budget about £20 for two, including a bottle of wine, though certain specials are only available for four or more. The cavernous interior can be a bit dreary, however, unless they're reasonably full.

## Beylerbeyi (Béllapais)

A couple of kilometres inland and uphill from Ozanköy on a secondary road, the village of **BEYLERBEYİ** (Béllapais, Bellabayıs) occupies a sloping natural terrace overlooking the sea, a ravine to the east providing some definition. **Lawrence Durrell**'s sojourn here during the mid-1950s put it on the literary and touristic map, and his former house – more or less in the centre of the village – sports an ornamental ceramic plate over the door, reading: "Bitter Lemons: Lawrence Durrell lived here 1953–56". Here he finished *Justine*, the first volume of the Alexandria Quartet, and entertained a succession of British literati who had already made – or subsequently went on to make – their mark as travel writers or chroniclers of the eastern Mediterranean. Since his time both the interior and exterior of this large house has been somewhat tastelessly revamped by several successive owners, but out front the mains-water standpipe which figured so prominently in the drama of Durrell's purchase of the property still protrudes from the pavement.

Frankly there are more attractive villages in the Kyrenia hills than Beylerbeyi: there's little greenery (especially since the bush fire) and open space compared with Kármi or Lapta, and cobbles have long since vanished from the lanes. The glory of the place resides definitively in the nocturnally illuminated Lusignan **abbey of Béllapais**, at the northern edge of the village.

## The history of the abbey

Béllapais abbey was originally founded as St Mary of the Mountain just after 1200 by Augustinian canons fleeing Palestine. Almost immediately the brethren changed their affiliation to the Premonstratensian order under Thierry, the man behind the construction of Ayía Sofía cathedral in Nicosia, and adopted the white habits which gave the place its nickname of the "White Abbey". Lusignan King Hugh III richly endowed it later the same century; he also conferred on the abbot the right to wear a mitre, sword and golden spurs, which only puffed up the abbey's pretensions in its frequent squabbles with the archbishopric of Nicosia – as did a gift of a supposed fragment of the True Cross in 1246.

Subsequent Lusignan kings were benefactors, and some even lived in the abbey, but it provided a tempting target for the Genoese plunderings of 1373, after which it spun into both moral and physical decline; the friars' reputation became scandalous on account of their concubines, and the fact that they would accept only their own children as novices. The Venetians shortened the long-standing name, Abbaye de la Pais (Abbey of Peace), to De la Pais, from which it was an easy elision to Béllapais.

The Turks dispersed the community in 1570 and handed the abbey over to the Orthodox Church, while a village – apparently populated by descendants of the monks – grew up around the monastery. The site subsequently suffered from being used as a quarry by villagers and even the British, who despoiled the buildings in various ways before their embryonic antiquities department began repairs under George Jeffrey, first curator of the Lapidary Museum in north Nicosia, early last century.

## Visits to the abbey

You approach through a promenade of palm trees that lend an exotic touch to the Gothic ambience, though the cloister's courtyard is still garnished with the robust cypresses planted by Durrell's Mr Kollis in the 1940s. **Admission** policies are somewhat flexible (nominally daily: summer 9am–7pm; winter 9am–1pm & 2–4.45pm; £2), since the (not especially recommended) *Kybele* restaurant operates within the grounds until 11pm, so in practice you can see much of the complex (at a slight distance) from the restaurant's access path.

Except for its western arcade, where the vaulting has vanished, the graceful fourteenth-century **cloister** is intact and enlivened by carvings of human and monster heads on the corbels. Just south of this, the thirteenth-century **church**, used by the Greek Orthodox community here until its last members were forced out in 1976, is now open for visits. The interior is much as the Greeks left it, with intricately carved pulpit, *témblon* and bishop's throne still intact in the dim glow of five fairly restrained chandeliers. Over the entrance, a horse-shoe-shaped wooden *yinaikonítis* seems to defy gravity; the rib-vaulted ceiling is rather more substantially supported by four massive columns. Underfoot, several Lusignan kings are thought to be entombed beneath the floor pavement. A stairway outside leads to a rooftop **parapet** that's the best vantage point for the ruined chapterhouse to the east of the cloister, and leads also to a small treasury, atop the church's north aisle, and the upper-storey dormitory, of which only one wall survives.

On the north side of the cloister, a Roman sarcophagus once served the monks as a washbasin before they trooped into the magnificent **refectory** (which now hosts the local music festival, every late May to early June). Six bay windows frame the sea, with a thirty-metre drop below them along the edge of the escarpment on which Béllapais was built. A raised pulpit in the north wall, from where scriptural selections would be read during meals, is accessible by a narrow spiral stairway. During the late 1800s, British forces barbarically used the refectory as a shooting range – hence the bullet holes in the east wall, where a higher rose window admits more light. A stairway leads from the ruins of the kitchen at the refectory's west end down to an **undercroft** with magnificent "palm" vaulting sprouting off low columns; it's currently used as an exhibition venue.

### Practicalities

Lest he accomplish nothing all day, Durrell was warned away from the "Tree of Idleness" (a now-sickly mulberry) shading its attendant *Ulusoglu* **café** on the square southwest of the abbey. Across the street, the *Huzur Ağaç* ("Tree of Repose" in Turkish) **restaurant** is a modern full-service outfit with tolerable food, but tackily souvenir-festooned and tour-oriented – besides Kyrenia harbour, the abbey's surroundings are the only place in the North that could be deemed rampantly commercialized. For better eating, head down the main street out of town – past overpriced and overrated *Aged House* – to unpretentious but wholesome *Paşa* (dinner only; closed Sun), where under £5 will see you to *ayran*, soup and either *pirohu* (vegetarian ravioli) or a *pide*. For excellent set-price kebabs and *meze*, try *Ayna* at the village's western edge, in the Terzioğlu district, in sleek, large premises at the top of the lane past various luxury villas of London Cypriots made good.

The best two among several short-term **accommodation** options in Beylerbeyi are almost adjacent. The excellent *Bellapais Gardens* (☎815 60 66, ⓦwww.bellapaisgardens.com; ⓖ), just below the abbey refectory and north wall, is a well-executed, human-scale bungalow cluster with its own, guests-only restaurant. The galleried one-bedroom units have more character than the studios, but all were refurbished in 2000–2002 with new bathrooms, marble floors and bedroom furniture; the level of service from Steve Abit and family, breakfast quality and attractive garden pool guarantee a loyal repeat clientele.

Immediately west of the abbey grounds is Aydın Öngül's *Abbey Inn* (☎815 94 44, ⓕ815 94 46, ⓔabbeyinn@kktc.net; ⓸), a small, self-confessed "boutique hotel" where again service is paramount. The view from the balconied, upper-floor units encompasses much of the coast, while the rooms themselves have genuine antique furnishings and wood-veneer floors, let down only by rather average bathrooms. Many guests opt for half-board since chef Graham, former proprietor of the now-closed *Abbey House* restaurant, is one of the best cooks in the North.

## Panayía Absinthiótissa monastery

The **monastery of Panayía Absinthiótissa** enjoys a grand setting amid juniper forest on the south flank of the range, gazing out across the Mesarya. Founded in late Byzantine times, it was taken over by Latin monks in the fifteenth century, and well restored during the 1960s – only to suffer comprehensive vandalization since 1974.

Despite its condition, Absinthiótissa still merits a visit, perhaps as a detour on the way between Kyrenia and north Nicosia. **Getting here** is fairly easy: from the divided highway linking those towns, turn east towards Aşağı Dikmen (Káto Dhíkomo) and Taşkent (Vounó); after about twenty minutes of mostly single-lane driving, you'll reach the latter village, just after the giant Turkish-Cypriot flag and Atatürk slogan painted on the hillside. At the junction opposite the central shop, head north uphill along an initially paved lane, which forks after 500m; take a right, away from the gravel pit, and another right at a water tank.

The monastery is in sight most of the way, so there's little chance of getting badly lost, but you'll be more comfortable with a 4WD vehicle to skirt the yawning quarry pits.

The enormous, twelve-windowed drum and dome of the **church** are visible from afar, but as you approach you'll notice the peculiar narthex which the Catholic monks added, with apses at each end; inside, there's marvellous Gothic rib-vaulting. Any frescoes have been defaced or stolen since 1974; the only other thing to admire is the **refectory**, north across the courtyard, with shallow ceiling vaulting and unusual lancet windows outlined in 1960s brickwork.

## Buffavento castle

**Buffavento** (variable access), the least well preserved but most dramatically sited – and at 940m the highest – of the Kyrenia hill-castles, requires considerable effort to reach, but will appeal to those who like their ruins wild and slightly sinister. There is no guard or admission, but entry days permitted by the Turkish Army have varied in recent years; sometimes Monday, Wednesday and Friday from 9am to 5pm, though in other years the castle was open daily, all day.

### Getting there

To **get there**, first take the inland turning, following the signs for Famagusta (not Esentepe), just past Çatalköy; the good surfacing is a legacy of the Greek Cypriots having bulldozed this route in 1969–70 to get around the Turkish-Cypriot enclave at St Hilarion.

The only local village, reached by a slip road partway along, is scruffy **Arapköy** (Klepíni, Klebini). A curious legend once held that no more than forty families could reside in the place, or the Angel of Death would cull the surplus within the year; there are still only about 150 people here, a mix of native Turkish Cypriots, Anatolian settlers and a few foreigners attracted by the views.

At the very top of the grade, when the Mesarya comes into view and the road (until late 2006) worsens markedly, sits the simple but convenient *Bufavento Beşparmak* **restaurant**, the area's only amenity. Just opposite this, take the rough track heading west, marked "Bufavento Kalesi" – you'll know it's a "no entry" day if a metal barrier is down. The first 400m, which deteriorate further with each winter's rains, are fortunately the worst; thereafter the surface improves along a total of 6km through unscathed forest and scrub to a circular area where vehicles without four-wheel drive must park (you'll in fact be lucky to get an ordinary car even this far). A jeep track, indicated by a sign pointing right (left leads to a Turkish military area), continues 250m of zigzags further up to the true trailhead, where an olive tree grows in a stone planter ring across from a trilingual marble memorial to victims of a 1988 air crash: a small aircraft, approaching Ercan in misty conditions, failed to clear the ridge above and disintegrated nearby.

From the lower parking area, it's a 25-minute walk up through junipers alive with birds to the castle, which blends well into the rock on which it's built; though the path is in good condition, there's a consistent southern exposure, so you'll bake to death in summer unless you go early or late in the day.

Incidentally, don't believe maps – either internationally published ones, or those issued by the North Cyprus tourist office – which imply that the easiest way to get up to the castle is from the south, via Güngör (Koutsovéndis) and the tempting-looking monastery of **Áyios Ioánnis Khrysóstomos**. Beyond Güngör all tracks are unmarked, and a giant army camp blocks the way, placing

△ Buffavento castle, Kyrenia hills

the deconsecrated monastery off-limits as well. (In fairness, the Greek-Cypriot National Guard was using the grounds as a barracks before 1974, though you could still visit the main church.)

## The site

Buffavento probably began life as a Byzantine watchtower in the tenth century and was surrendered to Guy de Lusignan in 1191. The Lusignan kings used it mostly as a political prison, in particular Peter I who – warned reluctantly by his friend John Visconti of Queen Eleanor's infidelity – repaid the favour by locking Visconti up here to starve to death.

Decommissioned by the Venetians, the vaulted buildings, almost all fitted with cisterns, are in poor-to-fair condition, and home now only to bats; they're a pretext, really, for a nice walk in the hills. You can follow the stair-path (fitted with handrails) from the graffitied **gatehouse** up ten minutes through the jumble of walls to the highest tower, where a natural terrace affords superb views, and would have been the site of signal fires to communicate with St Hilarion and Kantara castles.

Up top here, you'll usually learn how the place got its name (Buffavento means "wind gust"), and be treated to the best views on Cyprus: Kyrenia, Nicosia and Famagusta are all visible in the right conditions, as are the Tróödhos mountains and indeed half the island. If you're allowed up here at dusk, you'll be treated to the spectacle of Nicosia's lights blazing to life.

## Around Beşparmak (Pendadháktylos)

Coming up from the north coast, you can't help noticing the sculpted bulk of **Beşparmak** (Pendadháktylos), the "Five-Finger Mountain", just to the east of the Kyrenia–Nicosia bypass road. Although of modest elevation at 740m, its suggestive shape has engendered legend: the Greeks say the Byzantine hero Dhiyenís Akritas left the imprint of his hand here after leaping across the sea from Anatolia.

### Sourp Magar monastery

You can get a good view of the peak's south flank by turning left at the watershed along the signed Alevkaya (Halévga) forest road (away from the marked Buffavento turning and restaurant); the first kilometre or so is dirt, but the rest of the way is paved after a fashion with chippings or tarmac. Downhill to the north after 7km, you'll glimpse the roofless, thoroughly vandalized remains of the Armenian monastery of **Sourp Magar**, or St Makarios of Egypt. Founded by Copts in the eleventh century, it became the property of the island's Armenian community four hundred years later, and hosted an important festival every May until 1974.

Driving in this direction, take a hairpin left from a shady clearing with two round picnic tables, a water spout and a blank green placard. Just under a kilometre's bumpy, rutted driving brings you to the gate of the irregularly shaped monastery enclosure. Beside a withered orchard stands the tiny church, with pilgrims' cells lining the east and south perimeter walls. Absolutely nothing has been left intact by the Turkish army, venting its fury on a shrine of its historic enemies, and it's only worth visiting for the setting amidst dense, unscathed forest.

In 1998 considerable outrage was engendered in the small Armenian community of the South when it was learned that the northern authorities intended to hand over the ruins to a local businessman for restoration as a hotel; prevailing economic realities have put the scheme on indefinite hold.

## The North Cyprus Herbarium

Just 100m east of the turning for Sourp Magar, the forestry track emerges onto a secondary paved road up from the Nicosia–Ercan airport expressway; turn right to reach, after 300m, the vast picnic grounds around the forestry station at **Alevkaya (Halévga)**. In 1989 the main building here was refurbished and opened as the **North Cyprus Herbarium** (daily 8am–4pm; free) under the direction of Dr Deryck Viney of Kármi. With over a thousand preserved specimens of plants endemic to the island, pressed in folders or pickled in spirit, this is really more of a library and research facility than tourist attraction; however, it is a handy place to pick up a number of flora guides offered for sale, including Dr Viney's two-part manual of Cypriot plant life. The keeper of the small snack bar in the middle of the picnic grounds is very keen for custom, and will sell you a guide or fizzy drink with equal alacrity, and may (if around) open the herbarium doors after-hours.

## Antifonítis monastery

The twelfth-century **monastic church of Antifonítis** (Antifonidis), tucked into a piny valley northeast of Alevkaya, was once the premier Byzantine monument of the Kyrenia hills. It takes its name – "He Who Answers" – from the foundation legend, in which a rich man and a poor man met at the place. The pauper asked for a loan from the grandee, who retorted, "Who will act as witness that I have loaned you the money?", to which the penniless one replied, "God". At once a celestial voice was heard sanctifying the transaction, and the monastery grew up around the miracle.

### Getting there

There are two usual approaches, with a 4WD vehicle pretty much essential on either. From the herbarium and recreation area, proceed northeast on the paved road, shunning the turn down to Karaağaç (Khárcha) and leaving the tarmac above Esentepe in favour of a very rough dirt track contouring along just north of the watershed. Some 14km from Alevkaya, at an X-shaped junction, ignore the hairpin down and left to Esentepe (5km) in favour of a gentler left bearing down a steep but marked ("Antifonidis") track – 4WD mandatory here – and at the foot of this valley look out for the dome of the monastery church peeking above dense foliage.

From the coast road east of Kyrenia, turn off at the large village of **Esentepe** (Áyios Amvrósios, Aykuruş), once known for its apricots and crafts, and now resettled partly by natives of Áyios Nikólaos village in the Páfos hills. Traverse to the high end of Esentepe, following signposting to Alevkaya and Lefkoşa, but at the next junction, marked by a derelict forestry placard, go straight onto the dirt surface, rather than right with the pavement. The tiny monastic **church of Apáti**, not to be confused with Antifonítis and not worth the trouble of getting up to, is soon seen above and to the right among pines. Shortly you'll reach the crossroads described above.

### The site

You can drive to within a few paces of the church, which is guarded and **open for visits** daily except Thursday; nominal hours are 9am–4.45pm, but you'd be pushing your luck to show up after 2pm. A neglected, overgrown courtyard surrounds the twelfth-century *katholikón* which, while appealing, wins no prizes for architectural purity: the vaulted Lusignan narthex on the west side dates from the fourteenth century, and the Venetians added an arched loggia to the south in the following century.

Although Greek graffiti go back two centuries, most of the heartbreaking vandalization of the church's interior has occurred since 1974. Of its once-vivid and notable frescoes, only the magnificent *Pandokrátor* survives undamaged in the huge irregularly shaped dome – supported by eight columns and covering the entire nave – plus the occasional saint or apostle out of reach on arches and columns. Although the building is now locked at dusk, and the dome windows secured against birds or bats, it's very much a case of too little, too late.

**Leaving Antifonítis**, you can continue eastwards on the forestry track system; within a minute or two there's another major junction at a pass with an abandoned building. Heading down to the south leads towards Tirmen (Trypiméni) and Gönendere (Knodhára), a straight course keeps following the crest, while down and left proceeds rather perilously on a deteriorating track (even jeeps may founder) to the rather poor village of Bahçeli (Kalogréa), just above the coast road.

# East of Kyrenia: the coast

In contrast to the shoreline west of Kyrenia, the coast to the east was historically undeveloped and even deserted, any villages being built some way inland, out of reach of pirates. All that changed with the 2004 opening of a wide, well-graded road to the district boundary (and soon beyond), now just over half an hour distant rather than nearly twice that long. Villas are sprouting all the way to Tatlısu (Akanthoú), formerly one of the few areas where carob trees were still lovingly pruned and ploughed. Tucked between rocky headlands beyond the *Acapulco Holiday Village* are the best (if exposed) beaches in the district, lonely except on summer weekends.

## Karakum (Karákoumi)

The first beach of any significance east of town is at **KARAKUM** (Karák-oumi), accessible by a side road opposite the inland turning for the *Courtyard Inn* and then left at the first T-junction: two tiny, dark-sand coves either side of

---

### Pay beaches

You may find, if you're not staying at shorefront hotels, that you will be charged a fee (£1.50–4 per person) for use of many beaches either side of Kyrenia, artificially strewn or otherwise. In 1991 the government, in an effort to keep "riff-raff" (meaning mainland Turkish conscripts and local picnickers) off beaches frequented by tourists, instituted the charges along with a ban on bringing one's own food and drink onto the sand. While the fees (except for the £4 charged by Acapulco) may not seem excessive to a foreigner, they are well beyond the means of the miserably paid soldiers, and represent a considerable hardship for a typically large family of mainland settlers, intent as well on doing its own barbecuing and not giving the beach-side snack-bars much custom.

The local uproar was so great that the tourism ministry was forced to set aside various sandy but undeveloped bays east of Lara as *halk plajları* or "public beaches". They are accordingly very popular on weekends in season when large groups of Cypriots descend on them, though you should have the water almost to yourself as they're not especially keen swimmers. The main advantages of patronizing a fee beach will be guaranteed presence of certain amenities (umbrellas, snack-bar) and a much higher degree of cleanliness owing to regular raking and rubbish collection.

a promontory, the last few hundred yards for jeeps only. The *Courtyard Inn* itself, one of the longest established of Kyrenia's international-cuisine restaurants, is Pakistani-managed, so the pub-style menu is now dominated by good curries (£5.50) and other subcontinent specialities, though English-style Sunday off-season lunch is still a big draw.

A bit further east, about halfway to the turning for Çatalköy, a seaward driveway leads a few hundred metres to the *Paradise,* a not-too-hyperbolic name for the poolside **restaurant** (☎824 43 97 or 0542/851 76 66 for reservations; closed Nov–March) run by the amiable Ahmet Derviş and family. A large mixed *meze,* strong on such vegetarian items as *molehiya,* braised spinach, unusually succulent *hellim,* beans with courgettes or stuffed aubergine, may also include *bumbar* (skinny sausages), calamari rings, plus a portion of fish, the whole thing running to about £8. Saturday nights feature live music, when the place can get packed. Son Mustafa is responsible for twelve adjacent self-catering **bungalows** (phone as above, ⓦwww.paradisebungalows.50megs.com; £125 per week for two).

## Tomb of Hazreti Ömer

A bit east of the Çatalköy turning, the tomb of **Hazreti Ömer**, another Durrellian locale extensively renovated since the 1950s, is signposted as "Hazreti Ömer Türbesi" from the coast road. The tomb is reputed to be the final resting place of not one but seven warriors or holy men, and possibly dates from the Arab raids of the seventh century, though there was almost certainly a local pagan shrine before then. In typical Cypriot fashion, the *tekke* or dervish convent which grew up around the tombs was venerated by both Orthodox and Muslim communities (as "Áyii Fanóndes" in the former case) before 1974. Its setting on a sea-lashed rocky promontory is the thing, with views back towards the mountains. Posted visiting hours (daily except Fri 9am–4pm) should not be trusted implicitly, but if you gain entrance you'll be treated to a glimpse of the dazzlingly kitsch interior: day-glo wall tapestries of Mecca, gaudy rugs in all shapes and sizes, piled books (not all of them religious) obscuring the tomb of the seven.

One cove to the west, **Fortuna** – the house originally built by Durrell's friend Marie – still stands among greenery, but inaccessible today, as it falls within a fenced-off military area. Signposted from the main highway as "Villa Fırtına", it's now the Turkish ambassador's residence.

## The main eastern beaches

Unless you're staying here, it's best to skip **"Acapulco" Beach** with its resort complex (characterized by some as "Butlins without the redcoats"), completely surrounded by barbed-wire army installations and incorporating the Neolithic site of Vrysi (finds from which are featured in a Kyrenia castle exhibition). **Lara Beach**, 3km east, has unfortunately been withdrawn from public use, with access barred by a private club leasing the bay from the *vakıf.* The closest local **restaurant**, up on the main road back towards "Acapulco", is the *Valley View,* with seating overlooking the piny ravine of the name, and a good following among both locals and tourists for the sake of its *meze,* seafood and fruit for dessert.

Beyond Lara the coast road has been straightened and speeded up, though exits to some choice bays were not provided. A Siemens-designed power plant, the subject of considerable controversy spurred by its obsolete and polluting technology, was completed just east of Lara at **Teknecik** in 1993 to eliminate the North's dependence on electricity from the Dhekélia generator in the

South. Turbine-fuel reserves are still problematic, but the weekly power-cuts of 1994–1996 have now decreased to about one monthly since another turbine came on-line.

## Alagadi ("Turtle Bay")

Four **restaurants** – *Hoca*, *Benöz*, *Esenyalı* and *St Kathleen's* – plus a rapidly multiplying villa complex – signal your arrival at the sand-and-shingle "Esenyalı Halk Plajı". Of these, *St Kathleen's* (named after a ruined medieval church of Ayía Ekateríni just behind) and *Benöz* have the largest local following and the most durable operating record; fried or grilled fish, kebab and basic *meze* is the stock-in-trade at either, with £7 buying a simple meal with beer.

For beaches, it's better to continue – either on the new inland road, or the coast-hugging track – just over a kilometre to **Alagadi** (**Alakáti**), well marked at a sharp curve where a sign for the "Alagadi Halk Plajı" points to a 500-metre dirt side track. This ends at two separate car parks serving this vast sandy bay over a kilometre long, with no facilities aside from toilets and the sporadically operating *Green Turtles Beach Bar*. As it's a *halk plajı*, there's no clean-up of rubbish – predominantly from the permanent "island" of Arab rubbish reported by yachtsmen off Syria, judging from product labels – that washes up here; the western half is more protected and thus apt to be cleaner. The cove here is best known to expats as "Turtle Bay", after its status as a sea turtle egg-laying site, but between the rubbish, the enlarged power plant whose stacks jab the horizon, the firepits of weekend barbecuers and the manoeuvring jeeps (despite signs prohibiting the practice), the hatchlings' life expectancy was historically rated as low. This has improved in recent years, through the efforts of a local protection society (see box below).

## Onüçüncü Mil

The headland to the east of "Turtle Bay" is possibly the site of ancient Alakadi; beyond this promontory is yet another bay, **Onüçüncü Mil** ("Thirteenth Mile" after its distance from Kyrenia), no longer accessible from the main road since its improvement. To reach it, head east on the track system beginning from the 'STOP' sign on the "Turtle Bay" access drive; the track winds through olives, past shed-like brick structures (a stillborn holiday village) to the top of a not

### Sea turtles in North Cyprus

In North Cyprus, **sea turtles** – predominantly green but also a few loggerhead – lay their eggs at a number of beaches, but especially at Alagadi and "Golden Beach" on the Karpaz peninsula. (For a full description of the sea-turtle life cycle, see the box on p.192). In 1990, through the combined efforts of Kutlay "Jimmy" Ketço and an expat couple, the Society for the Protection of Turtles – SPOT for short – was founded locally. Together with researchers from Glasgow University, they formed a new umbrella group, the Marine Turtle Research Group, now based at the University of Wales, Swansea. Their most signal accomplishments to date have included persuading builders not to remove sand from nesting beaches, tagging turtles so that their movements can be followed, and placing mesh over fresh nests to discourage predators.

During the nesting season (May–Oct), SPOT maintains a **visitors' centre** (☎815 51 35) behind Alagadi Beach, which operates principally from 6pm onwards; on the appropriate nights, turtle-watching tours – of either nesting or hatching – are conducted in total darkness (any landward light source can be fatally disorienting to hatchlings). At other times, contact "Jimmy" at the *Grapevine Restaurant* (☎815 24 96) – see p.350.

especially sharp descent to the beach, much the best on the Kyrenia coast (though devoid of facilities). At either end of Onüçüncü Mil's sandy crescent, eerie jumbles of eroded limestone rear up like ruined fortifications, making it difficult to distinguish between them and man-made ancient masonry.

# Travel details

## Buses

**Kyrenia** to: Famagusta (hourly; 1hr 30min); Güzelyurt (several daily; 1hr); Nicosia (every 15min; 30min). Daily out-and-back minibus services exist for most villages between Bahçeli in the east and Tepebaşı on the Kormakíti peninsula, but there are usefully frequent schedules only for Çatalköy, Ozanköy, Beylerbeyi and Lapta.

## Ferries and catamarans

**Kyrenia** to the following Turkish ports: Taşucu, at least 1 car ferry daily around noon (4–5hr); plus at least 2 daily passenger-only catamarans, weather permitting, at around 9.30 & 10am (2–3hr); Alanya, 3–7 weekly catamarans (3–5hr). See pp.34–35 for a complete discussion of companies and fares.

# 8

# Famagusta and the Karpaz peninsula

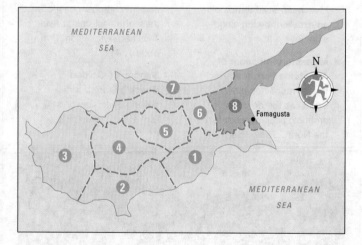

# CHAPTER 8

# Highlights

✳ **Venetian walls of Famagusta** Among the strongest and most complete medieval fortifications in the Mediterranean. See p.385

✳ **Lala Mustafa Paşa Camii** Formerly the cathedral of St Nicholas, this church-mosque is the most sumptuous Gothic monument on Cyprus. See p.389

✳ **Ancient Salamis** Ancient frescoes and mosaics, Mycenean-style tombs plus an excellent beach alongside. See p.394

✳ **Monastery-museum of Apóstolos Varnávas** The former monastery now serves as the de facto archeological museum for the North. See p.399

✳ **Panayía Theotókos** Contains exquisite Byzantine frescoes, the only intact ones surviving in the North. See p.402

✳ **Kantara castle** At the base of the **Karpaz** peninsula, Kantara castle completes a satisfying trio begun by St Hilarion and Buffavento. See p.404

✳ **Karpaz peninsula** This remote area has numerous ancient churches, best of these the basilicas at Ayía Triás and Áyios Fílon. See pp.407, 411

✳ **Nangomí ("Golden Beach")** Superb turtle-nesting beach beyond Dipkarpaz. See p.412

△ Ayía Triás basilica

# 8

# Famagusta and the Karpaz peninsula

The Mesarya (Turkish for Mesaoría) plain, hummocky and relatively confined around Nicosia, opens out to steppe-like dimensions as it approaches the long gradual arc of Famagusta Bay. This coast has been advancing slowly east over millennia, courtesy of silt brought down by the Kanlıdere River (the Pedhiéos in Greek), in recent centuries flowing intermittently at best – though after winter rains it becomes a raging torrent more than seven feet deep near Nicosia. Amazingly, the Mesarya was densely wooded, and a favourite hunting ground for the Lusignans, until the sixteenth century; climate change and Ottoman neglect of the landscape are together responsible for its present appearance.

At the southeast corner of the Mesarya, just as the land begins to rise appreciably to bluffs beyond the Attila Line, the town of **Famagusta** rears up, a Turko-Gothic chimera with no equal on Cyprus. Before the Ottoman era, the de facto capital of Cyprus had always been in the immediate environs of Famagusta, with a combination of geology and military history determining its precise location in each era. The present-day city is the successor to ancient **Salamis**, a few miles north on the far side of bird-haunted wetlands fed by the here-sluggish Kanlıdere and fringed by beaches. Salamis in turn replaced older **Enkomi-Alasia** as the main port of the region; the narrow strip of plain between the two is peppered with **tombs** of various eras, one – supposedly that of the Apostle Barnabas – Christianized and still venerated. A **monastery** which honoured him now serves as the North's archeological museum. Famagusta town presents a stark contrast to its featureless surroundings, which, particularly at twilight, take on a sinister aspect, perhaps from the numerous ancient dead in the graves of the Bronze Age and Roman cities.

The sandy shoreline of Famagusta Bay and the hotel-riviera at Varósha, south of Famagusta, saw the first mass tourism in Cyprus after independence, but now that Varósha is off-limits, the little fishing port of Boğaz marks the end of the functional row of resorts extending north of Salamis. It's also the gateway to the long, narrow **Karpaz peninsula**, the island's panhandle and likened by Winston Churchill, and more than one demagogic Turkish politician, to a "dagger aimed at the underbelly of Anatolia". Today it is in fact almost insignificant militarily – depopulated, remote, and sprinkled with traces of past importance, especially at the early Christian sites of **Ayía Triás**, **Áyios Fílon** and

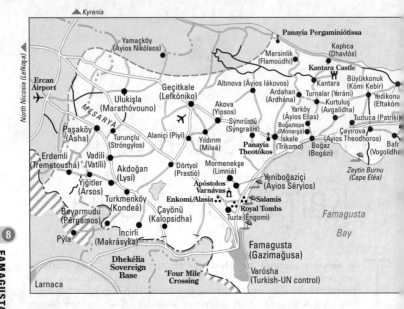

**Aféndrika.** The **castle of Kantara** effectively marks the base of the peninsula; the **monastery of Apóstolos Andhréas** sits near the far end, between one of the finest beaches on Cyprus and the desolate cape itself.

# Famagusta (Gazimağusa)

Its Venetian walls now enclosing almost nothing, and the silhouettes of its exotic Gothic churches colliding in your field of vision with palm trees and upturned fishing boats, **FAMAGUSTA** (Gazimağusa, Mağosa – pronounced, approximately, "mouse-uhh") is the architectural equivalent of a well-behaved houseplant gone to seed in its native jungle. Its official Greek-Cypriot name, *Ammókhostos*, means "sunken in sand" in Greek: its ramparts and deep harbour protect the old town from such a fate, but to the north, sand piles up in dunes, while offshore Maymun Adası (Monkey Island) is essentially a shifting spit. The climate is nearly subtropical, the sea air eating away metal and stone alike; in the years before swamp drainage, malarial mosquitoes had a similar effect on the people. All told, not much of a prospect for greatness.

Yet this was, briefly during the fourteenth century, the wealthiest city on earth, of sufficient romance for Shakespeare to make it purportedly part of the setting for *Othello*, a theory based on the brief stage instruction "a seaport in Cyprus". Today Famagusta is a double city: the compact, ghostly walled town, a crumbling Lusignan-Venetian legacy, and the sprawling, amorphous new

The character of Othello appears to be based on a historical Venetian soldier serving in Cyprus, most probably Francesco de Sessa, known as Il Moro for his dark complexion and banished in 1544 for an unspecified offence – along with two subordinates, possibly the models for Iago and Cassio.

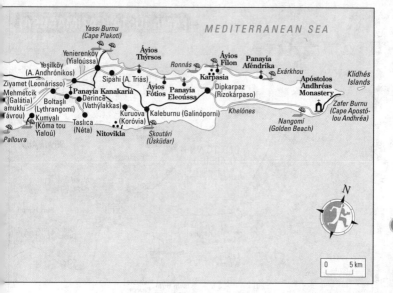

town, similarly derelict since 1974. If conditions do not change on Cyprus, it is easy to imagine both portions living up to the epithet of "sunken in sand" within decades.

## Some history

By Cypriot standards Famagusta is a young settlement, though not quite so new as Limassol. Some historians spuriously derive the name from "Fama Augusta" after the Emperor Augustus, implying an imperial Roman foundation, but the place is really first heard of only after the seventh century, when the survivors of Arab-sacked Salamis drifted here. It pottered along as a **Byzantine** fishing port, taking advantage of the only natural deep-water harbour on the island.

All that changed suddenly in 1291, after Palestinian Acre fell to the Saracens; **Christian merchants** poured in as refugees from a dozen entrepots on the Middle Eastern mainland. The pope forbade any trafficking with the infidel on pain of excommunication, thus guaranteeing Famagusta's **monopoly** as a trans-shipment point – and its spectacular growth. Every commodity of East and West changed hands here; the city became a babel of creeds, tongues and nationalities, reducing the native residents to a minority. Fortunes were made overnight, engendering spectacular exhibitionism and vulgarity: merchants' daughters wore more jewels at their weddings than certain European monarchs, and the prostitutes were as wealthy as the merchants, one of whom legendarily ground up a diamond to season a dish at table in full view of his guests.

Foreigners were fascinated and horrified in equal measure; Saint Bridget of Sweden, preaching in front of the cathedral in 1371 on her way back from the Holy Land, railed against the immorality of the city. The multiplicity of sects (and perhaps guilty consciences) resulted in scores of churches being built, supposedly one for every day of the year – many of them still standing.

But Famagusta's heyday lasted less than a century, for in 1372 a diplomatic contretemps triggered its decline. At the coronation of the Lusignan boy-king

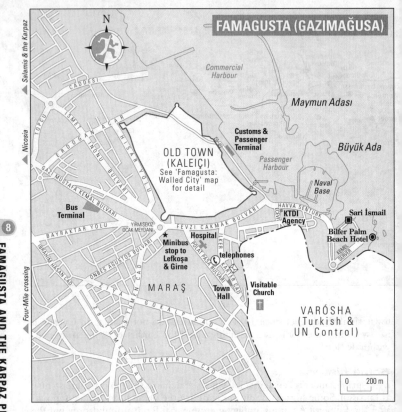

**Peter II**, a tussle between the Genoese and Venetian envoys as to the protocol of leading the royal horse degenerated into a brawl with massive loss of Genoese life and property. In revenge a Genoese expedition ravaged Cyprus over the next year, occupying Famagusta and inducing its traders to leave for Nicosia. James II expelled the Genoese in 1464, but it was already too late, and his Venetian widow, **Queen Caterina Cornaro**, presided over a diminished town before abdicating at the behest of her Venetian minders in 1489.

Anticipating the growing Ottoman threat, the **Venetian** military governors busied themselves improving and thickening Famagusta's **fortifications** just as they had at Nicosia and Kyrenia. So when the Turks appeared in October 1570, having taken the rest of the island with relatively little resistance, it required a ten-month siege to reduce the city, where the Venetian garrison put up a heroic defence, though outnumbered twenty to one.

Under **Ottoman rule**, walled Famagusta became an emblem of decay; with almost every building levelled or severely damaged, for centuries the space within the walls lay desolate and weed-choked, inhabited only by garrisons under the command of soldiers disgraced elsewhere. Ottoman sultans favoured it as a **place of exile** for political prisoners, most famously (both during the nineteenth century) the Turkish nationalist poet Namik Kemal and Suphi Ezel, founder of the Ezeli sect (like its rival faith Bahaism an offshoot of Persian

Babism). Christians were forbidden entry to, let alone residence in, **Kaleiçi** (the area within the ramparts), so that the predominantly Greek Orthodox town of **Varósha** (Maraş in Turkish) sprang up just south.

With independence and the subsequent **communal troubles**, old Famagusta again acquired significance as a Turkish stronghold. Greek Cypriots who had early in the twentieth century ventured into Kaleiçi to live were expelled in 1964, while **Turkish-Cypriot refugees** streamed into the town from vulnerable villages on the Mesarya. This trend accelerated during the tense weeks between July 20 and August 15, 1974, when the EOKA-B-dominated National Guard attacked any Turkish Cypriot they found outside the walls; the luckier ones entered Kaleiçi via a network of pre-dug tunnels, joining both besieged civilians and the small TMT garrison holding down the port and walled town. Old Famagusta was relieved by the advancing Turkish army on August 15, after the Greek Cypriots **abandoned Varósha** in the face of intense Turkish air raids. After the ceasefire went into effect the next day, the Turkish army pushed forward into Varósha, which, except for a few UN observation posts, they have effectively controlled ever since (see box on p.392).

## The City

Famagusta is usually visited as a full day-trip or two shorter outings from a beachfront base further north. Interest is confined almost entirely to the Kaleiçi, but don't raise your expectations too high. What you get are the walls, built to last by the Venetians, and such churches as escaped Turkish ordnance and British vandalism. It's claimed that the Ottomans bombarded the town with more than 100,000 cannonballs during their siege, and many of these are still to be seen lying about. The devastated neighbourhoods were mostly never rebuilt, leaving vast expanses of desolate ground that can have changed little since the day the Ottomans entered the city. Since 1996, the historic centre has been partly and attractively pedestrianized, especially the immediate environs of the Lala Mustafa Paşa mosque.

### The city walls

More complete than İstanbul or Antioch, stronger than Fez,
Jerusalem and even Avila, [a] prince of walled cities...

So enthused Colin Thubron in 1972 – and well he might, given the **walls'** average height of fifteen metres, thickness of eight metres, their fifteen bastions and five gates. The Venetians gradually raised them atop the existing Lusignan fortifications between 1489 and 1540, according to the latest precepts of engineering and ballistics. Yet they were ultimately proved an exercise in futility, considering the Ottoman victory, though structurally they mostly withstood the siege.

The ramparts are still dry-moated on their three landward sides, overgrown with prickly bushes on top, and impossible to walk completely around owing to partial occupation by the Turkish army. Content yourself instead with a stroll up the ramp near the southwestern **Land Gate** to the most spectacular bit, the **Ravelin** or **Rivettina Bastion** (open Mon–Fri only; token admission). This vast complex of guard houses and galleries was protected by a double moat, the main one now crossed by an alarmingly rotten wooden bridge. The Ottomans knew it as the *Akkule* or "White Tower", from the Venetians' waving of the white flag of surrender from this point.

At the southeast corner of the perimeter, the **Canbulat Bastion** (sometimes Canpolat or Cambulat) takes its name from an Anatolian bey who,

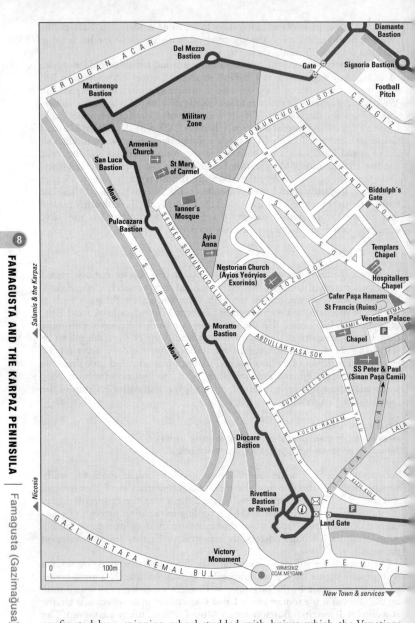

◄ Salamis & the Karpaz

◄ Nicosia

New Town & services ▼

confronted by a spinning wheel studded with knives which the Venetians had mounted in the gate here, charged it with his horse. Both were cut to ribbons, but the infernal machine was also destroyed. For years Turkish women used to come to his tomb in the bastion, from which a fig tree grew, to pray for sons as valiant as Canbulat, and to eat the fruit to ensure conception.

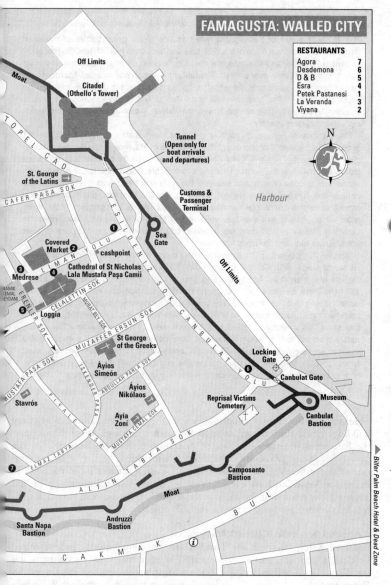

## FAMAGUSTA: WALLED CITY

**RESTAURANTS**

| | |
|---|---|
| Agora | 7 |
| Desdemona | 6 |
| D & B | 5 |
| Esra | 4 |
| Petek Pastanesi | 1 |
| La Veranda | 3 |
| Viyana | 2 |

Off Limits

Moat

Citadel
(Othello's Tower)

Tunnel
(Open only for
boat arrivals
and departures)

TOPEL CAD

St. George
of the Latins

CAFER PASA SOK

Customs &
Passenger
Terminal

*Harbour*

Covered
Market ❷

cashpoint

❶

Sea
Gate

LIMAN YOLU

❸
Medrese

Cathedral of St Nicholas
Lala Mustafa Paşa Camii ❹

NAMIK
KEMAL
EYDANI

CELALETTIN SOK

ERENLER SOK

MURAT BEY SOK

Off Limits

❺
Loggia

MUZAFFER ERSUN SOK

St George
of the Greeks

Locking
Gate

❻

Canbulat Gate

MUSTAFA PASA SOK

ISKENDER PASA

ABDULLAH PARLA SOK

Áyios
Simeón

PIYALE PASA

Áyios
Nikólaos

Reprisal Victims
Cemetery

Museum

Stavrós

Ayía
Zoni

MUSTAFA CEMAL SOK

Canbulat
Bastion

ELMAZ TABYA

Camposanto
Bastion

❼

ALTIN TABYA SOK

Moat

CANBULAT YOLU BUL

Santa Napa
Bastion

Andruzzi
Bastion

ℹ️

CAKMAK

N

**8**

FAMAGUSTA AND THE KARPAZ PENINSULA | Famagusta (Gazimağusa)

▶ Bilfer Palm Beach Hotel & Dead Zone

Today the interior is home to a small **museum** (daily: summer 8.30am–5pm;
winter 9am–1pm & 2–4.45pm; £1.25). The admission fee isn't money terribly well spent, as the collection is merely an assemblage of mediocre pottery,
traditional dress, Ottoman weaponry, amphorae and Iznik tiles. On the wall, a
famous engraving by Stephano Givellino of the siege, its text translated into
English, somewhat redeems the collection.

The **1570–71 siege of Famagusta** ranks as one of the great battles of medieval times: for ten months a force of 8000 Greeks and Venetians held off an Ottoman army of almost 200,000, and the outcome might have been different had promised relief from Venice and Crete ever arrived. The brilliant Venetian commander, **Marcantonio Bragadino**, was as resourceful with the limited means at his disposal as could be expected; Lala – "The Mentor" – Mustafa Paşa, his Ottoman counterpart, was a seasoned if unimaginative campaign veteran with an explosive temper as an overriding weakness of character.

The entrance of Famagusta harbour could be chained shut, starting from a salient of the Othello Tower; the opening at the south end of Maymun Adası (Monkey Island) didn't then exist. Thus the Turks concentrated on assaults of the south and west land walls, avoiding the north wall with its formidable Martinengo Bastion. Armenian sappers dug coils of trenches towards the ramparts deep enough to completely conceal the Turkish soldiery except for the tops of their turbans; the main evidence of their presence on the plain around the city was a forest of campaign tents, three miles wide. The sappers also burrowed under the walls, setting off mines, while the Ottoman artillery of 150 guns (as opposed to the 90 small-bore weapons of their adversaries) reduced the walls from afar.

Despite this pounding, little progress was made by the attackers over the initial winter of siege, with Bragadino organizing bold sorties to create the impression that he had manpower to spare – and also to raid for necessary food. On July 7, 1571 the Turks gained a foothold on the Rivettina bastion, and started to scale the walls. Seeing that the structure was useless for its intended purpose, the Venetian command detonated a mine of their own prepared for such a moment, burying a thousand Turks (and a hundred of their own men) in the resulting rubble, which partly blocked further enemy advance. The defenders fell back behind hastily improvised barricades of earth-filled carts and sandbags; the relief fleet had failed to materialize, and the situation inside the city became increasingly desperate, with plague spreading and rats or cats figuring in the diet. On August 1, having

Heading northwest on Canbulat Yolu from the namesake bastion, most of the buildings facing the wall are devoted to warehousing and customs brokerage; the harbour is just the other side of the ramparts, formerly accessible by the now-boarded-up **Sea Gate**, which along with the Citadel (see below) was one of the earliest Venetian improvements. Beside it squats a more-naturalistic-than-usual **Venetian lion**: a legend says that once a year the mouth opens, and anyone lucky enough to be there at the unpredictable moment can stick their hand down its throat and extract a valuable object.

### Around Namik Kemal Meydanı

Entering Kaleiçi through the **Land Gate** and along mostly pedestrianized İstiklal Caddesi, you pass a concentration of basic tradesmen's restaurants and jewellery shops before you see the mid-fourteenth-century church of **SS Peter and Paul** (later the Sinan Paşa Camii) on the left. Supposedly built by a merchant from the profits of a single business transaction, it's a rather inelegant, workaday building, its good condition assured by its former role as a mosque, public library, and state theatre (it is currently disused).

Just north across the street, the Venetian governor's palace is little more than a shell, much of the site ignominiously cleared for use as a car park. The remaining east façade is admittedly impressive, facing pedestrianized **Namik Kemal Meydanı**, the town's central square, named after a dissident Ottoman writer of

lost nearly three-quarters of his forces, Bragandino ran up the white flag, and negotiated a surrender whereby civilians were to be unmolested and he and his men were to be given safe conduct to Crete in Turkish ships.

When the remnant of the garrison emerged from the smoking ruins and staggered over to the Turkish lines, the besiegers were amazed that so few men had been able to mount such courageous resistance against hopeless odds, and were moved to pity by their woebegone appearance. At first the defeated were received with kindness and all courtesy, even by the volatile Lala Mustafa himself, but the flouting of Turkish might for so long – and his own casualties of over 50,000 – must have preyed on the general's mind, for Bragadino's audience with him suddenly turned sour.

Lala Mustafa abruptly demanded retention of the Venetian officer Quirini as security against the safe return of the Turkish fleet from Crete; when Bragadino protested that this hadn't been part of the agreed surrender, Lala Mustafa accused him of murdering fifty civilian prisoners in the last weeks of the siege. Working himself up into one of the towering rages he was known for, the Turk summoned his executioner and before Bragadino's horrified eyes Quirini and two other assistant commanders were hacked to bits. Then came Bragadino's turn: his nose and ears were sliced off, and he was thrown into a dungeon for ten days before being retrieved, publicly humiliated in various ways, and finally chained between two pillars in front of the cathedral and flayed alive. Eyewitness accounts agree that Bragadino bore all these torments in dignity and silence, and that even many Turks disapproved of these and other atrocities perpetrated by their frenzied leader.

But Lala Mustafa Paşa was not to be mollified: he gutted the body, stuffed Bragadino's skin with straw, and paraded it around the city on a cow, under the red parasol which the Venetian had jauntily used when marching out to give himself up. The stuffed skin was later ransomed from İstanbul at considerable cost by Bragadino's descendants, and it now rests in an urn at the Venetian church of SS Giovanni e Paolo.

the late nineteenth century; a bust of the man stands outside, near the *medrese* now housing the Faisal Islamic Bank. His **dungeon** (open sporadically Mon–Fri as a museum; £0.25), where he spent 38 months at the sultan's pleasure for writing a seditious play, incorporates a surviving bit of palace, which overlooks a pleasant outdoor café. North of the palace precinct, the equally ruined church of **St Francis** abuts a set of Turkish baths, the Cafer Paşa Hamamı, now occupied by the partly subterranean, vaulted *Hamam Inn*, besides *Desdemona* (see p.393) the old town's only proper bar.

## Lala Mustafa Paşa Camii (St Nicholas Cathedral)

Dominating the eastern side of the square, the **Lala Mustafa Paşa Camii** (£0.80 "donation" required, and headscarves or leg-coverings provided, when warden present) is the most magnificent and best-preserved Lusignan monument in town, and arguably in all Cyprus. Completed between 1298 and 1326 to a design resembling the cathedral at Rheims, it outshines its sister church in Nicosia; here the Lusignan royalty received the honorary crown of lost Jerusalem after their coronation in the official capital, and here too Queen Caterina Cornaro formally abdicated in 1489.

Regrettably, the twin towers were decapitated during the bombardment of 1571; after seizing Famagusta, the Ottomans perpetrated more deliberate alterations. As at Nicosia they emptied the floor-tombs, including presumably those of James II and his infant son, last of the Lusignan dynasty; destroyed all accoutrements of Christian worship; and added the minaret which – lower than the pair on Nicosia's Selimiye Camii – happily detracts little from the building's appeal.

The church-mosque reveals itself to best advantage from the **west**, where the gables of three magnificent porticoes point still higher to the fine six-paned window with its circular rose. Pedestrianization of the plaza has cleared away all of the former obstacles and traffic, with the outdoor tables of two café-eateries affording vantage points to admire the façade at leisure. Two series of six columns stalk the **interior** of the nave, supporting superb vaulting; as at Nicosia, the austere, whitewashed decor allows an appreciation of the cathedral's elegance, undistracted by the late-medieval clutter which would have accumulated had the building remained a church. In the **courtyard** out front, a giant sycamore fig is rumoured to be as old as the building; to one side, a small Venetian **loggia** has been converted to an Islamic ablutions fountain. The Faisal Islamic Bank, across the courtyard from the loggia, occupies what was formerly a *medrese* or Koranic academy, in front of which (moved from their original location by the loggia) stand a pair of granite columns from Salamis, between which the hapless Bragadino was flayed (see box on pp.388–389). Across Liman Yolu, unsung in most tourist literature, the **covered market** occupies a building at least partly Venetian.

### The Citadel (Othello's Tower)

The treasure-lion in front of the Sea Gate, at the seaward end of Liman Yolu, is complemented by a larger relief lion of St Mark above the entry to the **Citadel** (daily: summer 9am–4pm; winter 9am–1pm & 2–4.45pm; £2), 100m north across the oval roundabout. A Lusignan fort, which was extensively remodelled by the Venetians between 1489 and 1492, this strongpoint is popularly known as **"Othello's Tower"**, after Famagusta's Shakespearean connections. On the far side of the courtyard, partly taken up by a stage used for folkloric performances, the Great Hall, 28m long, has fine vaults whose limestone rib vaulting, however, has mostly been eaten away by the all-corroding sea air.

From the **northeast tower**, you can peer over the industrial harbour; you'll get no closer, as the protruding citadel mole is as militarily important today as in medieval times. Up on the perimeter parapet, **ventilation shafts** or cistern mouths alternate with rooms whose roofs were stove in by the bombardment. Some of these shafts lead down to Lusignan passages and chambers which the Venetians either filled up or simply sealed at one end, giving rise to the persistent theory that somewhere in this citadel is hidden the fortune of the Venetian merchants, who were only allowed to leave the city empty-handed by the victorious Ottomans. This legend has exercised the Turkish imagination ever since, with investigations conducted periodically; similar hollows in the Martinengo bastion served as a bomb shelter for two thousand civilians during August 1974.

### Minor churches: the north of town

Just southwest of Othello's Tower, **St George of the Latins** is one of the oldest Famagustan churches, originally part of a fortified monastery which may predate the Lusignan ramparts. Today it's merely a shell, but a romantic one; on the surviving apse and north wall, a group of carved bats peer out of a column capital. Nearby on Naim Effendi Sokağı, **Biddulph's Gate** is a remnant doorway of a vanished mansion and named in honour of an early high commissioner who made it an exception to the pattern of British destructiveness.

Naim Effendi leads towards the northwest corner of Kaleiçi, a military zone since 1974; the Martinengo bastion in the wall here was never stormed by the Turks in their first campaign, and the returning modern Turkish army seems to have taken the hint of impregnability. Access to the churches of **Ayía Ánna**, **St Mary of Carmel**, the **Armenian Church** or the (converted) **Tanners Mosque** is therefore restricted at present, with photography out of the question, though they are no longer fenced off and you can at least drive by them.

One church which you can at least approach is the fourteenth-century Nestorian church of **Áyios Yeóryios Exorinós**, usually locked but used as an occasional cultural centre by the local university, and also for Sunday-evening religious services by the tiny local expatriate community. Built by one of the fabulously wealthy Lakhas brothers, he of the jewel-sprinkling incident (see p.383), it was before 1964 the parish church of the small Greek Orthodox community. The epithet *exorinós* means "the exiler", after a strange legend, reminiscent of the one pertaining to Áyios Misitikós in Páfos (see p.172): dust gathered from the floor and tossed in an enemy's house would cause them to die or leave the island within a year.

Nearby on Kışla Sokağı, on the way back to Namik Kemal Meydanı, the adjacent box-like churches of the **Knights Templar** and **Knights Hospitaller**, both fourteenth-century, enjoy a proximity which those rival orders never had in their day. The chapel of the Templars is distinguished by a small rose window out front, and is now used as a theatre and art gallery; the Hospitallers' chapel serves as a music rehearsal hall. If you manage to get in (the door of one is often ajar, and a modern passage interconnects them), you'll find that they're bare in the extreme, enlivened only by fine ceiling vaulting.

## More churches: the southern quarter

The otherwise unremarkable Lusignan church of **Stavrós**, two blocks south of Namik Kemal Meydanı, marks a small concentration of **arched lanes** and **medieval houses** on Lala Mustafa Paşa Sokağı and perpendicular Erenler Sokağı, all that survived the siege and later developers. A few steps east, half-demolished **St George of the Greeks**, an uneasy Byzantine-Gothic hybrid whose three rounded apses clash with the two rows of column stumps, stands cheek-by-jowl with the purer Byzantine but equally dilapidated **Áyios Simeón**, tacked onto its south wall.

Two more tiny but exquisite late Byzantine chapels stand to the south amid palm-tree greenery: battered **Áyios Nikólaos**, and intact **Ayía Zoní**, which make a satisfying duo seen juxtaposed.

## Maraş (Varósha)

Polat Paşa, the commercial main street of the inhabited portion of **Maraş**, currently parades grandiosely to nowhere; behind the oil-drum-and-sand-bag barricades at its south end, where it detours abruptly, rusty street and shop signs in Greek and the dome of a church (see below), are visible. About halfway down, in front of the courthouse, a parked locomotive, built in 1904 by a Leeds company, seems far less derelict than anything in the dead zone. It plied the now-vanished Lefke–Famagusta railway from 1907 until 1951: the tracks were to have been extended to Larnaca, but the mayor vetoed the plan to protect local camel-drivers from the competition. At the time he was roundly jeered for the decision, but in the event the camel caravans outlasted the trains by over a decade.

The only part of Varósha ever open to foreign civilians is a modern **Orthodox church** (theoretically open Mon–Fri 9am–1.30pm; £1), clearly visible about

Only a small fraction of the new town, called Maraş by the Turks, is currently inhabited; the rest, by the terms of the 1974 ceasefire, is technically UN territory but effectively under Turkish army control, a ghost town entered only occasionally by UNFICYP forces since then. Their patrols, and specially escorted journalists, reported light bulbs burning for years, washing in tatters on the line and uncleared breakfast dishes, so precipitous was the Greek Cypriots' departure.

Behind the barricade of wire and oil drums, weeds have attained tree-like dimensions on the streets and inside buildings, while cats, rats and snakes prowl as in Nicosia's dead zone. The fate of the Famagusta Archeological Museum's contents is unknown, but unlikely to be happy in light of how the magnificent, private Hadjiprodhromou archeological collection was looted and dispersed for sale quite openly on the international market. In contrast to the automotive "time capsule" in Nicosia, the Turks here helped themselves to the contents of an automobile showroom, with the exception of a single Alfa Romeo that remains inside to this day.

The disposition of Varósha has figured high on the agenda of nearly every intercommunal negotiating session since 1974. Greek Cypriots see its return to use as an initial gesture of good faith for progress on any other issue: the town has practical as well as symbolic significance, since with nearly 40,000 former Greek inhabitants its **resettlement** could solve a goodly fraction of the South's refugee problem.

With bed capacity elsewhere in the North generally outstripping demand, the Turkish Cypriots have never had much need for the row of 33 decaying, far-from-state-of-the-art **hotels** which line Varósha's six-kilometre-long Glóssa beach, but they have periodically proposed that a limited number of Greek Cypriots return to renovate and manage the 4000-bed resort – which apparently is built on land leased from the island's *vakif* or Islamic trust. The South has refused, objecting that these offers are always couched in such a way as to make it clear that the hotels would be run largely for the financial benefit of the North. Meanwhile, most of Varósha has attained write-off condition, and it's hard to avoid the suspicion that the Turkish side has always maintained the area for use as a **bargaining chip** at some crucial stage of negotiations.

150m into the restricted zone, accessed off İlker Karter Caddesi. A military guard here will phone ahead to ascertain if the church is staffed, and then allow you to drive in and park by the church. This is now home to a collection of icons, few of any significant artistic interest.

Out on the shore, the *Bilfer Palm Beach Hotel* is virtually the last occupied building in Maraş before the dead zone; beyond sheet-metal barricades, emblazoned with no-photography signs, begins the long, Benidorm-like row of abandoned 1960s hotels, many bearing marks of shelling, and the northernmost one partly bulldozed to form a clear zone.

## Practicalities

Coming **by boat** from Mersin, Turkey, you'll dock at the customs and passenger terminal, just east of the Sea Gate leading into the heart of the old town and open only for ferry arrivals. Arrival **by land** is equally uncomplicated; both the road from Salamis (İsmet İnönü Caddesi once within city limits) and the Nicosia highway (Gazi Mustafa Kemal Bulvarı, where the **bus terminal** is) converge on Yirmisekiz Ocak Meydanı, the victory-monument roundabout directly opposite the Land Gate of the old city. So too does the way in from the Four-Mile Crossing, along Onbeş Ağustos Bulvarı. Generally, **parking** within the old town presents few problems, though in addition to pedestrianization, various traffic-control barriers and a one-way system complicate matters along and to either side of İstiklal Caddesi. If necessary, drive to the thinly populated areas around St George of the Greeks, the Canbulat Gate or Othello's Tower.

The **tourist information** bureau (nominally Mon–Fri 8am–5pm, Sat–Sun 10am–6pm) is housed inside the Rivettina Bastion; as at Kyrenia, don't expect much.

## Accommodation

Since nearly all of the pre-1974 hotels were in now-inaccessible Varósha, there is next to no **accommodation** in or immediately around Kaleiçi – almost all visitors stay out on the beaches near Salamis. On the shoreline next to the dead zone is the pastel-pink, nominally five-star *Bilfer Palm Beach Hotel* (☎366 20 00, ⓦwww.bilferhotel.com; ⓺); the *Constantia Hotel*, pre-1974, is offered by most UK package-tour operators, but is overpriced on a walk-in basis, and caters largely to the business and casino trade. The rooms are also small, though the grounds do offer several (exorbitantly priced) bars, beachfront watersports, tennis courts and a gym.

## Eating, drinking and nightlife

Paralleling the dearth of accommodation within the actual city limits, eating and drinking options are similarly limited – you can count the **restaurants** of distinction on one hand, and simple affairs for local tradesmen on the other. However, there's certainly enough choice for a well-priced midday meal, though pickings can be slim in the off-season. As for consistent **nightlife**, you're pretty much restricted to the nightclub, casino and discotheque inside the *Bilfer Palm Beach Hotel*, the aforementioned *Hamam Inn*, or a few of the livelier student-patronized cafés and snack-bars opposite the Eastern Mediterranean University campus, on the way out of town along İsmet İnönü Bulvarı.

**Agora** Elmaz Tabya 17. Long-running specialist in *fırın kebap*; it's best to order a double portion, however, as this dish contains a high proportion of bone and gristle. Closed Sun.
**D&B Café** Namik Kemal Meydanı. Popular student hangout, placed unimprovably opposite the west façade of Lala Mustafa Paşa Camii, with outdoor tables in season. The fare is Western snack food, vaguely hankering after *Californian Bar & Grill* in Lefkoşa.
**Desdemona Restaurant & Bar** Canbulat Yolu 3. Built into a vaulted bastion with no windows, this drippingly atmospheric outfit purveys high-quality, copious *meze*, more Turkish-style than Cypriot, for about £10 a head. Especially out of season, it doubles as the locals' bar, with piped mainland-Turkish music.
**Esra** Liman Yolu 6, opposite covered market. Narrow-fronted premises where cheap and salubrious *lahmacun* (Arabic pizza), *pide* (Turkish pizza), *döner* and *ayran* are the stock-in-trade.

**Sarı İsmail** Approach road to *Bilfer Palm Beach Hotel*. All of eight tables in a glorified shack poised right over the water – here is some of the best seafood in Famagusta, though many items are only seasonally available and staff aren't the friendliest.
**Petek Pastanesi** Liman Yolu, corner Yeşildeniz Sokağı. A cavernous, two-level oasis of glitz in the otherwise down-at-heel old town. Enjoy a slightly pricey pudding, sticky cake or ice cream at seating arrayed around an indoor, carp-stocked fountain, or (in winter) near the fireplace beyond the tempting sweet counters.
**La Veranda** Namik Kemal Meydanı, opposite the *medrese*. Mostly drinks at this café, but also light snacks; a few outdoor tables in warm weather.
**Viyana** Liman Yolu, opposite apse of Lala Mustafa Paşa Camii. Carniverous plates and salads with garden seating in summer; £4.50 maximum with a beer.

## Listings

**Airline** Cyprus Turkish Airlines, İlker Karter Cad 50, Maraş ☎366 77 99.

**Banks and exchange** ATMs are grouped around Namik Kemal Meydanı, plus one more a block northeast of Liman Yolu.

Car rental Benzincioğlu, Gazi Mustafa Kemal Bulvari ☎ 366 54 79; Sur, İsmet İnönü Cad 7 ☎ 366 47 96; Tab, İsmet Anönü Cad 7 ☎ 366 13 23. Also arrangeable through the *Bilfer Palm Beach Hotel.*

Camera repair Semih Erciyes at İstiklal Cad 18D ☎ 366 60 65 has proven very skilled and helpful, and speaks good English.

Ferry agency KTDI has its well-signposted sales office on Ecevit Cad ☎ 366 45 57, southeast of the Venetian walls near the naval base; you might also try in the passenger terminal itself a few hours before sailing.

Internet Highly subject to change, but at least one café opposite the university's main gate will be providing a service at any given time.

Post offices Main branch on İlker Karter Cad, Maraş (Mon–Fri 8am–1pm & 2–5pm), with a more convenient branch in the Ravelin.

Public toilets Easiest to find are those by the parking lot behind the Templars' chapel.

Telephones The Telekomünikasyon Dairesi on Polat Paşa Bulvari (daily 8am–1pm & 2–6pm) sells telecards; the most convenient pay phones are next to the Cafer Paşa baths, and on Liman Yolu near the *medrese.*

# Salamis

The most famous and important ancient city of Cyprus, **Salamis** remains the island's most prominent archeological site, for once living up to the tourist-brochure hype. Even if your interest is casual, you'll need a couple of hours to see the best-preserved highlights; a half-day can easily be spent on the site, especially if you allow for periodic intermissions at the wonderful beach that fringes Salamis to the east. Various monuments, mostly Roman and Byzantine, are widely scattered – it's well over a kilometre from the entrance to the ancient harbour, for example – and vehicles are no longer allowed past the amphitheatre, so you'll need stout footwear, sun protection and drinking water. Furthermore, leave nothing valuable in sight in your buggy, as Salamis is the one place on Cyprus with a consistent pattern of car break-ins and burglaries. Otherwise, any **bus** from Famagusta towards Boğaz or beyond to the Kárpas peninsula runs past the site entrance.

## Some history

To Salamis are ascribed quasi-mythical foundations in the twelfth century BC by the Trojan war hero **Teucer** (Tefkros), exiled by his father King Telamon from the **Greek isle of Salamis**. The young city shared not only the name but the Mycenaean culture of its parent – borne out spectacularly by the finds in the nearby royal tombs (p.397) – and quickly replaced nearby Enkomi-Alasia as the chief settlement on the coastal bight here. By the eighth century it was already the greatest of the ten Cypriot city-kingdoms, and within two hundred years Salamis was the first place on the island to mint coinage.

The city was the leader in the first fifth-century revolt against the Persians; **Onesilos** temporarily deposed his brother King Gorgos, a Persian collaborator, and commanded a hastily thrown-together Hellenic confederacy at the Battle of Salamis – lost mostly because of treachery on the part of the Kourion faction. Later that same century, native son **Evagoras** – a remarkable man for whom every other street in the South seems to be named – shrewdly united the Cypriot city-kingdoms in another, somewhat more durable, pro-Hellenic federation, with culture as well as politics oriented towards peninsular Greece. Despite his political and military ingenuity Evagoras could not actually prevail against Persia, but over a period of a decade fought the oriental empire to a standstill, finally negotiating a vassalage relationship.

Salamis actively assisted Alexander the Great and was subsequently rewarded with the copper revenues of Tamassos. But under the Ptolemaic kings, the city briefly fell on evil times. Its last king, **Nicocreon**, rather than surrender to the besieging Ptolemy I, committed suicide in 295 BC, as did all his surviving relatives, who set the royal palace alight before doing so.

During the **Roman** era, although Paphos was designated the official capital of Cyprus, Salamis remained the island's main commercial centre and figured prominently in early Christianity: another native son, the Apostle Barnabas, lived and died here (for the full story see "Monastery-museum of Apóstolos Varnávas", p.399). In the Jewish revolt of 116 AD, it is thought that the city's entire gentile population was slaughtered; after the Romans had put down the rebellion, Jewish residence on the island was forbidden, an edict not effectively countermanded until a small colony of European Jews settled nearby at the Mesaorian village of Koúklia (today Köprülü) late in the nineteenth century.

The **Byzantines** renamed Salamis as **Constantia** and designated it an archbishopric and capital of the island again, but the earthquakes and tidal waves of the mid-fourth century badly hurt the city, and the Arab invasions of the seventh century, along with the silting-up of its harbour, administered the final blow. From this time neighbouring Famagusta began its ascendancy. Bits of ancient Salamis, used as a convenient quarry throughout medieval times, are scattered throughout contemporary villages and towns of the Kanlıdere (Pedhiéos) River's flood plain which drains the region.

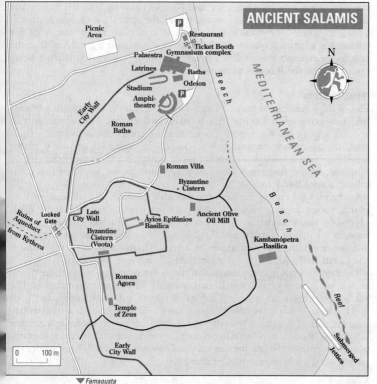

▲ Boğaz & the Karpaz peninsula

**ANCIENT SALAMIS**

Picnic Area

Restaurant
Ticket Booth
Gymnasium complex
Palaestra
Latrines    Baths
            Odeion
Stadium
Amphi-
theatre
Early City Wall
Roman Baths

Roman Villa
Byzantine Cistern

Ruins of Aqueduct from Kythrea
Locked Gate
Late City Wall
Byzantine Cistern (Vuota)
Áyios Epifánios Basilica
Ancient Olive Oil Mill
Kambanópetra Basilica

Roman Agora

Temple of Zeus

Early City Wall

Beach

MEDITERRANEAN SEA

Beach

Reef

Submerged Jetties

N

0    100 m

▼ Famagusta

Salamis had only been partially **excavated** by a Franco-Cypriot team before 1974, and assuming a future political settlement which permits further research, more archeological treasures can be anticipated under the dunes that have largely covered the city since its abandonment.

## The main site

The ruins lie eight to nine kilometres north of Famagusta between the main highway and the beach. More effectively than the small official "Salamis" signs, a placard for the *Bedi Restaurant* marks the one-kilometre side turning off the coast road, passing a piny picnic area to the north to reach the **site entrance** (daily: summer 9am–7pm; winter 9am–1pm & 2–5pm; £2), flanked by an "improved" beach and the aforementioned restaurant.

### The gymnasium

A sign directs you towards the walkway of the **gymnasium's east portico**, probably once covered over and still mosaic-paved in variegated Byzantine-era marble, with two rectangular plunge-pools at either end. The northerly one is ringed by a gallery of headless statues, decapitated by Christian zealots in a fury against pagan idolatry; some are now in the Cyprus Museum in south Nicosia, others have allegedly disappeared since 1974.

To the west, an impressive, photogenic **colonnade**, re-erected during the 1950s after being tumbled by earthquakes, stakes out the quad of the gymnasium's palaestra. The eastern series is taller, and the whole mismatched, because the Byzantines recycled Hellenistic and Roman columns from the theatre and another building without too much regard for symmetry or which capitals belonged where. The semicircular structure at the southwest corner of the palaestra is a latrine, capacity 44; the flush pipe and tank are still visible at the rear, as are armrests to one side. Privacy was not a concern, elimination being considered by the Romans as another social event.

### The baths

East of the palaestra and portico loom the **baths**, like the gymnasium a Byzantine reworking of Hellenistic and Roman predecessors. Just off the portico another set of cool-water pools – one nearly circular, one octagonal – sandwich the giant **west–central hall** (reckoned the *tepidarium* or mildly steamy anteroom) whose underfloor heating cavity is exposed. Over the south entry, a Christian **fresco fragment** shows two faces, one angelic, executed in a naturalistic, almost Buddhist style.

At the seaward end of the **east-central hall** (probably the *caldarium* or hot-plunge room) another, elevated, pool has been partially restored, and a dank, crypt-like cavity under its floor can be entered. This hall contains further mosaics: a patch of abstracts and floral motifs in a niche of the north wall, and another one of three pomegranates on a branch in the northerly semi-dome of the **north hall**, probably a hot-steam "sauna" chamber.

The best, most complete **mosaics** in the entire complex, however, are found in the south bays of the **south hall**, possibly an alternative entry way. The smaller one shows the river god Evrotas – part of a damaged version of Leda and the swan – while the other displays the shield and quiver of a fragmentary warrior, part of a scene whose identity is disputed: either Apollo and Artemis slaying the Niobids, or a battle between men and Amazons. Both are rare examples of work from the late third or very early fourth century AD, just before the advent of officially sponsored Christianity.

## The amphitheatre

Another paved and partly colonnaded way leads south from the palaestra, between a vaulted structure with banks of seats against its south wall – probably an **odeion** (concert venue) – and an unexcavated area to the west, thought to be a small **stadium**. Both are overshadowed by the fine Roman **amphitheatre**, dating from the reign of Augustus and not over-restored as these things go. From the top eighteen surviving rows of seats you have excellent perspectives over the site. Occasional performances still take place during the tourist season, though not attracting anything like the original capacity of 15,000.

## Áyios Epifánios basilica

As you continue southwest of the amphitheatre along the paved drive, there seems little left at first glance of the six-aisled **basilica of Áyios Epifánios** other than the stumps of four rows of fourteen columns, but at the rear (east) of the southernmost naves, mosaic flooring covers a **crypt**, the presumed tomb of the patron saint, emptied by Byzantine Emperor Leo for the sake of its holy relics. In the manner of so many post-Arab-raid churches on Cyprus, this shrunken area around the crypt was refurbished for use after the rest of the basilica was destroyed.

Nearby, an **aqueduct** bringing water from ancient Khytroi (today Değirmen-lik/Kythréa) ended at the giant Byzantine cistern or Vuota beside the Roman agora, at the far end of which are the negligible remains of a **Zeus temple**.

## Kambanópetra basilica

Most recently excavated, and perhaps more interesting, the romantically set fourth-century **Kambanópetra basilica** overlooks the sea from one curve of a dirt track leading towards the southeast corner of the archeological zone. Its western forecourt, with small rooms giving onto it, may have been a colonnaded agora or an early monastic cloister. The central apse of the three-aisled nave was provided with a synthronon or seats for church dignitaries, while a fourth aisle to the south contains half-a-dozen marble sarcophagi.

A handful of standing columns to the east belong to yet another set of **baths**, as suggested by some tumbled-over hypocaust bricks and a tank with a fill-hole. The highlight here is a magnificent *opus sectile* floor, consisting of concentric rings of alternating light and dark triangles, the most elaborate mosaic at Salamis.

## The beach

The **beach** fringing the entire site is particularly accessible just below Kambanópetra. A reef encloses a small lagoon, extending all the way south past a cape before subsiding; snorkelling in the metre-deep water, you see not only fish but long courses of man-made stone – the jetty or breakwater of the ancient port – on the sea floor. The wind is often brisk here, and the ancient harbour facilities were distributed to either side of the point, for use according to the weather. But there has been so much quake-generated subsidence, and silting-up courtesy of the river, that it's difficult to envisage the ancient shore profile.

# The Royal Tombs

Just 100m south of the disused, locked Salamis west gate, a side road heads off west for 500m to a yet smaller turning, signposted for the **Royal Tombs** (partially fenced; same nominal hours as Salamis site; £1.75, but free upon presentation of ticket for Salamis or Apostolos Varnavas). Two of the nearly 150 eighth- and seventh-century burial sites and graves here caused a sensation when discovered in 1957, because they confirmed Homer's descriptions of Late Bronze Age funerary rites, still being observed here five centuries after the original Mycenaean homeland on the Greek Peloponnese had passed its zenith.

Most of the tombs had already been looted in antiquity, but others, in particular **Tombs 47 and 79** east of the access drive, yielded the elaborate remains of several royal funerals. Hoards of precious metal or ivory objects, pottery, weapons and food containers were all intended to serve the dead in the underworld, and included the famous ivory-inlaid throne and bed – showing profound Phoenician/Egyptian influence – now in the Cyprus Museum.

All of the tombs save one opened to the east, and were approached by gently slanting *dromoi* or ramps – on which the most telling artefacts were unearthed. Over the years at least four ceremonial chariots bearing a king's bier had been drawn by pony-like horses to a certain point on the ramps, where the deceased was cremated after the horse (and frequently favourite human servants) were ritually sacrificed. East of three of the tombs the preserved, paired skeletons of the slaughtered horses have been left rather gruesomely in situ, protected by glass plates. A few of the terrified horses broke their own necks at the deadly moment by lunging in their tackle, and at least some of the attendants did not willingly follow their masters in death, as can be gathered by human remains in the *dromoi* discovered bound hand and foot.

Officially **Tomb 50**, the so-called "St Catherine's prison" became associated with the Alexandrian saint through a Cypriot legend proposing her as a native of Salamis, briefly imprisoned here by her father the Roman governor for refusing an arranged marriage. That this tomb didn't start life as a Christian place of worship is dramatically borne out by the well-preserved pair of fossilized horses found adjacent; the T-shaped subterranean interior, with a vaulted antechamber and tiny tunnel-like room that was the tomb, still bears some ecclesiastical trappings. The upper courses of masonry date from the Roman/Byzantine era, when they were built atop the tomb itself, hidden from Christian worshippers until the excavations.

Three tombs to the west of the access drive include a prominent tumulus concealing a mud-brick **"beehive" chamber** nearly identical in design to those at Greek Mycenae. South of these, less exalted citizens were interred in the Kellarka (*Shellarka* in dialect) complex, apparently used well into Christian times.

The small adjacent **museum** (Mon–Fri 8am–sunset, same ticket) displays plans and photographs of the tombs and excavations, plus a reconstruction of one chariot used to transport the dead kings to the necropolis: the brass fittings and horse ornamentations are original, remounted on facsimiles of the long-decayed wooden structures.

## Salamis area practicalities

In the immediate environs of Salamis various tourist amenities beckon. South of the ruins, once past a soldiers' beach, Glapsides and "Silver" **beaches** tout camping as well as swimming, though as ever in Turkish cultures "camping" seems merely to mean the pitching of sun-flaps for day use.

Between Salamis and Boğaz, the shoreline features intermittent sandy patches, occasionally ballooning out into respectably wide beaches; eucalyptus, planted by the British to drain the local marshes, thrive just inland, though there are still plenty of mosquitoes about on summer nights.

All international-standard **accommodation** on this stretch enjoys a beach-front location, though patronage is considerably down since the 2001 bankruptcy of İstanbul Airlines (and the near-disappearance of German clientele), a slump in casino tourism and the fitful marketing of the area by UK package operators. We recommend the hotels that are likely to continue to survive.

The colonial-era, three-star *Park* (℡ 378 82 13, ⓦ www.parkhotel.online.com; ❹) just north of ancient Salamis, with tennis courts, plus lots of stone and wood used in the common areas, gets excellent reports for service, restaurant food and cleanliness, with an unobtrusive casino.

The smallish, three-star *Mimoza* (℡ 378 82 19, ⓦ www.mimozabeachhotel .com; ❸), adjacent to the mammoth *Salamis Bay Conti*, never threw in its lot with casino tourism and seems content to get by on a family trade. The rooms are basic but clean, Turkish-Cypriot families are in attendance at weekends, and the pool abuts the excellent beach.

Right next to the *Mimoza* is one of the best beachfront **restaurants** in the North: the atmospheric, inexpensive *Kocareis Beach Bar*, excellent for a lunch (or supper) while touring, where £7 should net you a good portion of fish, unusual salad greens, chips and beer; two can eat for about £11. The restaurant also has adjacent self-catering beachfront **bungalows** (℡ 378 82 29, ⓔ kocareis@north-cyprus.net; ❷).

# Monastery-museum of Apóstolos Varnávas

Continuing 500m further on the same minor road that serves the Royal Tombs, you soon approach the former **monastery of Apóstolos Varnávas** (daily: summer 9am–7pm; winter 9am–1pm & 2–4.45pm; £2.50), refurbished during the 1980s as a museum, with a crafts shop and cafeteria added in 1997. A monastic community first grew up here in the fifth century following the discovery of the purported tomb of the Apostle Barnabas, with funds provided for its construction by the Byzantine emperor himself. The Arab raiders destroyed this foundation during their seventh-century pillagings; the present church and cloister date from 1756, though some ancient columns from Salamis are incorporated into the church.

Until 1974 Apóstolos Varnávas was a favourite goal of pilgrimage among Famagustans, with sequential baptisms being conducted by one of three look-alike, Santa-Claus-bearded monks: Barnabas, Stephanos and Khariton. Since 1917 these three (biological) brothers had presided over the monastery, restoring the belfry in 1958, supporting it through sales of honey and mass-produced icons popular with the nearby villagers, but of rather limited artistic merit. Somehow they contrived to stay after August 1974, but finally, too weak and old to combat Turkish harassment, gave up and moved to the South in 1976, living out their days at Stavrovoúni monastery near Larnaca.

## The museum

It's certainly not the **icon collection**, housed in the former *katholikón*, that justifies the entrance fee; the oldest and most artistically worthy is an unusual *Herod's Banquet* (1858), with John the Baptist being beheaded in the lower frame. Most seem scrabbled-together replacements for 35 more valuable ones which went mysteriously missing from the lightly guarded premises in 1982, with still more disappearing in 1997.

The former cells around the appealingly landscaped court have been converted into what is at present the North's best **archeological museum**;

**Barnabas** (Varnávas in Greek), a native of Salamis, was the companion of the Apostle Paul on missionary voyages around Cyprus and Asia Minor before their falling-out over whether or not Barnabas's cousin Mark was to accompany them overseas. He is generally credited with being the apostle most influential in introducing Christianity to the island, and – long after his demise – with perpetuating its independent status through a miraculous intervention.

His activities having aroused the ire of the Salamis Jewish community into which he had been born, Barnabas was martyred by stoning in about 75 AD; thereafter matters become apocryphal, with most accounts having Mark interring the corpse at an undisclosed location. There things would have rested (in all senses) had it not been for an ecclesiastical squabble four hundred years later.

Late in the fifth century the Church of Antioch, having been founded by Peter and thus being an apostolic see, claimed precedence over that of Cyprus, which retorted, initially unsuccessfully, that as a foundation of the Apostle Barnabas the island's Church was also apostolic and of equal rank. Subordination to the Syrian archbishopric was only avoided through the supernatural intervention of Barnabas himself, who appeared in a dream to Anthemios, Archbishop of Salamis, and bade him unearth the apostle's remains from a lonely spot on the Mesaoría marked by a carob tree. Following these instructions, the cleric indeed found a catacomb matching the description and containing what could well have been the bones of Barnabas, clasping a mildewed copy (in Hebrew) of the Gospel of St Matthew to his breast. Armed with these incontrovertible relics, the Cypriots went to Constantinople, where a synod convened by the Emperor Zeno was sufficiently impressed to grant special privileges to the island's Church.

Most importantly it was to remain autocephalous (autonomous), deferring only to the sees of Constantinople, Alexandria, Antioch and Jerusalem in importance, and in later centuries pre-eminent over larger autocephalous churches, such as those in Russia. Cypriot bishops retained the right to elect their own archbishop, who was permitted to sign his name in red ink in imitation of the Byzantine emperor's custom, wear imperial purple and wield a sceptre instead of a pastoral staff. When Cyprus fell to the Ottomans, these hitherto symbolic privileges acquired practical import inasmuch as the churchmen were charged with the civil as well as the spiritual administration of their Orthodox flock. Following independence, Archbishop Makarios revived the medieval term "ethnarch", further blurring the lines between secular and ecclesiastical power, with ultimately catastrophic consequences for the island.

how much, if any of it, is based on the looted Hadjiprodhromou collection or the holdings of the inaccessible Famagusta Archeological Museum (see box on p.392) is uncertain. Eras are presented slightly out of order, proceeding clockwise from the Bronze Age to the Venetian period, with a strangely mixed Ottoman/Classical Greek wing at the end. Labelling gives only dates, with few indications of provenance.

The Bronze Age room features incised red polished and white slip pottery, as well as bronze items. A model house and set of miniature plates appear in the Geometric room; Archaic jugs exhibit Mycenaean influence in their depiction of an archer and birds. Among terracotta votive figurines and chariots stands an unusual wheel-footed horse – definitely not a chariot – on which a lyre player entertains two other riders.

Star of the Classical section is a woman in a head-dress – possibly the goddess Demeter – holding a poppy; Cyprus was one of the earliest centres of opium production. Two stone lions squat, haunch to haunch, with their tongues out, near a perfectly formed sphinx; continuing the animal theme, some Hellenistic child's rattles are in the shape of wild boars.

## The tomb of Barnabas

To one side of the monastery car park stands a little mausoleum-chapel, shaded by a carob tree and erected during the 1950s over a catacomb that is the presumed **tomb of Barnabas**. Stairs (the light switch now works) lead down to two rock-cut chambers with room for half-a-dozen dead, similar to the crypt of Áyios Lázaros in Larnaca – and far older than Christianity. Since the barriers came down in April 2003, both monastery and catacomb are popular targets for weekend pilgrims from the South, who have reinstalled an assortment of inexpensive icons and offertory candles in the tomb. But even before then, candle drippings and floral offerings proved that local Muslims continue to revere the cave regardless of the departure of its Orthodox custodians. The stratum of simple, fervent belief runs deep in Cyprus, predating the monotheistic religions and not respecting their fine distinctions.

# Enkomi-Alasia

From the monastery-museum it's a short drive southwest to a T-junction. Take the right turn – just beyond the junction is the inconspicuously signed entry to the Bronze Age town of **Enkomi-Alasia** (unenclosed, but £1.25 admission when warden present, typically daily: summer 9am–7pm; winter 9am–1pm & 2–4.45pm), opposite a water tank. Founded in about 2000 BC, it first appeared historically four hundred years later on some Pharaonic tablets, referred to as "Alashya" (Éngomi is the modern Greek name of the nearest village). Alasia figured in Egyptian trade documents because from the sixteenth century BC onwards it acted as a thriving copper-exporting harbour, in an age when the coast was much closer and the river Pedhiéos more navigable than it is today. Mycenaean immigration had swelled the population to 15,000 by the twelfth century, but fire and earthquake mortally weakened the city during the eleventh century, after which it was abandoned in favour of Salamis.

## The site

Excavations sponsored by the British Museum began in 1896, revealing the most complete Late Bronze Age town on Cyprus, and were continued at intervals by French, Swedish and Cypriot missions until 1974. The town plan was a grid of narrow, perpendicular streets and low houses, surrounded by a wall; Alasia was initially thought to be a necropolis for Salamis, since human skeletons were discovered under each dwelling as at Khirokitiá.

Also found here was an as-yet-undeciphered tablet in Cypro-Minoan script; the famous "Horned God", possibly an avatar of Apollo whose worship was imported from Arcadia in the Peloponnese; and an exquisite silver bowl inlaid with ox-head and floral designs, whose only known equal also came from the same region. These and other treasures are distributed between the British Museum and the Cyprus Museum.

Notwithstanding these glories, the site, west of the eucalyptus-tufted hill where the excavation warehouses sit, is today of essentially specialist interest. Little remains above waist level, and there's absolutely no labelling; problems of interpretation are made more difficult by the fact that survivors of the eleventh-century earthquakes divided up damaged open-plan houses with crude rubble barriers. The walled precinct was originally entered via a north gate; west of the main longitudinal street, the "**Horned God**" was found in a namesake sanctuary marked by stone horns similar to those at Pigádhes, surrounded by the skulls of animals presumably worn as masks during the celebration of his cult. At the south edge of the exposed grid stands the so-called **House of Bronzes**, where many such objects were discovered in 1934.

## The cenotaph of Nicocreon

If you turn left at the T-junction towards Famagusta, you'll pass through the modern village of Tuzla (Engomi), at the far side of which stands the cut-open tumulus known as the **cenotaph of Nicocreon**, the last king of Salamis. Excavations revealed an elevated platform on which an ancient mock cremation had taken place; among the limited number of items recovered were various clay dummies, thought to represent the actual family of Nicocreon, who had killed themselves in their palace rather than surrender to Ptolemy I. Its burning, collapsing beams were their real pyre; just who conducted the memorial ceremony honouring the recently defeated dynasty remains a mystery.

# Boğaz

**BOĞAZ** (Bogázi) could make a fairly pleasant base with its fishing anchorage and small beach, though oil-storage tanks and a cement plant across the bay, built a stone's throw from the almost vanished Templars' castle of Stronglyos, are a bit disconcerting. Just one local **hotel** survives: the 2002-built, smallish *Exotic* (☎371 28 81, ⊛www.exotichotel.com; ❸), near the south end of the strip on the inland side of the road, slightly set back from the noisy cement trucks which rumble through here in the morning.

By contrast, a half-dozen seafood **restaurants** flank the road here; once reasonable value, they've become fairly touristy, expensive and much of a muchness, all the more so since trippers from the South began passing through. The fish is pretty fresh, but a main dish, salad and chips with a couple of tiny starter plates will run to £11 and up. Perhaps more worthwhile, just 2km south, is expat-run *Moon Over the Water* (Mon–Sat dinner only, plus Sun lunch; closed in winter; reserve on ☎371 32 97 or 0542/856 94 41), a beachside bistro-bar with consistently good reports.

# Iskele (Tríkomo)

Approaching Boğaz from Nicosia or Kyrenia, you'll almost certainly pass through **İSKELE** (Tríkomo), notable as the birthplace of notorious EOKA leader George Grivas and, less controversially, of Vassos Karageorghis, Cyprus's foremost archeologist. In the central square and roundabout, the diminutive fifteenth-century Dominican chapel of **Áyios Iákovos** (locked) seems plunked down like a jewel-box; supposedly the early twentieth-century Queen Marie of Romania was so taken with it that she had an exact replica built on the Black Sea coast as a royal chapel.

At the western edge of the village, on the way to Geçitkale (Lefkóniko), stands the double-aisled Byzantine church of the **Panayía Theotókos**, constructed from the twelfth to fifteenth centuries. It is now a so-called "**Icon Museum**" (daily: summer 9am–6pm, winter 9am–1pm & 2–4.45pm; £1.25) – though there have been allegations that at least one of the exhibits was spirited away from another, still-functioning church. In any case, the entirely modern icon collection is of negligible artistic merit; what makes the admission charge justifiable are the best surviving **frescoes** in the North, strongly related in style to those at Asínou in the Tróödhos.

The oldest are found in the south aisle, where scenes from the life of Joachim and Anna, the Virgin's parents, predominate, appropriately so for a church dedicated to the Virgin. In the arch of the south recess, below the dome, the *Prayer of Joachim in the Wilderness* faces the *Meeting of Joachim and Anna*, where the couple embrace while a maidservant looks on; the north recess arch features the *Prayer of Anna* (for offspring; the couple had been childless) and the pair's *Presentation of Gifts to the Temple*. In the apse, over the altar, a *Virgin Orans* presides below a fine *Ascension*, with Christ borne heavenward by four angels, while an archangel and six awed disciples look up from either side.

But the most arresting image is the severe *Pandokrátor* in the dome itself, where the frowning Christ averts his gaze towards a surrounding inscription, identifying him as "Overseer of All" who searches hearts and souls, concluding with the injunction: "Mortals, Fear the Judge!" Angels on bended knee worship all around, while below, the bust of Christ flanked by the Virgin and John the Baptist awaits the Throne of Judgement, with the instruments of the Passion.

# The Karpaz (Kárpas) peninsula

The remote "panhandle" of Cyprus, known variously as the **Karpaz**, **Kárpas**, **Kırpaşa** or **Karpásia peninsula**, presents a landscape of rolling hills and grain fields, partly domesticated with vineyards, tobacco fields or olive and carob trees – plus an ever-growing number of villa projects – but still fringed by some of the loneliest beaches on the island. In ancient times it was much more densely inhabited, something attested to by a surprising concentration of small **archeological sites** and **early Christian churches** which, taken together, are considerably more interesting than the celebrated **monastery of Apóstolos Andhréas** near the far cape. The inhabitants were once noted for relict traditions which had died out elsewhere, for their craftwork and for a smattering of blue or green eyes – and more finely chiselled features – that hinted at Frankish or Arab settlement.

Until 1974 the peninsula was an ethnic mosaic, Turkish villages such as Áyios Simeón, Koróvia and Galinóporni alternating with Greek ones like Rizokárpaso, Ayía Triás and Yialoússa. However only a handful, like Kómi Kebír and Áyios Andhrónikos, were actually mixed; Denktaş reportedly came through in 1964 to urge its Turks to segregate themselves. They refused then, though the small Turkish-Cypriot minority of Áyios Theódhoros moved to ethnically homogeneous Galátia when the troubles started, and a fortified enclave eventually formed around the kernel of Áyios Simeón, Koróvia and Galinóporni. The Republican government aggravated the problem, it is claimed, by routeing and paving the main road through the Orthodox villages, leaving the Muslim settlements to fend for themselves. Today the crumbling villages – certainly the smaller ones – seem at least fifty percent resettled by mainland Turks. But the peninsula, superfluous as it is to the argument of who controls the North, is no longer heavily garrisoned by the Turkish army.

In 1998 the Northern authorities widened and improved the road all the way to **Yenierenköy** (Yialoússa), thus greatly easing travel in the peninsula. This new road – now being extended beyond Yenierenköy – bypasses most of the villages discussed below, so slight detours are required to visit them and nearby attractions. **Buses** run from Famagusta to Yenierenköy, but are irregular and do not leave the main road, so you will almost certainly need a **car**. You can see the most interesting sights in a single, long day (beginning from a base near Salamis), but to really savour the area you'd want two, especially starting from Kyrenia – a fairly brutal, 250-kilometre round-trip drive by the shortest routes. An overnight at a simple *pansiyon* or hotel on the peninsula is highly recommended. Out of season local **petrol stations** – even along the main trunk route – close very early; the closest reliable one to the peninsula is in Akova (Yípsou), open until midnight.

Since the advent of all-but-unrestricted movement for Cypriots in April 2003, Karpaz has become a firm favourite with **Greek–Cypriot trippers**, who revel in empty landscapes, beaches and Orthodox monuments the likes of which are getting progressively harder to enjoy in the South. In response, tourist facilities are multiplying – as are establishment signs in often wonkily grammatical Greek, proudly proclaiming the proprietors' Cypriot origins – although, human nature being what it is, prices have climbed and quality dropped at many outfits.

## Kantara castle

Poised at the spot where the Kyrenia range subsides into rolling hills, **Kantara castle**, the easternmost and lowest of the Byzantine/Crusader trio, is as good a spot as any to call the base of the peninsula. Even here the Karpaz is so narrow that the castle simultaneously surveys impressive arcs of shoreline along both the north coast and the Bay of Famagusta. The name is thought to derive from the Arabic *qantara*, "arch" or "bridge", though it's difficult to pinpoint such a structure in either this citadel or the surrounding landscape.

Traditionally the castle is reckoned to be where Isaac Komnenos surrendered to Richard the Lionheart in 1191. Like St Hilarion, it figured prominently in the 1229–30 war between the supporters of the Holy Roman Emperor Frederick II and the Lusignan–Ibelin cartel, and again during the Genoese invasion, when the regent John of Antioch was smuggled out of prison in Famagusta to this hideout disguised as a pot-tinner. Kantara shared the fate of the other Kyrenia hill-castles at the hands of the Venetians early in the sixteenth century, but it is still the best preserved of the three.

From Boğaz you'll need the better part of thirty minutes' driving to get to the castle, climbing via dilapidated Yarköy (Áyios Elías); Turnalar (Yeráni) with a conspicuous, desecrated church on the point of collapse; and finally reaching, after a paved but narrow, curvy one-lane section, pine-swathed **Kantára village**, the closest thing to a hill-station in the Kyrenia range.

Among the boarded-up Greek summer villas and dried-up fountains, there's an abandoned hotel and a sporadically operating restaurant. From the central junction by the restaurant, turn right to follow the ridgeline, following signs for the castle and picnic grounds; the tarmac gives out shortly before the castle's car park, 4km east of the village.

### The site

Just over seven hundred metres above sea level, most of the complex (unenclosed but £1.75 admission when warden present, typically summer 10am–6pm, winter 9am–4.45pm) faces east, the only direction from which it is easily accessible. You enter the outer enceinte through a **barbican** flanked by a pair of towers, then climb steps to the inner ward. First stop here will probably be the massive **southeast tower**, its lower part a cistern which occasionally doubled as a dungeon. Further along the southeast wall are the **barracks**, a trio of rooms fitted with loopholes; adjacent, an obvious latrine was flushed by the castle's sophisticated plumbing system. Up to here the buildings are in good condition, down to the woodwork and rib-vaulted ceilings, and could be used tomorrow. Beyond this point, however, Kantara is quite ruinous until the southwest corner of the battlements, where one chamber contains a hidden **postern gate** for surprising besiegers.

Crossing the rubble of the inner bailey, or returning to the southeast tower, you can attain the **northern towers**; their design – two long galleries equipped with arrow slits and joined by a square chamber – is a remarkable piece of military engineering. Of the highest watchtower, once used to communicate with Buffavento to the west, just one wall and a Gothic window survive; the northeast bastion, by contrast, is impressively complete.

## Kaplıca (Dhavlós) and around

From either the castle or village of Kantára, you can plainly see **KAPLICA** (Dhavlós) and its bays just below on the north coast. To get here, return to the four-way junction in Kantára village for the sharp but brief descent. Kaplıca village, resettled by mainlanders, is actually 1km inland from the main beach, a more-than-decent, 400-metre stretch of sand, the first really good beach east from Onüçüncü Mil (see p.377). Dominating this cove is the *Kaplıca Restaurant*, enduringly popular at weekends (ring ahead then), with *woppa* and *şiş kebap* prominent on the menu. The management keeps equally busy **rooms** (T 387 20 32 or 0542/851 03 37, W www.kaplicabeach.8m.com; ❶) downstairs: basic but en suite, with fans and TV, opening right onto the sand. Just to the east there's an anchorage and a smaller beach, while another sandy patch (with a fish-fry shack) lies about 5km to the west.

Twelve kilometres west, near the boundary between Famagusta and Kyrenia districts, the lonely late Byzantine church of **Panayía Pergaminiótissa** (signposted) sits about 400m inland from the road. Once completely frescoed and the seat of a monastery, it's now bricked up to prevent further vandalism, and more evocative seen from afar.

## Zeytin Burnu to Kumyalı

The most obvious excursions from Boğaz go northeast, towards Zafer Burnu (Cape Apostólou Andhréa). For very private, sandy beaches relatively near Boğaz, two nameless strands to either side of **Zeytin Burnu** (Cape Eléa) fit the bill well. For the first one, head southeast out of the central crossroads in the village of **Çayırova** (Áyios Theodhóros) on the most prominent dirt track, always turning towards the sea when given the choice. Soon you emerge at an impromptu car park/turnaround area very near Zeytin Burnu; the shore below can be rubbishy and seaweed-strewn, but walk to the far end of the 400-metre beach and the litter thins out. Up on the headland closing off the cove are supposed to be the sparse remains of the ancient town of Knidos.

For the other local beach, bypass Çayirova in favour of **Bafra** (Vogolídha), from where another, briefer dirt road continues to decent **Palloúra** beach, deposited by a rather stagnant stream. An abandoned, half-built holiday village here testifies to the collapse of the Asil Nadir empire; instead, there is just a single, summertime "restaurant/camping" (really a day-use area). From Palloúra, you can return to the main trunk road at Pamuklu (Távrou).

Your next opportunity for a swim will be the small, reefy beach below **Kumyalı** (Kóma toú Yialoú), encroached on somewhat by another "restaurant/camping", the *Pelican*, and a fishing port. The village itself, sturdily built from local stone (the nearby quarries also supplied material for the walls of Famagusta), has two noteworthy churches: a sixteenth-century one about 1500m west, and a slightly older one on a flat-topped knoll close to Kumyalı.

## Panayía Kanakariá church and around

The intriguing fifth-to-twelfth-century monastic church of **Panayía Kanaka-riá** stands at the very western edge of Boltaşlı (Lythrangomí), reached via a side road east from the main Kırpaşa trunk route at Ziyamet (Leonárisso). Today it is locked – rather a case of bolting the stable door after the horse has fled (see box below), but enough can be seen of the design from outside to convince you of the building's merit. Nave and aisles represent an eleventh-century revamping of the original fifth-century structure, of which only the apse (former home of the mosaics) remains. The domed narthex was added shortly afterwards, while the high, drummed central cupola followed in the 1700s.

The narrow but paved side road beyond the village threads through the territory of this former Turkish-Cypriot enclave before ending at **Kaleburnu** (Galinóporni), a remarkable semi-troglodytic village wedged between two hills. Both slopes and the surrounding areas are riddled with rock-cut **tombs** and other ancient relics. Among the most striking of these are the enormous cliff-tomb at **Derince** (Vathýlakkas), the free-standing one at **Avtepe** (Áyios Symeón) hamlet and the seaside, Bronze Age fortress at **Nitovikla**, 3km south

### The theft of the Kanakariá mosaics

The sixth-century **mosaics** which formerly graced the apse of **Panayía Kanakariá** are contemporary with those at Ravenna; in situ, they consisted of a Virgin and precociously aged Child flanked by the archangels, while above the Virgin busts of various evangelists and apostles, particularly Matthew, Andrew, Bartholomew, Luke, James, Thaddeus and Thomas, ran in a curved band. Art historians disagree on their merit, but the expressiveness of the figures compensates somewhat for the crudeness of the tesserae (the pigmented or gilded glass cubes used to compose the mosaic).

Even before independence, the mosaics had suffered at the hands of superstitious villagers who believed that the tesserae were efficacious against skin disease. Much worse was to follow, however; at some undetermined moment between 1974 and 1979, thieves broke in through the windows of the drum, hacked four sections of mosaic off the wall, and spirited them off the island.

The whereabouts of the fragments were unknown until the late 1980s, when American art dealer Peg Goldberg purchased them for just over $1 million from a Turkish-Dutch duo, Aydın Dikmen and Michel van Rijn, who also brandished a dubiously legal export permit from the North Cyprus government. The mosaics were then offered for sale to the Getty Museum in California for twenty times that amount, but the museum management contacted the Los Angeles police, and by this point Cyprus's Autocephalous Orthodox Church and Department of Antiquities had also got wind of the dealings.

Acting jointly with the Church, the government of the Republic sued for the return of the mosaics in the US District Court of Indianapolis, finally winning their case in August 1989; the presiding judge essentially agreed with the Greek-Cypriot contention that an

by jeep track from Kuruova (Koróvia). Just before Kaleburnu, another seaward track leads to **Üsküdar** (Skoutári) beach, not utterly wonderful but acceptable for a dip. Dirt tracks head northwest to Yenierenköy and east to Dipkarpaz from here; shown rather optimistically on virtually every map, they are really only negotiable with a 4WD vehicle with high clearance, and even then at speeds hardly exceeding walking pace.

## Yenierenköy and the Ayías Triás basilica

**YENIERENKÖY** (Yialoússa, Yalusa), the second-largest village on the peninsula and centre of the local tobacco industry, has been resettled by the inhabitants of the Kókkina (Erenköy) enclave in Tillyría since 1975. To travellers it offers the last reliable petrol pumps you'll see before the end of the peninsula, a bank which (theoretically) will handle foreign exchange, and a seasonally functioning tourist information office (summer only, daily 9am–5pm). Just northeast, the small **beaches** and boat jetties of "Yenierenköy Halk Plajı" and "Malibu" lie almost within sight of the main coast road, to either side of **Yassi Burnu** (Cape Plakotí), but except for the namesake *Malibu* **restaurant** there seems no compelling reason to take advantage of them unless the south wind is up, when these coves will be more sheltered than usual.

The inland turning from the southern edge of Yenierenköy leads to **SİPAHİ** (Ayía Triás), noted for the handsome mosaic floor of the **early Christian basilica of Ayías Triás**. The signposted site (fenced but gate always unlocked; £1.50 if warden present) lies at the northerly exit of the village going downhill towards the sea, just west of the road.

The fifth-century, three-aisled basilica seems far too large for the needs of the modest early village partly excavated here. From their similar style, it

export licence granted by an internationally unrecognized state was invalid, and that the artwork remained the property of the Orthodox Church. Following a failed appeal by the dealers, the mosaics returned to the South in the summer of 1991, and are now displayed in a special wing of the Archbishop Makarios Cultural Centre (see p.286). Shortly after, a judgement in Texas concerning frescoes removed from the fourteenth-century church of Áyios Efimianós on the Mesarya also found in favour of their eventual return to the South (they are still in Texas pending a political settlement).

By the mid-1990s, Van Rijn had fallen out with his partner Dikmen and, ostensibly tired of a life of art-crime, approached the Greek-Cypriot authorities and offered to co-operate in retrieving more stolen mosaics and frescoes – for a small commission to cover "expenses" only. With money fronted by wealthy Cypriot businessmen, and the Greek-Cypriot consul in The Hague as his contact and paymaster, in September 1997 Van Rijn negotiated with Dikmen through intermediaries to buy the mosaics of Thaddeus and Thomas, plus considerable quantities of other religious art from the North, including several important frescoes lifted from the walls of Antifonítis monastery (see p.374). Under threat of arrest and prosecution, Van Rijn agreed to organize a sting operation to catch Dikmen, now in Germany; the trap was sprung at the Munich Hilton in October 1997, and Dikmen's basement was searched and found to contain several rooms full of treasures from the North, now all in South Nicosia.

With court orders, like UN resolutions, proven to be of limited efficacy as a precedent for other cases of antiquities theft, the authorities in the South have had to resort to such James-Bond-ish doings to obtain satisfaction – at a price of about half a million pounds, all of which (excluding Van Rijn's fee) was presumably also recovered in the sting operation.

△ Paleochristian fresco, Salamis

seems likely that the same craftsmen who decorated the annexe of Eustolios at Kourion are responsible for the **nave mosaics** here, which are entirely but engagingly geometric. An inscription at the west entry relates that three men contributed to the cost of the decoration in honour of a vow, while up by the apse another inscription informs that Iraklios the deacon paid for that section of the floor.

In the **north aisle mosaics**, there are several exceptions to the pattern of abstract imagery, including a cluster of pomegranates, diagonally opposite one of two pairs of sandals. This curious symbol, common in the early Christian Middle East but found nowhere else in Cyprus, may represent the pilgrimage through this world to the next. The baptistry, just southeast of the basilica, has a deep, marble-lined cruciform font, the largest on the island.

## The coast east of Yenierenköy

The inland detour to Sipahi and the coastal route join up again well before **Áyios Thýrsos** (Ayterisos), a tiny anchorage grouped around two namesake churches: the modern one up on the road, next to the namesake restaurant, is of little interest, but the older one down at sea level contains a crypt at the rear in which a healing spring once trickled. One or the other is still used for the saint's commemorative mass on July 23.

Less than 1km beyond Áyios Thýrsos, just seaward of the road, is one of the peninsula's best **accommodation/restaurant** options: the one-star *Theresa Hotel* (☎374 42 66 or 0533/863 27 87, ⓦwww.theresahotel.com; ①). The 24 rooms are very plain but clean, airy and en suite, with mains electricity and hot water. The courtly proprietor Erdoğan Özbalıkçı, nicknamed "Hoca" from his "day job" as a schoolteacher in Yenierenköy, speaks good English; just across the road, the salubrious restaurant offers a choice of decent *meze*, cooked dishes of the day or fish. Erdoğan doesn't much care for hunting, but winter-weekend hunters attend his diner once they've packed out *Çira'nin Yeri (Yiannakis)* just down the road. The "*Çira*" (Cypriot dialect for *kyría* or "the Mrs" is a Yialoússa Greek-Cypriot who elected to stay after 1974, was ill-treated by the Turkish Army for her stubbornness and lost various family members. Her endurance was rewarded, as she (and surviving son Yiannakis) can barely cope with the crowds, and the food is excellent.

Minuscule, tenth-century **Áyios Fótios**, the next church passed, is accessible by a non-motorable, 300-metre track some 5km past Áyios Thýrsos; after 3km more, a paved side-turning leads up through the pines to the sixteenth-century monastery church of **Panayía Eleoússa (Sína)**, beautiful, unusual and worth the slight detour. It's an asymmetrical two-apsed church rather than the usual three, with the smaller, narrower north aisle divided from the main one by a double archway a bit like that seen at Panayía Iamatikí in the Limassol foot-hills.

Such lopsided double churches are also found in the Greek islands where a Latin Catholic medieval ruling class has conceded some space of worship to the Orthodox peasantry, and it seems likely that something of the sort occurred here. The carved south portal (door always open) shows marked Lusignan influence, while the large ruined outbuilding adjacent suggests the church was once part of a monastery. During summer, a **restaurant** operates adjacent.

Panayía Eleoússa romantically overlooks the broad sweep of **Ronnás** bay. Here dunes give way to a fine beach possibly favoured by egg-laying turtles, but the prevailing north wind brings a lot of garbage, and even 4WD vehicles may founder in the sand-tracks towards the water.

## The Greeks of the Karpaz peninsula

The 1974 war effectively bypassed the peninsula, so that there was no panicky exodus of civilians in the path of the oncoming Turkish army. Thus of the nearly 20,000 **Greek Cypriots** who chose to stay in the North, most of them lived in the Karpaz. But since 1975, systematic harassment by the Turkish army and the North Cypriot government has reduced this population to a handful of middle-aged and older individuals. There were often forcible expulsions to the South when property was coveted by settlers or Turkish-Cypriot refugees, and the remaining Greek Cypriots required permits to travel outside their home village. Secondary education was no longer allowed after 1975, with only two Greek primary schools functioning thereafter, so any children over the age of 11 had to go to the South for continued education, without any right of return. Only if youths stay continuously do they have the right to inherit property, as houses can only be left to relatives still living in the North – the (desired) result is that as the Greeks die out, the North's government seizes their property and hands it to settlers. Similarly, no Greek-Cypriot doctor practises anywhere on this side of the Line, and while the right to private telephones was theoretically conceded in 1996 after UN pressure on the North, in practice few have been installed. Neither do the local Orthodox have the right to vote in local elections.

Not surprisingly, then, only about 400 stubborn Greeks continue to live on the peninsula: under 350 in Dipkarpaz (Rizokárpaso), fewer than 80 in Sipahi (Ayía Triás), plus a few scattered others. The UN post in Ziyamet (Leonárisso), which formerly existed to protect their interests, shut in the mid-1990s, after which UN lorries only visited periodically, primarily to bring food from the South, as their lack of facility in Turkish and their restricted participation in the local economy meant that most Greeks couldn't or wouldn't shop locally. The Greeks were allowed to visit doctors and relatives in the South on one-week visas, shuttled to the Ledra Palace crossing in Nicosia by Turkish-Cypriot authorities for a fee; relatives from the South were not allowed to make reciprocal visits.

Relations between the Greek Cypriots and goat-grazing Anatolian settlers are habitually strained, somewhat better with Turkish Cypriots or Bulgarian-Turkish immigrants used to farming, though the coffeehouses in Sipahi and Dipkarpaz remain ethnically segregated. The conditions of the Greeks' continued residence here are undeniably humiliating, a judgment endorsed officially on May 10, 2001 by the European Court of Human Rights; "We live like animals" can be an unsolicited local comment on the state of affairs. This is often voiced in tandem with the fatalistic, almost Byzantine belief that the invasion and its aftermath were God's punishment for their sins – sentiments expressed by Greeks at regular intervals since the Turks first appeared in Anatolia during the tenth century. Medieval-style harassment extends even to religious observance: the church bell in Dipkarpaz may not be rung lest it offend the Muslims, although the bells in Sipahi – with a proportionately higher Greek population – may be sounded. The icon of the Sipahi village church went missing in December 1991, allegedly appearing thereafter among the exhibits of the museum in İskele (Trikomo).

Under the circumstances, the opening of the "border" on April 23, 2003 was little short of a godsend for the enclave Greeks of the Karpaz. The secret police who used to dog their every public conversation with outsiders could no longer cope with the flood of Greek-Cypriot company; freedom of mobility and exponentially increased access to Cypriot pounds have brought a vastly improved standard of living, especially for the handful of restaurateurs and café-owners noted in the text. The most recent hopeful development, in September 2004, was the reopening (with the consent of the North's government) of the secondary school in Dipkarpaz. As with the Maronites of Kormakiti, it looks as if the patience of the holdouts is being rewarded.

# Dipkarpaz and around

From Ronnás the road turns inland to **DİPKARPAZ** (Rizokárpaso), the remotest and yet largest village on the peninsula, with a population of around three thousand, and a huge modern mosque overshadowing the triple-aisled church of the remaining Greeks. Once a prosperous place, Dipkarpaz has been reduced to the status of an Anatolian village, with added poignancy in the use of formerly imposing arcaded houses as poultry pens and hay barns. Besides its coffeehouses – the Greek one of Nikos Siambis is prominently signposted of late, and assiduously attended by Greek-Cypriot trippers and Turkish-Cypriot hunters alike – the main amenities for travellers are a filling station, and a worthwhile **accommodation** scheme. This, the 2002-built *Karpaz Arch Houses* (℡ 372 20 09, ℻ 372 20 07; B&B ❶), lies some 500m from the current centre, just off the route to Áyios Fílon. Here the old village high street has been pedestrianized and the arcaded houses flanking it restored as attractive studios, most of which interconnect to form family suites; breakfast is taken in the old coffeehouse, now the scheme's office.

## Áyios Fílon and Aféndrika

The early Christian sites of Áyios Fílon and Aféndrika both involve a slight but eminently worthwhile detour north from Dipkarpaz; from the modern village square with its mosque, church and coffeehouses, follow signs for both the *Karpaz Arch Houses* and the *Oasis* as the proper road snakes over the northerly of the two ridges enclosing the village.

The basilicas of **Áyios Fílon** (Ayfilon), 3km along this, are the most obvious remains of ancient Karpasia – even from the ridge you can easily spot the cluster of bedraggled washingtonia palms (with new sprouts coming up) and the resort buildings surrounding them. Typically, the half-ruined tenth-century chapel, of which only the apse and south wall are completely intact, sits amid foundations of a far larger, earlier basilica and baptistry, perhaps the seat of the saintly Philon, first bishop of Christian Karpasia. The bapistry's extensive *opus sectile* flooring includes an abstract ring design similar to that of Kambanópetra at Salamis. Just to the north, you can find the ancient jetty sticking 100m out to sea, its masonry furrowed where long-vanished iron pins held the stones together. The rest of Hellenistic and Roman **Karpasia**, which supplied building stone for church and baptistry alike, lies scattered to the west of the road in, but it's a long slog through thorn-bushes to never-excavated walls and a necropolis.

Immediately beyond the palm trees stands the *Oasis*, a combination **restaurant-inn** spread over several buildings (℡ 0533/867 36 85, 🌐 www.kayanacyprus .com; B&B ❷). The diner has unfortunately already come to take Greek-Cypriot clientele for granted, and is overpriced and perfunctory (weekend hunters stop in only for soup or a hot drink); the pastel-decor rooms are basic (non-en-suite) but cheerful, with solar showers in a separate building, all overlooking a "private" 30-metre beach lapped by a bay where turtles can often be seen in the water. But much the best swimming hereabouts is at the so-called **Dipkarpaz Halk Plajı**, a 700-metre fine-sand bay just 400m west, along a dirt track well signed from beside the church.

Beyond Áyios Fílon in the opposite direction, the mostly paved but narrow road swings east to follow the coast 5km more to **Aféndrika**, another important ancient town on an even larger scale than Karpasia. All that remains today are three contiguous ruined churches: Panayía Khrysiótissa, a twelfth-century ruin inside which is a smaller chapel two hundred years younger; formerly domed, double-apsed Áyios Yeóryios, its west end missing; and three-aisled

Panayía Asómatos, mostly roofless but still impressive. West of the group of churches is a necropolis, while in the opposite direction the chambers of the citadel were partly cut into the outcrop on which it was built.

The now-dirt road continues 1km to where a distinct path leads within 600m north across fields to sandy **Exárkhou** cove. Given the excellence (and usual cleanliness) of Dipkarpaz Halk Plajı, this isn't really worth the extra effort except for committed misanthropes.

### Beaches southeast of Dipkarpaz

Dipkarpaz is the last proper village on the peninsula; beyond supposedly stretches a "national reserve", posted as off-limits to hunting, though this doesn't seem to deter in the least the crowds of Sunday shooters who come here from all over the North to bag partridge from November to March. Other conspicuous "wild" life consists of large herds of skittish donkeys, descendants of domestic ones who escaped in 1974 when their Orthodox owners had to abandon them. They have since multiplied and become a nuisance, trampling seeded fields and eating crops, and plans have long been mooted to capture or if necessary cull them.

Some 5km east of Dipkarpaz, the road passes the solar-powered *Blue Sea* restaurant at the promontory known as **Khelónes**, an ideal lunch stop if touring these parts, offering fresh if unadorned fish from the adjacent anchorage. The proprietors (one of whom is from Andhrolíkou in from Páfos district) also keep a small, one-star hotel upstairs (☏372 23 93, 🖷372 22 55; B&B ❶); the rooms are cell-like, with saggy beds, though breakfast is good.

The closest alternative, about 1km further along, is the uncertified *Livana Hotel* (☏372 23 96; ❶), where accommodation consists of wooden huts on stilts, complete with proper bed and mosquito netting; at the base of the ladder up is another hut with toilet and shower. There's a tiny private beach on the shore of the well-sheltered inlet here, plus a fish-and-beer restaurant in a building with a few conventional rooms.

## Nangomí ("Golden Beach")

Continuing towards the cape, the road bears inland again for a while, passing through fields and pastures surprisingly well tended for such a deserted region. Some 12km beyond the *Blue Sea* begins the best beach in the North, if not the entire island, initially hidden behind a straight line of scrub-covered knolls halting the advance of vast dunes. Known officially in pre-1974 days as **Nangomí**, it has lately been dubbed **"Golden Beach"**, though the strand is of a distinctly reddish tint in full daylight.

Westerly access is provided by a dirt lane starting by some old stone foundations at the roadside; this track threads through a conspicuous gap in the barrier hillocks, leaving you with a ten-minute walk across the sand to the water. Behind the sand here you'll find *Hasan's Turtle Beach* (☏0533/864 10 63; ❶) and *Golden Beach* (☏372 21 46; ❶) both acting as combined rustic **bungalow clusters/campsites**, with attached **restaurants**. Hasan, the original entrepreneur here, offers a half-dozen or so huts and mans the grill himself.

Alternatively, you can proceed until the road skirts the edge of the hard-packed dunes, and the beach extends obviously southwest, though the walk in from several lay-bys here is no shorter. Here there's one more simple restaurant/"camping", *Big Sand*, with sweeping views back down to the base of the peninsula.

The five-plus kilometres of sand could easily accommodate most of the North's population on a summer weekend, and probably does on occasion.

Given the rather impermanent nature of development thus far – mains powers stops around Dipkarpaz – there's some hope for its preservation, as the tip of the peninsula has been declared a protected area: good news for the quail and other birds living in the dunes, and the **sea turtles** who lay eggs on this wild, spectacular beach. Just past *Big Sand* there's a checkpoint, presumably to screen for hunters, though it in fact rarely staffed.

## Apóstolos Andhréas monastery

The phone lines which have shadowed the road for miles end at the sprawling, barracks-like **monastery of Apóstolos Andhréas**, for decades a lodestone for Cypriot pilgrims. The spot has been revered since legend credited the Apostle Andrew with summoning forth a miraculous spring on the shore during a journey from Palestine, and using the water to effect cures. By Byzantine times there was a fortified abbey here, long since disappeared but a plausible alternative to Kantara as the site of Isaac Komnenos's capture by Richard the Lionheart.

The tradition of mass pilgrimage and popularity, however, only dates from the well-documented experience of one **Maria Georgiou**, an Anatolian Greek whose small son was kidnapped by brigands in 1895; seventeen years later the apostle appeared in a dream and commanded her to pray for the boy's return at the monastery. Crossing the straits from Turkey in a crowded boat, Georgiou happened to tell the story to a young dervish among the passengers, who grew more and more agitated as the narrative progressed. He asked the woman if her lost son had any distinguishing signs, and upon hearing a pair of birthmarks described, cast off his robes to reveal them and embraced her. The son – for he it was – had been raised a Muslim in İstanbul, but upon docking on Cyprus was rebaptized, to the general acclaim of the population.

Subsequent **miracles** – mostly cures of epilepsy, paralysis and blindness – at the monastery further enhanced its prestige and rendered it enormously wealthy in votive donations. But the faithful never missed the opportunity for a fun day out as well, eventually scandalizing the church into censuring the weekend carnival atmosphere.

All that came to an abrupt end **after 1974**, since when the pilgrims' hostel was long occupied by the Turkish army, and the monastery shrunk to a pathetic ghost of its former self. For some years the place was entirely off-limits to outsiders, but after the late 1980s it was signposted by yellow-and-black placards (Manastır) as a tourist attraction, run as a sort of zoo by the authorities to prove North Cyprus's religious tolerance. "Zoo" is not such an arbitrary characterization, with about fifty cats (still) far outnumbering the human population, plus (until 1999) several enormous pigs at any one time, raised for sale in the South, and incidentally (one assumes) to annoy the majority Muslim population in the North.

As of 1996, as part of various "confidence-building" measures instituted jointly by North and South, Greek-Cypriot pilgrims from the South were allowed day-trips to the monastery twice yearly (Aug 15 & Nov 30), coached in under Turkish-Cypriot and UN escort from the Ledra Palace checkpoint as a quid pro quo for Turkish Cypriots making occasional trips to the Hala Sultan Tekke near Larnaca. Not surprisingly, the complex deteriorated markedly over the decades when the northern regime refused to permit any maintenance, though in 2001 repairs finally began, funded under the presumably neutral aegis of the US and UN.

### Visiting the monastery

Since April 2003, things have changed at Apóstolos Andhréas, though not as radically as you'd think. Despite daily, unrestricted traffic from Greek-Cypriot pilgrims, and well-attended Sunday services, tourist facilities at the gate of the grounds are still limited to a drinks café, a *panayır* (a small forest of trinket stalls) and the larger, municipally-run *Manastır* **restaurant**. One of several remaining elderly Greek caretakers will show you (feed the donation box) the nineteenth-century **katholikón**, of little intrinsic interest since it's been fairly comprehensively stripped of its more valuable icons, though lately it's a bit sprucer inside, and full of *támmata* or tin votaries in the shape of the body part or object needing curing or acquisition. Finally, you may be taken down to the fifteenth-century seaside **chapel**, now essentially a crypt below the main church, where the **holy well** of the apostle flows audibly below a heavy stone cover; both Turkish and Greek Cypriots still esteem and collect the water for its therapeutic properties.

## Zafer Burnu (Cape Apostólou Andhréa)

From the monastery, 5km of rough track brings you to Cyprus's John O'Groats, **Zafer Burnu**, the definitive, if somewhat anti-climactic northeastern tip. A cave-riddled rock, the Neolithic village known as Kastros, was later the site of an ancient Aphrodite temple, of which nothing remains; the goddess was by most accounts in a savage aspect here, a siren-like devourer of men in the sea below. Beyond an abandoned guard house and around the offshore **Klidhés Islets** (the "Keys"), beloved of seabirds, many a ship has been wrecked; weather permitting, local scuba operators occasionally visit one as part of their programmes. Even modern shipping, often evident on the horizon, gives the cape a wide berth as it plies the sea lanes between Syria, Lebanon, Turkey and Cyprus.

# Travel details

| Buses |
|---|
| **Famagusta** to: Kyrenia (every 30min; 1hr 10min); Nicosia (every 30min; 1hr); Yenierenköy (several daily; 1hr). |

| Ferries |
|---|
| **Famagusta** to: Mersin, Turkey (3 weekly; 10hr). |

# Contexts

# Contexts

# History

With its critical location just offshore from the Middle East, the history of Cyprus can't help being long and chequered. The following summary is heavily biased towards antiquity and events of the twentieth century, enabling a reader to grasp what they are most likely to see in a museum – and on the street.

# Beginnings

Settlements of **round stone dwellings**, particularly along the north coast and at Khirokitia and Tenta near Larnaca, as well as graves near Parekklishá, indicate habitation in Cyprus as early as 8000 BC; the origins of these first **Neolithic** settlers are uncertain, but items in obsidian, a material unknown on the island, suggest the Middle Eastern mainland opposite. The first Cypriots engaged in hunting, farming and fishing, but were ignorant of pottery, fashioning instead rough vessels, idols and jewellery from stone. Religious observance seems to have been limited to **burial practices** – the dead were interred under or near dwellings in a fetal position, with their chests crushed by boulders to prevent them from haunting the living.

Following this initial colonization, a three-millennia-long hiatus in archeological evidence, so far unexplained, ensued until the so-called **Neolithic II** culture appeared after 4500 BC. Sites at Vrysi-Áyios Epíktitos (Çatalköy) on the north coast and Sotíra in the south yielded quantities of so-called "red combed" and abstractly painted ware, the first indigenous **ceramics**.

The **Chalcolithic** period, whose cultures emerged after 4000 BC in a gradual transition from the late Neolithic, was distinguished by the settlement of the previously neglected western portion of Cyprus. The era takes its name from the discovery of copper (*chalkos* in ancient Greek) implements, but more important, as indications of developing **fertility cults**, are the limestone female idols at Lémba and Kissónerga, and cruciform grey-green picrolite pendants at Yialiá, reminiscent of similar work in the west Aegean.

With the advent of the **Early Bronze Age** (reckoned from 2500 BC onwards), the focus of Cypriot life shifted to the Mesaoría and its perimeter, conveniently near the first **copper mines**, with the importation of tin permitting the smelting of bronze. Curiously, no confirmed habitation has yet been excavated, but settlement has been inferred from the distribution of elaborate subterranean chamber **tombs or shrines** and their contents, especially at Vounous near Kyrenia. Ceramics executed in red clay seem to have spread across the island from north to south; deeply incised, whimsical zoomorphic or composite ware, imaginatively combining humorous aesthetics with function, appeared along with cruder models of schematic figures engaged in elaborate religious ceremonies pertaining to a bull-centred fertility cult. The **bull**, imported from Asia, permitted for the first time the ploughing of hitherto unusable land, and models show this also.

Well into the second millennium BC, during the so-called **Middle Bronze Age** period, settlements appear on the south and east coasts of Cyprus, facing probable **overseas trading** partners; commerce with immediate neighbours, fuelled by the copper deposits, would by now have been well developed. The most important eastern port was Enkomi-Alasia, the second name soon to be synonymous with the island. Rectangular or L-shaped **dwellings** with flat roofs completely supplanted round ones, and, ominously, **forts** – their inland positioning indicative of civil conflict over the copper trade, rather than of threats from outside – sprang up at various sites around the Mesaoría. Both transport and warfare were facilitated by the recent importation of **horses**. In religious life, female **plank idols**, alone or nursing infants, and bird-headed, earringed figurines were important – the latter probably intended as symbolic companions for interred men, or manifestations of an earth goddess reclaiming one of her children.

# The Late Bronze Age and arrival of the Mycenaeans

As Cypriot political and commercial transactions became more complicated, a **writing script** became necessary: the earliest known Cypriot document, from the **Late Bronze Age**, is an incised clay sixteenth-century BC tablet unearthed at Enkomi-Alasia. Although the eighty still-undeciphered characters are called **Cypro-Minoan** after their supposed derivation from Cretan Linear A, their origins or language have not been proved. Pottery finds, however, at Toúmba toú Skoúrou and Ayía Iríni on the bay of Mórfou indicate the necessary contacts with Minoan culture. Fragmentary passages were inscribed frequently on cups, cylinder seals and loomweights, implying that the language was common throughout Cyprus, though the Enkomi-Alasia tablet remains the only known complete text. Variations of this script remained in use long after the arrival of the Mycenaeans, who did not impose the use of their own presumed form of Linear B.

Other people's records, especially those of the Egyptians, suggest that the island was consistently referred to as **Alashiya** (or Asy, or Alasia) by the fifteenth and fourteenth centuries BC and also imply that for the first time Cyprus formed a loosely united **confederation** of towns. Of these, **Kition** (modern Larnaca) and **Enkomi-Alasia** came to the fore, their high standard of living reflected in elaborate **sanitary facilities**, including bathtubs and sewers. Two new ceramic styles emerged: so-called "base ring", shiny and thin-walled in imitation of metal, usually with a basal ring; and "white slip", provided with a primer coat of white slurry on which brown or black patterns were executed.

## The Myceneans

But the most dramatic change in island culture was fostered by the first **arrival of the Myceneans** from the Greek Peloponnese, who replaced the Minoans as the main Hellenic influence in the east Mediterranean after 1400 BC. Their immediate influence was most obvious in **pottery** of that era – "rude style" pictorial *krater*s, showing mythological scenes and bestiaries (including the octopus, a Minoan favourite) – though it's still uncertain whether such items were brought by the Myceneans to trade for copper, or whether their production techniques were taught to local potters using wheels for the first time. From the same period date the notable enamelled *rhyton* (a horn-shaped drinking vessel – now in the Cyprus Museum in south Nicosia) from Kition, with three series of hunters and animals, and the famous silver bowl of Enkomi-Alasia, inlaid with a floral and bull's-head design.

Around 1200 BC, Mycenean civilization in its Peloponnesian homeland collapsed when confronted with invasion by the Dorian peoples, an event which had a profound knock-on effect in Cyprus. Rogue Mycenean survivors fled Greece via Anatolia, where others joined them to become the raiding "sea peoples" mentioned in Egyptian chronicles of the time. They established an initial foothold on Cyprus at **Maa** (Paleókastro) in the west of the island, choosing a headland easily defensible from both land and sea, and proceeded to destroy Enkomi-Alasia and Kition. Both were soon rebuilt with fortification walls reminiscent of the Mycenean Argolid, with ashlar blocks used for these and individual buildings.

**Religious shrines** were closely associated with the **copper industry**; in separate temple niches at Enkomi-Alasia were discovered the famous "Horned God", possibly a version of Apollo melded with aspects of the indigenous bull-cult, and the so-called "Ingot God", a spear-wielding figure poised atop an ingot shaped like an outstretched oxhide, then the standard form of copper export. While Kition was not so spectacularly rewarding in artefacts, the sanctuaries here formed a huge complex of multiple temples with more Middle Eastern characteristics, though again in intimate association with copper forges. Large numbers of **bull skulls** have been found on the floors of all these shrines, implying their use as ceremonial masks – and the retention of bull worship and sacrifice.

At this time the **Aphrodite** shrine at Palea Paphos first attained prominence. Her cult and that of the smithing deity were not so disparate as might seem at first: in mainstream Hellenic culture, Aphrodite was the consort of Hephaistos, the god of fire and metal-working. A voluptuous female statuette in bronze found at Enkomi-Alasia is thought to be the consort of the martial ingot deity, and terracotta figurines of the Great Goddess with uplifted arms were among archeological finds at the Kition temples.

In general, Mycenean influence was on the ascendant in Cyprus even as the same culture died out in its Aegean birthplace. But the immigrants introduced few of their religious practices and conventions wholesale, instead adapting their beliefs to local usage. Mycenean technology did, however, invigorate local **metallurgy**, permitting the fashioning of such exquisite objects as the square, often wheeled stands for libation bowls found at Enkomi and Kourion, their sides intricately decorated in relief figures. The concept of kingship and **city-states** with Hellenic foundation-legends became institutionalized, after another wave of Mycenean-Anatolian settlement around 1200 BC, at the seven "capitals" of Salamis, Lapethos, Marion, Soli, Palea Paphos, Kourion and Tamassos; pure or "Eteo-Cypriot" culture retreated to Amathus.

A violent earthquake finished off Mycenean Enkomi-Alasia and Kition around 1050 BC; Palea Paphos continued to be inhabited, but effectively the Bronze Age was over. Not, however, before the Mycenean-tutored island smelters had apparently mastered the working of **iron**, as borne out by large numbers of iron weapons appearing in excavated sites of the early eleventh century.

# The Geometric era

The beginning of the **Geometric era** in Cyprus was an echo of the "Dark Ages" in surrounding realms: the Mycenean homeland was now thoroughly overrun by the Dorians; the Hittite empire of Anatolia had collapsed; Egypt was stagnant. Cyprus was essentially **isolated** for around two centuries. Most Cypriots, now a mix of settlers and indigenous islanders, gravitated towards the Mycenean-founded city-kingdoms, such as Salamis; nearby Enkomi-Alasia was gradually abandoned after the mid-eleventh-century earthquake, which, along with silting up, rendered its harbour unusable.

Despite the cultural doldrums, early Geometric **pottery** is quite startling; cups and shallow dishes were popular, painted boldly in black rings, very occasionally with human or animal figures. **Funerary customs** show Mycenean habits, especially among the population descended from immigrants: chamber tombs were approached by long *dromoi* or passages, and slaves were occasionally sacrificed to serve their deceased master. Cremations took place at Kourion, while ossuary urns were used for old bones when reusing a tomb – an increasingly common strategy. In one grave at Palea Paphos, **syllabic Greek script** was found for the first time on a meat skewer, spelling the name of the deceased in Arcadian dialect – partial confirmation of the foundation myth of Palea Paphos by Agapinor, leader of the Arcadian contingent in the Trojan war.

Following stabilization in the west Aegean around 800 BC, trade and other **contacts resumed** between Greece – particularly Euboea – and the indigenous or Eteo-Cypriot centre of Amathus, more extroverted than the Myceno-Cypriot centres. Further fresh input was provided by the peaceful **Phoenician** resettlement of Kition, whose temples had never been completely abandoned even after the natural disaster of the eleventh century. The Phoenicians, an up-and-coming mercantile empire of the Middle East, rededicated these shrines to Astarte, the oriental version of Aphrodite; the **multiple sanctuary**, rebuilt after a fire in 800, was the fulcrum of Phoenician culture on Cyprus, with worship continuing until 312 BC. Not surprisingly, bichrome pottery of the eighth century BC throughout the island shows Phoenician characteristics of dress style and activities.

These exceptions aside, the Geometric culture of Cyprus was **deeply conservative** – Mycenean observances, whether or not melded with Eteo-Cypriot expression, maintained static or even retrospective forms, a trend accentuated by the two-century gap in communication with most of the outside world. The seven city-states were ruled by despotic monarchies, unmindful of the recent experiments in constitutional government in Greece; the Arcadian dialect continued to be written in syllabic script, rather than a true alphabet, until the fourth century BC.

No better demonstration of this traditionalism can be found than the **royal tombs** at Salamis of just before 700 BC, where the details of several burials seem to have been taken from public readings of Homer. The grave artefacts themselves are manifestly Oriental, in a blend of Phoenician and Egyptian styles, reflecting the royal taste of the time; but the numerous roasting spits (similar to the inscribed one at Palea Paphos), the skeletons of sacrificed chariot-horses at the entrance to tombs, and great bronze cauldrons containing the ashes of cremated royalty can only be accounted for in the light of the Homeric epics. Here was a perhaps politically motivated revival of the presumed funerary customs of the Trojan War character Teukros, the reputed Mycenaean founder of Salamis.

## Ancient zenith: the Archaic era

Some consider the start (750 BC) of the **Archaic era** on Cyprus to overlap the end of Geometric by half a century, but the signal event was the island's domination by the **Assyrians** between 708 and 669 BC; however, Cypriot kings were merely required to forward tribute regularly, and this episode left little trace on island life other than some suggestive beards and hairstyles in later sculpture. Upon the departure of the Assyrians, a century of **flourishing independence** followed, producing some of the finest ancient Cypriot art. Its genius was an innate inventiveness combined with a receptivity to surrounding influences and their skilful assimilation into styles that were more than the sum of their component elements.

## Art

Archaic Cyprus excelled for the first time in large-scale **sculpture** in limestone, which exhibited a strong similarity to the art of Ionia in Asia Minor. Figures were nearly always robed in the Ionian manner, rarely nude, with great attention paid to facial expression – contrasting with an often cursory rendering of body anatomy. Large almond-shaped eyes, prominent eyebrows and more than a trace of the celebrated "Archaic smile" were often conjoined with Asiatic hair- and-beard styles, bound by head bands or, later, elaborate head-dresses. A famous example is the **statue of Zeus Keraunios** (Thunderbolt-Hurler) from Kition. Female statue-heads were adorned with suggestions of **jewellery** matching in all respects some exquisitely worked gold and precious-stone originals which have been found. **Pottery** advanced from the abstract to bichrome figurative ware, especially the so-called "free-field" style, where single, well-detailed animal or human figures are rampant on a bare background.

## Religion

**Religious observance** in Archaic Cyprus varied considerably, a function of the increasing number of foreigners visiting or living on the island. In contrast to cosmopolitan ports where the Greek Olympian deities and other more exotic foreign gods like the Egyptian Bes or Phoenician Astarte competed for devotees, the important **rural shrines** of the seventh and sixth centuries were more conservative in their adoration of old chthonic gods, or localized variants of imported divinities. The Phoenicians had their own rural cult, in addition to the Kition temples: that of Baal Hamman at Méniko, in the middle of the island near the copper mines they controlled, though it displayed many elements – such as bull sacrifice – of native Cypriot religion. The other most important sanctuaries were that of Apollo Hylates near Kourion and the long-venerated shrine at Ayía Iríni (Akdeniz), where two thousand terracotta figurines were discovered.

Such **figurines** were typically arranged as ex votos around the altar of the usually simple courtyard shrines; in accord with Cypriot belief that the deity often resided in the temple, these clay figures served as permanent worshippers, ready for the divine presence. Some of the terracottas were realistically modelled for individual detail, and so have been taken to be gifts of a particular worshipper, made to order at workshops adjacent to the shrines. Figurines of musicians and women in various attitudes (including childbirth) accumulated logically enough at Aphrodite or mother-goddess shrines, while the preferred offerings to male deities were bulls, horse-drawn chariots or helmeted warriors such as formed the bulk of the finds at Ayía Iríni.

## The Persian influence

The sixth century BC saw a very brief interval of direct Egyptian rule which, while stricter than the Assyrian era, left a similarly subtle legacy in the form of more outlandish beards or head-dresses on statues. Monumentally, this time is characterized by the strange subterranean "house" tombs at Tamassos, possibly built by itinerant Anatolian masons. The newest Asian power on the horizon, the **Persians**, assumed control over Egypt in 545 BC; with their existing ties to the Middle East through the Phoenicians, and relatively weak military resources, it was easy (and prudent) for the Cypriot kingdoms to reach a vassal-age arrangement with King Cyrus in 545 BC. Yet for a while a measure of autonomy was preserved, and Evelthon, the late sixth-century king of Salamis, minted his own coinage.

In 499 BC, however, this *modus vivendi* dissolved as Persian rule under Darius became harsher and the non-Phoenician Cypriots joined the **revolt** of the Ionian cities. **Onesilos of Salamis** mutinied against his brother the Persian puppet-king and attempted to rally the other Myceno-Cypriot city-kingdoms, but this hastily patched-together confederation, despite land and sea reinforcements from the Ionians, was defeated in a major battle at Salamis, largely due to the treachery of the Kourion contingent. Onesilos' head was stuck on the city gate of pro-Persian Amathus as a warning to other would-be rebels, though after it filled with honeycomb an oracle advised the townspeople to bury it and revere his memory. After the battle, each of the remaining Cypriot city-kingdoms except Kition was besieged and reduced one by one, Soli and Palea Paphos being the last to capitulate in 498. Such prolonged resistance against the mighty Persian empire was made possible by vastly improved stone and mud-brick fortifications, which dwarfed the original designs of the Mycenean settlers. The **pro-Persian Phoenicians** took the opportunity to extend their influence northward, placing their kings on the thrones of Marion and Lapethos; in the aftermath of the revolt the hilltop palace of Vouni was also built by the king of Marion to intimidate nearby pro-Hellenic Soli. Never again, until the twentieth century, would Cyprus be both independent and united.

# Turmoil and decline: Classical Cyprus

By the start of the fifth century BC, Cyprus had ten **city-kingdoms**: Kyrenia, Idalion, Amathus and Kition were added to the Myceno-Cypriot seven, with Soli subsumed into Marion. The island now became thoroughly embroiled in the struggle between Greece and Persia; **Athens** repeatedly sent forces to "liberate" Cyprus, but the distance involved, plus pro-Persian factions on the island, made any victories transient. The Athenian general **Kimon** led three expeditions to various parts of Cyprus, especially against the pro-Persian strongholds of Marion, Salamis and Kition, dying at the hour of victory on his last attempt in 449 BC, outside the walls of Kition. Deprived of leadership, the Greeks sailed home, and the next year the Athenians signed a treaty with the Persians agreeing to drop the matter.

But if the political results of these campaigns were minuscule – the palace at Vouni was rebuilt to a nostalgic Mycenean plan, though oligarchic, dynastic rule continued at most city-kingdoms whether pro-Greek or not – profound **cultural effects** attended the five decades of contact with Greece. A craze for Attic art swept the island in everything from pottery – imported via Marion and Salamis – to coinage, to the marked detriment of local creativity. Sarcophagi and Attic-style memorial *stelae* began to rival rock-cut tombs in popularity; the worship of Heracles and Athena as deities came into vogue, and many Phoenician divinities acquired a Hellenic veneer.

Before the truce, however, the Phoenician regime at Kition, perennial allies of the Persians, had again struck northwards, taking Idalion in 470 BC. The Persians took the peace itself as a cue to tighten their control yet again on the island, and the stage was set for the emergence of a great Cypriot patriot and political genius, **Evagoras I of Salamis**. Born in 435, at the age of 24 he overthrew the Phoenician puppet-king of that city, but skilful diplomatic spadework and judicious payment of tribute to the Persians ensured no repercussions then or for a long time after, giving him the necessary breathing space to build up his defences and elaborate his sophisticated intrigues. Though fiercely pro-Hellenic, he was able to act simultaneously as a mediator between the Athenians and the Persians, even convincing the latter to lend him a fleet for use against the Spartans on behalf of Athens, which duly honoured him after the victory was accomplished. Evagoras' court became a haven for Attic artists and soldiers in exile, voluntary or otherwise, and he vigorously promoted Greek culture throughout his expanding dominions, including the introduction of the **Greek alphabet**, which slowly replaced the Cypriot syllabic script over the next century.

His conduct of domestic statecraft, however, tended towards the megalomaniac; in attempting to **unite** by force all the Cypriot city-kingdoms into one state, Evagoras alienated Kition, Amathus and Soli sufficiently that they appealed for help to the Persians. Evagoras had finally overreached himself; despite some aid from the Athenians, he failed to depose the king of Kition, and another treaty in 386 between Greeks and Persians, acknowledging the latter's hegemony over the island, left him to confront the eastern empire effectively alone. But with some support from Anatolian Greek city-states he managed to carry the fight to the enemy's home court, causing confusion by landing on the Syrian coast. Though the Persians returned to Cyprus in force in 381, sacking Salamis, Evagoras battled them to a stalemate and negotiated relatively favourable surrender terms, keeping his throne.

He and his eldest son were apparently murdered in a domestic plot at Salamis in 374 BC; he was a hard act to follow, and Evagoras' descendants were insignificant in comparison, not having his touch in handling the Persians – least of all in another abortive revolt of 351. Of his **successors** only Pytagoras salvaged a shred of dignity as a culturally pro-Hellenic vassal king of the Persians, ushering in the Hellenistic era.

# Recovery: Hellenistic and Roman Cyprus

When **Alexander the Great** appeared on the scene in 333, the Cypriot city-kingdoms responded unequivocally, furnishing 120 ships for his successful siege of Persian Tyre. But following his general victory in the east Mediterranean it soon became clear that, while finally rid of the Persians, Cyprus was now a subordinated part of the Hellenistic empire, without even the minimal freedoms which had been honoured under their old masters.

When Alexander died in 323, the island became a battleground for his successors **Ptolemy** and **Antigonus**; the city-kingdoms were split in their support, and **civil war** was the result. Ptolemy's forces initially prevailed, and the losing cities – Kition, Marion, Lapethos and Kyrenia – were razed or severely punished. **Nicocreon**, the pro-Hellenic king of Salamis, was promoted for his loyalty, but in 311 he was denounced for plotting with Antigonus, and Ptolemy sent an army under his deputy Menelaos to besiege Salamis. Rather than surrender, Nicocreon and his family set their palace alight and committed suicide, and the truth of the accusations remains uncertain; in any event the dynasty founded by Teukros died with them.

Antigonus's adherents were still very much in the picture, though, and the dynastic war continued in the person of his son Demetrios Polyorketes, who defeated both Ptolemy and Menelaos and single-handedly ruled the island from 306 to 294. The pendulum swung back one final time, however, for when Antigonid forces let their guard down momentarily, Ptolemy I Soter of Egypt – as he now styled himself – retook Cyprus, commencing two and a half centuries of relatively peaceful and prosperous Ptolemaic, **Egyptian-based rule**.

Cyprus became essentially a province of the Alexandria-based kingdom, exploited for its copper, timber, corn and wine, and administered by a military governor based first at Salamis, later at Nea Paphos. All city-kingdoms were now defunct, replaced by four **administrative districts** and uniform coinage for the whole island; its cultural life was now thoroughly Hellenized, with the usual range of athletic, dramatic and musical events. To existing religious life were added the cult of deified Ptolemaic royalty and a fresh infusion of Egyptian gods. Art was largely derived from Alexandrian models, with little in the way of originality. Portraits in the soft local limestone or terracotta made up the majority of statuary, with the marble work common elsewhere in the Greek world relatively rare. The only idiosyncratic expressions were in funerary architecture, especially at Nea Paphos, where the subterranean "Tombs of the Kings" were a blend of Macedonian and Middle Eastern styles.

During the first century BC, the decline in the Ptolemies' fortunes was matched by the growing power of republican **Rome**, which annexed Cyprus in 58 BC; with the see-sawing of events the island reverted to Egyptian control twice, but Roman rule was consolidated in the imperial period after 31 BC. The *Koinon Kyprion* or civic league of the Ptolemies continued under the Romans, charged with co-ordinating religious festivals, including emperor-worship. The four Ptolemaic districts were also retained, but Cyprus as a whole was administered as a senatorial province through a proconsul (one of the first was the orator Cicero), still based at Nea Paphos. Salamis, however, remained the most important town on the island, its commercial centre with a population of over a quarter of a million.

The Hellenistic pattern of **stability and prosperity** continued, permitting massive public works, some redone several times in the wake of earthquakes; Roman roads (except for traces), bridges and aqueducts have long since vanished, but their gymnasia, theatres and baths constitute most of the archeological heritage visible on Cyprus today. Wealthier private citizens also commissioned major projects, as borne out by the sophisticated villa-floor **mosaics** at Nea Paphos. Otherwise, however, not much effort was expended to Latinize the island – Greek, for example, continued to be used as the official language – and as a largely self-sufficient backwater, Cyprus took little part in the larger affairs of the Roman empire.

## Christianity

**Christianity** came early (45 AD) to Cyprus, which was evangelized by the apostles Paul and Barnabas, the latter a native of Salamis. The pair ordained

Iraklidhios of Tamassos as the island's first bishop, and supposedly converted Sergius Paulus, proconsul at Nea Paphos. Barnabas was subsequently martyred by the Jews of Salamis, who participated in the major **Jewish rebellion** which swept across all of the Middle East in 116 AD. Cyprus was particularly hard hit since, given its scant political and military importance, it was lightly garrisoned; some estimated that virtually the entire gentile population of Salamis was slaughtered by the rebels. The insurrection was finally put down by Hadrian, and a decree promulgated which expelled all Jews from Cyprus. Despite this removal of an obstacle to proselytizing, Christianity spread slowly on the island, as suggested by the enthusiastically pagan Paphos mosaics – executed on the eve of Emperor Constantine's designation of Christianity as the preferred religion of the eastern empire in 323.

The Roman empire had been divided into **western and eastern portions** in 284, and local Cypriot administration transferred to Antioch in Syria – a situation which would last until the fifth century, when the opportune discovery of the relics of Barnabas (see p.400) provided justification for Cyprus's **ecclesiastic and civic autonomy**, answerable only to the capital of the eastern empire, Constantinople. Cyprus's prestige in the Christian world was further enhanced by the visit in 324 of Helena, Constantine's mother, who legendarily left fragments of the True Cross and the cross of the penitent thief.

# The Byzantine era

The break with antiquity was punctuated not only by a new faith and governmental order, but by two cataclysmic **earthquakes** – in 332 and 365 – which destroyed most Cypriot towns. Rebuilt Salamis was renamed Constantia, and again designated the capital of the island. As elsewhere in **Byzantium** – that portion of the empire centred on Constantinople – some of the more inhumane pagan-Roman laws were repealed, and mass conversion to Christianity proceeded apace, as evidenced by the huge fifth- and sixth-century basilica-type cathedrals erected in all cities. Foundations and **mosaic floors** for many of these are the most attractive early Byzantine remains on Cyprus; little else survives, however, owing to the repeated, devastating **raids** of the **Arab caliphate**, beginning in the seventh century AD. Their intent was not to conquer outright but to pillage, and to neutralize Cyprus as a Byzantine strongpoint; the Arabs' only significant legacy is the Hala Sultan Tekke near Larnaca.

An immediate result of the raids was the **abandonment** of most coastal cities, which were far too vulnerable, as well as plague- and drought-ridden at this time. By the terms of an **Arab-Byzantine treaty**, the island was to accept Muslim settlers, remain demilitarized except for naval bases of each side and pay taxes equally to both the caliphate and the Byzantine empire. Except for occasional skirmishes, this strange agreement of condominium endured for three centuries, while Cyprus thrived on its silk trade and food exports, and served as a convenient place to exile dissidents from both Constantinople and the caliphate.

Only in 963 did Byzantine Emperor **Nikiphoros Phokas** permanently end Arab co-rule on Cyprus, and the Muslim colonists left or converted to Christianity. For another two centuries Cyprus had a peaceful, if heavily taxed, respite as a fully-fledged province of Byzantium, during which most of its **existing towns** – Kyrenia, Famagusta, Nicosia, Limassol – were founded or grew suddenly, with formidable **castles** raised against the threat of further attacks. At the same time, in the Tróödhos mountains, the first **frescoed chapels** were endowed by wealthy private donors.

# Western rule: the Lusignans and Venetians

Trouble loomed again in the eleventh century, however; the **schism** between the Catholic and Orthodox churches in 1054 fostered political antagonism between the Byzantine empire and most Latin principalities, and after their defeat of the Byzantines at the Battle of Manzikert in 1073, the **Seljuk Turks** were able to spread south and occupy the Holy Land. In response, the **First Crusade** was organized in western Europe during 1095, and Cyprus lay near or astride the Latin knights' path towards the infidels. Although the first two Crusades bypassed the island, the knights soon established mini-kingdoms in Palestine, and the Seljuks also occupied most of Anatolia, allowing a capricious, despotic Byzantine prince, **Isaac Komnenos**, to declare Cypriot independence from a fatally weakened Constantinople in 1184 and reign for seven years. Greedy, cruel and consequently unpopular, he was hardly an improvement on the succession of incompetent and unstable emperors in the capital; this misrule made Cyprus a ripe plum for the Crusaders.

In the spring of 1191 a small fleet bearing the sister and fiancée of **Richard the Lionheart** of England hove to off Limassol. Isaac, realizing their value as hostages, tried to inveigle the two women ashore, but they wisely declined; he then refused them provisions. When the English king himself appeared, he landed in some force, considering his kinswomen to have been gravely insulted. After an unsuccessful attempt to secure Isaac's co-operation in the Third Crusade, Richard and his allies pursued the Byzantine forces across the island, defeating them at the battle of Tremetoushá on the Mesaoría; Isaac surrendered at the end of May, sent away in silver chains upon his insistence that he not be put in irons.

Richard had never intended to acquire Cyprus, and was still keen to resume crusading; having plundered the island, he quickly sold it to the **Knights Templar** to raise more funds for his army. The Templars put forty percent of the purchase price down and had to raise the balance by confiscatory taxation; the Cypriots not unnaturally rebelled, with the knights quelling the revolt viciously to save their skins.

Having received rather more than they'd bargained for, the Templars returned Cyprus to Richard, who quickly resold it to **Guy de Lusignan**, a minor French noble who had been the last Crusader king of Jerusalem before losing the city to Saladin in 1187. Cyprus was essentially his consolation prize; Guy recreated the feudal system of his lost realm, parcelling out fiefs to more than five hundred supporters – principally landless allies without future prospects in what remained of Crusader Syria – and the **Knights Hospitallers of St John**, who soon displaced the Templars. Guy's brother and successor **Aimery** styled himself **king of Cyprus and Jerusalem**, the latter an honorary title used by all subsequent Lusignan rulers, though the Holy City went permanently back to Muslim control after 1244.

# The Lusignans

Under the **Lusignans**, Cyprus acquired a **significance** far out of proportion to its size. European sovereigns, including **Holy Roman Emperor Frederick II Hohenstaufen**, stopped off obligatorily on their way to subsequent Crusades, and the Lusignans – and their deputies the **Ibelins** – married into all the royal houses of Europe. **Regencies** for under-age princes were common, owing to the short life-expectancy of Crusader kings; an unusually long regency for Henry I in the early thirteenth century caused complications, obliging the Ibelin regents to defend Henry's title to the throne in a prolonged war against counter-claimant Frederick II Hohenstaufen.

Monumentally, the Byzantine **castles** of the Kyrenia range were refurbished, and new ones built around the capital Nicosia and the eastern port of Famagusta, which after the **1291 loss** of Acre, Sidon and Tyre, the last Crusader toeholds in the Holy Land, saw an influx of Christian refugees from all over the Near East. For barely a century **Famagusta** served as the easternmost outpost of Christendom, and became one of the wealthiest cities on earth owing to a papal prohibition on direct European trade with the nearby infidel. No longer having to siphon off resources to defend a slender Syrian coastal strip also improved the military and financial health of the Cypriot kingdom. The Lusignan royalty were crowned in two massive Gothic **cathedrals** at Nicosia and Famagusta: coronations for the Kingdom of Cyprus were conducted at Nicosia; at Famagusta, facing the Holy Land across the water, the honorary ceremony for Jerusalem took place. All major **monastic orders** were represented, though the sole surviving foundation is the abbey of Béllapais.

The **everyday life** of the nobility was notorious for its luxury and ostentation, a privilege definitely not shared by the common people. The Greek Orthodox population, which had initially welcomed the Crusaders, soon discovered that they were effectively shut out from power or material security. Most of them lived as **serfs** of the Catholic overlords, and by a papal edict of 1260 the Orthodox archbishops were effectively **subordinated** to a Catholic metropolitan and furthermore exiled to rural sees. Orthodoxy was constrained to a rearguard holding action, awaiting a change in its fortunes; yet during this time many of the finest frescoes were painted in rural chapels of the Tróödhos Mountains.

In general, the Lusignan **kings** were a visibly overweight, mediocre bunch, probably resulting from a combination of hereditary thyroid problems with "riotous and unclean living", as one historian of the time put it. The most extravagant and activist sovereign was **Peter I** (reigned 1358–69) who, in contrast to the live-and-let-live attitude of his lethargic predecessors, canvassed Europe for support for his mini-Crusades along the neighbouring Muslim coasts, culminating in a thorough sacking of Alexandria in 1365. Also an inveterate womanizer, he was in the arms of one of his two mistresses when certain nobles, tired of his increasingly erratic behaviour and disregard for feudal law, burst into the bedchamber and murdered him.

**Decline** followed Peter's murder, though that was more the last straw than the root cause. If the Lusignans governed the Cypriot kingdom, the Venetians and Genoese were rivals for supremacy in its commercial life; at the 1373 Famagusta coronation of Peter II, a dispute between the two factions as to who would have the honour of leading the young king's horse escalated into destructive anti-Genoese riots. Incensed, **Genoa** sent a punitive expedition to ravage the island. For a year a virtual civil war raged, ending with the return of the throne to the Lusignans only upon payment of a huge indemnity – though the royal family was actually held prisoner in Genoa for eighteen years – and the retention of Famagusta by the Genoese. But the damage had been done; both Cyprus and the Lusignans were in a disastrously weakened condition economically and politically.

A harbinger of worse "infidel" attacks to come took place in 1425–26, when the **Mamelukes** of Egypt, still smarting from Peter I's attack on Alexandria, landed on the south coast to plunder Limassol and Larnaca. **King Janus** confronted them near Stavrovoúni monastery, but was soundly defeated and taken prisoner; the Mamelukes marched inland to sack Nicosia before returning with their treasure to Egypt. Janus was only released three years later after payment of a crippling ransom and a humiliating promise of perpetual annual tribute to the Mamelukes.

With Janus's dissolute successor **John II**, the Lusignan saga entered its last chapters. He complicated matters by favouring his bastard son, **James II**, over his legitimate daughter **Charlotte**, and after John died in 1458 the two strong-willed offspring spent six years disputing the succession. Securing Mameluke aid – which in effect meant an extension of the onerous tribute – James returned from Egypt and deposed his sister; he matched this success by finally evicting the Genoese from Famagusta, though it was far too late to restore that town to its former importance. A roistering, athletic man, James was relatively popular with his subjects for both his daring exploits and his fluency in **Greek**; indeed the language had recently begun to replace French in public use.

James did not run true to family form in his own choice of consort, contracting marriage with a Venetian noblewoman, **Caterina Cornaro**. Both the king and his infant son died mysteriously within a year of each other (1473 and 1474) – a Venetian poisoning plot has been suggested – leaving Queen Caterina to reign precariously in her own right. Charlotte, in exile, intrigued ceaselessly against Caterina until Charlotte died in 1485. Besides her foiled plot to assassinate Caterina, there was a Catalan-fomented rebellion in 1473. All this, and the growing **Ottoman threat**, convinced the Venetians that Caterina was better out of the way, and she was persuaded to **abdicate** in 1489, being given as a sop the town and hinterland of Asolo in the Veneto, where she continued to keep a court of some splendour.

## The Venetians

Three centuries of Lusignan rule were over and the **Venetians** now governed the island directly through a *proveditore* or **military governor**. Their tenure was even more oppressive than the Lusignan one from the point of view of ordinary people; Cyprus was seen simply as a frontier fortress and money-spinner, the island otherwise being neglected and inefficiently administered. The Lusignan nobility retained their estates but were excluded from political power. The Venetians devoted most of their energy to overhauling the fortifications of Kyrenia, Nicosia and Famagusta in anticipation of the inevitable Ottoman attack. In the end, however, the undermanned Venetian forces were no match for the Turkish hordes, especially when relief failed to arrive from Venice: Nicosia fell after a seven-week **siege** in 1570, with almost half its population subsequently massacred, while Famagusta held out for ten months until July 1571 in one of the celebrated battles of the age (see box on p.388). The victor, **Lala Mustafa Paşa**, perhaps irked at having been so valiantly defied by the tiny garrison, reneged on his promises of clemency, flaying commander **Marcantonio Bragadino** alive after butchering his lieutenants.

Surrounded on three sides by Ottoman territory, it was almost certain that Cyprus should eventually fall to the Muslim power, but the specific impetus for the 1570–71 campaign is interesting. The incumbent sultan, **Selim the Sot**, had a particular fondness for Cypriot Commandaria wine; his chief adviser, **Joseph Nasi**, was a Spanish Jew whose family had suffered at the hands of the Venetians during their long exile after the 1492 expulsion, and who longed to take revenge on the Serene Republic – and perhaps secure a haven for Jewry. In fact the invasion plan was hatched over the objections of the grand vizier and others, who considered it unfeasible, and feared the wrath of the European powers. Selim died just three years later, fracturing his skull by slipping in his bath – while drunk on Commandaria.

# Stagnation: Ottoman rule

Because the Lusignans had never made any attempt to bridge the gap between ruler and ruled, they remained an unassimilated upper crust, all trace of which was swept away by the Turkish conquest. By 1573 most of the monasteries and Latin churches had been destroyed, and most surviving **Catholics** had departed or converted to Islam; the tiny "Latin" minority on the island today is all that survives from this era. Some other ancestors of the present **Turkish population** date from the year of the conquest, when Ottoman soldiers and their families formed the nucleus, some twenty thousand strong, of initial settlement, later supplemented by civilians from Anatolia (see box p.430). Their relations with the native Greek population were, if not always close, usually cordial.

The Greek Orthodox peasantry, perhaps surprisingly in the light of later events, actually **welcomed** the Ottomans at first; both were united in their hatred of the Franks, whose feudal system was abolished and lands distributed to the freed serfs. The Greeks also appreciated Ottoman **recognition of their Church:** not only were certain Catholic ecclesiastical properties made over to Orthodoxy, but in 1660 the archbishop was officially acknowledged as the head of the Greek community in accord with prevailing Ottoman administrative practice, with the right of direct petition to the sultan. This was followed in 1754 by the revival of the role of **ethnarch**, with comprehensive civil powers, and in 1779 by the stipulation for a **dragoman**, a Greek appointed by the ethnarch to liaise with the island's Turkish governor. The most powerful and famous dragoman was **Hadjiyeorgakis Kornesios** (see p.283).

None of this, however, was done in a spirit of disinterested religious tolerance; the Ottomans used the ecclesiastical apparatus principally to collect onerous **taxes**, and the clerics, who eventually all but ran the island together with the dragoman, made themselves every bit as unpopular as the Muslim governors. In fairness the clergy often attempted to protect their flock from the more rapacious exactions of the various governors, who – minimally salaried and having paid huge bribes to secure their short-term appointments – were expected to recoup their expenses with exactions from the populace. People unable to meet assessments forfeited **land** in lieu of payment, the original source of the Orthodox Church's still-extensive real-estate holdings.

If the Greeks had hoped for a definitive improvement in their lot with the end of Frankish rule, they were thoroughly disillusioned, as Cyprus became one of the **worst-governed and neglected** Ottoman provinces. Almost all tax revenues went to İstanbul, with next to nothing being spent to abate

## Who are the Turkish Cypriots?

The number of Muslims on Cyprus, even during the most vigorous periods of Ottoman rule, has never exceeded about one-third of the population, and had already declined to about one-quarter when the British arrived in 1878. The word "Muslim" is used deliberately, since religious affiliation, and not race or ethnicity, was the determining civic factor in the Ottoman empire; the present-day Turkish Cypriots are in fact descended from a variety of sources.

At the time of the 1571 conquest, Ottoman **civil servants** arrived with their families, whose descendants tend to preserve their aristocratic consciousness to this day. Some twenty thousand **janissaries**, by definition of Anatolian or Balkan Christian origins and adherents of the Bektashi dervish order, took as wives the widows of the defeated Venetians, as well as a number of Orthodox Christian virgins. Roughly another ten thousand civilian transportees from Anatolia consisted of skilled, town-dwelling craftsmen, landless farmers, **Turkmen** nomads brought over for the sake of their reed- and textile-weaving skills, **Alevî** mountaineers, and various prison convicts transported to a more comfortable exile on Cyprus. **Blacks** from Sudan also arrived, mostly working as porters in and around Larnaca and Limassol, and obliged by local colour consciousness to marry less desirable, "low-class" women. Muslim **Gypsies** tagged along from Anatolia, and while allowed to settle, they were (and are) discriminated against as much as anywhere else in the Balkans – despite taking the Turkish-Cypriot side in the battles of recent decades.

The so-called **Linovamváki** (Cotton-Linen) sect, which practised Islam outwardly but maintained Christian beliefs (including baptism) in private, arose mainly among Venetian civilians (names like Mehmet Valentino occur in old archives); curiously, they spoke Greek in preference to Turkish, and many villages such as Áyios Ioánnis, Monágri, Louroujína (today Akıncılar in the North), Vrécha and most of the Tillyría region were once almost exclusively inhabited by *Linovamváki*. After 1878, evangelization of this group by both Muslim and Christian clerics, and the resulting assimilative marriages, resulted in a hitherto unknown polarization in island society; in the North today, many of the more fanatical nationalists are in fact of *Linovamváki* background, eager to deny a practice – propitiation of all local deities without prejudice – which was once common in the Ottoman empire.

Another more recent development is proselytization by the **Bahai** faith, with approximately five hundred adherents in the North. It was founded by the adoptive son of the holy man Mirza Ali Mohammed (Al-Bab), who was hanged as a troublemaker by the Iranian shah towards the end of the nineteenth century. Al-Bab's biological son, Süphi Ezel, was exiled first to Edirne, then to Famagusta, and while the **Ezeli** rite is no longer a vital religion in the North, his tomb is still a focus of pilgrimage for Iranian believers.

There are also a number of **"Palestinian"** – or rather part-Palestinian – northerners, the descendants of Turkish-Cypriot women who, in the depths of the 1930s Depression, amidst dire conditions on the island, were married off to Arab Muslim grooms in Palestine; after its partition in 1948, many returned with their husbands and families.

Given these motley, often "heretical" origins of the Turkish Cypriots (the janissaries and Alevîs being particularly tolerant of alcohol consumption), it's hardly surprising that observance of orthodox Islam on Cyprus has always been famously lax – despite recent Saudi agitation – and that fervent Turkish nationalism has had to be whipped up by outsiders since World War II.

the drought, plagues and locusts which lashed the island, or on other local improvements; Turkish medieval monuments are rare on Cyprus, with most large mosques merely churches adapted for Muslim use. Between 1571 and the late 1700s the population dropped sharply, with many Greeks **emigrating** to

Anatolia or the Balkans despite administrative reshuffles aimed at staunching the outflow.

These conditions ensured that the three Ottoman centuries were punctuated by regular **rebellions**, which often united the Muslim and Christian peasantry against their overlords. The first occurred in 1680; in 1764 the excesses of the worst governor, **Çil Osman**, precipitated a longer and bloodier revolt in which he was killed, the Turkish commander of Kyrenia mutinied, and the Greek bishops appealed to İstanbul for the restoration of order. With the rise of Balkan nationalism later that century, the *Filikí Etería* (Friendly Society), the Greek revolutionary fifth column, was active on Cyprus after 1810. To forestall any echo of the mainland Greek rebellion, Governor **Küçük Mehmet** got permission from the sultan in 1821 to execute the unusually popular **Archbishop Kyprianos**, his three bishops and hundreds of leading Greek Orthodox islanders in Nicosia, not so coincidentally confiscating their considerable property and inaugurating another spell of unrest on the island, which ended in the revolt of 1833.

Such incidents were not repeated after European powers established more trading posts and watchful consulates at Larnaca, and the Church's power **waned slightly** with the suspension of its right to collect taxes and the emergence of an educated, westernized class of Greek Cypriot. As the nineteenth century wore on, **Britain** found itself repeatedly guaranteeing the Ottoman empire's territorial integrity in the path of Russian expansionism; in 1878, this relationship was formalized by the **Anglo-Turkish Convention**, whereby the Ottomans ceded occupation and administrative rights of Cyprus – though technically not sovereignty – to Britain in return for having halted the Russian advance outside İstanbul during the 1877–78 Russo-Turkish war, and for a continued undertaking to help defend what was left of Turkish domains. Curiously, Britain's retention of Cyprus was **linked** to Russia's occupation of Ardahan, Kars and Batumi, three strongpoints on Turkey's Caucasian frontier; Kars and Ardahan were returned to republican Turkey in 1921, but in the NATO era Turkey's and Britain's continued alliance against the Russian threat still served as ostensible justification for the latter's occupation of Cyprus.

# British rule

British forces landed peacefully at Larnaca in July 1878, assuming control of the island without incident; ironically, the British acquisition of Egypt and the Suez Canal in 1882 made Cyprus of distinctly secondary importance as a **military base**, with civilian high commissioners soon replacing military ones. The Greek Orthodox population, remembering Britain's cession of the Ionian islands to Greece in 1864, hoped for the same generosity here, and the bishop of Kition (Larnaca)'s greeting speech to the landing party alluded directly to this. Free of the threat of Ottoman-style repression, the demand for **énosis** or union with Greece was to be reiterated regularly by the Greek Cypriots until 1960 – and beyond. From the very outset of the colonial period the Turkish Cypriots expressed their satisfaction with the status quo and their horror at the prospect of being Greek citizens.

What the Cypriots got instead, aside from separate Greek- and Turkish-language education, was a modicum of **better government** – reafforestation, an end to banditry and extralegal extortion, an English legal system, water supplies, roads and a stamping out of disease and locusts – combined with a continuance of **crushing taxes**, which militated against any striking economic growth. An obscure clause of the Anglo-Turkish Convention mandated that the excess of tax revenues (appreciable) over local expenditures (almost nil) during the last five years of Ottoman rule was theoretically to be paid to the sultan's government, a rule which pressured colonial administrators to keep programmes modest so as to have some sum to forward – or to squeeze the Cypriots for more taxes. The practice was widely condemned by Cypriophiles and Turkophobes in England, including Gladstone and Churchill, but amazingly continued until 1927. Worse still, the monies went not to İstanbul, but to bond-holders of an 1855 loan to Turkey on which the Ottoman rulers had defaulted. So while Cyprus regained its former population level, the British-promised prosperity never appeared, the islanders in effect being required to **service an Ottoman debt**. The only apparatus of self-government was a very rudimentary **legislative council**, numerically weighted towards colonial civil servants and with limited powers in any case.

## Cyprus as colony

Following Ottoman Turkey's 1914 entry into World War I as one of the Central Powers, Britain declared most provisions of the Anglo-Turkish Convention void, and formally **annexed** Cyprus. The next year she secretly offered the island to Greece as a territorial inducement to join the war on the Allied side, but Greece, then ruled by pro-German King Constantine I, declined, to the Greek Cypriots' infinite later regret. In the 1923 Treaty of Lausanne, republican Turkey renounced all claims to Cyprus, but the island did not officially become a British Crown Colony until 1925, by which time calls for *énosis* were again being heard. These increased in stridency, leading in **1931** to the first serious **civil disturbances**: the Greek-Cypriot members of the legislative council resigned, and rioters burned down the Government House, a rambling bungalow diverted from use in Ceylon. The Cypriots' anger was not only sparked by the *énosis* issue, but derived from disappointment at the thus-far modest level of material progress under British rule, especially the woebegone state of agriculture.

## Advent of the Left

The British **response** to the mini-rebellion was predictably harsh: reparations levies for damages, bans on publications and flying the Greek flag, proscriptions of existing political parties (especially the KKK or Communists, who had organized strikes in 1929 at the Tróödhos asbestos mines), and imprisonment or deportation of activists – including two bishops. The legislative council was abolished, and Cyprus came under the nearest thing to martial law; only the **PEO** or Pancyprian Federation of Labour, though driven underground until 1936, remained as a pole of opposition to the colonial regime, and a haven for left-wing Turkish and Greek Cypriot alike. **AKEL**, the new **communist party**, grew out of it in 1941, and has remained an important faction in the Greek-Cypriot community to this day. Municipal elections were finally held in 1943, and served as a barometer of public sentiment through the balance of the colonial period; the British could not very well profess to be fighting fascism while simultaneously withholding basic political freedoms.

During **World War II**, Cyprus belied its supposed strategic value by escaping much involvement other than as an important supply depot and staging post. The island suffered just a few stray Italian raids from Rhodes, and German ones from Crete; after the German difficulties on Crete, Hitler had forbidden another paratroop action to seize Cyprus. About 28,000 Cypriots, both Greek and Turkish (plus hundreds of Cypriot donkeys), fought as volunteers with British forces in Europe, the Middle East and North Africa, and the Greeks at least expected some political reward for this at the war's end.

The extent of this was the 1947 offer by Governor Lord Winster of a **limited constitution** of self-rule, similar to that tendered in other colonies at the time. It was summarily rejected by the enosist elements, principally the Orthodox Church, who proclaimed that anything less than *énosis* or at least provision for its eventual implementation was unacceptable – a stance which probably guaranteed later bloodshed. AKEL was lukewarm on the idea; they were busy mounting the inconclusive but distinguished 1947–48 **strike** in the American-run copper mines of Soléa district. The Americans had at least one other toehold on the island: an electronic listening post at Karavás (now Alsancak) on the north coast near Kyrenia, opened in 1949 to monitor all radio broadcasts from behind the Iron Curtain, and the first of several local facilities designed to keep tabs on Soviet doings in the incipient Cold War.

# The postwar years

By 1950, demands for *énosis* had returned to the fore; in a **referendum** campaign organized by newly elected Archbishop and Ethnarch **Makarios III**, results showed 96 percent support for *énosis* among Greek Cypriots. They seemed to ignore the fact that Greece, dominated by far-right-wing governments and still a stretcher case after the rigours of German occupation and a civil war, was a poor candidate as a partner for association; yet so great was the groundswell for union that even the PEO and AKEL subscribed to it after 1950, though they could both expect a fairly unpleasant fate in a rightist "Greater Greece". In general outsiders did, and still do, have trouble understanding the enormous emotional and historical appeal of *énosis*, whose advocates readily admitted that Cypriot living standards would drop sharply once the island was out of the sterling zone and yoked to chaotic, impoverished Greece.

Soon the at least theoretical possibility of *énosis* dawned on the island's **Turkish minority** – some eighteen percent of the population – who began agitation in opposition, advocating either the status quo or some sort of affiliation with Turkey rather than becoming a truly insignificant minority in a greater Greece. As the Turkish Cypriots were scattered almost uniformly throughout the island, forming nowhere a majority, the option of a separate Turkish-Cypriot province or canton was not available without painful population transfers.

Many Greek Cypriots retrospectively accused the British (and to a lesser extent the Americans) of **stirring up** Turkey and the Turkish Cypriots against them, and while there is some truth to this – divide-and-rule was very much a colonial strategy – mainland Turkey itself would probably have eventually become involved without cues from Britain, and the Turkish Cypriots were certainly not quiescent. Greek Cypriots saw the situation as a non-colonial problem of the island's wishing to transfer its allegiance to the "mother country"; Britain, in their view, transformed matters into a general Greco-Turkish dispute under the guise of "harmony in the southeast flank of NATO", ensuring that Turkey would forcefully block any move towards *énosis*.

After Egyptian independence in 1954, **British Mid-East Military HQ** was moved to Cyprus over a period of twenty months, making self-determination far less likely, and the British position increasingly inflexible – thanks to such intemperate Tory personalities as Anthony Eden, and increasing murmurs of support for such a policy by the Americans. In July of that year, the minister of state for the colonies declared that "certain Commonwealth territories, owing to their particular circumstances, can never expect to be fully independent" – and went on to express fears of a pro-Soviet AKEL dominating an independent Cyprus. To the Greek Cypriots this utterance seemed ludicrous in the light of independence being granted to far less developed parts of Asia and Africa. That "never" closed off all avenues of communication with more moderate Greek Cypriots, and came back repeatedly to haunt the British over the next five years.

In **Greece** the government encouraged a shrill, anti-British media barrage in support of *énosis*, available to any radio set on Cyprus. For the first time Greece also tried to internationalize the Cyprus issue at the **UN**, where it failed to get a full hearing, though Turkey bared its teeth in the preliminary discussions, a promise of trouble in the future. Only the Greek ambassador to London astutely saw that the mainland Turks were now an interested party and would have to be included, or at least mollified, in any solution.

## The EOKA rebellion

In conjunction with **General George Grivas** (see also box on p.284), code-named "Dhiyenis" after the hero of a Byzantine epic, Archbishop Makarios in 1954 secretly founded **EOKA**, *Ethnikí Orgánosis Kypríon Agonistón* or "National Organization of Cypriot Fighters", as an IRA-type movement to throw off British rule. Late that year several clandestine shipments of arms and explosives were transferred from Rhodes to the deserted Páfos coast, though the archbishop initially shrank back from advocating lethal force against persons, restricting Grivas to sabotage of property. EOKA's campaign of violence on Cyprus began spectacularly on April 1, 1955 with the destruction of the Government radio transmitter, among other targets.

Overseas, a hastily scheduled **trilateral conference** in July 1955, convening representatives of Greece, Turkey and Britain, flopped miserably; Makarios remarked that Greece's attendance at it had merely legitimized Turkish involvement in the Cyprus issue. Two months later, massive, Turkish-government-inspired **rioting** in İstanbul caused staggering loss to Greek property and effectively dashed any hope of a reasonable future for the Greek Orthodox community there. Greek government recourse to the UN was again futile.

Newly appointed **High Commissioner John Harding**, a former field marshal, pursued a hard line against EOKA; ongoing negotiations with Makarios, who distanced himself at least publicly from the armed struggle, were approaching a breakthrough when Grivas set off more strategically timed bombs. Talks were broken off and the archbishop and two associates **deported** in March 1956 to comfortable house arrest in the Seychelles. Deprived of its ablest spokesman, EOKA now graduated to murderous **attacks** on Greeks who disagreed with them, as well as on British soldiers and civilians. The island terrain was ideal for such an insurgency; despite massive searches, internments, collective punishments for aiding EOKA and other now-familiar curtailments of civil liberties in such emergencies, the uprising couldn't be quelled. An estimated three hundred guerrillas, based primarily in the Tróödhos, tied up twenty thousand regular British Army troops and 4500 special constables. The latter were overwhelmingly composed of Turkish-Cypriot auxiliaries – who often applied **torture** to captured EOKA suspects under the supervision of British officers, an assigned task which perceptibly increased intercommunal tensions. These auxiliaries were attracted by pay rates of £30 a month, a small fortune on the island at the time, and the fact that no Greek Cypriot could expect to last long in such a post without being done away with as a traitor by EOKA. Spring and summer of 1956 also saw the **hangings** of nine convicted EOKA men, touching off violent protests in Greece and plunging British-Greek relations to an all-time low. When Harding issued an ultimatum for the surrender of insurrectionist weapons, EOKA responded contemptuously by parading a riderless donkey through downtown Nicosia, emblazoned with banners reading (in Greek and English) "I surrender" (see p.458 for the role of the donkey in Cypriot society).

International pressure in **1957** – and Britain's realization that no other Greek-Cypriot negotiating partner existed – brought about Makarios's release, just after Greece finally managed to get Cyprus on the UN agenda, resulting in a resolution accepting independence "in principle". Harding was replaced with the more conciliatory civilian **Governor Hugh Foot**, and a constitutional commissioner, Lord Radcliffe, was dispatched to make more generous proposals for limited self-government than those of 1947. These were again rejected by the Greek Cypriots, because they didn't envision *énosis*, and by the Turkish Cypriots – represented by the **Turkish National Party**, headed by future vice-president **Fazil Küçük** – since it didn't specifically exclude that possibility.

## TMT

After isolated intercommunal incidents post-1956, the **TMT** or *Türk Mukavemet Teskilati* (Turkish Resistance Organization) was founded early in **1958** to counter EOKA's goals and work for *taksim* or partition of the island between Greece and Turkey. TMT's cell structure was modelled on EOKA, and it also duplicated EOKA's rabid **anti-communism**, killing various left-wing Turkish personalities and pressurizing Turkish Cypriots to leave PEO and AKEL, virtually the last unsegregated institutions on the island. TMT also organized a boycott of Greek-Cypriot products and shops, just as EOKA was presiding over a Greek-Cypriot boycott of British products.

## Intercommunal clashes – and resumed rebellion

A June 1958 bomb explosion outside the Turkish press office in Nicosia – later shown to have been planted by TMT provocateurs – set off the first serious **intercommunal clashes** on the island. In Nicosia, Turkish gangs expelled Greeks from some mixed neighbourhoods, and induced some of their own to abandon villages in the south of the island in favour of the north – a forerunner of events in 1974. Shortly after, in what became known as the **Gönyeli incident**, seven EOKA suspects were released from British custody to walk home through a Turkish-Cypriot area, where they were duly stabbed to death – as was presumably the British intent. EOKA retaliated by targeting Turkish-Cypriot policemen, and also stepping up assaults on the British after a year's lull. The resumed war of attrition between EOKA and the British army became increasingly dirty and no-holds-barred, with the latter nursing a racial loathing for their adversaries; the **death toll** for the whole insurrection climbed to nearly six hundred. Of these almost half were left-wing or pro-British Greek Cypriots killed by EOKA, while eventually 346 UK squaddies were laid to rest in a special military cemetery, today found in the buffer zone. **Truces** were declared in late summer by both TMT and EOKA, with many displaced Cypriots returning to their homes in mixed areas. The EOKA truce did not, however, extend to members of AKEL, who now favoured independence again – and continued to suffer fatal consequences.

One last mainland Greece-sponsored UN resolution for Cypriot "self-determination" (by now a code word for *énosis*) failed in 1958 to muster the necessary two-thirds majority in the General Assembly, so Makarios began to accept the wisdom of independence, especially as both the British, in the person of Prime Minister Harold Macmillan, and the Turkish Cypriots were threatening to revive the option of partition and massive population movements. The bloody July 1958 anti-royalist coup in Iraq, hitherto one of Britain's staunchest allies in the Middle East, and the subsequent loss of unfettered use of its two airfields, had also reinforced British (and American) resolve not to let Cyprus with its valuable military facilities fall into "unreliable" hands.

Throughout the later 1950s, EOKA, Greece and most Greek Cypriots had failed to take seriously the **mainland Turkish position**: that Turkey would take steps to prevent strategically vital Cyprus becoming Greek territory, as Crete had after a fifteen-year period of supposed independence at the start of the century. Less genuine, perhaps, was Turkey's new-found concern for its "brothers" on the island; programmes broadcast regularly over Radio Ankara agitated feelings in its communal audience just as mainland Greek programmes did in theirs. The British, now faced with hostility from the Turkish Cypriots as well as from the Greeks, and contemplating the soaring costs of containing the rebellion, desperately sought a way out. Various proposals were briefly mooted by the British and Americans, including NATO administering Cyprus, or a joint Greek-Turkish-British tridominium over the entire island, or an "orderly" partition into mainland-Greek- and Turkish-administered cantonments, all with the express intent of preventing any military use of the island by the Communist bloc.

# The granting of independence

In February 1959, the foreign ministers of Greece and Turkey met in **Zurich** to hammer out some compromise settlement, with a supplementary meeting including the British and Cypriots in **London** a few days later. The participants agreed on the establishment of an independent Cypriot republic, its **constitution** to be prepared by an impartial Swiss expert. Of its 199 clauses, 48 were unalterable, with *énosis* or *taksim* expressly forbidden. The two ethnic communities were essentially to be co-founders, running the republic on a 70:30 Greek:Turk **proportional basis** that slightly favoured the Turkish minority. A single fifty-seat House of Representatives – with fifteen seats reserved for the Turks, two separate communal chambers funded partly by Greece and Turkey, and a Greek-Cypriot president plus a Turkish-Cypriot vice-president elected by their respective communities was also envisioned. After considerable hesitation and misgivings – and, allegedly, threatened blackmail by the British secret services with compromising material of a sexual nature – Makarios gave his assent to the constitution.

The meetings also produced three interrelated **treaties**, which in turn were incorporated as articles of the constitution. Britain, Turkey and Greece simultaneously entered into a **Treaty of Guarantee**, by which they acted as guarantors to safeguard Cypriot independence. A **Treaty of Establishment** stipulated the existence of two main British military bases, their extent to be determined, and other training areas. The **Treaty of Alliance** provided for the stationing of Greek and Turkish military forces, at Yerólakkos (Alaykoy) and Gönyeli respectively, and the training of a Cypriot army, presumably as an arm of NATO; this provision was roundly denounced by AKEL, and indeed in the long run this treaty was to prove the most destabilizing element of the package.

Makarios, who had been in Greece since 1957, was finally permitted to **return to Cyprus**, where an amnesty was declared for most EOKA offenders. Grivas and the more hard-line enosists, excoriating Makarios for his supposed betrayal of the cause, flew off to self-imposed exile in Greece, while certain supporters stayed behind to punctuate most of 1959 with fulminations against the independence deal. They and others induced the bigotedly anti-Turkish-Cypriot **Mayor Themistoklis Dhervis of Nicosia** to form the first opposi-tion party, the **Democratic Union**, which contested the presidential elections of December 1959 against the archbishop's **Popular Front**. Makarios won handily with two-thirds of the vote, while Fazil Küçük ran unopposed for the vice-presidential seat.

**Elections** for the **House of Representatives** in February 1960 were poorly attended, with absenteeism and abstention rates of up to sixty percent in some districts reflecting popular disgust at the civic arrangements – and a poor omen for the future. The Popular Front took thirty seats, its coalition partners AKEL five, while Küçük's National Party got all fifteen Turkish seats. Polling for the powerful **communal chambers**, charged with overseeing education, religion, culture and consumer credit co-ops, showed a similar profile, though in the Greek chamber one seat each was reserved for the Armenian, Maronite and "Latin" communities.

**Final independence**, which had been set for no later than February 1960, was postponed until **16 August 1960**, as the Cypriots and the British haggled over the exact size of the two sovereign bases. By coincidence, Venetian and British rule lasted exactly the same duration: 82 years.

## Dr Fazil Küçük (1906–1984)

The first official leader of the Turkish-Cypriot community, Dr Fazil Küçük was a man of many parts – a prodigious drinker, foul-mouthed frequenter of *meyhane*s with large groups of friends, and a journalist, in addition to being a politician and medico. He founded the still-existing *Halkın Sesi*, in pre-Asil Nadir days the main Turkish-Cypriot newspaper, and often used it as a platform to indulge his bent for elaborate practical jokes. Although Küçük started his political career as an instrument of Turkish mainland policy on the island, he increasingly stood up for long-term Turkish-Cypriot interests, and was forced into early retirement in 1973 by TMT for not being malleable enough in the eyes of his "handlers". When Ahmet Berberoğlu was similarly given a non-refusable offer, Rauf Denktaş was appointed unopposed as leader of the community. Unlike Denktaş, however, "Doktor" – as he was universally known – was also universally loved; about 100,000 people, virtually the entire Turkish-Cypriot population in the North (and then some), attended his funeral in 1984. Küçük's last oral "will" to his lawyer was for regular libations of Peristiany 31, "Doktor"'s favourite tipple, to be poured over his grave in Hamitköy (Mándhres). This was done just once, with such alarming results for the Turkish-army guard of honour posted there that the grave was cemented over to prevent recurrences.

# The unitary republic: 1960–1964

The Republic of Cyprus seemed doomed from the start, with EOKA and TMT **ideologues** appointed to key cabinet positions. Neither organization completely disbanded, but maintained shadowy existences, waiting for the right moment to re-emerge. They and others made Makarios's life difficult: the enosists considered that he'd sold them out, the Turks and Turkish Cypriots were convinced that he was biding his time for an opportunity to impose *énosis*, and many Communists felt he was too accommodating to the West.

On a **symbolic** level, communal iconography, street names, etc all continued referring to persons and events in the "mother" countries; the respective national flags and national days were celebrated by each community, and while there was (and still is) a Cypriot flag, there never was a national anthem. Such institutionalized separatism was inimical to fostering a national consciousness. The **constitution**, an improbably intricate one for a population of just over half a million, proved unworkable in application. The Greek Cypriots chafed at it because it had been imposed from outside, while the Turkish Cypriots took every opportunity to exploit its numerous clauses benefiting them. It was, as several outside observers remarked, the only democracy where majority rule was explicitly denied by its founding charter. It did not seem to have occurred to any of the drafters of the constitution that, by not providing for cross-communal voting (whereby, for example, presidential and vice-presidential candidates had to secure a majority of votes in *both* Greek-Cypriot and Turkish-Cypriot communities), Cyprus was condemned to rampant tribalism.

The **70:30 ratio**, running through all civil service institutions, could not be reached within the five months prescribed, and the **army**, supposed to be set up on a 60:40 ratio with ethnic mix at all levels, never materialized, since the Turks insisted on segregated companies; instead Makarios eventually authorized the establishment of an all-Greek-Cypriot **National Guard**. Both the president and the vice-president had **veto power** over foreign affairs, defence and internal matters, exercised frequently by Küçük. Laws had to clear the House of Representatives by a majority of votes from **both communal factions**: thus eight of the fifteen Turkish MPs could defeat any bill. When agreement could not be reached in the first two years of the republic's life, colonial rules were often extended as **stopgaps**.

For much of 1962, Cyprus had no uniform income tax or customs excise laws, the Turks having obstructed them in retaliation for Greek foot-dragging on implementation of separate municipalities for the five largest towns. Another concession to the Turkish Cypriots was the maintenance of **separate municipalities**, first set up in the 1950s, for each community in those five towns – something which the Greek Cypriots considered to be an incredibly wasteful and time-consuming duplication of services, as well as (correctly in light of later events) stalking horses and seedbeds for island-wide partition. Yet the Greeks did not hesitate to pass **revenue** laws through their own communal chamber when frustrated in the parliament, thus perpetuating the apartheid by providing services only to the Greek-Cypriot community and those Turks choosing to acknowledge its jurisdiction.

Among the hardline elements, the TMT struck first, against its own community: on April 23, 1962 gunmen murdered **Ahmet Gurkan and Ayhan Hikmet**, leaders of the only Turkish-Cypriot political party to oppose Küçük's National Party, promoting closer co-operation between two communities. It was a reprise of numerous such attacks in 1958, and, now as then, no action was taken against TMT or its backers; **Rauf Denktaş**, protégé of Küçük, even managed to get Emil Dirvana, Turkish ambassador to Nicosia and one of many to condemn the murders, recalled. There would be no other significant Turkish-Cypriot opposition group until the 1970s.

In late November 1963, Makarios proposed to Küçük **thirteen amendments** to the constitution to make bicommunal public life possible. These included the abolition of both the presidential and vice-presidential right of veto, the introduction of simple majority rule in the legislature, the unification of the municipalities and justice system, and an adjustment of communal ratios in civil service and the still-theoretical army. Apparently, this proposal had been drafted with the advice of the British high commissioner; the mainland Greeks subsequently deemed the bundle incredibly tactless, even if such reforms were worth introducing gradually. Turkey was sent the suggestions and denounced them, threatening military action if introduced unilaterally, even before Küçük had finished reading them, leaving him little room to manoeuvre. The infamous thirteen proposals are alleged to be part of a secret Greek-Cypriot strategy known as the **Akritas Plan**, whereby political obstacles to *énosis* were to be eliminated incrementally and discretely – and Turkish Cypriot objectors eliminated physically if necessary. It was, and remains, a Turkish codeword for enosist perfidy, and widely distributed printed copies of the supposed plan have never been convincingly demonstrated to be a hoax.

## Further intercommunal fighting

Reaction to the Turkish refusal was swift: on **December 21, 1963** shots were exchanged between a Greek-Cypriot police patrol and a car full of Turkish Cypriots – the precipitating factor, as so often in Cypriot violence, was prostitution – and within hours EOKA and TMT took to the field again. EOKA struck at Turkish neighbourhoods in Larnaca, and also in the mixed Nicosia district of Omórfita (Küçük Kaymaklı), with an EOKA detachment under **Nikos Sampson** rampaging through, seizing seven hundred hostages. In retaliation the Armenian community, accused of siding with the Greek Cypriots, was expelled by the Turks from north Nicosia on 23 December, and mainland Turkish troops left their Gönyeli barracks next day to take up positions along the Nicosia–Kyrenia road, with more forces concentrated on the Turkish mainland opposite; the mainland Greek force at Yerólakkos also deployed itself. Barriers, known as the **Green Line** after an English officer's crayon mark on a map, were set up between Greek and Turkish quarters in Nicosia after a UK-brokered ceasefire was effected on Christmas Day.

Already, all Turkish Cypriots had **resigned** from the government and police forces, to begin setting up a parallel administration in north Nicosia and in the rapidly growing number of **enclaves**. Denktaş and the TMT promulgated a communal law making it "treasonous" for any Turkish Cypriot to have commercial or administrative dealings with Greek Cypriots, a ban enforced by ostracization, beatings or worse. Any Turkish Cypriot who might have thought to continue at his post in south Nicosia would have to run a gauntlet of both his own co-religionists, enforcing the sequestration, and Greeks who might shoot first and ask questions later. The enclaves in fact constituted a deliberate policy of laying the physical basis for later partition. The Turkish-Cypriot position from now on asserted that the 1960 constitution was **defunct**, and there were merely two provisional regimes on the island pending the establishment of a new arrangement. Makarios agreed that the 1960 constitution was hopeless – but differed in his conclusions: namely that majority rule would prevail as per his suggested amendments, with minority guarantees, whether the Turks liked it or not.

## International repercussions

Because of the superpower interests involved, the Cyprus intercommunal dispute again took on **international** dimensions. The Greek Cypriots preferred, as they always had done, the UN as a forum; the US, UK and both mainland Turkey and the Turkish Cypriots pressed for **NATO intervention**. Turkish opinion, expressed by Küçük's and Denktaş's rightist Turkish National Party, helped plant the seeds of implacable American hostility to Makarios by successfully painting him with a pink (if not red) brush, calling attention to his forthright espousal of the **Non-Aligned Movement** and purchase of arms from the USSR and Czechoslovakia. In the event, the Cypriot government, with the support of the Soviets and Greek Premier George Papandreou, had its way: in February 1964, a UN resolution dispatched **UNFICYP** (UN Forces in Cyprus) for an initial three-month peace-keeping assignment – extended later to six months and renewed since then without a break. In addition, a **tripartite truce force**, composed of Greek, Turkish and British (from the sovereign bases) soldiers, was formed, under the partial leadership of Lieutenant Commander Martin Packard, and a UN civilian mediator was also appointed. George Ball, who as the US under-secretary of state had unsuccessfully tried to persuade Makarios to accept occupation by a NATO landing force, was later overheard to say "that son of a bitch [ie Makarios] will have to be killed before anything happens in Cyprus."

Little was accomplished immediately by UNFICYP; the death toll in the communal disturbances in the six months after December 1963 reached nearly six hundred, with the Turkish Cypriots suffering disproportionately. The presence of ten thousand **mainland Greek troops**, who had also landed on the island, gave EOKA and Greek Cypriots a false sense of being able to act with impunity. After TMT occupied St Hilarion castle and the Kyrenia–Nicosia road to form a core enclave, US President Lyndon Johnson sent Turkish Premier İnönü a letter, in his inimitably blunt style, warning him off plans to invade. At the same time the US administration pressurized Greece to follow its prescription or possibly face Turkey alone on the battlefield; heads were to be knocked together, if necessary, to preserve NATO's southeast flank.

The UN mediator having reached a dead end (and himself soon dying anyway), the **Acheson Plan** – named after the incumbent US secretary of state – was unveiled in mid-1964. It amounted to double *énosis*: the bulk of the island to Greece, the rest (plus the cession of the tiny but strategic Greek isle of Kastellórizo) to Turkey – effectively partition and the disappearance of Cyprus as an independent entity. After initial mulling over by both Greece and Turkey, the Greeks rejected the idea because of vociferous objections from Nicosia.

## The Turkish-Cypriot enclaves

The **Kókkina incident** (see p.204) made world headlines in August 1964, when the newly formed National Guard, commanded by a returned Grivas, attacked this coastal enclave in an effort to halt the landing of supplies and weapons from Turkey. Guarantors Greece and Turkey were again brought to the brink of war as Turkey extensively bombed and strafed the Pólis area, causing numerous casualties, and Makarios threatened to sanction attacks on Turkish Cypriots throughout the island unless Turkey ceased its air strikes. It was the first, but not the last, time that US-supplied NATO weapons were used in contravention of their ostensible purpose.

Since January 1964, **Martin Packard** – one of the few British military personnel to emerge with much credit from the post-independence period – had been conducting an all-but-one-man, increasingly successful campaign to rebuild trust between the two communities, persuading combatants to disarm, and proposing to dissolve the newly formed enclaves and escort the inhabitants back to formerly mixed villages, with UN protection where necessary. But his reintegrationist campaign seems to have been opposed by his superiors and other interested parties, who succeeded in securing Packard's removal from the island in June despite objections from both Greek- and Turkish-Cypriot community leaders with whom he was uniformly popular. (His memoirs of the time are shortly to be published; exact information is not available as of writing.)

Any residual trust between the two island communities was destroyed by the end of 1964, with the Turkish Cypriots well **barricaded** in their enclaves, the central government responding by placing a ban on their acquisition of a wide range of essential materials deemed militarily strategic. The enclave inmates, numbers swelled by Turkish army personnel, retaliated by keeping all Greeks out, setting up a TMT-run state-within-a-state with its own police, radio station and other services, which provocation EOKA could not resist on numerous occasions.

Despite all this, Cypriot **economic progress** post-independence was considerable – though heavily weighted towards the Greek Cypriot community, whose attitude towards the Turkish Cypriots at best resembled sending naughty children to bed without supper. The first of many **irrigation dams** to ease chronic water problems began to appear on the slopes of the Tróödhos range and Kyrenia hills. Tourism became important for the first time, primarily on the sandy coast to either side of Famagusta and to a lesser extent around Kyrenia.

# A twilight zone: 1965–1974

The new UN mediator **Galo Plaza** submitted his report in March 1965; it astutely diagnosed the shortcomings of the 1960 constitution and made forthright suggestions for a new one, principally that the Greek Cypriots must decisively renounce *énosis* and that the Turkish Cypriots must acquiesce to majority rule, with guarantees for certain rights. This did not go over well with them or with the mainland Turks, who arranged to send Plaza packing.

After April 1967 Greece had been taken over by a **military junta**, anxious – with American approval – to remove the "Cyprus problem" from the global agenda. However, secret summer meetings with Turkey, exploring variations of the Acheson Plan, came to nothing. In November, Grivas's National Guard attacked **Kofínou**, another enclave between Limassol and Larnaca, with considerable loss of Turkish life; Greece and Turkey both mobilized, Ankara again tendered an ultimatum to Athens and American diplomats got little sleep as they shuttled between the two capitals. Despite its soldierly composition, the Greek regime meekly complied with Turkish demands; **Grivas** and most of the ten thousand smuggled-in mainland soldiers were shipped back to Greece. The National Guard, however, remained – a Trojan horse for future plots.

In 1968, the UN sponsored direct **intercommunal negotiations**, which sputtered along until 1974, with **Glafkos Clerides**, president of the House of Representatives, and Rauf Denktaş as interlocutors. Substantial agreement on many points was actually reached, despite the Turks pressing for implementation of a high degree of local communal power in place of a spoiler role at the national level, and the Greek side holding out for more comprehensive central control. But Makarios never made the necessarily dramatic, generous concessions, and Clerides repeatedly threatened to resign in the absence of what he saw as a lack of consistent support from Makarios.

The Turkish enclaves were, though, finally **opened** to the extent of supplies going in and Turks coming out; with UN mediation, local arrangements – such as joint police patrols – were reached for a semblance of normal life in less tense areas of island. But in most details the leaders of the Turkish-Cypriot community still enforced a policy of **self-segregation** as a basis for a federal state. But whether they meant a federation as most outsiders understood it, or merely federation masquerading as partition, was highly moot. The Turkish Cypriots, biding their time in cramped and impoverished quarters, perhaps knew something that the Greek Orthodox islanders didn't or wouldn't realize: that the mainland Turks were in earnest about **supporting** their cause materially and militarily as well as morally.

Both Makarios and Küçük were overwhelmingly re-elected early in 1968, though Makarios's three bishops had repudiated him for dropping *énosis* as a realistic strategy. This was just one aspect of his **deteriorating relations** with the Greek colonels, who – with the approval of the CIA – instigated repeated **plots** to eliminate him through the medium of the Greek regular army officers, who by now controlled most of the National Guard.

A bizarre **counterplot** of the same year deserves mention: **Polycarpos Yiorgadjis**, a former EOKA operative and minister of interior, provided one Alekos Panagoulis in Greece with the explosives for an abortive attempt to kill junta chief Papadopoulos. Exactly why Yiorgadjis would do this – considering that EOKA and junta aims were now identical – remains a mystery; he was also implicated in a later attempt on Makarios's life, and was himself assassinated by forces loyal to the archbishop, in March 1970 (his widow, interestingly, later married Tassos Papadopoulos, the current president of Cyprus).

Grivas slipped back into Cyprus during 1971 and founded **EOKA-B** with the express intent of resuming the struggle for *énosis*, but the old trouble-maker, now in his seventies, died in January 1974, still in hiding. EOKA-B and its allies set in motion various devices to destabilize the elected government of Cyprus, reserving – as had its predecessor – special venom for AKEL. Publicly, the Greek junta demanded, and eventually got, the resignation of **Spyros Kyprianou**, long-time foreign minister and future president. The three dissident bishops of 1968, still acting as junta placemen, claimed at one point to have defrocked Makarios, reducing him to lay status. Makarios retaliated by getting the **three bishops dismissed** with the help of other Middle Eastern prelates, and by creating three new, subordinate bishoprics – those of Mórfou, Nicosia and Limassol – to reduce the chances of such a revolt in the future. He was re-elected as president in 1973 unopposed; in the same year Küçük was replaced as nominal vice-president by Rauf Denktaş.

# 1974: coup and invasion

The Greek junta, by early 1974 tottering and devoid of any popular support at home, now tried a Falklands-type diversion, with the encouragement – if not outright connivance – of CIA agents in Athens. Makarios, well aware of the intrigues of the junta's cadres in his National Guard, had proscribed EOKA-B in April 1974, and wrote to the Greek president on July 2 demanding that these officers be withdrawn. The junta's response was to give the go-ahead for the **archbishop's overthrow**, which, despite advance knowledge, Makarios's primarily left-wing and poorly armed supporters proved powerless to prevent.

Early on **July 15**, National Guard troops attacked the archiepiscopal palace, gutted it and announced the archbishop's demise. But Makarios, in another building at the time, escaped to loyalist strongholds in Páfos district; on hearing of this, a US diplomat was overheard to remark, "How inconvenient." With British help, the archbishop left the island for Britain, which offered lukewarm support, and then the US, where he was refused recognition as head of state by Henry Kissinger, a man who had done as much as anyone to oppose – and possibly depose – him. He got a warmer reception, as usual, at the UN.

Unfazed, the coup protagonists proclaimed as president **Nikos Sampson**, long-time EOKA activist, Turkophobe warlord and head of the (anything but) Progressive Party. A contemporary foreign correspondent characterized him as "an absolute idiot, though not quite illiterate – a playboy gunman. He spends every night in cabarets getting drunk, dancing on tables, pulling off his shirt to show his scars." A widely circulated photo showed him in full battle regalia, one foot atop the corpse of a Turkish Cypriot he'd killed as a "hunting trophy". Small wonder, then, that his term of office and EOKA-B's direct rule would last exactly one week.

On reflection (obviously not their strong point), the EOKA-B people might have realized that their coup would give Turkey a perfect **pretext** to do what it had long contemplated: partition the island, claiming as guarantor to be acting as protectors of the threatened minority. Indeed many Turkish-Cypriot fighters resident in the North pre-1974 recall receiving coded messages weeks before the coup, telling them to prepare for action. Post-coup international opinion initially favoured Turkey, whose prime minister **Bülent Ecevit** went through the proper legalistic motions on July 16–17 of flying to Britain to propose joint action for protecting the Turkish minority, restoring Cypriot independence and demanding that Athens withdraw its officers. While Sampson was indeed quoted as saying "Now that we've finished with Makarios's people, let's start on the Turks," EOKA-B in the end killed more Greek opponents – estimates run to several hundred interred in mass, unmarked graves, including many wounded buried alive – than the almost three hundred Turkish Cypriots slaughtered at Tókhni and three villages around Famagusta.

## "Phase I"

Just before dawn on July 20, Ecevit authorized the **Turkish invasion** of Cyprus, entailing amphibious armoured landings, napalm strikes, bombing raids on many towns and paratroop drops around Kyrenia and Nicosia. **"Phase I"** of the campaign lasted from **July 20 to July 30**: despite the demoralizing coup, and being outnumbered four to one, the Greek Cypriots managed to confine Turkish forces to a lozenge-shaped bridgehead straddling the Nicosia–Kyrenia road. The initial Turkish landing west of Kyrenia, the first time its forces had fought since the Korean War, was a near-fiasco, as were many supporting naval and air force operations. For starters, Turkey was expecting little or no resistance from the Greek Cypriots, and threw poorly equipped, trained and disciplined conscripts into the opening battles. Soldiers disembarked without water bottles in the July heat, and tanks rolled ashore with no ammunition and insufficient fuel. Turkish air-force jets managed to sink two of their own landing craft, while completely missing the contents of a Cypriot National Guard tank camp (though the Greek Cypriots also mistakenly shot down two Hercules transports bringing reinforcements from Greece). A Greek naval fleet, a radar phantom as it turned out, was reported southwest of Cyprus; three Turkish destroyers sailed to meet it, but Turkish jets attacked and sank one of these when the captain failed to give the right password (the US had supplied Greece and Turkey with identical vessels). The brigadier general in charge of operations was killed as he came ashore, with the next-highest-ranking officer, for some days, being a captain. UN observers subsequently estimated a ratio of seven Turkish to every Greek casualty over the entire war; much of this can be attributed to pre-landing lectures by Turkish religious leaders, who assured the raw recruits that death in battle with the infidels ensured a direct path to Paradise. To such pep talks – and not (as often alleged) the ingestion of drugs – was owed the repeated and oft-corroborated spectacle of human wave attacks by wild-eyed Turkish cannon fodder, marching zombie-like into Greek-Cypriot machine-gun fire, until the latter ran out of ammunition and had to retreat.

In Greece, the junta chiefs ordered the Greek army to attack Turkey across the Thracian frontier; its officers refused, precipitating the collapse of the junta on **July 23**, the same day Sampson fell from power. Glafkos Clerides replaced him as acting head of state in Makarios's absence, as a civilian government took power in Athens. The first round of hastily arranged **negotiations** between the Greek, Turkish and British foreign ministers convened in **Geneva**, resulting in the ceasefire of July 30. On August 8, talks resumed, with Clerides and Denktaş additionally present. The Turkish military, with little to show for the heavy casualties sustained during Phase I, and with their forces increasingly vulnerable as the Greek Cypriots began to comprehensively mine the perimeter of their toehold, began to pressurize their civilian leaders to be given a freer hand. Accordingly, on the night of August 13–14, the Turkish foreign minister gave Clerides an effective **ultimatum** demanding approval of one or the other Turkish plans for "federation": either six dispersed cantons or a single amalgamated one under Turkish-Cypriot control, adding up to 34 percent of Cyprus. Clerides asked for 36 hours to consult his superiors, which was refused at 3am on August 14; ninety minutes later, the Turkish army resumed its offensive.

## "Phase II"

**"Phase II"** was a two-day rout of the Greek Cypriots, who had insufficient armour and no air support to stop the Turkish juggernaut, this time manned by crack troops. The Greek Cypriots – as opposed to the Greek officers, whom the Turks regarded with contempt from the start – had acquitted themselves splendidly during "Phase I", far exceeding their brief to hold the line for 36 hours until massive aid arrived from Greece, which never did; come "Phase II", they were completely exhausted, demoralized and literally out of fuel and ammunition.

The behaviour of the Turkish infantry in both phases of the war featured sporadic, **gratuitous violence** against Greek-Cypriot civilians unlucky enough to lie in their path; word of the rapes, murders and widespread looting which marked their advance was enough to convince approximately 165,000 Greek Cypriots to flee for their safety. Had they in fact not done so, the entire purpose of the campaign – to create an ethnically cleansed sanctuary for the Turkish Cypriots – would have been confounded.

At a second ceasefire on August 16, the areas occupied by the Turkish army totalled 38 percent of the island's area – slightly more than Turkey had demanded at Geneva – abutting a scalloped boundary, henceforth the **Attila Line**, extending from Káto Pýrgos in Tillyría to Famagusta. The Greek-Cypriot **death toll**, including combatants and civilians, rose to 3850. The **missing** supposedly numbered 1619, though now it seems likely that several hundred of these were leftists killed by EOKA-B activists and Greek junta officers, as noted above, or – as Turkish army units often found them – chained to their gun emplacements or shot in the back. Others – probably over two hundred National Guardsmen – were shown by Greek-Cypriot journalists in spring 1998 to have been killed by the Turkish army and buried in unmarked graves by the Southern government, to be exploited for propaganda purposes. Turkish Cypriots living in the South were put in an untenable position by the Turkish "peace action", as it was termed; EOKA-B units occupied or cleared out most of their enclaves, with reprisal killings at several points.

Since July 15, a flurry of **UN Security Council resolutions**, calling on all concerned to desist from warlike actions and respect Cypriot independence and territorial integrity, had been piling up, blithely disregarded then and in the years since. With the benefit of hindsight, UK parliamentary and US congressional committees duly condemned the timidity, lack of imagination and simple shamefulness of their governments' respective past policies towards Cyprus, specifically the absence of any meaningful initiative to stop the Turkish war machine. The **British** claimed that with just over five thousand men on the sovereign bases, there was (despite their role as guarantor) little they could have done – other than what they actually did, which was to half-heartedly interpose a small fleet between Cyprus and Anatolia as a deterrent in the four days before July 20, eventually ferry tourists to safety out of the North, and to shelter in Sovereign Base territory Turkish Cypriots fleeing EOKA-B gunmen in the South. In retrospect, though, it seems the UK had been content to follow American dictates rather than pursue an independent course.

On the part of the **US**, there was more of a failure of will than inability to do something. President Nixon, on the point of resigning over Watergate, had deferred to the archpriest of *realpolitik*, **Henry Kissinger**, who made no secret of his "tilt" towards Turkey rather than Greece as the more valuable ally in the Aegean – once the colonels' junta had served its purpose – or of his distaste for Makarios. Thus the integrity of Cyprus was sacrificed to NATO power politics. The only substantive American congressional action, over Kissinger's objections, was the temporary **suspension of military aid** to Turkey as a wrist-slap punishment.

During anti-American riots in Nicosia on **August 19**, the **US Ambassador Rodger Davies** and a Cypriot embassy employee were gunned down by EOKA-B hitmen aiming deliberately from an unfinished building opposite. Periodic assertions that Davies was the CIA paymaster and handler for the EOKA-B coup do not hold water, as he was an Arabist by training and had been in the job for less than two months – though this does not rule out "conduct incompatible with diplomatic status" on the part of his predecessor, for whom the gunmen may have mistaken him. Eleven days later, **Vassos Lyssarides**, head of the socialist **EDEK** party supporting Makarios, narrowly escaped death at the hands of the same bunch. These lurid events demonstrated that clapping Sampson in jail – where he remained until 1992 – wouldn't cause his associates to simply disappear.

# De facto partition: Cyprus 1974–1991

While still acting head of state, Clerides acknowledged that the Greeks and Greek Cypriots had been acting for years as if Turkey did not exist, and that some sort of **federal republic** was the best Cyprus could hope for. Makarios returned on December 7, 1974 to a diminished realm, and contradicted Clerides: the Greek Cypriots should embark on a "long-term struggle", using their favourite method of **internationalization**, to induce the Turkish army to leave and get optimum terms from the Turkish Cypriots. This prefigured a final break between the two men the following year. In his homecoming speech in Nicosia, with half the South turned out to welcome him, Makarios also forgave his opponents – not that he had much choice, with EOKA-B operatives still swaggering about in full battledress. But others, especially those who had lost relatives at the hands of either the rebels or the Turks, were not in such an accommodating mood; three decades on, assessing blame for the fiasco of 1974 still occupies a certain amount of the South's agenda, and few people are willing to discuss it publicly (the main reason it took three editions of this guide to recruit a Greek-Cypriot viewpoint for the next section, "The events of summer 1974").

Top priority was given to **rehousing the refugees** from both communities: the Turkish Cypriots simply occupied abundant abandoned Greek property in the North, but it took the South more than a decade to house adequately those who had fled the North. The international community, so disgracefully sluggish at the time the problem was created, was reasonably generous and prompt with **aid** to help reconstruct the island – aid which, however, went primarily to the South.

Strangely, **intercommunal negotiations resumed** almost immediately, though at first they centred almost entirely on the fate of Cypriots caught on the "wrong" side. Greeks in the South separated from relatives and homes in the North were at first allowed to rejoin them; the government initially attempted to prevent Southern Turks from **trekking north**, but by early 1975 this too had happened. This departure was not entirely voluntary, especially in the case of Turkish Cypriots with extensive properties or businesses in the South, or with Orthodox Christian spouses; accounts abound, especially in the Páfos area, of Turkish and British army trucks virtually rounding up Turkish Cypriots, with their neighbours compelled to rescue those – usually non-observant Muslims or converts to Orthodoxy – who wished to stay behind. Once these Turks were safely on the "right" side of the Attila Line, most remaining northern Greeks were expelled and the North pronounced, over the South's protests, that an equitable exchange of populations had been carried out.

The North declared itself the **Turkish Federated State of Cyprus** (TFSC) in February 1975, though as always what the Turkish Cypriots meant by federation, and with whom, was quite different from what the South had in mind. Clerides and Denktaş, brought together again by UN Secretary General **Kurt Waldheim**, made hopeful noises of peacemaking intent through much of 1975, but no substantive progress was registered. In 1977, Makarios and Denktaş met for the first time in fourteen years at the latter's request, agreeing on various **general guidelines** for a bi-communal, federal republic, the details of territorial jurisdiction to be determined later but envisioning a reduction in the amount of land held by the Turkish Cypriots.

After **Makarios died** in August 1977, **Spyros Kyprianou** replaced him as president and Greek-Cypriot representative at the on-again, off-again talks. As an initial goodwill measure, it was first suggested in 1978 that the empty **ghost town of Varósha** be resettled by its former Greek-Cypriot inhabitants: the Greeks wanted this to precede any other steps, while the Turks would only countenance it under limited conditions and as part of an overall settlement. The reopening of Nicosia international airport was also mooted periodically, though it is now obsolete and virtually unusable owing to post-1974 urban growth (and summer temperatures in the Mesaoría, which limit permissible payloads on modern jets). In 1981, Waldheim seized the initiative by presenting an "evaluation" of the talks thus far, and generating for the first time **detailed proposals** for the mechanics of a federal republic, which came to nothing.

In the international arena, the South increasingly protested against Turkish and Turkish-Cypriot practices in the North – specifically the **expulsion** of most Greek Cypriots and the denial of human rights to those remaining, the **settlement** of numerous Anatolian Turks to alter the demographic balance of the island and vandalism against Greek religious property. In short order a comprehensive and well-orchestrated embargo of the North was imposed with the assistance of most international agencies, which extended from declarations of its postal service and ports of entry as invalid, to consistent referral to the North's officeholders, civil servants and government as "so-called" or within inverted commas. Such boycotts of the North have ensured – among other things – that **archeological sites** are mostly neglected, since no archeologists would be permitted to work in a Greek-speaking country again if they were known to have visited the North, even just to inspect their old digs.

The North put another spanner in the works by unilaterally declaring full independence on November 15, 1983 as the **Turkish Republic of Northern Cyprus** (TRNC), generating the usual storm of pious UN resolutions of condemnation and widespread overseas support for the Greek-Cypriot position. To date no other state besides Turkey has recognized the TRNC. Yet talks towards a peaceful island-wide solution continued: early 1984 saw more proposals by Kyprianou to the UN, not significantly different from those before or since. **Javier Perez de Cuellar**, the new Secretary General, presented successively refined draft frameworks for a federal settlement between 1985 and 1986; first the South said yes, but the North no; then the Turks agreed, but Kyprianou wavered until the **opportunity was lost** – behaviour for which he was roundly pilloried, and which contributed to his loss of office in 1988. He returned from the political dead in the late 1990s, serving as president of the House of Representatives until his death early in 2002.

# 1991–1995: more fruitless talk

Late in 1991, Cyprus returned to the global picture; President George Bush, needing another foreign-policy feather in his cap prior to the 1992 US elections, called for **new peace conferences**, and visited both Turkey and Greece canvassing support for them – the first American presidential junket to either country in decades.

Intercommunal meetings did not actually materialize until mid-1992, with **Boutros Boutros-Ghali** now UN Secretary General. His "Set of Ideas" was similar in most respects to all previous proposals: Varósha and some or all of the

**Coalitions** have long been a fact of life among the Greek Cypriots, since no one party is strong enough to govern alone. And in such a small society horse-trading and flexibility are essential; stances or declarations of one campaign are cheerfully eaten in the presence of new coalition partners in the next elections. Even very small parties – the threshold for entry into the parliament is a 1.8 percent vote nationwide – often control swing votes, and are assiduously courted as partners. Shifts of party vote of even a percentage point or two are hailed as major victories, or catastrophes. The South has a **presidential** system, and considerable power resides in the executive office; there is no prime minister, the closest analogue being the president of the House of Representatives. Both presidential and **parliamentary** elections occur every five years, but are at present out of sync: the former in years ending in 8 and 3, the latter in years ending in 6 and 1.

*Tó Kypriakó* or the **"Cyprus Question"** – the most appropriate response to Cyprus's de facto partition – is theoretically the paramount electoral issue. In general, the centre-right party **DIKO** has stood for an idealistic solution, relying on cumulative international pressures from various quarters to get the Turkish army to depart and the Turkish Cypriots to come to terms. Centrist **DISY**, preferring a pro-NATO/EU alignment, has stressed pragmatic deal-cutting directly with the Turkish Cypriots to get as many of the refugees home as quickly as possible. **AKEL** and **EDEK** point to their track record of never having systematically harassed the Turkish-Cypriot community as a valuable asset for bridge-building in a theoretical federal republic. Left unarticulated is the necessity for massive concessions, with some politician(s) allotted the unenviable task of announcing which refugee constituents can go home to the North, and who will have to stay in the South. After 1974, the leftist parties were in a position to exert additional pressure, with many **social-welfare measures** introduced for the first time to alleviate some of the misery caused by the refugee influx.

In the House of Representatives elections of **1976**, AKEL, EDEK and Makarios's Popular Front combined to shut out Clerides' DISY party, owing this sweep to a first-past-the-post system. After Makarios's death in 1977, his groomed successor Kyprianou was designated to serve out the remainder of the archbishop's presidential term, then re-elected unopposed in **1978** in his own right as head of DIKO, an ostensibly new party, but still widely seen as Makarios's creature.

By **1981**, the parliamentary system had been changed to one of proportional representation; AKEL and DISY finished in a dead heat, with DIKO and EDEK holding the balance of power in the 35-seat House of Representatives; the **1983** presidential voting returned Kyprianou to office with AKEL backing, again shutting out Clerides.

In the **1988** presidential contest **George Vassiliou**, a professional businessman and political outsider, was elected, backed by AKEL and DISY who, despite their wide differences on domestic issues, agreed that the timely resolution of the "Cyprus Question" was imperative. The **1991** parliamentary polls showed a slight rightward swing in the House, now enlarged to 56 seats.

On his fourth try for the presidency in February **1993**, DISY candidate **Clerides** upset AKEL-supported incumbent Vassiliou by less than two thousand votes in run-off polling – a margin garnered, it is claimed, by numbers of hunters seduced by Clerides' (unfulfilled) promise to reinstate the controversial springtime bird-shoot. The result was primarily regarded as a rejection of the UN-sponsored negotiations to date and an endorsement of Clerides' intent to pursue EU membership more strongly.

The parliamentary elections of **1996** saw DISY and AKEL representation enhanced at the expense of DIKO and EDEK, yet DISY entered into a coalition with EDEK (dissolved in January 1999). Clerides was re-elected president in **1998** by another razor-thin margin, polling second in a crowded first-round field but besting independent George Iakovou in the run-off.

The House elections of May **2001** were on one level a reprise of 1981's, with AKEL and DISY again neck-and-neck, but with some startling differences. An unprecedented eight parties got parliamentary representation, 23 new deputies included six women among them, but the biggest surprise was the selection, with support from DIKO and EDEK (briefly renamed KISOS), of AKEL head Dimitris Christofias as president of the House, succeeding Kyprianou. This was an historic first occupation of high office by Cyprus Communists, in the teeth of DISY warnings that this would send the "wrong" message to the EU, and seen as a quid pro quo for AKEL's support of a DIKO or KISOS presidential candidate in 2003.

The presidential contest of February **2003** proved to be the biggest shocker yet. Clerides, despite a constitutional ban on a third run, announced in January that he would stand for a limited 16-month term. His opponent was Tassos Papadopoulos of DIKO, who gained the support of AKEL as promised, plus EDEK and the Greens as well, and went on to score a decisive first-round victory over Clerides, with over 51 percent of the vote.

The first **Euro elections** with Cypriot participation, in June 2004, saw four of the six seats at stake taken by DISY and AKEL. In theory two of the seats are reserved for Turkish Cypriots, should a settlement materialize before the next Euro elections in 2009.

## Greek-Cypriot political organizations

**AKEL** *Anorthotikón Kómma tou Ergazoménou Laoú* or "Regenerative Party of the Working People" – in plain English, the Communist Party of Cyprus; historically enemies of EOKA and conciliatory towards the Turkish Cypriots. Until the early 1990s unreconstructed as opposed to Euro-communist, but now bourgeois and "social-democratic". Currently chaired by Dimitris Christofias, also president of the House of Representatives.

**ADIK** *Agonistikó Dhimokrátiko Kínima*, a splinter party from DIKO, which gained a seat in the 2001 parliament; essentially a personality cult of its leader Dinos Michaelides.

**DIKO** *Dhimokratikó Kómma* or "Democratic Party", the centre-right party that's the successor of Makarios's Popular Front; pursues a relatively tough line in negotiations with the North. Long chaired by Spyros Kyprianou, currently headed by President Tassos Papadopoulos.

**DISY** *Dhimokratikós Synayermós* or the "Democratic Rally", formerly chaired by Glafkos Clerides, currently headed by Nicos Anastasiades; despite a right-wing domestic and foreign policy, advocates sweeping concessions to the North and was the only party to back the Annan Plan.

**EDEK** *Enoméni Dhimokratikí Énosis tou Kéndrou* or "United Democratic Union of the Centre" – despite the name, a socialist party headed since the 1960s by Vassos Lyssarides, perennial also-rans and coalition partners in national elections; briefly rechristened **KISOS** (*Kínima Sosialdhimokratón*) for 2001 elections, after which Lyssarides finally bowed out in favour of new chief Yiannakis Omirou.

**EOKA** *Ethnikí Orgánosis Kypríon Agonistón* or "National Organization of Cypriot Fighters", right-wing, IRA-type group co-founded by Makarios and Grivas to effect *énosis* or union of Cyprus with Greece. Continued to exist after independence, metamorphosing into the virulently anti-Makarios, pro-junta **EOKA-B**.

**Greens** The ecologists' party, which managed to get a parliamentary seat in the 2001 elections.

**Néi Orizóndes/New Horizons** Irredentist, anti-federation party, opposed to UN-brokered intercommunal negotiations; got a seat in the 2001 election.

As per the record of murderous suppression by TMT of its opponents, multiple parties or even factions were not actively encouraged in the Turkish-Cypriot community until after the founding of the Turkish Federated State of Cyprus in 1975. Even since, questionable tactics have been used to nip budding opposition – specifically against presidential candidate Ahmet Berberoğlu in 1975 and opposition party chief Özker Özgür in 1988 – though since the late 1990s conditions have more resembled genuine **pluralism.**

In North Cyprus, **the political designations "Left" and "Right" mean the opposite** of what they do elsewhere: leftist parties advocate economic liberalism, free trade and a positive attitude towards the EU, along with an unfettered press and a more flexible position on the "Cyprus Question", whilst conservative parties stand for heavy state intervention in commerce, token protectionism for select industries, complete deferral to Turkey rather than the EU, a swollen civil service and a hardline stance in negotiations with the South.

North Cyprus has a tiny electorate of about 125,000, with a high degree of **overlap** between government figures, business bigwigs, the habitual ruling parties and President Denktaş's personal acquaintances, with politicking inevitably personalized. Though the North's system provides for both a **president and a prime minister**, President Denktaş was always the dominant figure until his 2005 retirement. Presidential and parliamentary elections initially were held more or less together every five years, formerly in years ending in 6 and 1 but more recently 5 and 0.

The first elections in the North were held in **1976**: Denktaş won easily with three-fourths of the vote and a like percentage of seats for his **UBP** in a forty-seat Assembly. In **1981** the UBP victory margin diminished to just over half the votes; the party no longer enjoyed an absolute majority, sharing a hung parliament with the **TKP** and the **CTP**. Following an unstable period, the assembly was expanded to fifty seats, allowing Denktaş to fill ten vacancies with compliant appointees.

In the **1985** elections, only parties polling over eight percent were awarded seats, which forced splinter factions to disappear or join with others. The constitutional clause prohibiting more than two consecutive presidential terms was eliminated, and Denktaş ran as an **independent**. Although he retained office in an "above-party" role, the UBP's share of votes declined to just over a third, reflecting widespread disillusionment. Yet because of the various "reforms", its proportion of Assembly seats remained the same – about half.

Denktaş was re-elected again in the early **1990** presidential polls, and prior to the hard-fought May Assembly elections, more **changes in the election laws** were introduced. These included a bonus-seat system for high-vote parties and, most importantly, a prohibition against coalition governments. The opposition's response to this last condition was to combine into the **DMP** (Democratic Struggle Party). Composed of three smaller parties, it ran on a platform of ending corruption, better economic management and liberalization of the official electronic media. But with just under half the vote, the DMP received less than one-third of Assembly seats, because of the bonus-seat rule. Despite numerous irregularities – voter intimidation, the biased media – the UBP would probably still have won "fair" elections: DMP simply hadn't convinced enough voters that the UBP's glaring shortcomings overrode its guarantee of continued security vis-à-vis the Greek Cypriots.

In late 1992 Denktaş fell out with his prime minister Eroğlu, who accused the president of being (of all things) too "flexible" in dealings with the South. Ten MPs loyal to Denktaş defected, forming the *Demokrat Partisi* (**DP**), under the leadership of Hakki Atun and Serdar Denktaş. **December 1993** elections resulted in a near-tie between the UBP (17 seats), now headed by Eroğlu, and the DP (15 seats), a deadlock broken by DP's entry during 1994 into an unprecedented coalition with Özker Özgür's CTP (13 seats).

In **March 1995**, this coalition crumbled, which doubtless contributed to Denktaş's decision to stand yet again in presidential elections the following month, despite his announced intention to resign during 1995. In the event, Denktaş suffered the minor humiliation of a run-off against rival Eroğlu, which he won through the support of TKP and CTP members convinced Denktaş was the lesser of two evils. Shortly thereafter, the CTP–DP coalition was revived under PM Hakki Atun; but in January 1996, Deputy PM Özker Özgür threw in the towel, exasperated by Denktaş's continued obstructionism in negotiations with the South, and was replaced at the CTP helm by Mehmet Ali Talat.

In **December 1998** parliamentary elections, the DP's and TKP's vote share remained more or less stable, but Eroğlu's UBP increased its strength to 24 seats, mostly at the CTP's expense – with which, curiously, it entered into yet another coalition, lasting until June 2001, when the TKP bowed out and was promptly replaced by the UBP under Salih Çoshar as Deputy Prime Minister.

Presidential elections of **April 2000** saw a reprise of Denktaş vs. Eroğlu, and proved the most bizarre yet. Again Denktaş, with just over 43 percent of the first-round vote, would have been forced into a run-off against his perennial rival, except that Eroğlu mysteriously conceded before the second poll took place. No cogent explanation was given, and rumours abound that mainland Turkish pressure secured their desired result.

Prior to parliamentary polls of **December 2003**, the authorities attempted to pad the voter registration rolls by hastily granting North citizenship to settlers, who were presumably expected to vote for anti-settlement parties. The desired result was the CTP at 35.2 percent forced into a coalition with the DP; this duly collapsed in October 2004, with fresh elections in **February 2005** (after Turkey had received a green light from the EU to begin accession negotiations) rewarding Talat's CTP with 44 percent and exactly half the seats. The nationwide minimum for representation dropped to five percent, allowing a coalition to be formed with the pro-settlement **BDH**, (5.8 percent and 1 seat), headed by Mustafa Akıncı, prior to the presidential elections of April 2005, pending as of writing.

## Turkish-Cypriot political organizations

**CTP** Cumhuriyetçi Türk Partisi or "Republican Turkish Party", headed by Prime Minister Mehmet Ali Talat; cast in the image of the namesake centrist-secularist Anatolian party. Theoretically conciliatory towards the South, though has been ineffective in this respect in coalitions with the UBP or DP.

**DP** Demokrat Partisi, a personality-centred hiving-off from the UBP and leading component of recent coalition governments, run by Serdar Denktaş, second son of Rauf Denktaş, and Salih Çoshar.

**TKP** Toplumcu Kurtuluş Partisi or "Communal Liberation Party", headed by Mustafa Akıncı, a centre-left grouping strongly favouring rapprochement with the South. In June 2003, this combined with the United Cyprus Party to form the **BDH** (Barış ve Demokrasi Hareketi) or "Peace and Democracy Movement".

**TMT** "Turkish Resistance Organization", formed in 1958 to counter EOKA's activities; its ideology guided the North's government until very recently.

**UBP** Ulusal Birlik Partisi or "National Unity Party", established by Rauf Denktaş in 1974 and governing the North alone until 1993; now headed by Derviş Eroğlu. Pro-Anatolian, nationalist and against significant accommodation with the South.

**UHH** or "National Patriotic Movement", established in May 2001; thought by many to be the reincarnation of TMT, and the political face of the so-called Civil Defence Organization held responsible for attacks on many opposition figures.

**Patriotic Unity Movement**, centre-left faction, anti-settler and anti-Turkish Army, founded by Alpay Durduran along with veteran politicians Özker Özgür and İzzet Izcan; cooperates with the BDH.

Mórfou plain would revert to Greek-Cypriot control, and Turkish-Cypriot-administered territory would shrink overall to 28 percent of the island's surface area. Left discussable was the degree of Greek refugees' return to the North; by gerrymandering the boundaries of the Turkish-administered zone, a profile could be reached such that most Greek Cypriots could go home without complications – Varósha and Mórfou taking most of the total – and even if all Greeks formerly resident in the agreed Turkish zone decided to go back, they would still be in a minority there.

**Politically**, a joint foreign ministry and finance ministry was foreseen, with the Cyprus pound reintroduced throughout the island. Either a rotating or an ethnically stipulated presidency was suggested, plus a supreme court equally weighted ethnically, and a bicameral legislature, with the upper house biased towards the Turkish Cypriots in the sense that each federal unit would be represented equally rather than proportionately, as the states are in the US Senate.

July sessions between Vassiliou and Denktaş at the UN were inconclusive; Boutros-Ghali had circulated to certain interested parties a **tentative map** showing proposed adjustments of territory in a bizonal federation. When this circulated generally, many in the North reacted strongly: "We won't be refugees a third time" was a typical newspaper headline, referring to the previous compulsory shifts of 1964 and 1974.

October sessions in New York were again a washout; the Security Council passed yet another **resolution** in November 1992, the most strongly worded in years, laying most of the blame for their failure on Denktaş for his intransigence in refusing to accept the Boutros-Ghali settlement guidelines. Denktaş's reaction was to threaten immediate resignation rather than sign any agreement which he deemed unfavourable. Many began to suspect that Denktaş was content with the status quo, and had merely been humouring world opinion by his attendance at successive conferences.

Cyprus virtually disappeared from the international agenda during 1993 and 1994, except for the UN's recycling of the "Set of Ideas" as the so-called **"Confidence Building Measures"** (CBMs), in particular the rehabilitation of Nicosia airport and Varósha, and five "informal talks" between Denktaş and new Southern president Clerides in the presence of a UN mediator during October 1994. The UN announced that all essential elements for a solution were on the table, with only the political will lacking on each side to implement one.

Since his election in 1993, President Clerides had presided over a continuation of the **rightward tilt** in Southern politics. One particularly conspicuous instance of this, early in 1995, was the reinstatement with back pay of 62 coup supporters – educators, civil servants and police officers who'd been cashiered years before – and the exiling of their opponents to minor posts. This was done unilaterally by the Clerides administration, over the objections of his parliament.

Spates of terror **bombings** and **gangland crimes** convulsed the South during much of 1995. The campaign of terrorist group EKAS, the "Greek-Cypriot Liberation Army", to extort donations from wealthy businessmen for ostensibly patriotic purposes was cut short by its suppression in late April, but their activities were overshadowed by a series of car bombings, arson attacks and fatal shootings, all part of a battle to control the lucrative trade in cabaret girls, gambling dens and drugs. None of the crimes was solved, and in December President Clerides made the sensational announcement that this was hardly surprising, given the **police** force's involvement in the underworld, and demanded the resignations of the national police chief and his deputy. All this severely dented the South's overseas image of savouriness and safety, and constituted a propaganda windfall for the North, which was not slow to exploit it after years of being on the receiving end of a Southern slander campaign implying that North Cyprus was a dark and dangerous place heaving with Anatolian barbarians.

# 1996–1999: resurgent tensions

A cynical view has it that Cyprus only gets international attention when UNFICYP, balking at the cost of operations, threatens to leave; when it's a US presidential election year, with points to be scored by brokering yet another quick foreign-policy "fix"; or when the Cypriots themselves do something drastic to concentrate overseas minds. Before Bill Clinton, with Haitian, Bosnian and Israeli "successes" notched on his belt, could dispatch US special envoy Richard Holbrooke to the island in 1996, events overtook such an initiative.

Since the 1992 decision to greatly **scale down the UNFICYP presence**, a regular pattern of **border incidents** had arisen involving demonstrations by Southern refugee groups attempting to march to their old homes, counter-representations by Northerners and pitched battles on each side with their own police. Usually these were on or near the anniversary of the 1974 events, but every few weeks year-round a young (invariably male) Greek-Cypriot motorist rammed barriers at a checkpoint and led soldiers in the North on a merry chase before capture and a long prison term. The northern regime also began abducting or even killing Greek-Cypriot fishermen off Famagusta whom it claimed drifted into its territorial waters, as well as apprehending unarmed Greek Cypriots who strayed too far into the buffer zone.

But by far the worst and deadliest such episode was in **August 1996**. Nationalist Greek-Cypriot motorcyclists announced a "rally", beginning in no-longer-divided Berlin and finishing (hopefully) in Kyrenia, to "end" the partition of Cyprus. The Orthodox Church of Cyprus provided material and moral support to the bikers who, though prevented from crossing the Attila Line, caused considerable provocation by riding through the buffer zone near Dherínia, accompanied by hundreds of stone-throwing, shouting **demonstrators**, effectively unrestrained by Southern police. The Turkish Cypriots had got wind of the rally plans and invited a rent-a-mob of their own: ultra-nationalist, paramilitary Grey Wolves from the Turkish mainland, armed with batons and iron staves. Allowed into the buffer zone by the Turkish army, the Grey Wolves and similarly equipped Turkish-Cypriot policemen administered savage beatings to the Greek Cypriots, killing one – all action broadcast live on international television. Three days later, after the victim's funeral at nearby Paralímni, another riot erupted at the Line in Dherínia when the deceased's cousin attempted to scale a flagpole on the Turkish-Cypriot side of the buffer zone and pull down the Turkish flag; he was immediately shot dead by the Turkish Cypriots rather than arrested, and numerous UN peacekeepers were wounded in more Turkish gunfire as the crowds went berserk. The Greek-Cypriot ultra-nationalist fringe had two **martyrs** (as perhaps was intended); belligerent soundbites were heard in Ankara, Athens and Nicosia South and North; and the Southern government – despite never officially endorsing the motorcylists' rally – laid on a second, de facto state funeral at Paralímni cathedral, attended by major dignitaries in both cases. It took some weeks for cooler heads to prevail (the violence badly

## The Orthodox Church in Cyprus

Both Greek and Turkish Cypriots concede that the former are among the most religiously observant in the Orthodox Christian world, and much more devout than Muslim islanders; in no other eastern-rite country will you find, for example, *nistísima* or special vegetarian fare offered during Lent at local franchises of *McDonald's*. But the faithful have been poorly served in recent years, to put it mildly, by the Auto-cephalous Church of Cyprus, as ungodly an institution – once up the hierarchy from the often conscientious parish priests – as you would never hope to see: a (if not the) major obstacle to communal reconciliation, xenophobic, anti-semitic, homophobic, thoroughly corrupt, and often involved in enterprises (especially real estate) that would be the province of lay mafias in other countries. Much of the period from 1998 to 2003 was occupied by **scandals** which effectively forfeited the Church much of its previous authority; the local media, of course, made a meal of various events which occasionally descended into such farce that you couldn't make it up if you tried.

First there was the 1998 case of the deacon in the bishopric of Mórfou, a candidate for the office of bishop, who took the precepts of the New Testament at face value: succouring the poor and conducting baptisms and weddings free of charge. Bishop Khyrsostomos of Trimithi (Nicosia) and all Cyprus, apparently fearing depletion of the church's coffers, presided over a framing campaign whereby provocateurs tried to implicate the deacon in acts of buggery by throwing condoms into his cesspit, to be conveniently produced as evidence later (unfortunately they neglected to open the packets). When two essential "witnesses" fled abroad, the case was dropped, but the poor man had to retract his candidacy.

The former, mid-1990s **Bishop of Limassol, Khryssanthos**, was amongst the most hypocritical in the upper echelons of the church. He kept an American mistress and borrowed money from various sources to play the Nicosia stock market, and lost the bundle. His creditors blew the whistle, the fraud squad even flew out from Britain to interview him, and criminal proceedings against him were considered; he was defrocked, briefly banned from officiating at any service and made to do austere penances before leaving for America.

Khryssanthos had been instrumental in re-establishing at least two **convents** around Limassol; there are ten functioning convents on the island at present, up from just one in Makarios's time. In the current climate of the Church's disgrace, formerly murmured cynical sentiments are now openly voiced, to the effect that the convents exist partly to satisfy the "urges" of ecclesiastical higher-ups, who can't be seen to be visiting the traditional red-light districts or the modern "night clubs" which have replaced them. Assuming, of course, that the majority of the nominally celibate clergy are straight, which seems to be a moot point in Cyprus.

The **Limassol bishop** since 1999, **Athanasios**, is apparently a completely differ-ent sort from his predecessor, taking his pastoral mission seriously – and would be a strong candidate in an un-influenced election to succeed the namesake archbishop in Nicosia. Bishop Khrysostomos of Páfos, sensing his pre-eminent position was threatened, attempted during 2000 to repeat the dispatch of the unfortunate Mórfou deacon by accusing the new bishop of homosexual acts. Two archimandrites or senior priests, Andreas Konstantinides and Khrysostomos Argyrides, and two lay witnesses, Kostas Savva and Manolis Georgiou, duly came

hurt tourism) and the threat of further skirmishes to recede – but not before two Turkish-Cypriot soldiers had been shot, possibly in revenge, by persons unknown firing from the "Five Mile Crossing" of the Dhekélia SBA.

Denktaş broke off further official contact with his interlocutor Clerides in 1997, while Clinton's would-be envoy Robert Holbrooke opined that "this island is capable of exploding at any moment." In May 1998, the TRNC negotiating

forward to give evidence; a three-member **ecclesiastical tribunal**, split between the old guard and a reformer, failed to reach a necessarily unanimous verdict, but the two veterans refused thereafter to co-officiate with Athanasios. The Church was forced to call in bishops from abroad for a full, thirteen-member **synod** (the island can only muster nine), which found the Bishop of Limassol innocent as charged within a day in November.

A resourceful journalist then obtained phone records showing Savva and Georgiou to have been coached by the Bishop of Páfos and his crony, the Bishop of Arsinoë (Pólis), and the two civilians were prosecuted and jailed for conspiracy for three months in January 2001. Khrysostomos's reputation, already poor, lay in tatters; for a while it looked like he would face a **criminal court case**, but in the end only the two archimandrites were charged with conspiracy to defame and went to trial – which was mysteriously suspended in early April 2001 by Attorney General Alekos Markides after Athanasios, acting as a prosecution witness, publicly forgave the two conspirators in court. Cyprus at large was less indulgent; the already compromised Church, despite the mysterious halt in proceedings, had its dirty linen thoroughly washed in public, and its credibility lay at an all-time low. The main response, post-2001, has been a massive **recruitment** drive for monks and nuns in schools, an acceleration in the **reoccupation** of empty or derelict monasteries, and their ostentatious signposting despite a resounding lack of intrinsic interest.

Monastic premises are just a fraction of the huge amount of **property** owned by the Church, which it collects rents on, or sells outright as building sites, for everything from most foreign embassies to many coastal hotels. Increasingly murmurs are heard that taxes ought to be paid on all this, and that the Autocephalous Church is hardly a "charitable", not-for-profit institution any longer. But AKEL, the Church's old enemy, was unable or unwilling to obtain any satisfaction on this in the 2001–2006 House of Representatives.

Since 2002, Archbishop Khrysostomos of Trimithi and all Cyprus has become senile and wheelchair-bound; his staff and family members set to work forging his signature and thus managed to embezzle hundreds of thousands of pounds of church funds before being detected (one committed suicide, others were jailed). It is clear that a **successor** will have to be chosen while the incumbent is still alive (a Cypriot first), at some point after June 2005. By tradition, this ought to be the most senior from among the bishops of Kyrenia, Salamis, Mórfou, Arsinoë, Trimithi, Limassol, Kition and Páfos – who at present is the odious Bishop of Páfos, Khrysostomos. But in Cyprus bishops and archbishops are elected by a broad-based council of laymen and clerics, and the support of a civilian political party is essential. A very dark-horse candidate is the young **Bishop of Mórfou Neophytos**, who has distinguished himself from his fellows through his support for communal reconciliation and by remaining free from scandal. He braved strong political opposition in his long, ultimately successful campaign to have Áyios Mámas in Mórfou reopened for worship in September 2004, and in this he had the overwhelming support of his parishioners (and northern Prime Minister Talat, who attended the reconsecration). But precisely because of his humaneness and refusal to kowtow to political orthodoxy, his chances of being selected the next head of the Church must be rated as slim.

position in meetings with Holbrooke **hardened** still further; Denktaş declared dead the notion of two federated zones under one government, demanded international recognition of the North as a separate and equal state, with himself as official head of the same, prior to any further discussions with the South.

Alarmist scenarios of renewed, large-scale fighting on Cyprus were heard, given how each side was busily **stockpiling heavy weapons**: the Greek

Cypriots supplied by France, Greece, the Czech Republic and Russia, the Turkish Cypriots (of course) by Turkey. Although the South still commanded appreciable international sympathy and has tallied an impressive number of UN resolutions in its favour, they would still have come off worse in world opinion – not to mention militarily, outnumbered three to one in manpower – if they used this arms build-up to force the Turkish army off the island. The absence (except for August 1996) of overt clashes since 1974 should not, as the North's backers often do, be mistaken for true peace. Cyprus overall remains one of the most **militarized** territories on earth; it's calculated that there are nearly 90,000 men under arms on all sides (including UN and British personnel), versus about 250,000 civilian males of fighting age.

Amidst the resurgent jingoism in the South, a hard-learned lesson of 1974 was in danger of being forgotten: that Cyprus is essentially indefensible from Greece, despite a much-vaunted defence pact with Greece in effect since 1993, involving regular joint exercises with the Greek navy and air force. Without a significant air force of its own, the only offensive strategy for the South entails having permanent, Greek-equipped **air bases** on its territory – an option which continues to preoccupy the Turks as it did during the 1960s. Accordingly, a Greek air-force base for F-16 fighters has indeed been built right next to the Páfos civilian airport, but it's hardly impregnable and considered locally as something of a joke.

If the Páfos air base caused the Turks to at least pay attention, it was nothing compared to the disquiet provoked all around by the South's proposed 1997 purchase of sophisticated **Russian SS-300 surface-to-air missiles**. This highly mobile, truck-loaded defensive weapon, together with its state-of-the-art "Tombstone" radar guidance system, was publicly pooh-poohed by NATO members but privately admitted to be more effective than the Patriots used during the Gulf War. The integrated **radar system**, staffed partly by Russians and to be installed on Mount Olympus near the British site, would also be able to monitor NATO aircraft movements throughout the Middle East, not just Cyprus. From the moment the scheme was announced, Turkey threatened to use any means necessary – including intercepting the missiles while they sailed through the Bosporus Straits, or bombing them once delivered – to prevent installation. Apparently they had a healthier respect for the SS-300's potential to upset the local strategic balance than other NATO countries; the missiles were primarily intended to target not fighters but C-series transport planes full of Turkish paratroopers to be dropped on the South, a recurring nightmare scenario for the Greek-Cypriot command.

Throughout 1997 and 1998 considerable diplomatic pressure was brought to bear on President Clerides by the US, UK and others to **cancel** their deployment, while the cash-strapped Russians insisted that the deal was done and that somebody was going to have to cough up the purchase price. Finally, in late December 1998, Clerides knuckled under and announced that, after consultations with Greece, the missiles would be stationed on Crete instead, which only partly mollified the Turks. Although Clerides' spin doctors tried to cast this humiliating climbdown as a generous concession towards reducing tensions, the domestic uproar was such that EDEK withdrew its two ministers from the governing coalition in January 1999. In retrospect it seems that the threatened missile purchase was a clumsily handled bargaining chip, to be abandoned as a "concession" once international attention was again focused on the island; if the Southerners had really been serious about acquiring it as both a defence system and a negotiating tactic, they would have installed it secretly with no fanfare, presenting it to the world as an accomplished fact.

# 2000–2003: the North's economic and political meltdown

Matters might have continued indefinitely stalled in this way if domestic unrest in the North, coupled with the virtual collapse of the Turkish economy, hadn't reignited interest in an equitable settlement, not least among the Northern population.

On July 8, 2000, **Şener Levent**, editor of **Avrupa** (Europe), one of the few genuine opposition newspapers in the North, was detained, along with three of his staff, on charges of spying for the South and "instigating hatred against the Turkish Republic of North Cyprus and the Turkish army", facing potential penalties of five years in jail. Their release ten days later, following local and international pressure, was the occasion for opposition demonstrations 10,000 strong; on July 24, more street rallies protesting against the ongoing economic stagnation and the first in a wave of bank failures turned violent, with the arrests of organizers. Judicial harassment of *Avrupa* continued through the year, with contributing journalists (and politicians) Özker Özgür and İzzet Izcan hauled into court for sedition, and lawsuits by the Denktaş family for libel. On November 27 the premises of *Avrupa* were firebombed (an "electrical fault" was officially announced), on May 24, 2001 the printworks used by *Avrupa* were bombed, and by mid-December 2001 *Avrupa* had been closed down and its plant confiscated in lieu of civil damages to the victorious Denktaş. Levent managed to reopen the paper in early 2002, rechristened *Afrika* in line with his assessment of the Zimbabwe-type of public culture prevailing in the North, but also ended up serving a few months in jail after a fresh prosecution in August 2002. By late 2003, journalists at normally tame *Ortam* and *Kıbrıs* were also being hauled into court for stories deemed insulting by the powers that were.

Throughout this time, a free press was not always foremost in the minds of most Turkish Cypriots. The implosion of the mainland Turkish banking system during early 2001 took with it most North Cypriot **banks**; by the end of the year seven island-based financial institutions had failed outright, to the tune of $200 million worth of uninsured deposits. Unlike in Turkey, there were no bailouts whatsoever, and most of the rest were kept going on artificial life-support, existing primarily to launder money and hand out unsecured loans. Only those existing prior to 1974, such as the Vakıflar Bankası, and insured mainland-based banks like İşbank and Demirbank (part-owned by HSBC) survived. Observers were treated to the unedifying spectacle of ever-increasing destitution juxtaposed with an ever-growing range of consumer durables on sale to a tiny elite of UBP/DP-connected apparatchiks that could still afford them.

The mainland Turkish intervention, and its three-decade aftermath, was increasingly seen as a classic example of "Be careful what you wish for". Though unanimously acclaimed by Turkish Cypriots at the time, a growing proportion of Northerners deemed the mainlanders to have long outstayed their welcome, and to have become new, onerous masters replacing the Greek Cypriots. By paying to keep the North afloat, including directly employing an estimated 36,000, Turkey expected to call all the shots locally, down to the last detail. Long-simmering resentment of Turkish tutelage finally boiled over early in 2001, when, in response to an announced $350 million "aid" package from the mainland, the teachers' union took out a newspaper advert basically telling them what they could do with the money. For their troubles the union offices were raided, a court case instituted, and over the next year or so various individual instructors were sacked from their jobs for similar public statements. Despite this intimidation, they and several other unions, NGOs and opposition parties went on to form the Group of 41 by mid-summer, under the slogan "This Country is Ours", which would become the 92-member "**Common Vision**" within a year and be critical in coordinating street demonstrations over the next twenty months.

The ruling elite was not slow in reacting; the **UHH** (*Ulusal Halk Hareket* or National Patriotic Movement), seen by most as the reincarnation of TMT, was formed in May, and promptly took the lead in stepping up existing intimidation of anyone wishing to cross into the South, especially to attend communal reconciliation events in the buffer zone, at Pýla village or the Ledra Palace.

Most ominously from the Turkish nationalists' point of view, during 2001 there was sharp rise in the number of Turkish-Cypriot applications for **passports** issued by the **internationally recognized** Southern republic. Already, since the early 1990s, there had been an estimated four thousand northerners holding Republic of Cyprus passports, these individuals periodically subject to threats of prosecution from the TRNC authorities. By the end of 2003, the figure was 20,000 RoC passport-holders in the North, and growing. Essentially, obtaining such a document was a hedge against there being no settlement in the foreseeable future; should the South alone join the EU (as eventually happened), Turkish Cypriots counted among its citizens would be free to seek better lives either in the South or in western Europe. As the GDR's experience of its citizens fleeing to the West via Hungary in 1989 demonstrates, when a regime starts haemorrhaging its most talented and intrepid folk, its days are numbered.

To all this agitation, Rauf Denktaş had only the following retort: "Those who are against Turkey are wrong. There is no Cypriot culture, apart from our national custom of drinking brandy. There are Turks of Cyprus and Greeks of Cyprus. The only true Cypriots are its donkeys." The last sentence, unrecorded in the international media, was a calculated jibe at anyone advocating an island-based patriotism; in both Greek and Turkish, "donkey" (and additionally in Turkish, "son of a donkey") are exceptionally abusive insults.

Perhaps it was Denktaş's desire to go down in history as a great statesman; or pressure from Turkish businessmen feeling that the Cypriot tail had wagged the Anatolian dog long enough, and that their interests were being hurt; or maybe it was the IMF implying that bail-out aid to the prostrate Turkish economy would be more generous if Cyprus was sorted; or perhaps the looming June 2002 EU decision on Cypriot membership concentrated minds. In any event something – probably not Northern public opinion – prompted Denktaş to **renew communication** with Clerides after a four-year gap, under the aegis of new UN Special Cyprus Adviser Alvaro de Soto. On December 6, 2001 Clerides responded to an invitation from Denktaş to attend dinner in North Nicosia, the first visit by a Greek-Cypriot leader to the Turkish-Cypriot zone since 1974. After a reciprocal visit by Denktaş to the South on December 29, the two men – who had known each other since acting as prosecutor and defence respectively for EOKA suspects being tried in a colonial Crown Court during the 1950s – agreed to meet regularly from mid-January onwards to hammer out a solution.

Against a backdrop of continued harassment and prosecution of opposition figures in the North, **six rounds** of high-level talks occurred in Nicosia between January and September, but by October Denktaş was too ill with incipient heart failure to continue. Based on the talks to date, UN Secretary General Kofi Annan presented what became known as the first **Annan Plan** for a federal solution in mid-November. Turkish Cypriot opposition groups seized the initiative and organized **massive rallies**, sometimes comprising over half the adult population of the North, in central Nicosia every month from November until February, demanding a federal settlement and EU membership for the entire island. In February 2003, Clerides unexpectedly lost the southern **presidential elections** to the more hard-line DIKO chief Tassos Papadopoulos, and many observers rated the prospects of success in negotiations as slimmer than ever. In March 2003 Denktaş rejected the third version of the Annan Plan, earning himself yet another censure from the Security Council.

# Good Wednesday: the barriers come down

Denktaş's (indirect) response was another bolt from the blue – the announcement, on April 23 of Orthodox Holy Week, a date subsequently dubbed "**Good Wednesday**", of the **lifting of most restrictions on crossing the Green/ Attila Line** in either direction. Some speculated that Turkey had had a word in his ear; others that it was a safety valve for accumulated popular misery in the North, permitting routine shopping and employment in the South which had hitherto been done clandestinely – and a bonanza for northern tourist enterprises who suddenly found themselves with masses of new, Greek-Cypriot customers. Four official "border" points opened immediately, and thousands of islanders began crossing back and forth, with moving reunions a-plenty, visits to home villages, churches and mosques, and a general euphoria and conviction that "people power" had left the politicians far behind. By late 2003, well over half of each community had been to the "other" side at least once, with almost none of the violence or ugly incidents promised (or threatened) by ultra-nationalists in each camp. It was no longer necessary to attend organized bicommunal events in the buffer zone designed to show young Cypriots especially that they had more in common than they did differences.

The South, initially caught completely on the hop by Denktaş's sudden move, eventually reciprocated with a number of measures designed to facilitate trade and communications between the two parts of the island, and made it much easier for Turkish Cypriots to join professional organizations and get official paperwork done in the South. Both southern and northern bureaucrats and private outfits benefited handsomely by selling largely useless vehicle insurance to all parties crossing the line in either direction. Turkey responded by allowing Greek Cypriots to visit that country for the first time in 29 years, though official Turkish recognition of the South was (and still is) not yet on the table.

Closer to home, Greek-Cypriots resented the necessity of showing passports (a requirement later reduced to ID cards) at the barriers to travel as tourists into what they felt was their own country, and this prevented numbers from crossing the Line on principle. Among the others, some refused to spend a cent in the North, picnicking instead at the roadside; others ostentatiously made a point of patronizing only Turkish-, Maronite- or Greek-Cypriot businesses, whilst snubbing settler-run enterprises. Over the course of 2003 and 2004, the North became well established as the Las Vegas-style "**sin-bin**" for Greek

Cypriots, where they go in their off-hours for anything – hookers, casinos, wild mushrooms or asparagus, pickled songbirds, oriental sweetmeats – that's cheaper, better or more legal than at "home".

Less frivolously, the cracking of the walls awoke the North from its long developmental sleep. Sensing that a definitive settlement might come sooner rather than later, and resolved to create facts on the ground, contractors commenced a **building boom** (see p.57) which shows little sign of abating, disfiguring much of the north coast and promising to reduce the aesthetic and ecological differences between North and South to nil.

# 2003–2004: the end of Annan, the start of EU membership

(see p.57)

Negotiations for the **accession of Cyprus to the European Union** (EU) proceeded in parallel with the UN-sponsored peace-settlement talks throughout 2002 and the first third of 2003. As part of the South's incremental disengagement from excessive reliance on the UN to broker a settlement, membership of the EU had been vigorously pursued since the early 1990s as a way of forcing the issue: Europeanization versus Makarios's old strategy of internationalization. Turkey would thus legally be put in the position of occupying the territory of an EU member state, and denying universally accepted, pan-European rights of residence and commerce to its former Greek-Cypriot inhabitants. After considerable misgivings about inheriting an unsolved communal conflict, and the degree of penetration of both southern and northern economies by organized crime and money-laundering, the EU gave "Cyprus" a clean bill of health – and made it clear that, were there no final solution by May 1, 2004, the South alone would join along with nine other members. Although this was intended as a warning to the Euro-phobe TRNC (who declined to send any official delegation to Brussels to participate in accession negotiations, leaving it to opposition politicians and NGOs to talk to EU and mainland Greek officials), it actually had the effect of removing most incentives for the South to proceed meaningfully towards reunification.

**EU membership**, confirmed by the Treaty of Accession of April 16, 2003, promises to have profound, perhaps unintended, consequences. As elsewhere, thousands of resident foreigners would get voting rights in municipal and Euro-MP elections, conceivably in numbers sufficient to decide habitually close polls, a tricky possibility on an island with a history of being bullied by powerful outsiders. This supposed catalyst to a federal solution still risks backfiring badly, as accession of the South alone will just consolidate the island's partition, with or without Turkey actually acting on its periodic threat to **annex the North** outright if any part of Cyprus got into the EU, and Turkey didn't. In practice this is now far less likely to happen since Turkey itself got a date to begin accession negotiations in December 2004; besides the tremendous international opprobrium which would result from formal annexation, Turkey would find its own entry negotiations abruptly halted. Before December 2004, the Turks viewed EU membership, for either the South alone or the entire island, as backdoor *énosis*, since Greece is a member and Turkey for the immediate future will not be. Turkish partisans claimed that the Treaty of Guarantee forbade Cyprus joining the EU unless Greece and Turkey were both also members; in fact the clause in question was so vague as to defy strict application, and was clearly meant for Cold War conditions (to keep Cyprus and its surveillance facilities from "defecting" to the Soviet bloc).

By March 31, 2004, the **Annan Plan** had been through five versions, most of the successive changes designed to accommodate Turkish (and Denktaş's) objections. Versions three and above contained the interesting provision, never before featured in UN-sponsored plans, for Britain to cede half its SBA territory to any future federal republic (90 percent of this, however, to the Greek-Cypriot entity). Other territorial adjustments (amounting to 8 percent of the island's area) were roughly as expected, with land – including Varósha, most of the Mórfou plain and large numbers of formerly Greek Cypriot villages on the Mesaória – returned to the South over a three-year period along a curiously shaped border allowing up to 100,000 refugees to go home. However the rest of the complex document, running to over a thousand pages, had little appeal to most Greek Cypriots, merely repeating many of the mistakes of the ill-fated 1960 Constitution and adding some new ones (see overpage) which were manifestly contrary to the principles of both the UN and EU.

The UN compounded its errors by scheduling the **referendum on April 24, 2004**, just a week before EU accession, in the hope that a unified island would be able to join. Even given that various versions had been under serious discussion since October 2003, it was a hopelessly abbreviated campaign time to explain such a complex settlement, and frankly neither government on the island seemed to have much interest in doing so. "NO" forces in the South quickly mobilized their Black Arts Departments. President Papadopoulos made an impassioned three-hour address on April 7 condemning the Plan, which caught EU and UN negotiators off-guard. "YES" advocates, including UN envoy Alvaro de Soto, were intimidated, accused of being *Tourkófili* (Turk-lovers) and denied access to government media and private advertising, which were both put at the full disposal of the anti-Plan forces. Bishop Pavlos of Kyrenia threatened parishioners who voted "yes" with eternal damnation, while a fellow bishop stocked his fridge with champagne for a bash with his old EOKA mates in the likely event of the Plan's defeat. The only politicians of any stature to defend it were DISY and ex-presidents Clerides and Vassiliou, and the only major newspaper to do so was *Politis*. International figures were resigned to defeat in the South, but hoped that the margin would be narrow enough so that the referendum could be resubmitted to the electorate, after minor tinkering, later the same year. When AKEL – commanding nearly one-third of voters – withdrew its support on April 21, after having failed to get the poll delayed, the Annan Plan was doomed to a **crushing defeat**. On the day, Greek Cypriots voted against it by a margin of 3:1, while Turkish Cypriots (along with a large number of "naturalized" settlers) defied Denktaş and Turkish nationalist rent-a-mobs by favouring it by 2:1, but to no avail as both communities had to vote "yes". Turnout was nearly identical on both sides (87–88 percent), so the UN and EU couldn't say the poll was unrepresentative.

The **recriminations and post-mortems** began immediately. EU Enlargement Commissioner Gunter Verheugen accused President Papadopoulos of betrayal in so many words by pretending to accept the Annan Plan in principle but actively campaigning against it. Verheugen and others warned that the Turkish Cypriots would be substantially rewarded for their "yes" stance by direct "convergence" aid (259 million euros) to the North – not yet delivered as of writing – and the possibility of the end of its international embargo, leading to a sort of Taiwan status for the mini-state. South Cyprus alone entered the EU and went straight to the doghouse, whilst Turkey basked in the unaccustomed role of UN poster-child for its quiet support of the plan. UN Secretary General

Annan expressed his regret for the lost opportunity missed, made it clear that no other "alternative" plan was available, and essentially washed his hands of the island until Papadopoulos and Co. might have a change of heart. British special envoy Lord Hannay warned the same bunch that they "were doomed to frustration if they think the European Union will deliver things [ie a better deal] that it hasn't been possible to get from any other international forum."

Despite the thuggish conduct of the "NO" camp, it was undisputable that there were serious problems with the Plan, which would have suggested a prudent wait for polling whilst revisions made the acceptance of a later version more likely. **Reasons for a negative vote** were almost as numerous as voters, but they tended to fall mainly into the categories of inadequate security guarantees, economic iniquities, and derogation from Europe-wide human rights norms, with reservations about the viability of the proposed federal state and the status of mainland Turkish settlers important secondary considerations.

Most ominously, the Annan Plan required Cypriots to completely **disarm** themselves – including the painstakingly prepared air defence systems in the South – and accept an indefinite stationing of up to six thousand Greek and Turkish troops on the island. Turkey would have been largely responsible for air traffic control, and could exercise a veto on exploration for undersea oil in the Karamanian Straits (offshore oil-drilling rights was also suspected as a factor in the UK's retaining of some base territory). To succeed in the South, any new plan would have to provide for EU- or UN-staffed security forces. The Plan also in effect required the South to subsidize the **costs** of cleaning up the consequences of the 1974 intervention, a sum estimated at ten billion euros and, even allowing for some EU largesse, clearly beyond the capacity of the island's total economy (the North's is one-tenth the size of the South) now or in the foreseeable future. Neither Turkey, Greece, the UK or the US – all culpable to various degrees for the situation in Cyprus – were required to stump up any money to bring the North's infrastructure up to scratch, or to create a slush fund to compensate refugee property-owners who can't return home.

The Annan Plan foresaw the **limitation in population resettlement** in either direction to three percent annually of the total refugee population in either community, thus stringing out the process of theoretical resettlement for up to twenty years – something which sorely rankled on the Greek Cypriot side as a brazen opt-out from internationally accepted norms, but was expressly designed to prevent Turkish Cypriots who chose to stay in the North from being swamped. Although the Greek-Cypriots paid, and pay, full lip service to freedom of movement, in reality far more Turkish-Cypriots would have come south to reclaim now-hyper-valuable property than the reverse process. Thus the **potential of losing** what one had gradually accumulated over three decades loomed large. Tourism bigwigs in the South were not looking forward to a massive shift of clientele to the manifestly superior beaches of the North. Greek Cypriots who had been given, or squatted, abandoned Turkish Cypriot properties in the South faced the prospect of the original owners reclaiming them, with no compensation for any improvements made during the interim, and naturally voted "no". And as in the Turkish Cypriot community, there's a significant minority of ultra-nationalists – perhaps three percent – who simply don't like their opposite numbers and prefer to continue living separately.

The Plan also allowed 45,000 Turkish **settlers** to remain, to compensate for the approximately 40,000 native Turkish Cypriots who have left the island since 1974; Greek-Cypriot maximalists want most or all settlers to leave, but the North admits that it "naturalized" 64,000 settlers up to 2003, who were entitled to vote in the 2004 referendum. An accurate, island-wide **census** should have been conducted before the poll, and will be mandatory before any new attempt. **Cross-voting**, whereby critical office-holders in the mooted federal republic would have to receive a majority of votes from both ethnic communities, was expressly ruled out by Denktaş during negotiations, so the civic arrangements of the Plan merely guaranteed a reprise of the disruptive tribalism of the 1960 Constitution.

# Life after Annan: prospects for a settlement

Despite the April 2004 fiasco, everyone involved privately admits that a settlement to the longest-running international crisis (aside from Kashmir) is inevitable, and that it will, in general outlines, resemble the Annan Plan (and indeed every UN plan presented since 1992). This means a "**United Cyprus Republic**" comprised of two federal units, like the *autonomías* of Spain or the constituent republics of ex-Yugoslavia, with a single international personality and EU membership throughout. Border adjustments will closely resemble that of Annan, as this was one aspect about which few substantive complaints were heard. There will be a rotating presidency with a presidential council (cabinet) proportional to the population of both states, and a two-chamber parliament, with the upper house weighted towards the Turkish-Cypriot component state. A Supreme Court would be ethnically balanced, with three foreign judges casting tie-breaking votes as necessary. Ercan Airport on the federal border would be legitimized and upgraded as Nicosia's designated airport, with separate access to North and South (the way Geneva has French and Swiss exits).

The devil, as ever, is in the details, specifically concerning **property rights**. To outside observers it might seem that the Greek Cypriots especially were overly fixated on the economic and real-estate aspects of the problem and paid little heed to its civic aspects, but Cyprus is traditionally an agrarian culture, to which land is central. That said, surprisingly few refugees – except for those from Mórfou, Varósha, Larnaca and Limassol – would return to pre-1974 rural properties, even for use as a weekend home; life has changed too much in three decades, with a taste for the comforts of the bright lights. (As a counter to this increased urbanization, it would be useful for any eventual settlement to provide for the establishment of **national parks** in Akámas and Karpaz – one for each federal unit – as some token atonement for the rape of the Cypriot coasts.)

What refugees want at a bare minimum, however, is clear title to their original properties and the right, if not to occupy them, to sell them to whomever at going rates. In the past, cynics (including, most prominently, Denktaş) have argued that there would be no need or even impetus for a federal settlement if a title swap were to be arranged, with all refugees laying de jure claim to what they occupied, or if all refugees were paid market-rate compensation for property they lost. But estimates differ wildly as to the value of **abandoned property** – certainly Turkish-Cypriot real estate in the South is vastly undervalued officially compared to Greek-Cypriot property in the North – and integral to any fresh settlement attempt is the establishment of just assessments and a corruption-free property board to oversee compensation, long-term leases, swaps and the like.

In the absence of an equitable legal framework for dealing with the property issue, both Greek and Turkish Cypriots have pursued property feuds with **court**

**litigation**, both Cypriot and European, or other legal maneouvres centred on said property. 1995, for example, saw Denktaş threaten to distribute full, rather than provisional, title deeds of Greek-Cypriot properties to Turkish Cypriots and Anatolian settlers, a ploy that figured largely in various governing-coalition collapses. In 1989, a refugee from Kyrenia, Titina Loizidou, took Turkey to the European Court of Justice, asserting that her human rights were being violated by her inability to return to her home, while a Turkish-Cypriot family from the South, long resident in the UK but retaining Cypriot citizenship, sued in Cyprus to regain possession of their land near Limassol, which had been used for building refugee housing after 1974. The European Court eventually found for Loizidou in July 1998, awarding her substantial damages – which Turkey finally grudgingly paid (amounting to $1.1million, with interest) in December 2003, with the proviso that no more embarrassing cases be heard in Strasbourg, but only on the island itself. The latest building boom on Greek-Cypriot land in the North will, in the absence of a prompt settlement, doubtless prompt a new wave of cases, both in Cyprus and in Strasbourg.

In terms of **freedom of movement**, there will have to remain some artificial "protection" (ie restrictions on Greek-Cypriot ownership and residence) of a Turkish-Cypriot state in the medium term, to protect against token representation and forced buyouts of Turkish-Cypriot businesses; the number of major tourist enterprises owned or managed by Turkish Cypriots before 1974, for example, could be counted on one hand, and it seems undeniable that they faced de facto discrimination in the unitary republic. It also seems that proposed delays in implementation of full freedom of movement for Greek Cypriots in the North were designed in part to allow for those personally involved in EOKA and EOKA-B atrocities to pass away – though since "Good Wednesday" such individuals have kept a low profile, in the North at least.

It is difficult to overestimate the degree of **bitterness** which used to divide Greek and Turkish Cypriots, and which persisted unabated until the millennium. It could be said that for Greek Cypriots, 1974 was the beginning of history – for which read invasion, dispossession and expulsion – with a curiously selective memory enveloping the preceding years, while for Turkish Cypriots, 1974 marked the end of history – which for them had meant attacks, enclaves and disenfranchisement. Memorials to those killed by whomever between 1954 and 1975 remain lovingly tended in every village of the island; a spate of grandiose, post-1994 monuments glorify EOKA as part of a generally intensified Hellenic climate in the South. Children of each community are still raised to believe that their opposite numbers come equipped with horns and a curly tail – this last the fault of truly objectionable history textbooks used in both the South and North which, as elsewhere in the Balkans and Middle East, do much to fuel ill-feeling. To its credit, the Annan Plan provided for establishing a mutually agreed version of the truth (ie rewriting chauvinist history books), complete with shared symbols and institutions, and hopefully this will apply in any final settlement.

Particularly since "Good Wednesday", this bitterness has been largely replaced by **hope and goodwill** at street level, though as subsequent events showed, these are not substitutes for the hard graft of making an improbably complex bicommunal state function without hiccups. Realistically, there's little chance of a workable political solution until both Denktaş and Papadopoulos have departed the scene. From the point of view of southern solution advocates, one must come within the lifetime of those who can remember what it was like to live on an undivided island. Those born since 1970 or so and have never known anything else, and those who were not displaced by the events of 1974 have become habituated to a truncated realm, and couldn't care less about a settlement unless it's really made attractive to them. In the North, the opposite applies; it's the under-40s who have been marching at anti-Denktaş and reconciliation rallies, whilst their elders who lived through the EOKA days are warier. If you ask older people who suffered pre-1974 at the hands of Greek-Cypriots if they hate them, you may be told, "I don't hate the Greeks any more. But I still don't trust them."

To which most Greek Cypriots would reply that they have no reason to trust (mainland) Turks, and that everyone will have to wait some more, feeling (in the words of one) like "they're sharing the island with a stillborn twin".

# The events of summer 1974: personal accounts

T he following three accounts are intended mainly to illustrate the personal impact of events during July and August 1974. Their authorship – a Turkish Cypriot, a Greek Cypriot and an American expatriate – in no way constitutes an endorsement of any position, nor do they imply that any group suffered more than another. More accounts for use in future editions are most welcome.

## Dana Davies's story

Dana Davies is the daughter of the late American ambassador to Cyprus, Rodger Paul Davies. She now lives in California.

I was a twenty-year-old sophomore at Mills College in Oakland, California, in March 1974 when I first learned that we would be moving to Cyprus; I was also attending a Middle Eastern history seminar at UC Berkeley, where by coincidence we were actually studying Cyprus. My father was considered an Arab specialist and had spent most of his 28-year foreign service career working in the Bureau of Near Eastern and South Asian Affairs, having been stationed in Saudi Arabia, Syria, Libya and Iraq. A Mediterranean island seemed spectacular by comparison, so when Dad asked me if I could take time off from school and serve as his hostess, I jumped at the chance. I returned to Washington, DC three weeks before our departure date to pack up twelve years of life there, and also to attend a day-long crash course on how to run an ambassadorial residence: how to set a table, how to plan a meal that would not offend any of the religious dietary restrictions I might encounter, the proper protocol for determining seating. Nothing, however, prepared me for what actually lay ahead.

By the time July 15 came, I had lived in Nicosia for just sixteen days. The summer stretched before me with promises of new friends, diplomatic functions and learning to speak Greek. All that changed at 8.30am that day, when dull thumps accompanied by firecracker-like pops roused me from sleep in the embassy residence. I wondered briefly if I was hearing gunfire from the Green Line; during the past two weeks we had heard several brief bursts. This cacophony, however, continued, and sounded much closer than downtown. I had just about convinced myself that the sounds were coming from a building under construction across the street when the phone rang. In short, gruff phrases Dad informed me that a coup was under way. I was to get my brother John and move quickly to the den, which was the only room with no windows facing the street, and wait for further instructions. He answered my pleas for more information with "We just don't know anything. I'll call when we do."

For the next several hours we were alone in that room with little contact with the outside world. The television was useless: loud military music played over a frozen image of the Cypriot flag, broadcast continuously. The BBC and British Armed Forces stations were equally frustrating; news of the coup had not reached the rest of the world, judging from continuous talk of dreary London fog and ongoing reports on the Watergate scandal. From now until our evacuation on July 22, I was able to leave the embassy compound only twice, so my understanding of events relied heavily on what Cypriot embassy employees, foreign service officers and Marine guards told me.

My initial worry was for our household staff. Andreas lived in a village south of Nicosia and drove into town every Monday morning, stopping downtown to do our shopping; I was certain he must be trapped by the fighting. We also had two housekeepers who lived in Nicosia, whom we imagined must be in some danger out on the streets. We called downstairs and were told that they hadn't heard from anyone who wasn't actually in the building before 8.30am. Shortly before noon Antoinette Varnava, a Maronite Cypriot from Kormakíti village who was an administrative assistant for the embassy, came upstairs to help us prepare a tray of sandwiches and fruit for embassy personnel on the floors below. John and I had been obediently avoiding windows all morning, but Toni – already one of our favourite people there – was determined to view the city from our living room, so of course we joined her. This was the largest room in the residence, running the full length of the building. From the waist up, three walls were actually windows, from which we could see most of Nicosia and the Pendadháktylos range to the north. To our horror, the eastern window revealed a mushroom cloud rising from the skeleton of the presidential palace's domed roof. [*NB Ms Davies, along with other observers, was mistaken; it was the archiepiskopal palace which had been attacked, Makarios was actually in the intact presidential palace.*] I heard Toni swallow a sob and followed her gaze to the archbishop's residence; its majestic arcade had jagged black bites in the stonework and we could see flames licking at the yellow-and-white masonry. "How could they!" she cried. "Not a man of the cloth! He didn't have a chance." I clumsily tried to comfort her: "But Toni, I thought you were a Maronite Christian, not Orthodox." "Orthodox, Maronite, it makes no difference. Even if one does not agree with the politics, it is not right to kill a man of the cloth!" Later that night, when we learned that Makarios had escaped to Páfos, even those embassy staff who had voiced opposition to some of his policies expressed relief that he had not been killed.

Later that afternoon both Andreas and our housekeeper Anna made it to the residence. Andreas had been taking his two children to summer school when he found himself trapped for hours in a road-block line near the presidential palace, watching pillars of smoke pour from the building. After settling his children in a small room off the kitchen, Andreas sprang into action, whipping up meals for the 45 employees and embassy dependants we would be feeding three times daily for the next week. Embassy officers defied the curfew to check on other Americans trapped across the city, taking the opportunity to accumulate cooked chickens from the Hilton, bread from a favourite restaurant and a freezer full of meat from one of their own houses, defrosting since the power had been cut. Nicos, another assistant, also managed to run regular errands; much to our alarm, he drove Dad out to Béllapais to meet with the UN forces commander – which let us know that most of the trouble was confined to the capital. They also managed to find an open market selling fish and fresh vegetables.

Our other housekeeper, Anna, lived close by and so was able to go home sooner than other employees; it wasn't until she returned to work on Thursday that we learned she hadn't seen her son, a young National Guardsman, since breakfast time on Monday morning. From her we had our first accounts of trucks full of bodies driving out of the city. Also trapped in the embassy on Monday were two men – one a Turkish Cypriot, the other a member of Makarios' palace guard – who often travelled with my father as bodyguards. As John and I brought food to the buffet table in the living room, we saw these two huddled together, talking in low tones about their families and events outside; only later did I understand that these men in particular would both have been in extreme danger had they left the embassy before Wednesday or Thursday and been caught by EOKA-B members.

Dad stood by his promise of keeping us informed on developments; shortly after lunch he rang and told me to turn on the television. The coup leaders were expected to make an announcement naming their leader and declaring the status of their military exercise. The onscreen visuals had not changed from the static flag, but the martial music was now punctuated every thirty seconds with a brusque announcement. Dad and two of his officers who spoke fluent Greek arrived shortly, and translated the announcement as a reiteration of one on the radio instructing the public to stand by for important information. It was nearly half an hour before the big announcement came, but during that time these three gave me a good outline of the morning's events, learned in turn from an American staff member who was still at home a few blocks from the palace when the coup erupted. He had a portable two-way radio, and despite repeated orders to take cover, had spent the morning on his apartment building roof, relaying detailed reports of the attack on the palace, thus giving the embassy much-needed information about possible open roadways and enabling foreign service officers to reach Americans and embassy dependants stranded elsewhere in the city.

As time wore on, conversation turned to jokes about the coup leaders, and their lack of forethought as to who would assume leadership; someone even wondered if they were trying to bribe someone to take the position, and who might actually become the interim head of state. Their jokes halted when the blaring music stopped and a new voice filled the room with angry sounds. All three men leaned towards the set, and I watched my father straining to catch the rapid words in his newest language. Periodically the Greek statements were punctuated with American curses; finally the broadcast ended, and the quiet was interrupted only by a groaned "Oh, God!" from within the room and sporadic sounds of fighting from outside. Once the men had collected themselves, they gave us a quick summary of the broadcast and let us know that Nikos Sampson – the designated leader – would never be acceptable to anyone concerned. Also mentioned for the first time was their fear that this would guarantee Turkish intervention.

As it soon became evident that the coup against Makarios was not going to finish swiftly or neatly, our residence became an extension of the embassy itself. A strong sense of solidarity developed among this community of people who had been virtual strangers a week before. Over our daily group meals for up to 45, we learned of life beyond our compound. Pairs of foreign service officers ventured in cars out into Nicosia and beyond, asking, pleading or even demanding at the various curfew checkpoints for permission to pass. They made the rounds of hotels to check on American citizens, called on the two Americans wounded during the second day of fighting, and moved their own family members to safer lodgings.

When Dad managed to get away from his downstairs office, he would settle into the study just off the living room, usually with two or three other officers, for informal discussions. He always invited me and my brother to join them, as part of a lifelong habit of discussing his work in front of us, tolerating our interruptions and always answering our questions. With constant talk about the shuttle diplomacy that American envoy Joseph Sisco undertook between Greece, Turkey and Great Britain during the week after the coup, it seemed natural for us to discuss possible American involvement in the current crisis. Dad said bluntly that, except for diplomatic efforts aimed at influencing these three guarantors of Cypriot independence, America had no legitimate role at present. From watching the actions of my father and others, I firmly believe that the US took what diplomatic measures possible to prevent a Turkish intervention during the week after the coup. Relations between the US and Turkey were at low ebb during summer 1974, owing partly to a Turkish decision to resume growing opium poppies, and in the waning days of America's involvement in Vietnam, there would have been little political support for military action on Cyprus to stop the Turks.

I remember clearing dishes from that study long after midnight on the morning of Friday, July 19. Dad and several others were loudly discussing the best possible wording for a radio announcement. Nicosia airport was scheduled to reopen at 6am for the first time that week, and they were desperately trying to phrase the message in such a way that would encourage American visitors to leave the island without creating panic, while simultaneously ensuring that any public utterance would not in any way influence – or be interpreted as influencing – Cypriot politics.

I don't think I fully understood the sensitive nature of diplomatic statements or gestures until a number of years later, when I read in Christopher Hitchen's *Cyprus* that "In Nicosia, Ambassador Rodger Davies received [coup participant] Dimis Dimitriou as 'Foreign Minister' – the only envoy to do so." I can't be sure if it was that same night or the preceding one, but it was during the only supper that Dad managed to have with John and me. We had just sat down when someone rang Dad from downstairs. I had never seen him so angry before; he was yelling at the person on the other end of the phone. Finally he calmed down and said he would go downstairs, but to have whomever was waiting to remain in the lobby, at the Marine guard's desk – he did not want him received in the office. The visitor standing at the front gate was Dimis Dimitriou, demanding to see the ambassador. Most of us at the table were acquainted with Dimitriou, whose brother was the Cypriot ambassador to Washington, and by showing up he had put all the foreign service officers present, including the deputy chief of mission, in a compromising position. Dimitriou had just been appointed foreign minister of the EOKA-B regime, which no country had recognized. After several minutes of discussion, Dad felt he had no choice but to go down to the lobby and speak to him as briefly and informally as possible, without inviting Dimitriou to official premises. Unfortunately his actions were misconstrued.

\*\*\*

I was not actually present on August 19, 1974, when at least two men fired into the embassy from the building site across the street, killing my father and our friend Toni Varnava, but I have had extensive interviews with those who were actually there, and possess photographs of the bullet holes. So it amazes me to still hear – from Glafkos Clerides, among others – the theory that their deaths were accidental, a result of random shots from the ground-level riot. The only two locations to be struck by gunfire were my father's second-floor office, and his third-floor bedroom, precisely where he would most likely have been. The one random aspect of the deed was that Ambassador Davies chose to step into the hallway and phone Clerides to demand protection as the fighting outside escalated; the fatal bullets passed through the thick wooden shutters and glass of the office window, cleared the official reception room, and out into the hallway. One struck my father in the heart, and shortly after another hit Toni in the head as she ran to his aid. The identity of the assassins is in fact known; one actually served time in prison for a token charge of illegal firearms possession, and is now a security guard at the main Cypriot race track near Nicosia.

# George Demetriades

George Demetriades, originally from the village of Skoúlli in Páfos district, was 18 and on holiday from the American Academy in Larnaca when the events of July 1974 took place. His father was for some time the personnel and payroll manager at the Límni mines, and worked with many Turkish Cypriots. George has his own restaurant at the Páfos-Yeroskípou municipal boundary, which he runs with his wife Lara. Some names have been changed in the account below to protect individuals now living in the North from possible reprisals, but the incidents described are all factual.

It is so difficult to begin, almost impossible in fact. Where does one start to tell about such catastrophic days on such a beautiful island? In my mind these events are still intensely vivid, like a movie. I have strenuously tried to write down my memories and not my thoughts or opinions. I have also refrained from being overtly political, but at the same time I am a Greek Cypriot who has been through these difficult times, so they are inextricably part of my life.

I had just returned to my village Skoúlli, in Paphos district, near Pólis on the north coast, for the summer holidays. My involvement in politics was not considered of any importance by my elders, since back then, 18-year-olds didn't have the vote, but I could understand a few things. I told my mother at the beginning of July that something bad was going to happen in Cyprus. Over the past year or so, EOKA-B had, with the full co-operation of the Greek junta, increasingly stepped up its activities. Makarios continually warned the Cypriot public about the coming dangers which, unfortunately, most Cypriots could not (or would not) see.

On Monday morning, July 15, the inevitable happened. The National Guard, under the command of mainland Greek officers and EOKA-B cadres, carried out a coup d'état. Their main target was Makarios, the lawfully elected president of Cyprus, but also the combined presidential palace and Archbishopric, plus the *efedhrikó*, a special auxiliary police force which Makarios had formed to combat EOKA-B. The first thing I heard on the CyBC [Cyprus Broadcasting Corporation] radio station, after my mother woke me up in panic with tears in her eyes, was that Makarios was dead. The CyBC was already in the coup-plotters' hands, and soon they had taken over the presidential palace, having overwhelmed the guards with tanks. By the evening of the 15th, the putschists had gained control of the whole of Cyprus, except for Paphos district. Paphos, overwhelmingly pro-Makarios (it was his birthplace), refused to surrender and continued resisting. I went down to the Pólis central police station in order to help. The station was in uproar, with some EOKA-B members from the area under arrest; others had managed to escape.

All of a sudden some people started shooting in the air, smiling and laughing – word had come through that Makarios was alive. He had managed to escape from Nicosia and was in the monastery of Kýkko, heading towards Paphos. An impromptu army was formed by policemen and civilian volunteers, in order to go to Nicosia via Limassol to help resist the coup. But in Limassol they were ambushed, with many wounded and some killed, and had to retreat. By then Makarios was in Ktima Paphos, at the Bishopric. His first act was to order everybody to put their guns down. He did not want bloodshed or worse, an all-out civil war; resistance meant casualties. The most important thing at the moment was that Paphos was still free, and it had a radio station operated by Nikos Nicolaides, which was powerful enough to be heard across much of the

Mediterranean. Makarios going on the air was the best evidence that he was still alive and well.

Eventually it was decided that to guarantee Makarios's safety, he had to leave the island. He was smuggled abroad through the Akrotiri Sovereign Base to continue the fight to restore the legal government of Cyprus. That happened unexpectedly quickly, not necessarily through Makarios's efforts, but rather as a result of Turkey's invasion on July 20.

I would like to backtrack a few days to say one or two things about the activities of EOKA-B and the mainland Greek officers. Paphos eventually surrendered, the legal government was formally dismissed, Nikos Sampson was appointed President of Cyprus, and a band of his adventurist cronies were installed in the various ministries. Sampson had begun his career during his twenties as a fighter in the original EOKA against the British; he was now the owner-publisher of the extremist *Makhi* and *Tharros* newspapers, and above all a fanatical supporter of *énosis* (union of Cyprus with mainland Greece), a utopian vision which has cost the island dearly in many ways.

Around my area EOKA-B was by now in full swing. They began going around arresting people and collecting all weapons from absolutely everybody. I remember seeing one of them with a Kalashnikov hanging on his shoulder, and one in his hands. They came to our house in the village, found one of my uncles there, and arrested him. I think it's important to stress here that at this point no hostilities were directed against the local Turkish Cypriots.

On July 20 Sampson's "reign" was rudely interrupted by the initial Turkish invasion, which took place around Kyrenia, a considerable distance from the Pólis area where I was living. I remember sitting under the shade of the mulberry tree in our yard with my parents, Uncle George and Aunt Christina, and my cousin Steve from Australia – he was visiting Cyprus in order to avoid being drafted and sent to Vietnam, though ironically here he was stuck in another war. We could hear the bombs, most probably rockets or napalm clusters. The sky had a very different colour during those days, which I can still visualize: sometimes grey, other times white, while at night it turned a golden crimson from the burning of the beautiful forests of the Pendadháktylos and Tillyrian mountain ranges. The CyBC was continually broadcasting war bulletins, most of them untrue as it turned out. In a few days the Turks had managed to establish a bridgehead between Kyrenia and Nicosia. During this same time most of the Turkish-Cypriot enclaves in the southern part of the island were compelled to surrender to the National Guard, after pitched battles and casualties on both sides. These enclaves served a purpose by tying down Greek-Cypriot forces, thus allowing the mainland Turkish army to get on with its job. To be frank, though, the battle for the enclaves was a sideshow, and didn't really influence the outcome. The bulk of the Greek-Cypriot forces were in a state of chaotic disorganization. Antonis, a reservist from my village, and a number of others had to return to Skoúlli having seen no action, because they were taken to the front at Kyrenia to fight without guns.

On July 21 or July 22, I'm not sure which day, I vividly remember an enormous black cloud forming slowly over the sea southwest of Paphos. From the explosion of shells in the air, I realised that a naval-air battle was raging. Later on I found out that Turkish jets had bombed some of their own ships and sunk one. An Israeli ship picked up quite a number of survivors, but a lot of sailors were killed.

On Tuesday July 23, Sampson was replaced by Glafkos Clerides, the legal successor to Makarios and still [at the time this account was written in December 2001] the current president of Cyprus. He resumed talks with Turkey in

Geneva and by month's end a ceasefire was established. A new round of August talks collapsed after a few days owing to Turkish intransigence; as the victors, they could dictate terms. On August 14 the mainland Turks resumed their self-described "peace operation". Everything went according to plan: having secured their bridgehead during the ceasefire, the few days after the 14th saw nearly forty percent of Cyprus fall into their hands, with the well-known consequences in refugees and fatalities. With the second-largest standing army in NATO after the US, it was like running over a mouse with a road roller.

Over the next seven months or so there was a population transfer, with scenes painful for me to remember. The Turkish Cypriots did not have an alternative to leaving, and it is true that some had to be forced into waiting lorries and buses bound for the North. One day during the transfer, a bus full of Turkish Cypriots going to the North from a nearby village stopped outside our house. Binaz stepped off it for a moment, put her arms around my mother and would not let go. In tears, she said "We do not have an alternative. We must go, but I hope we come back soon." Redif kissed my dad and said, "How can we leave our property, our house, the place we were born? We are being forced to move."

Another woman came to our house with two boxes containing glassware and a couple of cooking pots. She said to my mother, "Please take these. I do not want anybody else to have them." The articles are still in those boxes; my mother kept them for her. If this woman ever comes back, she will get them back. [She did in fact come back in 2003, but mainly to visit; she insisted George's mother keep the utensils.]

I believe that the Turkish Cypriots lost a lot as well, not just kitchenware, especially taking into consideration today's conditions in the northern part of the island. The number of native, resident Turkish Cypriots has diminished; where have they all gone? In spite of the increasing self-imposed isolation and numerous provocations by Denktaş, ordinary Turkish Cypriots and Greek Cypriots have kept in contact.

Based on my personal experience, I want to elaborate a bit on this central aspect of our pre-1974 life, the everyday relationship between Greek and Turkish Cypriots. One must remember that after late 1963, the Turkish Cypriot internal regime had prohibited commerce and indeed any kind of transaction with the Greek Cypriots, as a deliberately political ploy leading up to formal partition. But how can you stop personal exchanges between people who used to live next door to each other, ate together and worked together? The mining company that my dad used to work for had a mixed staff of just over three hundred people, one-third of them Turkish Cypriots. In 1965, my entire family was invited to a wedding in a Turkish village. It was already an enclave but we were allowed in; my father and the bridegroom Kâmil were very good friends. When that family came to say farewell to us in 1974 the atmosphere was as if we were attending a funeral.

My Uncle George's village house had been built by Turkish Cypriots. He had a bulldozer, and used to terrace fields and open farm tracks. Many Turkish Cypriots employed George for this kind of rural work. Jemal, from a nearby village, owed him C£125 for a job like that. Forty-eight hours before leaving for the North, Jemal came by with a giant load of wheat as payment. He too had tears in his eyes; he did not want to leave his home. Jemal could have gone off without paying, but he didn't. This was typical of the respect and friendship which existed between Turkish and Greek Cypriots. In and around Skoúlli at least, we lived in harmony in spite of the violence and political machinations elsewhere.

I would like to ask anyone who reads this memoir not to consider it a domestic political account – and to also bear in mind that it is very difficult to elaborate enough in a few paragraphs so as not to be misunderstood. We all agree that the Cyprus Question cannot be analysed in a few words; this complex issue involves a mountain of facts, centuries of history and many states with enormous political and financial interests. Of course there were Cypriot extremists on both sides who did a lot of damage, but the larger powers have the lion's share of the blame. They should start thinking about human factors as well – in this case the Cypriots, Turkish and Greek – and revise their policies which blight the lives of people in small nations.

# Küfi Birinci's story

Küfi Birinci, a businessman and former TKP politician in North Cyprus, was 16 at the time of the Turkish invasion of Cyprus. While he was experiencing the events described below, his future business partner and his twin brother both narrowly escaped death before an EOKA-B firing squad in their home village, only through the intervention of a widely respected Turkish-Cypriot policeman.

On the night of July 19, 1974, I heard on the BBC 7pm news that the Turkish fleet had "sailed towards an unknown destination". I didn't know exactly why, but this time I was sure that Turkey was really coming. Early next morning, my uncle came by, in a really excited state, and woke us up: "Wake up, they came!" I didn't even have to ask who "they" were. Within a few minutes we were all in the streets, singing and dancing, as we watched the Turkish parachutists landing on the fields of Hamitköy [Mándhres, a village just north of Nicosia]. It crossed nobody's mind that this was the start of a fierce war; we only came back to our senses after the shooting started, and our great joy gave way to panic as people started thinking about the safety of their loved ones. (I myself had no news of my twin brother, trapped in our home village of Áyios Nikólaos, until after August 1.)

Caught up in the general excitement, I was nearly half a mile from home when I decided to go back, but it was too late. A police Land Rover stopped next to me and a police sergeant told me to jump in; I replied that I had to go home, but he said that he knew better where I should be going. So we went around the streets of Turkish Nicosia, collecting some other young lads who were not old enough to fight, but suited for other services.

On the first day our job was easy; we filled potato-sacks with sand for use as cover for Turkish-Cypriot fighters against gunfire from the Greek-Cypriot National Guard. But on the second day we were taken to Tekke Bahçesi, site of a Turkish martyr's cemetery, given the necessary hand tools and ordered to start digging. There were about twelve of us, all teenagers except for one older, partly disabled man unfit for military service. Over the next two days and nights, we dug countless graves; we weren't given proper food, and had to sleep rough in the building site of what is now called the Vakıflar Çarşısı. There was another sergeant in charge of us, who was very rude and cruel; perhaps he felt he had to be like that in order to keep us under control.

On July 23, while we were having a bit of a rest at lunchtime, an open lorry pulled into the cemetery and turned around; with it came a horrible, unbearable stench. I could see that the back payload area was covered with a white sheet, now stained a dirty mud-and-blood colour. On top of the sheet was somebody we all easily recognized: Hami the sandwich-maker, who sold sandwiches next to the Zafer cinema. Sitting with his legs crossed, he had cigarettes in each hand, which he was chain-smoking, looking really nervous. When he jumped off the lorry and pulled the dirty sheet off, immediately a huge swarm of flies and a horrible smell spread around. I'd never smelt anything worse, anywhere, in my entire life, but the stink was nothing compared to the scene before my eyes. The lorry was full of dead soldiers who had been killed during the landing [near Kyrenia]; the driver used the lorry dumper to sling them off as if the corpses were sand or pebbles at a building site. The bodies were in an awful state: three days old, and all blown up like balloons in the July heat. Some of them were without heads, or sometimes the head was lying separate next to the body; others had hands missing, and some were badly burned.

Hami the sandwich man sat by the pile of corpses and started to take their boots off with a huge knife; since then I've never been able to buy a sandwich from him, imagining he still uses the same knife. According to Muslim belief, war martyrs (şehitler) go directly to heaven and so can be buried with their clothes on; however their shoes must be removed to make them more comfortable. After removing their boots, Hami checked the soldiers' pockets, collected their personal belongings and put them each in a nylon bag together with their künye [ID dogtag worn around the neck]. We just watched him, astonished, holding our breath; we couldn't breathe that stinking air anyway. Hami and everyone else who'd arrived with the lorry had cologne-drenched handkerchiefs to hold over their noses – we didn't. We just stood there terrified and shocked, not knowing what to do next; I was praying to God to get out of there, without knowing how I might do that. While we waited there with these feelings, the sergeant ordered us to go and bury the soldiers. He shouted at us but we still wouldn't move, so he came over and hit us one at a time. Those whom he hit snapped out of it and ran to bury the bodies. I thought to myself, "We'll have to do it anyway, better to do it before the bastard hits you," so I ran off to bury them before he got to me.

There was a hoca [Islamic prayer leader] present, reciting the necessary last rites for the dead soldiers and ensuring that they were buried in accordance with Islamic rules. My first body was the most difficult; I tried, together with another boy, to carry and bury it, but since we were both so disgusted, not wanting to touch the corpses, we couldn't get a proper grip. I was trying to grab him by the end of his trousers, while my companion was trying to hold the soldier by his shirtsleeves; it was a difficult task because the swollen body weighed much more that it would have when alive. We just managed to bring it to a ready-dug grave, and threw him inside. The hoca saw us and shouted angrily: "You must not *throw* him in, you must *put* him in gently." He then came and inspected the body in the grave and said: "You laid him out in the wrong direction. His head is not facing the kible [the direction of Mecca]. Jump in and do it right." So I had no choice but to jump into the grave and turn the corpse to the right orientation. Neither Turkish nor English is adequate to explain in words my feelings at that moment.

Lorries and transit vans arrived one after the other that day; the pile of dead bodies got bigger and bigger. We hadn't dug enough graves to bury them all, so on the advice of the hoca we started putting three corpses to a hole. Soon this wasn't enough either, so the hoca gave us permission to make it five in each grave. In the end I recall being allowed to bury them eight to a grave, and still we didn't have enough space to bury them all. We spent that night next to a pile of unburied corpses, plus those in the many open graves which we hadn't had time to cover with soil.

The next morning someone brought a bulldozer abandoned by the Greek Cypriots. We were very happy to see it, because we were really at our physical and psychological limits. The dozer made things much faster, and helped us finish the job – I would guess that by that second afternoon, we boys had buried almost 1500 corpses.

My grandmother had a house with one door opening onto this cemetery, and another looking towards Girne Caddesi [the main commercial street of north Nicosia]. I pointed out her house to the sergeant, and got permission to go and get a handkerchief for the smell; he gave me fifteen minutes' leave. So I entered my grandma's house through the back door, and immediately ran out the front door to my own house, which was about a mile away. When I got home, I went straight to our basement toilet, where I hid for 48 hours until I was convinced that the sergeant was not following me.

I write of this terrible experience to show everybody how war and nationalism are the worst enemy of mankind. Why do we Cypriots have to distinguish ourselves as Turkish or Greek? Cyprus our homeland has more than enough for both communities; all we have to do is recognize that it's our country and that we can share everything it offers us. We must stop running after other countries as our motherland; if we deny our real home in favour of other nations, then the day will come when we won't have a motherland of our own. Didn't the Turkish Cypriots already lose one part of it and the Greek Cypriots the other? If we don't come back to our senses, one day soon we will lose all of it.

# Wildlife

Cyprus's location has made it a "collecting basket" for wildlife from Asia Minor, Africa and the Mediterranean countries, and the island offers a rare chance to see plants and animals which could otherwise only be found by making separate journeys further afield.

Cyprus escaped the ravages of the Ice Ages, which wiped out so many species in northern Europe, so within its territory there's a staggering diversity of rock types and natural habitats. The island supports a varied **flora**, with some 1350 different species of flowering plants – comparable to the total number of wild species listed in Britain, but concentrated within an area about the size of Wales.

The current political division of Cyprus has parallels in the island's **geological history**. Until the Pleistocene period around one million years ago, the Tróödhos to the south and Kyrenia mountains to the north stood as the hearts of separate islands, with the primordial Athalas Sea in between. This became silted up to form the central plain (Mesaoría) at a time coinciding with the "dawn of man" and the most recent Ice Age in much of mainland Europe. Today, wherever winter streams cut through the plain, they expose fossil shells. from that era which look like scallops, mussels and oysters.

Long-term isolation from neighbouring land masses such as Turkey has meant that some plants have had time to evolve into **distinct species**; currently over ninety plants rank as endemics (species found only in Cyprus). To a lesser extent this is true for animals, and there are insects, birds and even races of shrews, rats and mice that the island can claim as its own. Even the separation of the southern and northern mountain ranges has been long enough for plants in the Tróödhos to have relatives in the Kyrenia hills which evolved separately from a common ancestor – for example, purple rock cress (*Arabis purpurea*) is abundant on volcanic rocks in the South, while the similar Cypriot rock cress (*Arabis cypria*) grows on the northern limestones.

Away from intensive cultivation and over-enthusiastic use of insecticides, the **insect fauna** is as diverse as the flora: butterflies, hawkmoths, beetles and mantids are abundant. The impact of **human activity** has changed Cyprus in the same way that much of the rest of the Mediterranean has been changed. Eratosthenes (275–195 BC) writes of a very different Cyprus where innumerable streams flowed year-round and even the Mesaoría was thickly forested. The Phoenicians and other traders up until the Venetians were attracted to the island by an abundance of timber suitable for ship-building; the destruction of the forests has contributed to drastic local climatic change since antiquity.

From the early days of British administration through to the present, forestry departments in Cyprus have been enlightened enough to manage and establish new forests throughout the island. Thus, about eighteen percent of Cyprus's territory is covered with "forest", although it's a much more open, park-like woodland than northern Europeans associate with the word. It is easy to remember only the negative side of human impact on the vegetation, but the commercial history of Cyprus has resulted in horticultural exotics such as the palms, agaves, cacti, mimosas, eucalyptus and citrus trees which are a familiar part of today's landscape. Even the olive (*Olea europaea*) originated in the Middle East, and today its range is taken to broadly define the limits of Mediterranean vegetation and climate in Europe.

**Birdlife** is diverse, especially in the mountains, and the island lies astride spring and autumn migration routes. Though having comparatively few

**mammals** (sixteen species, including eight kinds of bat), Cyprus has a surprising range of **reptiles and amphibians** – in spite of the age-old association of snakes with evil, which seems to require that every snake crossing a road be crushed by car tyres.

# When to come

To sample the wildlife at its most varied, the **hot summer** months should be avoided: the ground is baked in the lowlands, sensible life-forms are hidden well away from the sun, and there's no birdsong – though crickets and cicadas make up loudly for the absence. However, many native flowers persist in the mountains through June and July, bulbs start to flower with the first rains in October and November, anemones are in bloom by Christmas, while orchids appear in abundance in the lowlands from February (even December in some years) through to early April. **Springtime** sees the real explosion of colour on the plains and lower hills.

In the winter, **weather** is unpredictable: until late March, days can change quickly from pleasantly warm to cloudy and windy in the space of a few hours. In recent years, a serious shortage of winter rains has left water levels in mountain reservoirs way below what is needed to cope with the summer tourist influx, though since the millennium there have been torrential storms almost annually between November and March. By the end of April the plains are getting hot (summer temperatures in Nicosia reach 40°C and above, with a more tolerable 35°C or so on the coast). In May, June and again in late September and October the mountains are a delight for the walker: warm, sunny and not another soul for miles.

# Habitat types

Geographically, the island can be split into three broad regions: the **northern mountains**, which are mainly limestone; the **southern mountains** of igneous rocks which have erupted from deep in the earth through younger sedimentary rocks, leaving volcanic mountain heights with flanks of chalks and limestone; and the **central plain** of comparatively recent deposits with schists forming conical hills at its edges. This geological diversity creates added interest in the **four main habitat types**: coastal habitats, cultivated land, low hillsides less than 1000m and mountains above 1000m.

## Coastal habitats

**Coastal scenery** is varied. Some **flood plains**, such as those in the north around Güzelyurt (Mórfou) which continue along the coast to Cape Koruçam (Kormakíti), and those in the south stretching westwards from Limassol, are kept moist much of the year. Water reaches them from the mountains in seasonal streams, or from deep wells. This enables them to support vast citrus orchards and, more recently, avocado groves. Reedy river mouths are rare nowadays, since inland reservoirs hold back much of the winter rainfall, reducing some watercourses to little more than a trickle. The wide, stone-strewn bed of the Xerós stream between Páfos and Koúklia shows that river's former extent before the Asprókremos Dam was built.

Undeveloped **coastal wetlands** are found north of Famagusta, in pockets in the Güzelyurt and Pólis hinterland, and in a limited area east of Xylofágou, near Ayía Nápa. Little of the once-extensive marshland at Asómatos, north of the Akrotíri salt lake, remains untouched and what is left can be hard to find because of drainage for vast fruit orchards.

Most resorts boast so-called "beaches", but some are just shingle or dirt-grey sand and hardly deserve the status. Naturalists and connoisseurs should try the west coast from Coral Bay to Lára and beyond, which takes in some interesting fossil-rich chalk (shark's teeth and sea urchins), which the sea has eroded into a stark lunar landscape. Further to the northwest, there are small **sandy beaches** on the Akámas peninsula. In the north, excellent beaches run from Famagusta to İskele (Tríkomo) on the east coast and on the north coast to the east of Kyrenia and on the Karpaz (Kárpas) peninsula.

Much of the coastline, however, consists of **low cliffs** of clay or limestone with rocks plummeting down to the sea; high cliffs occur between Episkopí and Pétra toú Romioú. Coastal plantations of eucalyptus date from attempts to control mosquitoes by draining swamps; those of funeral cypress or Aleppo pine are more recent and form extensive **open woodlands** – near Hala Sultan Tekke and the Péyia forest, for example. These plantations provide essential shelter and are rapidly colonized by all sorts of insects, birds and plants (orchids in particular, though the latter take some years to actually flower).

## Cultivated land

Large areas of **cultivated land** are maintained clinically free of weeds and insect pests by drastic measures such as deep ploughing, insecticides and fertilizers. But smaller areas on the Mesaoría – orchards near villages, olive groves (even in Nicosia) and carob orchards – can be very colourful in the spring with numerous annuals. A direct consequence of the diverse plant life is a rich population of insects, lizards and occasional snakes; in the early morning orchards are also good places to wander with binoculars and see small migrant birds.

Numerous species of flowering plants thrive in badly tended mountain vineyards and even at the edges of well-tended ones. One family of plants, always well represented, is the *Leguminosae* (vetches and wild peas) – which also includes many commercially important food plants such as peas, chickpeas, beans of all types and lentils. In Cyprus, these crops often play host to another family of plants, the parasitic broomrapes (*Orobanchaceae*); when present in large numbers these are a highly damaging pest.

## Low hillsides

**Low hillsides** (slopes up to 1000m) occur over much of Cyprus away from the central and coastal plains. They take on a markedly different character according to whether the underlying soil is limestone (alkaline) or volcanic (neutral to slightly acidic). Over-grazing by **goats** is another factor affecting large areas of the island. These voracious animals leave pastures with few flowering plants other than the tall spikes of white asphodels, one of the surprisingly few plants they find distasteful in a diet which can include woody and spiny shrubs. Government policy in the North has allowed settlers from the Turkish mainland to bring in their flocks, so that meadows which a few years ago were ablaze with flowers now have the goat-grazed look of their southern counterparts.

In the Mediterranean region, low hills are extensively covered with a dense, low scrub composed of spiny, often aromatic shrubs. It forms a type of vegetation widely known as **garrigue** – in the Greek-speaking world it's called *frýgana* (often written *phrygana*), literally "toasted". Left to grow, it may well become maquis, with bushes and low trees a few metres high. The final, or "climax", stage is the evergreen forest which once covered the island. In general, garrigue and maquis often blend into one another on the same hillside.

On limestone or chalk, shrubby thymes, sages and a wickedly spined member of the rose family, *Sarcopoterium spinosum*, form an often impenetrable scrub. Numerous bulbous plants grow between and below the bushes, sheltered from the full glare of the sun and protected from all but the most determined goats. As you climb higher in the Tróödhos foothills the ground changes quite dramatically in nature from white chalks to a range of brown soils owing to underlying serpentines and pillow lavas, with noticeable shifts in vegetation accompanying the change in geology.

Whatever the underlying rock types, garrigue can slowly evolve into a dense **maquis** – look over any hillside covered in bushes and the range of shades of green will show the sheer variety of species. In a limited area you can find **lentisk** (*Pistacia lentiscus*), **terebinth** (*Pistacia terebinthus*), **storax** (*Styrax officinale*), **myrtle** (*Myrtus communis*), the red-barked **strawberry tree** (*Arbutus andrachne*) and several kinds of evergreen oaks, more like holly bushes than the stately oaks of Britain.

Many of the plants in the garrigue are **aromatic** and, on a warm day, their oils vaporize to scent the air. In spring, after a few days outdoors, you may well find yourself almost absent-mindedly picking a leaf and gently crushing it before smelling it. Anyone venturing off paths and brushing shrubs will find their clothing has taken on the scent of the island where tiny amounts of fragrant essences – thyme, oregano or lavender – have rubbed off. Some of the plant oils are highly volatile and, on a really hot day, have been known to ignite spontaneously: the origin of Moses' burning bush, perhaps.

**Aspect** – the direction a slope faces – can make a great difference in the vegetation present because it determines how much sun and, on higher hills, how much rain the land will get. In Cyprus, there is an obvious change when you cross either mountain range and leave behind the rich, almost lush vegetation of the north-facing slopes to find the dry southern slopes, with their xerophytic (drought-adapted) species clinging to life in the "rain shadow".

**Woodlands** on the northern limestone hills are largely composed of **funeral cypress** and **Calabrian pine** (*Pinus halepensis* ssp. *brutia)* grading into maquis, a pattern also repeated in the far west on the Akámas peninsula. In the Tróödhos, woodlands in the low and middle regions are mainly extensive open pine forest of two varieties, with less lofty specimens of **strawberry tree**: this wood has an attractive natural sheen and was traditionally used for making village chairs. Another characteristic small tree is the endemic evergreen **golden oak** (*Quercus alnifolia*) – the leaves have a leathery, dark-green upper surface but are golden-brown on the lower side. Beneath the trees, a dense **understorey** of assorted shrubs – cistus, lavender, thyme and honeysuckle – completes the picture.

## The High Tróödhos

The **High Tróödhos** – land over 1000m – is extensively forested and much reafforestation has been carried out using both native and introduced species. Lower woods of Calabrian pine yield to **black** or **Caramanian pine** (*Pinus nigra* var. *caramanica*) mixed with **stinking juniper** (*Juniperus foetidissima*) and,

near the summit of Khionístra, trees of both species appear gnarled as a consequence of their age, attained in a rigorous climate of long, dry summers and
cold, snowy winters. On Khionístra you will also see trees where the trunk
is violently twisted or split – the cause is lightning strikes which boil the sap
almost explosively to vapour. Under these tremendous pressures the trunks
split, but such incidents are seldom fatal to resilient trees and they continue to
grow, albeit with an unexpected change of direction. In open areas there are
low bushes of ankle-tearing **gorse** (*Genista fasselata*), a spiny **vetch** (*Astragalus
echinus*) and a **barberry** (*Berberis cretica*). The native **cedar** (*Cedrus libani* sp.
*brevifolia*) is being extensively propagated after becoming largely confined to
the so-called "Cedar Valley" in the course of the past century, especially after
destructive fire-bombing of the forests by the Turkish air force during the invasion of 1974.

# Flowers

Even though something, somewhere, is in bloom throughout the year, things
begin in earnest when the first rains of autumn relieve the summer drought and
moisten the hard-baked soil. It only seems to take a few drops percolating into
the parched soils of the plains to activate the bulbs of a tiny, light-blue **grape
hyacinth** known locally as "Baby's Breath" (*Muscari parviflorum*), or the delicate,
white **autumn narcissus** (*Narcissus serotinus*). In the mountains, under bushes
of golden oak, you can find the **Cyprus cyclamen** (*Cyclamen cyprium*), with
distinctive pink "teeth" to its otherwise white flowers. The flowering sequence
continues with **friar's cowl** (*Arisarum vulgare*), a curious candy-striped arum.
The first of the **crown anemones** (*Anemone coronaria*) appears at Christmas
time near the coast, followed by pink, then red varieties. Growing close by will
be the highly scented **polyanthus narcissus** (*Narcissus tazetta*) and the royal
purple stars of the **eastern sand crocus** (*Romulea tempskyana*).

Cyprus is justifiably famous among **orchid** enthusiasts for its unique assemblage of species – a good example of the "collecting basket" role mentioned
earlier. The first orchids to appear are the robust, metre-high spikes of the **giant
orchids** (*Barlia robertiana*). Look closely and you see flowers like tiny "Darth
Vader" figures and perhaps catch a hint of its iris-like scent. Already by late
December these orchids are blooming near Hala Sultan Tekke, close to Larnaca
airport, along with the fleshy-stemmed **fan-lipped orchid** (*Orchis collina*).
Come late February to early March the season is in full swing, with an abundance of bee orchids including the remarkable endemic **Cyprus bee orchid**
(*Ophrys kotschyi*), the pick of a fascinating bunch of insect mimics – this one
has a fat black and white lip forming the insect "body". It occurs in scattered
populations in the South near Larnaca, but is more common in the North.

In the **lowlands**, especially on the limestone soils of the northern slopes of
the Kyrenia mountains, the Akámas peninsula and the southern Tróödhos, the
early **spring wildflower** display is staggering, with a profusion of **turban
buttercups** (*Ranunculus asiaticus*) in white, yellow, various shades of pink, scarlet and even occasional bi-coloured forms. Less obvious to the eye, but equally
diverse in colour, are the small pea and vetch family members with over 170
species listed in the island's flora, many of them endemic to Cyprus. Two in
particular stand out: the **veined vetch** (*Onobrychis venosa*), with white flowers
and marbled leaves which spread over dry limestone, and the yellow-and-violet

crescent vetch (*Vicia lunata*) which flourishes on volcanic soils – around the church at Asínou, for example.

Snow melting on the heights of Tróödhos reawakens one of the island's three endemic species of **crocus**, the **Cyprus crocus** (*Crocus cyprius*), followed by a **pink corydalis** (*Corydalis rutifolia*), an endemic **golden drop** (*Onosma troodi*) and numerous other local flora from **dandelions** to the **garlics** and **dead-nettles**. Cyprus has two other species of crocus: the winter-flowering late crocus (*Crocus veneris*), especially frequent on the northern slopes of the Kyrenia range, and **Hartmann's crocus** (*Crocus hartmannianus*), usually encountered in early spring if you happen to be walking on peaks near Makherás.

By mid-March, many of the bulbous plants will already be dying back. The **annuals**, however, more than make up for the loss by providing sheets of colour, often created from surprisingly few species: scarlet **poppies**, the golden yellow of **crown marigolds** (*Chrysanthemum coronarium*), pink **Egyptian catchfly** (*Silene aegyptiaca*), perhaps tempered with white **camomile** (*Anthemis chia*). In the days before intensive cultivation and deep ploughing, **field gladiolus** (*Gladiolus italicus*) made corn fields magenta with its stately spikes, and people still talk of looking down on a Mesaoría scarlet with tulips. Today, in the South, **wild tulips** (*Tulipa agenensis*) still survive under fruit trees near Stroumbí, north of Páfos, but to see the endemic **Cyprus tulip** (*Tulipa cypria*), with its dark red, almost purple flowers, you either have to visit bean fields and orchards around Çamlıbel (Mýrtou) or chance upon it in the wilder parts of the Akámas peninsula.

Two **coastal displays** of wildflowers are not to be missed. First appearing in late January and February, the **Persian cyclamen** (*Cyclamen persicum*) cascades over rocks on the north slopes of the Kyrenia mountains. You will also find them forcing their way through cracks and crevices around the Tombs of the Kings in Páfos, but the most spectacular display is on the natural rockery of the Akámas peninsula where they grow in white, pink and magenta shades waiting to be photographed with an azure blue sea below. A couple of months later, towards the beginning of April, there's another display: the **three-leaved gladiolus** (*Gladiolus triphyllus*) with scented pink and white flowers, growing in countless thousands, virtually all around the coast of the island.

The unmistakable, two-metre-high stalks of the **giant fennel** (*Ferula communis*) with their umbrels of yellow blossoms are out in full force in March, but have largely disappeared by April. In legend, Prometheus concealed the fire he stole from the gods in one of these stalks; the slow-burning pith inside is still used as tinder, and the sturdy husks for making furniture.

In the **Tróödhos mountains** things are slower off the mark. As you travel north from the coast, however, two new orchids – the yellow **Roman orchid** (*Dactylorhiza romana*) and the pink **Anatolian orchid** (*Orchis anatolica* ssp. *troodi*) – become noticeable as soon as the soil changes from chalk to volcanic. From late May onwards, an unusual saprophytic orchid, the **violet limodore** (*Limodorum abortivum*), with purple stems and large purple flowers, is a common plant of the woodlands, usually growing beneath pines or close to them. It occurs in some abundance not far from Tróödhos resort itself, with three other orchid companions: **Cyprus helleborine** (*Epipactis troodi*), **Holmboe's butterfly orchid** (*Platanthera holmboei*) and **red helleborine** (*Cephalanthera rubra*).

When the plains are burnt dry, **pink oleander** (*Nerium oleander*) brings a welcome touch of colour to dried streambeds. It has been widely planted as a flowering "hedge", and at the right season you can travel the Nicosia–Tróödhos road flanked by the colourful flowers of these bushes. Few other flowering plant species now relieve the grey and brown shades of a dessicated landscape.

There are thistles – the **cardoon** (*Cynara cardunculus*), a wild artichoke growing several metres tall, is quite spectacular – and also a yellow dandelion relative forming sticky-leaved bushes, often covered in dust. This plant is one of those you see everywhere but rarely find in field guides: it's called **aromatic inula** (*Dittrichia viscosa*), and this is one of those cases where "aromatic" does not mean pleasantly so.

In the middle heights of the Tróödhos massif, where the road climbs up to Pródhromos, May is the time to see the white, lupin-like flowers of **Lusitanian milk vetch** (*Astragalus lusitanicus*), with **purple rock cress** (*Arabis purpurea*) in pink cushions hanging over rock faces above. Late in the day, shafts of sunlight on an open glade might illuminate scarlet **peonies** (*Paeonia mascula*), almost making the flowers glow. During April or May acres of **French lavender** (*Lavandula stoechas*) flower on the pillow lavas, the blossoms sticky to the touch, and whole hillsides can seem to be in bloom with one or another of the local **rock rose** varieties: white (*Cistus salvifolius* and *C. monspeliensis*), pale pink (*C. parviflorus*) and deep pink (*C. creticus*).

In only a few places in the Tróödhos does water run all the year round, but locate it and there, in early summer, you can find the rare **eastern marsh helleborine** (*Epipactis veratrifolia*), the **marsh orchid** (*Dactylorhiza iberica*) and an indigenous **butterwort** (*Pinguicula crystallina*), a plant that traps insects on its sticky leaves. By July, even plants in the mountains find it too hot, and only spiny things such as various gorses, brooms and barberry provide a bit of colour.

Surprisingly, it's only when the sand gets too hot to stand on during the day that delicate white **sea daffodils** (*Pancratium maritimum*) bloom: they were once so numerous on the east coast that they were called Famagusta lilies. Under these same "desert" conditions, in coastal and other lowlands all over the island, you find tall spikes of starry-white flowers emerging leafless straight out of hard-baked ground. These are **sea squills** (*Drimia maritima*) and are what becomes of the huge bulbs you might have wondered about, in spring, when you saw them half-pushed out of the ground, topped by long, strap-like, leathery leaves. The bulbs were once used as the source of both a rat poison and a cough remedy.

When little else is left in flower near the sea, you will find **carline thistles**, favourites of flower arrangers for their long-lasting flower heads. The tiny one with scarlet, daisy-like flowers found near Southern beaches is yet another Cypriot endemic – the **dwarf carline thistle** (*Carlina pygmaea*).

# Exotic and edible plants

**Introduced exotic plants**, noted in the introductory section, now play an important part in the island's **food production**. The climate has favoured the introduction of subtropical species which are now widely cultivated: **palms** (from North Africa, Asia and the Americas); **agave**, **avocado**, **prickly pear**, **tomatoes**, **potatoes**, **peppers** and **aubergine** (the Americas); **mimosa** and **eucalyptus** (Australasia); **citrus** (originating in Asia) and **pomegranate** (Iran). The British administration introduced flowering trees from other colonies which, in maturity, have become a colourful feature of the parks and gardens in towns and cities: **orchid tree** (*Bauhinia variegata*), **bougainvillea** (*Bougainvillea spectabilis*) and **silk oak** (*Grevillea robusta*).

Cypriots north and south of the Attila Line are essentially pragmatic people when it comes to natural resources, readily recognizing **edible "weeds"** while remaining indifferent to or disparaging of less "useful" plants. Even town-dwellers will head for the countryside in spring, perhaps to gather shoots of woody-stemmed *agrélia* (**wild asparagus** – *Asparagus acutifolius*) or of the **bladder campion** (*Silene vulgaris*), called *strouthkiá* – "little sparrows". Both are fried with eggs to make a kind of omelette. In much of the lowlands it's possible to ask for *spatziá* (pronounced "spajá") or *faskómilo* – a tea made from leaves of a bitter-tasting **wild sage** (*Salvia cypria*). In autumn, the slightest of bumps in woodland leaf-litter can lead the sharp-eyed and knowledgeable villager to edible wild **fungi**. Outside private gatherings with Cypriot families, it is almost impossible to try most of these foods: only *kápari,* whole, spiny **caper stems** softened by pickling, are readily available in tavernas.

Over the centuries, Cypriots have employed many plants as natural remedies for every imaginable ill; with increasing Westernization much of this lore has been forgotten. If you're interested in further study, some of the botanical field guides listed in the bibliography at the end of this article will be useful.

# Birds

Cyprus no longer has anything like the numbers of resident **birds of prey** it once had – thanks to the mania, North and South, for the gun, along with the use of poisoned carcasses by misguided goatherds, anxious to protect their flocks and their meagre income. Vultures in particular are scavengers, and will only feed on animals already dead. The black vulture had become extinct across the island by the mid-1990s, and the North's small population of **griffon vultures** in the Kyrenia hills were all shot by hunters in 1996. Griffons have fared little better in the South: 37 of the colony of 40 in the Xerós valley were poisoned by laced carcasses in 1998, and only three nests have been recorded lately in the Akámas area. A planned dam in the Dhiárizos valley will destroy nesting sites there, and just six nests have been counted recently at the cliffs west of Episkopí. A "conservation" programme has been supposedly implemented, but when native numbers fall this low, breeding is not viable and complete extinction will only be avoided by introducing individuals from Greece and Spain.

**Kestrels** are still common, but nesting peregrine only survive in remote strongholds in the Kyrenia range and offshore on the Klidhés islands at the tip of the Karpaz peninsula. **Bonelli's eagle** is far from common nowadays in either northern or southern mountain ranges, whereas in the past it was even known to have nested in the walls of Buffavento castle.

Other raptors seen over the island are usually migrants: transient visitors on passage to nesting grounds in spring, returning in autumn. They tend to be seen as they hunt over reservoirs and salt lakes for prey to sustain them on their journey, or when flying over the peninsulas of Akámas and Karpaz. Species regularly observed include the **red-footed falcon** and the **hobby**, a small falcon which looks like a large swift in flight and which has the turn of speed and agility in the air to take swallows, martins and even swifts on the wing. There are also broad-winged raptors such as **marsh harrier**, **common buzzard** and **black kite** which can be seen soaring above scrub-covered hills or hunting low over reedbeds.

**Eleonora's falcons** breed late in the year in colonies on the cliffs at Akrotíri, safely protected within the Episkopí Sovereign Base. They favour Cape Gáta at the tip of the peninsula and nest late, timing the hatching of their chicks to coincide with the autumn migration of exhausted hoopoes, orioles, swifts and sandmartins, exploiting these passerines' misfortunes. Once you have witnessed their mastery of flight, as they scythe through the air, you may forgive their opportunism.

In the Tróödhos massif there are permanent nesting populations of familiar species such as **raven**, **jackdaw**, **rock dove** and **wood pigeon**. Less familiar to those used to watching birds in northern Europe will be **crag martin**, **Cretschmar's bunting** and the colourful **hoopoe** with pink body, black and white crest and a call which can be heard from afar. In the northern range, Kantára has always been a favourite place for birdwatchers in spring; in the course of a couple of hours you might see **blue rock thrush**, **alpine swift**, **black-headed bunting** and **spectacled warbler**.

The **chukar**, an attractive rock partridge, survives as a ground-nester in dense scrub, in spite of its being the favourite target of hunters North and South: just enough seem to escape the hunters to maintain the population in a fragile equilibrium. The **black francolin**, exterminated in much of southern Europe by thoughtless hunting, just managed to recover from the brink of extinction in Cyprus when the British administration revoked gun licences during the EOKA troubles of the 1950s. For some years it was still hunted in one of its main strongholds in the Karpaz, to the east of Dipkarpaz (Rizokárpaso), though recently a protective reserve has (in theory) been established here.

**Rollers** and **bee-eaters** are the most colourful of the spring migrants seen each year on passage through the island. Both species are known to breed locally, choosing suitable holes in sandy riverbanks or soft cliffs for the purpose. Being vividly coloured, they attract the attention of hunters, and have been regarded as articles of food. Cyprus suffered habitually in the past from depredation by **locusts** – government reports for the years 1878 and 1879 record how villagers were expected to catch locusts to be bagged up and weighed. Failure to comply with the directive or even to collect minimum weights brought fines and sometimes imprisonment. Ironically, locusts form part of a roller's diet – if these insects are around then they will eat nothing else.

**Salt lakes** provide both food (tiny brine shrimps siphoned up in their millions) and a resting place for the **greater flamingoes** which winter at Akrotíri and Larnaca. Together with reservoirs, the salt lakes and marshes constitute the main areas of open water on the island and regular visitors have a chance to observe a changing variety of **water birds** in the course of a year. There are various species of duck (**mallard**, **shoveler**, **teal** and **wigeon**), **black-necked grebe** and larger birds such as several members of the heron family (**squacco heron**, **night heron**, **little bittern**, **little** and **cattle egrets**). Shallow waters at the edges of reservoirs and salt lakes provide the mud in which waders probe incessantly for their food. Occasionally, one can be lucky and see **glossy ibis**, **black-winged stilt** or **black-tailed godwit**. The migratory routes of storks do not pass over the island but, occasionally, individual **black** or **white storks** and even **pelicans** can be blown off course and spend a few days in the island, before resuming their journey.

Cyprus has several endemic bird species, distinct enough from their nearest relatives that they can be properly thought of as species; others are only regarded as distinct "races". The best-known of the endemics is the **Cyprus warbler**, with a wide distribution in scrubby areas throughout the island. It closely resembles the Sardinian warbler but differs in having underparts marked with black – it also lacks the red ring around the eye and the red iris which are the trademarks of the Sardinian species. Only one other endemic is widespread and that is the **Cyprus Scops owl**: the others – **pied wheatear**, **coal tit**, **jay**, **crossbill** and the **short-toed treecreeper** – are confined to the High Tróödhos pine forest.

Both **demoiselle** and **common cranes** spend the winter months in the Sudan but migrate via Cyprus – en route to the demoiselle's breeding sites in Asia Minor and southern Russia in March and April, while the common crane flies in the opposite direction, leaving the Balkans, Turkestan, Asia Minor and northern Europe in August and September. They are often seen following the line of the Akámas peninsula in spring, but particularly evocative are hot, late-August nights over Nicosia: the birds are far out of sight, only the wing beats and trumpeting metallic calls identifying their passage.

# Mammals – past and present

The Mediterranean Sea has had a chequered history, and geological evidence shows that it has even dried out on several occasions, enabling plants and animals to migrate to mountain peaks which have since become islands. The basic shape of the **Mediterranean basin** was formed about 40 million years ago, but until around 20 million years ago it was open at either end to the Atlantic and Indian oceans respectively. First the eastern channel closed up, isolating sea life but still allowing land animals to cross between continents, and then the western outlet closed, effectively sealing it off.

Some six million years ago the land-locked sea **evaporated** almost completely; the Mediterranean became an arid, inhospitable basin with a few shallow salt lakes on its floor and some of today's islands standing as **forested oases**, in which animals congregated and developed. Drilling has revealed salt deposits which show that the Atlantic breached the debris dam at the present-day Straits of Gibraltar on several occasions over a 700,000-year period. Finally, the "dam" gave way for good and the basin was filled in about a century by a gigantic cascade of Atlantic water, isolating the forested hilltops and their inhabitants.

Excavations on the Mesaoría have revealed **fossil bones** showing that Cyprus, in Pleistocene times, was the home of mammals such as pygmy elephants, pygmy hippopotamus, ibex, genet and wild boar. Today the largest mammal on the island is the **Cyprus moufflon** (*Ovis musimon*), possibly a survivor from those times. Although hunted almost to the point of extinction, it has been saved by a captive breeding programme in the forests of the southern mountains, and is widely used as a symbol of the island – visitors first meet it as the symbol of Cyprus Airways.

Although **foxes** are rarely seen in the open, they are not uncommon in the Akámas and Karpaz peninsulas. They have paler coats than north European races and blend easily with the browns and greys of the landscape. **Cyprian hares** (*Lepus cyprius*) can sometimes be seen as they break cover, but they are justifiably shy creatures barely able to sustain small populations between successive hunting seasons. Other small animals include the **Cyprian shrew**, a race of **spiny mouse** and **brown tree rats**, enormous (for rats anyway) arboreal beasts which live by preference on almonds and carob pods. **Long-eared hedgehogs** look like the animal equivalent of an old Renault 4, with their long back legs keeping their rear end higher than the front. For years, hedgehogs were persecuted because of a reputation for climbing into chicken coops and trying to have their spiny way with the inhabitants. As laughable as it's physically impossible, this strongly held superstition did the welfare of these creatures no good at all.

Of the eight species of bat recorded in Cyprus, the **fruit-eating bat** (*Rousettus aegyptiacus*) is the most spectacular, with a powerful bird-like flight. They can sometimes be seen on the outskirts of Pólis and in villages along the northern coast, when they come in the evening to feed on ripe fruit. They live and breed in limestone caves and so are confined to the Akámas (where they were filmed for David Attenborough's TV series on the Mediterranean) and the Kyrenia mountains. Their visits to orchards have made them the target of hunters, but in the wild they have an important role to play because hard-coated fruit seeds pass undamaged through their digestive systems. Thus fruit-eating bats have played an unwitting but essential role in the propagation of trees by spreading seeds in their droppings.

# Reptiles and amphibians

Saint Helena, mother of the Byzantine emperor Constantine, apparently visited Cyprus on her return voyage from Jerusalem to Constantinople after a successful venture to discover the Holy Cross. She found an island gripped by the ravages of drought, but what really perturbed her was that it seemed to be infested with snakes and lizards. Her answer to the problem was to return with a shipload of cats to hunt them down, and these were landed at the tip of the Akrotíri peninsula, henceforth known as Cape Gáta (*gáta* means "she-cat"). Although feral cats in cities continue to take an enormous toll of lizards (and small birds), **reptiles** and **amphibians** still occur in numbers sufficient to interest those who want to see them.

Spring and autumn are the times to see the island's eight endemic species of snake: in winter they hibernate and in summer they are hidden, virtually comatose, from the unremitting heat. Looking like a glossy earthworm, the **worm snake** is the smallest; at a length which can easily exceed two metres, the large **whip snake** just qualifies as the longest, edging out its cousin the **Cyprus whip snake**. The former is easily recognized by its almost black back – it wriggles away when disturbed in vineyards or at field edges and will also climb trees. The **coin snake** has distinctive lozenge markings on its back; it and the 1992-rediscovered but still endangered aquatic "**grass**" snake (see p.256) are harmless. The **cat snake** and **Montpellier snake** feed on small lizards and produce venom which can paralyse or kill their prey in a matter of minutes. Humans fare better if bitten by either, since the inward-pointing fangs are set far back in the throat, but a large Montpellier snake can still inflict a wound which is slow to heal, with local swelling and headache as an accompaniment. The **blunt-nosed viper** (*Vipera lepetina lepetina*), fortunately quite rare, is the only really dangerous serpent on Cyprus. Called *koúfi* locally, it has a distinctive yellow, horn-like tail and can inflict a bite which is highly **poisonous**: its fangs remain embedded in the tissue and the venom is pumped into the wound by movements of the jaws. Infant vipers are, if anything, more toxic as their venom is more concentrated; in autumn 2000 they were shown to be oviparous (hatched from eggs) rather than, as was long believed, vivaparous (born live from the mother's body where the eggs are incubated).

During the years of the British administration, problematically large numbers of rodents led to the idea of importing more Montpellier snakes from southern

France as a biological control. Some were undoubtedly brought in to bolster the local population, but as to numbers involved, the period of time and the ultimate success of the venture, nobody seems certain. In Cyprus all snakes have a bad press, based almost entirely upon superstition – none of the island's species is aggressive and individuals will only bite in a desperate attempt to defend themselves.

Small **lizards** seem to be everywhere. You will see tiny **geckos** coming out at night to feed on insects attracted to wall lights, and agile **sand lizards** racing over rocks or even dashing suicidally across roads. The largest lizard in Cyprus is the **starred agama** (*Agama stelio*), which grows up to 30cm long. It has a disproportionately large head, and if you see one at close quarters it's like looking back in time to the age of dinosaurs. They are shy creatures, often seen scuttling into cracks in walls or the trunks of ancient olive and carob trees. In Cyprus, the politest of the local names means "nosebiter", inspired by the oversized head.

In summer, **tree frogs** (*Hyla arborea*) are usually heard rather than seen when they call, often at night and far away from water, with a volume out of all proportion to their small size. In winter, they return to water to breed and can be found on bushes or reeds close to streams, ponds and rivers, where you might be lucky enough see their acrobatic climbing. **Marsh frogs** and **green toads** are considerably larger and, thus, correspondingly easier to find.

**Stripe-necked terrapins** can still be found, even in surprisingly murky pools, although they have suffered badly from the effects of pollution – mainly from agricultural chemicals. A plop into a muddy pool as you approach will usually be a large frog – occasionally it might be a terrapin, which will surface several metres away to survey you, the intruder, with quiet confidence.

## Sea turtles

Cyprus is one of the few places in the Mediterranean where **sea turtles** still come ashore to breed, at certain sandy beaches east of Kyrenia and also along the Karpaz and Akámas peninsulas. Tourism has driven them from the sands of the south coast, though there may still be some nesting on "Lady's Mile" beach southwest of Limassol. Since the late 1970s, the Fisheries Department has run a camp at Lára, near Páfos, with the express purpose of protecting nests and collecting hatchlings in order to transfer them to the water, safe from predation by crows and foxes. Simultaneously, a running battle has been fought between conservationists and the developers who see the obvious tourist potential of this superb, sandy beach.

Both **loggerhead turtles** (*Caretta caretta*) and less common **green turtles** (*Chelonia mydas*) haul themselves ashore at night, landing from June onwards on beaches to the northwest of Páfos. Conversely, in the North more greens than loggerheads come ashore to lay eggs on sandy beaches east of Kyrenia and also on the Karpaz peninsula. Both species mate at sea.

The green turtle is the larger of the two species, with mature adults attaining a length of some 100–140cm. They are smooth-shelled herbivores, feeding on sea grasses and seaweeds and, in the nesting season, a female can produce several clutches of eggs at two-week intervals – they tend to breed every two to three years. Loggerheads, reaching 75–100cm in length, have a tapered shell or carapace, a short muscular neck and powerful jaws which can crush the shells of the molluscs – one part of the varied diet, along with jellyfish, crabs, sponges and aquatic plants. Numbers of them die yearly from mistaking plastic carrier bags floating at sea for edible jellyfish. They breed every other year and will lay three or four clutches in a season.

A popular local belief maintains that turtles will only lay on the two or three nights to either side of the full moon. What is certainly true, however, is that turtles the world over prefer to emerge on bright, **moonlit nights**. The laborious journey up the beach, the digging of a nest, followed by egg-laying and then covering with sand, is an exhausting business which takes several hours. Turtles disturbed as they come ashore will simply return to the sea, but when laying has started they carry on until virtually drained of energy – behaviour that has made them extremely vulnerable to hunters.

**Temperature** plays a very important part in the development of the embryo within the parchment-skinned turtle egg, as it not only controls the incubation rate, but also determines the sex of the offspring. Instinctively, the female selects a place on the beach and lays her eggs at such a depth (about 40cm) that the ambient temperature will stay fairly constant during the incubation period. Since sea turtles have evolved from land-based ancestors, their eggs will not develop in water; to survive, they need the air trapped between the grains of sand that surround them in the "nest".

**Hatchlings** appear some six to nine weeks after the white, ping-pong-ballish eggs are laid in batches of 75–120; in Cyprus most nests are established in June, and hatchlings emerge throughout August into September. The deeper in the sand an egg is placed, the cooler it is and hence the slower the development – and the more males result. Thus hatchlings emerge at different rates, a batch each day from the same nest. Immediately after biting and wriggling their way out from the egg, they still have part of the yolk-sac attached and will have to wait beneath the sand until that has been absorbed into the body. The young struggle the final few centimetres to the surface and make directly for the sea around dawn or in the evening when it's cool. Occasionally, their internal clocks go wrong and they try to emerge onto hot sand with fatal consequences.

In some countries, hatchlings have to run a gauntlet of seabirds to reach the sea; in Cyprus, foxes have been the major **predators**. The hope is that the immediate danger of predation at Lára is removed by placing wire cages over nests, ensuring one less peril in the ten years it will take them to reach "adolescent" status. It is very difficult to assess the success of conservation ventures with sea turtles because of other hazards they have to face: predation from other sea creatures when small, deliberate killing by fishermen or being left to die trapped in drift nets. The good news is that numbers have certainly not decreased in the south of Cyprus in the three decades that a conservation programme has been operational.

# Insects

As soon as the sun comes out, butterflies are in evidence as they fly over patches of open ground in scrub or hotel gardens. Here, often for the first time, visitors see the glorious **swallowtail butterfly** (*Papilio machaon*), rare in Britain yet common here, where its larvae thrive on fennel plants. Strawberry trees along the south and north coasts are the food-plant of the magnificent **two-tailed pasha** (*Charaxes jasius*), a powerful flier which defends its territory against infiltrators by flying at them. When seen at close quarters a complex and beautiful striping of the underwings is revealed.

Cyprus has several unique species of butterfly, including the **Paphos blue** (*Glaucopsyche paphia*) and **Cyprus festoon** (*Zerynthia cerisyi* ssp. *cypria*), a swallowtail relative with scalloped margins to the wings. It has curiously spiked caterpillars which feed on a plant with a similarly bizarre appearance, the Dutchman's pipe (*Aristolochia sempervirens*), found thoughout the island's hills on chalk and volcanic soils. **Cleopatras** (*Gonepteryx cleopatra*) fly through sunny glades in the mountain woods, heralding the arrival of spring; the males are a deep sulphur yellow, with a splash of orange just visible on the forewings in flight.

In summer, numerous species usually referred to collectively as "browns" (*Satyrids*) and "blues" (*Lycaenids*) are found all over the island wherever weeds grow. In spite of heavy use of insecticides, enough weeds are left to enable caterpillars to thrive. Some larvae are very particular and restrict their diet to one species of plant, while others are virtually omnivorous, even resorting to cannibalism if there is nothing else to eat.

One of the things you notice in pine trees are hanging nests of gossamer, spun by **caterpillars** after they hatch from their eggs. They feed on tender pine needles within the nest and then drop to the ground in a wriggling mass until one sets off and the others attach themselves in a nose-to-tail migratory arrangement. So successful are these processionary caterpillars of **pine beauty** and **gypsy moths** that they have become a forest pest, causing serious damage to trees; it seems they arrived on the island late in the 1980s, and no drastic measures were taken at the time to control them. They are covered in hairs secreting a highly irritant substance, so neither they nor any surface they've recently crawled on should be touched – dogs which attempt to ingest them invariably develop necrosis of the tongue and may have to be put down.

Many moths could be grouped under the heading "small, brown and boring", but the **hawkmoths** rival butterflies in terms of colour, and are superbly equipped for fast, powerful flight with strong forewings and small hindwings. Their caterpillars are often more gaudily coloured than the parents and can assume a curious posture to frighten off predators – a habit which has given them the common name of **sphinx moths**. In Cyprus, the most common member of the family is the **hummingbird hawk** (*Macroglossum stellatarum*), which can be cheeky enough to approach on whirring wings and, with long, thin tongue, sample the liquid from the edges of your drink glass as you enjoy an evening meal outdoors. Less frequently seen are the beautiful **oleander hawk** (*Daphnis nerii*) with olive-shaded wings and the **death's-head hawk** (*Acherontia atropos*) whose large yellow-and-violet-striped caterpillars feed on potato plants and were quite common crop pests before the use of insecticides. **Praying mantids** are curious creatures and, in Cyprus, range from the small brown species to the larger **crested mantid** or *empúsa*, named after a Greek demi-goddess who visited men in their beds and made love with them until they expired: the insect males have to be fast to avoid becoming the main item in the post-coital breakfast.

Not strictly insects, but coming into the general category of "creepy-crawlies", most Cypriot **spiders** are small except for the **European tarantula** which lives in burrows on open hillsides venturing out to catch any suitable prey passing its way. **Scorpions** are not as common as they once were, primarily owing to destruction of habitat and to the use of agricultural chemicals. By carefully turning up stones in chalky areas or looking in the cracks in old limestone walls you can still find them. They are shy, pale-coloured creatures, but in defence of their brood they will inflict a very painful sting. The large black **millipedes** are harmless, but orange **centipedes** pack a nasty, venomous bite: when in rural areas, shake out your shoes or slippers carefully in the morning, and your bedding before retiring.

# Marine life

The sea turtles mentioned above are the most spectacular of the marine creatures regularly seen in the waters around the island. Although **dolphins** are
infrequently sighted off the north coast, their true haunts are much closer to
Turkey's southern shore where there are more fish. The lack of tidal movement,
coupled with very few streams providing nutrients to enrich the coastal water,
keep plankton levels on the low side. Also, the building of Egypt's Aswan High
Dam has drastically reduced the outflow of nutrient-rich Nile water into the
southeastern end of the Mediterranean. Consequently, fish numbers around the
coasts are not as high as might be expected, but there is still a surprising diversity of colourful species – scuba-diving is a very popular activity because the
absence of plankton makes the waters very clear.

A visit to a quay when a fishing boat comes in is also a recommended
experience. As the catch is unloaded you see a great mixture of fish, including
**peacock** and **rainbow wrasse**, **parrot fish**, **red soldier fish** and **red** or **grey
mullet**. Many of these are visible from the surface if you're lazily snorkelling, in
addition to the ubiquitous **sea urchins**, **starfish**, **anemones** and the occasional
**octopus**. Further out to sea are small, harmless **sharks** and several species of
**ray** (including electric and thornback), making a total of around two hundred
species of fish recorded in the seas off the island. However, owing to overfish-
ing and high tourist levels in the south, the squid you dine on probably came
in boxes from southeast Asia or the North Sea, and nowadays boats have to sail
almost to the Libyan coast in order to catch swordfish.

# Sites

## The salt lakes: Larnaca and Akrotíri

If you arrive in Cyprus in winter or spring and collect a rental car at Larnaca
airport, the first taste of the island's wildlife is only a short drive away at the
**Larnaca salt lake**, right next to Hala Sultan Tekke, burial place of Muhammad's aunt. From the mosque here, you can see rafts of pink flamingoes and
from January onwards contemplate a walk under the pines to the west in
pursuit of orchids. Luck might allow for the flamingoes, feeding on brine
shrimp, to be near the road when you visit. They're here all winter in thousands, adults arriving first, with juveniles following later from Turkey, Iran and
even further afield. They start to leave by late March, with small flocks flying at
low levels; the last stragglers quit in June for their nesting areas.

Near Limassol, **Akrotíri** is a reed-fringed lake which, with crossed fingers
and a good map, you can try to approach on small roads from the north, but
it's easier to take the road to the RAF base and turn left before reaching the
gates. To prevent problems, always carry your passport when in this area and
avoid pointing cameras at any obvious installations. On a good day in spring,
it's possible to find scorpions, green toads, tree frogs and Cyprus bee orchids in
the scrub around the lake. Throughout the year, it's a magnet for migrating birds
and thus a favourite bird-watching site for off-duty military personnel, visiting
ornithological tour parties and increasing numbers of local enthusiasts.

On maps, another salt lake is marked **near Paralímni**, but it only fills after heavy rains. It has always been a good area in which to observe migrant birds but, distressingly, was long also a centre for the trade in tiny pickled birds caught on lime sticks (see "Conservation", p.496).

## The Akámas peninsula

The **Akámas peninsula** was the first area in Cyprus to have been proposed as a national park, intensifying ongoing controversy as to its fate. The peninsula forms the western tip of the island and its geology is varied, with outcrops, cliffs and deep gorges of limestone in addition to serpentine and other igneous rocks. This allows for a diversity of soil types and a rich plant life as a direct consequence – there is even an endemic alyssum (*Alyssum akamasicum*), for example, as well as the endemic tongue orchid (*Serapias aphroditae*).

Although once an inhabited area, as extensive remains of ancient settlements show, its separation from present concentrations of population, plus its long-time use as a practice range by the British Forces, means it has remained largely unspoiled. Scattered pine groves constitute the nearest thing to virgin forest the island can offer, but considerable tracts of land have suffered the depredations of feral goats. Where grazing has been controlled, the plant life is rich and, should completely protected status ever be conferred, the whole peninsula could eventually be similarly vegetated.

In February and March, coastal walks here take you over hillsides of cascading cyclamen, and you might see the first rollers and bee-eaters to have arrived on the spring migration. **Gorges** hidden from view provide cave roosts – especially near **Faslí** and **Andhrolíkou** – where you might discover some of the island's fruit bats. Green and loggerhead turtles use the beaches such as Lára for breeding, as discussed previously. There are orchids too, although these have suffered as much as other plant species because of over-grazing. Encouragingly, numbers increase by the year and include the rare yellow-flowered punctate orchid (*Orchis punctulata*).

From Káthikas, at the more populated southern base of the Akámas, a road descends through Péyia to the coast and is worth travelling for the views alone. As a bonus, you pass through an area planted with pines – the **Péyia forest** – where orchids grow in both abundance and astonishing variety. High above the sea, it is a cool place that has become something of a haven for small birds.

## The High Tróödhos

High on the mountains, snow can remain in pockets until April – one meaning of the summit's name, **Khionístra**, is "snow-pit". Thus, spring starts late but with a choice series of plants: crocus, corydalis, various vetches, an endemic buttercup (*Ranunculus cyprius* var. *Cadmicus*) – no large-scale displays, more like a huge rock garden with many plants unique to the island. In colonial times the British established a network of paths, mostly on a contour, so that walks around Mount Olympus can be as long or as short as you like. Wherever the paths pass through the open forests of black pine you can look for the endemic coal tits, pied wheatear, jay, crossbill and short-toed treecreeper.

Another nature trail follows the Krýos river past **Caledonian Falls**, just southwest from and below Tróödhos resort, and numbered posts indicate plants of interest; both Greek and scientific names are given. In early summer there are various endemic plants – many of them with *troodi* as part of the Latin name. Look out for groups of marsh orchids (*Dactylorhiza iberica*), near the streams, and eastern marsh helleborines (*Epipactis veratrifolia*) around the Caledonian Falls near the end of the trail. Here, well out of reach on wet rocks behind the falls, grows the rare Cyprus butterwort (*Pinguicula crystallina*).

The extensive forests to the northwest below Khionístra offer peonies (*Paeonia mascula*) in May near Pródhromos; a curious red parasite, the Cyprus broomrape (*Orobanche cypria*), and a seemingly endless network of dirt roads, usually well maintained, which take you far from other visitors. Better, paved roads run to Kýkko Monastery (the area has its very own buttercup – *Ranunculus kykkoënsis*) and beyond to **Stavrós tís Psókas**, a forestry station where it's possible to stay by prior arrangement, falling asleep to the sound of nightingales and waking to the scent of pines.

Several rather dejected-looking **moufflon** are kept penned here and, for most visitors to the island, they will be the only ones seen, even though the Páfos forest is their stronghold. The exact origins of this wild sheep are uncertain but remains have been found in Neolithic settlements, dating to around eight thousand years ago. It could well have been a domesticated animal then, either brought to the island by settlers, or the direct descendant of creatures trapped when the Mediterranean filled for the last time. In Greco-Roman times, moufflon were plentiful throughout the Tróödhos and in the Kyrenia mountains, but hunting, especially during the Middle Ages, reduced the population drastically. In 1878, the first year of British rule, only twenty animals were counted, a situation which persisted until 1939 when game laws were strengthened and the Páfos forest became a game reserve. At the same time goat-grazing was banned in the reserve, removing competition for the available food; subsequently, numbers began to increase steadily, with counts of 100 animals in 1949, 200 in 1966 and 800 in 1982.

The moufflon is a very agile animal, but shy and not readily seen – let alone approached. Its closest relatives are island races of wild sheep (*Ovis orientalis*) in Sardinia and Corsica, which tend to live in open, rocky territory. The Cypriot race, however, has found its "niche" as a forest-dweller, although for fodder it prefers grasses to bush or tree shoots. When the uplands are snow-covered, it descends to lowland valleys, always relying on the cover provided by the forest. Mating takes place in November when competitive males become aggressive: the dominant male in a group sires the lambs, and the gestation period is five months. In both males and females the summer coat is short and pale brown, becoming white on the underparts; in winter they grow a coat of dense brown hair.

The "**Cedar Valley**" is much advertised as a tourist attraction. It is certainly pleasant woodland with a rich flora and some attractive birds – Cyprus cyclamen (*Cyclamen cyprium*), various orchids and hoopoes for example – but not quite deserving its hype in tourist brochures. The particular attraction, for naturalists who like to wander, is the ease with which you can get off the beaten track – dirt (and in one case paved) roads from here to the coast are tortuous but negotiable. Allow time to linger as you travel from volcanic to limestone soils and pass interesting collections of roadside plants, see butterflies or notice birds. Cultivated fields in the area still sport collections of colourful cornfield weeds such as field gladiolus, corn marigold and a royal-purple poppy (*Roemeria hybrida*), so delicate that its petals seem to fall as soon as a camera is pointed its way.

Near Agrós looms **Mount Adhélfi**, at 1612m the second highest peak in the island. On its slopes and also on nearby hills grow some of the rare endemic bulbs of Cyprus, such as Hartmann's crocus (*Crocus hartmannianus*) and chiono-doxa (*Scilla lochiae*). From Agrós you can explore the Pitsyliá region which is known for its fruit and nut trees, but thus far little explored by tourists. The roadsides and field edges are particularly interesting for a rich assortment of "weeds" – "candlesticks" of *Sedum lampusae*, various parasitic broomrapes and whole banks of purple vetch, for example.

Mount Adhélfi can also be approached from **Kakopetriá** where one of the few **permanent streams** in Cyprus is located. It runs close to the famous church of Áyios Nikólaos tís Steyís through a wild valley with abundant flowers (Cyprus broomrape, orchids, Cyprus butterwort). This wealth of flora inevitably attracts butterflies such as cleopatras and the southern white admiral (*Limenitis reducta*) – as the latter sups nectar from tree honeysuckle you will see its open wings, and two rows of large white spots relieving the jet-black surface. Dutchman's pipe, food-plant of the larvae of the Cyprus festoon butterfly, straggles over ancient vines near here with its hanging rows of striking brown and yellow flowers – close by will be the butterflies themselves.

This little river is also the home of a curious, olive-green, freshwater crab (*Potamon fluviatilis*) which was once common around the island, especially in brackish streams near the coast. Sadly, numbers have dwindled as a direct consequence of pollution caused by agricultural chemicals running off into streams. In this, one of its last strongholds, it survives by hiding under stones but comes out at night onto the bank to feed. Locals regret the disappearance since it was regarded as a good *mezé* or taverna snack.

## The Tróödhos foothills

Although the core of the Tróödhos range is igneous, overlying chalks were deposited on top of the volcanic rocks, when seas covered the land. Upheavals have pushed the underlying serpentines and pillow lavas through the chalk, and you can move confusingly between the two types of strata, noticing the dramatic changes in plant life. The road from Áyios Iraklídhios (southwest of Nicosia) to Makherás monastery epitomizes these transitions. The route first takes in a cultivated area with great telegraph-pole spikes of agave, then a dry chalk valley with orchids and grape hyacinths wherever the slightest humus builds up from fallen needles beneath the pines. Where the rocks change, the cistus and lavender bushes form a roadside scrub, with yellow Roman and pink Anatolian orchids protected beneath them.

**Around Makherás** itself, the woods are worth exploring since they are typical forest of the lower Tróödhos with their eastern strawberry trees and golden oak. Early in the year, you find an occasional Hartmann's crocus, and in autumn the Cyprus cyclamen. Birdlife is varied, with Scops owl frequently heard but seldom seen; chukars prefer to run for cover through the bushes rather than fly.

**From Limassol**, journeys to Yermasóyia and its dam, to Léfkara and further west through Pákhna to Malliá and Vouní cut through country with dry, chalky soils which have proved good for viticulture. Even with abundant vines there are still pockets of scrub rich in the shrubby herbs that make up the *frýgana*, giving protection to numerous plants such as yellow Star of Bethlehem, grape hyacinths, "naked man" orchid, and giant and dense-flowered orchids, as well as turban buttercups in whites, creams, yellows or even with a reddish tinge. You can see and hear stonechats and the Cyprus warbler standing sentinel on bushes, while dry chalk, with its high reflectance of light and heat, always seems particularly attractive to numerous small lizards and the occasional snake lazily sunning itself. If your eyesight is particularly acute you might spot a chameleon: they are fairly common but stay well hidden from view, camouflaged by their ability to match the mottled browns and greens of their surroundings.

## Rivermouths and reservoirs

Extensive natural wetlands near Güzelyurt (Mórfou) in the North and near Limassol in the South proved ideal for establishment of the extensive citrus groves that now occupy them, being fed by mountain waters and kept moist all year round. Death from malaria was common until early in the British period, when malarial swamps were drained by planting thirsty eucalyptus. In recent years, diversion of streams to fill the newly built and much-needed reservoirs is another factor which has cut down water flow. Thus reedbeds – other than those planted as windbreaks – are a rarity in Cyprus.

In the South, try **east** and **west of Pólis** or **north of Akrotíri salt lake**; in the North, for the birdwatcher, there is **Glapsides** just to the north of Famagusta, where a popular beach is backed by a freshwater lake and wetland vegetation.

Also in the North are large **reservoirs** at **Köprülü** (Koúklia) and at **Gönyeli** on the northern perimeter of Nicosia, which are important sites for over-wintering wildfowl (ducks, grebe and heron). They are also attractive to smaller lowland and mountain birds throughout the year, since insects always hover near water. Consequently, indigenous and migrating raptors patrol the reservoirs and their immediate environs, regarding these smaller birds as a readily available "in-flight" meal. Areas of open water are attracting growing numbers of people, both visitors and locals, interested in the changing variety of birds throughout the year.

## The coast around Cape Koruçam (Kormakíti)

Although **Cape Koruçam** (Kormakíti) itself can be bleak in the winter months, being openly exposed to the prevailing winds, its spring wildflowers – anemones in particular – are delightful. Coastal rocks at first sight seem to provide an inhospitable environment, but fleshy-leaved stonecrops grow in the crevices together with another succulent – *Mesembryanthemum crystallinum*, a relative of the colourful Livingstone daisies grown in gardens.

In Cyprus, dunes – however modest in size – will probably reveal flowering sea daffodils during the hotter months. They survive their arid environment by having a bulb buried so deeply that it would need an excavator to get to it. Even where the sand meets low cliffs, and debris washed down by winter rains bakes dry to form a rock-like surface, these resilient plants are able to grow. Butterflies always seem to be abundant on Cape Koruçam and it's a good place to visit with binoculars and observe the arrival of spring migrants, which might include the occasional kingfisher providing an iridescent diversion as it darts over the rocks below you.

Between Güzelyurt (Mórfou) and Lapta (Lápithos), the road passes through cultivated fields, always tinted with splashes of colourful annuals, especially at their edges. However, the loveliest of the island's "weeds" of cultivation must be the native Cyprus tulip (*Tulipa cypria*). It has blackish-purple flowers and is abundant enough to colour cornfields on the road from Çamlıbel (Mýrtou) to Nicosia; it also grows among the broad-bean plants in fields around the Maronite village of Koruçam (Kormakíti).

Unfortunately the best **beaches** along Mórfou bay are now off-limits because of the Turkish military presence. You can get to Akdeniz (Ayía Iríni), where pygmy hippo fossils have been found, but no further; as a consolation prize, try exploring **near Yayla** (Syrianokhóri).

## The Kyrenia mountains (Beşparmak or Pendadháktylos range)

The sculpted limestone pinnacles of the **Kyrenia range**, whose Greek and Turkish names both mean "Five Fingers", have an appropriately "Gothic" look, mimicking the three medieval castles tucked among them. Their northerly and southerly aspects are quite different: the northern slopes are much lusher, receiving more rain and less of a baking, so that in spring there are cyclamen, anemones and turban buttercups everywhere. What's left of the native vegetation after the massive 1995 fire is mainly Aleppo pine with funeral cypress and dense maquis; the southern slopes have sparse, xerophytic (drought-tolerant) vegetation.

A mountain road built during the colonial period runs from **St Hilarion** westwards along the range for 29 kilometres via the highest peak Selvili Dağ (Kyparissóvouno: 1024m), offering stupendous views right and left plus birds, butterflies, lizards and flowers in abundance. Avoid detours because of the heavy military presence on the south side of the route.

Only the eastern approach to **Buffavento** is open to the public; here you can see a host of the mountain birds mentioned earlier, such as the blue rock thrush. Around St Hilarion, Buffavento and Alevkaya, shaded limestone cliffs are the places to look for endemic plants of the northern range, such as Cypriot rock cress (*Arabis cypria*), Cypriot sage (*Phlomis cypria*) and St Hilarion cabbage (*Brassica hilarionis*), an ancestor of the cultivated cauliflower, which was supposedly first bred at nearby Değirmenlik (Kythréa) during the seventeenth century.

At **Alevkaya** (Halévga), the old forest station is the site of the North Cyprus Herbarium, open since 1989 and housing a collection of more than eight hundred preserved plant specimens plus line drawings. This offers an opportunity to identify what you have seen and also to find out what else there is to spot. The area around Alevkaya has long been known for its orchids, especially the tiny insect-mimicking **bee orchids** (*Ophrys* spp.) which have a lifestyle as bizarre as their appearance. They produce scents which are chemical cocktails with the power to fool tiny male solitary wasps into thinking they have found a female – each orchid produces a subtly different blend to delude a particular species of wasp. When they land they try to mate with the flower, eventually get frustrated and fly off in disgust, carrying pollen to the next orchid flower; fortunately for the plant, memory is not an insect's strong point. The **Cyprus bee orchid** (*Ophrys kotschyi*) and **Lapithos bee orchid** (*Ophrys lapetheca*), both found growing here, are exclusive to the island.

## The Karpaz (Kárpas) peninsula

Long, sparsely populated, but well cultivated in parts, the **Karpaz (Kárpas) peninsula** is a continuation of the limestone ridge of the Kyrenia range, which makes its final Cypriot appearance as the Klidhés islands before re-emerging as the Amanus range in southeast Turkey. Its spine is gently hilly, rising to 383m at Pámboulos. You can approach the peninsula from the northern side of the Kyrenia mountains by heading east from Kyrenia along the coast road, then turning south via Kantára, or by turning off further along, through Büyük-konuk (Komí Kebír). Alternatively, south of the hills, you can travel the coast road north from Famagusta with giant fennel lining your route. Whatever the choice, take your time – the main trunk roads are good but the wayside flowers in spring are superb and well worth lingering over.

In springtime, on reaching the peninsula itself, you will find multicoloured displays of anemones, turban buttercups, poppies and gladioli. Here, the *terra rossa* soil derived from limestone is often a rich red thanks to traces of iron compounds; although it has long proved excellent for cultivating tomatoes, fruit trees and bananas, you can find numerous uncultivated pockets on the peninsula, where orchids and other lime-loving plants thrive on it. The long "panhandle" of the Karpaz provides a flight path into the island for numerous colourful migrants such as rollers, golden orioles and bee-eaters. Rollers are a familiar sight, perching on telegraph wires before taking off across country with a distinctive buoyant flight; they get their name from the way they somersault on the wing as part of their courtship displays.

Turtles – mainly loggerheads – come ashore to lay their eggs on sandy beaches to the east of **Yası Burnu (Cape Plakotí)**, not far from the sixteenth-century monastic church of Panayía Eleoússa. All along this coast, where rocks gently shelve to the sands, grow white sea daffodils in the height of the summer. At **Dipkarpaz (Rizokárpaso)** the land is well cultivated by the remaining Greek-Cypriot population, but a choice of roads beyond the village leads into wilder country, close to the shore. By keeping to the main, paved route you pass the site of ancient Khelónes (meaning "turtles" in Greek) and shortly thereafter the amazingly **long beach**, of Nangomí, stretching nearly to Zafer Burnu (Cape Apostólou Andhréa), where sea turtles have also been known to breed.

The **Klidhés islands** mark the remotest outpost of Cyprus to the east and are one of the few places where sea birds such as shag and Audouin's gull can nest undisturbed. The cliffs also provide one of the last strongholds for nesting peregrine falcons, which breed in March or April and are both fast and strong enough to make doves and pigeons a favourite prey for themselves and their ever-hungry nestlings.

# Conservation

After the trauma of the 1974 invasion, when over 200,000 islanders lost homes and (often) family members, and the Cypriot sense of security was shattered, many on the island felt that they could not afford the luxury of being Green. Thanks to the joint efforts of comparatively few Cypriots and resident "foreigners", people are finally becoming conscious of what has been lost environmentally by unbridled development since 1974 and, moreover, that remedial action has to be immediate and drastic. Dedicated **conservationists** in the Cyprus Biological Society, Cyprus Conservation Foundation, Cyprus Wildlife Society, Friends of the Earth, Green Party and the Ornithological Society, as well as individuals in governmental departments such as education, fisheries and forestry, have all fought an at-times-difficult battle to alert people to what is in imminent danger of being lost for ever.

There have been exhibitions, lectures, sets of stamps and avidly followed broadcasts of David Attenborough's TV series, all part of the exercise to **increase public awareness**. Although still not officially a national park, such publicity has up to the present saved the Akámas peninsula from an unholy alliance of the Orthodox Church and big business which hoped to realize its potential for development. Extensive coverage of the Akámas in the media awakened more and more people to the frightening rate at which other areas in the Cyprus countryside are being changed in the name of development. One of the main "arguments" from opponents to the Akámas conservation venture was that the Pafiot villagers, like their counterparts in Ayía Nápa, had an inalienable right to make money. To try and ensure the prosperity of the area but simultaneously avoid the seemingly inevitable destruction of the last wilderness in the South, the **Laona Project** was set up to encourage **sustainable tourism** (see p.194).

The impact of **hunting** on birds, particularly migrants, is devastating. In Cyprus, North and South, the sanctity of hunting is inviolate: this, not Christianity or Islam, is the national religion, the main thing held in common on both sides of the Attila Line amongst the atheists and the godly, adolescents and geezers, with the "kill" definitely secondary to the social aspect of a Sunday in the country with the boys. The right to have a hunting licence is passionately defended – probably best not to waste breath objecting to it – and although the Southern government ratified the Berne Treaty on endangered species, two weekly days of shooting are allowed during the autumn migratory season (the traditional spring shoot was banned in 1995). Another seldom-considered factor is that the weight of lead shot, falling annually on the land, presents a tangible pollution hazard.

Cypriots sometimes claim that it was western Europeans, in particular the Templars, who introduced **bird-liming** to the island. During the 1980s conservative estimates claimed that millions of small passerines were taken annually in mist nets and on sticks coated with the sticky "lime"; exhausted migrants were trapped and their necks wrung, the pickled carcasses regarded as a delicacy in the Arab Middle East as well. Cyprus is certainly not alone among Mediterranean countries as an offender, and has at least passed legislation to outlaw lime sticks and the import and use of fine-filament "mist" nets. It is now far less socially acceptable than it was, and since accession of the South to the EU in fact completely illegal, but there is still a ready market for the birds, and the main centre of "production" has now shifted from Paralímni to Yeniboğaziçi (Áyios Séryios) in the North, near Salamis. At close to £2 per bird, there's a tangible cash incentive, and it is one of the more notorious contraband items smuggled from North to South at present.

Conservationists in Britain, particularly those concerned with ornithology, have often called upon naturalists to **boycott** the island. When tourism is as important to the economy as it is in Cyprus, considerable pressure can indeed be brought to bear by the threat of lost revenue. However, national pride over "outside intervention" – an understandably touchy subject, given the history of Cyprus – will merely provoke a stubbornly defiant reaction. Perhaps the worst thing that armchair activists unwittingly manage to achieve is the effective isolation of those people on Cyprus, such as Friends of the Earth (Limassol), working at the cutting edge. However, local campaigns are considerably strengthened by support for their efforts from visiting outsiders – sabotage methods include ripping mist nets and urinating on lime sticks (a technique which renders them useless). And if you see things you don't like while in Cyprus, complain in writing to the Cyprus Tourism Organisation and the government: it counts if enough people do it.

**In the North** there is now an active North Cyprus Society for the Protection of Birds (its initials KKKKD in Turkish). **Hunting** is as much a problem in the North as in the South, with a large number of gun licences for the size of the population. Another pressing concern is the level of **grazing** permitted by the enormous herds of goats brought in by Anatolian settlers. Visiting botanists, especially Germans working on a detailed mapping of the orchid flora, have voiced great concern over changes seen over a two- or three-year period in the late 1980s: once flower-filled hillsides now host little but grass, thistles and white asphodels. The only portion of the Karpaz (Kárpas) peninsula which enjoys any protection from hunting or over-grazing is the far tip, near the monastery of Apóstolos Andhréas.

# Wildlife books

Cyprus falls just outside the loose definition of Europe used in field guides, other than those for birds. Thus, it's not easy to find good illustrations of its special plants or butterflies, and a well-nigh impossible task for many of the insects, snails and other creatures which have a lower rating in the popularity stakes. Since a significant proportion of the Cypriot flora and fauna is found around much of the Mediterranean, you can make considerable headway with popular guides, but identifying endemic species is often difficult.

Many of the better natural history works are now out of print, but the Hogarth Press ones are periodically reprinted, while others appear fairly regularly in catalogues of specialist secondhand and antiquarian booksellers, who advertise in the natural history press. One in particular to aim for is A. C. Campbell's very useful *The Hamlyn Guide to the Flora and Fauna of the Mediterranean*; this was also published as *The Larousse Guide to the Flora and Fauna of the Mediterranean*. That said, there were massive changes in taxonomic conventions during the early 1990s, so anything with an imprint before that will be out of date in that respect.

In case of difficulty obtaining titles listed below from conventional booksellers, there is a reliable mail-order outlet for wildlife field guides within the UK. **Summerfield Books** (☎017683/41577, ☏41687, ✉atkins@summerfieldbooks .com) not only has new botanical titles, but also rare or out-of-print natural history books on all topics.

## Flowers and plants

**Marjorie Blamey and Christopher Grey-Wilson** *Mediterranean Wild Flowers*. Comprehensive field guide with colour drawings that includes the lowlands of Cyprus; recent and thus taxonomically up to date.

**K. P. Buttler** *Field Guide to the Orchids of Britain and Europe*. A wealth of colour pictures and modern nomenclature.

**Takis C. Tsintides, Georgios N. Hadjikyriakou, Charalambos S. Christodoulou** *Trees and Shrubs in Cyprus* (A. G. Leventis Foundation, Nicosia). Not exactly portable, but useful photos and authoritative text.

**Lance Chilton** *Plant Checklists: Akamas & Cyprus*. Personal and literature records for this peninsula – order from ☻www.marengowalks .com.

**Yiannis Christofides** *The Orchids of Cyprus* (self-published, through Hotel Minerva, Platres, Cyprus). As it says: covers all the endemics, with full descriptions, flowering-season and habitat charts, phylogenetic minutiae, and lavish colour photos justifying the fairly high cover price.

Sonia Halliday and Laura Lushington *A Photographer's Eye View of the Flowers of Northern Cyprus* (o/p). As much a close-up photo-essay as field guide.

Anthony Huxley and William Taylor *Flowers of Greece and the Aegean* (o/p). Helpful in conjunction with other general works – but does not specifically cover Cyprus, and taxonomy is now slightly dated.

Anthony Huxley and Oleg Polunin *Flowers of the Mediterranean*. A classic book on Mediterranean flora; coverage is general but surprisingly useful, and the scientific nomenclature has been updated.

R. Desmond Meikle *Flora of Cyprus* (Bentham Trust; available from the Royal Botanic Gardens, Kew, Richmond, Surrey). Pricey, two-volume work for the serious plant freak who jettisons clothes from the luggage in favour of books. A model of clarity and erudition – whatever you'll find is in here. No colour pictures, but plenty of line drawings.

Gizela & Karlheinz Morschek *Orchids of Cyprus* (Steijl, The Netherlands). Bilingual (English–German) text describing all known species on the island, with colour photos; affordable paperback.

V. Pantelas, T. Papachristophorou and P. Christodoulou *Cyprus Flora in Colour: The Endemics* (Botanical Society of the British Isles). Good photos of endemic plants; cheaper in Cyprus than in Britain.

Oleg Polunin *Flowers of Greece and the Balkans*. Useful for plants generally distributed in the eastern Mediterranean; get the 1997 reprint.

I. and P. Schoenfelder *Wildflowers of the Mediterranean*. General, but includes many of the ordinary Mediterranean species in Cyprus.

Deryck E. Viney *The Illustrated Flora of North Cyprus* (vol 1, Koeltz Scientific Books, US; vol 2, Gantner Verlag, Germany). Two-volume, affordable paperback series with line drawings; vol. 2 has errata for vol 1, and covers sedges, grasses and ferns.

## Birds

Lucas Christophorou *Birds of Cyprus* (Chr. Nicolaou & Sons, Nicosia). Brief, not overly technical text, excellent colour plates.

Peter Flint and Peter Stewart *The Birds of Cyprus*. Available from the British Ornithological Union, British Museum Press, Tring, Herts. A thorough checklist with details of good sites for birdwatching.

Dave Gosney *Finding Birds in Cyprus* (Gostours, UK). Inexpensive and fairly recent handbook.

Heinzel, Fitter and Parslow *The Birds of Britain and Europe with North Africa and the Middle East*. Another useful item in your bag.

Hollom, Porter, Christensen and Willis *Birds of the Middle East and North Africa*. Very thorough, with good illustrations and distribution maps.

Lars Jonsson *Birds of Europe with North Africa and the Middle East*. Very good coverage and excellent illustrations.

Arthur Stagg, Graham Hearl and James McCallum *Birdwatching Guide to Cyprus*. With 92 illustrations by McCallum and a modest price tag, perhaps the best choice for specific coverage of the island.

J. M. C. Took *Birds of Cyprus*. Very good descriptions, though the colour plates could be better.

## Insects

**Christodoulos Makris** *The Butterflies of Cyprus* (Bank of Cyprus Cultural Foundation). In large coffee-table format and weighing in at several kilos, this isn't your average handy field guide but it's a gorgeous, erudite volume, worth the high price tag and ideal for either casual or expert use.

**Lionel Higgins and Norman Riley** *A Field Guide to the Butterflies of Britain and Europe.* A very detailed classic which contains most of the Cyprus butterflies except the handful of indigenes.

## Reptiles, amphibians and marine life

**Arnold, Burton and Ovenden** *A Field Guide to the Reptiles of Britain and Europe.* Most, but not all, species – again this stops well short of the Middle East.

**Jiri Cihar** *Amphibians and Reptiles* (o/p). Selective in coverage, but has many species from Asia Minor and is useful for Cyprus.

**B. Luther and K. Fiedler** *A Field Guide to the Mediterranean Seashore* (o/p). Very thorough, and includes much of what occurs around the Cyprus coast.

**Paul H. Davies,**
amended and updated by Lance Chilton, David Whaley and the author.

# Books

As befits a former Crown Colony, there are a huge number of books on Cyprus in English. Many worthwhile classics have been reissued since the millennium, and out-of-print but still worthwhile books (indicated by o/p) are easily available through online rare book-dealers, foremost ⓦwww.abe.co.uk/.com or ⓦwww.bookfinder.com. When a title is published outside the English-speaking world, or in Cyprus only, this has been indicated. Titles marked ☆ are particularly recommended.

One of the best walk-in UK sources for English-language books on Cyprus is the **Hellenic Bookservice**, 91 Fortress Rd, Kentish Town, London NW5 1AG (☏020/7267 9499, ☏7267 9498, ⓦwww.hellenicbookservice .com): knowledgeable and well-stocked specialist dealers in new and out-of-print books on all aspects of Greek Cyprus. Rivals **Zeno's**, 57A Nether St, North Finchley, London N12 7NP (☏020/8446 1985, ☏8446 1986, ⓦwww .thegreekbookstore.com), have more of an antiquarian stress, with their own line of reprints, especially classics and educational texts. For materials with a specifically Turkish-Cypriot slant, **Daunt Books** (83 Marylebone High St, London W1M 3DE; ☏020/7224 2295) makes an effort to stock products of the Eothen Press. **Moufflon Books** in south Nicosia (see p.295) has also begun its own line of selected reprints.

Useful **bookstores in Cyprus** are detailed in the town listings for Larnaca, Limassol, Páfos, Kyrenia and Nicosia.

## Archeology and ancient history

☆ **Bank of Cyprus** (Nicosia). This is the sponsor for a series of generally excellent, affordable (C£3.50–5) guidelets for an assortment of archeological sites and indoor attractions, often written by the supervising archeologists and collection curators. Places covered thus far include: Amathus, Khirokitia, the Paphos mosaics, the Hadjiyiorgakis Kornesios mansion, Tenta, Lemba, Palea Paphos, the church at Asinou and Kourion.

**Porphyrios Dikaios** *Khirokitia* (o/p). By the long-time excavator of the site. See also his *Enkomi Excavations 1948–1958* (o/p) and *A Guide to the Cyprus Museum* (Nicosia, reissued regularly).

**Jane Fejfer** ed. *Ancient Akamas: Settlement & Environment* (Århus UP,

Denmark). Pricey, illustrated account of a Danish archeological expedition to the peninsula in 1988.

**Einar Gjerstad** *Ages and Days in Cyprus* (Paul Åströms Förlag, Göteborg). An anecdotal record of travels, personal encounters and life on site digs by the head of the Swedish Cyprus Expedition active on the island during the 1920s and 1930s.

☆ **Vassos Karageorghis** *Early Cyprus: Crossroads of the Mediterranean*. Definitive, well-written introduction by one of the foremost Cypriot archeologists, long director of the island's Antiquities Department. Other available titles wholly or partly by the same author, all lavishly illustrated, include *Kition, Mycenaean and Phoenician Discoveries in Cyprus*; *Salamis in Cyprus: Homeric,*

*Hellenistic and Roman* (o/p); *Cyprus Before the Bronze Age: Art of the Chalcolithic Period*, with Edgar Peltenburg; and *Paphos, History and Archaeology* (A. G. Leventis Foundation, Nicosia), with Franz Georg Maier.

★ **Demetrios Michaelides and W. A. Daszewski** *Mosaic Floors in Cyprus* (Ravenna, Edizioni del Girazole). More precisely, part I covers the magnificent Roman mosaics of Paphos; part II describes the mosaic floors of Christian basilicas across the island. Michaelides' *Cypriot Mosaics* (Cyprus Department of Antiquities, Nicosia) is a lot cheaper and easier to find, and is adequate for most levels of interest.

**Louis (Luigi) Palma di Cesnola** *Cyprus: Its Cities, Tombs and Temples* (Star Graphics, Cyprus). A reprinted classic – the rogue diplomat and archeologist/plunderer in his own shameless words, including fascinating vignettes of everyday life on the eve of British rule.

**David Soren and Jamie James** *Kourion, the Search for a Lost Roman City* (o/p). Despite its American-pop style, a valuable account of 1980s finds at Kourion, particularly evidence of the mid-fourth-century earthquake. Soren's *The Sanctuary of Apollo Hylates at Kourion, Cyprus* may also be of interest.

★ **Veronica Tatton-Brown** *Ancient Cyprus*. Good illustrated introduction to the island's past, from Neolithic to late Roman times, by a distinguished archeologist with years of dig experience on Cyprus. Organized by topic ("Jewellery", "The Human Form in Cypriot Art") rather than chronologically, and extremely readable. Her *Cyprus in the Nineteenth Century: Fact, Fancy and Fiction* is an entertaining chronicle of the procession of late-Ottoman, European and American visitors to Cyprus, all eager to find a treasure, locate an acropolis or demonstrate a connection with Bronze Age Greece.

# Pre-1955 history

**Doros Alastos** *Cyprus in History*. Two massive tomes covering all periods up to 1955; unfortunately the author died before finishing vol. III.

★ **Peter W. Edbury** *The Kingdom of Cyprus and the Crusades, 1191–1374*. Plumbs the intricate power struggles of the relatively little-known Lusignan period, but frustratingly stops short of the Venetian tenure.

**Ahmet C. Gazioglu** *The Turks in Cyprus: A Province of the Ottoman Empire (1571–1878)* (o/p). Useful, if exceedingly tendentious history, of which the main thrusts are how beneficent and tolerant the sultan's rule supposedly was, and how perfidious and deserving of their

defeat were the Venetians. That said, full of fascinating data, and worth the price alone for one reprinted 1954 essay: "The Turks of Cyprus", by C. F. Beckingham.

**Sir George Hill** *A History of Cyprus* (4 vols; o/p). The standard, if sometimes flawed, pre-independence reference work – rare and pricey.

**David and Iro Hunt** *Caterina Cornaro, Queen of Cyprus* (o/p). Picks up more or less where the Edbury volume left off, but concentrates mostly on the life and times of the last sovereign of the island, a Venetian married into the Lusignan line.

**Sir David Hunt** ed. *Footprints in Cyprus, an Illustrated History*. Lavishly illustrated anthology covering all eras, more literate than the usual coffee-table book; most easily found in Cyprus.

**Sir Harry Luke** *Cyprus Under the Turks, 1571–1878*. Extensive quotations from documents of the era, not as expository or interesting as it could be – but virtually the only source in English.

**Ioannis Stefanidis** *Isle of Discord: Nationalism, Imperialism and the*

*Making of Cyprus*. Specialist diplomatic history by a respected Greek scholar, focusing on the period 1945 to 1954. Shows how British and American bungling, together with nationalist extremism on the island and in Greece, precluded a peaceful compromise and fuelled the rise of EOKA. Despite the author's status, relies much more on British source material than on the famously stingy Greek archives.

# Monumental art and photo portfolios

**Philippe Delord** *Cyprus: In the Footsteps of Louis-François Cassas* (Gallimard-Hathas, France). Retracing, by a talented young artist, of Cassas' 1785 visit to the island; additional captions by Christine Damillier. Widely available in the South.

**Camille Enlart** *Gothic Art and the Renaissance in Cyprus*. Translated from the French, this highlights the magnificent architecture and exterior decoration left behind by the Lusignan rulers.

**Cyprus: Memories and Love – Through the Lens of George Seferis** (Popular Bank Cultural Department, Nicosia). The Greek Nobel-laureate poet was also a keen photographer, and this well-priced album contains 288 photos from his sojourns here in the mid-1950s.

**Rupert Gunnis** *Historic Cyprus, A Guide to its Towns and Villages, Monasteries and Castles* (o/p). Gunnis visited most sites of interest on the island over a five-year period in the 1930s; this is the result, good for the legends accruing to various spots, but a little uncritical in its evaluations, and misses out a surprising number of villages.

**George Jeffrey** *A Description of the Historic Monuments of Cyprus*. Just that, by the founder of the eponymous museum. Exhaustive, and rather less dry than the *Blue Guide*.

**Michael Radford** *The Railways of Cyprus* (Laïki Group Cultural Centre, Nicosia). An amazing photo-illustrated monograph of all the railways extant on the island 1905–51, including those used for archeological digs. An absolute must for train-spotters, but fascinating for ordinary folk as well.

**Rita Severis** *Travelling Artists in Cyprus, 1700–1960*. More or less as the title says: watercolours and sketches from the beginnings of the Grand Tour to modernity.

⭐ **Andreas and Judith Stylianou** *The Painted Churches of Cyprus* (A. G. Leventis Foundation, Cyprus). The last word on the Tróödhos country churches especially, by a couple who made this subject their life's work; only to be faulted for the scanty number of colour reproductions. Widely available and reasonably priced in Cyprus.

**John Thomson** *Through Cyprus with the Camera in the Autumn of 1878* (o/p). First-ever photos of the island – showing how exotic it was at the start of British rule.

**Reno Wideson** *Cyprus: Images of a Lifetime* (o/p) and *Portrait of Cyprus* (o/p but reasonably priced copies available from Hellenic Bookservice, see p.501). Forty-two years of stunning pictures by the top Cypriot photographer, the former a recently (mid-1990s) published colour study.

# Travel and memoirs

**Sir Samuel Baker** *Cyprus as I Saw it in 1879* (o/p). By turns scathing and rapturous, with plenty of white-man's-burden stuff – including proposals to raze what remained of old Famagusta – from the first year of British administration.

**Patrick Balfour** *The Orphaned Realm* (o/p). Impressionistic and anecdote-laden account from the late 1940s; the title is taken from a famous passage by Leontios Makhairas.

⭐ **Oliver Burch** *The Infidel Sea* (o/p). North Cyprus as it was in the mid-1980s, before tourism had become a significant factor; excellent as a portrait of the Northern community.

**Anne Cavendish** ed. *Cyprus 1878: The Journal of Sir Garnet Wolseley* (Popular Bank Cultural Department, Nicosia). The memoirs of the first British High Commissioner, republished in 2000 at a modest price.

**Claude Delaval Cobham** *Excerpta Cypria, Materials for a History of Cyprus.* An engaging, landmark endeavour: pithy snippets from travellers' and local protagonists' views of Cyprus from biblical times to the nineteenth century, diligently mined by all subsequent writers on Cyprus. But with the price-tag at well into three figures, you'd have to be a rather dedicated researcher.

**Lawrence Durrell** *Bitter Lemons.* Durrell's lyrically told experiences as an English teacher, minor colonial official and bohemian resident of the Kyrenia hills in the EOKA-shadowed mid-1950s have worn remarkably well despite the intervening years.

**Sheila Hawkins** *Back of Beyond* and, *Beyond our Dreams, Beyond Compare, Anthology from the Akamas* (Cyprus Mail Publications, Cyprus). In which a naïve expat and husband make a go at living in a rustic, remote village of the Akámas peninsula; light beach reading, but evocative and widely available on the island.

**Leontios Makhairas** *Recital Concerning the Sweet Land of Cyprus.* Another rare and expensive medieval classic, translated by R. M. Dawkins.

**Giovanni Mariti** *Travels in the Island of Cyprus.* A wonderful eighteenth-century account, translated by Cobham; this edition includes Umberto Foglietta's useful seventeenth-century *The Sieges of Nicosia and Famagusta.*

⭐ **Kyriacos Markides** *The Magus of Strovolos; Homage to the Sun; Fire in the Heart.* Hard to classify: Markides, author of *The Rise and Fall of the Cyprus Republic* (see p.507), becomes involved in the circle of the late mystic and spiritual healer "Daskalos", resident in the Nicosia suburb of Stróvolos; the resulting, late-1980s trilogy is rather sounder than Castaneda's *Don Juan* series, to which it's been compared. His more recent *Riding with the Lion* may also be of interest.

**David Matthews** *The Cyprus Tapes* (Kemal Rüstem, Nicosia). Unashamedly pro-North memoirs by a former BBC producer, for some years a regular columnist for *Cyprus Today* in the North; intimations of Greek-Cypriot skulduggery, and good detail on UN operations.

★ **Ludwig Salvator, Archduke of Austria** *Levkosia, The Capital of Cyprus* (o/p). Nicosia as it was in 1873, delightfully described by one of the Belle Epoque's great eccentrics – though his command of Greek and Turkish terminology was shaky at best, which can make identifying monuments difficult.

★ **Colin Thubron** *Journey into Cyprus*. Account of a three-month trek round the island during 1972 – and in terms of history in context, and a finger on the pulse of (then) contemporary Cyprus, arguably one of the single best books on the place ever written. Widely available in southern Cyprus.

# Independence and after

Most new titles since the early 1990s concern themselves with analysis and post-mortems of events from the late 1950s to the 1980s, often taking advantage of documents released from British archives under the thirty-year rule.

**Rebecca Bryant** *Imagining the Modern: The Cultures of Nationalism in Cyprus*. Current (2004) and incisive, if controversial, dissection of the topic as stated.

**Cynthia Cockburn** *The Line: Women, Partition and the Gender Order in Cyprus*. Patriarchy, nationalism and militarism have been instrumental in keeping women at the margins of power in Cyprus; this is demonstrated, but also the pre-2003 role of bicommunal women's groups in breaching the divide.

**Nancy Crawshaw** *The Cyprus Revolt: An Account of the Struggle for Union with Greece* (o/p). Factual but highly readable, this was long the standard reference work on the rebellion.

★ **David Hannay** *Cyprus: The Search for a Solution*. Lord Hannay was Britain's special envoy to Cyprus from 1996 to 2003, and pulls no punches in this assessment of the failed 2002–03 negotiations and 2004 referendum; both Denktaş and "Tassos" get the roasting they deserve.

★ **Christopher Hitchens** *Hostage to History: Cyprus from the Ottomans to Kissinger*. Given a new preface in 1997, this lively and provocative polemic from 1984 is essential reading, whether you agree with Hitchens or not. Broadly similar conclusions to Stern (see below) as to responsibility for the 1974 catastrophe, but Britain and extremists both Greek- and Turkish-Cypriot get their share of blame as well. Unhappily, some copies are missing crucial maps – check on purchase.

**Robert Holland** *Britain and the Revolt in Cyprus, 1954–1959*. Now considered the classic account, treating events as an instance of decolonization; Holland had access to all the pertinent archives, so authoritative.

**Joseph S. Joseph** *Cyprus: Ethnic Conflict and International Politics – From Independence to the Threshold of the European Union*. Good and fairly current (1999) round-up of all the communal and international issues contributing to the island's status.

★ Keith Kyle *Cyprus, Minority Rights Group Report No. 30* (MRG, UK/Cultural Survival, US). One of the excellent series of pamphlets by this organization, though the summary ceases in 1984; his *Cyprus: In Search of Peace* (MRG, UK), compiled in late 1997, somewhat updates matters, at the price of somewhat condensing earlier events.

★ Diana Weston Markides *Cyprus: From Colonial Conflict to Constitutional Crisis 1957–1963: The Key Role of the Municipal Issue*. Falls into the category of post-mortems on what went wrong early on, but as such one of the best; among other things, explodes the TMT-promoted myth of the Turkish-Cypriot community's monolithic-ness, and shows how the concepts of ethnically separate municipalities were the seedbeds for partition.

Stanley Mayes *Makarios* (o/p). Still the best biography of the man.

Farid Mirbagheri *Cyprus and International Peacemaking, 1964–1986*. Summarizes UN initiatives for a solution; pricey, specialist and rather dated considering its 1998 imprint, but very readable.

★ Brendan O'Malley and Ian Craig *The Cyprus Conspiracy: America, Espionage and the Turkish Invasion*. If you've absorbed Stern and Hitchens, this puts it all together into one coherent thesis: that NATO's numerous electronic surveillance facilities on Cyprus, which date back to the 1940s, have sealed the island's fate. The conspiracy in question is that, following the UK's relegation to second-echelon power after the Suez debacle, and her further inability to guarantee an abiding presence on the island, guiding US policy was to ensure that these spying devices remained out of the hands of any pro-Soviet or even neutral Cypriot regime – first by encouraging Greek moves to undermine Makarios, and subsequently when the junta proved insufficiently reliable, by designating the Turks to take their place. If partition was the price for maintaining NATO's grip on the island, so be it; Kissinger (who gives a grudging, paraphrased interview as an appendix) again emerges in a bleak light. Essential reading, and fairly up to date; even if you disagree with the thesis, the footnoted, recently released UK/US government documents are all there to check up on.

John Reddaway *Burdened with Cyprus: The British Connection* (Kemal Rüstem, Nicosia). General apologia for the UK's colonial and 1960–74 actions (and inactions) by a former high colonial official. Convinced of Makarios's enosist perfidiousness, and gives numerous examples of the archbishop's inflammatory early 1960s utterances (as well as the full text of the infamous Akritas Plan). Though broadly sympathetic to the Turkish Cypriots, Reddaway admits that the UK High Commission may have egged Makarios on to propose his tactless "thirteen amendments", and also concedes that the second phase of the 1974 Turkish invasion was completely unjustified by existing treaties.

★ Laurence Stern *The Wrong Horse* (o/p). The "wrong horse" of the title which the US "bet on" was the 1967–74 Greek military junta and parastate, which under its last leader Ioannides engineered the July 1974 coup resulting in Cyprus's partition. Makes clear just how loopy and self-destructive Ioannides was, and good on the blinkered American Foreign Service/CIA culture of the time in Athens, but a bit absorbed in the minutiae of US congressional politics, and written too soon (1977) after the events described to benefit from declassification of critical papers.

Still, he's barking up the right tree, and despite being relatively polite towards villain of the piece Henry Kissinger (compared to Hitchens, O'Malley and Craig), it provoked the globe-trotting Doctor into supposedly buying up and destroying most of the press run. Thus a rare antiquarian item, difficult to find even in libraries.

# The Greek-Cypriot viewpoint

Especially in the aftermath of 1974, Greek Cypriots were quite successful in monopolizing historiography; the following are some of the more durable and objective sources.

★ Michael Attalides *Cyprus: Nationalism and International Politics* (Moufflon Books, Nicosia). A wide-ranging and readable, if slightly dated, discussion of all aspects of the problem, by a former high-ranking diplomat (ambassador to the UK and France); still considered by many to be the best one-stop summary of all the issues.

★ Peter Loizos *The Heart Grown Bitter: A Chronicle of Cypriot War Refugees* (o/p). Describes Argáki (lately Akçay), a village on the Mórfou plain, and the fate of its inhabitants after the Turkish invasion; moreover an excellent introduction to the complexities of Cypriot communalism and politics, by a London professor with roots in Argáki. His *The Greek Gift: Politics in a Cypriot Village*, demonstrating how Greek-junta meddling impinged on Argáki party politics, has recently been reissued.

Kyriacos Markides *The Rise and Fall of the Cyprus Republic* (o/p). The excellent standard history, still fairly easily found.

Stavros Panteli *A New History of Cyprus: Foreign Domination to Troubled Independence*. This is the second, 2000-updated edition of a choppy and partisan 1984 volume, but nevertheless one of the best sources for the colonial period.

Polyvios Polyviou *Cyprus, Conflict and Negotiation 1960–80* (o/p). Dry but detailed – and relatively objective.

P. N. Vanezis *Cyprus: The Unfinished Agony*, and *Makarios: Life and Leadership* (o/p but Hellenic Bookservice may have copies). These two relatively balanced works are preferable to his Makarian hagiographies *Faith and Power* (again, Hellenic has a stock) and *Pragmatism versus Idealism*.

# The Turkish-Cypriot viewpoint

For decades, the North's position got less of a hearing in the international arena, but since the early 1990s there has been a veritable flood of material, much of it generated by two publishers: Kemal Rüstem in north Nicosia, and the Eothen Press in the UK (☏01480/466106), who should be contacted directly in case of difficulty in ordering from local booksellers.

★ Mehmet Ali Birand *30 Hot Days* (o/p). Hour-by-hour, fairly objective account of the 1974 war by a top Turkish journalist; especially revealing on why the Geneva peace talks failed.

**Clement H. Dodd** ed. *The Political, Social and Economic Development of Northern Cyprus*. Collection of scholarly articles on everything you could possibly want to know about the "non-existent" TRNC. Objective, and frank about the North's problems, though inevitably made obsolete by the crises of 2000–2001, and the events of 2003–04.

**Süha Faiz** *Reflections and Recollections of an Unknown Cyprus Turk*. In which a Turkish Cypriot who has been sent to British public school in the 1930s, married an English woman, become a passive Anglican and served in the colonial civil service unassimilates by rediscovering his Turkic (and Sufi) heritage in late middle age. Overly mannered, and not much specifically on Cyprus, but still worthwhile as a portrait of self-discovery by an upper-crust islander, and for its views on medieval Sufi poet Yunus Emre.

**Pierre Oberling** *The Road to Bellapais: The Turkish Cypriot Exodus to Northern Cyprus*. Useful study, if rather lenient on mainland Turkey, written just before the UDI of 1983; Hitchens (see above) has characterized it as "generally speaking the most naïvely pro-Turkish account of the Cyprus problem yet published." Best secure a copy (expensive) and judge for yourself.

**Vamik Volkan** *Cyprus – War and Adaptation; A Psychoanalytic History of Two Ethnic Groups in Conflict* (o/p). Heavy going through the Freudian jargon, but the Turkish-Cypriot/American author does outline the stresses and adaptive neuroses of the island's beleaguered Turks, pre- and post-1974. His more recent *Turks and Greeks: Neighbours in Conflict*, co-authored with Norman Itzkowitz, was a needed first step in putting both island cultures on the shrink's couch, but proves ultimately disappointing.

# Specific guides

**Adrian Akers-Douglas** *Discover Laona: Walks, Strolls and Drives in "Undiscovered" North-western Cyprus*. As the title says: a delightful small booklet covering the villages, monuments and legends of the Akámas in great detail, though it has not been updated since 1993, and is only easily found at Terra Books, Páfos.

**Lance Chilton** *Walks in the Akamas Area*. A 2001-current guide focusing on the best hikes out of Pólis, Latchí and Neokhorió. Order through ⓦwww.marengowalks.com.

★ **Eileen Davey** *Northern Cyprus: A Traveller's Guide*. Somewhat

misleadingly named, this is actually an excellent archeological survey of Northern sites and monuments from all periods, with useful site plans and well-written potted histories; especially good for the medieval monuments. Easily available at Green Jacket Books in Kyrenia.

★ **Gwynneth der Parthog** *Byzantine and Medieval Cyprus: A Guide to the Monuments* (Moufflon Books, Nicosia). Obsessively detailed guide to churches, castles and other monuments in the South; excellent plans and sketches, far superior to the *Blue Guide* for its chosen period.

# Cypriot fiction in English

These titles can be most easily found through the recommended bookshops in England, and/or Moufflon Bookshop in Nicosia.

**Marian Engel** *Monodromos* (o/p). Probably the only novel (expat-written) with Nicosia as its setting, capturing perfectly the atmosphere of the old town.

**Christakis Georgiou** *Archipelagos: Twenty Years in Labour* (o/p). Landmark novel written in English, set against a background of the miners' strikes and insurrection as Cyprus lurches towards independence. Chronicles a peasant girl's rise from grinding poverty in a hill village, and the sleazy demimonde of the cabarets, to become – through marriage to the heir of the American-managed mines at Léfka – one of the most powerful and wealthy women in the land: the thinly fictionalized story of Zena Gunther, who has a street named for her in Nicosia. The prose is staccato and frankly amateurish, but the tale itself, redolent of atmosphere, would make an excellent film script.

**Niki Marangou** *The Doctor from Vienna*. Essentially her father's life and times, fictionalized, with loads of 1930s-to-1950s period detail of Limassol. To be published in 2006.

**Costas Montis** *Closed Doors*. A fictive portrait of Lawrence Durrell's years, and milieu, in Cyprus.

**G. Philippou Pierides, tr. by Donald E. Martin & Soterios G. Stavrou** *Tetralogy of the Times: Stories of Cyprus*. A collection of modern short stories, part of the growing University of Minnesota Modern Greek Studies series.

# Food and wine

**Yiannos Constantinou** *The Cyprus Wine Guide*. Highlights a score or so of the best wineries in the South, with top picks from each and extensive coverage of Commandaria and *zivanía*.

**Gill Davies** *The Taste of Cyprus*. A seasonally organized look at Cypriot cooking.

**Amaranth Sitas** *Kopiaste*. A good background and overview of island cuisine, preceding a selection of recipes.

**Stanna Wieclawska** *Stop Whining, Start Wining* (Kyriakou Books). The latest word, by a woman with fifteen years of experience reviewing wines for local publication. To be published in 2006.

# Films

Rather tellingly, the first two works cited are banned from screening in both North and South for telling the unvarnished truth about the events of 1963–67 and 1974 (they have only been shown in UN territory at the Ledra

Palace). However, these, and most of the other films listed below, tend to make the rounds of international film festivals, especially in London, Thessaloníki and İstanbul.

**Our Wall** (directed by Panikos Khrysanthou and Niyazi Kızılyürek). Superb, unflinchingly honest feature-length documentary from the late 1990s by two instructors at the Cyprus University in South Nicosia. Besides the experiences of the two film-maker-narrators, it follows the effect of post-independence events on the bereaved of the 1974 war, and on two Turkish Cypriots – Hasan Mustafa and Fatma Mehmet – who elected to stay behind in the South, and who effectively steal the show.

**Parallel Trips** (directed by Derviş Zaim and Panikos Khrysanthou). Shot in late 2002 with Zaim (resident in the North) and Khrysanthou having to work separately, this documentary contains some unflinching personal testimony about atrocities committed by both communities, together with some humbling attitudes of forgiveness from those directly affected. After "Good Wednesday" in 2003, Zaim and Khrysanthou were able to edit together and made only small changes. The natural outgrowth of this was their equally controversial feature, *Mud* (*Çamur*), an allegory about a conscript soldier's search for a cure to the "Cyprus disease", which won the UNESCO Prize at the 2003 Venice Film Festival but also ran foul of censors on the island.

**Living Together Separately** (directed by Elias Demetriou). A 2003 account of bicommunal living, after a fashion, in Pýla.

**Which Cyprus?** (directed by Rustem Batum). Courageous film by Turk Rustem Batum, who exposes the links between the cynical Denktaş regime and military/intelligence figures in the so-called Turkish "deep state", who have together prolonged the island's agony far longer than necessary; banned from, of all places, the 2003 Thessaloníki Film Festival as the Greeks were keen not to offend Turkey.

# Language

# Language

# Language

I asked in Greek and was answered in English. I asked again in Greek and was once again answered in English. It was a long moment before I recollected why. I was in the presence not, as I thought, of Turks who either knew no Greek, or would not condescend to speak it: no, I was in the presence of babus. To lapse into Greek with anyone who was not a peasant would involve a loss of face. It was rather sad.

Lawrence Durrell

D urrell's experience still applies, and to a great extent in the Turkish-Cypriot community as well. Speaking English in Cyprus is a badge of sophistication, and despite Greek's official pre-eminence in the South and similar rank for Turkish in the North, the road to advancement in tourism, education and the private professions if not the civil service. In touristed areas, your Greek or Turkish will have to be nearly perfect to get a reply in kind. Most tourists can and will get by on the island without learning a word of either local language; leave the beaten track, however, especially in the North, and you'll be surrounded by a monolingual culture.

Both Cypriot Greek and Cypriot Turkish are strong dialects – some might argue almost separate languages from the standard phrasebook fare – and familiarity with the latter is not as much of an advantage as you'd think. You will be understood if you utter Athens or İstanbul pleasantries, but you may not catch the reply the first time round – and you won't be alone, since before the homogenizing effect of metropolitan Greek and Turkish television, islanders could carry on conversations virtually incomprehensible to visitors from the "mother" country. About fifteen percent of the day-to-day vocabulary of each community is still peculiar to Cyprus, and the distinctive island accent tends to make Cypriot Greek and Turkish sound almost identical to the untrained ear.

# Greek

So many Greek Cypriots have lived or worked abroad in Britain, and, to a lesser extent, North America and Australia, that you will find numbers of people speaking English even in the remotest village. Add to this the fact that any adult over 55 grew up under British administration, that English is all but compulsory at school, and the overriding importance of the tourist industry, and it's easy to see how many British visitors never bother to learn a word of Greek.

You can certainly get by this way, but it isn't very satisfying, and the willingness and ability to say even a few extra words in Greek will upgrade your status from that of dumb *touristas* to the honourable one of *xénos*, a word which can mean foreigner, traveller and guest all rolled into one.

## Learning basic Greek

Greek is not an easy language for English-speakers – translators' unions in the UK rate it as harder than German, slightly less complex than Russian – but it is a very beautiful one, and even a brief acquaintance will give you some idea of the debt owed to it by western European languages.

Greek **grammar** is predictably complicated: nouns are divided into three genders, all with different case endings in the singular and in the plural, and all adjectives and articles have to agree with these in gender, number and case. To simplify life for beginners, all adjectives are arbitrarily cited in the neuter form in the boxed lists on pp.517–519. **Verbs** are even more complex; they come in two conjugations, in both active and passive voices, with passively constructed verbs often having transitive sense. As a novice, the best thing is simply to say what you know the way you know it, and dispense with the niceties.

## Language-learning materials

### Teach-yourself Greek courses

**Breakthrough Greek** (Pan Macmillan; book and four cassettes). Excellent, basic teach-yourself course; no Greek lettering, but good for classicists who need to unlearn bad habits.

**Greek Language and People** (BBC Publications, UK; book and two cassettes available). More limited in scope but good for acquiring the essentials, and the confidence to try them.

**Anne Farmakides** A Manual of Modern Greek (Yale UP; McGill UP; 3 vols). If you have the discipline and motivation, this is one of the best for learning proper, grammatical Greek; indeed, mastery of just the first volume will get you a long way.

**Hara Garoufalia** Teach Yourself Holiday Greek (Hodder & Stoughton, UK; book and cassette available). Unlike many quickie courses, this provides a good grammatical foundation, but you'll need a dictionary to supplement the scanty vocabulary lists.

**David Hoton et al** Greek: A Comprehensive Grammar of the Modern Language (Routledge). A bit technical in terminology, so not for rank beginners, but it covers just about every conceivable construction.

**Peter Mackridge** The Modern Greek Language. Analysis, by one of the tongue's foremost scholars, of contemporary "standard" Greek; the best resource if you get really interested.

**Niki Watts** Greek in Three Months (Hugo, Dorling Kindersley; book and four cassettes). Delivers as promised; equals or exceeds Breakthrough Greek.

### Phrasebooks and dictionaries

**Greek, A Rough Guide Phrasebook** (Penguin, UK & US). Up-to-date and accurate pocket phrasebook with useful expressions. The English-to-Greek section is sensibly transliterated, though the Greek-to-English part requires basic mastery of the Greek alphabet. Feature boxes fill you in on do's and don'ts and cultural know-how.

**The Oxford Dictionary of Modern Greek** (Oxford UP, UK & US). A bit bulky in its wide format, but generally considered the best Greek–English, English–Greek paperback dictionary.

**Collins Pocket Greek Dictionary** (HarperCollins, UK & US). Very nearly as complete as the Oxford and better value for money. The inexpensive **Collins Gem Greek Dictionary** (UK only) is palm-sized but exactly the same in contents – the best handbag or day-pack choice.

**Oxford Greek-English, English-Greek Learner's Dictionary** (Oxford UP, UK & US). If you're planning a prolonged stay, this pricey, hardbound, two-volume set is unbeatable for usage and vocabulary. There's also the more portable one-volume **Oxford Learner's Pocket Dictionary**.

## Idiosyncrasies of Cypriot Greek

**Consonants** on the island are often at complete variance with what you may know from metropolitan Greece. The "b" sound of standard Greek (ΜΠ, ) is often delivered as a simple "p": thus *parpoúni* for the tasty reddish fish, not *barboúni*; *tapélla* for "sign, placard", not *tabélla*. The letter pi (Π,) is in turn rendered as "b" rather than "p", as in *baboútsia* (shoes) rather than *papoútsia*, the town of Báfos rather than Páfos. Kappa (K, κ) before an "e" or "i" type vowel will sound like the "tch" of Crete rather than "k", as in *Yerostchípou* for the village near Páfos (Yeroskípou). When initial before "a" or "o", kappa sounds more like "g"; the letter tau (T, τ) often sounds more like "d" than "t"; thus, *káto* comes out more like *gádo*, *tavás* as *davás*. Where it's meant that the initial tau is to be pronounced "t" not "d", the letter is doubled (eg Ttákkas Bay); the same has been done with kappa in this word to make it a "k" rather than a "g" or a "tch" sound.

Strong sibilants, lacking to most peninsular Greek-speakers, are also a feature of the dialect: the letter combination sigma-iota (ΣI, σι) is pronounced, and transliterated (though no longer in officialese), as "sh" rather than "si". The letter khi (X, χ), when medial, is often pronounced the same way – *éshi*, not *ékhi*, for "there is" or "he/she/it/ has". The combinations delta-iota-alpha (ΔIA, δια), theta-iota-alpha (ΘIA, θια) or delta-ypsilon (ΔY, δυ) have unpredictably bizarre results in sound and accent: the first two, as in the bridge of Roúdhias, come out as *thskiá*, while the latter, as in dhýo, "two", emerges as *thskió*. Iota after rho (PI, ρι) becomes a "g" sound: eg *horgó* rather than standard Greek *horió*, "village", or *Tillyrgá* rather than Tillyría, the remote western region. Especially in Páfos district, Turkisms in the vocabulary abound: examples include *chakí* instead of the standard *souyiás* for "pocketknife", *chatália* (literally, "forks") for "trousers". Many final iota-ni (-IN, -ιν) syllables, not found in metropolitan Greek, have been added to words of Turkish or Venetian origin.

If you know Greek passably well, there is one small learning aid designed for continental Greeks attempting to cope with Cypriot dialect: Konstantinos Yiangoullis's *Lexiko-Etymoloyiko ke Ermineftiko tis Kypriakis Dhialektou* (Etymological and Interpretative Dictionary of the Cypriot Dialect), easily available in the South, which lists thousands of words derived from ancient Greek, medieval French, Italian, Turkish (and even English), often with short examples of use in folk ballads or poetry. There is unfortunately nothing available to assist the English-speaking novice – the local dialect is apparently considered beneath serious consideration by the linguistic powers that be.

## The Greek alphabet: transliteration and accentuation

On top of the usual difficulties of learning a new language, Greek presents the additional problem of an entirely separate alphabet. Despite initial appearances, this is in practice fairly easily mastered within a few days – a skill that will help enormously if you are going to get around independently (see box on overpage, and the Greek-alphabet lists of place names at the end of each chapter of Southern Cyprus). In addition, certain combinations of letters have unexpected results – especially compared to peninsular Greek; see the remarks on Cypriot dialect preceding. This book's transliteration system should help you make intelligible noises, but you have to remember that the correct **stress** (marked throughout the book with an acute accent or sometimes a dieresis) is crucial. With the right sounds but the wrong stress people will either fail to understand you, or else understand something quite different from what you intended. There are numerous pairs of words with the same spelling and phonemes, distinguished only by their stress.

The **dieresis** is used in Greek over the second of two adjacent vowels to change the pronunciation that you would expect from the table on p.516; sometimes it can function as the primary stress. In the word *kaïki* (caique), the presence of the dieresis changes the pronunciation from "cake-key" to "ka-ee-key" and additionally the middle "i" carries the primary stress. In the place Kaïmaklí (near Nicosia), the dieresis again changes the sound of the first syllable from "kay" to "Ka-ee", but in this case the primary stress is on the third syllable. It is also, uniquely among Greek accents, used on capital letters in signs and personal-name spellings in Cyprus, though for simplicity our city street maps are unaccented.

Set out below is the Greek alphabet, the system of transliteration used in this book, and a brief aid to pronunciation.

| Greek | transliteration | pronounced |
|-------|-----------------|------------|
| Α, α | a | a as in father |
| Β, β | v | v as in vet |
| Γ, γ | y/g | y as in yes, except before consonants, α, o or ου, when it's a breathy g, approximately as in gap |
| Δ, δ | dh | th as in then, except before i/y |
| Ε, ε | e | e as in get |
| Ζ, ζ | z | z sound |
| Η, η | i | i as in ski |
| Θ, θ | th | th as in theme, except before i/y |
| Ι, ι | i | i as in ski |
| Κ, κ | k | nominally k sound, usually 'tchí if medial, 'gí if initial, unless doubled |
| Λ, λ | l | l sound |
| Μ, ∝ | m | m sound |
| Ν, ν | n | n sound |
| Ξ, ξ | x | x as in box, medial or initial (never z as in xylophone) |
| Ο, ο | o | o as in toad |
| Π, π | p | p sound |
| Ρ, ρ | r | xr sound |
| Σ, σ, ς | s | s sound, except z sound before μ or γ; |
| | | note that single sigma has the same phonetic value as double sigma |
| Τ, τ | t | t sound, but more like d unless doubled |
| Υ, υ | y, i | y as in barely |
| Φ, φ | f | f sound |
| Χ, χ | kh | harsh h sound, like ch in loch, but often sh when medial |
| Ψ, ψ | ps | ps as in lips |
| Ω, ω | o | o as in toad, indistinguishable from o |

## Combinations and diphthongs

| | | |
|---|---|---|
| ΑΙ, αι | e | e as in hey |
| ΑΥ, αυ | av/af | av or af depending on following consonant |
| ΕΙ, ει | i | long i, exactly like ι or η |
| ΕΥ, ευ | ev/ef | ev or ef, depending on following consonant |
| ΟΙ, οι | i | long i, exactly like ι or η |
| ΟΥ, ου | ou | ou as in tourist |

516

| ΓΓ, γγ | ng | ng as in angle; always medial |
| ΓΚ, γκ | g/ng | g as in goat at the beginning of a word; ng in the middle |
| ΜΠ, μπ | b/mb | b at the beginning of a word; mb in the middle, but see note p.514 |
| ΝΤ, ντ | d/nd | d at the beginning of a word, nd in the middle |
| ΣΙ, σι | sh | sh as in shame |
| ΤΣ, τσ | ts | ts as in cha-cha |
| ΤΖ, τζ | tz | j as in jam |

# Greek words and phrases

## Basics

| | |
|---|---|
| Né | Yes |
| Málista | Certainly |
| îhi | No |
| Parakaló | Please |
| Endáxi | Okay, agreed |
| Efharistó (polý) | Thank you (very much) |
| (Dhén) Katalavéno | I (don't) understand |
| Parakaló, mípos miláte angliká? | Excuse me, do you speak English? |
| Signómi | Sorry/excuse me |
| Símera | Today |
| Ávrio | Tomorrow |
| Khthés | Yesterday |
| Tóra | Now |
| Argótera | Later |
| Anikhtó | Open |
| Klistó | Closed |
| Méra | Day |
| Nýkhta | Night |
| Tó proï | In the morning |
| Tó apóyevma | In the afternoon |
| Tó vrádhi | In the evening |
| Edhó | Here |
| Ekí | There |
| Aftó | This one |
| Ekíno | That one |
| Kaló | Good |
| Kakó | Bad |
| Megálo | Big |
| Mikró | Small |
| Perisótero | More |
| Ligótero | Less |
| Lígo | A little |
| Polý | A lot |

| | |
|---|---|
| Ftinó | Cheap |
| Akrivó | Expensive |
| Zestó | Hot |
| Krýo | Cold |
| Mazí (mé) | With (together) |
| Horís | Without |
| Grígora | Quickly |
| Sigá | Slowly |

## Other needs

| | |
|---|---|
| Trógo/píno | To eat/drink |
| Foúrnos, psomádhiko | Bakery |
| Farmakío | Pharmacy |
| Takhydhromío | Post office |
| Gramatósima | Stamps |
| Venzinádhiko | Petrol station |
| Trápeza | Bank |
| Leftá/Khrímata | Money |
| Toualéta | Toilet |
| Astynomía | Police |
| Yiatrós | Doctor |
| Nosokomío | Hospital |

## Requests and questions

To ask a question, it's simplest – though hardly elegant – to start with *parakaló*, then name the thing you want in an interrogative tone.

| | |
|---|---|
| Parakaló, o foúrnos? | Where is the bakery? |
| Parakaló, ó dhrómos yiá ...? | Can you show me the road to ...? |
| Parakaló, éna dhomátio yiá for two – dhýo átoma | We'd like a room for two |
| Parakaló, éna kiló portokália? | May I have a kilo of oranges? |

| | |
|---|---|
| Poú? | Where? |
| Pós? | How? |
| Póssi, pósses or póssa? | How many? |
| Póso (káni)? | How much (does it cost)? |
| Póte? | When? |
| Yiatí? | Why? |
| Sé tí óra . . . ? | At what time . . . ? |
| Tí íne/pió íne . . . ? | What is/Which is . . . ? |
| Tí óra aníyi? | What time does it open? |
| Tí óra klíni? | What time does it close? |

## Talking to people

Greek makes the distinction between the informal (*essý*) and formal (*essís*) second person, as French does with *tu* and *vous*. Young people, older people and country people often use *essý* even with total strangers, though if you greet someone familiarly and they respond formally, it's best to adopt their usage as the conversation continues, to avoid offence. By far the most common greeting, on meeting and parting, is *yiá sou/yiá sas* – literally "health to you". Incidentally, as across most of the Mediterranean, the approaching party utters the first greeting, not those seated at sidewalk *kafenío* tables or doorsteps – thus the occasional silent staring as you enter a remote village.

| | |
|---|---|
| Hérete | Hello |
| Kalí méra | Good morning |
| Kalí spéra | Good evening |
| Kalí nýkhta | Good night |
| Adío | Goodbye |
| Tí kánis/Tí kánete? | How are you? |
| Kalá íme | Iím fine |
| Ké essý/essís? | And you? |
| Pós sé/sás léne? | What's your name? |
| Mé léne . . . | My name is . . . |
| Kýrios/Kyría | Mr/Mrs |
| Dhespinís | Miss |
| Parakaló, miláte pió sigá | Speak slower, please |

| | |
|---|---|
| Pós léyete stá Elliniká? | How do you say it in Greek? |
| Dhén xéro | I don't know |
| Thá sé dhó ávrio | See you tomorrow |
| Kalí andámosi | See you soon |
| Kaló taxídhi | Bon voyage |
| Páme | Let's go |
| Parakaló, ná mé voithíste | Please help me |

## Greek's Greek

There are numerous words and phrases which you will hear constantly, even if you rarely have the chance to use them. These are a few of the most common.

| | |
|---|---|
| Éla! | Come (literally) but also Speak to me! You don't say! etc |
| Oríste! | Literally, "Indicate!"; in effect, "What can I do for you?" |
| Embrós! or Léyete! | Standard phone responses |
| Tí néa? | What's new? |
| Tí yínete? | What's going on (here)? |
| Étsi kiétsi | So-so |
| Ópa! | Whoops! Watch it! |
| Po-po-po! | Expression of dismay or concern, like French "o là là" |
| Pedhí moú | My boy/girl, sonny, friend, etc |
| Maláka(s) | Literally "wanker", in mainland Greek; not often heard in Cyprus and best not used by foreigners |
| Palavós | A nutcase, a loony – much more used in Cyprus than *malákas*, and more socially acceptable |
| Sigá sigá | Take your time, slow down |

## Accommodation

| | |
|---|---|
| Xenodhohío | Hotel |
| Xenón(as) | Inn |
| Éna dhomátio . . . | A room . . . |
| yiá éna/dhýo/tría átoma | for one/two/three people |
| yiá mía/dhýo/trís vradhiés | for one/two/three nights |
| mé megálo/dipló kreváti | with a double bed |
| mé loutró | with en-suite bath |
| Zestó neró | hot water |
| Krýo neró | Cold water |
| Klimatismós | Air conditioning |
| Anamistíra | Fan |
| Boró ná tó dhó? | Can I see it? |
| Kámping/ Kataskínosi | Campsite |

## Travelling

| | |
|---|---|
| Aeropláno | Aeroplane |
| Leoforío, púlman | Bus, coach |
| Aftokínito, amáxi | Car |
| Mihanáki, papáki | Motorbike, scooter |
| Taxí | Taxi |
| Podhílato | Bicycle |
| Mé tá pódhia | On foot |
| Monopáti | Trail |
| Stássi | Bus stop |
| Limáni | Harbour |
| Ti óra févyi? | What time does it leave? |
| Ti óra ftháni? | What time does it arrive? |
| Póssa hilióimetra? | How many kilometres? |
| Pósses óres? | How many hours? |
| Poú pás? | Where are you going? |
| Páo stó . . . | I'm going to . . . |
| Thélo ná katévo stó . . | I want to get off at . . . |
| O dhrómos yiá . . . | The road to . . . |
| Kondá | Near |
| Makriá | Far |
| Aristerá | Left |
| Dhexiá | Right |
| Katefthía, ísia | Straight ahead |
| Éna isitírio yiá . . . | A ticket to . . . |

| | |
|---|---|
| Paralía | Beach |
| Spiliá | Cave |
| Kéndro | Centre (of town) |
| Eklissía | Church |
| Thálassa | Sea |

## Days of the week, months and seasons

| | |
|---|---|
| Kyriakí | Sunday |
| Dheftéra | Monday |
| Tríti | Tuesday |
| Tetárti | Wednesday |
| Pémpti | Thursday |
| Paraskeví | Friday |
| Sávato | Saturday |

NB You may see katharévoussa (formal Greek), or hybrid, forms of the months written on schedules or street signs; these are the spoken demotic forms.

| | |
|---|---|
| Yennáris | January |
| Fleváris | February |
| Mártis | March |
| Aprílis | April |
| Maïos | May |
| Ioúnios | June |
| Ioúlios | July |
| Ávgoustos | August |
| Septémvris | September |
| Októvrios | October |
| Noémvris | November |
| Hekémvris | December |
| Therinó dhromolóyio | Summer schedule |
| Himerinó dhromolóyio | Winter schedule |

## Numbers

| | |
|---|---|
| énas/éna/mía | 1 |
| dhýo | 2 |
| tris/tría | 3 |
| tésseres/téssera | 4 |
| pénde | 5 |
| éxi | 6 |
| eftá | 7 |
| okhtó | 8 |
| ennéa (or more slangy, enyá) | 9 |

519

| | | | | |
|---|---|---|---|---|
| dhéka | 10 | | hílies/hília | 1000 |
| éndheka | 11 | | dhýo hiliádhes | 2000 |
| dhódheka | 12 | | éna ekatomírio | 1,000,000 |
| dhekatrís | 13 | | próto | First |
| dhekatésseres | 14 | | dhéftero | Second |
| íkossi | 20 | | tríto | Third |
| íkossi éna | 21 | | | |
| triánda | 30 | | | |

## Time

| | |
|---|---|
| Ti óra íne? | What time is it? |
| Mía íy óra/dhýo íy óra/trís íy óra | One/two/three o'clock |
| Tésseres pará íkossi | Twenty minutes to four |
| Eftá ke pénde | Five minutes past seven |
| Éndheka ke misí, endhekámisi | Half past eleven |
| Se misí óra | In half an hour |
| Siéna tétarto | In a quarter-hour |
| Sé dhýo óres | In two hours |

Additional number entries:

| | |
|---|---|
| saránda | 40 |
| penínda | 50 |
| exínda | 60 |
| evdhomínda | 70 |
| ogdhónda | 80 |
| enenínda | 90 |
| ekató | 100 |
| ekatón penínda | 150 |
| dhiakóssies/ dhiakóssia | 200 |
| pendakóssies/ pendakóssia | 500 |

# Turkish

It's worth learning as much Turkish as you can while you're in North Cyprus; if you travel far from the tourist centres you may well need it, and Cypriots will always appreciate foreigners who show enough interest and courtesy to learn at least basic greetings. The main advantages of the language from the learner's point of view are that it's phonetically spelt, and (98 percent of the time) grammatically regular. The disadvantages are that the vocabulary is completely unrelated to any language you're likely to have encountered, and the grammar – relying heavily on suffixes – gets more alien the further you delve into it. Concepts like vowel harmony further complicate matters. Trying to grasp at least the basics, though, is well worth the effort.

## Vowel harmony and loan words

Turkish generally adheres to the principle of **vowel harmony**, whereby words contain either the so-called "back" vowels a, ı, o and u, or the "front" vowels e, i, ö and ü, but rarely mix the two types. Back and front vowels are further subdivided into "unrounded" (a and ı, e and i) and "rounded" (o and u, ö and ü), and again rounded and unrounded vowels tend to keep exclusive company, though there are further nuances to this. A small number of native Turkish words (eg, *anne*, mother; *kardeş*, brother) violate the rules of vowel harmony, as do compound words, eg *bugün*, "today", formed from *bu* (this) and *gün* (day).

The main exceptions to vowel harmony, however, are foreign **loan words** from Arabic or Persian, and despite Atatürk's best efforts to substitute Turkish or French expressions (the latter again failing to follow vowel harmony), they still make up a good third of the modern Turkish vocabulary. Most words beginning with f, h, l, m, n, r, v and z, or ending in d, t, b or p are derived from Arabic and Persian.

# Dictionaries and phrasebooks

For a straightforward **phrasebook**, look no further than *Turkish: A Rough Guide Phrasebook* (Rough Guides) – though based on the mainland dialect, it has useful two-way glossaries and a brief and simple grammar section. If you want to **learn** more, Geoffrey L. Lewis's *Teach Yourself Turkish* (Hodder) still probably has a slight edge over Yusuf Mardin's *Colloquial Turkish* (Routledge); or buy both, since they complement each other well. Alternatively, there's Geoffrey Lewis's *Turkish Grammar* (OUP), a one-volume solution. If you're serious about learning Turkish when you get to Cyprus, the best series is a set of three textbooks and tapes, *Türkçe Öğreniyoruz* (Engin Yayınevi), available at Rüstem's Bookshop in Nicosia.

Among widely available Turkish **dictionaries**, the best are probably those produced by Langenscheidt in miniature or coat-pocket sizes, or the *Concise Oxford Turkish Dictionary*, a hardback suitable for serious students. The Redhouse dictionaries produced in Turkey are the best value: the affordable four-and-a-half-inch *Mini Sözlük* has the same number of entries as the seven-and-a-half-inch desk edition and is adequate for most demands; the definitive, two-tome version even gives Ottoman Turkish script and etymologies for each word, but it costs the earth and isn't exactly portable.

## Idiosyncrasies of Cypriot Turkish

Pafiot Turkish in particular, as long as it lasts as a separate sub-dialect, shows the effects of long cohabitation with Cypriot Greek. There is no indicative tense as in standard Turkish, the indefinite mood being used on most occasions; nor are there interrogative particles as in Turkey, a question being indicated by voice inflection as in Greek.

Moreover, refugees from Páfos (*Baf* in Turkish, incidentally) frequently use *etmek*, normally only an auxiliary verb in Anatolian Turkish, in place of *yapmak* for "to do, to make". Slurred pronoun constructions are common and confusing: *ba* for *bana* (to/for me), *sa* for *sana* (to/for you), *gen* for *kendíne* (to/for oneself). *Naípan*, the standard colloquial greeting, is an elision of *Ne yaparsın* (approximately, "Whaddya up to?" or "Whatcha doin'?")

That last translation gives a fairly accurate idea of the casualness of Cypriot linguistic mores; the islanders derive some amusement from the painfully polite diction of İstanbul people, who in turn consider the island dialect just plain slovenly. However, Turkish television plus nearly two decades of army occupation, mainland settlers and refugee status are steadily eroding these peculiarities, which could disappear over the next generation unless there's a settlement which permits substantial social mixing with Greek Cypriots.

## Pronunciation and accentuation

Pronunciation in Turkish is worth mastering, since once you've got it, the phonetic spelling and regularity helps you progress fast. The following letters differ significantly from English pronunciation.

| | | | |
|---|---|---|---|
| Aa | short a, similar to that in far | Oo | as in note |
| Ee | as in bet | Öö | like ur in burn |
| İi | as in pin | Uu | as in blue |
| Iı | unstressed vowel identical to the vestigial sound between the b and the l of probable | Üü | like ew in few |
| | | Cc | like j in jelly |
| | | Çç | like ch in chat |

| | | | |
|---|---|---|---|
| Gg | hard g as in get | Hh | as in hen, never silent |
| Ğğ | generally silent, but lengthens the preceding vowel, and between two vowels approximates a y sound | Jj | like the s in pleasure |
| | | Şş | like sh in shape |
| | | Vv | soft, between a v and a w |

The **circumflex** (^), found only over the letters a, u and i in loan words from Arabic or Persian, has two uses. It usually lengthens the vowel it crowns, eg Mevlâna sounds like 'Mevlaana', Alevî is pronounced 'Alevee', but when used after the consonants g, k or l the affected vowel sounds like it's preceded by a faint y, and distinguishes words that are otherwise homonyms: eg *kar* (snow) versus *kâr* (profit). Although its meticulous use in the modern language is dwindling over 'i', news of the circumflex's demise has been greatly exaggerated, and you still commonly see it in media as diverse as THY publicity and newspaper headlines – while its use in historical or religious texts remains universal.

## Turkish words and phrases

### Basics

| | | | |
|---|---|---|---|
| Bey | Mr; follows first name | (Sağol) İyiyim/ İyilik sağlık | I'm fine (thank you) |
| Bayan | Miss; precedes first name | İngilizce biliyormusunuz? | Do you speak English? |
| Hanım | Mrs (literally lady) polite Ottoman title; follows first name | Anlamadım/Türkçe anlamıyorum | I don't understand (Turkish) |
| | | Bilmiyorum | I don't know |
| | | Affedersiniz | I beg your pardon, sorry |
| Usta | Half-humorous honorific title bestowed on any tradesman; means "master craftsman" | Pardon | Excuse me (in a crowd) |
| | | Geziyorum/ Dolaşıyorum | I'm sightseeing |
| Hacı | Honorific of someone who has made the pilgrimage to Mecca | İngilizim/İsko/ yalım/ | I'm English/Scottish |
| | | İrlandalıyım/ Avustralyalım | Irish/Australian |
| Günaydın | Good morning | . . .'de/da oturuyorum | I live in . . |
| İyi Günler | Good afternoon | Bugün | Today |
| İyi Akşamlar | Good evening | Yarın | Tomorrow |
| İyi Geceler | Good night | ...bür gün/Ertesi gün | The day after tomorrow |
| Merhaba | Hello | | |
| Allahaısmarladık | Goodbye | Dün | Yesterday |
| Evet | Yes | Şimdi | Now |
| Hayır | No | Sonra | Later |
| Yok | No (there isn't any) | Bir dakika! | Wait a minute! |
| Lütfen | Please | Sabahleyin | In the morning |
| Teşekkür ederim Mersi/Sağol | Thank you | Öğleden sonra | In the afternoon |
| | | Akşamleyin | In the evening |
| Bir şey değil | You're welcome, that's OK | Burda/Burda/Orda | Here/there/over there |
| Nasılsınız? Nasılsın? Ne haber? Napan? | How are you? | İyi/Kötü, Fena | Good/bad |
| | | Büyük/Küçük | Big/small |
| | | Ucuz/Pahalı | Cheap/expensive |

LANGUAGE | Turkish

| Erken/Ge | Early/late |
|---|---|
| Sİcak/Soğuk | Hot/cold |
| Yakİn/Uzak | Near/far |
| Boş/Dolu | Vacant/occupied |
| Hızlı/Yavaş | Quickly/slowly |
| (Süt)lu/(Süt)suz | With/without (milk) |
| (Et)li/(Et)siz | With/without (meat) |
| Yeter | Enough |

## Driving

| Sol | Left |
|---|---|
| Sağ | Right |
| Doğru, direk | Straight ahead |
| Sola dön/Sağita dön | Turn left/right |
| Park yapılır/Park yapılmaz | Parking/No parking |
| Tek yön | One-way street |
| Araç giremez | No entry |
| Çıkmaz sokak | No through road |
| Yavaşla | Slow down |
| Yol kapalı | Road closed |
| Dörtyol | Crossroads |
| Yaya geçidi | Pedestrian crossing |

## Some signs

| Giriş/Çıkış | Entrance/exit |
|---|---|
| Giriş ücretsiz/ Ücretlidir | Free/paid entrance |
| Baylar | Gentlemen |
| Bayanlar | Ladies |
| WC/Tuvalet/Umumî | WC |
| Açık/Kapalı | Open/closed |
| Varİş/Kalkış | Arrivals/departures |
| Çekiniz/Ğtiniz | Pull/push |
| Arızalı | Out of order |
| İçilebilir su | Drinking water |
| Kiralık | To let/for hire |
| Kambiyo | Foreign exchange |
| Dikkat | Beware |
| İlk yardım | First aid |
| Sigara İçilmez | No Smoking |
| Çimenlere basmayınız | Don't tread on the grass |
| Dur | Stop/halt |
| Askeri bölge | Military Area |
| Girmek yasaktır | Entry Forbidden |

| Lütfen ayakkabılarınızı çıkartınız | Please take off your shoes |
|---|---|
| Yaya giremez | No entry on foot |

## Requests and questions

| ...nerede? | Where is the . . . ? |
|---|---|
| Ne zaman? | When? |
| Ne/Ne dir? | What/What is it? |
| Ne kadar/Kaça? | How much (does it cost?) |
| Kaç tane? | How many? |
| Niye? | Why? |
| Saatınız var mı? | What time is it? (polite) |
| Saat kaç ? | (informal) |
| 'ia/e nasıl giderim? | How do I get to . . . ? |
| 'ia/e ne kadar uzakta? | How far is it to . . . ? |
| Beni . . . 'a/e götürebilirmisiniz? | Can you give me a lift to...? |
| Kaçta a ılıcak? | What time does it open? |
| Kaçta kapanacak? | What time does it close? |
| Türkcesi ne dir? or, Turkçe nasıl söylersiniz? | Whatís it called in Turkish? |

## Accommodation

| Hotel/Otel | Hotel |
|---|---|
| Yakında otel var mı? | Is there a hotel nearby? |
| Boşodanız var mı? | Do you have a room? |
| Tek/Çift/Üç kişilik | Single/double/triple |
| Bir/İki/Üç gecelik ift yataklı odanız var mı? | Do you have a double room for one/two/ three nights? |
| Bir/İki haftalık | For one/two weeks |
| İlave yataklı | With an extra bed |
| Fransiz yataklı | With a double bed |
| Duşlu | With a shower |
| Havuzlu | With a bathtub |
| Sicak su | Hot water |
| Soğuk su | Cold water |
| Bakabilirmiyim? | Can I see it? |
| Reservasyonim var | I have a booking |

## Travelling

| Uçak | Aeroplane |
|---|---|

| Otobus | Bus |
|---|---|
| Araba | Car |
| Taksi | Taxi |
| Bisiklet | Bicycle |
| Feribot | Ferry |
| Deniz otobüsü | Catamaran |
| Yaya | On foot |
| Otogar | Bus station |
| İskele | Ferry terminal/jetty |
| Liman | Harbour |
| ...a bir bilet | A ticket to... |
| Kaçta kalkıyor? | What time does it leave? |
| Bir sonraki otobus/ vapur kaçta kalkıyor? | When is the next bus/ ferry? |
| Nereden kalkıyor? | Where does it leave from? |
| Kaç mildir? | How many miles is it? |
| Ne kadar sürerbilir? | How long does it take? |
| Hangi otobus... 'a gider? | Which bus goes to...? |
| Hangi yol ... 'a çıkar? | Which road leads to...? |
| Müsait bir yerde inebilirmiyim? | Can I get out at a convenient place? |

## Days of the week, months and seasons

| Pazar | Sunday |
|---|---|
| Pazartesi | Monday |
| Salı | Tuesday |
| Çarşamba | Wednesday |
| Perşembe | Thursday |
| Cuma | Friday |
| Cumartesi | Saturday |
| Ocak | January |
| Subat | February |
| Mart | March |
| Nisan | April |
| Mayıs | May |
| Haziran | June |
| Temmuz | July |
| Ağustos | August |
| Eylül | September |
| Ekim | October |
| Kasım | November |
| Aralık | December |

| İlkbahar | Spring |
|---|---|
| Yaz | Summer |
| Sonbahar | Autumn |
| Kış | Winter |

## Numbers

| 1 | Bir |
|---|---|
| 2 | İki |
| 3 | Üç |
| 4 | Dört |
| 5 | Beş |
| 6 | Altı |
| 7 | Yedi |
| 8 | Sekiz |
| 9 | Dokuz |
| 10 | On |
| 11 | On bir |
| 12 | On iki |
| 13 | On üç |
| 20 | Yirmi |
| 30 | Otuz |
| 40 | Kırk |
| 50 | Elli |
| 60 | Altmış |
| 70 | Yetmiş |
| 80 | Seksen |
| 90 | Doksan |
| 100 | Yüz |
| 140 | Yüz kırk |
| 200 | İki yüz |
| 700 | Yedi yüz |
| 1000 | Bin |
| 100,000 | Yüz bin |
| 500,000 | Beşyüz bin |
| 1,000,000 | Bir milyon |

## Time

| Saat üç (ta) | (At) 3 o'clock |
|---|---|
| İki saat | 2 hours (duration) |
| Yarım saat | Half hour (duration) |
| Beş büçük | Five-thirty |
| Sekizi on geçiyor | It's 8.10 |
| On bire çeyrek var | It's 10.45 |
| Sekizi on geçe | At 8.10 |
| On bire çeyrek kala | At 10.45 |

# A Greek and Turkish food glossary

In the following lists, the words are given in this order – **Greek/Turkish, English**. If the dish or drink is not found in the particular community, or there is no known Greek or Turkish equivalent, a dash is shown.

## Basics

| | |
|---|---|
| neró/su | water |
| aláti/tuz | salt |
| eliés/zeytin | olives |
| pítta/pita | flat Arab bread |
| psomí/ekmek | bread |
| elióti/– | olive bread |
| piláfi/pilav | cooked rice |
| pourgoúri/bulgur | cracked wheat |
| makarónia/şehriye | (thin) noodles |
| yiaoúrti/yoğurt | yogurt |
| gála/süt | milk |
| méli/bal | honey |
| voútyro/tereyağ | butter |

## Appetisers (mezédhes/mezeler) and picnic items

| | |
|---|---|
| talatoúra/talatur, cacık | yogurt, cucumber, garlic and herb dip; Turkish-Cypriot *talatur* has more mint and cucumber, less garlic |
| taramás/tarama | pink fish-roe paté |
| húmmos/humus | hummus |
| tashíni/tahin | sesame seed paste |
| –/eşeksiksin | tahini with lemon juice or other souring agents |
| loœntza/– | smoked pork loin slabs |
| shirómeri/– | cured local ham, like parma or prosciutto |
| tsamarélla/samarella | lamb- or (better) goat-based salami; made from flesh just under the skin |
| halloúmi/hellim | minty ewe's or goat's cheese, often fried |
| anarí/nor | soft, crumbly sweet cheese, byproduct of above |
| fétta/beyaz peynir | white goat's or ewe's cheese |
| kasséri/kaşar | kasseri cheese |
| moúngra/moungra | pickled cauliflower |
| tsakistés/çakistes | split olives, usually green, marinated in coriander seed, lemon and garlic |

## Meat and game entrees

| | |
|---|---|
| kléftigo/küp kebap, fırın kebap | lamb baked in an outdoor oven |
| souvlaáki/şış kebap | meat chunks grilled on a skewer |
| rífi/– | whole lamb on a spit |
| –/kuyu kebap | meat baked in an underground vessel |
| sheftália/şeftalya, şeftalı kebap | grilled mince-and-onion pellets in gut casings |
| keftédhes/köfte | meatballs |
| pastourmás/pastırma, sucuk | greasy sausage or cured dry meat |
| glykádhia/– | sweetbreads |
| zalatina/– | brawn |
| kotópoulo/pili | chicken |
| gourounópoulo/– | suckling pig |
| peristéri/güverçin | pigeon |
| kounélli/tavşan | rabbit |
| ortítchia/bildirçin | quail |
| ambelopoúlia/amberobulya | pickled songbirds |
| karaóles/salyangoz | land snails |
| lougánigo/bumbar | skinny home-made sausages, the latter often with a high proportion of rice filling |

## Soups

| | |
|---|---|
| avgolémono/düğün | egg and lemon |
| trakhanás/tarhana | grain, yogurt, spices |
| patsás/işkembe | tripe |

## Preparation terms

| | |
|---|---|
| tís óras, stá kárvouna/kömürde, ızgarada | grilled |
| tiganitó/yağda | fried |
| stifádho/yahni | stewed in a sweet onion-and-tomato sauce |
| parayemistá/dolması | stuffed |
| plakí/pilaki | vinaigrette, marinated |
| oftó/fırında | baked |

## Fish and seafood

| | |
|---|---|
| péstrofa/– | trout (farmed) |
| parpoúni/tekir | red mullet |
| koutsomoúra/ barbun | dwarf red mullet |
| sorkós/sargoz | bream |
| ballás/– | large-eyed dentex |
| melána, melánes/– | saddled bream |
| lithríni/mercan | red bream, pandora |
| marídhes/smirida | picarel |
| wóppes/küpes, woppa | bogue |
| parakoúdha/– | barracuda |
| lakérdha/lakerda | white-flesh bonito, marinated |
| mayátiko/mineri | amberjack |
| lagós/lahoz | small (golden) grouper |
| rofós/orfoz | large (dusky) grouper, rather bony |
| stýra, vláhos/vlahos –/sokan | stone bass, wreckfish cheapish medium-size fish |
| fangrí/mercan | common bream |
| spáros/karagöz | two-banded or ringed bream |
| skathári/sarıgöz | black bream |
| tsipoúra /çipura | gilt-head bream |
| synagrídha/sinagrit | dentex |
| khános/asıl hani | comber |
| smérna/merina | moray eel |
| garídhes/karides | small prawns |
| khtapódhi/ahtapod | octopus |
| kalamarákia/kalamar | small squid |
| karavídhes/ karavidler | crayfish |

| | |
|---|---|
| kolokythás/– | "sea mole", a meatier crustacean than crayfish |

## Greens

| | |
|---|---|
| saláta/salata | any salad |
| maroúli/marul | lettuce |
| koliándhros/kolandro | coriander |
| maïdhanós /maydanos | parsley |
| glystirídha/semizotu | purslane |
| sélino/kereviz | celery |
| lapsána/lapsana | wild mustard greens |
| rókka/rokka | rocket greens |
| –/gömec | mallow greens |
| louvána/– | pea-plant leaves |
| strouthondhiá/– | wild baby spinach |
| khristangáthi/– | dockweed |
| pangáli/– | another Lenten green |
| ostés/ostes | artichoke-like thistle |
| molehíya/molohiya, mulihiya | a mint-like leaf used as meat flavouring, or served steamed on its own, mostly in the North |
| kírtamo/kırtama | rock samphire |
| agrélia/ayrelli, kuşkonmaz | (wild) asparagus |
| kapária/gebre | pickled caper plants |
| angináres/enginar | globe artichokes |

## Other vegetables

| | |
|---|---|
| krambí/lahana | cabbage |
| domátes/domates | tomatoes |
| kremídhi/soğan | onion |
| skórdho/sarmısak | garlic |
| repánia/turp | radish |
| kouloúmbra/ kouloumbra | kohlrabi |
| (kafteró) pipéri/ (acı) biber | (hot) pepper |
| manitária/mantar | mushrooms, often wild |
| spanáki/ispanak | spinach |
| patátes/patates | potatoes |
| tzips/çips | chips |
| kolokássia/kolokas, bules, yer elmasi | taro root |
| kolokythákia/kabak | courgettes |

| | |
|---|---|
| bámies/bamya | okra |
| bezélia/bezelye | peas |
| fasólia/fasulye | beans |
| goutsiá/bakla | broad beans |
| gounoupídhi/ çiçek lahanası | cauliflower |
| louviá/börülce | black-eyed peas |
| óspria | generic for any pulse |

## Typical dishes

| | |
|---|---|
| davás/dava | sweetish stew, usually of lamb, with onions |
| afélia/– | pork cooked with red wine and coriander seeds |
| réssi/– | cracked wheat and meat dish, served at weddings |
| moussakás/musaka | aubergine and potato slabs overlaid with mince and white sauce |
| –/karnıyarık | similar to preceding but no sauce or potato |
| kolokótes/– | turnovers stuffed with pumpkin, raisins and bulgur |
| koupépia/yaprak dolması | vine leaves filled with rice |
| koúppes | torpedo-shaped fried turnovers filled with onions and mincemeat |
| pourétcha/börek | turnovers filled with meat or cream cheese |
| –/laz böreği | meat-filled cr pes topped with yogurt |
| –/mantı | ravioli, filled with mince and served with yogurt and chili |
| –/tatar böreği | similar meat-stuffed pasta, served with cheese and mint |
| –/pirohu | ravioli, filled with cheese |

## Nutty snacks

| | |
|---|---|
| soushoúkou/ soudzouki | almond string dipped in rosewater and grape molasses |
| –/köfter | as above, but with no nuts |
| pastelláki/– | sesame, peanut and syrup bar |
| fistíkia/fıstık | peanuts |
| halepianá/şam fıstığı | pistachios |
| amýgdhala/badem | almonds |

## Desserts and sweets

| | |
|---|---|
| loukoúmi/lokum | "Cyprus" delight: varying proportions of sugar, pectin, gelatin, rosewater or citrus extract, nuts, boiled then solidified |
| pagotó/dondurma | ice cream |
| baklavás/baklava | filo pastry layers with nut-honey filling |
| kataïfi/kadayıf | same as above but with "shredded wheat" instead of pastry sheets |
| katméri/katmer | crepe stuffed with banana, honey and clotted cream (kaïmáki or kaymak yağ) |
| loukoumádhes/lokma | deep-fried batter rings |
| halvás/helva | grainy paste, semolina- or tahini-based |
| shamísi/şamişi | semolina-based granular sweet |
| krem karamel/krem karamel | creme caramel |
| mahallebí/muhallebi | cherry-pit flour and rosewater pudding |
| palouzé | grape-must pudding |
| kalopráma | syrup-drenched sponge cake |
| glyká/macun | sweet preserved fruit |

**Types of glyká or macun include:**

| | |
|---|---|
| výssino/vişne | sour morello cherry |
| kerási/kiraz | Queen Anne-type cherry |
| petrokéraso/– | dark red cherry |
| kitrómilo/neranci | Seville orange |
| vazanáki/– | baby aubergines |
| sýko/incir | fig |
| karýdhi/ceviz | walnut |

## Fruit

| | |
|---|---|
| fráoules/ ilek | strawberries |
| moúsmoule/ muşmula | medlars |
| méspila/yeni dunya | loquats |
| kaïsha, khryssó mila/kayısı | apricots |
| rodhákina/şeftali | peaches |
| bastésha, batíha/ karpuz | watermelon |
| gouáva/guava | strawberry guava |
| pepóni/kavun | dessert melon |
| paraméles/erik | plums |
| kerásia/kiraz | cherries |
| papoutsósyko/ frenk inciri | prickly pear |
| sýka/incir | figs |

| | |
|---|---|
| stafýlia/üzüm | grapes |
| mila/elma | apples |
| akhládhia/armut | pears |
| portokália/portakal | oranges |
| lemónia/limon | lemons |
| mandarínia/mandalin | mandarins |
| gréypfrout/grepfrut | grapefruit |
| banánes/muz | banana |

## Drinks

| | |
|---|---|
| kafés/kahve | Oriental coffee, served: |
| pikrós/sade | unsweetened |
| métrios/orta | medium sweet |
| glykós/şekerli | very sweet |
| tsáï/çay | tea |
| spadjá/spaca | sage tea |
| býra/bira | beer |
| brandy/brandy | brandy |
| krasí/şarap | wine |
| áspro/beyaz | white |
| mávro/kırmızı | red |
| kokkinélli/roze | rosé |
| aïráni/ayran | diluted yogurt with herbs |
| khymós/meyva suyu | fruit juice |

# Glossary of words and terms

For glossaries of acronyms of political parties, see p.449 and p.451.

## Archeological, artistic and architectural terms

**Acropolis** Ancient fortified hilltop.

**Agora** Market and meeting place of an ancient Greek city.

**Amphora** Tall, narrow-necked jar for oil or wine.

**Aniconic** Abstract, non-figurative, dating from the Iconoclast Period – see "Iconoclasm" below – when the Orthodox Church forbade figural representation.

**Apse** Polygonal or curved recess at the altar end of a church.

**Archaic period** An era (c. 750–475 BC) when Cypriot artistic expressiveness was most developed in its own right, though heavily influenced by the Middle East.

**Ashlar** Dressed, squared masonry in an ancient structure, either free-standing or facing a rubble wall.

**Atrium** Open, inner courtyard of a Hellenistic or Roman dwelling.

**Basilica** Colonnaded, "hall"- or "barn"-type church adapted from Roman public buildings, common in Cyprus.

**Betyl** Bullet-shaped stone, sacred object of the Aphrodite cult and anointed like a Hindu Shiva lingam.

**Bronze Age** Early (2500–1900 BC) to Late (1650–1050 BC); the latter eras show marked cultural influence of the Mycenaean migration from the Greek Peloponnese.

**Byzantine empire** The Greek-speaking Christian state, ruled from Constantinople (modern Istanbul), which developed out of the eastern Roman empire after its division from the west in the fourth century AD. Byzantine rule on Cyprus ended in 1191.

**Capital** The top, often ornamented, of a column.

**Chalcolithic period** Cultures (3900–2500 BC) distinguished by advanced ceramic and worked-stone artefacts, and by the first smelting of copper – from which Cyprus probably takes its name.

**Champlevé** In architecture, the technique of chiselling reliefs onto a flat stone surface; the recesses so created might be filled with glass or coloured wax for contrast.

**Classical period** In Cyprus, from the start of the fifth century BC to the rule of the Macedonian kings late in the next century; a period of destruction at the hands of the Persians, and thus poor in home-grown artefacts.

**Conch** Curved wall surface at the top of an apse.

**Dromos** Ramp leading to the subterranean entrance of a Bronze Age tomb.

**Forum** Market and meeting place of a Roman-era city.

**Frigidarium** Cold plunge-pool room of a Roman or Byzantine bath.

**Geometric** Archeological era (c. 1050–750 BC) so named for the abstract designs of its pottery.

**Hellenistic era** Extending from 325 to 50 BC, this meant for Cyprus rule by the Ptolemaic kings, based in Alexandria.

**Hypocaust** Underfloor space, with brick supports, for hot-air circulation, especially below ancient baths.

**Iconoclasm** Eighth- and ninth-century Byzantine movement whereby the veneration of icons was forbidden as idolatrous; during this time many figurative frescoes were destroyed as well.

**Ierárkhi** The Church Fathers (codifiers of Christianity and monastic life), a common fresco subject.

**Ierón** Literally, "sacred" – the sanctuary between the altar screen and the apse of a church, reserved for priestly activities.

**Katholikón** Central church of a monastery.

**Krater** Large, usually two-handled ancient wine goblet.

**Lusignan dynasty** Mostly French, Catholic nobility who ruled Cyprus from 1191 until 1489, a time typified by monumental Gothic architecture, the introduction of feudalism and the suppression of the Orthodox Church.

**Machicolations** Openings at the edge of a castle's parapet or above its doorway, usually between corbels, for dumping noxious substances on invaders.

**Mandorla** An almond-shaped or sometimes star-shaped aura often used by fresco-painters to emphasize the sanctity of the risen Christ.

**Mitrópolis** Orthodox cathedral of a large town.

**Naos** The inner sanctum of an ancient temple; also, any Orthodox Christian shrine.

**Narthex** Vestibule or entrance hall of a church, traditionally reserved for unbaptized catechumens; also exonarthex, the outermost vestibule when there is more than one.

**Nave** Principal lengthwise limb of a church.

**Necropolis** Concentration of above-ground tombs, always outside the walls of an ancient city.

**Neolithic period** Earliest era of settlement on Cyprus, divided into Neolithic I (7000–6000 BC), as at Khirokitiá, and Neolithic II (4500–3800 BC).

**Odeion** Small Hellenistic or Roman theatre, used for musical performances, minor dramatic productions or municipal councils.

**Opus sectile** Roman technique for wall or floor mosaics, using thin, translucent sections of marble, mother-of-pearl or glass set in adhesive, framed when necessary by metal clamps.

**Orans** Term for depiction of the Virgin with both arms aloft in an attitude of prayer.

**Pandokrátor** Literally "The Almighty", but generally refers to the stern portrayal of Christ in Majesty frescoed or in mosaic in the main dome of many Byzantine churches.

**Pediment** Triangular wall space between roof and wall of a chapel.

**Pendentive** Any of four triangular sections of vaulting with concave sides, positioned at a corner of a rectangular space to support a circular or polygonal dome. In churches, often adorned with frescoes of the four Evangelists.

**Rhyton** Vessel, often horn-shaped, for libations or offerings.

**Rib vaulting** Series of projecting curved stone ribs marking the junction of ceiling vaults; common feature of Lusignan monastic and military architecture.

**Roundel** Decorative painted medallion in a church, on flat or curved surface.

**Soffit** Inner surface of an arch, often frescoed.

**Stele** Upright stone slab or column, usually inscribed; an ancient tombstone.

**Stoa** Colonnaded walkway in ancient marketplaces.

**Synthronon** Semicircular seating for clergy, usually in the apse of a Byzantine church.

**Témblon** Wooden altar screen of an Orthodox church, usually ornately carved and painted and used to display icons.

**Temenos** Sacred precinct, often used to refer to the sanctuary itself.

**Tepidarium** Warm anteroom of a Roman or Byzantine bath.

**Tesserae** Cubes used to compose a mosaic, made either of naturally coloured rock or of painted or gilded glass.

**Tholos** Conical or beehive-shaped building, especially a Bronze Age tomb.

**Transept** The "arms" of a church, transverse to the nave.

**Tympanum** In Orthodox use, the semicircular space over a church door reserved for dedicatory inscriptions, dates, frescoes, etc.

**Xenon** Hostel for pilgrims at an ancient shrine; the tradition continues at modern Cypriot Orthodox monasteries, though such inns are more accurately *xenónes* in modern Greek.

**Yinaikonítis** Women's gallery in an Orthodox church, almost always at the rear.

## Common Greek-Cypriot terms

**Áno** Upper; as in upper town or village.

**Áyios/ayía/áyii** Saint or holy (m/f/pl). Common place name prefix (abbreviated Ag or Ay.), often spelt AGIOS (the official version) or AGHIOS.

**Exokhikó kéndro** Rural taverna, often functioning only in summer or at weekends.

**Kafenío** Coffeehouse or café; in a small village the centre of communal life.

**Káto** Lower; as in lower town or village.

**Kinotárkhis** See *múkhtar*, below.

**Mesaoría** The broad plain between the Tróödhos and Kyrenia mountains; site of Nicosia.

**Moní** Monastery or convent.

**Múkhtar** Village headman.

**Néos, néa, néo** "New" – a common part of a town or village name.

**Paleós, paleá, paleó** "Old" – again, common in town and village names.

**Panayía** Virgin Mary.

**Paniyiri** Festival or feast – the local celebration of a holy day.

**Platía** Square, plaza; *kendrikí platía*, central square.

## Common Turkish-Cypriot terms

**Ağa** A minor rank of nobility in the Ottoman empire, and still a term of respect applied to a local worthy – follows the name (eg Ismail Ağa).

**Bahçe(si)** Garden.

**Bedesten** Covered market hall for textiles, often lockable.

**Bekçi** Caretaker at an archeological site or monument.

**Bey** Another minor Ottoman title, like Ağa, still in use.

**Camı(ı)** Mosque.

**Çarşı (sı)** Bazaar, market.

**Dağı, dağları** "Mount" and "mountains", respectively.

**Eski** "Old" – frequent modifier of place names.

**Ezan** The Muslim call to prayer.

**Halk plajı/plajları** Free-of-charge public beach(es).

**Hamam(ı)** Turkish sauna-bath.

**Han(ı)** Ottoman-era hostel for travellers, or tradesmen's hall.

**Hastane(sı)** Hospital.

**Hoca** Teacher in charge of religious instruction of children.

**İmam** Usually just the prayer leader at a mosque, though it can mean a more important spiritual authority.

**Kale(sı)** Castle, fort.

**Kapı (sı)** Gate, door.

**Kervansaray(ı)** Strategically located "hotel", for pack animals and men, on the main trade routes; few survive in Cyprus, most of them heavily modified. Some overlap with *hanı*.

**Kılıse(sı)** Church.

**Konak** Large private residence, also the main government building of a province or city; genitive form *konatı*.

**Kule(sı)** Tower, turret.

**Mabet** Temple, common signpost at ancient sites; genitive form *mabedi*.

**Mahalle(sı)** District or neighbourhood of a larger municipality.

**Mesarya** Turkish for the Mesaoría; officially renamed İçova.

**Meydan(i)** Public square or plaza.

**Meyhane** Tavern serving alcohol and small platters of seasonal delicacies on an equal footing; similar (but often superior) to the *mezé* houses of the South.

**Mezar(ı)** Grave, tomb; thus *mezarlık*, cemetery.

**Mıhrab** Niche in mosque indicating the direction of Mecca, and prayer.

**Mımbar** Pulpit in a mosque, from where the imam delivers homilies.

**Mınare** Turkish for "minaret", the tower from which the call to prayer is delivered.

**Müezzın** Man who pronounces call to prayer from the minaret of a mosque; the call is often taped these days.

**Muhtar** Village headman; *muhtarlık* is the office, both in the abstract and concrete sense.

**Namaz** The Muslim rite of prayer, performed five times daily.

**Paşa** Ottoman honorific, approximately equivalent to "Lord"; follows the name.

**Sarniç** Rain cistern, often partly subterranean and domed.

**Sufı** Dervish – more properly an adherent of one of the heterodox mystical branches of Islam.

**Tabya** Bastion (on walls of north Nicosia or Famagusta).

**Tapınak** Alternative term for "temple" at archeological sites; genitive form *tapınağı*.

**Tarikat** Any one of the various Sufi orders.

**Tekke(sı)** Gathering place of a Sufi order.

**Vakıf** Islamic religious trust, responsible for social welfare and religious buildings; holds extensive property, often donated or willed posthumously by believers, across Cyprus.

**Vizier** The principal Ottoman minister of state, responsible for the day-to-day running of the empire; in Turkish *vezir*.

**Yenı** "New" – common component of Turkish-Cypriot place names.

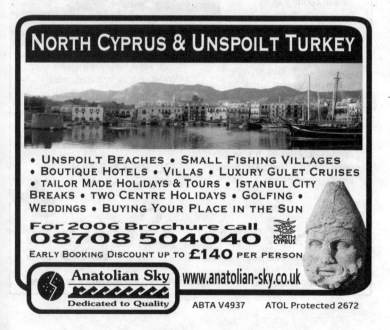

# A Rough Guide to Rough Guides

In the summer of 1981, Mark Ellingham, a recent graduate from Bristol University, was travelling round Greece and couldn't find a guidebook that really met his needs. On the one hand there were the student guides, insistent on saving every last cent, and on the other the heavyweight cultural tomes whose authors seemed to have spent more time in a research library than lounging away the afternoon at a taverna or on the beach.

In a bid to avoid getting a job, Mark and a small group of writers set about creating their own guidebook. It was a guide to Greece that aimed to combine a journalistic approach to description with a thoroughly practical approach to travellers' needs – a guide that would incorporate culture, history and contemporary insights with a critical edge, together with up-to-date, value-for-money listings. Back in London, Mark and the team finished their Rough Guide, as they called it, and talked Routledge into publishing the book.

That first *Rough Guide to Greece*, published in 1982, was a student scheme that became a publishing phenomenon. The immediate success of the book – with numerous reprints and a Thomas Cook prize shortlisting – spawned a series that rapidly covered dozens of destinations. Rough Guides had a ready market among low-budget backpackers, but soon also acquired a much broader and older readership that relished Rough Guides' wit and inquisitiveness as much as their enthusiastic, critical approach. Everyone wants value for money, but not at any price.

Rough Guides soon began supplementing the "rougher" information about hostels and low-budget listings with the kind of detail on restaurants and quality hotels that independent-minded visitors on any budget might expect, whether on business in New York or trekking in Thailand.

These days the guides – distributed worldwide by the Penguin Group – offer recommendations from shoestring to luxury and cover more than 200 destinations around the globe, including almost every country in the Americas and Europe, more than half of Africa and most of Asia and Australasia. Our ever-growing team of authors and photographers is spread all over the world, particularly in Europe, the USA and Australia.

In 1994, we published the *Rough Guide to World Music* and *Rough Guide to Classical Music*; and a year later the *Rough Guide to the Internet*. All three books have become benchmark titles in their fields – which encouraged us to expand into other areas of publishing, mainly around popular culture. Rough Guides now publish:

- Travel guides to more than 200 worldwide destinations
- Dictionary phrasebooks to 22 major languages
- History guides ranging from Ireland to Islam
- Maps printed on rip-proof and waterproof Polyart™ paper
- Music guides running the gamut from Opera to Elvis
- Restaurant guides to London, New York and San Francisco
- Reference books on topics as diverse as the Weather and Shakespeare
- Sports guides from Formula 1 to Man Utd
- Pop culture books from *Lord of the Rings* to Cult TV
- World Music CDs in association with World Music Network

Visit www.roughguides.com to see our latest publications.

# Rough Guide credits

**Text editor**: Jules Brown
**Layout**: Ajay Verma
**Cartography**: Katie Lloyd-Jones
**Picture editor**: Mark Thomas
**Proofreader**: Stewart Wild
**Editorial**: **London** Kate Berens, Claire Saunders, Geoff Howard, Ruth Blackmore, Gavin Thomas, Polly Thomas, Richard Lim, Clifton Wilkinson, Alison Murchie, Sally Schafer, Karoline Densley, Andy Turner, Ella O'Donnell, Keith Drew, Edward Aves, Nikki Birrell, Chloë Thomson, Helen Marsden, Joe Staines, Duncan Clark, Peter Buckley, Matthew Milton, Daniel Crewe; **New York** Andrew Rosenberg, Richard Koss, Steven Horak, AnneLise Sorensen, Amy Hegarty, Hunter Slaton
**Design & Pictures**: **London** Simon Bracken, Dan May, Diana Jarvis, Jj Luck, Harriet Mills, Chloë Roberts; **Delhi** Madhulita Mohapatra, Umesh Aggarwal, Jessica Subramanian, Amit Verma, Ankur Guha
**Production**: Julia Bovis, Sophie Hewat, Katherine Owers

**Cartography**: **London** Maxine Repath, Ed Wright; **Delhi** Manish Chandra, Rajesh Chhibber, Jai Prakash Mishra, Ashutosh Bharti, Rajesh Mishra, Animesh Pathak, Jasbir Sandhu, Karobi Gogoi
**Online**: **New York** Jennifer Gold, Suzanne Welles; **Delhi** Manik Chauhan, Narender Kumar, Manish Shekhar Jha, Lalit K. Sharma, Rakesh Kumar
**Marketing & Publicity**: **London** Richard Trillo, Niki Hanmer, David Wearn, Demelza Dallow; **New York** Geoff Colquitt, Megan Kennedy, Milena Perez; **Delhi** Reem Khokhar
**Custom publishing and foreign rights**: Philippa Hopkins
**Finance**: Gary Singh
**Manager India**: Punita Singh
**Series editor**: Mark Ellingham
**Reference Director**: Andrew Lockett
**PA to Managing and Publishing Directors**: Megan McIntyre
**Publishing Director**: Martin Dunford
**Managing Director**: Kevin Fitzgerald

# Publishing information

This fifth edition published September 2005 by
**Rough Guides Ltd**,
80 Strand, London WC2R 0RL
345 Hudson St, 4th Floor,
New York, NY 10014, USA
14 Local Shopping Centre, Panchsheel Park,
New Delhi 110017, India.
**Distributed by the Penguin Group**
Penguin Books Ltd,
80 Strand, London WC2R 0RL
Penguin Putnam Inc,
375 Hudson Street, NY 10014, USA
Penguin Group (Australia)
250 Camberwell Road, Camberwell
Victoria 3124, Australia
Penguin Books Canada Ltd,
10 Alcorn Avenue, Toronto, Ontario,
Canada M4V 1E4
Penguin Group (New Zealand)
Cnr Rosedale and Airborne Roads
Albany, Auckland, New Zealand

Typeset in Bembo and Helvetica to an original design by Henry Iles.
Printed and bound in Italy by LegoPrint S.p.A.

© Marc Dubin 2005

No part of this book may be reproduced in any form without permission from the publisher except for the quotation of brief passages in reviews.

552pp includes index
A catalogue record for this book is available from the British Library

ISBN 1-84353-456-8

The publishers and authors have done their best to ensure the accuracy and currency of all the information in **The Rough Guide to Cyprus**, however, they can accept no responsibility for any loss, injury, or inconvenience sustained by any traveller as a result of information or advice contained in the guide.

3   5   7   9   8   6   4   2

SMALL PRINT

# Help us update

We've gone to a lot of effort to ensure that the fifth edition of **The Rough Guide to Cyprus** is accurate and up to date. However, things change – places get "discovered", opening hours are notoriously fickle, restaurants and rooms raise prices or lower standards. If you feel we've got it wrong or left something out, we'd like to know, and if you can remember the address, the price, the time, the phone number, so much the better.

We'll credit all contributions, and send a copy of the next edition (or any other Rough Guide if you prefer) for the best letters. Everyone who writes to us and isn't already a subscriber will receive a copy of our full-colour thrice-yearly newsletter. Please mark letters: "**Rough Guide Cyprus Update**" and send to: Rough Guides, 80 Strand, London WC2R 0RL, or Rough Guides, 4th Floor, 345 Hudson St, New York, NY 10014. Or send an email to **mail@roughguides.com**

Have your questions answered and tell others about your trip at
**www.roughguides.atinfopop.com**

## Acknowledgements

The author would like to acknowledge, on the ground in the South: the managements of Cyprus Villages and Cydive for various facilities; the "ground crew"" at Sunvil Páfos for insights and assistance; Yiannis Christofides for his usual gracious hospitality and insights, for four editions now; George and Lara Dimitriades for their usual good food and conversation; Romos Christodoulides for restaurant tips and material on the Annan Plan; Ruth Keshishian for book updates, more restaurant recommendations, and good company; Christofis Kykkas for his usual stimulating perspective; Richard and Alison Sale at Monágri for multiple corrections, hospitality and general lowdown; Roxanne Koudounari and friends for restaurant- and bar-crawling in Limassol; Stavros Stavrou Karayanni for arranging the terrific night out; and Zitsa for sharing the last three days. In the North, tip of the hat to Bryan Balls of the Green Jacket Bookshop, Steve Abit at Bellapais Gardens, and once again Küfi and Şirin Birinci for another season of nocturnal safaris and (as ever) the Secret History of Cyprus. Back in London, thanks again to Dudley der Parthog at Sunvil Travel, and Karen Brown at Anatolian Sky. Last but not least, editor Jules Brown managed the near-impossible of discreet pruning without blunting the impact of the text.

## Readers' letters

Thanks to all the readers who have taken the time to write in with comments and suggestions (and apologies if we've inadvertently omitted or misspelt anyone's name):

Sylvia Barnard, John Bartlett, R. D. Beckley, H. Bowes, Stan & Irene Cambers, C Collins & Lesley Phillips, Michael & Ruth Cork, Iain Cottingham, Athol Cowley, Louise Dando, Ann Doré, Christopher Elliott, Katrina Fisher, Ursula FitzGerald, Sheila & Tony Forrester, Yvonne Fox, Ruth Anne French, Martin Garvey, Michael & Ann Gill, Michael Hall, Peter Hancock, Patricia Harrison (twice), Anne Headdon, Philip Hodgson, Mark & Emma Horstall, Steve Howard, Colin Ingram, Tim Jellings, Alix Jones, Zane Katsikis, Bill & Jean Lacey, Rob Lambie, Mark & Irene Lawrence, Clifford Lewis, Carlo Longino, Umberto Manassei & Piervincenzo D'Angelo, Carol McGrath, Duncan Mitchell (twice), Marc Munden, Ronen Numa, Janet Patterson and Angus Mcleish, Charles Orange, A. M. & A. K. Pearson, David Pedlow, Sheila and Barney Perkinson, Julia Prior & Friend, Malcolm Punnett, Mike Quigley, Gloria Rawle, Leatrice Reid, Carola Scupham, Paul Snell, Jim Stewart, Geoff Taylor, Janet & Denis Thornton, Georgina Troman, M. K. Tucker, Sue Turl, Denis Vanderveld, Stephanie West and Sabine Wichert.

## Photo credits

All images © Rough Guides except the following:

# Index

Map entries are in colour

**INDEX**

**INDEX**

# Map symbols

maps are listed in the full index using coloured text

| | | | |
|---|---|---|---|
| – – – – | Chapter boundary | 〰 | Waterfall |
| — ·· — | District boundary | ∿ | Spring |
| ▬▬▬ | Motorway | 🏖 | Beach (regional maps) |
| ▭▭▭ | Dual carriageway | ∴ | Ruins |
| ═══ | Main road | ⚠ | Campsite |
| ═══ | Minor road | ⅜ | Picnic area |
| ╤╤ | Blocked road | 🚻 | Toilets |
| ─── | Dirt road | 🅿 | Parking |
| ▥▥▥ | Steps | ★ | Transport stop |
| ▭▭▭ | Pedestrianized street | ℂ | Phone office |
| - - - - | Path | ⓘ | Tourist office |
| ─── | River | ✉ | Post office |
| — — | Ferry | ⊞ | Hospital |
| ⬧ | Point of interest | ◉ | Accommodation |
| ✈ | Airport | ◼ | Restaurant |
| ♕ | Castle | ▬ | Building |
| ‡ | Church (regional maps) | ⊞ | Church (town maps) |
| ⛪ | Monastery | ⌐⊦ | Cemetery |
| ☪ | Mosque | ▦ | Park |
| ▲ | Mountain peak | ▨ | Beach (town maps) |
| ⌁ | Lighthouse | | |